FIRST CENSUS
OF THE UNITED STATES
1790

MAINE

DEPARTMENT OF COMMERCE AND LABOR

BUREAU OF THE CENSUS

S. N. D. NORTH, DIRECTOR

HEADS OF FAMILIES

AT THE FIRST CENSUS OF THE

UNITED STATES TAKEN

IN THE YEAR

1790

MAINE

WASHINGTON

GOVERNMENT PRINTING OFFICE

1908

> ### *Notice*
>
> In many older books, foxing (or discoloration) occurs and, in some instances, print lightens with wear and age. Reprinted books, such as this, often duplicate these flaws, notwithstanding efforts to reduce or eliminate them. The pages of this reprint have been digitally enhanced and, where possible, the flaws eliminated in order to provide clarity of content and a pleasant reading experience.

Heads of Families at the First Census of the United States Taken in the Year 1790:

Maine

Originally published
Washington D. C.
1908

Reprinted by:

Janaway Publishing, Inc.
2412 Nicklaus Dr.
Santa Maria, California 93455
(805) 925-1038
www.JanawayGenealogy.com

(2001), 2007

ISBN 10: 1-59641-090-6
ISBN 13: 978-1-59641-090-9

Made in the United States of America

HEADS OF FAMILIES AT THE FIRST CENSUS
1790

INTRODUCTION.

The First Census of the United States (1790) comprised an enumeration of the inhabitants of the present states of Connecticut, Delaware, Georgia, Kentucky, Maine, Maryland, Massachusetts, New Hampshire, New Jersey, New York, North Carolina, Pennsylvania, Rhode Island, South Carolina, Tennessee, Vermont, and Virginia.

A complete set of the schedules for each state, with a summary for the counties, and in many cases for towns, was filed in the State Department, but unfortunately they are not now complete, the returns for the states of Delaware, Georgia, Kentucky, New Jersey, Tennessee, and Virginia having been destroyed when the British burned the Capitol at Washington during the War of 1812. For several of the states for which schedules are lacking it is probable that the Director of the Census could obtain lists which would present the names of most of the heads of families at the date of the First Census. In Virginia, state enumerations were made in 1782, 1783, 1784, and 1785, but the lists on file in the State Library include the names for only 39 of the 78 counties into which the state was divided.

The schedules of 1790 form a unique inheritance for the Nation, since they represent for each of the states concerned a complete list of the heads of families in the United States at the time of the adoption of the Constitution. The framers were the statesmen and leaders of thought, but those whose names appear upon the schedules of the First Census were in general the plain citizens who by their conduct in war and peace made the Constitution possible and by their intelligence and self-restraint put it into successful operation.

The total population of the United States in 1790, exclusive of slaves, as derived from the schedules was 3,231,533. The only names appearing upon the schedules, however, were those of heads of families, and as at that period the families averaged 6 persons, the total number was approximately 540,000, or slightly more than half a million. The number of names which is now lacking because of the destruction of the schedules is approximately 140,000, thus leaving schedules containing about 400,000 names.

The information contained in the published report of the First Census of the United States, a small volume of 56 pages, was not uniform for the several states and territories. For New England and one or two of the other states the population was presented by counties and towns; that of New Jersey appeared partly by counties and towns and partly by counties only; in other cases the returns were given by counties only. Thus the complete transcript of the names of heads of families, with accompanying information, presents for the first time detailed information as to the number of inhabitants—males, females, etc.—for each minor civil division in all those states for which such information was not originally published.

In response to repeated requests from patriotic societies and persons interested in genealogy, or desirous of studying the early history of the United States, Congress added to the sundry civil appropriation bill for the fiscal year 1907 the following paragraph:

The Director of the Census is hereby authorized and directed to publish, in a permanent form, by counties and minor civil divisions, the names of the heads of families returned at the First Census of the United States in seventeen hundred and ninety; and the Director of the Census is authorized, in his discretion, to sell said publications, the proceeds thereof to be covered into the Treasury of the United States, to be deposited to the credit of miscellaneous receipts on account of "Proceeds of sales of Government property:"

Provided, That no expense shall be incurred hereunder additional to appropriations for the Census Office for printing therefor made for the fiscal year nineteen hundred and seven; and the Director of the Census is hereby directed to report to Congress at its next session the cost incurred hereunder and the price fixed for said publications and the total received therefor.

The amount of money appropriated by Congress for the Census printing for the fiscal year mentioned was unfortunately not sufficient to meet the current requirement of the Office and to publish the transcription of the First Census, and no provision was made in the sundry civil appropriation bill for 1908 for the continuance of authority to publish these important records. Resources, however, were available for printing a small section of the work, and the schedules of New Hampshire, Vermont, and Maryland accordingly were published.

The urgent deficiency bill, approved February 15, 1908, contained the following provision:

That the Director of the Census is hereby authorized and directed to expend so much of the appropriation for printing for the Department of Commerce and Labor allotted by law to the Census Office for the fiscal year ending June thirtieth, nineteen hundred and eight, as may be necessary to continue and complete the publication of the names of the heads of families returned at the First Census of the United States, as authorized by the sundry civil appropriation act approved June thirtieth, nineteen hundred and six.

In accordance with the authority given in the paragraph quoted above, the names returned at the First Census in the states of Connecticut, Maine, Massachusetts, New York, North Carolina, Pennsylvania, Rhode Island, and South Carolina have been published, thus completing the roster of the heads of families in 1790 so far as they can be shown from the records of the Census Office. As the Federal census schedules of the state of Virginia for 1790 are missing, the lists of the state enumerations made in 1782, 1783, 1784, and 1785 have been substituted and, while not complete, they will, undoubtedly, prove of great value.

THE FIRST CENSUS.

The First Census act was passed at the second session of the First Congress, and was signed by President Washington on March 1, 1790. The task of making the first enumeration of inhabitants was placed upon the President. Under this law the marshals of the several judicial districts were required to ascertain the number of inhabitants within their respective districts, omitting Indians not taxed, and distinguishing free persons (including those bound to service for a term of years) from all others; the sex and color of free persons; and the number of free males 16 years of age and over.

The object of the inquiry last mentioned was, undoubtedly, to obtain definite knowledge as to the military and industrial strength of the country. This fact possesses special interest, because the Constitution directs merely an enumeration of inhabitants. Thus the demand for increasingly extensive information, which has been so marked a characteristic of census legislation, began with the First Congress that dealt with the subject.

The method followed by the President in putting into operation the First Census law, although the object of extended investigation, is not definitely known. It is supposed that the President or the Secretary of State dispatched copies of the law, and perhaps of instructions also, to the marshals. There is, however, some ground for disputing this conclusion. At least one of the reports in the census volume of 1790 was furnished by a governor. This, together with the fact that there is no record of correspondence with the marshals on the subject of the census, but that there is a record of such correspondence with the governors, makes very strong the inference that the marshals received their instructions through the governors of the states. This inference is strengthened by the fact that in 1790 the state of Massachusetts furnished the printed blanks, and also by the fact that the law relating to the Second Census specifically charged the Secretary of State to superintend the enumeration and to communicate directly with the marshals.

By the terms of the First Census law nine months were allowed in which to complete the enumeration. The census taking was supervised by the marshals of the several judicial districts, who employed assistant marshals to act as enumerators. There were 17 marshals. The records showing the number of assistant marshals employed in 1790, 1800, and 1810 were destroyed by fire, but the number employed in 1790 has been estimated at 650.

The schedules which these officials prepared consist of lists of names of heads of families; each name appears in a stub, or first column, which is followed by five columns, giving details of the family. These columns are headed as follows:

Free white males of 16 years and upward, including heads of families.
Free white males under 16 years.
Free white females, including heads of families.
All other free persons.
Slaves.

The assistant marshals made two copies of the returns; in accordance with the law one copy was posted in the immediate neighborhood for the information of the public, and the other was transmitted to the marshal in charge, to be forwarded to the President. The schedules were turned over by the President to the Secretary of State. Little or no tabulation was required, and the report of the First Census, as also the reports of the Second, Third, and Fourth, was produced without the employment of any clerical force, the summaries being transmitted directly to the printer. The total population as returned in 1790 was 3,929,214, and the entire cost of the census was $44,377.

A summary of the results of the First Census, not including the returns for South Carolina, was transmitted to Congress by President Washington on October 27, 1791. The legal period for enumeration, nine months, had been extended, the longest time consumed being eighteen months in South Carolina. The report of October 27 was printed in full, and published in what is now a very rare little volume; afterwards the report for South Carolina was "tipped in." To contain the results of the Twelfth Census, ten large quarto volumes, comprising in all 10,400 pages, were required. No illustration of the expansion of census inquiry can be more striking.

The original schedules of the First Census are now contained in 26 bound volumes, preserved in the Census Office. For the most part the headings of the schedules were written in by hand. Indeed, up to and

INTRODUCTION.

including 1820, the assistant marshals generally used for the schedules such paper as they happened to have, ruling it, writing in the headings, and binding the sheets together themselves. In some cases merchants' account paper was used, and now and then the schedules were bound in wall paper.

As a consequence of requiring marshals to supply their own blanks, the volumes containing the schedules vary in size from about 7 inches long, 3 inches wide, and ½ inch thick to 21 inches long, 14 inches wide, and 6 inches thick. Some of the sheets in these volumes are only 4 inches long, but a few are 3 feet in length, necessitating several folds. In some cases leaves burned at the edges have been covered with transparent silk to preserve them.

THE UNITED STATES IN 1790.

In March, 1790, the Union consisted of twelve states—Rhode Island, the last of the original thirteen to enter the Union, being admitted May 29 of the same year. Vermont, the first addition, was admitted in the following year, before the results of the First Census were announced. Maine was a part of Massachusetts, Kentucky was a part of Virginia, and the present states of Alabama and Mississippi were parts of Georgia. The present states of Ohio, Indiana, Illinois, Michigan, and Wisconsin, with part of Minnesota, were known as the Northwest Territory, and the present state of Tennessee, then a part of North Carolina, was soon to be organized as the Southwest Territory.

The United States was bounded on the west by the Mississippi river, beyond which stretched that vast and unexplored wilderness belonging to the Spanish King, which was afterwards ceded to the United States by France as the Louisiana Purchase, and now comprises the great and populous states of South Dakota, Iowa, Nebraska, Missouri, Kansas, Arkansas, and Oklahoma, and portions of Minnesota, North Dakota, Montana, Wyoming, Colorado, New Mexico, Texas, and Louisiana. The Louisiana Purchase was not consummated for more than a decade after the First Census was taken. On the south was another Spanish colony known as the Floridas. The greater part of Texas, then a part of the colony of Mexico, belonged to Spain; and California, Nevada, Utah, Arizona, and a portion of New Mexico, also the property of Spain, although penetrated here and there by venturesome explorers and missionaries, were, for the most part, an undiscovered wilderness.

The gross area of the United States was 827,844 square miles, but the settled area was only 239,935 square miles, or about 29 per cent of the total. Though the area covered by the enumeration in 1790 seems very small when compared with the present area of the United States, the difficulties which confronted the census taker were vastly greater than in 1900. In many localities there were no roads, and where these did exist they were poor and frequently impassable; bridges were almost unknown. Transportation was entirely by horseback, stage, or private coach. A journey as long as that from New York to Washington was a serious undertaking, requiring eight days under the most favorable conditions. Western New York was a wilderness, Elmira and Binghamton being but detached hamlets. The territory west of the Allegheny mountains, with the exception of a portion of Kentucky, was unsettled and scarcely penetrated. Detroit and Vincennes were too small and isolated to merit consideration. Philadelphia was the capital of the United States. Washington was a mere Government project, not even named, but known as the Federal City. Indeed, by the spring of 1793, only one wall of the White House had been constructed, and the site for the Capitol had been merely surveyed. New York city in 1790 possessed a population of only 33,131, although it was the largest city in the United States; Philadelphia was second, with 28,522; and Boston third, with 18,320. Mails were transported in very irregular fashion, and correspondence was expensive and uncertain.

There were, moreover, other difficulties which were of serious moment in 1790, but which long ago ceased to be problems in census taking. The inhabitants, having no experience with census taking, imagined that some scheme for increasing taxation was involved, and were inclined to be cautious lest they should reveal too much of their own affairs. There was also opposition to enumeration on religious grounds, a count of inhabitants being regarded by many as a cause for divine displeasure. The boundaries of towns and other minor divisions, and even those of counties, were in many cases unknown or not defined at all. The hitherto semi-independent states had been under the control of the Federal Government for so short a time that the different sections had not yet been welded into an harmonious nationality in which the Federal authority should be unquestioned and instructions promptly and fully obeyed.

AN ACT PROVIDING FOR THE ENUMERATION OF THE INHABITANTS OF THE UNITED STATES

APPROVED MARCH 1, 1790

SECTION 1. Be it enacted by the Senate and House of Representatives of the United States of America in Congress assembled, That the marshals of the several districts of the United States shall be, and they are hereby authorized and required to cause the number of the inhabitants within their respective districts to be taken; omitting in such enumeration Indians not taxed, and distinguishing free persons, including those bound to service for a term of years, from all others; distinguishing also the sexes and colours of free persons, and the free males of sixteen years and upwards from those under that age; for effecting which purpose the marshals shall have power to appoint as many assistants within their respective districts as to them shall appear necessary; assigning to each assistant a certain division of his district, which division shall consist of one or more counties, cities, towns, townships, hundreds or parishes, or of a territory plainly and distinctly bounded by water courses, mountains, or public roads. The marshals and their assistants shall respectively take an oath or affirmation, before some judge or justice of the peace, resident within their respective districts, previous to their entering on the discharge of the duties by this act required. The oath or affirmation of the marshal shall be, "I, A. B., Marshal of the district of ———, do solemnly swear (or affirm) that I will well and truly cause to be made a just and perfect enumeration and description of all persons resident within my district, and return the same to the President of the United States, agreeably to the directions of an act of Congress, intituled 'An act providing for the enumeration of the inhabitants of the United States,' according to the best of my ability." The oath or affirmation of an assistant shall be "I, A. B., do solemnly swear (or affirm) that I will make a just and perfect enumeration and description of all persons resident within the division assigned to me by the marshal of the district of ———, and make due return thereof to the said marshal, agreeably to the directions of an act of Congress, intituled 'An act providing for the enumeration of the inhabitants of the United States,' according to the best of my ability." The enumeration shall commence on the first Monday in August next, and shall close within nine calendar months thereafter. The several assistants shall, within the said nine months, transmit to the marshals by whom they shall be respectively appointed, accurate returns of all persons, except Indians not taxed, within their respective divisions, which returns shall be made in a schedule, distinguishing the several families by the names of their master, mistress, steward, overseer, or other principal person therein, in manner following, that is to say:

The number of persons within my division, consisting of ———, appears in a schedule hereto annexed, subscribed by me this ——— day of ———, 179–. A. B. *Assistant to the marshal of* ———.

Schedule of the whole number of persons within the division allotted to A. B.

Names of heads of families.	Free white males of 16 years and upwards, including heads of families.	Free white males under 16 years.	Free white females, including heads of families.	All other free persons.	Slaves.

SECTION 2. And be it further enacted, That every assistant failing to make return, or making a false return of the enumeration to the marshal, within the time by this act limited, shall forfeit the sum of two hundred dollars.

SECTION 3. And be it further enacted, That the marshals shall file the several returns aforesaid, with the clerks of their respective district courts, who are hereby directed to receive and carefully preserve the same: And the marshals respectively shall, on or before the first day of September, one thousand seven hundred and ninety-one, transmit to the President of the United States, the aggregate amount of each description of persons within their respective districts. And every marshal failing to file the returns of his assistants, or any of them, with the clerks of their respective district courts, or failing to return the aggregate amount of each description of persons in their respective districts, as the same shall appear from said returns, to the President of the United States within the time limited by this act, shall, for every such offense, forfeit the sum of eight hundred dollars; all which forfeitures shall be recoverable in the courts of the districts where the offenses shall be committed, or in the circuit courts to be held within the same, by action of debt, information or indictment; the one-half thereof to the use of the United States, and the other half to the informer; but where the prosecution shall be first instituted on the behalf of the United States, the whole shall accrue to their use. And for the more effectual discovery of offenses, the judges of the several district courts, at their next sessions, to be held after the expiration of the time allowed for making the returns of the enumeration hereby directed, to the President of the United States, shall give this act in charge to the grand juries, in their respective courts, and shall cause the returns of the several assistants to be laid before them for their inspection.

SECTION 4. And be it further enacted, That every assistant shall receive at the rate of one dollar for every one hundred and fifty persons by him returned, where such persons reside in the country; and where such persons reside in a city, or town, containing more than five thousand persons, such assistants shall receive at the rate of one dollar for every three hundred persons; but where, from the dispersed situation of the inhabitants in some divisions, one dollar for every one hundred and fifty persons shall be insufficient, the marshals, with the approbation of the judges of their respective districts, may make such further allowance to the assistants in such divisions as shall be deemed an adequate compensation, provided the same does not exceed one dollar for every fifty persons by them returned. The several marshals shall receive as follows: The marshal of the district of Maine, two hundred dollars; the marshal of the district of New Hampshire, two hundred dollars; the marshal of the district of Massachusetts, three hundred dollars; the marshal of the district of Connecticut, two hundred dollars; the marshal of the district of New York, three hundred dollars; the marshal of the district of New Jersey, two hundred dollars; the marshal of the district of Pennsylvania, three hundred dollars; the marshal of the district of Delaware, one hundred dollars; the marshal of the district of Maryland, three hundred dollars; the marshal of the district of Virginia, five hundred dollars; the marshal of the district of Kentucky, two hundred and fifty dollars; the marshal of the district of North Carolina, three hundred and fifty dollars; the marshal of the district of South Carolina, three hundred dollars; the marshal of the district of Georgia, two hundred and fifty dollars. And to obviate all doubts which may arise respecting the persons to be returned, and the manner of making the returns.

SECTION 5. Be it enacted, That every person whose usual place of abode shall be in any family on the aforesaid first Monday in August next, shall be returned as of such family; the name of every person, who shall be an inhabitant of any district, but without a settled place of residence, shall be inserted in the column of the aforesaid schedule, which is allotted for the heads of families, in that division where he or she shall be on the said first Monday in August next, and every person occasionally absent at the time of the enumeration, as belonging to that place in which he usually resides in the United States.

SECTION 6. And be it further enacted, That each and every person more than 16 years of age, whether heads of families or not, belonging to any family within any division of a district made or established within the United States, shall be, and hereby is, obliged to render to such assistant of the division, a true account, if required, to the best of his or her knowledge, of all and every person belonging to such family, respectively, according to the several descriptions aforesaid, on pain of forfeiting twenty dollars, to be sued for and recovered by such assistant, the one-half for his own use, and the other half for the use of the United States.

SECTION 7. And be it further enacted, That each assistant shall, previous to making his return to the marshal, cause a correct copy, signed by himself, of the schedule containing the number of inhabitants within his division, to be set up at two of the most public places within the same, there to remain for the inspection of all concerned; for each of which copies the said assistant shall be entitled to receive two dollars, provided proof of a copy of the schedule having been so set up and suffered to remain, shall be transmitted to the marshal, with the return of the number of persons; and in case any assistant shall fail to make such proof to the marshal, he shall forfeit the compensation by this act allowed him.

Approved March 1, 1790.

FIRST CENSUS OF THE UNITED STATES.

Population of the United States as returned at the First Census, by states: 1790.

DISTRICT.	Free white males of 16 years and upward, including heads of families.	Free white males under 16 years.	Free white females, including heads of families.	All other free persons.	Slaves.	Total.
Vermont	22,435	22,328	40,505	255	[1] 16	[2] 85,539
New Hampshire	36,086	34,851	70,160	630	158	141,885
Maine	24,384	24,748	46,870	538	None.	96,540
Massachusetts	95,453	87,289	190,582	5,463	None.	378,787
Rhode Island	16,019	15,799	32,652	3,407	948	68,825
Connecticut	60,523	54,403	117,448	2,808	2,764	237,946
New York	83,700	78,122	152,320	4,654	21,324	340,120
New Jersey	45,251	41,416	83,287	2,762	11,423	184,139
Pennsylvania	110,788	106,948	206,363	6,537	3,737	434,373
Delaware	11,783	12,143	22,384	3,899	8,887	[3] 59,094
Maryland	55,915	51,339	101,395	8,043	103,036	319,728
Virginia	110,936	116,135	215,046	12,866	292,627	747,610
Kentucky	15,154	17,057	28,922	114	12,430	73,677
North Carolina	69,988	77,506	140,710	4,975	100,572	393,751
South Carolina	35,576	37,722	66,880	1,801	107,094	249,073
Georgia	13,103	14,044	25,739	398	29,264	82,548
Total number of inhabitants of the United States exclusive of S. Western and N. territory	807,094	791,850	1,541,263	59,150	694,280	3,893,635

	Free white males of 21 years and upward.	Free males under 21 years of age.	Free white females.	All other persons.	Slaves.	Total.
S. W. territory	6,271	10,277	15,365	361	3,417	35,691
N. "						

[1] The census of 1790, published in 1791, reports 16 slaves in Vermont. Subsequently, and up to 1860, the number is given as 17. An examination of the original manuscript returns shows that there never were any slaves in Vermont. The original error occurred in preparing the results for publication, when 16 persons, returned as "Free colored," were classified as "Slave."

[2] Corrected figures are 85,425, or 114 less than figures published in 1790, due to an error of addition in the returns for each of the towns of Fairfield, Milton, Shelburne, and Williston, in the county of Chittenden; Brookfield, Newbury, Randolph, and Strafford, in the county of Orange; Castleton, Clarendon, Hubbardton, Poultney, Rutland, Shrewsbury, and Wallingford, in the county of Rutland; Dummerston, Guilford, Halifax, and Westminster, in the county of Windham; and Woodstock, in the county of Windsor.

[3] Corrected figures are 59,096, or 2 more than figures published in 1790, due to error in addition.

HEADS OF FAMILIES—MAINE.

Summary of population, by counties, towns, etc.: 1790.

CUMBERLAND COUNTY.

TOWN.	Number of families.	Free white males of 16 years and upward, including heads of families.	Free white males under 16 years.	Free white females, including heads of families.	All other free persons.	Total.	TOWN.	Number of families.	Free white males of 16 years and upward, including heads of families.	Free white males under 16 years.	Free white females, including heads of families.	All other free persons.	Total.
Bakerstown plantation	110	292	364	613	.....	1,269	Otisfield plantation	32	56	46	95	.....	197
Bridgton	60	100	81	147	1	329	Plantation No. 4	77	89	101	154	.....	344
Brunswick	197	355	328	660	14	1,357	Portland	366	564	537	1,123	16	2,240
Bucktown plantation	68	96	146	211	.....	453	Raymondtown plantation	52	81	92	170	3	346
Butterfield plantation	35	49	55	85	.....	189	Rusfield gore	20	22	30	50	.....	102
Cape Elizabeth	231	341	324	683	8	1,356	Scarborough (see Gorham and Scarborough)						
Durham	116	163	214	344	3	724	Shepardsfield plantation	83	126	140	261	1	528
Falmouth	446	648	814	1,504	28	2,994	Standish	123	183	186	346	1	716
Flintstown plantation	37	54	48	88	.....	190	Turner	57	87	104	158	.....	349
Freeport	230	322	342	654	2	1,320	Waterford plantation	36	55	32	73	.....	160
Gorham and Scarborough	786	1,108	1,134	2,186	47	4,475	Windham	152	228	265	444	1	938
Gray	290	148	139	290	.....	577							
Harpswell	217	253	268	539	11	1,071	Total	4,342	6,214	6,633	12,557	156	25,560
New Gloucester	207	320	338	694	6	1,358							
North Yarmouth	314	474	505	985	14	1,978							

HANCOCK COUNTY.

TOWN.	Number of families.	Free white males of 16 years and upward, including heads of families.	Free white males under 16 years.	Free white females, including heads of families.	All other free persons.	Total.	TOWN.	Number of families.	Free white males of 16 years and upward, including heads of families.	Free white males under 16 years.	Free white females, including heads of families.	All other free persons.	Total.
Barrettstown	53	61	44	68	.....	173	Orrington	86	114	128	234	1	477
Belfast	43	64	55	126	.....	245	Penobscot	189	249	251	542	6	1,048
Bluehill	55	69	79	125	1	274	Sedgwick	100	144	155	270	.....	569
Camden	69	93	85	153	.....	331	Small Islands not belonging to any town	18	19	17	30	.....	66
Canaan	27	34	39	59	.....	132	Sullivan	92	126	123	254	1	504
Conduskeeg plantation	103	145	170	249	3	567	Trenton (including township No. 1, east side of Union river)	54	75	92	144	1	312
Deer Isle	129	175	181	318	8	682	Township No. 1 (Bucks)	62	85	81	148	2	316
Ducktrap	53	78	82	118	.....	278	Township No. 6 (west side of Union river)	46	69	49	120	1	239
Eastern River township No. 2	54	59	63	118	.....	240	Vinalhaven	108	131	154	292	1	578
Eddy township	19	19	32	59	.....	110							
Frankfort	169	235	235	419	2	891	Total	1,796	2,436	2,531	4,544	38	9,549
Gouldsborough	45	78	64	116	9	267							
Isleborough	67	90	114	177	1	382							
Mount Desert	132	191	207	345	1	744							
Orphan Island	25	33	31	60	.....	124							

LINCOLN COUNTY.

TOWN.	Number of families.	Free white males of 16 years and upward, including heads of families.	Free white males under 16 years.	Free white females, including heads of families.	All other free persons.	Total.	TOWN.	Number of families.	Free white males of 16 years and upward, including heads of families.	Free white males under 16 years.	Free white females, including heads of families.	All other free persons.	Total.
Balltown	156	229	258	425	.....	912	Pittston	102	135	281	281	7	704
Bath	140	235	257	450	7	949	Pownalborough	330	535	535	969	4	2,043
Boothbay	164	247	248	499	3	997	Prescotts and Whitchers plantation	13	12	8	11	1	32
Bowdoin	203	237	264	468	15	984	Rockmeeko, east side of river	26	28	7	24	.....	59
Bowdoinham	73	109	127	218	1	455	Sandy river, first township	98	141	127	224	2	494
Bristol	75	115	143	257	1	516	Sandy river, from its mouth to Carrs plantation	67	77	96	160	1	334
Canaan	81	99	132	221	.....	452	Sandy river, middle township	14	17	15	33	.....	65
Carratunk	25	31	35	39	.....	105	Sandy river, upper township	10	18	17	24	.....	59
Carrs plantation, or Unity	27	32	33	62	.....	127	Seven Mile Brook	40	41	34	62	1	138
Chester plantation	15	24	19	27	.....	70	Smithtown plantation	109	142	126	240	1	509
Cushing	160	256	235	451	.....	942	Starling plantation	53	58	31	77	.....	166
Edgecomb	133	183	159	413	.....	755	Thomaston	139	207	209	379	4	799
Fairfield	98	122	114	222	.....	458	Titcomb	29	34	36	76	.....	146
Georgetown	206	345	322	655	11	1,333	Topsham	118	215	203	398	10	826
Great Pond plantation	30	43	52	69	.....	164	Twenty-five Mile Pond	30	33	27	59	.....	119
Greene	92	102	100	173	.....	375	Union	42	52	50	94	3	199
Hallowell	184	344	285	553	12	1,194	Vassalborough	197	301	317	624	11	1,253
Hancock	61	83	64	130	1	278	Waldoborough	269	429	454	821	13	1,717
Hunts Meadow	11	15	21	32	.....	68	Wales plantation	92	115	120	204	.....	439
Jones plantation	40	63	63	119	11	256	Warren	105	307	148	178	13	646
Lewistown and gore adjoining	73	127	145	260	.....	532	Washington	149	169	139	312	.....	620
Little River	13	17	15	32	.....	64	Winslow, with its adjacents	169	204	225	367	1	797
Littleborough plantation	58	71	69	127	7	274	Winthrop	252	304	329	591	2	1,226
Livermore, east side of Androscoggin river	11	15	8	21	.....	44	Woolwich	128	206	189	391	1	787
Meduncook	49	89	79	153	.....	321	Between Norridgewock and Seven Mile Brook	26	28	46	73	.....	147
New Castle	131	223	222	443	8	896							
New Sandwich	64	91	65	140	.....	296	Total	5,309	7,769	7,751	14,052	151	29,723
Nobleborough	234	312	347	544	3	1,206							
Norridgewock	83	91	89	152	1	333							
Norridgewock, settlement east of	11	11	12	20	.....	43							

WASHINGTON COUNTY.

TOWN.	Number of families.	Free white males of 16 years and upward, including heads of families.	Free white males under 16 years.	Free white females, including heads of families.	All other free persons.	Total.	TOWN.	Number of families.	Free white males of 16 years and upward, including heads of families.	Free white males under 16 years.	Free white females, including heads of families.	All other free persons.	Total.
Bucks Harbor Neck	12	14	18	29	.....	61	Plantations west of Machias—						
Machias	177	229	210	372	7	818	No. 4	40	71	59	103	.....	233
Plantations east of Machias—							No. 5	33	45	49	83	.....	177
No. 1	15	18	16	32	.....	66	No. 6	46	56	55	96	.....	207
No. 2	33	41	30	67	6	144	No. 11	16	22	24	49	.....	95
No. 4	11	16	13	25	.....	54	No. 12	3	4	1	3	.....	8
No. 5	14	24	26	34	.....	84	No. 13	48	51	61	105	6	223
No. 8	54	75	60	109	.....	244	No. 22	31	43	44	87	1	175
No. 9	7	9	7	14	.....	30							
No. 10	11	14	5	23	.....	42	Total	564	754	708	1,277	20	2,759
No. 11	7	8	10	19	.....	37							
No. 12	10	13	15	26	.....	54							
No. 13	1	1	5	1	.....	7							

Summary of population, by counties, towns, etc.: 1790—Continued.

YORK COUNTY.

TOWN.	Number of families.	Free white males of 16 years and upward, including heads of families.	Free white males under 16 years.	Free white females, including heads of families.	All other free persons.	Total.	TOWN.	Number of families.	Free white males of 16 years and upward, including heads of families.	Free white males under 16 years.	Free white females, including heads of families.	All other free persons.	Total.
Arundel	259	367	380	700	11	1,458	New Penacook	18	23	13	41		77
Berwick	665	983	922	1,947	42	3,894	Parsonsfield	132	174	169	311		654
Biddeford	169	273	235	504	6	1,018	Pepperellborough	229	342	358	650		1,350
Brownfield township	26	39	37	68	2	146	Porterfield	16	23	14	34		71
Brownfield township—in the gore adjoining	4	6	5	9		20	Sanford	316	450	473	876		1,799
Buxton	238	357	402	746	3	1,508	Shapleigh	227	310	371	630	9	1,320
Coxhall	106	165	229	371		765	Sudbury-Canada	60	82	89	153		324
Francisborough plantation	76	98	101	210		409	Sudbury, settlements adjoining	12	17	13	21		51
Fryeburgh	88	141	138	270	1	550	Suncook	16	22	25	36		83
Hiram	18	22	29	41		92	Washington plantation	58	72	51	138		261
Kittery	611	769	714	1,736	40	3,259	Waterborough	174	229	277	465		971
Lebanon	224	310	344	642		1,296	Waterford	31	45	35	74		154
Limerick	71	99	110	200		409	Wells	504	827	733	1,495	15	3,070
Little Falls	115	159	147	301		607	York	504	751	605	1,518	26	2,900
Little Ossipee	120	144	200	318		662	Total	5,087	7,299	7,219	14,505	155	29,178

Assistant marshals for the state: 1790.

DISTRICT.	NAME.
Cumberland county (part of)......................... Bridgton, Standish, and Turner towns; Bakerstown, Bucktown, Butterfield, Flintstown, No. 4, Shepardsfield, and Waterford plantations; and Rusfield gore.	None given.
Cumberland county (part of)......................... Brunswick, Durham, Freeport, Harpswell, and North Yarmouth towns.	Henry Dearborn.
Cumberland county (part of)......................... Cape Elizabeth, Falmouth, Gray, and New Gloucester towns.	William Hobby.
Cumberland county (part of)......................... Gorham and Scarborough towns.	Samuel Pierson.
Cumberland county (part of)......................... Windham town; and Otisfield and Raymondtown plantations.	David Barker.
Cumberland county (part of)......................... Portland town.	John Hobby.
Hancock county......................... Barrettstown, Belfast, Bluehill, Camden, Canaan, Deer Isle, Ducktrap, Frankfort, Gouldsborough, Isleborough, Mount Desert, Orrington, Penobscot, Sedgwick, Sullivan, Trenton (including township No. 1 east side of Union river), and Vinalhaven towns; Eastern river township No. 2, Eddy township, township No. 1 (Bucks), and township No. 6 (west side of Union river); Conduskeeg plantation; and Orphan Island, and small islands not belonging to any town.	David Howe.
Lincoln county (part of)......................... Balltown town and Great Pond plantation.	Stuart Hunt.
Lincoln county (part of)......................... Bath, Boothbay, Bowdoinham, Edgecomb, Georgetown, Hallowell, Hunts Meadow, New Castle, Pittston, Pownalborough, Topsham, and Woolwich towns.	Henry Dearborn (marshal).
Lincoln county (part of)......................... Bristol, Nobleborough, and Waldoborough towns.	John Polerezcky.
Lincoln county (part of)......................... Bowdoin, Canaan, Carratunk, Fairfield, Hancock, Lewistown and gore adjoining, Little River, Norridgewock, Seven Mile Brook, Twenty-five Mile Pond, and Winslow (with its adjacents) towns; Sandy river, first, Sandy river, from its mouth to Carrs plantation; Sandy river, middle, Sandy river, upper, and Titcomb townships; Carrs or Unity, Chester, and Prescotts and Whitchers plantations; and settlement east of Norridgewock; and between Norridgewock and Seven Mile Brook.	John Chandler.
Lincoln county (part of)......................... Cushing, Meduncook, Thomaston, Union, and Warren towns.	Thurston Whiting.
Lincoln county (part of)......................... Greene, Livermore (east side of Androscoggin river), New Sandwich, Rockmeeko (east side of river), Washington and Winthrop towns; and Littleborough, Smithtown, Starling, and Wales plantations.	Simon Dearborn.
Lincoln county (part of)......................... Vassalborough town and Jones plantation.	Samuel Grant.
Washington county......................... Bucks Harbor Neck, and Machias towns; plantations east of Machias, Nos. 1, 2, 4, 5, 8, 9, 10, 11, 12, and 13; and plantations west of Machias, Nos. 4, 5, 6, 11, 12, 13, and 22.	Jas Avery.
York county (part of)......................... Arundel, Biddeford, Little Falls, Little Ossipee, Wells, and York towns.	Henry Dearborn (marshal)
York county (part of)......................... Berwick, Lebanon, Limerick, Parsonsfield, and Shapleigh towns; and Francisborough, and Washington plantations.	Daniel Wood.
York county (part of)......................... Hiram, New Penacook, Porterfield, Sudbury-Canada, Suncook, and Waterford towns; Brownfield township, gore adjoining Brownfield, and settlements adjoining Sudbury.	Philip Page.
York county (part of)......................... Buxton town.	Peter Ayer.
York county (part of)......................... Coxhall, Sanford, and Waterborough towns.	Abraham Annis.
York county (part of)......................... Kittery town.	Jeremiah Leavitt.
York county (part of)......................... Pepperellborough town.	Humphrey Pike.
York county (part of)......................... Fryeburgh town.	None given.

HEADS OF FAMILIES—MAINE.

CUMBERLAND COUNTY.[1]

NAME OF HEAD OF FAMILY.	Free white males of 16 years and upward, including heads of families.	Free white males under 16 years.	Free white females, including heads of families.	All other free persons.	Slaves.
BAKERSTOWN PLANTATION.					
Davis, Zebulon	1	2	2		
Rollins, Stephen	1	4	6		
Nevins, John	1		6		
Bailey, Samuel	1		3		
Bailey, Edmund	2	2	5		
Dunn, Josiah	2	5	2		
Strout, Nehemiah	1	1	5		
Bray, Henry	1	3	4		
Wescot, Daniel	1	4	1		
Strout, Jacob	1	1	4		
Davis, Aaron	1	1	4		
Strout, Joshua	1		1		
Davis, Wm	1		3		
Davis, Moses	1		3		
Marble, Ebenezer	1	3	1		
Dunn, Joshua	1	3	2		
Camel, Elexander	1	2	2		
Mores, William	1	2	2		
Denning, Samuel	3		1		
Downing, Saml	1		2		
Griffin, John	1	3	2		
Wilcot, Solomon	1	4	3		
Morgan, Saml	1	4	4		
Yeaton, Saml	3	2	3		
Yeaton, Stephen	1		3		
Hagget, Moses	1	2	3		
Haskel, Wm	1	1	1		
Hodge, John	2	2	3		
Harves, Joseph	2		1		
Tucker, Job	2		1		
Brook, Mary			3		
Hall, Hezekiah	1	2	2		
Hall, Job	1	1	2		
Lane, Benjamin	1	3	4		
Richardson, Benjn	1	3	2		
Woodman, John	1	1	1		
Woodman, True	1	1	3		
Watson, John	1	3	3		
Harris, Wm	1	3	1		
Waterman, John	3	3	2		
Waterman, Robert	1	1	1		
Davis, Elias	1	5	4		
Allen, John	1	1	1		
Manwell, Samuel	2		4		
Washburn, Eliab	1	1	4		
Goff, James	1	2	2		
Eaton, Ziba	1	4	3		
King, Ichabod	1	2	1		
Bray, Ebenezer	3	1	1		
Hagget, Elijah	1	3	2		
Rines, Ambrose	4	4	7		
Cotton, Thomas	1	2	1		
Hammon, Bebia	1	2	1		
Coy, John	3	3	7		
Millet, David	1	5	6		
Clefford, Benjamin	2	3	5		
Millet, John	1	3	6		
Roe, John	1	2	3		
Roe, Benjn	1		1		
Harris, Amos	1	3	6		
Densmore, David	1	3	6		
Bradbury, Benjn	1	3	5		
Safford, Stephen	1	3	3		
Bryant, Baldwin	1		2		
Parker, James	1	2	4		
Chickering, Zechariah	1	3	7		
Fisher, Elijah	1	1	4		
Briggs, Rufus	1		4		
Briggs, Danl	2	2	1		
Safford, Moses	1	1	1		
Castle, Simeon	1	1	3		
Hood, David	1	1	2		
Holmes, Gershom	1		3		
True, William	1		2		
Dillingham, John	1		5		
Allen, Abel	1	3	1		
Dillingham, Jeremiah	1		3		
Pilley, John	1		2		
Leavit, Jacob	1	2	1		
Bowen, Saml	1	1	2		
Staples, John	1				
Haskel, Israel	1		1		
Castle, Wm	1	2	3		
Andrews, Perez	1	1	2		
Castle, Squire	1		2		
Bray, Nicholas	1	3	5		
Perry, Dimon	2	2	3		
Castle, Job	1	2	2		
Simmons, Joel	1	1	1		
Sampson, Seth	1		2		
Varrel, Jeremiah	1		1		
Bradbury, Moses	2	3	3		
BAKERSTOWN PLANTATION—continued.					
Allen, Isaac	1	1	4		
Harlow, Ebenezer	5	3	1		
Bradbury, Joseph	1	1	2		
Allen, Joshua	1	2	2		
Merrill, Giles	1	2	2		
Pecker, Nehemiah	1	1	3		
Dwinell, Amos	4	1	3		
Dwinell, Jacob	2	2	3		
Chipman, Wm	1	2	1		
Dwinell, Aaron	1		4		
Waterman, Joseph	1	2	5		
Waterman, Noah	1	2	2		
Hawk, Edward	1	3	4		
Buckman, Danl	1	2	2		
House, Moses	2	2	4		
Brigham, Joseph	1	1	1		
Brigham, Willard	1		2		
Brigham, John, Jr	1	3	2		
Brigham, John	3		2		
Chandler, Reuben	1	1			
Chandler, Ichabod	1	2	2		
Chandler, Nathl	1	3	3		
Freeman, Joseph	1	1	2		
Freeman, Chandler	1	2	2		
Bradford, Peabody	1	1	2		
Bradford, Jonathan	1		2		
Austin, George		1	2		
Crooker, Joshua	1	2	4		
Crooker, Isaac	1	1	2		
Gardiner, John	1	1	1		
Benson, Caleb	1	1	7		
Noyes, Nicholas	1	1	1		
Hassa, Noah	1	2	2		
Hassa, James	1	3	2		
Beals, Benjamin	1	2	2		
Hapa, Amos	1		2		
Jackson, Henry	1	3	3		
Gurney, Thos	1	4	3		
Gurney, Jona	1	3	2		
Bates, Jacob	1	2	3		
Poole, Samuel	1	1	1		
Poole, Joshua	1	2	2		
Noyes, Bella	1	3	3		
Davis, Allen	1		3		
Willis, James	1	1	3		
Nash, Jona	1	2	5		
Chandler, John, Jr	1	1	4		
Chandler, John	1		2		
Lander, Edmund	1		2		
Seabury, Paul	5		3		
Davis, Zebulon, Jr	1	3	3		
Fuller, Jesse	1	4	4		
Chubb, Jabez	2		1		
Downing, John	1	1	2		
Sottel, Nathl	3	1	2		
Wilcom, Michael	1	3	5		
Elwell, Wm	1	2	2		
Varrell, Saml	1	1	3		
Varrel, Saml, Jur	1	3	2		
Varrel, Davis	1	3	3		
Varrel, Wm	1	1	2		
Prince, John	1	2	2		
Hodgkins, Ebenezer	1	2	3		
Hodgkins, Joseph	1	1	1		
Hodgkins, James	1		1		
Jumper, Edward	1	4	3		
Hill, James	2	1	2		
Leach, Joseph	1		2		
Shaw, Saml	1	3	3		
Shaw, Levi	1		1		
Sottle, Henry	2				
Leach, John	1	2	3		
Bray, Israel	1	4	2		
Herrick, John	1	4	2		
Hodgkins, James, Jur	1	2	4		
Cordwell, Wm	1	2	5		
Jumper, Danl	1	2	2		
Varrel, Joseph	1		1		
Tod, John	1		1		
Richardson, Elijah	1	1	2		
Pettingall, Saml	1	2	3		
Emmory, Moses	1	3	3		
Bailey, Thos	3	3	3		
Emmerson, Saml	2		2		
Coombs, Benjn	1	4	2		
Nason, John	1	5	3		
Stevens, Jacob	1	1	3		
Libby, James	1		3		
Starboard, Samuel	1	3	3		
Small, David	3		1		
Holmes, Gresham	2	2	2		
Jackson, Danl	1	3	2		
BAKERSTOWN PLANTATION—continued.					
Merrill, Edmund	7	4	13		
Varrel, Richard, Jur	1	2	2		
Varrel, Richard	2	3	3		
Wilson, Gonen	4	2	7		
Allen, Wm	1	4	4		
Proctor, Wm	1	1	4		
Pote, Saml	1		3		
Pote, Thos	1		1		
Merrill, Nathan	2	3	10		
Merrill, James	2	1	4		
Chipman, Benjn	1	2	3		
Chipman, Daniel	1		2		
Stinchfield, Josiah	1	3	2		
Martin, Ezekiel	1	1	1		
Hodgdon, Moses	1	2	1		
Parsons, Eleazer	1		3		
Varney, Ichabod	1	1	4		
Holmes, Joslah	3	3	4		
Thurrill, Davis	1	2	3		
Jordan, Saml	1	2	6		
Ring, Eliphus	5	3	9		
Holmes, Simeon	2	1	6		
Thurrill, Asaph	1	1	2		
Briggs, Ephraim	4	2	6		
Briggs, Barnabas	3	3	4		
Farnall, John	1	1	1		
Haskell, Wm	1	3	5		
Parsons, Edward	1	5	3		
Elly, Saml	2	1	2		
Worcester, John	1	1	1		
Tripp, Richard	1		3		
Saunders, Jona	1	3	3		
Shillings, Daniel	1	3	3		
BRIDGTON TOWN.					
Kibbon, John	1	3	2		
Clough, Josiah	1	3	1		
Yates, Timothy	1	3	4		
Sandbourn, John	1	2	1		
Emerson, Theodore	2	2	3		
Jewet, Ephraim	2	2	6		
Gibbs, Alpheus	1		1		
Farnsworth, Saml	2				
Knap, Jesse	3		4		
Church, Nathan	2	1	2		
Stevens, Jacob	3	3	6		
Kimball, Saml	1		4		
Kimball, Richard	1	1	4		
Barnam, Simeon	3		3		
Oliver, Wm	3		1		
Porter, David	3	2	3		
Stevens, Jacob, Jr	3		3		
Flint, James	1	3	3		
Keresland, Abraham	1		1		
Broadstreet, David	2		1		
Johnson, Isaac	3	1	3		
Perley, Enoch	3	2	3	1	
Peabody, John	1	3	3		
Howe, Moses	1		2		
Andrews, Robert	1		2		
Ingalls, Nathan	1	5	2		
Hale, David	1	2	3		
Ingalls, Asa	1		2		
Perley, Danl	1		4		
Bernard, Danl	1	1	2		
Hale, Nathl	1	1	4		
Ingalls, Isaih	1	4	2		
Ingalls, Phineas	1	3	1		
Mead, George	1		2		
Foster, Asael	3	3	4		
Chaplin, John	1	4	1		
Simons, Thos	2		1		
Simon, Francis	2	1	1		
Ingalls, Francis	1	2	2		
Burnam, Jeremiah	1	2	2		
Howe, Danl	1	1	1		
Brockelbank, Joseph	1		2		
Kimball, Benjn, Jur	1	2	2		
Styles, Enoch	1	1	4		
Styles, Noah	2		2		
Gates, Stephen	2	4	3		
Brigham, Daniel	2		2		
Gibbs, Ezra	1	1	2		
Porter, David	2		2		
Styles, Ezra	1		2		
Lowel, Thos	3	1	2		
Emerson, Wm	4	1	3		
Morrison, David	2	2	5		
Clark, David	1		2		
Kimball, Asa	4		3		

[1] No attempt has been made in this publication to correct mistakes in spelling made by the deputy marshals, but the names have been reproduced as they appear upon the census schedules.

FIRST CENSUS OF THE UNITED STATES.

CUMBERLAND COUNTY—Continued.

NAME OF HEAD OF FAMILY.	Free white males of 16 years and upward, including heads of families.	Free white males under 16 years.	Free white females, including heads of families.	All other free persons.	Slaves.
BRIDGTON TOWN—continued.					
Kimball, Asa, Jnr	1		1		
Davenport, Abner	1	1	1		
Davenport, John	2		1		
Beaman, Aaron	1		1		
Kimball, Benja	2		1		
BRUNSWICK TOWN.					
Stanwood, Willm, Junr	2	3	4		
Minot, John	2	2	5		
Kennady, Patrick	2	2	4		
Scofield, Thomas	2	5	4		
Grafton, Ephraim	3	2	5	3	
Miller, Margaret	2	2	4		
Simpson, Lewis	1	2	5		
Stanwood, Willm	5	2	7		
Simpson, Josiah	3	1	3		
Clark, Nathan	1		5		
Clark, David	1	1	3		
Hugh, Saml	2	1	8		
Givens, Daniel	2	1	7		
Pennel, Thos	1	5	6		
Givens, Robert	2	2	3		
Givens, John, Junr	1		4		
Givens, John	2		2		
Moseley, Willm	1	1	5		
Scofield, Joseph	5		2		
Spear, Robert	3	1	6		
Jordan, Robert	2	2	4		
Simons, John	2		4		
Cotton, Willm	3	3	4		
Ferren, John	1		2		
Ferren, John, Junr	1	2	4		
Doughty, Willm	1		2		
Gitchel, John	1		4		
Pennel, John	1		5		
Marriner, Saml	1		1	3	
Woodward, Saml	2	5	4		
Ferren, Richd	1	1	1		
Danforth, Willm	1	1	1		
Gitchel, Saml	3	3	4		
Gitchel, Stephen	2	1	3		
Wallace, John	1	1	6		
Gitchel, Willm	2	1	4		
Gitchel, Stephen, Junr	2	1	1		
Gitchel, Willm, Junr	2		2		
Marriner, John	1	1	2		
Merriner, John, Jur	1	2	1		
Winslow, George	1	2	3		
Mariner, Willm	1	3	1		
Cooms, Nathan	1	1	3		
Woodward, Peter	1	2	5		
Cooms, Asa	1	2	2		
Cooms, Peter	1	1	2		
Stickney, Bailey	1	2	2		
Snow, Joseph	2		3		
Thomas, Concider	1	5	4		
Thomas, Charles	2	2	5		
Jordan, Peter	1	3	3		
Cowen, Charles	2	4	5		
Cooms, Thomas	1		2		
Cooms, Caleb	1	1	4		
Gross, Saml	2	2	4		
Lewis, Thos	1	1	1		
Snow, Isaac	4	4	6		
Cooms, Joseph	1	2	4		
Hunniford, David	1	1	3		
Godfrey, Thomas	1	2	5		
Laraba, Benja	4	3	4		
Melcher, Saml	2	2	7		
Peterson, John	25	4	5		
Hinkley, Aaron	3		2		
Dwinnels, John	1	3	3		
Heyden, George	2		4		
Michaels, James	1		3		
Friend, John	1	2	3	7	
Andrews, John	2	2	4	3	
Blackmore, Joseph	1		3		
Cox, Artemas	1	1	2		
Cowen, Betsy		2	3		
Cox, Ely	1	1	2		
Bates, Mercy			2		
Laraba, Nathl	3	1	2	1	
Harden, Hezekiah	2	3	4		
Cornish, John	1	1	3		
Harden, Saml	1	5	2		
Curtes, James	3	2	4		
Hinkley, Edmund	4	1	3		
Weston, Jacob	2	4	3		
Sprague, Nathl	3	2	5		
Gray, Grace	1		2		
Ham, Joseph	1	2	5		
Ham, Tobias	2	3	6		
Keith, Cornelius	1	2	2		
Crafford, James	1	4	6		
BRUNSWICK TOWN—continued.					
Bates, Hozea	2	3	6		
Thomson, Alexander	1	2	4		
Baker, Elisha	1		3		
Doughty, Daniel	2	4	3		
Thompson, Cornelius	1		1		
Thompson, Robert	2	1	5		
Lowe, Willm	2	2	4		
Latherby, Stephen	1	2	3		
Brown, Ezekiel	1	4	3		
Crowel, Thomas	1	1	2		
Ward, Nehemiah	1	2	1		
Story, John	1				
Hinkley, Ruth		3	1		
Cook, Stephen	2	1	2		
Mitchel, Willm	1	1	1		
Marten, Thomas	1	1	2		
Clark, Archibald	1	2	3		
Ross, Eliphalet	2	2	3		
Stanwood, Ebenezer	3	1	6		
Sullivan, Amos	1		2		
Weymouth, Timo	1		1		
Thomas, Lewis	1	3	2		
French, Willm	1				
Hunt, Mary			2		
Lowel, Paul	1	2	4		
Dunning, David	1	2	4		
Hunt, Ephraim	1	4	4		
Dunning, Robert	2	1	4		
Chase, Judah	5	1	5		
Stanwood, Robert	2	3	5	4	
Goss, Ebenezer H	2	4	6		
Starboard, Willm	1		2	5	
Dunning, Andw	5	2	7		
Woodside, Anthony	4	1	3		
Chase, James	1	2	3		
Woodside, Willm	3		4		
Dunning, Willm	1	4	5		
Swett, John	2	2	4		
Morse, Joseph	2	3	7		
Melcher, Joseph	5	2	4		
Woodside, Vincent	4		6		
Chase, Benja	3	1	4		
Ross, Willm	1	3	6		
Elliot, James	4	2	6		
Anderson, Jacob	1	2	6		
Woodside, Willm, Junr	1	1	6		
Hunt, Saml	1	1	4		
Kincaid, Peter	2	2	5		
Linscut, David	1	1	1		
Ross, Joseph	1	1	1		
Gross, Mich1, Junr	1	3	2		
Toothaker, Abraham	1	3	4		
Stanwood, Saml	1	4	7		
Eaton, Daniel	2		2		
Ryan, Charles	1	2	2		
Dunning, Andrew	2	1	8	1	
Dunning, John	1	4	4		
Dunning, David	1		2		
Stanwood, Willm	4	3	6		
Stone, Benjs	4	1	2	1	
Lunt, Amos	5	1	3		
Cary, James	2	1	2		
Hunt, Daniel	1	1	3		
Gorden, James	1	1			
Nunan, John	1		4		
Hobbs, Obed	1	1	4		
Thompson, Thomas	3		4		
Cotton, Thomas	2		3		
Dunlap, John	1	1	4		
Morse, Anthony	1	1	4		
Crips, John	3	2	5		
Dunlap, John	2	4	4		
Brooks, ——	1				
Gross, Michael	1	4	5		
Gross, Jacob	1	1	1		
Gross, George	1	1	1		
Melcher, Noah	2		1		
Merriman, Thomas	1	2	1		
Chase, John	1	3	2		
Morse, Paul	1	2	2		
Burrel, Humphry	1	2	3		
Philbrick, George	1	2	5		
Rogers, Josiah	2	4	1		
Pierce, ——	1		5		
Spaulding, Saml	1	1	2		
Dana, Gardiner	1		2		
Jones, Edward	1	2	2		
Hacker, Jereh, Jun	1	1	4		
Hacker, Jereh	2		4	1	
Jones, Lemuel	3	1	2		
Jones, Caleb	1	4	4		
Owens, Willm	4	2	6	1	
House, Gershom	2	3	2		
Eaton, Saml	2	3	2		
Eaton, Daniel	2		1		
BRUNSWICK TOWN—continued.					
Danforth, Abner	1	2	1	8	
Willee, Edward	1	2	1		
Hogan, Mich1	1		5		
Higgins, Willm	1	2	2		
Orr, Richard	1	2	2		
McMahan, Daniel	3	2	1		
Mallet, John	1	3	2		
Toothaker, Roger	1	4	4		
Toothaker, Gideon	1	4	3		
Owens, Philip	3	2	4		
Dunlap, Hugh	1	2	3		
Dunlap, Saml	1	3	6		
Flahartha, Daniel O	1		2		
Spark, David	1		2		
Eaton, Moses	1	2	2		
BUCKTOWN PLANTATION.					
Hodgdon, Jeremiah	2	1	2		
Smith, Israel	1	2	1		
Rich, Joel	1	3	4		
Gammon, Nathl	1	3	3		
Roberts, Joseph	2		3		
Irish, John, Jur	1	1	6		
Irish, John	1	1	2		
Parsons, Phillemon	1	3	3		
Lowel, Thos	1		2		
Sweet, John	1	2	1		
Thurlo, John	1	5	2		
Coburn, Jonas	1	3	4		
Matthews, Volatiah	1	1	1		
Lowel, Willm	1	1	1		
Mathews, John	1	4	4		
Teague, Benj	1	2	3		
Crooker, Lemuel	1	2	6		
Young, Joshua	1		1		
Irish, Joseph	2	1	3		
Doble, Willm	2	4	4		
Records, Simon	1	4	4		
Records, David	1	3	2		
Irish, Thos	2	3	3		
Coburns, Thos	1	1	4		
Records, Jona	1	2	2		
Warren, David	1		3		
Spaulding, Benjn, Jr	1		1		
Lowel, Stephen	1		1		
Packer, Danl	1	2	5		
Packer, Job	1	3	1		
Taylor, Samuel	3		1		
Buck, Abijah	1	2	3		
Foster, Joel	1		1		
Tilson, Josiah	1	1	2		
Josselin, Thos	1	2	2		
Warren, John	1	3	3		
Hathway, Ichabod	1	1	1		
Mayhew, James	1	2	2		
Warren, Tristram	1	3	2		
Buck, John, Jur	1		1		
Farron, David	1	4	3		
Buck, Nathl	2	3	5		
Allen, Thos	1	3	4		
Brown, John	1		1		
Elliot, John	1		1		
Smith, Seabury	1	1	1		
Stevens, Moses	1	1	1		
Harlon, Andrew	1	2	3		
Davis, Joshua	1		1		
Damon, Jona	1		1		
Broch, John	1		1		
Clay, John	1		1		
Hussey, John	1		1		
Irish, Ebenezer	1	1	1		
Spaulding, Benjn, Senior	1	3	4		
Buck, John	1	2	6		
Berry, Willm	1	3	5		
Filbrick, Jonathan	1	2	4		
Foster, Isaac	1	2	3		
Records, Dominicus	1	2	3		
Chandler, Edmund	1	2	5		
Davis, Gershom	1	2	4		
Spaulding, Benj, second	2	2	3		
Ricker, Abias	1	2	2		
Wescot, Joshua	1	2	4		
Forbes, Jonah	1	3	3		
Hall, Enoch	1	2	2		
Smith, Nathl	1	1	3		
Young, Cabel	1	1	1		
Shaw, Jotham	1		1		
Roberts, Jonathan	1	1	1		
Jordan, James	1	3	3		
Leathers, Enoch	1	1	1		
Roberts, Joseph, Jur	1	3	5		
Brown, Amos	1	4	3		

HEADS OF FAMILIES—MAINE.

CUMBERLAND COUNTY—Continued.

NAME OF HEAD OF FAMILY.	Free white males of 16 years and upward, including heads of families.	Free white males under 16 years.	Free white females, including heads of families.	All other free persons.	Slaves.
BUCKTOWN PLANTATION—con.					
Chase, Joseph	2		3		
Chase, Nathl	1	1	2		
Tilly, Wllm	4		2		
Taylor, Saml, Jr	1	2	2		
Crocket, Danl	1	2	2		
Roberts, Joseph	1	1	3		
Whitman, Jacob	1	6	1		
BUTTERFIELD PLANTATION.					
Cummins, Oliver	1	1	2		
Ford, Joshua	1	1	3		
Fletcher, Thos	1		2		
Bisby, Moses	1		2		
Fletcher, John	1		2		
Parlin, Saml	1	1	2		
Briggs, John	1	2	3		
Sturdivant, David	1	3	1		
Sturdivant, Isaac	1	1			
Robinson, Increase	3		3		
Robinson, Asa	1		3		
Jennings, Eliphalet	1	1	1		
Jennings, Benjn	1		2		
Heffords, Wllm	1	1	2		
Allen, Seth	1	1	1		
Beasse, Wllm	1		2		
Doane, Ebenezer	1	1	1		
Bisby, Charles	5		1		
Oldham, Danl	1	5	7		
Cane, Lemuel	1		2		
Ford, Charles	1	2	2		
Bonney, Isaac	1	3	3		
Tucker, Wllm	1		3		
Bisby, Elisha	1	2	4		
Bosworth, Noah	4	2	1		
Robinson, Joseph	2		4		
Cane, Mesheck	1	1	4		
Cane, James	1	3	2		
Stetson, Hezekiah	1	5	2		
Hale, Benjn	1	1	3		
Crocke, John	5	5	3		
Hall, Enoch	1	2	2		
Buck, Moses	1	4	2		
Barret, Simeon	1	4	4		
Cane, John	1	2	3		
CAPE ELIZABETH TOWN.					
Dyer, Nathaniel	2	2	6		
Sawyer, Ebenezer	2	2	5		
Dyer, Micael	2	1	4		
Smally, Edward	1		1		
Roberts, Mary			2		
Dyer, Benjamin		1	5		
Dyer, Abigail		1	1		
Ray, William	1	1	1		
Simonton, Ebenezer	1	5	2		
Dyer, Joshua	1	3	7		
Randal, Stephen	1	1	2		
Dyer, Caleb	1	3	4		
Amory, John	2	3	4		
Sawyer, Joseph	1				
Ryon, John	1		3		
Sawyer, Jacob	1		1		
Mariner, Moses	1	1	6		
Woodberry, Israel	1	3	5		
York, Jacob	1		1		
Alden, Elisabeth	2		3		
Lovett, James	1	1	1		
Webb, Sarah	2		3		
Pilsbery, Hannah		2	1		
McCaning, Elisabeth			2		
Woodberry, Peeter	1	1	2		
Hatch, Ezekiel	1		4		
Hoole, William	2	3	3		
Simonton, Thomas	1	3	2		
Thompson, Robert	1		1		
Robinson, Samuel	1	3	2		
Simonton, Mary	2		3		
Thrasher, Benjamin	1		2		
Thrasher, Ebenezer	3	1	3		
Wallace, Jonah	1		2		
Webster, John	1	2	2		
Stout, Nathaniel	3	3	4		
Delano, Bezilla	5	1	4		
Richards, Humphrey	1	1	2		
Jorden, Samuel	1	4	3		
Richards, John	1		1		
Webster, James	1				
Robertson, Samuel	1	1	2		
Robertson, Joshua	2	3	4		
Miller, James	2	3	5		
Miller, Hugh	1		1		
Miller, David	1		2		

NAME OF HEAD OF FAMILY.	Free white males of 16 years and upward, including heads of families.	Free white males under 16 years.	Free white females, including heads of families.	All other free persons.	Slaves.
CAPE ELIZABETH TOWN—continued.					
Miller, Joshua	1	1	1		
Maxwell, James	2		2		
Marrs, John	3	3	4		
Jorden, Secomb	1	1	2		
Jorden, Noah	1		2		
Jorden, Noah	1	1	2		
Jorden, Rachel	1		2		
Jorden, Benjamin	3	2	6		
Johnston, Samuel	1	2	4		
Trundy, George	3	1	3		
Clark, Robert	2	3	3		
Davis, Simeon	1	1	3		
Abbot, James	1		2		
Atwood, Stephen	1	2	2		
Leach, James	3	1	3		
Wheeler, John	1	3	9		
Dyer, James	3	6	1		
Staples, Nathaniel	2	1	2		
McKenny, Jonathan	1	2	4		
Maxwell, James	2	1	3		
Irish, Partrick	2	1	4		
McCreat, William	1		2		
Crowley, Jeremiah	2	2	3		
Wallace, John	1	1	2		
Simonton, Thomas	1		2		
Davis, Daniel	1		4		
York, John	2		1		
Sawyer, Peeter	2	4	3		
Sawyer, Reubin	1		1		
Small, Timothy	1	2	3		
Allen, David	1	1	2		
Dyer, Paul	1	1	2		
Sawyer, Daniel	1		2		
Dyer, Ephraim	4	1	3		
Dyer, Isaac	1	2	4		
Dyer, Henry	2	3	5		
Parker, Ebenezer	1		7		
Thorndike, Ebenezer	3		2		
Jorden, Samuel	1	4	3		
Simonton, London				2	
Flint, Thomas	1	2	2		
Davis, Christopher	1		2		
Willard, Jesse	1	2	3		
Simonton, Andrew	3	2	2		
Simonton, Matthew	1	1	5		
Thorndike, Christian			3		
Clarke, Ephraim	3	1	6		
Deakes, George	1	2	6		
Welch, James	1	2	1		
Cobb, Joseph	1	1	3		
Webster, James	2	3	4		
Richards, Bezilla	1	1	4		
Armstrong, John	1	2	4		
Small, Elisha	1	3	4		
Crockett, Samuel	1		2		
Dyer, Samuel	1	3	6		
Stout, George	1		4		
Stout, Levi	1	1	2		
Bowa, George	1	6	2		
Stout, Eleazer	1	2	2		
Stout, Eleazer	1		5		
Cash, Nathaniel	1	2	2		
Stout, George	2		2		
Stout, Levi	2	2	2		
Brown, Jacob	3	2	5		
Cash, Samuel	1	2	3		
Elder, George	2	1	2		
Elder, Ellis	1		2		
Elder, John	1		2		
Elder, Joshua	1	2	1		
Babb, James	2		2		
Gent, Ephraim	1		1		
Hayes, George	1		2		
Weston, Beniah	1	2	8		
Dyer, Hannah		4	4		
Roberts, Hannah	1	2	2		
Dyer, Isaac	1		2		
Friket, Benjamin	3		3		
Dyer, Samuel	2	2	4		
Turner, James	1		2		
Douglis, Archbald	1		2		
Friket, John	3		4		
Friket, William		3	2		
Baley, William	3	2	5		
Leatherby, Jonathan	2	5	4		
Frikit, John	1	3	4		
Stanford, Benjamin	1	2	4		
Friket, Nathaniel	1	2	4		
Higgins, Massy	4	1	4		
Dyer, William	1		3		
Gammon, William	2		3		
Calif, Samuel	4	2	1	1	
Wuman, Volentine	1		2		
Jorden, Nathaniel	2	2	4	1	
Jorden, Ezekiel	1	4	5		

NAME OF HEAD OF FAMILY.	Free white males of 16 years and upward, including heads of families.	Free white males under 16 years.	Free white females, including heads of families.	All other free persons.	Slaves.
CAPE ELIZABETH TOWN—continued.					
Jorden, Trustim	2	1	3		
Bucks, Abraham	1		1		
Jorden, John	1	1	3		
Jorden, Abraham	1	1	3		
Jorden, Isaac	1	2	3		
Barnsbotom, James	1		1		
Dyer, Robert	1	2	6		
Robertson, John	1	1	3		
Woodberry, John	2	1	6		
Plummer, Robert	1		1		
Hatch, John	1	2	1		
Roberts, Ephraim	2	5	2		
York, Joseph	1	1	2		
Woodberry, Lucy		1	2		
Sawyer, Mary	2		4		
Stanford, Abigail			3		
Cushing, John		1	1		
Thomas, Abigail	1	2	3		
Stout, David	1		2		
Blake, John	1	1	1		
Stanford, Christopher	1		2		
Surline, John	1	1	2		
Mayew, Whitewood	2	1	2		
Sawyer, Jonathan	1	7	3		
Cushing, Abigail		1	1		
Stanford, Joseph	1		1		
Stanford, Sarah	1		5		
Stanford, John	2	3	1		
Sawyer, Jeremiah	1		2		
Mariner, Joseph	1	4	2		
Mariner, John	1	4	4		
Bryant, Abraham	1		2		
Westcot, Josiah	1	3	3		
Millet, Elisha	2	1	2		
Plummer, Jesse	1	5	2		
Crocket, Richard	1	1	5		
Doane, Edward	4		4		
Shillings, John	1	2	3		
Shillings, Samuel	2		4		3
Shillings, Joseph	1	4	3		
York, Samuel	1		1		
Doane, Ebenezer	1	1	1		
Shillings, Nehemiah	1		1		
Westcot, Samuel	1	1	4		
Libby, Jotham	1	2	4		
Dunn, Enoch	2	1	3		
Trickey, Zebulon	3		4		
Jackson, Thomas	1	1	2		
Bigford, Joshua	1		1		
Nason, Uriah	3	2	4		
Thombs, Benjamin	1		1		
Shillings, Samuel	5	6	7		
Shillings, Simeon	2	3	6		
Cummings, Thomas	1	1	2		
Shillings, Josiah	2		3		
Pratt, Zenas	4	3	3		
McKenny, Eleazer	1	3	3		
Fogg, John	1	2	1		
Jorden, Richard	1		1		
Jorden, Solomon	1	2	4		
Jorden, Stephen	1	3	5		
Jorden, Jonathan	3	1	5		
Jorden, Elisha	1		4		
Beal, Ebenezer	1	1	2		
Maxwell, Thomas	4	2	4		
Maxwell, William	1	2	6		
Maxwell, Joseph	3	3	5		
Dingly, William	1	2	7		
Jorden, Joshua	4		2	1	
Jorden, Dominicus	3	2	2		
Jorden, Jeremiah	2	1	2		
Cushing, Loring	1	1	4		
Jorden, Nathaniel	1		4		
Dyer, Jabes	2		2		
Mitchell, Jonathan	2	1	7		
Small, Edward	2	4	5		
Jorden, Jeremiah	2	2	2		
Clarkes, John R	2	2	4		
Pollock, Deliverance	1		5		
Welch, Mary		2	5		
Jorden, Elisha	2		3		
Hunscom, Moses	3		2		
Jorden, Nathaniel	1		4		
Jorden, Timothy	1		2		
Robertson, Joshua	3	2	6		
Maxwell, Patrick	2	4	1		
Jorden, Thomas	1		2		
Jorden, Samuel	3	1	5		
Jorden, John	1	3	5		
Avery, Jane	1		2		
DURHAM TOWN.					
Goodwin, Saml	3	2	1		
Adams, Andw	1	1	5		

FIRST CENSUS OF THE UNITED STATES.

CUMBERLAND COUNTY—Continued.

NAME OF HEAD OF FAMILY.	Free white males of 16 years and upward, including heads of families.	Free white males under 16 years.	Free white females, including heads of families.	All other free persons.	Slaves.	NAME OF HEAD OF FAMILY.	Free white males of 16 years and upward, including heads of families.	Free white males under 16 years.	Free white females, including heads of families.	All other free persons.	Slaves.	NAME OF HEAD OF FAMILY.	Free white males of 16 years and upward, including heads of families.	Free white males under 16 years.	Free white females, including heads of families.	All other free persons.	Slaves.
DURHAM TOWN—con.						**DURHAM TOWN—con.**						**FALMOUTH TOWN—con.**					
Cushing, John	2	3	3			Duglas, Cornelius	1	2	3			Rand, Lazarus	1	3	4		
Neal (Widow)			2			Jones, Noah	1	2	3			Small, Zachariah	1		3		
Bavage, James	1	1	2			Mitchel, Thomas	1	1	1			Small, John	2	2	3		
Wag, John	1	2	2			Pinkham, Andw	1	3	6			Haskell, Thomas	1	2	3		
Studson, Elisha	2	1	3			Esthers, Edward	1	1	2			Swett, Israel	1	1	3		
Lewis, Nathan	1	1	2			Gitchel, Hugh	1	4	3			Partridge, David	2	2	3		
Lincoln, John	1	4	2			Dudley, Micajah	1	3	7			Grant, James	2	2	5		
Gerrish, Charles	1		2			Duglas, Joseph	1	2	4			Farthingham, John	1		1		
Gerrish, George	1	3	2			Fisher, Thomas	3		4			Elder, John	1	2	3		
Pearson, Thomas	2		2			Crossman, Solomon	1	2	2	1		Cobb, Peeter	1	2	4		
Webb, Saml	1	2	1			Welch, Patrick	3		1			Cobb, Joseph	1	5	3		
Warren, Pelatiah	1	3	4			Esthers, Joseph	1		2			Small, Jeremiah	1	4	1		
Studson, Elijah	1	1				Esthers, Caleb	2	5	5			Bracket, John	1	2	2		
Jones, Ezekiel	2		2			Varney, Nicholas	4	3	4			Huntriss, Pearson	1	2	3		
Duran, Matthew	2	4	3			Tuttle, Reuben	3	1	4			Thombs, Benjamin	1	6	3		
Roberts, Ebenezer	2	4	2			Collins, Saml	3	1	9			Baley, Benjamin	3	4	6		
Sanborn, Simeon	1	1	3			Clough, Saml	2	2	6			Riggs, Enoch	1	3	4		
Snow, Joshua	1	2	2			Ring, Batcheldor	2	3	3			Riggs, Joseph	1		4		
Bagley, Enoch	1	2	1									Riggs, Jeremiah	1		3		
Bagley, Israel	2	1	3			**FALMOUTH TOWN.**						Frost, Johanna	2		4		
Weston, Stephen	1	3	4			Merrell, Elias	1	4	1			Means, James	1	1	3		
Warren, Henry	1	1	1			Merrell, James	1	1	3			Smith, John H	1	2	4		
Currier, Sarah		3	3			Merrell, Adam	2	2	2			Cox, Josiah	1	1	6		
True, Willm	3	3	4			Merrell, James	1		3			Quimby, John	1	5	3		
True, Abel	1	1	3			Swett, Moses	1	3	3			Partrick, William	1	4	3		
Osgood, Aaron	2	3	2			Watts, Edward	1	2	2			Stevens, Trustum	4	4	5		
Randal, John	2	3	4			Knights, George	5	3	6			Low, Esther		1	2		
Roberts, Willm	2	1	6			Knights, Jacob	1	2	3			Brooks, Daniel	1	2	3		
York, Saml	2	2	4			Knights, Benjamin	2		2			Partridge, Jesse	1	1	3		
Turner, Isaac	1		2			Sawyer, Anthony	4	5	4			Dole, Daniel	3		5		
Roberts, Vincent	1	6	3			Graves, Crispus	1	1	3			Titcomb, Andrew	1		3		
Blake, Will	1	2	2			Merrell, Joseph	1		2			Tate, George	5			1	
Davis, Joseph	2		2			Barber, John	4	1	3			Lewis, Archelas	2	1	3		
Holt, John	2	2	5			Sawyer, Thomas	1	2	3			Dyer, Josiah	1	3	6		
Davis, Isaac	1	1	4			Sawyer, Zachariah	1	1	2			Pierce, Thomas	1	1	2		
Fifield, Edward	1	2	1			Blake, John	4	1	4			Porter, Benjamin J	1		3		
Osgood, Nathl	1	3	2			Waite, Benjamin	2					Bartlett, Caleb	1	3	4		
Vening, Benja	3	1	4			Shaddock, Moses	1		2			Murrey, James	1	1	1		
Beman, Joseph	1	2	2			Blake, James	1	1	1			Brooks, John	1	2	5		
Fogginson, George	1	2	4			Noyes, Peeter	5	2	2			McDonald, John	2		3		
Ayers, Ebenr	1	2	2			Noyes, Amos	1	2	2			Billings, Mary			1	5	
Goodwin, George	1	2	1			Lunt, Joseph	1	2	2			Thombs, Samuel	1	3	4		
Warren, Ebenr	1	1	1			Sawyer, Benjamin	1	2	6			Ticket, Jonathan	3	3	3		
Tarr, Henry	1		2			Knights, Amos	1	2	2			Webb, Henry	1	3	3		
Tarr, Henry, Junr	1		1			Hilton, Emma	2		1			Ticket, Benjamin	4	1	3		
Brown, Saml	1	2	4			Noyes, Noah	1	1	2			Waterhouse, William	1	1	3		
Pall, Joseph	1	1	1			Ilsley, Jonathan	1	1	2			Waterhouse, William	2		3		
Bragdon, Ebenezer	1		1			Blake, John	1	2	3			Waterhouse, John	1	1	1		
Cushing, Charles, Junr	2	2	4			Berry, Obediah	2	1	4			Baley, Joseph	1		3		
Gerrish, Nathl	2	2	6			Berry, Josiah	1	1	5			Slimmons, William	1	1	4		
York, Joseph	1	3	4			Sawyer, Obediah	3	1	4			Hagerty, Jane	1		4		
Roak, Martin	1	1	2			Knights, Mark	1	2	1			Maxwell, William		1	3		
McGra, Will	2	2	2			Knights, Henry	1	2	3			Chapman, Shadrack	1	4	4		
Nichols, Saml	2	4	6			Sawyer, Isaac	1	1	5			Webb, James	1	2	4		
Spafford, Phinehas	1	2	3			Googin, Simon	1		1			Herrick, Daniel	1	3	3		
Stoddard, Willm	1	3	7			Reed, Jonathan	1		3			Barker, Jeremiah	1	3	4		
Willson, James	1	2	2			Stevens, Joshua	2	4	8			Laten, Jedediah	5	3	4		
Mitchel, Richd	1		2			Adams, Jacob	4	1	7			Staples, Joseph	1	1	4		
Procter, Saml	1	2	3			Night, Thomas	1	2	2			Merrell, James	1	2	3		
Stout, Joshua	2	4	6			Sawyer, Merrel	1	3	2			Winslow, William	2	7	5		
Plummer, Robert	1	1	3			Bishop, Mary			2			Hall, Jedediah	3	4	5		
Jordan, Secomb	1	1	3			Bracket, Thomas	2		2			Abbot, Nathaniel	1	1	3		
Dyer, Michael	1	4	6			Bracket, Peter	1	2	3			Allen, Isaac	2	1	5		
Dyer, David	1	3	2			Bracket, William	2	2	4			Steward, Peeter	1	2	3		
Parker, John	3	3	4			Baley, Benjamin	1		2			Baker, William	1	1	2		
Merril, Roger	1	2	2			Bracket, John S	1	5	4			Gerrish, Nathaniel	1	2	2		
Jones, Joshua	1	3	2			Whitney, Samuel	1	4	1			Laten, Joseph	2	2	6		
Newal, Ebenr, Junr	1	1	1			Hicks, Samuel	1	2	3			Willson, Ichabod	1	1	4		
Duglas, John	1		1			Baley, James	2	3	6			Winslow, Samuel	1		4		
Newal, Ebenezer	2	3	2			Knights, Merrell	1	2	9			Williams, Nathaniel	2	1	1		
McIntosh, John	1		4			Lord, James	1	2	3			Winslow, Hezekiah	1	2	3		
Gerrish, Willm	3	3	4			Winslow, Ebenezer	3	2	6			Laten, Robert	1	3	4		
Bailey, Timothy	1	2	2			Winslow, John	2	4	4			Laten, Peitiah	1	4	4		
Skinner, John	1	2	3			Cobb, Chitman	1	4	3			Woodson, Caleb	1	1	3		
Mitchel, Jeremiah	1	2	1			Cobb, James	1		3			Hall, Nicholls	2	3	6		
Parker, James	1	2	2			Cobb, Jonathan	1	1				Tripp, Abner	1	3	5		
Farrow, John	1	3	2			Pride, Isaac	1	2	3			Hicks, James	1	2	4		
Vining, John	1		2			Minot, Thomas	1	2	4			Fry, Benjamin	1		4		
Woodbury, Ebenezer	1	1	5			Procter, John	3	1	2			Roberts, Thomas	1	2	4		
Hibbart, James	1	2	5			Bracket, James	1	3	5			Creesy, Benjamin	1	1	3		
Hibbart, John	1		1			Bracket, Anthony	1	3	6			MGill, William	1		1		
Tracey, Christopher	1	2	4			Moody, Dorcas			2			Hall, Andrew	2	4	5		
Bliffen, James	1	1	2			Mumford, Samuel	2	1	2			Hall, Hatevil	3	2	6		
Beal, Jona	2	2	3			Winslow, Nathan	4	2	6			Frank, Thomas	3	2	2		
Night, Joseph	1	3	2			Howell, Silas	1	3	4			Field, Daniel	3	1	4		
Gitchel, Nathl	1	1	5			Procter, Nathaniel	1	2	3			Field, Zachariah	3	3	6		
Fasset, Richd	1	4	2			Moody, Josiah	1	2	4			Mumford, Edmund	3	1	6		
Tracey, Solomon	2	1	4			Winslow, James	2	4	3			Mastin, Ephraim	1	3	6		
Gitchel, Robert	1	4	3			Cobb, Peeter	1	3	3			Mastin, Benjamin					
Gitchel, John	1		3			Crandall, Philip	1		1			Stout, William					
Duglas, Elijah	2		1			Baley, Daniel	1	5	5			Merrel, Edmund	6		3		
Gitchel, Joseph	1		3			Baley, Josiah	1	3	3			Merrel, James	3	5	6		
Crossman, David	1	3	7	1		Thomson, David	3	1	2			Lunt, Benjamin	3	4	6		
Bliffen, Job	1		4			Rand, Benjamin	1	2	5			Worster, Luke H	1	4	4		
Day, Josiah	3	4	4	1								Hobbs, Jonathan	2	2	6		

HEADS OF FAMILIES—MAINE.

CUMBERLAND COUNTY—Continued.

NAME OF HEAD OF FAMILY.	Free white males of 16 years and upward, including heads of families.	Free white males under 16 years.	Free white females, including heads of families.	All other free persons.	Slaves.
FALMOUTH TOWN—con.					
Hall, William	3	3	2		
Laten, George	3	2	2		
Winslow, Thomas	2	2	4		
Baker, Jonah	2	1	4		
Hanson, Ruth		1	2		
Crocket, Simon	1		2		
Winslow, Benjamin	1	1	3	1	
Winslow, Olive	1	4	7		
Morrel, William	1	1	2		
Morrel, Stephen	2	1	6		
Winslow, Samuel	2	3	4		
Torrey, James	1	2	5		
Frost, Charles	1	2	4		
Tripp, Nathaniel	1		7		
Tripp, Peleg	1		2		
Cook, John	2	1	4		
Night, Job	1	6	3		
Pope, Elijah	2	7	5		
Morrell, John	1	3	5		
Night, Richard	1	3	4		
Night, Peeter	1	1	5		
Willson, Mark	2	5	1		
Pride, Benjamin	1		2		
Berry, George	1	2	3		
Doubty, Thomas	4		1		
Thurstin, Paul	1	5	4		
Gibbs, William	2		2		
Armstrong, Jonathan	1	2	2		
Night, Samuel	2	1	3		
Sawyer, Unis	2	1	3		
Merrel, Joseph	2		1		
Moss, Anthony	4	1	3		
Willson, Nathaniel	2	3	6		
Night, Amos	1	2	2		
Night, Joseph	1	4	4		
Night, George	1	7	7		
Night, Jonathan	1		3		
Cutter, Ebenezer	1		3		
Night, Stephen	1	1	2		
Walte, John	1	3	5		
Toby, Page	1	2	7		
Colley, John	1	1	2		
Colley, William	1	5	3		
Carll, Nathaniel	3	1	4		
Bracket, Abraham	3	1	3		
Allen, Zacheus	3	3	3		
Field, Stephen	2	4	3		
Fields, Zachariah	1	1	2		
Merrel, Moses	3	2	7		
Allen, Isaac	4	1	4		
Anderson, John	1	3	3		
Adams, Moses	1	5	2		
Watts, Samuel	1	3	4		
Merrel, Silas	1	1	9		
Merrel, Edmund	1	4	5		
Merrel, Humphrey	2	4	4		
Hutchins, Joseph	1	1	1		
Fields, Benjamin	1		1		
Fields, Joseph	1	2	3		
Lunt, Nathan	1	1	3		
Cobb, Benjamin	2	3	4		
Hustead, Robert	2	5	4		
Sawyer, Jonathan	1	4	5		
Small, Daniel	1	1	3		
Barber, Adam	1	4	6		
Bracket, John	1	2	1		
Cobb, Ephraim	1	2	4		
Purington, Abraham	1	2	2		
Purington, Elisha	1	3	2		
Hustin, Stephen	1	1	2		
Conant, Bartholomew	1	1	2		
Conant, Joseph	1	3	4		
Twamley, Daniel	1	2	2		
Woodberry, Joshua	1		1		
Lord, Nathan	1	2	5		
Abbot, George	2	3	4		
Morrison, Robert	1	7	2		
Bacheldor, Joseph	1	1	1		
Knights, Moses	1	4	4		
Webb, John	1	1	7		
Hale, Nathaniel	4	2	5		
Pride, Henry	1		4		
Pride, Joseph	1	1	2		
Austin, Benjamin	1	4	9		
Pride, William	1	5	3		
Walker, William	1	3	3		
Walker, Charles	1	2	2		
Lunt, William	2	3	1		
Pride, Joseph	1	2	2		
Grant, John	1	1	2		
Webb, Elisabeth			3		
Lunt, Daniel	2	4	2		
Irelsh, John	1	1	4		
Winslow, Job	2		8		
Merrel, Jacob	2	1	4		
FALMOUTH TOWN—con.					
Latin, Hatevil	1	4	1		
Hayes, John	1	2	1		
Broad, Thaddeus	2	5	6		
Rand, James	1	2	3		
Ward, Elijah	1		3		
Slemmons, Thomas	2		1		
Smith, William	1		3		
Trickey, David	2	3	5		
Johnston, Robert	3		2		
Johnston, John	3	2	5		
Porterfield, William	3	2	6		
Slemmons, Robert	1	3	3		
Burns, John	1		2		
March, Samuel	2		2		
Knights, George	2	3	5		
Saloan, Adam	3				
Parkes, Anna		4	4		
Knights, Nathaniel	1	1	6	1	
Andrews, Samuel	1	1	2		
Babb, Rhoda		2	1		
Wright, Boston				3	
Johnston, James	4	2	4		
Tate, Robert	2	1	6		
Warren, John	2	3	2		
Porterfield, Elisabeth		3	6		
Thompson, Jonathan	1	2	5		
Check, Nathan			5		
Check, Peeter	1	1	1		
Foss, Job	1	1	2		
Starberd, Anthony	1		2		
Starberd, John	1	3	5		
Walker, Josiah	1	1	2		
Starberd, John	1	1	1		
Ticket, Mary			4		
Starberd, Thomas	1	4	3		
Lincoln, Thomas	1	2	4		
Adams, Jonathan	2		4		
Babb, William	3	4	2		
Baley, David	3	4	4		
Haskel, Solomon	5		5		
Webb, Jonathan	3	2	6		
Gage, Isaac	1				
Chadwick, William	1				
March, Edmund			4		
Pike, Timothy	1	5	5		
Conant, William	1	2	4		
Bigsby, John	1	2	4		
Westcot, Eliakim	1	3	4		
Jorden, Joseph	1	2	5		
Quimby, Joseph	1	2	5		
Quimby, Benjamin	4	3	5		
Quimby, Nathan	1	2	2		
Conant, Samuel	2		4		
Woodberry, Hugh	1		2		
Partridge, Anna		1	2		
Webb, William	2	3	4		
Millikin, Benjamin	1		2		
March, Peltiah	1	2	5		
Freeman, Enoch	2	1	2		
Clark, Morris	3	1	2		
Wise, Amaziah	2	3	4		
Johnston, George	2	1	2		
Haskel, William	1	2	4		
Cobby, John	1	3	6		
Lamb, William	2	3	6		
Swett, Stephen	1	1	2		
Partridge, Jotham	1	2	3	4	
Frost, Cato				4	
Jorden, Cezar				2	
Riggs, Stephen	1		3		
Riggs, John	1	1	2		
Riggs, James	1		4		
Harper, William	2	1	2	6	
Gould, John	1	2	6		
Pennel, Thomas	1	1	3		
Knight, Joshua	1		2		
Noyes, Joseph	3	1	4		
Gould, Gardner	2	3	4	1	
Frost, Pepperell	1	4	6	1	
Epes, Daniel	1		5		
Frost, James		1	2		
Westcot, Richard	2	2	2		
Storer, Johanna			2		
Kimball, John	2	3	2		
Reed, Ichabod	1	1	7		
Whettum, Martha	1	1	4		
Brown, Thomas	3	1	9		
Sampson, Micael	2	2	7		
Higgins, Elisha					
Thombs, Cezar				7	
Stevens, Isaac S	2	4	5		
Wyer, Elijah	1		2		
Thompson, Joseph	1	1	3		
Davis, Roland	2	1	3		
FALMOUTH TOWN—con.					
Davis, Roland	1	1	2		
Merrel, Enoch	1	2	4		
Jones, Jabes	2	3	6		
Jones, Francis	1	1	3		
Honeyford, Thomas	1	1	2		
Foster, Charles	1	1	2		
Toppin, John	1		1		
Grant, William	1		2		
Pote, William	1		6		
Pote, Samuel	1	2	1		
Roughf, Sarah		3	1		
Pote, Greenfield	1	3	1		
Pote, Gamaliel	1	4	7		
Little, Sarah			2		
Richardson, William	1	2	6		
Allen, Hannah			3		
York, Samuel	1		3		
Wormwell, Nathaniel	1	2	2		
Pote, Jeremiah	1		2		
Lowell, Mary		1	2		
Jackman, Anna		1	5		
Bartlett, Thomas	1		1		
Delano, Thomas	1	5	3		
Dodd, Thomas	1		2		
Dodd, Stephen	1		3		
Williams, Ebenezer	3	4	4		
Moody, Benjamin	3	1	7		
Lock, Josiah	1	1	5		
Sawyer, Elisha	1	1	3		
Lunt, Benjamin	2		1		
Lunt, Daniel	1	2	1		
Cobb, Olive		3	4		
Lock, Abijah	1		4		
Bennet, Phineas	1	4	4		
Moss, Jethniel	1		3		
Merrell, Joshua	1	3	4		
Merrell, Adam	5	2	5		
Merrell, Jacob	1	4	4		
Merrell, Humphrey	1		1		
Pettengill, Benjamin	1	2	6		
Merrell, Amos	1	1	4		
Doubty, James	1		2		
Lunt, Ephraim	1	1	5		
Noyes, Samuel	1	3	4		
Merrell, Daniel	1	3	5		
Buckman, Samuel	1	6	5		
Tukesberry, John	1	6	3	2	
Thrasher, Joseph	1	3	6		
McIntire, Benjamin	1	2	6		
Buxton, William	1		4		
Buxton, James		4	4		
Chase, William	1	3	4		
Johnston, Joseph	1	2	5		
Malcom, Joseph	2	1	3		
Turner, Melzer	1	2	5		
Buxton, William	1	3	3		
Jones, Edward	1	1	1		
Pomeroy, Joseph	3		5		
Underwood, Joseph	1	1	5		
Underwood, David	1		2		
York, William R	1	2	4		
Titcomb, William	1	3	2		
Knight, William	1	3	2		
York, Joseph	1	2	4		
Lock, John	1	2	3		
Mason, John	1	3	1		
Clark, Ichabod	1	1	3		
Lock, Jonathan	2	1	2		
Buckman, Jeremiah	2	4	6	1	
Pote, Increase	1	2	3		
Kilpartrick, Iland	1	3	2		
Grover, Andrew	1	2	6		
Hinshaw, Sarah			2		
Prince, Benjamin	1	3	3		
Prince, Amos	1	2	1		
Buckman, Nathan	1	2	7	1	
Kilpartrick, Daniel	1		2		
Bangs, Joshua	1	2	2		
Wormwell, John	1	2	7		
Blackstone, Benjamin	4	3	4		
Noyes, Samuel	2	1	4		
Noyes, James	1		4		
Noyes, Nathan	3	3	3		
Merrel, Stephen	3	1	6		
Thompson, Nathaniel	2		2		
Thompson, William	1		4		
Swett, Samuel	1	1	2		
Thompson, Edward	1		2		
FLINTSTOWN PLANTATION.					
Larribee, Zebulon	2	2	2		
Mullikin, Josiah	1	2	3		
Bandford, Wllm	1	1	2		

FIRST CENSUS OF THE UNITED STATES.

CUMBERLAND COUNTY—Continued.

NAME OF HEAD OF FAMILY.	Free white males of 16 years and upward, including heads of families.	Free white males under 16 years.	Free white females, including heads of families.	All other free persons.	Slaves.
FLINTSTOWN PLANTATION—continued.					
Brown, David	2	1	2		
Whittum, Jedadiah	1	3	1		
Sweet, Benjn	1	1	2		
Fitch, Willm	2		2		
Roe, Benja	1	3	4		
Flint, Eleazer	1				
Thorn, Bartholomew	3	1	5		
Thorn, Joseph	1		3		
Sabine, Lewis	1	1	2		
Sandbourn, David	3	2	3		
Noble, Christopher, Ju	1	2	1		
Noble, Christopher	2		1		
Roe, Webber	1	1	1		
Roe, Lazarus	1		3		
Roe, Noah	1	1	3		
Sandbourn, Jona	6		5		
Philbrick, Michael	1	1	2		
Richardson, Joseph	1	2	3		
Burnal, John, Jr	1	1	1		
Burnal, John	1	2	3		
Fly, Isaac	1	1	3		
Fly, James	1	2	3		
Korah, Stephen	1	3	2		
Bachelor, Saml	1	1	2		
Flint, Cummins	1				
Harding, Simon	2	3	3		
Lowel, Moses	2	1	3		
Lowel, Jona	1	3	2		
Fitch, Richard	1		2		
Pierce, Josiah	1		4		
Bachelor, Ephraim	1	4	3		
Ingalls, Benja	2	2	4		
Laiken, Joseph	2	2	3		
Howe, Jacob	1	2	3		
FREEPORT TOWN.					
Jamerson, James	5	1	3		
Mann, John, Jr	2	1	4		
Dunham, John	1	2	4		
Duning, John	1	2	1		
Wentworth, Silas	3		2		
Carless, Willm	2		2		
Peckman, Bettey	1		5		
Rogers, Willm	1		2		
Kendal, Benja	1		3		
Rogers, George	2		3		
Mans, Thos	1	3	3		
Mans, John	5	1	5		
Anderson, Jacob	3		4		
Anderson, James	1	2	1		
Anderson, Joseph	2	2	6		
Anderson, James	5	1	3		
Anderson, Robert	1	3	3		
Anderson, John	1		3		
Robarts, James	1	4	1		
Pote, Green	3	1	6		
Moore, Elkins	1		2		
Adridge, Nathl	1	1	6		
Gookins, Richd	1		1		
Sole, Willm	1		2		
Cobb, Thos	4	1	4		
Bruer, Curried	1		3		
Day, Mehitable	1	1	2		
Day, Catherine	1		2		
Lake, Benja	1	1	2		
Lake, Lydia	2		2		
Anderson, John	1	1	1		
Brewer, Edward	2	1	2		
Brewer, Dan	2	3	4		
Brewer, Joseph	1	1	3		
Merrill, Jacob	1	2	1		
Leechfield, Nathl	1		2		
Leechfield, Saml	1	1	5		
Leechfield, Noah	1	3	3		
Leechfield, Willm	1		1		
Carter, Danl	2		2		
Carter, Danl, Junr	1	1	3		
Austin, Ruth		3	2		
Grant, Abram	2		2		
Curtis, Danl	3		3		
Dennison, Ame					
Cohon, John	1		3	2	
Townsend, Joseph	1		1		
Lufkin, Aaron	2	2	6		
Richardson, Benja	1	3	3		
Dennison, Abner	1	3	1		
Dennison, Gideon	1	3	2		
Curtis, Thomas	1	1	1		
Curtes, Thomas, Junr	1	4	5		
Turner, Lemuel	3		4		
Randall, Rebecca	1	3	3		
Silvester, Thos	1	1	3		
Evans, Willm	1		2		
Mitchel, Willm	2	5	3		
FREEPORT TOWN—con.					
Dennison, David	2	3	5		
Silvester, Amos	1	1	4		
Silvester, John	1		2		
Frost Phinehas	2	3	6		
Townsend, John	1		3		
Silvester, Abner, Jur	1		3		
Prout, James	1	1	3		
Silvester, Abner	4		2		
Silvester, Caleb	1		4		
Silvester, Joseph	1	1	3		
Silvester, Hinhman	1		2		
Scales, Samuel	1	2	2		
Scales, Nathl	1		2		
Brown, Francis	1		1		
Lambart, Isaac	2	4	5		
Hooper, David	2	2	2		
Sole, Ichabod	2	1	3		
Sole, Robert	1		1		
Byram, David	1		1		
Byram, Melcher	1	1	4		
Lotter, Robert	1	1	4		
Rogers, Mark	2	3	2		
Dunham, Danl	1		2		
Curtes, James	3	2	7		
Townsend, Benja	2	1	3		
Kilby, Richd	1	3	4		
Sole, James	1	2	4		
Sole, Jedediah	1	1	4		
Bicknal, Thos	2		2		
Buzzel, Noah	1	2	2		
Prat, Noah	1	4	2		
Curtis, Obadiah	1	1	2		
Curtis, David	1	1	1		
Lane, Gideon	1	1	3		
Curtis, Benja	2	1	3		
Bennet, Job	2	1	4		
Atkinson, Moses	3	1	2		
Gardiner, —	1	2	4		
Gurney, Eliab	1	3	3		
Townsend, Robert	1	1	1		
Grant, Richard	3	1	3		
Woodman, Jona	4	3	5		
Curtis, Joshua	1	1	3		
Tolbart, Saml	1				
Byram, Jona	1		4		
Dunham, Amaziah	1	2	1		
Tolbart, Ambros	1		2		
Woodworth, James	1	1	3		
Woodworth, James	1		1		
Pinkham, Elijah	2	1	4		
Pinkham, Stephen	1	1	5		
Sole, Jona	1	1	2		
Burbank, John	1	2	1		
Chapman, Mary	1		2		
Merril, Susanna	1	1	4		
Griffen, Jona	1	2	3		
Griffen, Saml	2	3	6		
Bailey, Seth	1	2	1		
White, Jacob	2	3	4		
Sawyer, Benja	2	2	6		
Dennison David, Jr	1	2	3		
Dennison, George	1		2		
Gorden (Widow)			2		
Dillenham, Melatiah	1	1	2		
Stockbridge, John	1	3	1		
Edes, Joseph	1		2		
Edes, Gideon	1		2		
Dugias, Job	1	4	3		
Merrill, John	1		2		
Silvester, Bester	1	2	2		
Rogers, James	1		2		
Johnson, Revd Alfred	1	2	2		
Townsend, Beley	1	3	2		
Dillenham, Saml	3	1	4		
Bartlett, George	1	2	6		
Porter, Seward	4	6	3		
Kimbal, Peter S	2	3	2		
Curtis, Stephen	1		2		
Bartlet, John	1	4	3		
Bartlet, Willm	2	2	7		
Carvar, Reuben	1		2		
Carver, Seth	1		1		
Sole, Moses	3	1	3		
Griffen, Ephraim	1		2		
Griffen, Seth	1	1	8		
Mitchel, Abraham	1	4	3		
Weston, Nathan	1	1	3		
Mitchel, Joshua	1	2	3		
Mitchel, John	1		2		
Cumings, Josiah	1		1		
Millet, Thos	1	1	2		
Read, John	1	3	1		
Read, Josiah	1	1	3		
Carver, Amos	1	1	6		
Sole John	1	1	2		
FREEPORT TOWN—con.					
Wilson, David	1		4		
Doughty, David	1	1	6		
Tory, Elisha	1	1	2		
Stockbridge, Joseph	1	1	3		
Winslow, John	1	1	1		
Porter, Benja	1		3		
Cummins, Abram	1	1	2		
Sole, John	2	5	2		
Mitchel, Abram	1	4	8		
Griffen, Ephraim	4	2	2		
Tolbart, Ambros	2	1	2		
Tolbart, Trecott	1		1		
Sherman, Margaret	1	1	4		
Parker, Benja	1		2		
Carver, Calvan	1	2	2		
Lowe, Willm	2		2		
Curtis, Ezra	2	1	9		
Welch, Thos	2	1	4		
Pratt, David	2	5	4		
Cromwell, Joshua	1	2	5		
Coffin, Stephen	2	6	4		
Fitts, John	2	1	2		
Welch, Molley			1		
West, Peleg	2	1	4		
Mitchel, Danl	1	1	4		
Mitchel, Joseph, Junr	4	1	2		
Holbrook Silas	1	2	4		
Brown, Willm	2	3	3		
Grant, John	2	1	2		
Crocker, James	5	1	3		
Fogg, Benja	1	3	4		
Fogg, Benaiah	2		2		
Penley, Joseph	1	1	2		
Fogg, Saml	1	1	2		
Cushing, John	2	2	2		
Staples, Joseph	3	3	3		
Stockbridge, Michael	1	3	1		
Tholl, Jeremiah	2	3	4		
Alden, Nathl	1	1	2		
Sole, Saml	1		4		
Sole, Barnabas	1	3	3		
Chandler, Edmond	1		2		
Brown, Peter	1	2	3		
Winslow, Gilbart	1	1	1		
Sole, Cornelius	3	3	4		
Harvey, David	1	4	4		
Winslow, Saml	1	4	3		
Walker, Jeremiah	2				
Godard, Robert	1	4	3		
Todd, Willm	3	3	6		
Reid, Bartholomew	2	1	2		
Bran, Ebenezer	1		2		
Reid, Abram	1	1	6		
Knight, Jeremiah	1	1	2		
Winslow, Benja	1	2	2		
Brown, Reuben	1		5		
Nason, Jeremiah	2	3	5		
Harvey, Enoch	1	2	3		
Mann, Joseph	2	1	7		
Small, Edward	1	3	4		
Lovell, Josiah	1	5	1		
Roberts, George	1		3		
Grant, Saml	2	3	4		
White, Elias	1		2		
Lawrance, Willm	2	3	4		
Barber, Robert	1	4	3		
Tuttle, Libius	1	1	1		
Reid, Stephen	1		1		
McCormal, James	1		1		
Whitney, Barnabas	1	1	1		
Marston, Danl	1		3		
Whitney, Ellas	1	1	2		
Johnson, Jesper	1		3		
Wench, Joseph	1	2	2		
Tuttle, Libius	1	3	2		
Godard, Silas	1	5	1		
Sawyer, James	1	3	4		
GORHAM AND SCARBOROUGH TOWNS.					
Alden, Austin	1				
Alden, Josiah	1	4	4		
Adams, Joshua, Jr					
Adams, Benja	4	1	2		
Akers, Moses	1	1	2		
Adams, Joshua	1	4	4		
Akers, James	1	1	3		
Ashley, Abner	1		2		
Andrews, Jona, Jr	1	3	5		
Andrews, Amos	3	4	5		
Andrews, Jona	2		2		
Andrews, Stepn	1	5	2		
Alden, Abiather	1		2		
Anderson, John	1				

HEADS OF FAMILIES—MAINE.

CUMBERLAND COUNTY—Continued.

GORHAM AND SCARBOROUGH TOWNS—con.

NAME OF HEAD OF FAMILY.	Free white males of 16 years and upward, including heads of families.	Free white males under 16 years.	Free white females, including heads of families.	All other free persons.	Slaves.
Bolton, Wm.	1		3	1	
Burnel, Jno, Jr.	2	2	4		
Brown, Simeon	1	4	2		
Brown, Benja.	2	2	6		
Bacon, Nathl, Junr.	1	3	5		
Bangs, Barns.	2		2		
Bremhall, Sylva.	1	1	4		
Bangs, Herman	2	1	5		
Blake, Ithiel	3	3	5		
Blake, Nathl	1	5	4		
Bracket, James	2		8		
Bangs, James	1	5	4		
Blake, Benja.	1		2		
Bangs, Barns, Junr.	1	2	4		
Bangs, Thos.	2	1	5		
Blanchard, Jno.	1	1	1		
Blake, Benja, Junr.	1	2	1		
Bishop, Enos	2		3		
Bacon, Josiah	1		2		
Bacon, Timy.	1	1	2		
Butler, John	1	1	3		
Bangs, Ebenr.	1		1		
Beverly, Farnham	1				
Brimhall, Corns.	1	1	2		
Blake, Jno.	1	1	4		
Bowman, Nathl.	2		2		
Bolton, Thos.	2	4	2		
Barton, Wm.	1		3		
Bacon, Nathl, Senr.	1		2		
Brown, Luthur.	1		2		
Bragdon, Jona.	1	3	4		
Brown, Hon. Jno Josha.	2	1	3		
Bragdon, Gideon	1		1		
Bragdon, Jno.	1	2	1		
Beals, Isaiah	1	1	3		
Bragdon, Solo	2	2	4		
Burnam, Aaron	3	5	7		
Boothby, Nathl.	1	5	4		
Burbank, Silas	3	1	4		
Burbank, David	1	1	1		
Burbank, Eleazer	1	1	1		
Boothby, Joseph	2		3		
Boothby, James	1		2		
Burnum, Solo.	1	2	5		
Burnum, Thos (Widow)	1		3		
Burnum, Robt.	1	2	4		
Burnum, Danl.	3	1	3		
Boothby, Richd	1		2		
Bragdon (Widow)			1		
Crocket, Saml, Jr.	1	5	4		
Crocket, Ephm	1	1	1		
Crocket, Palatiah	1	1	1		
Cates, Joseph	2	1	2		
Cobb, Elisha	4	1	3		
Cobb, Andrew	3		4		
Carsley, Jno.	2	2	4		
Crocket, Josha, Junr.	3	2	4		
Cates, Benja.	1	4	3		
Crocket, Jona.	1	3	5		
Crocket, Peter	1	3	3		
Cobb, Jedediah	3	2	7		
Chadburn, Silas	1	3	6		
Chamberlain, Benja	1				
Cobb, Elisha, Jr.	1				
Creasey, Joseph	3	4	3		
Cates, Ebenr.	1				
Cotton, Ebenr.	2	1	2		
Clemons, —	1		2		
Cloutman, Timy.	2	5	2		
Carsley, Jno, Jr.	1		1		
Crocket, Joshua, Jr.	1	1			
Coffin, Isaac	2	2	5		
Crocket, James	1	1	1		
Cates, Andrew	1	3	1		
Caverno, Charles	1		1		
Clark, Jacob	1				
Clemons, Jeremiah	1	3	3		
Cobb, Chitman	1		2		
Crocket, Joshua, Senr.	1		1		
Chadburn, James	1	1	1		
Crocket, Saml.	1		1		
Cotton, John	1	3	3		
Cutler, Timy.	1		1		
Chadwick, Benja.	2		5		
Colebroth, George	1	3	3		
Colebroth, Jos.	1	1			
Colebroth, Saml.	1	1	3		
Carter, Benja.	1				
Carter, Benja, Jr	2	3	5		
Carter, Richd	1	3	1		
Collins, Jona	1	2	4		
Carl, Saml.	1	3	4		
Carl, Ebenr.	1		3		
Colebroth, Danl.	1	1	1		
Carl, Ebenr.	1	2	4		
Davis, Saml.	1	1	4		
Dyer, John	2	2	3		
Davis, prince	3		3		
Dyer, Wm.	1				
Davis, Josiah	3	2	3		
Dan, Nathl.	1	4	3		
Dyer, John, Jr.	1		1		
Dun, Christopr.	1	1	3		
Davis, John	1		2		
Darling, Jno.	1	3	2		
Davis, David	1	2	1		
Dorset, Jereh.	1				
Davis, Ebenr.	3	1	1		
Davis, prince, Junr.	1				
Davis, Sylva.	1		1		
Dyer, Levi	1	1	4		
Duggins, Mrs.			2		
Dresser, John	1	1	3		
Dresser, Mindwell	3		3		
Day, James	1		1		
Dresser, Wentworth	1				
Dresser, Mark	1	1	1		
Downing, Dennit	1				
Dearing, Isaac	4	1	4		
Eldridge, Danl.	1		4		
Edwards, Richd.	2	3	4		
Elder, Saml.	3	4	5		
Elder, Reuben	2		4		
Elder, Isaac	2	3	2		
Elwel, Jona.	3	1	2		
Emory, James	1	2	2		
Edwards, Joshua	1		4		
Edwards, Nathl, Jr	1	3	3		
Edwards, Nathl.	2	2	5		
Emmerson, Jos.	1	3	5		
Edgcomb, Gideon	2	1	7		
Edgcomb, Robert	2	4	2		
Farnham, Simeon	1	2	2		
Frost, Nathl.	2	1	4		
File, Wm.	3	1	4		
Frost, Benja.	1				
Frost, David	3	4	5		
Frost, Peter (Widow)		1	3		
Frost, Enoch	1	1	3		
Freeman, Jona.	3	1	3		
Freeman, Nathl, Jr.	1				
File, Ebenr.	1	3	2		
Fogg, Seth	1	3	2		
Fogg, Jereh.	2	2	6		
Fogg, Joseph	2	4	1		
File, Wm, Jr.	1	1	2		
File, Wm	1	1	4	2	
Freeman, Benja.	1	1	2	2	
File, George	1		3		
Frost, Abm.	1	2	3		
Freeman, Nathl.	2	1	7		
Fogg, Moses	1		2		
Fenderson, Pelatiah	1	1	2		
Fitz, Obadiah	2		2		
Foss, Joseph	1				
Fabin, Joshua	6	2	5		
Foss, Wm	1		7		
Fenderson, Nathl.	2		2		
Fenderson, Nathl, Jr.	3	4	4		
Fogg, Jona.	2	6	4		
Fogg, Seth	3	3	5		
Foss, Peter	1	1	3		
Fabin, John	2		3		
Foss, Saml, Senr.	1	2	2		
Foss, Zechr.	1		5		
Fitz, Simeon	2		3		
Fogg, James	3	2	3		
Fogg, Nelson	1		1		
Foss, Saml, Junr.	1	2	1		
Fitz, Wm.	1	1	2		
Foss, Wm, Jr.	1		2		
Foss, Uriah	1	3	2		
Fogg, Reuben	1		2	1	
Fogg, Reuben, Jr.	2	1	4		
Fogg, Wm.	1	1	2		
Foss, Danl.	1		2		
Fogg, Moses	3	2	6		
Foss, Abner	1		2		
Fogg, Hannah (Wm)	1		2		
Fogg, Aaron	1	2	1		
Ficket, Vincent	1		2		
Gorham, Wm.	2	2	3	2	
Gammon, Jos.	2	2	4		
Gilkey, James	1		4		
Gilkey, Jos.	2	4	6		
Green, Thos.	1	1	2		
Gammon, Jos., Jr.	1				
Gammon, Danl, Jr.	1	3	2		
Gammon, Jona.	1		3		
Gammon, Benja.	1		3		
Gilkey, Jno.	1		1		
Gammon, Moses	1	2	2		
Gilkey, Isaac	1				
Green, Josiah	1				
Greenlaw, John	1	2	1		
Gammon, Philip	1		1		
Green, John	1	2	1		
Green, Jona.	1	2	3		
Gray, Tabitha	2		2		
Gustin, Thos.	1				
Grace, Jno.	1	2	1		
Grace, Wm.	1		2		
Grace, Wm, Jr.	1				
Gilford, Jno.	1		3		
Graffam, Josiah	2	2	4		
Gilford, Jno, Jr.	1	1	3		
Hanscomb, Moses	1		3		
Huston, Simon	3	2	4		
Hamblin, Danl.	1	2	5		
Hamblin, Timy.	2	6	4		
Haskel, John	1	1	4		
Hamblin, Prince	1		5		
Hamblin, Jos.	2	1	2		
Hicks, Leml.	1	4	3		
Hunt, Ephm	2	2	5		
Hamblin, Gershom	1	5	4		
Harding, Martha	2	1	2		
Hall, Ebenr.	2	3	4		
Harding, Zepha.	1	3	4		
Hanscomb, George	3	1	2		
Hanscomb, Nathan	1	6	2		
Hamblin, Ebenr.	1	3	5		
Hamblin, Saml, Jr.	2	4	4		
Hamblin, Jacob	1	3	5		
Hamblin, George	1	6	4		
Harding, Seth	3		2		
Hanscomb, Geo., Jr.	1	1	6		
Higgin, Jos.	2	4	5		
Hunt, Ichabod	1	3	2		
Haskel, Jacob	1	1	2		
Harding, Nichl.	1	1	1		
Harding, David	1		2		
Harding, Jno.	2	3	5		
Harding, Elkanah	1	2	1		
Harding, David, Jr.	1	1	4		
Hatch, Nathl.	1	1	5		
Hatch, Asa	1	2	2		
Hatch, Ebenr.	1				
Hamblin, Nathan	1				
Harris, Stepa.	1	2	3	1	
Hall, Abm.	1		1		
Hopson, Wm.	1		2		
Hamblin, Seth	1				
Harding, Jno, Jr.	1				
Hines, Richd.	1	2	4		
Hodgsden, Jos.	1		1		
Harding, David, Senr.	1		2		
Holmes, —	1		1		
Hasty, Wm.	2	1	4		
Hasty, Nathl.	1	3	3		
Higgin, Edmd	1	1	1		
Hunniwel, Richd.	1	1	1		
Hunniwel, Sarah	1		3		
Hanscomb, Elisha	1				
Hanscomb, Ketarah	1		2		
Hanscomb, Humpy.	1	1	3		
Hicks, prout Timy	1				
Hunniwel, Roger	2		2		
Hunniwel, Benja.	1	4	4		
Holmes, Epha.	1		3		
Hodgsden, John	1	4	2		
Harman, George	3	1	5		
Hearne, Nicha.	2	1	4		
Holmes, Jno.	3	1	3		
Holms, Wm.	2	2	3		
Harman, Wm.	1			1	
Harman, Elias	1	2	2		
Hains, Danl.	2	2	4		
Harman, Zechr.	1	1	7		
Harman, Danl.	1	1	1		
Harman, Benja.	1	1	5		
Harman, Eliza.	2	2	2		
Harman, Jno.	2	1	8		
Hodgsdon (Widow)			1		
Harman, James, Jr.	1	2	4		
Harman, Saml.	3	5	3	1	
Hasty, Robt.	2	3	6		
Harman, Jona.	1	6	6		
Harman, Moses	2	2	3		
Harman, Jas.	2		1		
Harford, Solo.	1	3	7		
Harman, Abner	1				
Harman, Joseph	1	2	4		
Hoit, George	2	1	2		
Haines, Timy.	2		1		

CUMBERLAND COUNTY—Continued.

NAME OF HEAD OF FAMILY.	Free white males of 16 years and upward, including heads of families.	Free white males under 16 years.	Free white females, including heads of families.	All other free persons.	Slaves.	NAME OF HEAD OF FAMILY.	Free white males of 16 years and upward, including heads of families.	Free white males under 16 years.	Free white females, including heads of families.	All other free persons.	Slaves.	NAME OF HEAD OF FAMILY.	Free white males of 16 years and upward, including heads of families.	Free white males under 16 years.	Free white females, including heads of families.	All other free persons.	Slaves.
GORHAM AND SCARBOROUGH TOWNS—con.						**GORHAM AND SCARBOROUGH TOWNS—con.**						**GORHAM AND SCARBOROUGH TOWNS—con.**					
Hunniwel, Zerubbael	1	1	5			Libby, Cpˢ	1					Meserve, Gideon	1	4	4		
Higgins, Edmᵈ	3	2	4			Libby, Allison	2	3	3			March, Samˡ	3		4		
Irish, James	2	1	2			Libby, Edwᵈ	1		2			Myrick, Isaac	2	4	5		
Irish, Thoˢ	3		6			Libby, Joshua	3		4			Marshall, Isaac	2		1		
Jones, Henry	1		2			Libby, Matthias	1		3			Marshall, Wᵐ	1		1		
Irish, James, Jr	2	1	5			Libby, Samˡ	1	2	2			Moody, Mary		1	4		
Irish, Stepⁿ	2	2	6			Libby, Ichabod	2	3	2			Meserve, Danˡ, Senʳ	1		1		
Jordan, Benjⁿ	1	4	7			Libby, James	1		1			Moses, Danˡ	1		5		
Irish, Isaac	1	1	2			Libby, Hanson	1		3			Morris, Chˢ	2	2	6		
Jones, Joseph	1	2	1			Larrabee, Stepⁿ	2	2	1			Matthews, John	1	3	3		
Johnson, Jnᵒ	2		4			Larrabee, Philip	1	3	6			McLellan, Jnᵒ	1		2		
Johnson, Robᵗ	1		2			Libby, Phinˢ	1	1	3			McKenny, Margᵗ			1	5	
Johnson, Matthew	1		1			Libby, Ebenʳ	2	1	4			McDonald, Timʸ, Jr	2	2	5		
Johnson, Ephᵐ	1					Lowel, Lydia	1		3			McDonald, Timʸ, Sr	1	1	1		
Jenkins, Josiah	1		4			Libby, Amos	1					McKenny, Elizᵃ			3		
Jenkins, Samˡ	2	1	4			Libby, Skilling Jnᵒ	1	1	2			McKenny, Samˡ	1	4	4		
Jordan, Moses	1		5			Libby, David	1		2			Millikan, Lemˡ	2	2	5		
Jewett, Caleb	1	2	4			Lancaster, Revᵈ	1	2	4			Moulton, Jonᵃ, 3ᵈ	1	1	1		
Johnson, Stepⁿ	1	2	5			Lovet, Abᵐ	3	2	4			Millikan, John	3	1	5		
Jones, Samˡ	1	1	1			Lovet, Richᵈ	1	1	4			Millikan, Samˡ	1	3	1		
Jones, Wᵐ, Junʳ	1					Lovet, Joseph	1	3	1			Millikan, Joˢ	2	2	7		
Jones, Wᵐ	1		2			Libby, Richᵈ	2	3	3	1		Millikan, Isaih	1	1	2		
Jones, Stepⁿ	1					Libby, Roger	2	2	3			Millikan, M. John	3	2	5		
Jones, James	1	1	2			Libby, H. Richᵈ	1	2	5			Millikan, Wᵐ	2	1	3		
Jones, Jˢ, Jr	1		1			Libby, Eliakim	1	1	3			Merril, Danˡ	1	1	4		
Jones, Wᵐ, 3ᵈ	1	1	2			Libby, Peter	1	4	3			Merril, Levi	1	3	2		
Jordan, Benjⁿ	1	4	6			Larrabee, Wᵐ	4		3			Merril, Bradley	1	2	4		
Jose, Nathˡ	2	2	4			Libby, Theoˢ	2	2	5			McKenny, Robᵗ	1	1	2		
Jose, Wᵐ	1	3	4			Libby, Jereʰ	1	2	5			McKenny, Robᵗ, Jr	1	3	3		
Jackson, Robᵗ				5		Libby, Neheʰ	2	2	6			Moulton, Danˡ	3		4		
Jordan, Lemˡ	1	3	4			Libby, Theoˢ, Junʳ	1	3	2			Moulton, Jnᵒ	2	3	3		
Jackson, Reuben				2		Libby, R. Hubᵈ	1	2	2	1		Moulton, Danˡ, Jr	3		4		
Keniard, Thoˢ	1					Libby, Isaac	1					Moulton, Charles	2	4	5		
Knights, Nathˡ	1		2			Libby, Enoch	3		2			Moulton, Jos	2	1	3		
Kemp, Ebenʳ	1	2	5			Libby, Zebulon	1	2	4			Moulton, Jonᵃ, Jr	2	2	3		
Knights, Joseph	2	3	2			Larrabee, Wᵐ, Junʳ	1	1	1			Moulton, Jos	1				
Kirkwood, Alexʳ	2		2			Letherbe, Tom				7		Moulton, Jonᵃ	2		4		
Killum, Ivory	1	2	2	1		McLellan, Thoˢ	2	3	4			Millikan, Edwᵈ	2	1	3		
Kelly, Chrisʳ	2	2	3			McLellan, Wᵐ	2	2	1	1		Millikan, Joshua	1		4		
King, Mary			4	1		Mosher, Jˢ	2	2	4			Millikan, Benjⁿ	2	2	3		
King, Richard	1	1	1	1		Murch, John	3		3			Millikan, Jonᵃ	3	3	3		
King, Willᵐ	1					Murch, Walter	3	1	3			Millikan, Thoˢ	2		4		
Kelly, Peter	1	2	4			Murch, Ebenʳ	2	3	4			McLaulan, Robᵗ	1		1		
Lewis, George	3	2	5	2		McLellan, Jˢ	2	2	3			Mains, Thoˢ	1	3	8		
Lombard, Richᵈ	3	2	3			Miller, Jnᵒ	2	2	4			McLaulan, Wᵐ	2	2	6		
Libby, Edwᵈ	1		1			McDusle, David	1		1			Meserve, George	1		3		
Longfellow, Stepⁿ	2	2	5			McCullister, Jˢ	4	1	7			Meserve, John	3	1	3		
Lombard, Solᵒ	1	2	3			McDonald, Jos	1	4	1			Meserve, Wᵐ	1		3		
Lombard, Calvin	2	2	4			Murray, Anthʸ	1	4	5			Moses, George	2	1	3		
Libby, Simeon	1	2	3			Morton, James	1	2	5			Moses, Nathˡ	1	1	4		
Libby, Joseph	2		3			Morton, Jabez	1	2	6			Millikan, Polly			1		
Larry, Stepⁿ	2	1	2			Mann, Daniel	1					Moses, George	1		3	1	
Lombard, Butler	1		3			Morton, Ebenʳ, Jr	1	2	5			Meserve, Thoˢ	1	1	3		
Lombard, Nathˡ	1	1	5			McDonald, Pelatiah	1	3	2			Meserve, Elizᵃ	1		3		
Lamb, John	1	3	1			McLellan, Wᵐ, Jr	1	2	5			Marston, Lemˡ	2	5	3		
Lombard, Jnᵒ, Jr	2	3	3			Murch, Ebenʳ, Jr	1		2			McKenny, Abner	1	1	3		
Libby, Reuben	1	4	3			Murch, Samˡ	1		4			Meservy, Clement	3	4	3		
Libby, Lemˡ	1	2	5			Mains, Nichˢ	3	1	3			Maxwell, Willᵐ	1		5		
Lakeman, Wᵐ	1		2			Morton, David	1	3	2			Morris, Charles	1	3	7		
Lombard, Jnᵒ	2		1			McLellan, Cary	1	3	4			Nason, Uriah	1		3		
Lakeman, Josiah	2	2	3			Murch, James	1	3	2			Newcomb, Enos	1	1	4		
Libby, Reuben, Jr	1		2			McGuily, Jnᵒ	1	2	2			Nason, Ephᵐ	1	1	5		
Libby, Jnᵒ	1	3	2			Moody, Joseph	2	2	4			Nason, Abᵐ	1				
Libby, Allison	1	3	2			Murch, Matthias	1	1	3			Nason, Wᵐ	1				
Lombard, Joseph	2		3			Morton, Thoˢ	1	1	1			Newcomb, Samˡ			1		
Libby, Wᵐ	1	1	2			McDonald, Abner	1	1	3			Newbegin, Jnᵒ	1	3	2		
Libby, Mark	1	1	2			Morton, Isaac	1					Nell, John	2	3	3		
Libby, Jethro	2		2			Moody, Robᵗ	1					Phinny, Edmᵈ	3		3		
Lombard, Thoˢ	1	2	1			Mosher, Jaˢ, Jr	1					Phinny, Jnᵒ	2	1	3		
Libby, Edmᵈ	1		2			Murch, Jeremiah	1	1	1			Phinny, Jaˢ	3		3		
Libby, Richᵈ	1	2	1			Murch, Joseph	1					Pain, Richᵈ	1		3		
Libby, Matthew	2		3			Morse, —— (Clothier)	2	2	1			Pain, Wᵐ	2	1	5		
Libby, Mark	1	1	4			Murch, Isaac	1	1				Pain, Jnᵒ	2	4	2		
Libby, Jonᵃ	2	3	3			Mains, David	1					Phinny, Decker	2	3	4		
Libby, Nathˡ	2	3	3			Morton, Reuben	1					Patrick, Charles	2	5	6		
Libby, Robᵗ	1	1	2			Murray, Anthʸ, Jr	1	1	1			Phinny, Joˢ	1	3	4		
Libby, Josiah	3	2	5			Morton, Bryant	1		3			Phinny, Edmᵈ, Junʳ	1	3	3		
Libby, Anthʸ	3	1	3	1		Merril, Daniel	1	5	4			Pain, Thoˢ	2		6		
Libby, Simon	1	1	7			Melvil, Jnᵒ	1	1	5			Plummer, Aaron	1	2	4		
Libby, Thoˢ	2	3	4			McLellan (old Mrs.)		1	2			Phinny, Jnᵒ, Jr	1	1	2		
Larrabee, Benjⁿ	2	2	4			Merril, Danˡ	1	5	4			Phinny, Ebenʳ	1	3	3		
Larrabee, Thoˢ	1		1			Mitchel, Job	2	1	3			Plummer, Isaac	1	3	3		
Libby, Danˡ	2	4	3			Moody (Widow)		1	4			Parsons, Jonᵃ	1	1	1		
Libby, Dominicus	1	3	3			Mitchel, Jereʰ	1					Phinny, Joˢ, Jr	1				
Larrabee, Nathˡ	2	1	6			Marr, Danˡ	1		1			Patrick, Benjⁿ	1				
Libby, Seth	1	1	6			Marr, Lydia		1	3			Prentiss, Samˡ	5	2	6		
Libby, Stepⁿ	4	1	3			Marr, James	1	1	3			Plummer, Chrisʳ	1		4		
Libby, Abner	1	1	3			Mitchel, Wᵐ	1		1			Poland, Moses	1		1		
Libby, Josiah	1	4	3			McKenny, Moses	1	2	7			Phinny, Stepⁿ	1		4		
Libby, Elisha	1	1	5			McKenny, James	3	2	3			Perkins, John	2		3		
Libby, Benjⁿ	1	1	1			Meserve, Elisha	1	2	4			Peabody, Samˡ	1		3		
Libby, Hezekiah	1		3			Meserve, Elisha, Jr	1					Perkins, John	1		1		
Libby, Nathan	1					Matthews, Jnᵒ	1	3	3			Parker, Hannah (Widʷ)		1	4		
Libby, John	1	1	1	1		Morris, Dennis	3	1	4			Parker, Johns (Widʷ)		3	3		
Libby, Jethro	2	1	4			Meserve, Solᵒ	1	2	4			Plummer, Moses	1		1		

HEADS OF FAMILIES—MAINE.

CUMBERLAND COUNTY—Continued.

NAME OF HEAD OF FAMILY.	Free white males of 16 years and upward, including heads of families.	Free white males under 16 years.	Free white females, including heads of families.	All other free persons.	Slaves.	NAME OF HEAD OF FAMILY.	Free white males of 16 years and upward, including heads of families.	Free white males under 16 years.	Free white females, including heads of families.	All other free persons.	Slaves.	NAME OF HEAD OF FAMILY.	Free white males of 16 years and upward, including heads of families.	Free white males under 16 years.	Free white females, including heads of families.	All other free persons.	Slaves.
GORHAM AND SCARBOROUGH TOWNS—con.						**GORHAM AND SCARBOROUGH TOWNS—con.**						**GORHAM AND SCARBOROUGH TOWNS—con.**					
Plummer, Saml	1	4	6			Smith, Peter		1	1	3		Burnum, Jona	1		2		
Plummer, Jesse	1	6	3			Shepherd, Lewis				6		Babb, Thos	2	1	3		
Prout, Joseph	3		2			Thatcher, Josiah	3	2	3			Beal, Simeon	1		3		
Prout, John	1					Thomas, Saml	1	4	3			Berry, Josiah	1		2		
Plummer, Jereh	2	4	4			Thomas, Charles		1	1			Berry, Ephm	1				
Perry, Corns	2	2	3			Thomas, Turf	1	1	1			Berry, Enoch	1		1		
Plummer, Saml, Jr	1					Tyng, Wm	3	1	5	1		Brown, Ellison	1	1	2		
Plaisted, Andrew	1		3			Tole, Jereh	1					Berry, Richard	1	3	2		
Pilsberry, Jos	1	1	2			Thomas, Geo	1	4	4			Berry, Zebulon	1		3		
Pilsberry, Jona	1	1	1			Tryon (Widow)		2	2			Berry, David	1				
Rich, Amos	2	3	5			Thomas, Thos			2			Berry, Timy	1		2		
Ross, Alexr	1		2			Tomson, Wm	2		2			Rand, Christopher	1	3	4		
Roberts, Jos	1	2	4			Tyler, Abm	2	4	2			McIntosh, William	1	2	4		
Roberts, Benja	3	2	5			Tyler, Abm Jr	2		4			**GRAY TOWN.**					
Rand, Jereh	2	1	3			Tyler, Abm, 3d	1	1	1			Moss, Mark	1		2		
Roberts, Jos., Jr	1	2	4			Tomson, Jno & Thos	3	1	2			Greely, William	1	1	3		
Ross, James	1		3			Thurston, Thos	1	4	3			Sprage, John	2	4	4		
Roff (Widow)		2	3			Tomson, Paul	2	4	2			Moss, John	3	2	5		
Roberts, ——	3	2	5			Whitney, Abel	2	1	4			Delano, Ameziah	1	3	2		
Rice, James	1	1	3			Whitney, Amos	2	1	3			White, Thomas	1	2	1		
Rindse, Jotham	2	1	4			Waterhouse, George	1	3	4			Libby, Benjamin	1	1	4		
Rand, Philemon	2		4			Whitney, Joseph	3	3	6			Austin, Stephen	1	3	4		
Robison, Jas	1	1	3			Whitney, Phinehas	2	2	4			Jackson, Francis	1	3	4		
Rice, Matthias	1	3	2			Whitney, Uriel	1		3			Libby, Andrew	4	1	2		
Runnels, Chs	1					Watson, Danl	2		2			Libby, Moses	1	2	1		
Richards, Saml	1	2	3			Whitmore, Saml		2	6			Davis, William	1		5		
Richards, Joseph	1	1	2			Wood, Wm			3			Dutton, Sarah		1	3		
Richards, Jos. (Dumb)	1	1	1			Whitney, Zebulon	2	3	5			Frank, James	1	2	3		
Richards, Jos., Jr	1	1	3			Watson, Ebenr	2	4	4			Fogg, Timothy	2		2		
Rice, Mehitable		1	2			Warren, Jas	1	4	3			Libby, Asa	1		1		
Rice, Richd	1	2	4			Whitney, Danl	1	1	3			Libby, Arther	1	1	2		
Rice, Gideon	1	3	3			Watts, David	1	3	3			Humphrey, Oliver	1	1	1		
Rice, Leml	1	4	2			Whitney, Asa	3	3	5			Libby, Asa	1		4		
Rice, Saml	2	3	4			Whitney, Isaac	1	6	4			Foster, Isaac	1		2		
Skillings, Benja	2		3			Williams, Jereh	1	2	5			Moss, Nathan	2	2	2		
Sylly, John	1	1	2			Ward, Joseph	3		1			Jorden, David	1	4	1		
Stuart, Joseph	1	2	4			Warren, Saml	1	2	3			Doubty, George	1	4	7		
Strout, George	1	1	2			Ward, John	2	4	4			Stevens, Joel	1	2	3		
Stephens, Nathl	3	2	1			Whitney, Nathl	1		4			Stowel, Samuel	3	3	4		
Skilling, Jno	1	1	2			Webb, Eli	2	2	4			Pearly, Samuel	3	2	4		
Skilling, Thos	2	4	2			Weeks, Wm (Widw)		2	1			Jorden, Elijah	1	1	6		
Stephens, Joseph	1	2	2			Whitney, Micah	1	2	4			Nights, Josiah	1	1	3		
Snow, Thos	2	2	2			Whitney, Jotham	1					Cummings, Isaac	1	2	3		
Stevens, A. Hovey	2		1			Watson, Elipht	1	1	1			Young, Nathaniel	1		1		
Snow, Wm	1	2	3			Whitney, Moses	2	3	3			Young, Abraham	1	2	2		
Sawyer, Joel	1		6			Weston, Joseph	1	1	2			Lunt, John	1	3	1		
Strout, Elisha	1	2	5			Warren, Nathl	2	1	3			Coley, James	3	2	3		
Sturgis, Jona	2	5	4			Wescot, Reuben	2	3	2			Stevens, Jonathan	1	1	1		
Swett, Stepn	1	2	5			Williams, Hart	2		2			Small, James	4	3	3		
Swett, Josiah	2	1	1			Webb, Edward	1	1	2			Nash, John	2	1	2		
Smith, Ephm	2	2	4			Wood, Charles	1	1				Haney, Daniel	5		4		
Smith, Hezekiah	1	1	2			Watson, John	2	3	7			Merrel, Nathan	2	2	2		
Stone, Jona	1	3	2			Whitney, Jas	1	3	1			Weeks, Joseph	5		5		
Stephens, Benjn, Jr	1	3	2			Whitney, Priscilla			4			Russel, James	3	2	3		
Stimpson, Alexr	1	2	3			Whitmore, Wm	1	2	6			Merrel, Joseph	1	2	4		
Stuart, Wentworth	1					Whitmore, Danl	1	2	2			Swicker, Richard	1	1	5		
Sawyer, Zechr	2	4	2			Waterman, Malchr	1		3			Fowler, John	1	2			
Stephens, Benja	1		1			Weymouth, Cathr		2	4			Matthews, Jabez	4	4	8		
Snow, Gideon	1	1	1			Wakefield, Jos	1	1	2			Ford, Nathaniel	1	2	3		
Smith, Saml	1	1	2			Weeks, Wm (Widw)		2	1			Sole, Asa	1	3	2		
Sawyer, Stepn	1		2			Weeks, Benjn	1		1			Webster, William	8	3	4		
Sanborn, Mrs	1		1			Wescot, Wm	3		5			Latham, George	1		1		
Swett, Moses	1		2			Wescot, Zebulon	1					Soaper, Salter	3	2	4		
Stevens, Mary			1			Wescot, Richd	2	2	2			Latham, Eliab	2	2	2		
Starbord (Widow)			1			Watson, Jno	1	2	2			York, Robert	1	3	4		
Sawyer, Jno	1	5	2			Wilber, Jno, Jr	1	2	4			Cummings, Joseph	3	3	5		
Skillings, Simeon	1	6	4			Warren, Walter	1		2			Humphreys, James	2	3	11		
Small, Saml	1		2			Waterhouse, Jos	1		1			Frank, Thomas	1	2	3		
Small, James	1	3	3			Waterhouse, Nathl	1	4	6			Cummings, Daniel	3	1	4		
Sevy, Nathl	3	2	4			Waterhouse, Timy	2	4	3			Dolley, John	3		2		
Sevy, Ebenr, Jr	1	2	1			Waterhouse, Saml	2	2	2			Libby, Moses	1		1		
Steward, Jno	1		1			Waterhouse, Jno	1	2	4			Doubty, Joseph	1		5		
Steward, Saml	1	1	6			Waterhouse, Theos	1	4	1			Young, John	1	2	3		
Steward, Timo	1	3	2			Warren, Benja	3	3	6			Young, Job	1	2	6		
Sevy, Ebenr	1		3			Wingate, Jona	1		1			Libby, Daniel	3	1	8		
Sevy, Reuben	1	3	2			Wingate, Jona, Jr	1	1	3			Libby, Joel	1	1	3		
Sevy, Thos, Jr	1	2	2			Watson, Jona	2	1	2			Hayden, Jeremiah	1		1		
Sevy, Thos	3	3	4			Witten, Thos	1	1	3			Nash, Samuel	1	3	4		
Smith, Rachel			2			Wilbert, John	1		4			Twitchel, Jeremiah	1		1		
Steward, Jno, Jr	3		6			Webster (Widow)			2			Thompson, Samuel	3	1	5		
Shute, George	1	1	3			Vickery, David	2	1	5			Ramsdel, Gideon	2	4	5		
Steward, Joseph	3	3	6			Young, Joseph, Senr	1		1			Buker, Israel H	1	3	1		
Shute, Js	2	3	3			Young, Joseph, Jr	1	2	3			Libby, William	1	1	3		
Stone, Sol	3	3	3			Berry, Wilm						Hunt, David	3	2			
Staple, Jere	2	3	6			Burnam, Danl, Jr, (Widw)		1	2			Cooley, Richard	1		2		
Sawyer, David	1		1			Berry, Benja	2	3	5			Moss, Levi	1				
Southgate, Robt	3	1	8			Berry, Jno	2	3	2			Merrel, John		1	2		
Staples, Saml	2	2	6			Berry, Jona	2		5			Pennel, Clemuel	1		3		
Staples, Saml, Jr	1	2	2			Bryant, Jno	2	3	4			Starberd, Jethro	1	3	3		
Shute, Wm	1	2	2			Bryant, Eleazer	2	1	3			Dyer, Jedediah	1				
Shute, Hannah	1		1			Berry, Sol	1	1	5			Small, Isaac	1	5	6		
Smith, Josiah	1		5			Berry, Elisha, Jr	1		2			Moody, Daniel	1	3	2		
Snow, Paul	1	1	2			Banks, Moses	3	1	2			Barber, Lucy					
Swicher, Wm	1	2	1			Banks, Bracy	1	1	1								
Sevy, David	1	1	1														

CUMBERLAND COUNTY—Continued.

GRAY TOWN—con.

NAME OF HEAD OF FAMILY.	Free white males of 16 years and upward, including heads of families	Free white males under 16 years.	Free white females, including heads of families.	All other free persons.	Slaves.
Cobb, Jedediah	2	1	6		
Merrel, Abel	1		4		
Berry, Pellatiah	1	2	2		
Pennel, Joseph	1	3	4		
Nason, Isaac	3	1	6		
Fletcher, Zachariah	2		3		
Nash, David	1	3	5		
Merrel, John	2		2		
Libby, Andrew	1	2	4		

HARPSWELL TOWN.

NAME OF HEAD OF FAMILY.	Free white males of 16 years and upward, including heads of families	Free white males under 16 years.	Free white females, including heads of families.	All other free persons.	Slaves.
Allen, Ephraim	3	1	4		
Clark, Josiah	2		2		
Clark, John	1	1	4		
Allen, Elisabeth			2		
Allen, Elisha	1		2		
Allexander, Hugh	1	4	3		
Allexander, Jane	1		3		
Merriman, Thomas	4		3		
Alexander, David	2	2	5		
Booker, Josiah	1	3	3		
Curtes, Ezekiel	4	2	4		
Childs, John	1		3		
Dunning, Andw	1	1	3		
Dunning, Benja	4		3		
Stackpole, John	1	3	5		
Doil, James	1	1	4		
Ewing, Joseph	2		3		
Ewing, Alexander			4		
Ewing, Joseph, Junr	1	2	3		
Ewing, James	1	2	4		
Springet, Nathl	1		1		
Snow, Isaac	3	1	4		
Snow, Willm	1		1		
Merril, Henry	1	4	4		
Snow, John	2	2	3		
Snow, Aaron	1	1	1		
Snow, Abizah	1		2		
Birthright, Peter	2	1	2		
Carr, Joseph	2	1	1		
Simscott, Joseph	1		3		
Simscott, Moses	1	2	3		
Snow, Saml	2		2		
Snow, John	1	2	2		
Dingley, Levi	1	2	3		
Small, Taylor	1	1	2		
Thompson, John	1		3		
Small, Mark	1	2	4		
Holbrook, John	2		2		
Matthews, John	1	2	2		
Purnton, Stephen	3	1	5		
Obins, Philip	2	2	4		
Easman, Nathl	2	1	3		
Hopkins, Simeon	2		3		
Ridley, Mark	1	4	3		
Jones, John Stephen	1	2	3		
Bankins, John	2		2		
Williams, Saml		1	2		
Otis, Saml	1	2	2		
Williams, Benja	1	2	2		
Thompson, Willm	2	1	7		
Easman, Kingsbury	3	2	5		
Ridley, James	1		2		
Snow, Isaac	1		2		
Totman, Joseph	1	4	1		
Cooms, Anthony	3	3	5		
Cooms, Joseph	1	2	7		
Doughty, James	1		2		
Whaling, Patrick	2		2		
Blake, Jacob	1		6		
Toothaker, Joanna			3		
Randal, Paul	2	1	4		
Thomas, James	1		3		
Stovar, Johnson	2	5	5		
Curtes, Paul	1	4	5		
Webber, David	3	3	4		
Stover, John	1		4		
Clever, Harrison			4		
Randal, Daniel	2	3	3		
Johnson, James	1		3		
Curtes, Michl	2	6	3		
Bibber, Lemuel	2	4	3		
Haskel, Ward	1	3	2		
Haskel, Ruth			3		
Toothaker, Seth	1	1	3		
Pinkham, Ebenr	2	1	3		
Haskel, Willm	1		6		
Pinkham, Nathl	1	3	3		
Haskel, Willebe	1		2		
Johnson, Jacob	3		5		
Johnson, Jona	1	2	4		
Johnson, David	1	4	2		
Weber, Daniel	3	3	4		
Bibber, James	1	4	4		

HARPSWELL TOWN—con.

NAME OF HEAD OF FAMILY.	Free white males of 16 years and upward, including heads of families	Free white males under 16 years.	Free white females, including heads of families.	All other free persons.	Slaves.
Bailey, Jacob	1	3	3		
Webber, Mary	1		2		
Atherton, Jona	1	5	3		
Booker, James	1		6		
Curtis, Caleb	1	2	4		
Curtes, Benja	1	1	2		
Curtes, Ambros	1	1	1		
Allen, Elijah	2		3		
Wheeller, David	2		1		
Buker, Daniel	1	1	3		
Duglas, Daniel	1	1	3		
Wheeler, David	1		1		
Eaton, Saml	2	1	2		
Farr, Thos	2	1	5		
Merriman, James	1	2	6		
Redock, John	2		7		
Stover, Alcot	2	5	4		
Easters, John	3	2	4		
Blake, John, Junr	1	2	5		
Duglas, Elijah	1	1	2		
Blake, John	5	3	4		
Orr, Clement	1	4	3		
Orr, John	1	3	4		
Sinnet, Michl	2		3	4	
Smith, John	1		3	2	
Bishop, Luke	2		4		
Reid, John	2	2	3		
Butler, James	1	3	3		
Weare, Robert	1	4	3		
Sinnet, Stephen	1	1	3		
Gardiner, Seth	1	2	3		
Smith, Jeremiah	1	1	3	2	
Alexander, Saml	2	1	6		
Wilson, Willm	1	2	8		
Allen, Elijah	1		2		
Wilson, David	1		2		
Bishop, Abner		1	2		
Curtes, Jacob	1	3	4		
Scofield, Clement	2	4	4		
Tinney, Seth	2		1		
Brown, John	1	3	1		
Jordan, John	1		4		
Martin, Matthias	1	1	2		
Booker, Joseph	2		5		
Goodridge, Jewett	1		3		
Nelson, Thos		1	3		
Wilson, James	2	3	4		
Alexander, Willm	1	3	6		
Doile, Elijah	1		2		
Merriman, Walter	3	3	6		
Silvester, Willm	3		4	2	
Jordan, John	2	1	4		
Doile, Elisha	1		1		
Dyer, James	2		3		
Curtes, Nehemiah	2		3	1	
Curtes, Mercy	1		3		
Merriman, Walter	1	1	2		
Merriman, Michl	1	2	2		
Gardiner, James	1		3		
Town, Willm	2	3	3		
Merriman, Hugh	2	2	4		
Merriman, Timo	1	2	1		
Scofield, Stephen	1		3		
Browner, John	1	2	2		
Gardiner, Luther	1	2	5		
Wilson, Alexander	1		2		
Ward, Nehemiah	2	3	2		
Cooms, Willm	1	1	2		
Holbrook, Jona	2	2	5		
Haynes, David	1	3	3		
Leavitt, Naphthali	1	5	3		
Anderson, Daniel	1	3	4		
Cooms, John	1	3	2		
Finney, Seth	1		3		
Brown, Daniel	1	2	6		
Small, Saml	2	2	4		
Totman, Josiah	1	2	2		
Dinslow, Benja	1	3	3		
Snow, Hannah			3		
Totman, Henry	1	3	2		
Ridley, Mark	1		2		
Hersey, Willm	1	1	3		
Toothaker, Ebena	1	1	1		
Toothaker, Ebena	1		4		
Toothaker, Nathl	1	1	3		
Ross, Thos	1	3	3		
Linscott, John	1	3	3		
Morse, Mary	1		2		
Purnton, Joshua	1	1	2		
Hall, Nathl	1		2		
Hall, Joseph	2	2	1		
Purnton, Joshua, Jur	1	4	3		
Hall, John	1		6		
Purnton, Robert	1	3	3		

NEW GLOUCESTER TOWN.

NAME OF HEAD OF FAMILY.	Free white males of 16 years and upward, including heads of families	Free white males under 16 years.	Free white females, including heads of families.	All other free persons.	Slaves.
Pierce, Samuel	2		3		
Baley, Robert	2		2		
Harris, John	1	4	3		
Yetton, James	1		1		
White, William	1	4	3		
Witham, Thomas	1	3	4		
Pierce, Joseph	1		3		
Merrell, Joshua	3	2	7		
Metguin, John	1	2	2		
Metguin, William	1		1		
Emmory, William	1	2	2		
Allen, Joseph	1	1	1		
Pierce, Joseph	1	1	3		
Witham, Thomas	2	5	6		
Gore, Joshua	2	5	6		
Witham, Jeremiah	3	4	5		
McIntire, David	2	2	5		
Titcomb, John	1	3	6		
Stinchfield, Ephraim	1		4		
Bennet, Isaac	1	2	2		
Stinchfield, John	3		3		
Penny, Thomas		4	4		
Honeyford, Robert	2	3	4		
Haskell, John	2	5	5		
Blake, James	3		5		
Bennet, Jonathan	3		8		
Bennet, Nathaniel	4	2	7		
Woodman, Joseph	1		2		
Tufts, John	1	1	7		
Rains, Joseph	1	4	5		
Forbush, Robert	3	1	3		
Woodman, David	3	1	1		
Nights, Phebe		2	4		
Haskel, Job	1		1		
Pierce, Joseph	2	1	4		
Irish, William	1	1	1		
Haskel, Jonathan L	1		2		
Smith, Josiah	4	3	5		
Harris, William	2	2	3		
Washborn, Stephen	3	3	3		
Harris, Simeon	1		3		
Parsons, William	1	1	5		
Hearsy, Elisabeth			3		
Stinchfield, James	1	4	4		
Stevens, Paul	1		3		
Winslow, Barnabas	2	2	7		
Foxcroft, Samuel	3		5		
Allen, Nathaniel C	3	1	4		
Arnold, Bildad	1	2	3		
Allen, James	1	2	3		
Ayers, Thomas	2		6		
Allen, Nehemiah	2	1	3		
Allen, Isaac	1		2		
Atwood, Solomon	2	3	2		
Bradberry, Jabes	3		2		
Bridgham, William	2	3	4		
Bradberry, Benjamin	2		4		
Baley, John	1	5	2		
Bryant, Balden	1	5			
Chandler, Peleg			1	6	
Collins, Ebenezer	1	1	3		
Davis, Ebenezer	3		4	5	
Dyer, Lemuel	1		3		
Day, Zebedee	1	1	3		
Bishop, James	1	3	4		
Bradford, Ephraim	1	5	4		
Bennet, Francis	1	5	2		
Campbell, Andrew	3		3		
Cushman, Jabes	2	1	6	1	
Bradberry, Samuel	1	3	4		
Bradberry, Moses	1	2	3		
Cotton, Adam	2	2	3		
Davis, Abel	1	2	4		
Evelith, Nathaniel	3	4	3		
Collins, Philemon	1				
Cobb, Joseph	1		4		
Chandler, Philip	1	3	3		
Fogg, Enoch	1		3		
Graffam, Mary			4		
Glass, Ezekiel	1	1			
Haskell, Jacob	2		5		
Grover, William	1	1			
Soames, Jonathan	1		1		
Black, Boston				5	
Philip, Eliphus	1		2		
Nevus, Samuel	1	4	5		
Haskell, Mary			5		
Ryall, Eli	1		2		
Haskell, Nathaniel	2	4	5		
Gerrish, Joseph	1	2	2		
Sergeant, Daniel	1		1		
Paul, David	1	1	1		
Taxbox, Samuel	1	1	4		
Woodberry, Joseph	1	1	4		
Royal, Eli	1	1	3		

HEADS OF FAMILIES—MAINE.

CUMBERLAND COUNTY—Continued.

NAME OF HEAD OF FAMILY.	Free white males of 16 years and upward, including heads of families.	Free white males under 16 years.	Free white females, including heads of families.	All other free persons.	Slaves.	NAME OF HEAD OF FAMILY.	Free white males of 16 years and upward, including heads of families.	Free white males under 16 years.	Free white females, including heads of families.	All other free persons.	Slaves.	NAME OF HEAD OF FAMILY.	Free white males of 16 years and upward, including heads of families.	Free white males under 16 years.	Free white females, including heads of families.	All other free persons.	Slaves.
NEW GLOUCESTER TOWN—con.						**NEW GLOUCESTER TOWN—con.**						**NORTH YARMOUTH TOWN—con.**					
Bradberry, William	2	3	4			Toby, Richard	3	2	8			Mitchel, Daniel	1	4	2		
Cleaves, Ebenezer	1	1	3			Toby, Page	1	2	3			Lewis, Asa			2		
McGuire, John	1	2	3			Trew, William	1	2	6			Brown, Moses	2		1		
Stinchfield, John	2	1	3			Trew, Jabes	2	4	5			True, Willm	2	3	3		
Haskell, John	2	4	8			Ryder, James	1		2			Brown, Ephraim	1	1	2		
Ingersol, Nathaniel	1	2	3			Raymond, Lemuel	1		3			Weare, Peter	1		5		
Low, Nicholls	1	4	4			Pierce, Abraham	1	2	3			True, Jona	1		2		
Lane, Ebenezer	1	1	4			Forbush, Samuel	1		2			Brown, Joseph	1	2	3		
McQuin, Edmund	1		2			Woodman, Joseph	2	1	6			Brown, Jacob, Junr	1		4		
Mastin, Robert		1	2			Webber, John	1		2			Videto, Joseph	1	1	2		
Morgan, John	1	1	1			Woodman, John	2	3	4			Humphry, Benja	2	2	2		
Noyes, Simeon	2		3			Stinchfield, John	1		3			Staple, Daniel	2		3		
Parsons, Isaac	3	2	8			Hearsy, Elisabeth		1	5			Hobbs, Willm	1	3	2		
Rearson, Luke	3	4	5			Haskell, Eliphalet	2	4	5			Moxy, Mercy	1	2	7		
Stevens, Paul	1		2			Herrin, Robert	1	4	3			Tuttle, Burrel	1	3	2		
Stinchfield, Mary	1	5	4			Haskell, William	1	4	4			Mitchel, David	1	2	3		
Tufts, John	1	1	7			Lane, Ebenezer	1	3	4			Mitchel, Loring	1	2	1		
Tucker, William	1	2	5									Drinkwater, David	1	5	3		
Toal, Micael	2		4			**NORTH YARMOUTH TOWN.**						Mitchel, Jona	4	1	4		
Witham, Benjamin	1	1	1									Currey, Mehltable	1	1	2		
Washborn, Stephen	3	1	4			Davis, Timothy	3		3			Melcher, Ammi	4	3	2		
Davis, Sarah			1			Davis, Thomas	1		1			Loring, Ance		1	4		
Bartlett, Josiah	1	3	5			Davis, John	1	3	5			Dinsmore, John	1		2		
Bartlett, Malchi	3		1			Lawrence, John	1	4	2			Young, Joseph	4		7		
Emmory, Mark	1		2			Parker, Saml	2	2	6			Sark, Polly			1		
Buxton, Samuel	1	2	1			Chandler, Joshua	1	2	2			Gilman, Revd Tristram	3	3	5		
Allen, Nehemiah	1	6	2			Worthley, Daniel	1	2	4			Gorden, Nathl	2	1	3		
Bennet, Nathaniel	1	1	1			Parker, Joseph	1	2	1			Sanborn, Benja	3	4	3		
Welch, Joseph	1	2	2			Mitchel, Horton	1	4	2			Sanborn, Paul, Junr	1	2	5		
Cotton, Adam	2	3	5			Ross, Isaac	1	1	3			Buxton, Willm	2	1	4		
Cleaves, Ebenezer	1	1	1			White, Abel	1		2			Titcomb, Edmund	5	1	3		
Cleaves, Edmund	2	2	4			Winslow, Benja	1	2	2			Titcomb, Joseph	1	1	5		
Cobb, Silvenus	1	2	4			Worthley, Saml	1		1			Switcher, Seth	4		4		
Evelith, Nathaniel	1	1	1			Seberey, Saml	3	4	1			Blanchard, Bezaiah	1				
Evelith, Isaac	1		3			Moore, Joanna	1		3			Blanchard, Nathl	4		3		
Fogg, Samuel	2	2	4			Mitchel, Saml	1	1	2			Switzer, John	3		3		
Fogg, Edmund	1	4	4			Mitchel, Benja	1	5	3			Merril, Nathan	2	1	2		
Mason, Ebenezer	1	5	4			Sebry, Elizabeth	1	2	3			Prince, Thomas	1	2	5	5	
Merrel, Peeter	1	2	4			Mitchel, Mehltable			1	1		Switzer, Benja	1	1	2		
Loring, Asa	1					Tusk, Lemuel	2	4	3			Noyes, Moses	3	2	3		
Lane, Benjamin	2	1	3			Elwel, Pain	2	4	4			Noyes, Zebulon	1		1		
Loring, Bezeliel	3	3	3			Elwel, Henry	1	2	4			Noyes, Willm	1		3		
Haskel, Moses	1		3			Elwel, Pain, Junr	1	1	1			Stubs, Jona	1	1	4		
Haskel, Benjamin	1	1	2			Russel, Hannah	1		4			Harris, Amos	3	1	3		
Groce, Isaac	1		2			Cutter, Saml	4	1	4			Merril, Sarah		4	3		
Glover, John	2	1	3			Mitchel, Seth	2	2	5			Thorn, Ebenezer	1	1	2		
Forbush, John	1		4			Humphry, Ebena	1	3	4			True, Israel	2	4	6		
Honeyford, Robert B	3	3	4			Foster, Nathl	1		3			Drinkwater, Silvanus	2	4	5		
Haskell, Moses	4	1	4			Batcheldor, Peter	2	2	2			Stubs, Richd	1	4	4		
Hutcherson, William	1	1	6			Bysom, Oliver	2	6	1			Stubs, Benja	1	3	4		
Hammon, Samuel	1		4			Prat, Sherebiah	3	3	6			Stubs, Jera	1	3	5		
Hatch, Fisher	1	3	1			Sargeant, Willm	1		1			Spear, Joshua	1	2	3		
Haskell, Gideon	1	3	2			Blaisdel, Jeremiah	1	2	6			Allen, Ebenezer	1	2	2		
Lane, Ebenezer	1	1	4			Mitchel, Willm	1	2	2			Stubs, Moses	1	2	2		
Lukes, Elkany	1		6			White, Luther	1		1			Reid, Willm	1	2	5		
Lukes, Ebenezer	1		3			Thompson, Saml	1	1	4			Wyman, Josiah	1		4		
Loring, Ezekiel	3		2			Humphrys, Joseph	1	3	2			Weeks, Nathl	2	3	2		
Morgan, Luke	2	1	4			True, John	1	2	3			Sawyer, Joseph	5	1	3		
Merrell, Elias	1	4	5			Young, Joseph	4		7			Clough, Amos	2	3	2		
Merrell, Moses	1	3	4			Perry, Ezra	1	2	2			Maxwell, Robert	1	2	1		
Merrell, Samuel	1	1				Ross, Peter	1		1			Drinkwater, Saml	1		7		
Haskell, Joel	2	2	2			Videto, Comfort	1	1	2			Tuttle, Elijah	1		2		
Haskell, Nathan	2	6	6			Brown, Joseph	1	2	2	5		Sawyer, John	1		1		
Harthaway, Seth	1	3	2			Corless, Ebenezer	2	1	1			Guerney, Lemuel	2		1		
Hayes, John	1	3	1			Lowe, Solomon	1	1	4			Prince, James	2	3	7		
Merrell, John	4	2	6			Johnson, David	1	1	3			Blanchard, Ebenezer	2	2	3		
Merrell, Ezekiel	3		4			Loring, Saml	1		1			Lowel, Stephen	2	1	4		
Neilson, David	1	1	2			Loring, Richmond	1		1			Blanchard, Nathl	1		4		
Parsons, William	1	1	5			Hix, Joseph	3	3	7			Prince, David	1	6	2		
Prince, John	3	1	3			Mitchel, Jona	3	2	2			Shaw, Daniel	1		1		
Row, Jonathan	2	1	4			Marston, Levi	1	2	3			Shaw, Joseph	1		1		
Webber, Micael	1	2	3			Rider, James	2	2	2			King, Eliab	1	4	2		
Whorfe, Joseph	1	3	4			Johnson, Thos	1	1	1			Hobbs, Josiah	1	3	1		
Walker, James	1	2	1			Marston, Simeon	1		3			Allen, Jacob	1	1	3		
Tylor, Joseph	1	2	3			Chandler, Jona	1	3	4			Hill, Thomas	2		2		
Shaw, Benjamin	1	2	3			Jones, David	2	2	6			Field, Zachariah	1		1		
Hall, William	1		2			Hatch, Abijah	3	1	3			Harris, Amos	1		1		
Ramsdel, Kimball	1		2			True, Hannah		1	2			Blanchard, Hozea	4	4	4		
Wells, Simeon	1	3	4			True, David	1		2			Buxton, Benja	2	4	5		
White, William	1	3	2			Ludon, Joseph	2	3	7			Prat, Thomas	1	3	4		
Parsons, Edward	3	4	3			Brown, Jacob	1		2			Wyman, Willm	1	1	1		
Penny, Thomas	2	4	4			Brown, John	1	2	3			Prince, Paul	1	3	5		
Pierson, Samuel	2		1			Noyes, Nathl	1	2	3			Black, Joab	1	1	2		
Widgery, William	1	2	2			Weare, Elijah	1		3			Skillens, Isaac	2			1	
Walker, Micael	3	5	3			Videto (Widow)			3			Goodwin, John	1		1		
Robertson, Solomon	1		2			Latherby, Saml	1	1	6			Bracket, Jeremiah	1	3	2		
Parsons, Moses	1		3			Fellows, Saml	1		2			Leighton, Andw	2	2	2		
Row, William	2	3	5			Field, James	1	3	4			Ridout, Willm	2	2	1		
Row, Zebedee	1	1	4			Mitchel, Solomon	4		6			Ridout, Nicholas	1		3		
Stevens, Nathaniel	4		3			Winslow, Else			2			Gurney, Lemuel, Junr	1	1	1		
Sawyer, John	1	2	3			Woodward, Davis	2	6	2			Cleaver, Willm	1		1		
Sawyer, Parker	1	1	3			Wortley, John	2	3	3			Reed, Zebulon	1		1		
Tylor, John	3	3	7			Ryal, Winthrop	3		3			Knight, Enoch	1	3	5		
Tucker, Lemuel	4	1	3			Lewis, John	3		1			Small, John	1	3	3		
Smith, Jonah	3	2	3									Martin, Willm	3	3	7	1	

FIRST CENSUS OF THE UNITED STATES.

CUMBERLAND COUNTY—Continued.

Name of head of family.	Free white males of 16 years and upward, including heads of families.	Free white males under 16 years.	Free white females, including heads of families.	All other free persons.	Slaves.
NORTH YARMOUTH TOWN—con.					
Dilleno, Ezekiel	3		9		
Prince, Paul	2		2		
Prince, Ammi	1		1		
Sturdivant, John	1				
Sturdivant, David	2	3	4		
Blanchard, Nathl	5		8		
Drinkwater, Danl	1	4	2		
Prince, Pyan	1	1	2		
Blanchard, John	3	3	2		
Maugridge, Benja	1	1	2		
Fisher, Joseph	1		2		
Farrow, John	1		3		
Farrow, Nathan	1	1	3		
Seales, Elizabeth	2		4		
Loring, Solomon	1	2	5		
Greely, Eliphalet	3	5	3		
Prince, Cushing	1	3	5		
Fisher, Onesiphorus	1	2	4		
Blanchard, Joshua	2	2	5		
Blanchard, Seth	1	5	2		
Loring, Richmond	3	2	4		
Mason, Saml	2	3	4		
Moore, Edmond	1	2	3		
Kimbal, Nathl	1	2	2		
Drinkwater, John	1	2	2		
Loring, Mary	1		2	1	
Prince, John	1	3	1		
Chase, Humphry	1	4	6		
Whitehouse, Zadock	2		8		
Chase, Willm	1		1		
Parker, Benja	2	1	4		
Parker, James	2		3		
Mirach, Willm	1	1	2		
Molton, Elizabeth	2		3		
Webster, John	1	2	6		
Gardner, Elisha	1	1	2		
Haze, John	3	3	4		
Buckman, Willm	1	3	7		
Drinkwater, Joseph	3	1	4		
Hill, Kiah	1	4	3		
Hamilton, Roland	2	1	5		
Weeks, Willm	2		5		
Shaw, Benja	1	2	3		
Carman, Francis	3	1	6		
Hill, Eleazer	1		3		
Greely, Stephen	1	3	3		
Hammond, Peter	2	3	5		
Eaton, Obadiah	2		3		
Trough, Solomon	4	1	3		
Haze, Amos	1	1	3		
Gray, Joseph	3	4	3		
Bates, Edsel	2	3	5		
Bennett, Nathl	2	1	3		
Gray, Andrew	2	2	9		
Pattinger, Arthur	2		3		
Gray, Jabiah			1		
Miller, Mary			2		
Drinkwater, Perris	1	2	2		
Robin, Thaddeus	1	1	2		
Gray, John	2	2	3		
Drinkwater, John	2	2	7		
Barnwell, Edward	1	2	4		
Prince, Elizabeth	1	1	3		
Pettee, James	1	4	4		
Chandler, Elisabeth			4		
Southworth, John	1	1	7		
Gooch, John	3	2	5		
Gooch, Benja	1		2		
Gooch, Nathl	1	3	2		
Russel, Thos Chandler	2	2	9		
Lawrence, Saml	1	2	3		
Brown, Danl	1	3	1		
Mitchel, Jonathan, Jr	2	1	2		
Safford, Nathan	1	2	2		
Gipson, Thos	4	3	4		
Cutler, John	1		2		
Mitchel, Jacob, Jr	1	2	5		
Storer, Matthias	2	2	5		
Stubs, Saml	1	3	5		
Colyer, Joshua	1		2		
Byram, Theos	1		1		
Mills, Alexander	1		3		
Biles, Charles	1		3		
Merrill, Saml	2	1	2		
Merrill, Saml, Junr	1	1	1		
Merrill, Nathl	1		1		
Wood, Bethuel	2		7		
Loring, John	1	2	3		
Baker, Saml	3		6		
Milekin, John	3		4		
Besto, Joseph	1	1	2		
Hammond, Saml	1		7		
Barton, Winthrop	2	3	3		
Barton, Ammy	1	3	2		
Ring, Eleazer	2	3	3		
NORTH YARMOUTH TOWN—con.					
Chandler, David	1	2	4		
Wait, Daniel	1	1	3		
Chandler, Rufus	1		2		
Oaks, John	1	3	3		
Prince, Thos	2	2	3		
Loring, Levi	2	6	3		
Ring, Andw	1	2	2		
York, Saml	4	1	6		
Cushman, Isaiah	1	1	5		
Switcher, Willm	2	3	3		
Lowing, Thos	2	3	3		
Haze, Jacob	1	2	4		
Hamilton, John	3	1	6		
Hammond, John	1		1		
Baker, Saml	1	2	4		
Johnson, Nathan	2	2	4		
Prince, Stephen	1	3	2		
Simpson, Thos	1	4	5		
Baker, Saml, Junr	1		2		
True, Winthrop		1	1		
Harris, Stephen	2	3	3		
Skillens, Josiah	1	3	5		
Libbey, Reuben	1	2	2		
Porter, Nehemiah	1	1	4		
Hamilton, Willm	1	1	3		
Lufkin, Nathl	1	4	2		
Porter, Nehemiah	1		2		
Marston, Jesper	1		4		
Marston, John	3	4	6		
Marston, Joshua	2		2		
Allen, Job	1	1	3		
Chandler, David	1	2	4		
Wait, Danl	1	1	2		
Chandler, Rufus	1		2		
Sele, Jessa	1	3	2		
Ricker, Wintworth	1	2	4		
Webber, Jona	1	3	2		
Sawyer, Solomon	1		3		
Sawyer, Solomon, Jur	1	1	5		
Hamilton, John	2		1		
Hamilton, Ambros	2	4	7		
Johnson, James	1	3	3		
OTISFIELD PLANTATION.					
Pierce, George	2		2		
Bartlett, Eleazer	3	1	3		
Gammon, William	1	3	4		
Thurston, Thomas	3		2		
Thurston, David	1		1		
Knight, Mark	4	1	2		
Knight, Jonathan	1	1	2		
Spurr, Joseph	3	1	3		
Spurr, Enoch	1		2		
Hancock, Joseph	2	1	5		
Patch, Benjamin	1	1	4		
Kneeland, David	2	3	2		
Gammon, David	1	3	3		
Pray, David	2		4		
Cobb, Daniel	1	4	3		
Moss, Joseph	2	2	2		
White, Joseph	4	1	5		
Edward, Nathaniel	1	2	4		
White, Joseph	1	2	2		
Reed, Mary	1	1	4		
Gammon, Samuel	1	3	3		
Brition, Jonathan	1		12		
Turner, Elisha	3	2			
Harnock, Elias	2		2		
Knight, Zebulon	2	1	4		
Bride, John	1		2		
Cates, Joseph	2	2	5		
Haskell, Catharine	2	1	3		
Green, Benjamin	1	4	3		
Mores, Jonathan	2	3	3		
Mayberry, Thomas	1	1	5		
Mayberry, David	1	1	4		
PLANTATION NO. 4.					
Jackson, Levi	1	1	4		
Twichel, Moses	1	3	4		
Jackson, Lemuel	2		15		
Jackson, Isaac	1	2	5		
Jackson, Lemuel, Jnr	1	4	2		
Staples, Daniel	1	1	2		
Cushman, Caleb	1	2	3		
Jackson, Barnabas	3	3	2		
Nelson, Nathan	1	1	3		
Rawson, Ebenezer	1		1		
Whitney, Clark	1				
Barrows, Malaga	1	2	2		
Dean, Edmund	1	2	2		
Andrews, David	3	2	1		
PLANTATION NO. 4—continued.					
Hubbard, Levi	1	2	1		
Warren, Abijah	1		1		
Gray, John	1		1		
Pratt, Luther	1		2		
Fewell, John	2	2	2		
Young, Nathl	1	1	3		
Smith, Josiah	1		2		
Hammond, Benjn, Jnr	1	2	3		
Chesley, David	1	2	3		
Dean, Jacob	1		1		
Stowel, Elias	1		1		
Stowel, Nathl	1		1		
Fuller, Aaron	1	2	2		
Bisby, Ruben	1	1	2		
Cole, John	1		1		
Bray, Ezekiel	1		1		
Gardiner, Nathl	1		3		
Dureld, Saml	1		1		
Billings, John	1		1		
Gorham, David	1		1		
Bessee, Thos	1		1		
Knight, Daniel	1	3	3		
Pratt, Nathl	1	1	3		
Wightman, Robert	1		3		
Sturdivant, Frances	2	3	3		
Sturdivant, Asa	1	1	2		
Dunham, Asa	1		3		
Bessee, John	1	2	5		
Baker, James	1	1	2		
Rerce, Nathan	1	4	2		
Perry, Joseph	1	2	2		
Ricket, John	2	2	5		
Ricket, Isaac	1		1		
Botster, Isaac	2	4	1		
Whitney, Danl	1		2		
Morse, James	1		3		
Hall, Jona	1	1	4		
Hall, Abijah	1		1		
Haskel, Nathl	1	1	1		
Robinson, Stephen	1		1		
Stowel, Daniel	1	1	2		
Stowel, Willm	1	2	2		
Dwella, Allen	1	3	3		
Briggs, Seth	1	3	3		
Cummins, Elisha	1	3	4		
Morse, Seth	1	1	3		
Buck, Peter	1	3	3		
Hubbard, Reuben	1		1		
Stevens, Thos	1	2	2		
Cole, Eleazer	1	2	6		
Smith, Merodick	2		1		
Swift, Joseph	1	2	1		
Swan, William	1		2		
Gardiner, Saml	1	1	1		
Gardiner, Wllm	1	1	1		
Shirtliff, Jona	2		1		
Shirtliff, Jona, Jr	1	2	2		
Barrows, Asa	2	3	3		
Washburn, Jacob	2	3	4		
Duval, Peter	1	2	3		
Bryant, Soloman	3	2	3		
Brooks, Peter	1	2	2		
Daniels, John	2	5	4		
PORTLAND TOWN.					
Smith, Thomas	1	2			
Dean, Samuel	4		3	1	
Stephenson, John	2	4	5		
Thorlo, John	2	1	7		
Cammet, Dudley	3		5		
Jorden, James	2	2	6		
Wheeler, Mary			2		
Crosby, Lydia	1		8	1	
Rice, Lettice			1		
Mumford, Samuel	2	2	3		
Haynes, Matthias	1	1	6		
Walte, Benjamin	1		2		
Weeks, Joseph	3	2	7		
Weeks, Lemuel	3	5	6		
Ramsey, John	1		2		
Hall, Moses	2	1	2		
Cobb, William	1	5	1	5	
Bradbury, Jacob	1	4	2		
Bradbury, Thomas	3	2	4		
Bradbury, Samuel	1	1	8		
Plummer, Moses	2		2		
Thomas, Stephen	1	2	2		
Ilsly, Enoch	2	2	4	1	
Williams, Joseph	1	1	2		
Cumings, Thomas	1		1		
Fox, John	4	3	7	6	
Deering, Nathaniel	2	1	2	3	
Sanford, Thomas	3	2	7		

HEADS OF FAMILIES—MAINE.

CUMBERLAND COUNTY—Continued.

NAME OF HEAD OF FAMILY.	Free white males of 16 years and upward, including heads of families.	Free white males under 16 years.	Free white females, including heads of families.	All other free persons.	Slaves.	NAME OF HEAD OF FAMILY.	Free white males of 16 years and upward, including heads of families.	Free white males under 16 years.	Free white females, including heads of families.	All other free persons.	Slaves.	NAME OF HEAD OF FAMILY.	Free white males of 16 years and upward, including heads of families.	Free white males under 16 years.	Free white females, including heads of families.	All other free persons.	Slaves.
PORTLAND TOWN—con.						**PORTLAND TOWN—con.**						**PORTLAND TOWN—con.**					
Harden, Stephen	1	4	3			Robinson, Joshua	1	3	4			Hana, John	1		1		
Cox, Lemuel	2		4			Hassack, Charles	1	2	3			Thompson, Thomas	1	1	1		
Stout, William	1	1	4			Lunt, James	4	1	4			Moore, John	1		2		
Starberd, Ebenezer	1	2	3			Phillips, John	1	1	1			Barber, Joseph	1	1	5		
Knights, John	1		2			Toby, Sarah	1		4			Newell, Zachariah	1	1	1		
Childs, Mary		1	6			Kenney, Thomas	2	2	2			Knight, Robert	1	2	4		
Mailen, John	1		4			Shaw, Samuel	1		2			McKensie, Mary		1	2		
Winslow, Samuel	1	5	4			Tukey, John	2		3			Hilton, Isaac	3	1	2		
Beeman, Abraham	1	1	2			Ingraham, William	1	2	1			Weldridge, James	5		3		
Jones, John	3	1	4			Tukey, William	1		1			Codman, Richard	3		5	1	
Thombs, Joseph	1		1			Googings, Samuel	1	1	2			McLellan, Arthur	4	3	7		
Thombs, Joseph	1		3			Haskel, Josiah	1	1	2			Bradberry, Abigail			2		
Boynton, Theophilus	1	1	2			Ilsley, Hosea	1		4			Wyer, Daniel	1		2		
Biggs, Josiah	1		2			Farrington, William	1		4			Riggs, Rebecca			2		
Pool, Abijah	2	2	3			Tukey, Hannah			1			Cross, Nathaniel	2		2	1	
Moss, Eliphalet	1	1	1			Cootman, Stephen	1	1	3			Thomas, Peeter	1	5	6		
Moss, Eliphalet	1	2	2			Vezie, John	1	4	4			Sawyer, Philip	1	1	1		
Price, Elisabeth		2	3			Ayers, Jemime		3	3			Clark, Elisabeth			1		
Noyes, David	3		5			Burns, George	1	1	5			Clough, John	1	3	5		
Hood, James	1	4	4			Riggs, Joseph	1	1	3			Turner, Elisha			1		
Baker, John	1	1	2			Freeman, Samuel	2	3	6			Pervish, Adam	1		1		
Wyley, James	1	1	1			Purington, William	4	2	7			Greenleaf, Joseph	1	1	2		
Berry, Jeremiah	3	2	6			Swett, Jonathan	1	3	2			Childs, Rebecca	1		2		
Newman, Thomas	3	1	4			Greenleaf, Amos	2	2	2			Pierson, Samuel	1	4	2		
Thrasher, John	3	2	5			Young, Abraham	2		3			Hall, Stephen	1	4	2	1	
Barret, James	2		3			Jewett, Joseph	1	3	4			Higgins, Samuel	1	4	5		
Brewster, William	1		1			Jewett, James	1	2	3			Poge, Robert	1		2		
Gustin, Ebenezer	1	1	3			Lowther, John	3	1	3			Pollard, Hezekiah	1		2		
Pennel, Matthew	1	2	4			Berry, Joshua	1	1	2			Jones, James	1		4		
Moody, William	2	1	2			Clap, Asa	3	1	1	1		Dinsdell, Henry	3	1	4		
Brazier, Sarah	1	1	5			Atkins, Nathaniel	5	2	4			Cox, James	1		4		
Brazier, Enoch	1	1	2			Bryant, Jonathan	2	7	5			Haite, John	1	3	2		
Paine, Jonathan	2	1	7			Owens, James	1		5			Goodwin, John	1	1	5		
Cobb, Ebenezer	1		1			Pool, Thomas		1	3			Davis, Ebenezer	3	1	2		
Cluston, Alexander	1		1			Bailey, Nathaniel	1	2	2			Shaw, Nathaniel	1	1	4		
Pool, James	1	1	2			Hore, Philip	1		1			Sherman, Barnabas	2	2	2		
Cobb, Smith	2	1	3			Stone, Benjamin	1	1	2			Bailey, Hudson	1	2	2		
Cobb, Enoch	1	3	1			Walker, Peeter	3	2	2			Webb, Micael	1	1	5		
Knights, John	1	2	5			Marble, Nancy	1		1			Lowell, Mary			1		
Lowell, John	1	4	3			Mussy, Daniel	1	3	3			Kelley, Mary			1		
Maston, Daniel	1	2	1			Motley, Alexander	1	2	3			Hance, John	2	2	1		
Bootman, Broadstreet	1	2	3			Starrot, David	1		1			Lunt, Job	1		3		
Sweetser, John	1		2			Emmons, John	1	1	3			Majory, John	1		1		
Ross, David	1	5	2			Leatherby, Benjamin	3		3			Chamberlain, Aaron	1	4	2		
Ilsly, Joshua	1		1			Green, Daniel	1	3	5			Gould, Joseph	1	4	4		
Tuckfield, Mary			2			Green, William			2			Marwick, Hugh	1	2	5		
Waite, Thomas B	2	4	5			Drake, Robert	1		2			Green, Casiah		2	3		
Bryant, Samuel	2	1	2			Bracket, Joshua	1		2			Coley, Noah	2		2		
Berry, Thomas	1	6	3			Lunt, Micael	1	4	3			Sawyer, Ezekiel	1		5		
Wadsworth, Peleg	2	5	6	1		Vaughn, William	2		4			Wiswall, Enoch	1	3	5		
Noyes, Moses	1	1	4			Rutburgh, John	1		1	1		Roff, Benjamin	1	3	5		
Procter, Samuel	1		1			Hagget, William	1	1	2			Broadstreet, Dudley	1		1		
Motley, William	1		3			Robinson, Thomas	7	3	8			Richardson, Edward	1		1		
Nichols, Elisabeth			2			Smith, James	1	1	2	1		Bryant, William	1	2			
Low, Benniah	1	1	4			Bracket, Joshua	2	1	2	1		Brackett, John	1		1		
Rollins, Betheah	1	1	3			Green, Henry	1	1	1			Sawyer, James	1	1	2		
Laroch, Thomas	1		1			Molton, William	1	1	2			Sawyer, Samuel	1	1	4		
McLellan, Joseph	2	1	3			Cook, John	1	1	4			Plummer, Asa	2	1	5		
McLellan, Hugh	4	1	5			Barton, James	1	2	2			Dole, John	2	2	4		
McLellan, Joseph	3	2	3			Brackett, Thomas	1		4			Coffin, Nathaniel	1	3	8		
McLellan, Samuel	1		2			Waterhouse, Jacob	3	4	5			Hustin, Mary	1		1		
Tinney, Samuel	2	1	4			Vezies, Jeremiah	3	1	3			George, Daniel	1		1		
Cohoon, Daniel	2	1	2			Knights, Benjamin	2	4	3			Moss, Nathaniel	1	3	3		
Barton, Robert	4	1	5			Burnham, John	1	2	5			Tucker, Daniel	3	1	4		
Preble, Ebenezer	3	2	3	1		Kent, John	1		2	2		Stover, Hannah	2	1	5		
Preble, Mehitable	4		2	1		Scott, John	1	1	4			Moss, Jonathan	2		2		
Deering, James	1	1	3			Owens, Ebenezer	3	4	6			Baker, Josiah	2	3	4		
Deering, Elliot	1		4			Cushing, Apolos	1	1	2			Thrasher, Sarah		1	1		
Mussy, Daniel	1	3	3			Rogers, Joshua	3	1	2			Cammet, Thomas	1	2	2		
Tukey, John	1	3	2			Bester, Timothy	1		4			Woodman, Sarah		1	2		
Smith, David	6	1	4			Tukey, John	1		3			Rich, Zephaniah	1	4	2		
Ingraham, Joseph	1	3	4			Jenks, William	2	4	4			Oxnerd, Thomas	1	5	5		
Tucker, Jonah	1	2	3			Tukey, Stephen	1	2	5			Fosdick, Nathaniel	1	1	3		
Randall, Isaac	1					Snow, Ebenezer	1	2	4			Fosdick, Thomas	1	2	3		
Nichols, John	2	2	6			Bailey, John	1	3	3			Bradish, David	3	2	7		
Titcomb, Joseph	1	1	5			Pettengill, Daniel	2	1	4			Fernald, Peltiah	3		4		
Moody, Nathaniel	4		3			Goodwin, Samuel	2	3				Stodard, David	1		7		
Poland, Benjamin	2	4	4			Brazier, Moses	1	1	4			Bagly, John	1		2		
Toby, William	3	3	3			Barr, Alexander	2	2	5			Moody, Benjamin	2	1	2		
Beck, Thomas	2	2	4			Stevens, Abraham	3	1	5			Chase, Francis	1	1	4		
Waite, Stephen	3	1	5			Shattuck, Moses	1		2			Lowell, Abner	4	2	5		
Dean, Eliphalet	2	1	4			Warren, George	1	2	5			Warren, Peeter	3	5	5		
Ingalls, Ephraim	2	1	2			Correy, James	1	1	2			Newman, Thomas	1		4		
Dean, John	3	3	4			Webber, Samuel	1		3			Woodman, David	1	1	1		
Davis, Daniel	2	1	3			Bradbury, Wyman	1		3			Constable, James	1		4		
Hardin, William	3	1				Storer, Woodberry	3	1	5			Sylvester, Joseph	3		4		
Campbell, William	1		2			Shattuck, Summers	1	2	2			Pinkham, Daniel	1		1		
Ilsly, Daniel	5	2	2			Lunt, Moses	1	2	6			Cox, William	1	1	2		
Titcomb, Benjamin	2	4	4			Day, George	1		2			Swan, John	1	1	3		
Stevens, Asa	1	1	5			Waldo, Samuel	1	1	3			Cobham, Sarah			3		
Woodman, Merry	4	2	2			Frazier, Alexander	2	1	2			Mitchell, Robert					
Hussy, Samuel	3	1	5			Codman, Richard	1	1	2			Pounder, William	1	1	2		
Butts, Samuel	3	2	3			Deering, Eunice	1	3	4			Hobby, John	2	1	4		
Barber, Solomon	2	4	3			Waite, John	5	4	5			Hobby, William	1	3	2		
Greeley, Elisabeth			2			Erving, Shirley	2	4	4			Frothingham, John	1	2	4		

FIRST CENSUS OF THE UNITED STATES.

CUMBERLAND COUNTY—Continued.

NAME OF HEAD OF FAMILY.	Free white males of 16 years and upward, including heads of families.	Free white males under 16 years.	Free white females, including heads of families.	All other free persons.	Slaves.
PORTLAND TOWN—continued.					
Poor, Samuel	1	1	2		
Toby, Samuel	1	2	5		
Shaw, Josiah	1	2	4		
Patterson, John	1	2	2		
Chellis, Joseph	2	2	5		
Prior, James	1	4	1		
Brown, William	2	2	4		
Seymour, John	4	2	2		
Baker, John	1	1	3		
Fabree, Peeter	1	5	3		
Harn, Shadrick	3		4		
Bailey, Joseph	1		2		
Daily, Emour	1		3		
Motley, Thomas	5	6	6		
Stone, Hannah		2	3		
Bond, William	1	2	4	1	
Goodwin, Richard	2	2	3		
Broad, Ephraim	1		2		
Webster, Thomas	1	2	3		
Hopkins, Thomas	2	4	8		
Blasdell, Susanna	1	1	5		
Kimbal, Jeremiah	2	2	2		
Clemmons, Joseph	1	1	2		
Cross, Ralf	4	2	2		
McLellan, William	2	3	5		
Storer, Ebenezer	1	1	5		
Mussy, John	3	3	2		
Titcomb, Benjamin	2	1	3		
Leatherby, John	1	6	3		
Cole, John	1	1	1		
Cox, Sarah		1	2		
Crandall, Philip	1		2		
Aspinwall, Caleb	1	2	2		
Brazier, Daniel	1	1	2		
Wiswall, John	1	1	2		
Churchwell, Seth	1		1		
Fosdick, James	1	4	3		
Oxnerd, Edward	1	1	2		
Willson, Joseph	1	4	2		
Curtis, John	1	3	5		
Riggs, Daniel	1		1		
Bancroft, John	1				
Oneal, John	1		2		
Pettingall, Eliphalet	1		1		
Freman, Joshua	6	3	1	1	
Knights, Samuel	1	4	3		
Cammet, Paul	1	2	2		
Mumford, Daniel	1		2		
Trott, Benjamin	2	1	2		
Woodberry, Samuel	2	1	3		
Cushing, Ezekiel	1	3	2		
Cushing, Jeremiah	2	3	2		
Cushing, Mehitable			3		
RAYMONDTOWN PLANTATION.					
Dingley, Joseph	2	1	2		
West, Desper	2	1	7		
Leach, Mark	3	1	2		
Ring, Josiah	3		3		
Staples, Pertor	1	5	3		
Jackson, Henry	1	1	5		
Dingly, Samuel	2	3	2		
Jorden, James	1	1	2		
Jorden, Jonathan	1		4		
Welch, James	1	1	3		
Fowler, Moses	1		2		
Silvester, Zachariah	1	2	3		
Brackett, Daniel	1	1	5		
Whitney, Moses	2	1	4		
Gray, Lewis	1	3	3		
Mitchell, John	1	3	7		
Mann, Obediah	2	2	4		
Willbee, Thomas	1	1	2		
Tinney, Samuel	1	1	3		
Starbird, Moses	1	3	3		
Small, Daniel	1	3	2		
Small, George	3	3	4		
Small, James	1	1	1		
Jorden, Samuel	3	4	1		
Simonton, Jonathan	1	2	6		
Cash, John	2		5		
Smith, Benjamin	1	2	4		
Barton, Isaac	1	3	3		
Dyer, Ezekiel	1	2	2		
Crisp, Thomas	2	1	1		
Jorden, Roger	1	3	2		
Davis, John	3		5		
Davis, Gideon	1	2	5		
Davis, Daniel	1	5	2		
Jordan, Hezekiah	1	2	2		
Small, Daniel	1	2	1		
Brown, Joseph	1	1	4		
Brown, Joshua	1	5	4		
Brown, Andrew	1	5	4		
RAYMONDTOWN PLANTATION—continued.					
Mayberry, Richard	2	1	3	2	
Jorden, Dominicus	3	2	7		
Lowell, Daney	1	2	2		
Sawyer, Jonathan	3	3	6		
Lomberde, John	1		4		
Jorden, Timothy	1	3	3		
Westson, James	1	1	2		
Edes, Thomas	1	1	2		
Spurr, William	1		2		
Beverly, David	3	1	1		
Rich, Ezekiel	5	3	6		
Anderson, Robert	1		2	5	
Greeley, John	2	2	5		
RUSFIELD GORE.					
Dicker, Willm	1	2	2		
Lasly, George	1	2	1		
Hobbs, Amos	1	1	3		
Stevens, Joseph	1	2	4		
Stevens, Jonas	3	2	6		
Stevens, Nathl	1	1	2		
Hobbs, Jeremiah	1	2	6		
Millet, John	1				
Witt, Benja	1		2		
Lucus, Warren	1				
Perkins, Saml	1	2	1		
Ames, Saml	1		5		
Cowen, Thos	1	3	3		
Pike, John	1	1	2		
Pike, Dudley	1	3	3		
Twichel, Moses	1	2	4		
Parsons, John	1	1			
Parsons, Willm	1			3	
Herring, Benjn	1	2	3		
Noble, Nathan	1	2	2		
SHEPARDSFIELD PLANTATION.					
Western, John	2		1		
Randall, Seth	1	1	4		
Fuller, Barzilla	1		3		
Cushman, Isaac	1	1	3		
Bearce, Asa	4	1	3		
Whittemore, Isaac	1	1	4		
Greenwood, John	3	1	5		
Mireck, Bazaliel	2	2	2		
Cushman, Caleb	1	1	2		
Cushman, Sarah		1	1		
Bignal, John	4	1	3		
Churchill, Josiah	1		1		
Pratt, Thaddeus	1	2	3		
Parish, Samuel	1	1	2	1	
Churchill, Jabez	1	3	3		
Brigham, Saml	1		3		
Bearce, Gideon	2	1	3		
Keene, Joshua	3	1	6		
Keene, Snow	2		8		
Cox, Benja	2	2	5		
Merrill, Jabesh	1	1	3		
Cobb, Pelatiah	1	3	4		
Benson, Elnathan	4	3	3		
Benson, Jepthah	1	1	3		
Roo, Zaccheus	1	3	4		
Drake, Ebenezer	1	2	2		
Drake, John	1	2	2		
Craft, Saml	1		2		
Packer, Edward	1		2		
Churchill, Willm		1	2		
Buckman, Danl	1	2	3		
Robinson, Elijah	6		4		
Dean, Abraham	1		3		
Dean, Zadock	1		1		
Sole, James	1	2	1		
Perkins, Joseph	1	2	2		
Thayer, Ruth		4	1		
Holmes, Job	3	1	4		
Richmond, Eliab	1	4	6		
Cordwell, John	3	1	4		
Cushman, Zebadiah	2	2	3		
Cushman, Job	2	2	7		
Fuller, Nathl	3	1	5		
Cushman, Joseph	1		2		
Bullings, Danl	1	1	2		
Heaton, Elijah	1	2	3		
Tucker, Lemuel	1	2	2		
Heaton, Richard	1	2	2		
Bartlet, Danl	1	1	3		
Bartlet, Asa	1		1		
Lucus, Elkanah	1		3		
Lucus, Elnathan		2	3		
Thomas, Holmes	1	3	4		
Holmes, Jona	1	2	2		
Holmes, James					
SHEPARDSFIELD PLANTATION—continued.					
Mason, Broadstreet	1	3	3		
Cushman, Gideon	1	4	4		
Packer, Reuben	2		3		
Packer, Ichabod	1	3	1		
Washburn, John	1	1	4		
Baker, Samuel	1	2	1		
LeBroke, James	1	2	2		
Barrows, Willm	2	3	5		
Barrows, Joseph	1		5		
Baker, Edmund	1		3		
Tobb, Jacob	1	3	3		
Glover, Robert	1	2	2		
Cary, Danl	1	2	3		
Lebarran, James	1	1	2		
Landers, Stephen	1				
Jordan, James	1		1		
Ryals, Danl	1	1	2		
Dudly, Nathan	1		4		
Pharis, James	1	3	2		
Fuller, Jesse	1	3	4		
Dunham, James	1	2	4		
Cane, Joshua, Jur	1	2	2		
Bearce, Asa, Jur	1		2		
Hill, Thos	1	1	3		
Curtis, Noah	1	3	3		
House, Moses	1	3	3		
Perkins, Ebenezer	1	1	2		
Wilborn, Robert	2	5	4		
Whitmore, Saml	1	2	2		
Bumpus, Morris	1	3	2		
Bumpus, Willm	1	3	2		
Bumpus, John	1		2		
Barrows, Ephraim		2	2		
Barrows, Benja	1				
Barrows, Benja, Jur	1		4		
Bumpus, Shubael	1	3	4		
Churchill, Joseph	1	1	2		
Curtis, Ashley	1	2	4		
STANDISH TOWN.					
Butterfield, Joseph	1	6	5		
Berry, Timothy	1	1	4		
Bolter, Nathl	2	1	3		
Bolter, Nathl, Jur	1		2		
Bolter, Benja	1		1		
Cram, Danl	4		2		
Cram, Danl, Jur	2	5	2		
Cummins, John	1	1	3		
Cummins, Willm	1	1	4		
Cummins, Thos	1	1	4		
Chase, Joseph	1	4	3		
Croxford, John	1	2	2		
Cookson, Reuben	2	3	7		
Camel, Phillip	4	2	5		
Dean, John	2	1	4		
Davis, James	1		6		
Dow, Jabez	1	2	2		
Dow, Joseph	1	3	2		
Dow, Abner	2	2	4		
Decker, John	1	2	2		
Eastman, Job	1	1	2		
Freeman, George	2	2	4		
Haskel, Benja	1	2	2		
Haskel, Jona	1				
Hasty, Danl	1	5	2		
Hasty, James	1	3	1	1	
Higgins, Ebenezer	1	2	5		
Higgins, Timothy	2	2	4		
Higgins, Robert	1	1	1		
Higgins, Willm	1				
Harmon, Danl	1	4	3		
Harmon, Willm	1		4		
Harmon, Elliot	1	1	1		
Hopkins, Theodore	3		2		
Hall, John	1	5	4		
Hall, Willm	1		2		
Hall, Charles	1	1	4		
How, Danl	3		2		
Jones, Ephraim	2	1	5		
Jones, Willm	1		3		
Jones, Ephraim, Jur	1		2		
Lowel, Danl	4	1	5		
Lowel, Jona	2	3	3		
Linnel, Enoch	3		5		
Linnel, Saml	1	1	2		
Libby, Isaac	1	3	2		
Moulton, Peter	3	2	2		
Mussey, Theodore	2	2	4		
Morcan, John	2	3	1		
Moody, James	1	1	3		
Moody, Joshua	1	1	1		
Mitchel, Dominicus	2	3	5		
Martin, Bryan	1	1	3		
McGill, John	2	2	3		

HEADS OF FAMILIES—MAINE.

CUMBERLAND COUNTY—Continued.

NAME OF HEAD OF FAMILY.	Free white males of 16 years and upward, including heads of families.	Free white males under 16 years.	Free white females, including heads of families.	All other free persons.	Slaves.	NAME OF HEAD OF FAMILY.	Free white males of 16 years and upward, including heads of families.	Free white males under 16 years.	Free white females, including heads of families.	All other free persons.	Slaves.	NAME OF HEAD OF FAMILY.	Free white males of 16 years and upward, including heads of families.	Free white males under 16 years.	Free white females, including heads of families.	All other free persons.	Slaves.
STANDISH TOWN—con.						**TURNER TOWN—con.**						**WINDHAM TOWN—con.**					
Moses, Josiah	1	2	3			Briggs, Jotham	1		1			Dennis, Andrew	1		1		
Philbrick, Jonª	2	1	4			Briggs, Jotham, Jnr	1	1	2			Mayberry, James	1	1	1		
Philbrick, Michael	2	1	3			Bradford, Ezekiel	1	2	2			Brown, Ezra	1	5	5		
Philbrick, Wllm	1	1	2			Bradford, Chandler	1	3	1			Millens, Robert	2		3		
Philbrick, Gideon	1					Elliot, Andrew	2	1	2			Millens, Thomas	1	1	1		
Parker, Aaron	1	1	3			Blake, Samuel	3	4	2			Stevens, Jonathan	1	3	6		
Pierce, John	1	1	2			Blake, Caleb	1					Barker, Thomas	2	1	4		
Pierce, Richard	1		2			Bradford, Jesse	2	3	1			Elder, William	4	2	2		
Paine, Joseph	3	5	5			Smith, Laban	1		1			Toler, Samuel	1	1	1		
Paine, Thoˢ	1	1	3			Smith, Josiah, Jur	1		1			Young, Martha	1	1	1		
Plaisted, John	1		1			Gilbert, Elijah	1	4	2			Chesley, Joseph	2	1	8		
Rockley, Chandler	2		3			Gilbert, Nathl	1	4	6			Little, Paul	2	3	3		
Rich, James	1	2	5			Jones, Benjamin	1	6	1			Brown, John	1	2	2		
Rich, Lemuel	4	4	3			Brown, John	1	1	2			Jelleson, John	1	3	4		
Row, Caleb	3		4			Merrill, Levi	1	4	4			Hooper, Joseph	1	2	3		
Row, Ephraim	2	2	2			Merrill, Jabesh	1	2	5			Purington, David	3	1	2		
Richardson, David	1	2	6			Phillips, Richard, Jr.	1	4	3			Merrell, Ebenezer	1		1		
Richardson, Moses	2	2	5			True, Benjª	1	3	5			Mayberry, Richard	1	1	1		
Richardson, Jonª	1		1			Bradford, Ezekiel, Jur	2		1			Hanson, Elijah	2	1	4		
Robinson, John	1	1	3			Dellingham, Jeremiah	1		1			Hutchinson, Ann			1		
Shaw, Josiah	3	1	2			Dellingham, John	1	3	1			Hutchinson, Samuel	2				
Shaw, Serjant	2	1	7			Childs, Daniel	2	3	5			Hutchinson, Joseph	1	5	3		
Shaw, Ebenezer	2	3	4			Bryant, Hezekiah	3	2	3			Starberd, Hannah			1		
Shaw, Thoˢ	2	2	2			Jones, Henry	1	3	6			Cook, Daniel	2	2	1		
Shaw, Joseph	1	3	3			Bradford, Wllm	2	2	1			Procter, William	3	1	3		
Sandbourn, John	3		4			Andrews, Mark	1		1			Ham, Benjamin	1		1		
Sandbourn, John, Jur	1	1	4			Andrews, Saml	1	2	4			Shane, Richard	1		3		
Sandbourn, David	1		2			Bonney, Ichabod	2		4			Hall, Stephen	1		1		
Sandbourn, Jeremiah	1					Bonney, John	1	1	1			Hodgdon, Israel	2	2	4		
Sandbourn, Simeon	2	3	2			Bonney, Ichabod, Jur	1		2			Jones, Samuel	1	3	3		
Sandbourn, Mary			2			House, Caleb	2		6			Hanson, Samuel	1		1		
Sawyer, John	2	2	5			Bradford, Martin	1		2			Hanson, William	1	2	1		
Smith, Archibald	1	2	5									Elliot, Jacob	1		3		
Sweet, Jonª	1	1	4			**WATERFORD PLANTATION.**						Pettingill, Moses	1	4	2		
Sparrow, Stephen	3		3									Elliot, Jacob	2		3		
Thorn, Israel	2	2	2			Jewet, Stephen	4	1	5			Hall, Winslow	2	2	2		
Thompson, Isaa S	1	2	2			Green, Thoˢ	3	1	6			Hall, William	1	1	2		
Topping, Luther	1	1	2			Warren, Saml	1					Gould, Benjamin	1	4	4		
Thombs, Amos	1	4	2			Gates, Wllm	1	1	2			Pettingill, Daniel	1	1	4		
Waterhouse, Joseph	1	2	5			Johnson, Asa	2		3			Hanson, Jonathan	1	5	1		
Wood, John	3	1	5			Orr, Philip	4		2			Lord, Samuel	1		1		
Whitney, David	1					Bryant, Richard	1		2			Osgood, Abraham	1	3	4		
Whitney, Joshua	1	1	3			Sampson, Phineas	1		2			Mayberry, John	1		2		
White, Peter	1	4	2			Whitcomb, David	1					Craige, Thomas	3	2	5		
Wiley, Wllm	2	1	2			Chamberlain, John	1					Elkins, William	2	3	3		
York, Isaas	1	1	2			Longley, Ely	1	1	3			Winslow, Joseph	1	1	2		
York, Jacob	1	1	3			Brown, Silas	1	2	2			Swett, Samuel	1	1	2		
York, Job	1		1			Brown, Thaddeus	1	2	2			Robinson, Stephen	1	3	2		
Yates, John	1	3	1			Chamberlain, Ephraim	1	1	2			Bolton, Rachel	3	2	5		
Chase, Isaac	1	2	2			Russ, John	2		3			Estis, Samuel	1	4	3		
Phinney, Stephen	1		1			Whitney, Phineas	1	2	3			Robinson, John	4	2	4		
Row, Robert	1	2	1			Stickney, Jonª	2					Haskell, John	2	3	2		
Parker, Eliphalet	1		1			Homan, Jonas	1	2	1			Rogers, Nathaniel	1	1	1		
Higgins, Elkanah	2		2			McWane, David	1					Mugford, Nathaniel	1		3		
Lombard, Thoˢ	1	1	1			Longley, Jonª	1	2	3			Purington, Sarah			3		
Lombard, Jedadiah	1	1	2			Hamblen, Africa	3	1	2			Hooper, Robert	1	1	3	1	
Woods, Joseph	1	3				Hamblen, America	3	1	2			Mugford, Joseph	1	1	5		
Eaton, Israel	1	1	6			Jewel, Ezra	1	2	3			Lovett, Jonathan	2	6	4		
Woodman, Nathan	1	1				Hale, Israel	1	2	3			Cobb, Isaac	1	3	2		
Whetcomb, Silas	1	2	4			Hapgood, Oliver	1	1	3			Hooper, Abigail	1	2	3		
Wiley, David	1	1	1			Robbins, Jonª	1	1	1			Mugford, John	1	2	3		
York, Ebenezer	1		1			Hale, Oliver	1	1	3			Estis, Simeon	1	3	4		
Parker, Moses	1	3	2			Gibson, Jacob	1	1	3			Graffam, Enoch	1	2	3		
Beaman, Noah	1	1	5			Barker, Daniel	3		2			Anderson, Edward	4	5	2		
Harmon, John	1	1	2			Holland, John	2	1	3			Dorrey, Timothy	4	1	2		
Harvey, John	3	1	2			Brown, Asaph	2		3			Anderson, Nancy	1	1	4		
Cookson, Elizabeth		2	2			Houghton, Jonª	1	1	3			Mayberry, William	1		2		
						Jewel, John	1		2			Dorrey, Jonathan	1		2		
TURNER TOWN.						Saunderson, Stephen	2	2	2			Dorrey, Elijah	1	2	4		
Copelin, Joseph	1	1	2			Chamberlain, Nathl	2					Tombly, Andrew	2		3		
Niles, Beniah	2		4			Hale, Benjª	1					Austin, Jonas	1	1	3		
Smith, Jasael	1		4									Lord, Simeon	1	2	4		
French, Daniel	1	4	1			**WINDHAM TOWN.**						Hanson, Ezra	1		1		
Gorham, Samuel	1	5	2									Lord, Charles	1	1	1		
Phillips, Mary		2	4			Ingersoll, John	2	1	4			Hanson, Ichabod	3	3	4		
Heffords, Wllm	1	4	1			Craige, Eveleth	2	6				Anthine, Nicholis	1	2	2		
Bryant, Stephen	1	2	9			Mayberry, John			4			Hanson, Ichabod	1	2	1		
Keene, John	2	1	5			Graffam, Caleb	1	3	4			Crockett, Daniel	1	1	3		
Merrill, Danl	2	4	4			Hawkes, Amos	3	1	5			Hawkes, Nathaniel	1	2	2		
Leavit, Jacob	3	1	2			Hawkes, Ebenezer	3		5			Hawkes, James	2	5	3		
Leavit, Joseph	1	4	3			Honeywell, Elijah	3	3	8			Dolley, John	1	3	3		
Stevens, Moses	1	1	2			Anderson, Ann	1		2			Dolley, Samuel	1		2		
Davis, Jacob	1	1	1			Anderson, Abraham	2	1	3			Jorden, Jeremiah	1	2	2		
Strickland, John	4	3	6			Walker, John	1		3			Rand, John	3	5	4		
Niles, Nathan	3	2	5			Hall, Hatevil	2	2	4			Fields, William	1	2			
Pratt, Jonª	3		1			Hardy, Isaac	2	2	3			Hutchinson, Stephen	1				
Young, Job	1					Campbell, Elisabeth		1	5			Elder, Joseph	2	3	6		
Bonney, Isaiah	5		2			Knights, John	1	2	2			Kennard, Samuel	2	3	6		
Staples, Josiah	1	3	3			Gammon, Pilip	1	2	2			Legro, Elias	2	1	3		
Phillips, Abner	1	4	4			Knights, John	1	2	4			Baker, Josiah	1		1		
Smith, Asa	1		1			Whitehouse, Pomphrit	1		2			Dorrey, David	3	2	4		
Phillips, Richard	2		3			Morrell, Benjamin	1		3			Clark, Gershom	1	1	1		
Briggs, Daniel	2	2	4			Mayberry, John	1	2	2			Manchester, Stephen	2	1	1		
Haskel, Israel	3	1	5			Mayberry, William	2	2	5			Manchester, Gershom	1	2	4		
												Allen, Joseph	1		4		

CUMBERLAND COUNTY—Continued.

NAME OF HEAD OF FAMILY.	Free white males of 16 years and upward, including heads of families.	Free white males under 16 years.	Free white females, including heads of families.	All other free persons.	Slaves.	NAME OF HEAD OF FAMILY.	Free white males of 16 years and upward, including heads of families.	Free white males under 16 years.	Free white females, including heads of families.	All other free persons.	Slaves.	NAME OF HEAD OF FAMILY.	Free white males of 16 years and upward, including heads of families.	Free white males under 16 years.	Free white females, including heads of families.	All other free persons.	Slaves.
WINDHAM TOWN—con.						**WINDHAM TOWN—con.**						**WINDHAM TOWN—con.**					
Morrell, Jedediah	1		1			Tobin, Matthew	3		1			Lowell, Joshua	2	1	4		
Morrell, Benjamin	1		3			Dole, Richard	1	1	3			Hawkes, Amos	2	2	5		
Morrell, Peeter	1	1	1			Windship, Ephraim	1	1	3			Allen, Pelatiah	4	2	6		
Pray, James	1	3	3			Chute, John	1	1	1			Mayberry, William	1	6	5		
Stevens, Richard	1	1	2			Chute, Josiah	1	3	2			Roberts, Jonathan	2	6	4		
Webb, Josiah	1	1	2			Swett, John	3		2			Mitchell, Benjamin	1	2	5		
Rea, Caleb	2	2	4			Willson, Jonathan	3		2			Rogers, Gershom	3	1	3		
Knights, George	3		3			Chute, Thomas	1	3	2			Stevens, Chase	1	7	2		
Waite, Enoch	1	2	2			Andrews, John	2	5	5			Jorden, Nathaniel	1	1	5		
Bodge, John	2	1	5			Smith, Peter F	4	7	1			Crockett, George	1	3	7		
Swett, Joseph	1		5			Chase, John	1	1	3			Hawkes, Amos	1	1	2		
Windship, Gershom	3	3	2			Trott, Thomas	2	1	7								
Windship, John	1		2			Barker, David	2	1	4								

HANCOCK COUNTY.

NAME OF HEAD OF FAMILY.	Free white males of 16 years and upward, including heads of families.	Free white males under 16 years.	Free white females, including heads of families.	All other free persons.	Slaves.	NAME OF HEAD OF FAMILY.	Free white males of 16 years and upward, including heads of families.	Free white males under 16 years.	Free white females, including heads of families.	All other free persons.	Slaves.	NAME OF HEAD OF FAMILY.	Free white males of 16 years and upward, including heads of families.	Free white males under 16 years.	Free white females, including heads of families.	All other free persons.	Slaves.
BARRETTSTOWN TOWN.						**BELFAST TOWN—con.**						**BLUEHILL TOWN—con.**					
Whitcomb, Abner	1					Willson, Jonathan	1		3			Candish, James	1	3	3		
Whitcomb, Ebenezer	1		1			Tufts, John	3	1	5			Hinkley, Susannah			1		
Bartlett, Isaac	1					Stephenson, Solon	2	1	3			Day, James	1	2	7		
Bartlett, Noah	1					Durham, Talford	1	3	4			Carter, Henry	1	2	2		
Bartlett, Daniel	1					Dolliff, John	1		2			Carter, James	2	4	5		
Sofford, Reuben	1					Durham, John	1	4	2			Carter, James, jun	1				
Mansfield, Jacob	1					Patterson, Nat¹	3	2	4			Carlton, Moses	1	3	2		
Kendall, Chever	1	1	3			French, Nathaniel	1	4	5			Carlton, Edward	1		3		
Barrett, Daniel	1					Patterson, William	2	2	6								
Pease, Aaron	1	1	2			Ames, Jacob	1	2	3			**CAMDEN TOWN.**					
Pease, James	3		2			Clark, Isaac	1		3			Corthall, Peletiah	2	2	4		
Symonds, Oliver	1	1	1			Clark, Abraham	1	2	2			Gibbs, Elisha	1	1	4		
Robbins, Jacob	1		3			McKean, Ephraim	2		1			Hosmer, Nathaniel	1	1	1		
Symonds, Peleg	1	3	3			McKean, Samuel	2		2			Hosmer, Nathaniel, junʳ	1	1	2		
Messerve, Benjᵃ	1	2	2			Dolliff, Daniel	1	4				Hogeman, Job	1	1	1		
Payson, Ephraim	1	2	2			Miller, James	3		2			Hosmer, Asa	1				
McClane, Fergus	1	2	2			Weeks, Lemuel	1	1	4			Harrington, David	1				
Katon, William	1	1	1			Coffran, John	1	1				Leavensellers, Jacob	1				
Davis, John	1	2	1			Crooks, William	2		3			Mansfield, Daniel	1				
Collamore, Isaac	1					Nesmith, Benjᵃ	3	1	4			Blodgett, David	1	1	2		
Temple, Nathaniel	1					Robinson, John	2	1	1			Derry, Lewis	1	2	4		
Pease, Prince, junʳ	1	2	4			Cochran, John	2	3				Bailey, Joseph	1	2	1		
Pease, Prince	3	1	2			Alexander, John	1		3			Wadsworth, Sedate	2	2	4		
Collamore, Joshua, junʳ	1	2	1			Stimpson, Richard	2		3			Thompson, John	1	1	3		
Collamore, Elisha	1											Whitney, John	1	1	1		
Pease, Shubael	1	1	1			**BLUEHILL TOWN.**						Cook, Paul	1	2	1		
Ripley, Abraham	1	3	3			Holt, Nickolas	1		1			McGlathry, William	3	5	2		
Thompson, John	3	1	2			Clough, Asa	1	1	1			Richards, James	3	5	4		
McMurphy, William	1					Pilsbury, Phineas	1	1	1			Metcalf, Leonard	1	2	3		
Wentworth, Shubael	1					Coggins, Samuel	1	1	2			Thorndike, Paul	2	4	3		
Wentworth, Sion	1					Coggins, Thomas	1		3			Harkness, John	1	2	3		
Messerve, Joseph	1		2			Wood, Israel	1	2	5			Ott, Peter	1	1	2		
Easinsy, Henry	1		2			Wood, Joseph	1		2		1	Ott, Peter, junʳ	1	2	2		
Suchfort, Andrass	1	2	2			Parker, Robert	3	4	2			Bradford, Elijah	1	4	3		
Jacobs, Andrew	1	2	1			Holt, Jedediah	1	5	2			Upham, William	2		1		
Thompson, Robert	1		1			Johnson, Obed	1	5	2			Porterfield, Wᵐ	1	1	1		
Wentworth, Lemuel	1	3	2			Parker, Nathan	3	1	6			Nutt, David	2		5		
Martin, Samuel	2	1	3			Wood, Joseph, junʳ	1	3	3			Jones, Abraham	1	3	5		
Crooker, Francis	2		1			Wood, Robert H	1	2	3			Gordon, John	3	1	1		
Jones, Windsor	1	2	3			Horton, Joshua	3	2	6			Buckling, Barrack	1	4	5		
Maddocks, Ichabod	1	1	3			Parker, Joseph	1		3			Gregory, William, junʳ	1	2	4		
Newbet, John	2	2	4			Peters, John	3	4	6			Jeminson, Alexander	1	4	3		
Smith, Charles	1	2	2			White, John	1	3	2			Jones, James	1	2	3		
Barrett, Timothy	1					Darling, Jonathan	2	4	3			Gregory, William	4	2	3		
Ames, Jacob	1	2	3			Clough, Benjᵃ	1	1	1			Cobb, Thomas	1		2		
Hewit, William	1	2	3			Dodge, Elisha	1	2	2			Spring, Thomas	3		4		
Hilt, Margaret		3	2			Faulkner, Daniel	1					Reed, Frederick	1	1	5		
Hilt, John	1					Hinkley, Isaiah	1					Dunbar, Hannah			2		
Barrett, Nathan	1					Parker, Ezra	1					Gay, Ephraim	1		2		
Barrett, Simon	1					Floyd, Ebenezer	1					Gordon, John, junʳ	1	2	1		
Miles, Nathan	1					White, Edward	1					Conklin, Samuel	1		1		
Bartlett, Samuel	1					White, Daniel	1					Mace, Thomas	1		1		
Brooks, Silas	1					Clay, Jonathan	2	4	3			Harup, Thomas	1		2		
						Hinkley, Ebenezer	1	1	2			Nutt, John	1	3	2		
BELFAST TOWN.						Hinkley, Nehemiah	1		2			Tibbitts, Thomas	1				
Mudgett, John	1		7			Spofford, Daniel	1					McLaughlin, Samuel	2				
Gilmore, John	1		2			Robinson, Israel	1					Thorndike, Robert	3	1	4		
Smith, Winthrop	1	3	4			Osgood, Ezekiel	1	5	5			Shays, Michael	1				
Patterson, Wᵐ	1	1	3			Osgood, Daniel	3	1	4			Simonton, James	1	3	2		
Clark, Alexander	1		4			Osgood, Phineas	1	3	4			Simonton, James, jun	1				
Houston, Samuel, junʳ	1	1	4			Holt, Nickolas, junʳ	1	2	1			Simonton, William	1				
True, Henry	1	2	3			Lecraw, Susannah						Gross, John	1	3	6		
Gilmore, James	1	1	2			Osgood, Christopher	1	1	2			Harrington, Isaac	1	2	4		
Houston, Samuel	3	1	2			Osgood, Nathan	1		1			Ogler, Abraham	1		1		
Houston, Robert	1		2			Osgood, John	1					Everton, Thomas	1	1	3		
Patterson, Robert	1	4	3			Dodge, Sarah	2		1			Jacobs, Samuel	2	1	2		
Brown, John	2	1	5			Parker, Peter	2	2	4			Eaton, Joseph	2	1	4		
Clark, Ichabod	1		3			Gra, Reuben, junʳ	1	2	2			Richards, Dodefer	1		5		
Clark, Elisha	1		3			Candish, John	1	1	3			Richards, Joseph	1		5		
Steel, Robert	2		1			Rounday, John	2	1	5			Richards, Jonathan	1	2	2		
McMullen, Alexander	1					Crabb, Jonathan	1	1	1			Demorse, Charles	1		3		
Patterson, James	1	3	4			Day, Jonathan	1	2	3			Young, Gideon	5		5		
Stephenson, Jerom	2	2	5			Candish, Joseph	1	2	3			Dillingham, Joshua	1	1	2		
Mitchell, Robert	1		2														

HEADS OF FAMILIES—MAINE.

HANCOCK COUNTY—Continued.

NAME OF HEAD OF FAMILY.	Free white males of 16 years and upward, including heads of families.	Free white males under 16 years.	Free white females, including heads of families.	All other free persons.	Slaves.	NAME OF HEAD OF FAMILY.	Free white males of 16 years and upward, including heads of families.	Free white males under 16 years.	Free white females, including heads of families.	All other free persons.	Slaves.	NAME OF HEAD OF FAMILY.	Free white males of 16 years and upward, including heads of families.	Free white males under 16 years.	Free white females, including heads of families.	All other free persons.	Slaves.
CAMDEN TOWN—con.						**CONDUSKEEG PLANTATION—continued.**						**DEER ISLE TOWN—con.**					
Dillingham, Lemuel	1		1			Tibbetts, Abner	1	4	2			Marshall, Ephraim	1	5	1		
Palmer, Nathaniel	1		2			Cook, Croell	1	1	1			Haskell, Francis	1	1	3		
Sherman, Joseph	1	2	2			Davis, William	1		2			Haskell, Jonathan	1	2	3		
Palmer, Joshua	1					Mann, Amos	1	2	4			Carman, Levi	3	1	4		
Palmer, Benj^a	1					Tozier, Lemuel	1	6	2			Eaton, Theophilus	2		2		
Hewell, Henry	1					Clark, Joseph	4	2	2			Dow, Nathan	1	1	3		
CANAAN TOWN.						Casey, William	1		1			Carlton, Jonathan	1	3	4		
Thomas, Charles	1	4	1			Nevers, Elisha	1	1	5			Haskell, Nathan	1	1	2		
Raredan, David	1					Tibbitts, William	3		4			Dow, Nathan, jun^r	1	1	3		
Miller, Noah	4	3	3			Mayo, James	1		1			Haskell, Abijah	1	2	3		
Knights, Nathan	2	1	5			Boober, Benj^a	1	3	2			Eaton, William	1	2	4		
Norton, John	2	2	3			Webber, Richard	1					Eaton, Eliakim	1	3	4		
Heal, Isaac	1	4	5			Banks, John	1		3			Howard, John	1	3	2		
Heal, Chesley	1					Harlow, Nathaniel	2	1	2			Eaton, Jeremiah	1	2	3		
Ogier, Lewis	1	2	3			Smart, John	1	3	7			Hardy, Peter	2	2	6		
Smith, Peleg	1	1	3			Tibbitts, Daniel	3	5	3			Scott, Nathaniel	3		4		
Smith, Isaac	1	1	3			Hichborn, Robert, jun^r	1					Closson, John	1	1	3		
Shelden, Ephraim	1		3			Plympton, William	1					Closson, Josiah	1	1	2		
Atkins, Cornelius	1					Lowe, Thomas	2	1	1			Thomas, Richard	1	1	3		
McFarlin, William	1	1	2			Lowe, Charles	1					Thompson, Thomas	1	3	5		
Dean, Joseph	1					Burges, Peter	1	1	3			Staples, Joshua	1	1	3		
Lamb, Joshua	2	4	3			Crosby, Simon	2	1	4			Sheldon, Nathaniel	1	2	1		
Pottle, Daniel	1	1	3			Cary, Samuel	1	3	2			Willson, Samuel	1	2	2		
Nason, John	1	5	3			Cary, Richard	1	1	2			Linn, Robert	1		1		
Dunton, John	1		1			Emery, John, jun^r	1	5	4			Staples, Moses	1	5	4		
Thomas, Joseph	2	3	6			Patten, William	1	3	4			Torrey, Jonathan	1	6	5		
Whitham, Joshua	1	3	4			McKenzie, Kenneth	1	1	2			Torrey, David, jun^r	1				
Gray, Levi	1		1			Crosby, Abner	1	4	4			Torrey, David	1				
Quin, James	1	1	3			Gorton, Simeon	1	2	5			Foster, William	3	2	4		
Millikin, Abner	1	1	2			Dole, Amos	1	3	2			Dexter, William P.	1				
Moody, William	1	2	1			Smith, Zebulon	1					Hamblin, Nathaniel	2		1		
Fletcher, Ephraim	1					Sweat, Shebna	1	1	5			Campbell, John	1	5	3		
Fletcher, Jonathan	1					Crosby, John	1	3	3			Joice, James	1	2	5		
Hilton, Nathaniel	1		1			Blasdell, Sanburn	1	2	2			Greenlaw, William	1	4	2		
CONDUSKEEG PLANTATION.						Emery, Nahum	1	1	4			Bray, William	1	1	3		
						Emery, James	1					Bray, Nathaniel	2	4	4		
Budge, James	1	3	4			Wheeler, Benj^a	9	2	4			Lane, Oliver	1	1	1		
Lovett, Francis	1	1	1			Graves, Moses	1					Frees, John	1		3		
Capers, John	1					Phillbrooks, James	2	3	4			Robbins, Nathaniel	1	1	2		
Tibbitts, John	3	3	5			Tarr, William	2	1	2			Babbige, Courtney	1	1	2		
Noble, Seth	1	3	3			Patterson, Andrew	2	2	3			Warren, Thomas	1	2	1		
Bussell, Jacob	2	1	1			Patten, John	2	4	2			Frees, George	2	1	2		
Howard, Thomas	2	2	5			Pickard, Jonathan	1	4	1			Frees, Isaac	1				
Hasey, William	1	1	2			Hewes, Eliu	3		1			Babbige, Stephen	1	2	2		
Mayo, Nathaniel	4		2			Blagden, Charles	2		3			Tyler, Joseph	2	3	2		
Griffin, Jacob	1					Pomroy, Joseph	2	5	4			Tyler, George	1				
Smith, Elijah	1					Swan, Gustavus	1	4	5			Tyler, Belcher	1	3	4		
Bayley, Samuel	1	4	1			Pierce, Lettice		1	1			Colby, Joseph	2	1	3		
Webster, Andrew	2	6	4			Garrish, Jack				3		Silvester, Edmund	1	1	2		
Treat, James	1		6			**DEER ISLE TOWN.**						Webb, Hannah	1		4		
Harthorn, Ashbell	1		5									Colby, Joseph, jun^r	1	2	1		
Allen, Abraham	1	1	2			Sellers, Joseph	1	1	2			Stinson, Thomas, jun^r	1	3	2		
Harthorn, David	1		1			Crockett, Josiah	2	2	2			Smith, David	1	2	2		
Harthorn, Silas	1	3	4			Torrey, William	1					Robbins, Thomas	1	1	4		
Treat, Robert	3	4	4			Smally, Job	3	2	2			Robbins, Thomas, jun.	1	1	1		
Page, Joseph	1	1	5			Smally, Thomas	2	3	5			Stinson, Thomas	2		2		
Frees, Isaac	1	2	6			Smally, Thomas, jun^r	1					Stinson, Samuel	1	1	2		
Dugen, William	1		2			Webster, Ebenezer	2	3	5			Stinson, William	1	2	1		
McPhetres, Archibald	3	4	2			Raynes, Anna			1			Babbige, William	1		2		
Lovejoy, Phillip	1		2			Raynes, John	1	3	3			Hatch, Seth	1		1		
Tourtellott, Abraham	1	3	3			Raynes, Martha	1		2			Staples, Samuel	1				
Maddox, Ichabod	1	4	2			Raynes, William	1	2	1			Thurston, John	3	3	3		
Spencer, Daniel	1	4	2			Lunt, Michael	1					Lane, Hezekiah	3	2	2		
Madden, Owen	1					Jordan, James	3	1	4			Richards, William	1	1			
Bussell, Isaac	1	1	3			Trundy, Samuel	3	1	7			Stockbridge, Benj^a	1		6		
Tourtellott, Reuben	1	1	3			Emerson, Joshua	1	2	1			Toothaker, Elijah	1				
Loushon, Anthony	1	2	2			Boynton, Isaac	1	3	3			Whitmore, Joseph	1	3	3		
Page, James	1		2			Eaton, Jonathan	2	4	5			Smally, Andrew	1	2	3		
Page, Joseph, jun^r	1	1	3			Sanders, James	1		3			Crockett, Robinson	1	3	3		
McPhetres, Archibald, jun^r	1	1	1			Sanders, Timothy	1		6			Carpenter, William	2		4		
Page, Isaac	1	2	1			Pressy, John, 3^d	1	2	1			Sellers, Charles	1	2	4		
Inman, Joseph	1	5	1			Pressy, John	1	1	2			Smith, Joseph	2	1	2		
Plympton, Joseph	1	1	2			Pressy, John, jun^r	1		4			Weed, Benjamin	3	2	5		
Davis, Ezra	1	2	2			Pressy, Chace	1	4	4			Gra, Christopher	1		2		
Colburn, Jeremiah	2		2			Johnson, Nathan	1	1	3			Farrell, Peggy			3		
Colburn, William	1	1	1			Hooper, John	3	1	2			Howard, Samuel	1		3		
Marsh, John	1	6	1			Hooper, William	1					Billings, Timothy		1	3	1	
White, Samuel	1					Morey, Ezekiel	1	2	4			Harris, Joseph	1		2		
Stanley, David	1		4			Morey, Elias	1	3	1			Blastow, Noah	1	1	3		
Frees, Abraham	2	3	3			Haskell, Joshua	1	1	4			Conry, Thomas	2	5	5		
Frees, John	1	1	3			Cole, Benjamin	2		1			York, Benj^a	2		2		
Eayrs, Joshua	4	1	5			Cole, Benjamin, jun^r	1	3	3			Marchant, Anthony	2	2	7		
Dennett, Jacob	2	1	7			Powars, Peter	4		2			Kimball, Solomon	2	1	4		
Barns, Jotham	1					Colby, Ambrose	1	2	2			Moody, Moses	2	2	2		
Burrill, Philip	1					Howard, Ezra	3		2			Brickett, Moses	1				
Gross, Moses	1					Fullerton, William	1		2			Williams, Peter				4	
Denning, Jane		2	2			Dunham, Elijah	1	2	1			**DUCKTRAP TOWN.**					
Denning, James	1	2	2			Haskell, Mark	4		1	4		Burkmar, Thomas	4	3	2		
Campbell, Daniel	1	1	3			Haskell, Thomas	1					Presscott, Samuel	3	1	3		
Tibbitts, George	1		4			Haskell, Ignatius	1	3	4			Adams, John	2				
						Whitelaw, James	1					Miller, David	1	1	3		
						Haskell, Caleb	1	2	4			Knowlton, Reuben	3	1	2		
						Marshall, Ezekiel	3		2			Knowlton, William	1	1	5		
						Marshall, Joshua	1	1	2								

HANCOCK COUNTY—Continued.

NAME OF HEAD OF FAMILY.	Free white males of 16 years and upward, including heads of families.	Free white males under 16 years.	Free white females, including heads of families.	All other free persons.	Slaves.	NAME OF HEAD OF FAMILY.	Free white males of 16 years and upward, including heads of families.	Free white males under 16 years.	Free white females, including heads of families.	All other free persons.	Slaves.	NAME OF HEAD OF FAMILY.	Free white males of 16 years and upward, including heads of families.	Free white males under 16 years.	Free white females, including heads of families.	All other free persons.	Slaves.
DUCKTRAP TOWN—con.						**EASTERN RIVER TOWNSHIP NO. 2—con.**						**FRANKFORT TOWN—con.**					
Knowlton, Thomas	1	4	1			Gray, Mary		2	1			Oaksman, Tobias	2	1	5		
Pinkham, James	1	2	4			Gross, Ebenezer	3		3			Grant, Ephraim	2		2		
Clark, Jonathan	2	3	3			Gross, Ebenezer, jun^r	1					Grant, Adam	1	3	1		
Baty, John	1	3	4			Blasdell, James	1	1	3			Blasdell, Ebenezer	2	3	5		
Ring, Jacob	1	1	3			Darling, Eliakim	2		2			McIntyer, John	1		2		
Gibson, James	1	3	3			Lawrence, Abel	1	2	2			Clark, Jonathan	2	1	1		
Highser, Adam	1	1	1			Herryman, Joshua	1	2	1			Clark, James	2	1	1		
Welsh, John	1	3	1			Davis, Jesse	1		1			Clark, Lemuel	1	1	2		
Welsh, Mark	1	2	2			Herryman, Asa, jun^r	1	2	2			Kingsbury, Enoch	1				
Patterson, Adam	1	4	2			Evans, John	1		3			Pratt, Seth	1	1	3		
Harvey, John	1		2									Kingbury, Phineas	1	2	4		
McDermot, John	1		1			**EDDY TOWNSHIP.**						Parker, Oliver	2		3		
Lawrence, Zachariah	2	1	3									Treat, Joshua, jun^r		4	2		
McIntyer, Angus	1		1			Phillips, John	1	3	3			Littlefield, Moses	1		2		
Carter, Edward	2	3	2			Blackman, Eleazer	1		1			Bolton, Elisha	5		3		
Richards, Joseph	3	5	3			Eddy, Elias	1	1	3			Littlefield, James	1	1	1		
Calef, Allen	1	3	4			Eddy, Jonathan	1	1	1			Grant, William	1	2	3		
Smith, John	1	1	2			Nickolls, James	1	2	3			Carlton, John	1		5		
Harding, Josiah	1	1	1			Eddy, Ibrook	1	3	4			Littlefield, Samuel	1		3		
Pomroy, John	1		2			McMann, Thankful			5			Littlefield, Stephen	2	2	1		
Smith, Benj^a	2	3	4			Bussell, Stephen		1	7			Woodman, Benj^a	1	2	2		
Gatchell, James	1	3	3			Mahany, Patrick	1	5	3			Wentworth, Grant	1		1		
Drinkwater, Micajah	3	4	4			Rowell, Patience	1	2	2			Kenny, Paul	2	3	3		
Drinkwater, Zenas	1		1			Mann, Daniel	1	1	3			Tyler, Andrew	1		1		
Thomas, Joshua	1	4	1			Grant, Samuel	1	1				Lane, Daniel	1	5	3		
Knights, Thomas	2	3	4			Grant, Alexander	1		2			Danford, Phillip	1	1	1		
Adams, Joshua	1	1	1			Grant, Stephen		3	3			Woodman, Molly		3	3		
Wade, John	1	2	3			Oliver, Jacob	1	2	5			Treat, Joseph	1		1		
Clark, John	1		2			Spencer, Phillip	1		5			Downs, Ephraim	1	1	2		
Pitcher, Lewis	2		1			Spencer, Daniel	1	2	2			Clark, Isaac	1		1		
Ulmer, George	3	4	4			Spencer, Nathaniel, jun	1		1			Downs, Asa	1		1		
Collamore, Joseph	1		1			Spencer, Nathaniel	1	5	3			More, William	1	1	3		
Gammon, James	1											Wentworth, W^m	1		1		
Clary, Daniel	1					**FRANKFORT TOWN.**						Hatch, Joseph	1		1		
Ulmer, Phillip	1	2	4									Hyde, Ezra	3	1	4		
Studley, Lemuel	1		1			George, William	1	1	1			Tibbitts, Benj^a	2		3		
Studley, John	1	1	1			Grant, Gooding	1	1	4			Tibbitts, Solomon	2	1	1		
Dickrow, Daniel	1	1	1			Grant, Andrew	4		3			Page, William	1		2		
Dickrow, Zepheniah	2		1			Newcomb, Reuben	4	1	6			Grant, James	1	6	2		
Thayer, Lemuel, jun^r	1	1	6			Newcomb, Jonathan	1	1	1			McMann, Joseph	1		2		
Thayer, Lemuel	1		2			Mayo, Nathaniel	1	1	3			Coolier, Francis	4	2	5		
Turner, Samuel	1	2	2			Welsh, Henry	1		2			Tibbitts, Nathaniel	2	1	1		
Gay, David	3	3	4			Mayo, James	1		2			Carr, William	1	2	2		
Brooks, Martin	2	3	3			Mayo, Israel	1		1			Merithue, Roger	1	2	4		
Dickrow, Peleg	1					Young, Zebulon	1		2			Ames, John	1	1	3		
Harley, Ralph	1	1	1			Whitney, Thomas	2	1	2			Mudgett, Abraham	1				
Dunbar, Moses	2	1	4			Murch, Benjamin	1		2			Bassick, George	1		3		
						Whitney, Daniel	1		4			Rankins, Robert	1	1	1		
EASTERN RIVER TOWNSHIP NO. 2.						Murch, William	1	1	2			Garland, Ebenezer	1		3		
						Doan, Amos	1	2	1			McLaughlin, W^m	1	2	1		
Bowden, Paul, jun^r	1		2			Billington, John	1	2	2			Sweetser, John, jun^r	1		2		
Canfield, Ebenezer	2		5			Newcomb, Simeon	1	3	3			Partrige, David	1		2		
Sherburne, Samuel	1	3	2			Baker, Moses	1		3			Boyd, Joseph	1	1	5		
Boynton, William	1	4	6			Cobb, Ezekiel	1	1	3			Goodale, Daniel	2	5	2		
Sherburne, Jacob	1	2	5			Phillbrook, Jonathan	1	2	3			Partrige, Clark	1	4	3		
French, Dearbon	1					Hamblin, Perez	1	2	4			Shute, Benjamin, jun^r	1	2	1		
Partrige, Samuel	1					Harding, Jesse	2	3	3			Cozens, Nathaniel	2	2	2		
Gross, Joseph, jun^r			2			Snow, Harding	1	2	1			Lancaster, Daniel	1	2	4		
Hart, John	1		1			Knowles, Freeman	2	3	5			Staples, John	1	4	5		
Crage, Samuel	1	1	3			Hopkins, Isaac	1	5	4			Adam, John, jun^r	1	1	1		
Crage, Andrew	1					Hopkins, Nathan	1	3	1			Adam, John	1	2	5		
Crage, Moses	1	3	3			Smith, Simon	1	4	4			Sweetser, John	3	2	4		
Gross, Joseph	2	2	3			Mayo, Ebenezer	3		2			Black, Henry	1	5	4		
Viles, Joseph	2	1	5			Mirrick, Nathaniel	2	3	4			French, Zetham	3	5	4		
Soper, Samuel	1		2			Higgins, Benj^a	1	1	6			Pierce, John	2	2	5		
Turner, Calvin	1	4	2			Harding, Archibald	2	2	4			Stowers, Samuel	1		3		
Gilman, Peter	1	1	7			Ryder, Amos	2	2	2			Eustis, Jacob	1				
Viles, Joseph, jun^r	1	1	1			Higgins, Abisha	1	1	4			Shute, Benj^a	3	1	4		
Holt, Humphry	1	2	5			Knowles, Mary	1	1	2			Treat, Joshua	2	4	1		
Hancock, John	1	2	4			Snow, Thomas	1	1	4			Dickey, William	2	1	8		
Tower, Elizabeth			3			Ellingwood, Richard	2	1	1			Farley, William	1		1		
Hancock, Nathan	1	2	3			Holbrook, John	2	2	5			Fletcher, Thomas	2	2	3		
Smith, James	2	2	2			Cole, Pheobe	1	2	3			Cluley, Isaac	2	1	3		
Gross, John	1	1	1			Sullivan, William	1	4				Clifford, Nathaniel	1		3		
Gross, Zachary	1		2			Haldershaw, John	2		2			Clifford, Jacob	1	2	3		
Davis, Micah	1					Haldershaw, John, jun^r	1	1	2			Hichborn, William	1				
Partrige, John	1		1			Downs, Noah	1	4	3			Marten, Joseph	1		1		
Hamilton, William	1	1	4			Trebble, Joseph	1	1	1			Clifford, John	1	1	2		
Partrige, Thomas	1	2	1			Downs, Paul	1	2	1			Dwelly, John	1		2		
Morrill, Benj^a	1		1			Downs, Thomas	1		1			Ellis, Manoah	1		2		
Crage, Samuel, jun^r	1	1	3			Clark, Nathaniel	1	1	2			Ellis, Levi	1	1	2		
Crage, John	1	2	1			Stubbs, James	1		1			Staples, Miles	3	4	3		
Partrige, Daniel	1					Kempton, John	3	5	2			Lanpher, Langworthy	1	4	2		
Homes, Samuel	1					Kempton, Zacheus	1	2	2			Griffin, Samuel	6		2		
Treat, Samuel	1					Gibbs, Sally			1			Griffin, Nathan	1		1		
Blasdell, Moses, jun^r		2	3			Collson, James	1	4	4			Griffin, William	1		2		
Sanders, William	1					Collson, Hateevil	2		1			Young, Alexander	1		4		
Herryman, Peter	1	1	2			Higgins, John	1	1	3			Staples, William	1	3	1	1	5
Herryman, Ezekiel	1	3	2			Bolen, John	1	1	3			Staples, Jotham	1	2	5		
Herryman, Asa	1	4	2			Coolier, James	2	1	1			Pendleton, William	1				
Soper, Justus	1	2	3			Whitham, Benj^a	2	2	5			Young, Samuel	1				
Keyes, Samuel	2	1	6			Green, Thomas	1	4	3			Roff, James	1				
Rooks, Joseph	1	1	4			Hassan, William	1	4	4			Park, John	2	3	5		
Rooks, Benj^a	1		1			Johnson, Miller	1	1	1			Ellis, Sarah			1		

HEADS OF FAMILIES—MAINE.

HANCOCK COUNTY—Continued.

NAME OF HEAD OF FAMILY.	Free white males of 16 years and upward, including heads of families.	Free white males under 16 years.	Free white females, including heads of families.	All other free persons.	Slaves.
FRANKFORT TOWN—con.					
Pendleton, Peleg	2	1	4		
Crary, Joseph	1	2	3		
Nickolls, James	4	1	7		
Nickolls, James, junr	1				
Lords, Henry	1	3	4		
Porter, Robert	1	4	2		
Stimpson, Ephraim	2	1	2		
Corsson, Ichabod	1	2	5		
Black, Henry, junr	1		2		
Ames, Josiah	2	1	3		
Ellis, Berrick	1		4		
Nickerson, Reuben	1	6	4		
Kimball, William	1				
Nickerson, Aaron	1				
Hoyt, Solomon A				1	
Hoyt, Richard				1	
GOULDSBOROUGH TOWN.					
Smith, John	1		1		
Sargent, Benja	1				
Sargent, Diamond	1	1	3		
Bacon, Thomas	1	2	1		
Sargent, William	2	1	4		
Stephens, Abraham	1	1	1		
Sargent, Wm, junr	1				
Jones, Nathan	12	1	5		
Hill, Thomas	2	7	3		
Walker, John	1		2		
Newman, Joseph	1	3	2		
Young, Noah	2	1	2		
Gubtail, John	2	1	2		
Gubtail, Thomas	1	1	1		
Libbey, Samuel	2	1	5		
Godfrey, Benja	4	1	5		
Shaw, Hannah	4	1	2		
Allen, Tobias	2	1	2		
Noonan, Abigail		1	5		
Wright, Daniel	1	2	3		
Alline, Benja	1	1	3		
Shaw, William	4		1		
More, Joel	3	4	4		
Tracy, Asa	1	2	3		
Tracy, Jonathan	3		3		
Tracy, Samuel	1	1	4		
Gubtail, John, junr	1	2	3		
Cole, Abijah	1	1	1		
Allen, Nathaniel	1		1		
McDaniel, John	1	2	4		
Petty, Oliver	1	2	1		
Young, Samuel	1	2	1		
Perry, Jesse	1	1	2		
Simonton, William	3	2	4		
Gubtail, Abijah	1	4	2		
Pinkham, Tristam	1		2		
Spurlin, James	1	1	3		
Whitten, Phineas	1	4	6		
Joy, John	1	1	1		
Joy, Samuel	2	3	3		
Fernald, Clement	3	2	5		
Tracy, Elizabeth	1	2	5		
Ash, Benjamin	1		4		
Ash, Robert	1	1	1		
Frazer, Thomas					9
ISLEBOROUGH TOWN.					
Page, Simon	1	3	2		
Sprague, John	1	3	3		
Vezie, Samuel	1	4	4		
Coombs, Anthony, junr	1		3		
Coombs, Fields	1	1	3		
Woodward, Peter	1		1		
Woodward, Joseph	1	2	2		
Dodge, Noah	1	2	2		
Thomas, Benja	1	2	5		
Trim, Godfrey, junr	1	1	3		
Trim, Godfrey	3	1	5		
Marshall, Benja	2	2	2		
Marshall, Zachariah	1	1	3		
Dodge, Rathburn	1	1	1		
Lasdell, Ellison, junr	1	3	2		
Grinnall, William	1	1	4		
Coombs, Peter	1		2		
Coombs, Hosea	1	3	2		
Coombs, Anthony	3	3	1		
Williams, Samuel	1		3		
Williams, Shubael	3		3		
Cottrell, Silvester	2	4	3		
Hewes, Paoli	1	1	2		
Dodge, Simon, junr	1		2		
Pendleton, Samuel	3	3	6		
Dodge, Simon	1	5	3		
Bordman, Joseph	1	5	5		
Pendleton, Joshua	1	1	6		
ISLEBOROUGH TOWN—continued.					
Pendleton, Thomas, junr	1	3	4		
Pendleton, Oliver	1	4	5		
Pendleton, Thomas	2	2	4		
Pendleton, Gideon	1	1	3		
Ellwill, William	3	2	3		
Pendleton, John	2	3	3		
Carver, Benja	1				
Hill, John	1				
Pendleton, Jonathan	1	4	3		
Turner, Isaac	1				
Adams, Thomas	1				
Homes, Tilden	1				
Pendleton, Henry	2	2	3		
Pendleton, Wm	2		3		
Gatchall, Nathaniel	1	1	1	1	
Pendleton, Job	3	2	7		
Lasdell, Ellison	1	2	1		
Harthorn, Thomas	1	3	1		
Jones, Joseph	1		1		
Ames, Thomas	1	1	5		
Ames, Jabez	1		2		
Thomas, George	1		2		
Farrow, Josiah	1	2	2		
Gilkey, John	2	4	5		
McDonald, John	1				
Pendleton, Natl	1	1	10		
Thomas, David	2	2	1		
Hardy, Joseph	1	2	3		
Phillbrook, Wm, junr	1	5	1		
Holbrook, Prince	1	2	1		
Phillbrook, Joseph	1	1	4		
Phillbrook, Wm	2	1	1		
Griffin, William	2	1	3		
Hatch, Jeremiah	1	1	4		
Sherman, Valentine	3	1	3		
Coombs, Robert	1		1		
Williams, Amos	1	3	1		
Burns, William	1	1	2		
Warren, Samuel	2	5	4		
MOUNT DESERT TOWN.					
Robinson, John	2	1	3		
Tinker, David	1	2	3		
Noble, Reuben	1	1	5		
Reed, Jacob	2	1	4		
Heath, Richard	1	2	3		
Heath, William	1		2		
Appleton, Francis	1	1	2		
Wentworth, Enoch	1	4	1		
Norwood, Stephen	1	1	4		
Rich, John	4	2	5		
Barton, James	1	1	5		
Richardson, Stephen	4	1	3		
Gott, Daniel, junr	1	2	3		
Gott, Daniel	3	3	4		
Gott, Nathaniel	1		3		
Gott, Joseph	1		1		
Norwood, Joshua	2	4	4		
Richardson, Thomas	3	3	5		
Gott, Peter	1	3	4		
Richardson, Thomas, junr	1	3	1		
Ward, Benja	1	1	3		
Bowden, Samuel	1	1	3		
Mayo, Joshua	3		2		
Salisbury, Jabez	1	1	4		
Langley, Phillip	2	3	3		
Spurlin, Benja	1	4	2		
Rich, Jonathan	1	2	4		
Stanley, Sans	2	1	2		
Stanley, Thomas	1	1	3		
Bunker, Aaron	1		3		
Stanley, Margaret			2		
Stanley, Samuel	1				
Stanley, John	1	1	2		
Stanley, Peter	1	1	2		
Flinn, Thomas	1		2		
Peache, James	1	4	2		
More, Jeremiah	1	1	2		
Tucker, Andrew	1	4	3		
Rafanel, Augustus	1	2	4		
Emerson, Samuel	1	7	2		
Groo, Joseph, junr	1		1		
Groo, Joseph	1	1	1		
Brown, Jonathan	1	1	1		
Baker, William	1		1		
Whitehorn, William	1		1		
Salisbury, Reuben	1	2	5		
Bunker, John	1		3		
Bunker, Isaac	1	9	3		
Bunker, Benja	2	2	3		
Bunker, Mark	1				
Gilley, William	1	2	3		
MOUNT DESERT TOWN—continued.					
Scott, William	1		2		
Sommers, Thomas	1	1	1		
Tarr, Andrew	2	1	2		
Manchester, John	2	1	3		
Richardson, James, junr	1	1	1		
Manchester, John, junr	1		1		
Sargent, Stephen	2		1		
Hadlock, Samuel	1	2	3		
Richardson, James	2	1	4		
Somes, Abraham	4	3	2		
Reed, Samuel	1	3	4		
Massy, Nathaniel	1				
Richardson, George	1		3		
Gott, Stephen	1		1		
Dodge, Ezra H	1		2		
Richardson, John G	1	1	2		
Athenton, Benja	1	2	2		
Wescott, Davis	1	2	5		
Eaton, David	1	1	2		
Robinson, John, junr	1	2	1		
McKenzie, John	1	2	1		
Pray, Ephraim, junr	1	1	2		
Hodgdon, Joseph	1	4	4		
Lunt, Abner	1	4	2		
Pray, Ephraim	2	1	3		
Millikin, Samuel	1	2	4		
Freeman, Reuben	3		6		
Bartlett, Israel	1		4		
Bartlett, David	1	1	2		
Bartlett, Christopher	2	2	4		
Bartlett, Christopher, jun	1		2		
Bartlett, Elias	1				
Higgins, David	5	3	5		
Higgins, Jesse	2	4	3		
Chipar, John					
Mayo, Joseph	4	5	2		
Hinkley, Seth	1		2		
Higgins, Elkanah	1	2	1		
Thomas, Nickolas	1	4	3		
Thomas, John	1		2		
Thomas, John, junr	1	4	3		
Thomas, Amos	1				
Richardson, Daniel	1	2	2		
Hadley, Simeon	2	2	7		
Leland, Ezra	3	4	5		
Leland, Ebenezer	2	1	3		
Hopkins, Joseph	1	2	7		
Salisbury, Ebenezer	4	2	6		
Young, Eikanah	1	7	1		
Paine, Thomas	2		3		
Mason, William	1		1		
Doane, Seth	1	2	4		
Cozens, John	1	1	2		
Hamer, John	1	2	4		
Knowles, Henry	2	1	4		
Higgins, Levi	2	3	7		
Higgins, Jerusha	1		2		
Smellige, Timothy	1	2	7		
Smellige, Josiah	2		2		
Hamar, David	2	2	2		
Thompson, Peleg	1		1		
Cozens, Elisha	2	2	2		
Thompson, Cornelius	3	2	5		
Young, Ezra	2		2		
Young, Robert	1	2	2		
Stanwood, Benja	1	1	1		
Hodgkins, William	1				
Hodgkins, Joseph	1				
Day, John	1	5	2		
Wescott, Thomas	4		2		
Higgins, Solomon	2	2			
Higgins, Israel	2	5	2		
Rodick, Daniel	3	2	6		
Wescott, Thomas, jr	2	3	3		
Stanwood, Humphry	1		3		
Hopkins, Smith	1	1	1		
Bunker, Joseph	1	2	2		
Higgins, Stephen	1	1	1		
Gillcott, George	1	2			
Lynam, William	1		6		
Neptune, Junior				1	
ORPHAN ISLAND TOWN.					
Collins, Syrenus	2	1	4		
Hopkins, Bazilah	1	3	3		
Hearsy, Peleg					
Scott, James	2	2	3		
Nickerson, William	1				
Cunningham, James	2	2	2		
Buckley, James					
Mace, William	2	1	3		
Blasdell, Moses	1	1	2		
Sanders, Moses	1		1		

HANCOCK COUNTY—Continued.

NAME OF HEAD OF FAMILY.	Free white males of 16 years and upward, including heads of families.	Free white males under 16 years.	Free white females, including heads of families.	All other free persons.	Slaves.	NAME OF HEAD OF FAMILY.	Free white males of 16 years and upward, including heads of families.	Free white males under 16 years.	Free white females, including heads of families.	All other free persons.	Slaves.	NAME OF HEAD OF FAMILY.	Free white males of 16 years and upward, including heads of families.	Free white males under 16 years.	Free white females, including heads of families.	All other free persons.	Slaves.
ORPHAN ISLAND TOWN—continued.						ORRINGTON TOWN—con.						PENOBSCOT TOWN—con.					
Merrill, Caleb	1	2	2			Harthorn, Solomon	1	5	3			Costin, Daniel	1		1		
Haines, Frederick	1		1			Manssell, John	1		2			Magee, Neil	1		1		
Webber, Isaac	1		2			Manssell, Joseph	1	2	2			Lowe, Daniel	1	1	3		
Lillie, Benjª	2		1			Orcutt, Emerson	2	4	5			Howard, Benjª	3	1	4		
Walker, Eleazer	2	1	2			Knap, Samuel	1	3	5			Howard, Benjª, junʳ			4		
Perkins, Eliphalet	1	1	1			Gardiner, George	1		2			Orcutt, Jacob	2	3	3		
Abbott, James	1	3	4			Rowe, Zebulon	2	2	3			Orcutt, Malachi	3	1	2		
Grout, William	2	2	5			Lancaster, William	2	2	1			Condon, John	3	4	2		
Pomroy, William	1	2	2			Robshaw, Peter	2		1			Wasson, John	1	2	2		
York, Joseph	1	2	2			Mann, Hannah	1		8			Wasson, Thomas	1		1		
Crocker, John	1	3	6									Wasson, Samuel	1	2	5		
Rawlins, Benjª	1	1	3			PENOBSCOT TOWN.						Hawes, David	1	3	4		
Cummins, Thomas	1	1	1			Howe, David	1	1	1			Henry, Archibald	1	2	2		
Blake, Jonathan	1		1			Crawford, James	2		2			Perkins, Nathaniel	1	2	2		
Richards, Samuel	1	1	3			Halliburton, George	1					Slack, Thomas	1	1	2		
						Junin, Joseph	2		2			Perkins, Abraham	1	1	5		
ORRINGTON TOWN.						Hunewell, Richard	2	1	2	3		Lunt, Benjª	1	2	6		
Whelden, Ebenezer	2	1	3			Lee, John	3	1	3	1		Wardwell, Joseph	1	1	2		
Whelden, Joseph	1		2			Rogers, Samuel	2	1	3			Wardwell, Jeremiah, junʳ	1	1	2		
Smith, Thomas	2	2	2			Higgins, Barnabas	1	1	4			Butler, James	1		4		
Wentworth, Moses	1	3	6			Readhead, William	1	1	4			Lymburner, Cunningham	1	2	6		
Homes, Jeremiah	1	2	3			Mann, Oliver	1	1	6			Grindall, John	1		2		
Bartlett, Samuel	2	1	3			Orr, Debby	1	1	2			Varnum, Mathew	1	3	3		
Snow, Edward	3	3	5			Fields, Thomas	1		2			Jones, Jeremiah	1	2	2		
Freeman, Timothy	1	4	4			Pollard, Avis			2			Jones, Samuel	1				
Snow, Amasa, junʳ	1		1			Cook, Ephraim	1	1	2			Bowden, Jacob	1		6		
Cole, Henry	1		1			Robbins, Isaac	2	1	2			Stover, William	1	2	1		
Nickerson, Paul	1	2	3			Littlefield, Joseph	1		2			Stover, Isaac	1	1	4		
Nickerson, Eliphalet	1		2			Perkins, John	4	2	8			Tapley, Peletiah	1		4		
Nickerson, Eliphalet, junʳ	1	1	1			Bray, John	4	1	3			Webber, Joseph	3	2	4		
Nickerson, Warren	1	2	2			Hatch, Mark	3	3	5			Blodgett, Seth	1	4	3		
Nickerson, Daniel	1	3	2			Lawrence, Rogers	1		2			Allen, Peter	1	2	2		
Dean, Thomas	1					Parker, Mighill	1		1			Davis, Thomas	1		2		
Dean, Thomas, junʳ	1		2			Perkins, Joseph	6	3	6	1		Swain, Meriam		3	2		
Doane, Oliver	1	4	3			Banks, Aaron	3	2	5			Curtis, Benjª, junʳ	1	4	2		
Atwood, Jesse	1	5	5			Hayden, John	1		2			Parker, Oliver	2	3	3		
Brooks, George	1	2	6			Lowder, Jonathan	1	2	2			Morgrage, Peter	1	2	4		
Fowler, Simeon	2	2	6			Bishop, Hudson	1	1	3			More, John	2		1		
Freeman, James	1		2			Calef, Joseph	1		1			More, James	1		2		
Severance, Joshua	1		2			Cogswell, Sarah		1	3			Curtis, Benjª	2		3		
Sweat, Shebna	1		1			Hunt, Laban	1	2	2			Curtis, Charles	1		2		
Severance, Caleb	1	3	2			Douglas, James	1	2	3			Wescott, Elizabeth		1	3		
Rogers, Jesse	2	3	3			Hilton, Daniel	1		5			Wescott, William	1	2	2		
Rogers, Moses	1	3	2			Mathews, Abigail		3	4			Lowell, Eliphalet	1	4	4		
Pierce, Nathaniel	1	3	3			Maddox, Caleb	1					Lowell, Joseph	2	1	3		
Freeman, Samuel	1	2	4			Rea, Benjª	1	2	7			Woodman, Joshua	1				
Pepper, Mercy			1			Perkins, Stover	1	5	4			Herrick, Joseph	1				
Snow, Benjª	2	3	3			Willson, David	1	3	2			Binney, Joseph	2		5		
Snow, Amasa	1		2			Witham, Abraham	1	2	5			Powars, Battry	1		1		
Gould, Nathaniel	1	3	8			More, John, junʳ	1	1	2			Webber, William	3	1	3		
Sweat, Solomon	2	1	2			Steel, Andrew	1	1	4			More, David	1				
Baker, Joseph	3	4	5			Dolliver, William	1		1			Gooding, Luxford	2	1	2		
Ward, Nathaniel	1	1	1			Willson, John	1		2			Buckley, Daniel	1				
McCurdy, Robert	3		3			Vezie, Moses	3		3			Burges, John, junʳ	1	1	4		
Wiswall, Samuel	1		5			Bowden, Ebenezer	1	2	4			Blake, Moses	1		2		
Wiswall, David	1		3			Dobble, John	1	1	3			Avery, Thatcher	1	2	5		
Ginn, James	3	4	6			Curtis, Joseph	1	1	4			Freeman, Peletiah	3	1	5		
Brewer, John	2	2	6			Bowden, William	1		4			Stover, Nathaniel	2	2	2		
Rogers, John	1					Bowden, Abraham	1	3	3			Richey, Mathew	1	2	2		
Brewer, Josiah	1		1	1		Bowden, Lucy			2			Johonnot, Gabriel	2	1	2		
Tibbetts, John	1	2	4			Hibbert, Joseph	2	1	3			Grindall, Ichabod	3	2	2		
Kenny, Henry	1	2	3			Devereaux, Ralph	2	1	4			Eaton, Thirza			1		
Hutchins, John	1	2	5			Hibbert, Joseph, junʳ	1	1	3			Atkins, Nathaniel	1				
Emery, John	1	1	1			Bowden, Thomas	1	2	2			Kench, Thomas	1	1	1		
Fulman, George	1		3			Bowden, Ebenezer	3	1	4			Magee, Robert	2		3		
Skinner, Daniel	2	2	3			Bridges, Henry	1		2			Lord, Jeremiah	1	2	2		
Skinner, Elisha	1	4	2			Stover, Jeremiah	1	2	2			Vezie, Nathaniel	1	2	6		
Campbell, Thomas, junʳ	1					Stover, Abraham	1	1	4			Leach, Peletiah	2	4	4		
Holyoak, John	2	5	5			Stover, Jotham	1	2	1			Connor, Alice		3	6		
Perkins, Benjª	1		3			Bridges, Edmund	1					Webster, Daniel	1	2	4		
Mayew, Andrew	1		3			Heath, Eldad	1	3	5			Rhodes, Esther			2		
Johnson, Simeon	1	3	5			Bowden, Caleb	1	2	5			Hutchins, William	1	3	1		
Wall, David	1					Bowden, Paul	2		1			Grindall, John, junʳ	1		1		
Ryder, John	3	4	5			Basteen, Joseph	1	1	2			Gay, Moses	1				
Thomas, John	2	1	4			Bowden, Samuel	1	1	4			Perkins, Isaac	2	4	3		
Campbell, Thomas	3		8			Howard, Edward	1	1	6			Perkins, Sparks	1	3	4		
Bradley, Levi	1	2	2			Hopkins, Elisha	2	1	1			Wardwell, Daniel	1		2		
Jeminson, Daniel	1	2	2			Norton, Noah	1	4	3			Wardwell, Jeremiah	1	3	4	1	
Bradley, Bryant	1	2	2			More, William	1	1	4			Snowman, William	1		1		
Cluley, Isaac	1	1	2			Blake, Andrew	1	1	4			Perkins, Mary		3	3		
Jones, Elijah	1		2			Darrow, George	1	2	1			Stover, William	1	2	5		
Farrington, John	1		2			Radman, John	1	2	4			Littlefield, Elijah	1		4		
Mann, David	1	2	2			Blake, Ephraim	2	4	3			Leach, James	3		1		
Blake, John	1		2			Radman, Israel	1		3			Wardwell, Daniel, junʳ	1		4		
Gilmore, Samuel	1	1	1			Mayew, Reuben	2	3	6			Herrick, Andrew	3	4	4		
Blake, Solomon	1	1	1			Corsson, John	1	2	6			Nutter, Thomas	2	1	4		
Winchester, Silas	1	2	3			Radman, Benjª	1		2			Woollins, John	1	1	3		
Simpson, John	2		2			Young, Joseph	1	1	3			Vezie, Samuel	2	3	4		
Brastow, Thomas	1					Dyer, Michael	1	3	6			Wardwell, Josiah	1	1	4		
Brastow, Billings	1					Bakeman, John, junʳ	1	1	2			Winslow, Elijah	1		6		
Hollbrook, Calvin	1		1			Bakeman, John	2	3	4			Snowman, John	1	1	3		
Dupee, Elias	1					Holbrook, Jesse	2	2	5			Perkins, Daniel	1	2	6		
Gilmore, William	1					Hosmer, Abel	1	1	1			Nutter, William	1		6		1
						Adams, Francis	1		3								

HEADS OF FAMILIES—MAINE.

HANCOCK COUNTY—Continued.

NAME OF HEAD OF FAMILY.	Free white males of 16 years and upward, including heads of families.	Free white males under 16 years.	Free white females, including heads of families.	All other free persons.	Slaves.
PENOBSCOT TOWN—con.					
Grant, Alexander	1	4	4		
Wescott, Samuel	2	1	3		
Wescott, Andrew	1		1		
Johnson, Giles	1	2	4		
Grindall, Reuben	2		8		
Grindall, Daniel	1	4	2		
Varnum, Gershom	1	3	4		
Hill, Geofry	1				
Stevens, Thomas	1				
Larry, Michael	1				
Taylor, James	2				
Jenkins, David	1				
Mathews, Samuel	1		2		
SEDGWICK TOWN.					
Stanley, Kenny	1	2	4		
Herrick, Joshua	2		5		
Trussell, William	2	4	4		
Herrick, Joseph	1				
Hale, Samuel	4	1	3		
Holly, Joanna			2		
Friend, Benjᵃ	4	2	5		
Carlton, David	2	4	2		
Allen, Joanna	2	3	3		
Blasdell, Enoch	1	1	2		
Over, William	2	2	2		
Over, William, junr	1		4		
Dodge, Abner	4	3	2		
Dodge, Jonah	1	1	3		
Dodge, Amaziah	1	1	2		
Cole, Thomas	1	1	4		
Allen, Nehemiah	4	2	3		
Fly, James	1	4	4		
Dorothy, Robert	3		2		
Dorothy, David	1	1	1		
Freathy, Joseph	3		2		
Bunker, Silas	3	3	3		
Herrick, John	2	6	4		
Herrick, Samuel	3	4	3		
Herrick, Ebenezer	1	2	6		
Black, Daniel	1	1	4		
Freathey, Joseph, junr	1	2	2		
Reed, Abraham	1	1	4		
Black, John, junr	1	1	2		
Black, Samuel	1		1		
Reed, William	3		2		
Cozens, Thomas	1		3		
Mahoney, James	1				
York, Solomon	1		2		
Cozens, Samuel	2	1	1		
Cozens, Samuel, junr	1	2	1		
Hutchinson, Joseph	1				
Babson, Joseph	2	2	4		
Black, Moses	1		5		
Black, Sally			2		
Black, Anna			1		
Harper, William	1	1	2		
Ementon, Joseph	1	1	3		
Herrick, Shadrach	1	1	1		
Wells, Richard	1		2		
Wells, William	1		3		
Staples, John	1	1	1		
Hammond, John	1	2	2		
Bridges, Job	1	3	3		
Carter, James	1	3	4		
Gra, Joshua	1		3		
Cain, Samuel	1	1	2		
Harding, Josiah	1	2	5		
Carter, John	2		1		
Carter, John, junr	1	1	4		
Bridges, Daniel, junr	3	1	3		
Bridges, Daniel	2	1	2		
Bridges, Jonathan	1	2	3		
Eaton, Ebenezer	1	3	4		
Eaton, Moses	4	2	4		
Carter, Allen	1	2	2		
Norris, William	1		3		
Hooper, John	1	3	3		
Eaton, Jonathan	1		2		
Hutchinson, John	1	2	4		
Billings, Benjᵃ	1	4	4		
Billings, Abel	1	4	1		
Byard, Robert	2	5	4		
Billings, John	2	2	3		
Billings, Solomon	1		2		
Maker, Joseph	1	2	3		
Williams, Thomas	1	2	2		
Parker, Simeon	1		2		
Lymburner, John	1	2	3		
Grindall, Joshua	3	6	2		
Bartrick, Dolly			5		
Butler, George	1	4	4		
Douglas, John	1	2	4		
Snow, Nickolas	3		5		

NAME OF HEAD OF FAMILY.	Free white males of 16 years and upward, including heads of families.	Free white males under 16 years.	Free white females, including heads of families.	All other free persons.	Slaves.
SEDGWICK TOWN—con.					
Gra, Andrew	1	3	1		
Door, John	1	2	2		
Gra, James	3	5	4		
Walker, John	1	2	3		
Watson, Shadrach	1		1		
Black, John	1	2	3		
Gra, Reuben	2	3	3		
Gra, Samuel	2	1	7		
Gra, Samuel, junr	1	1	1		
Stuart, Charles	1		3		
Douglas, James	2	4	1		
Snow, Joshua	1	2	2		
Door, Benjᵃ	1		1		
Gra, Nathaniel	1	2	2		
Gra, Joshua, junr	1		2		
Knowles, Samuel	1		2		
Davis, Israel	1				
McCaslin, Alexander	1	1	2		
Grindall, William	1	3	6		
Dodge, Abraham	1	1	2		
Parker, Oliver, junr	1				
SMALL ISLANDS NOT BELONGING TO ANY TOWN.					
Blake, Daniel	1	3	1		
Webster, Andrew	1		2		
Russell, Samuel	2		1		
Corsson, Nathaniel	1	1	3		
Corsson, John	1	1	2		
Annis, Ralph	2	3	6		
Pickering, Samuel	1	2	3		
Pickering, Daniel	1		2		
Dow, John	1	4	3		
Prince, Joseph	1	1	4		
Prince, John	1				
White, Thomas	1				
Robinson, Daniel	1				
Cunningham, Thomas	1				
Orr, William	1				
Walker, Charles	1	1	1		
Woodhouse, George	1	1	1		
Green, Anna			1		
SULLIVAN TOWN.					
Buckley, John	1	1	4		
Bean, Samuel	1	2	3		
Bickford, Joshua	1		4		
Bickford, Joseph	1	3	3		
Dyer, Ephraim	1	1	2		
Johnson, John	3	1	5		
Marten, Phillip	1	4	3		
Bragden, Ebenezer	3	1	3		
Dyer, Sarah		3	3		
Ingalls, William	1	1	2		
Doyle, Thomas	1		2		
Simpson, Jabez	1	3	4		
Ash, Thomas	2		5		
Hammond, John	3		2		
Bean, John	2		2		
Bean, John, junr	1	1	1		
Sullivan, Abigail	2	1	3		
Bragden, Joseph	3	2	3		
Prebble, Nathaniel	2		3		
Bean, James	1	3	3		
Prebble, Samuel	1		4		
Urann, John	2	1	1		
Welsh, Benjamin	1	2	4		
Ingalls, Samuel	3		2		
Simpson, James	2	2	2		
Prebble, Nathaniel	1		2		
Prebble, John	1		3		
Downing, Richard	1	1	3		
York, Benjᵃ, junr	2		3		
Simpson, John	1		3		
Salter, Francis	1		2		
Sargent, Paul Dudley	2	2	9		
Bennett, Benjᵃ	1				
Simpson, Josiah	2		1		
Simpson, Paul	1	2	4		
Simpson, Samuel	1		2		
Gordon, John	1	3	2		
Miller, James	2	3	4		
Blasdell, Abner	1	5	3		
Springer, James	1		2		
Everett, Henry	1	1	2		
York, Bartholomew	1	1	3		
Hardison, Nathaniel	2	3	5		
Bragden, Jeremiah	2	1	2		
Bragden, John	1	1	1		
Bragden, Jeremiah, jun	1		2		
Clark, Benjᵃ	1	2	6		
Johnson, Dorcas			2		

NAME OF HEAD OF FAMILY.	Free white males of 16 years and upward, including heads of families.	Free white males under 16 years.	Free white females, including heads of families.	All other free persons.	Slaves.
SULLIVAN TOWN—con.					
Springer, Jacob	1	1	1		
Donnell, Abraham	1	3	4		
Card, Stephon	1		4		
Hooper, David	1	3	6		
Williams, John	1		1		
Barronock, John	1	1	2		
Scammons, Daniel	1	4	3		
Abbott, James	1		2		
Butler, Nathaniel	1	1	2		
Butler, Peter	1	2	2		
Springer, David	1	1	2		
Hardison, Stephen	2		1		
Clark, Elisha	1				
Clark, Stephen	1	2	6		
West, Judah	1	3	5		
Butler, Moses	2	1	2		
Butler, Moses, junr	1	3	3		
Abbott, Reuben	2	4	3		
Abbott, Reuben, junr	1	2	1		
Abbott, Moses	1		4		
Clark, Richard	1	1	3		
Grant, Francis	2	1	1		
Gatcomb, William	2	2	5		
Moon, Thomas	3	1	4		
Moon, Joseph	1		2		
Jones, Morgan	1				
Coates, Charles	1	1	1		
Crabtree, William	1	4	2		
Crabtree, Agreen	2	3	1		
Wooster, William	2	2	4		
Wooster, Oliver	2	3	4		
Wooster, David	1		1		
Pettingall, Edward	1	1	1		
Foss, Thomas	2		1		
Lunt, Joseph	1	2	4		
Hodgkins, Moses	1	1	2		
Hodgkins, Shemuell	2	3	4		
Hodgkins, Phillip	3	1	3		
Leland, James	1	1	2		
Young, Stephen	2	1	6		
Massy, Robert	1	1	1		
Cook, Betty		1	5		
Lancaster, Joseph	1	3	5		
Abram, Paddy				1	
TRENTON TOWN (INCLUDING TOWNSHIP NO. 1, EAST SIDE OF UNION RIVER).					
Wiggins, Benjᵃ	1	1	1		
Ford, John	1	1	2		
Hodgkins, Edward	2	2	2		
Googins, Rogers	3		2		
Killpatrick, Robert	1	1	1		
Berry, Edward	1	5	4		
Killpatrick, Marten	3	1	3		
Killpatrick, Samuel	1		1		
Lord, James	1	1	4		
Harding, John	1	3	2		
Coolidge, Silas	1				
Foster, Jacob	1	2	4		
Whitaker, Elisha	1				
Black, Edmund	1		1		
Bark, Joseph	1	1	1		
Haines, Ephraim	2		3		
Haines, Parley	1				
Haines, Peter	1				
Hopkins, William	2	1	6		
Murch, John	1		1		
Farrell, Farrington	1		1		
Murch, John, junr	1		2		
Anderson, Job	2	5	3		
Sinclair, Edward	1	2	1		
Hapworth, Thomas	1	1	1		
Green, John	1	1	3		
Farnsworth, Jonas	1				
Dutton, Jesse	2	1	2		
Jordan, Solomon	3	4	6		
Jordan, Ebenezer	2	4	3		
Morrison, Joseph	1	1	4		
Tinker, John	1		2		
Beal, Joanna	1	1	4		
Card, Joseph	1	2	1		
Lord, Isaac	1	7	2		
Jones, Theodore	2		2	1	
Hopkins, James	1	3	2		
Jealoson, Nathaniel	1	3	3		
Maddox, Henry	1	2	3		
Millikin, Robert	1	4	2		
Fletcher, William	2	2	6		
More, Joseph	1	2	4		
Smith, Nathaniel	1	7	3		
Debeck, Samuel	1				
Jealouson, John	1	3	3		
Jealouson, Wm	1	2	3		

HANCOCK COUNTY—Continued.

NAME OF HEAD OF FAMILY.	Free white males of 16 years and upward, including heads of families.	Free white males under 16 years.	Free white females, including heads of families.	All other free persons.	Slaves.	NAME OF HEAD OF FAMILY.	Free white males of 16 years and upward, including heads of families.	Free white males under 16 years.	Free white females, including heads of families.	All other free persons.	Slaves.	NAME OF HEAD OF FAMILY.	Free white males of 16 years and upward, including heads of families.	Free white males under 16 years.	Free white females, including heads of families.	All other free persons.	Slaves.
TRENTON TOWN (INCLUDING TOWNSHIP NO. 1, EAST SIDE OF UNION RIVER)—con.						**TOWNSHIP NO. 6 (WEST SIDE OF UNION RIVER)—continued.**						**VINALHAVEN TOWN—continued.**					
Haslem, George	2	1	3			Orcutt, John	1	1	6			White, George	1	3	5		
Jordan, Meletiah	1	2	7			Maddox, Samuel	1	1	3			Dyer, Anthony	1	2	7		
Lord, George	1		2			More, Edward	1	3	3			Bramhall, Cornelius	2	2	4		
McFarlin, James	1	1	5			Garland, Josiah	3	3	4			Wooster, David	1	1	3		
McFarlin, Thomas	3	3	3			Maddox, Joshua	4		3			Wooster, Nathaniel	1	2	2		
Smith, James	3	3	5			Maddox, Caleb	2	2	1			Wooster, Joseph	1	1			
Springer, John	1	2	2			Maddox, John	1		2			Perry, John	1	4	4		
Googins, Thomas	2	2	3			Tourtellott, Abraham, jun	1					Ames, Mark	2	3	3		
TOWNSHIP NO. 1 (BUCKS).						Smith, John	2	3	4			Barrick, William		2	3		
						Hammond, Moses	2					Brown, Cyrel	1		2		
Herryman, Daniel	1	1	4			Ross, Daniel	1		1	1		Parry, William		2	5		
Buck, Ebenezer	1	3	3			Gardiner, Joshua	1					Glover, James	1	2	5		
Buck, Jonathan, jun	2	3	5			Trueworthy, James	2	3	4			Cox, Ebenezer	1		4		
Herryman, Benja	1					Davis, James	2	1	2			Smith, Jonathan	1				
Herryman, Ahasael	2		3			Steward, John	1	1	3			Whaling, James	2		3		
Stanley, Nathaniel	1					Joy, William	1	1	5			Cooper, William	1	2			
Buck, Daniel	2	1	4			Trueworthy, Daniel	1		1			Whaling, William	1	2	5		
Adams, Isaac	1					Davis, Samuel		2	3			Beverege, Thomas			4		
Buck, Jonathan	1		1			More, Wyat	1	2	6			Foster, Jonathan	1	3	7		
Putney, Jonathan	1		1			More, Benja	2	2	4			Smith, Levi	3		3		
McDonald, Lauchlan	1	1	1			Wormwood, Benja	1		1			Lindsay, James	1	1	1		
McDonald, Roderick	2	1	2			Wormwood, Joseph	1		4			Roulstone, Benja	1				
Herryman, John	1	1	2			Lord, Jacob	1		2			Babrick, John		1	1		
Emes, Phineas	2	1	6			Wormwood, Eli	2	1	4			Annis, Benjamin	1	2	2		
Lanpher, Stephen	1	1	3			Fly, William	1		3			Calderwood, John	3		5		
Lanpher, Anson	2	4	1			Jordan, Nathaniel	1		2			Calderwood, Samuel	1	1	1		
Lawrence, William	1	1	5			Flood, Dominicus	1	1	2			Carver, Israel	3	2	3		
Murphy, Thomas	1					Means, Robert	1	2	5			Norton, Pheobe			1		
Patterson, John	1		3			Millikin, Elias	1	1	2			Norton, Sarah			1		
Cottrell, Ezra	1	3	5			Hammond, Nathaniel	1	2	2			Vinal, William	1	3	1	1	
Page, Benja	3	2	5			Pray, James	1	2	3			Scevy, James	1	1	2		
Page, Moses	1	2	1			Ray, Mathew	1		1			Calderwood, James	2				
Brown, Theophilus	1	1	4			Patten, James	1	1	7			Calderwood, John, jun	1	2	5		
Cole, Joseph	1	1	2			Patten, Susannah			2			Morey, Ezekiel	1		2		
Atwood, Nathan	1	3	3			Patten, John	1		1			Norton, Uriah	1		3		
Bassett, Ebenezer	1	3	2			Flood, Andrew	2		2			Luce, Bethuel	3	1	2		
Higgins, Jethro	3	1	2			Flood, Bartholomew	1		2			Daggett, Benja, jun	1	2	8		
Colson, Josiah	4	3	3			Green, Isaac	1	5	1			Daggett, Benja	1		1		
Lowell, Abner	1	2	6			Morgan, Benja	2	1	2			Young, Samuel	1	1			
Dones, Bangs	1	1	1			Hopkins, Allen	2	1	2			Phillbrook, Jeremiah	1	3	5		
Homer, William	1					Young, Samuel	3	3	4			Leadbetter, Increase	1		1		
Clements, James	2	1	4			Coggins, Josiah	1					Leadbetter, John	1		1		
Fowler, Levi	1	2	5			Sinclair, Edward	2		2			Leadbetter, Luther	1				
Kenny, Stephen	1	4	4			Coggins, Hezekiah	2	2	3			Crockett, Isaac	2	5	2		
Snow, Reuben	1	1	1									Burges, John	1	1	2		
Carr, Silvanus	1		1			**VINALHAVEN TOWN.**						Brown, Thomas	1	6	5		
Snow, Benja	1		5									Ginn, Thomas	1	1	3		
Coullard, Joshua	2	3	5			Newberry, John	1	2	4			Green, Joseph	1	5	5		
Curtis, Abel	2	2	1			Robbins, Benjamin	2	2	6			Stinson, James	1		2		
Harding, Ezekiel	1	3	3			Stewart, Charles	1					Lane, Benja	1		2		
Smith, Zoeth	1		2			Carver, Caleb	1	1	4			Fernalld, Nathaniel	1				
Kent, William	3		2			Cooper, James	1		1			Carver, Thadeus	1	1	7		
Stubbs, Samuel	2	1	2			Cooper, James, jun	1	1	1			Arey, Isaac	1	5	4		
Lowell, Benja	1	1	3			Cooper, Thomas	1		5			Leadbetter, Increase, jun	1	7	4		
Higgins, James	1	1	1			Douglas, Robert, jun	1		2			Jewell, James	1	3	7		
Palne, Joseph	1		4			Douglas, Joseph	1	3	2			Lane, Joseph	1		2		
Sears, Paul	1		1			McMullen, Archibald	1	2	3			Arey, Ebenezer	1		1		
Eldridge, James	3	3	2			Day, John	2		3			Jewell, James, jun	1				
Higgins, Josiah	1		2			Walton, Paul	1					Cain, John		1	3		
Ballard, Baze		2	3			Carver, Stephen	1		1			Phillbrook, Job	1	2	4		
Lewis, John	1		1			Kent, Susanah			1			Smith, John	1	4	4		
Lewis, Lathley	1	3	4			Winslow, Penelope		1	3			Phillbrook, Joel	1	3	4		
Colson, Ebenezer	1	3	3			Dyer, William	2	3	3			Coombs, Anthony	1	5	4		
Lowell, Nathaniel	1	3	1			Ames, Justus	2	3	4			Lane, Isachar	1		3		
Miller, Robert	1	2	1			Norton, Samuel	1		2			Hall, Ebenezer	2	4	6		
Carr, John B	1	1	2			Dyer, Benjamin	1		4			Young, Abraham	1	4	5		
Appleby, John	1					Ames, Margaret			1			Young, Joseph	1				
Miller, John	1	3	3			Kent, Benjamin	2	2	2			Cree, John		1	1		
Buck, Benjamin	1	1	2			Armstrong, Richard	1		1			McDaniel, James	1	3	1		
Stubbs, James	5			1		Thomas, Samuel	5	1	3			Tolman, Isaiah	1	2	3		
Black, Samuel				1		Winslow, Joseph	1					Nickolls, Alexander	1		4		
Sturgis, Edward				1		Waterman, Joseph	1	1	5			Andrews, Amos	1		4		
TOWNSHIP NO. 6 (WEST SIDE OF UNION RIVER).						Whitman, Abel	2		3			Young, Benja	1	4	5		
						Crabtree, Eleazer	2	4	3			Allen, Jonathan	1	2	4		
Joy, Benjamin	5	2	4			Bowen, Michael	1		2								
Murch, Joseph	1		2			Carr, Benja	2	3	3								
						Dunham, James	1	2	3								
						Heard, James	1	4	4								
						Sever, William	1										

LINCOLN COUNTY.

NAME OF HEAD OF FAMILY.	Free white males of 16 years and upward, including heads of families.	Free white males under 16 years.	Free white females, including heads of families.	All other free persons.	Slaves.	NAME OF HEAD OF FAMILY.	Free white males of 16 years and upward, including heads of families.	Free white males under 16 years.	Free white females, including heads of families.	All other free persons.	Slaves.	NAME OF HEAD OF FAMILY.	Free white males of 16 years and upward, including heads of families.	Free white males under 16 years.	Free white females, including heads of families.	All other free persons.	Slaves.
BALLTOWN TOWN.						**BALLTOWN TOWN—con.**						**BALLTOWN TOWN—con.**					
Bond, David	1	3	3			Trask, Thomas, Juner	1	2	3			Henry, Robert	2	4	3		
Whiten, Joseph	1	1	2			Hopkins, William	3		3			Cunningham, James	2	2	3		
Clark, James	1	1	3			Hopkins, William, Juner	1	3	3			Cambol, James	1	1	3		
Rice, John	1		1			Hopkins, Solomen	1	4	1			Jones, John	1	2	3		
Rice, John, Junier	1	1	1			McCollistor, Archable	3		1			fish, Jonathan	1	1	2		
Trask, Thomas	2	2	3			McCollistor, Richard	1	1	3			Jackson, Joseph	2		3		

HEADS OF FAMILIES—MAINE.

LINCOLN COUNTY—Continued.

NAME OF HEAD OF FAMILY.	Free white males of 16 years and upward, including heads of families.	Free white males under 16 years.	Free white females, including heads of families.	All other free persons.	Slaves.	NAME OF HEAD OF FAMILY.	Free white males of 16 years and upward, including heads of families.	Free white males under 16 years.	Free white females, including heads of families.	All other free persons.	Slaves.	NAME OF HEAD OF FAMILY.	Free white males of 16 years and upward, including heads of families.	Free white males under 16 years.	Free white females, including heads of families.	All other free persons.	Slaves.
BALLTOWN TOWN—con.						**BALLTOWN TOWN—con.**						**BATH TOWN—con.**					
Jackson, Samuel	2	3	3			Plumer, Joseph	2	3	3			Ewers, John	1	1	2		
Dow, Peter, Juner	1	1	2			Speed, Joseph	2	1	5			Thorn, Susanna		4	1		
fanders, Enoch	4	4	3			Gliden, Charles	1	4	3			McFarlen, John	3	2	4		
Kanadey, Thomas	3	3	3			Hutchens, Elisha	1	2	2			McHonnen, James	1		2		
Rollins, John	1	1	6			Richardson, Abather	1		3			Bracket, James	2				
Avrill, Samuel	1		7			Chenneston, Benjamen	1	1	1			Bean, Saml	1		1		
Perham, Rias	1	2	1			Hall, John	1	4	2			Colson, David	1	3	3		
Crumell, Thomas	1	1	3			Hall, Isac	1	2	2			Welsh, Saml	1	5	3		
farnan, Daniel	1	2	1			Hall, James	1	4	2			Lincoln, Zadoc	1	2	6		
Noys, Jonathan	2	6	4			Thomas, Henry	1	1	7			Marshal, Willm	1	1	3		
withouse, Samuel	2		2			Horks, Joseph	1	1	1			Robertson, John	1	2	6		
Whithous, Samuel, Ju	1	5	2			Johnson, John	2	2	2			Robertson, Alexander	1	3	5		
Whithouse, Jacob	1	1	3			Weaks, John, Juner	1	1	3			Pettingale, Edward	2		2		
Hatch, Zach	1	1	5			Weaks, Joseph	1	2	6			Trufaut, David	5	3	6		
Jones, Joseph	3	3	6			Weaks, Thomas	1	2	2			Whitmore, John	1	3	3		
Linsuit, John	2	2	6			Weaks, Mark	1	2	2			Cook, Isaiah	1	2	2		
Linsuit, Joshua	3		3			Weaks, John	3	2	2			Worster, Francis	1	2	3		
Clark, William	4	3	2			Rollins, Nathaniel	1	2	1			Davis, Jona	4		3		
Clark, Elisha	1		2			Rollins, Eliphlot	1	1	1			Page, Edward H	2	3	4		
Gliden, Adndrew	1	3	4			Parker, Joseph	2		2			Swanton, Willm	3	5	3		
Palmer, Simon	1	3	1			Ames, Jonathan	1					Summer, David	1	1	4		
Kain, John	1	1	3			Eams, Phinas	1	5	1			Swanton, Willm	1	1	5		
Heath, Abraham	1	1	2			Shepard, James	3	2	3			Ross, Willm	1	3	3		
Cunengham, Isacc	1		1			Day, Thomas	2	6	4			Cook, Elisabeth	6	1	4		
Starns, Ebennesor	2		2			Separd, Samuel, Juner	1		3			Fitts, Ephraim	1	3	6		
Dow, Peter	1	2	2			Shepard, William	1	1	2			Bradford, Isaac	2	1	2		
murphy, James	1	7	3			Brand, Isac	2					Sampson, Caleb	1	1	3		
Carr, Josiah	1	2	2			Johnson, Samuel	2	2	2			Pettingale, Summon	1	6	2		
ford, Abner	1		3			Plumer, Timothy	1	3	3			White, Joseph	2	1	3		
ford, Abner, Juner	1	3	1			Stickney, Benjamen	1	3	5			Cooker, Isaiah	4	4	3		
Ripley, Joslah	1	1	2			mcClary, Robert	1	2	3			Webb, Willm	1		5		
Trask, Jonathan	1	2	2			Decker, John	2		5			Wood, John	1	1			
Casten, Thomas	1		1			Waters, Samuel	2	4	5			Turner, Consider	1		5		
Cuningham, Samuel	1		3			mcCurdey, Samuel	1	1	2			McDaniels, Betsy			2		
Cuningham, David	1	1	1			Plumer, Benjemen	1		1			Emerson, Saml	2		4		
Howard, Andrew	3		2			Reaves, James	2	3	4			Berry, James	1	5	2		
Wire, John	1		1			Rowall, Jacob	3	3	4			Osgood, Jona	2		4		
Hilton, Isaac	1		3			Choat, Abraham	4	1	4			Berry, Saml	3	4	4		
Hilton, John	3		3			Trask, Joseph, Juner	1		3			Ring, David	1	3	4		
Boynton, John	1	1	1			ferrin, Timothy	1		1			Mitchel, Jona	5	2	6		
Boynton, John, Juner	2	2	3			Rogers, Joseph	1	3	4			Brown, James	1				
Cuningham, William	1		3			Rogers, Prince	1	3	2			Brady, John	1	1	4		
Cuningham, John	1	1	2									Mitchel, James M	1	4	2		
Glidon, Charles	1	4	3			**BATH TOWN.**						Lumber, Thos	1	1	3		
Weaks, Winteig	1											Clifford, David	1	2	3		
Balley, Joseph	1		2			Cooms, George	2	5	4			Williams, John	1	3	4		
Balley, Nathan	1		2			Eaton, Abel	2		2			Bridges, Isaac	1	5	2		
Potte, John	1	6	4			Williams, John	1	4	3			Clemmons, Ruth	1		2		
Woodman, John	3	2	2			Williams, George	2		5			Lumber, Samuel	2	1	4		
Little, Joshua	5		2			Higgins, Reuben	1	4	3			Lowel, Martha	1	1	4		
Toby, William	1	2	4			Holbrook, Abizah	3	2	3			Clefford, Benja	4	1	5		
Heath, Asa	1	4	5			Higgins, Philip	2	4	4			Williams, Thos	1		4		
Pesley, Olover	1	1	5			Pain, Joshua	3	3	3			Campbel, John	1				
Pesley, Ezekiel	1	3	3			Bailey, Christopher	1	6	2			Standish, Lemuel	1	1	4		
Peasley, Nathan	1	2	5			Cooms, Stephen	4	2	5			Hodgkins, Willm	2	2	4		
Gilman, Samuel	1		3			Higgins, Benja	3	4	6			Weeks, Silvanus	1	2	2		
Bartlet, Caleb	1	3	3			Higgins, Simeon	1	2	3			Low, Jacob	2	2	2		
Heath, Isaac	1					Mariner, Jona N	2		5			Soward, Theodore	1	4	5		
King, Benjamen	3	4	2			Brown, Benja	1		3			Lowel, John	1	1	1		
Ware, Nathan	1	1	4			Smith, Joseph	2	1	3			Lemont, Adam	1		2		
Noris, Benjamen	3	2	3			Andrews, John	2	1	2			Foot, Thos	1		2		
Choat, Aaron, Juner	1	1	2			Ham, Benja	3	2	3			Foot, John	1	3	2		
Carlow, Martin	1	2	3			Ham, John	2	3	5			Russey, David	3		4		
Cresey, Abel	1		2			Grace, Patrick	1		1			Runnel, Nathl	1	6	1		
Turner, Thomas	3		2			Purington, Joshua	2		3			Lemont, James	3	3	5		
Turner, Nichlass	1	2	2			Lemont, Thomas	1	1	5			Stanford, John	1	3	2		
Tarry, David	3		5			Howland, Arthur	1		3			Morse, Stephen	1	3	6		
durley, John	3		2			Foot, Thos, Jnr	1	2	2			White, Joseph	2	1	2		
Plumer, Daniel	1					Labree, James	1		1			Lemont, Samuel	1	3	1		
Wire, Obed	1	2	1			Williams, John	1	2	1			Purnton, Humphry	1	2	3		
Kinkade, Samuel, Jua	1	2	3			Whitney, Saml	3	2	2			Sargeant, Jona	1	1	2		
Winslow, Benjamin	1		6			Whitney, Ebena	1	3	1			Gould, Joseph	4	1	6		
Prible, Jedediah	1	3	3			Welch, Edward	4	1	2	7		Cooms, Joshua	1	2	4		
Cartton, Samuel	1	3	5			Crafford, Mary			3			Durnton, John	1	1	3		
Trask, Joseph	2	2	4			Grace, Jane	1		2			Brown, Willm	1	3	3		
Choat, Abraham	1	1	2			Crafford, Thos	1	4	1			Sargeant, Joseph	1		3		
Grover, Ebenezor	1		5			Crafford, John	1	4	1			Sargeant, Jona	1	1	2		
Milikin, John	1	3	2			Gran, Willm	1	1	2			Higgam, Philip	1	5	2		
Peasley, Jonathan	1	1	1			Clark, John	1	4	8			Higgam, Simeon	3	2	6		
Poor, Richard	3		4			Ranes, Joshua	2	1	2			Morrison, Nathl L	2	1	1		
Heath, Jonathan	1	1	4			Loring, Jeromy	3	3	3			Lemont, John	1	3	2		
Longfelow, John	3		2			Hodgkins, Francis	2	1	2			Woodward, Willm	1	3	4		
Kinkad, Samuel, Juner	1		3			Cushing, Christopher	1		3			Pray, Ebenezer	2	1	2		
Choat, frances	1		1			Marsh, Caleb	1	1	3			Shaw, David	1				
Philbrooks, Ebenezor	1	1	5			Foster, Mary	1	2	3			Shaw, Joshua	1	3	3		
Bartlet, Jonathan	1		2			Philbrick, Joshua	3	2	4			Berry, John	2	1	5		
Bartlet, James	1	3	3			Sewall, Dummer	3	1	3			Brown, Benja	2	3	6		
Peasley, Daniel	1	5	3			Sewall, Stephen	1	1	3								
Erykins, George	1		2			Kimball, Richard	2	1	6			**BOOTHBAY TOWN.**					
Tarr, Abraham	1	2	2			Sewall, Henry	2	2	5								
fowls, William	1		1			Lambert, Joseph	3	2	9			Brown, John	2		3		
fowls, Samuel	1	1	2			Lambert, Luke	2	1	4			Burnham, Solomon	1	3	2		
Philbrooks, Ebenezer	1		1			Moody, Saml	3	4	6			Brown, Margaret	1		3		
Philbrooks, John	2	3	7			Turner, Simeon	3	3	7			Burnham, Ephraim	1	1	1		
Potter, Solomon	1		4			Tod, Saml	1		5								
Vining, Jonah	2	4	4			Capon, Theos	1	1	3								

LINCOLN COUNTY—Continued.

NAME OF HEAD OF FAMILY.	Free white males of 16 years and upward, including heads of families.	Free white males under 16 years.	Free white females, including heads of families.	All other free persons.	Slaves.	NAME OF HEAD OF FAMILY.	Free white males of 16 years and upward, including heads of families.	Free white males under 16 years.	Free white females, including heads of families.	All other free persons.	Slaves.	NAME OF HEAD OF FAMILY.	Free white males of 16 years and upward, including heads of families.	Free white males under 16 years.	Free white females, including heads of families.	All other free persons.	Slaves.
BOOTHBAY TOWN—con.						**BOOTHBAY TOWN—con.**						**BOWDOIN TOWN—con.**					
Burnham, Solomon	1					Tibbits, Ichabod	1	5	3			Chace, Isaac	1	2	3		
Carlisle, Joseph	1	2	1			Preble, Ebenezer	1	1	2			Rideout, Benjamin	1	2	3		
Trask, Obadiah	1	1	2			Abbot, Henry	1	3	2			Wheeler, Hannah		1	4		
McPharlen, Benjᵃ	1	2	3			Abbot, John	1		1	6		Wheeler, Joseph	1	1	5		
Bryer, Elihu	1	2	5			Horn, Cornelius	1	4	6			Starbord, Samuel	1	1	4		
Perkins, Joseph	3	3	5			Poor, John	1	4	6			Grover, Andrew	1	3	2		
Burnham, Solomon	4		6			Langdon, Joseph	1	3	2			Grover, James	1				
Bowland, John	3	3	4			Decker, Abraham	1	3	2			Richardson, John	3	2	3		
McCobb, Samˡ, Jur	1	2	2			Ball, Samˡ	1	3	3			Wheeler, Joseph	1		3		
Kennady, James	3	2	6			Ball, Levi	1		2			Booby, Joseph	2		1		
Kelley, Benjᵃ	3		1			Reid, Robert	1	1	3			Booby, William	1		3		
Kennady, Willᵐ	2		3			Rand, John	2	2	5			Barrat, Benjamin	1	2	3		
Brier, Samˡ	5	3	4			Knight, Daniel	5	2	6			Sparks, Nicholas	2		2		
Boyd, Thomas	2	2	2			Knight, Pettishal	1	2	4			Booker, David	1	2	3		
Boyd, Thomas, Junʳ	2	3	6			Cross, Joshua	1	1	2			Luis, George	1				
Boyd, George	3	1	6			Cunningham, Ruggles	1	1	2			Whiting, William	1	1	3		
Booker, Joseph	1	2	3			Tibbits, James	1		1			Wheeler, John	1	1	2		
Adams, Samˡ, Junʳ	1	1	3			Kenny, Benjᵃ	1	1	1			Temple, Levi	1	3	3		
Booker, John, Junʳ	1	1	2			Lamson, Samˡ	2	1	2			Tibbits, Benjamin	1		1		
All, James	1	4	7			Lewis, Joseph	1	2	1			Flag, John	1	1	2		
Wall, Andʷ	1	2	6			Lewis, John	1	1	1			Marston, Nathaniel	1		1		
Beath, Jerᵉ	2		2			Dawes, Jonᵃ	1	1	8			Allen, Daniel	1	2	2		
Holton, John	1	2	4			Matthews, John	1	3	3			Jeleson, Nathaniel	1	1	2		
Dawes, John	1	1	2			Southard, John	1		5			Allexander, Robart	1		1		
McCobb, Willᵐ	2	2	4			Lamson, James	1	2	4			Combs, Leonard	1				
Reid, Joseph	2	5	4			Lewis, Stephen	2	3	3			Alexander, William	1		1		
Booker, John	1		1			Lewis, Willᵐ	1	5	2			Allexander, John	1	1	2		
Montgomery, Lydia		2	5			Carlton, Stephen	1	2	2			Richardson, John	2	2	2		
Montgomery, Samˡ	3		4			Sawyer, Ebenezer	1	2	3			Richardson, Joseph	1				
Race, George	1	1	1			Stover, John	1	1	2			Galloway, Job	2		1		
Farnham, Joseph	4	1	3			Webb, James	1	2	2			Baker, Judah	1	1	2		
Farnham, Ansel	1		1			Skidmore, Elias	1		2			Baker, Smith	1	2	4		
Farnham, Chapen	1	1	2			Reid, John	1	2	2			Baker, Barnard	1	5	1		
Farnham, Jonᵃ	1	1	3			Kenny Samˡ	1	2	4			Jones, Isaac	1				
Linnecon, Benjᵃ	3		3			Barter, Samˡ	1		1			Booby, Christlpher	1				
Alley, Samˡ	1	4	6			Barter, Joseph	2		3			Alexander, James	1	1	2		
Ratclif, John	1		2			Day, James	1		1			Shephard, John	1				
Wallace, David	1	2	2			Barter, John	1	3	4			Sheen, Jonathan	1				
Cooper, Philip	1		2			Pinkham, Calvin	1	2	3			Temple, John	1	1	3		
Reid, Paul	2	1	6			Kent, Benjᵃ	1	2	6			Smith, Joseph	1				
Lishman, John	3		4			Alby, Obadah	1	1	2			Booker, Zacheus	1	1			
Creamer, Edward	2	1	4			Tibits, Giles	1	1	2			Pain, Timothy	1				
McCobb, Samˡ	1		3			Lewis, Joseph, Junʳ	1	2	4			Myreen, John	1				
McCobb, David	1		3			Emerson, John	1	1	4			Hodgman, John	1	1	1		
Seargeant, Benjᵃ	3	2	2			Pinkham, Ichabod	6	1	7	1		Bramijon, Thomas	1	1	2		
McPharlen, Elizabeth	2	1	6			Cromett, John	1		2	2		Morey, Phillip	1	1	2		
McPharlen, Andʷ	1					Cromett, Jerebˡ	1		6			Jlluce, Joseph	2	1	2		
Fullerton, Ebenezer	1	1	4			Rollins, Stephen	1	2	2			Duncan, Robart	1		4		
Beath, John	1		1			Pinkham, Nathˡ	2	3	2			Hogings, William	1	1	4		
Beath, Joseph	1		4			Perkins, Samˡ	1	4	4	1		Rideout, Stephen	1	2	4		
McCobb, John	1	6	3			Alley, John	1	1	2			Hall, Lemuel	1	2	5		
Willee, Robert	1		2			Alley, John, Jnʳ	2		5			Varnum, John	1	1	4		
Willee, Martha			2			Sherman, Eleazer	2	6	3			Varnum, John, Jur	1				
Kenny, Abijah	1		2			Willey, Alexander	1	3	3			Varnum, Wanton Jnʳ	1				
Reid, David	5	1	4			Giles, Joseph, Junʳ	1		2			Truant, Job	2	3	7		
Reid, David, Junʳ	1	2	3			Kenny, Thoˢ	1	2	1			Potter, James	2	2	2		
Reid, David, 3ʳᵈ	1		5			Kenny, Henry	1		2			Wire, John	1	4	2		
Poor, Willᵐ	1	2	4			Train, Jonᵃ	1	3	3			Bishop, William	1		3		
Sawyer, Benjᵃ	2					Giddings, Joseph	1		3			Poores, Richard	2	5	4		
Sawyer, Jonᵃ	2		5			Giles, Joseph	2	1	4			Potter, Alexander	1				
Sawyer, Aaron	2	4	2			Pinkham, Solomon	2	1	5			Potter, David	1	3	2		
Sawyer, Jacob	1	1	2			Tibbits, Nathˡ	1	1	2			Kinnicum, Daniel	1	2	4		
Reid, Andʷ	1		2			Stover, Joseph	1		6			Kinnicum, Edward	1				
Reid, Andʷ, Junʳ	1	2	3			Webber, Gersham	1	2	4			Potter, James	4		4		
Greenough, Jonᵃ	1		5			Alley, Joshua	1	2	4			Rose, Prince	1	1	4		
Reid, Andʷ, 3ʳᵈ	1		6									Hinkly, Aaron	1	1	3		
Reid, Willᵐ	1		2			**BOWDOIN TOWN.**						Rose, George Potter	1				
Murray, John	1		2									Whitney, Isaac	1	1	5		
Hern, Patrick	1		3			Hewey, John	2	2	3			Mallet, John	1	2	7		
Hern, Daniel	4	4	3			Hewey, John, Jur	1					Alexander, James	2				
Adams, Samˡ	3	3	3			Hewey, James	1					Thompson, Amos	2	2	7		
Reid, Mary	3		2			Waymouth, Jonathan	1	4	5			Brown, Jonathan	1	1	3		
Reid, James	1	2	1			Whitney, Jonathan	1					Alexander, John	1	3	3		
Willee, Robert	1	2	5			Spokin, Joseph	1		2			Alexander, William	1				
Willee, John	1	1	1			Wood, Joseph	1	1	2			Wilson, David	1	4	4		
Decker, David	1	1	1			Waymouth, Edmond	3	1	5			Barnes, Benjamin	2	4	4		
Decker, Thomas	1	3	2			Ross, Robert	1	2	3			Gowel, William	2	3	4		
Brewer, John	2	3	5			Merril, Samuel	1	3	3			Hall, Luther	1	3	3		
McCown, Margara	1	1	3			Sanborn, Jethrow	1	2	4			Polley, Samuel	3	1	4		
Thomson, Samˡ	2	2	4			Macmanners, John	1	2	2			Jaquish, Richard	2				
Thomson, Joseph	3		1			Heath, William	1	1	1			Williams, William	1	3	3		
Harris, Samˡ	1	5	3			Gray, Alexander	1	4	4			Combs, John	2	4	3		
Emery, David	1	2	2			Hewey, Robert	1	5	2			Thompson, John	1				
Horn, Thoˢ	1		2			Freeman, Samson				5		Potter, Alexander	1	1	4		
Horn (Widow)			4			Gilpatrick, Nathaniel	1	3	1			Campbel, William	2	1	6		
Pierce, Silvester	2	2	4			Higings, Timothy	3	5	4			Truant, Stephen	1				
Pierce, Joseph	1	2	4			Handerson, Benjamin	1	2	2			Campbel, John	1	1	2		
Hamilton, John	2	3	4			Wilson, Samuel	1					Buker, Job	1				
Decker, Willᵐ	1					Wheeler, Joseph			1			Stinson, Robert	1				
Bird, Edward	2		2			Smith, Nathaniel	1		1			Robertson, William	1	1	5		
Nelson, David	1		1			Smith, John	1					Perry, David	1		3		
Clambo, Willᵐ	1	1	1			Temple, Ichabod	1	1	3			Townes, Noah	1	1	2		
Pierce, Ezekiel	1	2	3			Temple, Ebenezer	1	4	3			Townes, Isreal	1				
Barter, Samˡ, Jur	1	1	3			Emery, Joseph	1		2			Jaquish, Benjamin	1	1	4		
Pierce, Samˡ	2	3	8									Purrinton, Humphry	1	4	2		

HEADS OF FAMILIES—MAINE.

LINCOLN COUNTY—Continued.

NAME OF HEAD OF FAMILY.	Free white males of 16 years and upward, including heads of families.	Free white males under 16 years.	Free white females, including heads of families.	All other free persons.	Slaves.
BOWDOIN TOWN—con.					
Adams, John	2	3	5		
Purrinton, Nathl	2		4		
Tarr, Joseph	1	1	5		
Raymon, Samuel	1	2	3		
Small, Ephrom	1	3	3		
Dinslow, Joseph	1	2	3		
Hopkins, Elisha	1	1			
Randal, Joseph	1	1	2	1	
Thompson, Joseph	2	4	4		
Toothacher, Mary		1	3		
Ridly, James	1	2	4		
Buker, Joseph	1	1	5		
Adams, Samuel	1	1	3		
Buker, Dimmick	1	1	4		
Ridly, Daniel	1	2	3		
Boah, Alexander	1		3		
Ridly, George	1	2	2		
Williams, Jonathan	1	3	2		
Huff, Moses	1	1	1		
Williams, George	1	2	2		
Sparkes, James	1	1	3		
Cornish, Sipperon	1	1	1		
Smalley, David	2	3	3		
Rogers, James	2	3	2		
Small, Joseph	2	2	4		
Small, Taylor	2	2	6		
Townes, Joseph	1	1	3		
White, Hugh	1	1	4		
Stinson, William	1	1	3		
Jack, Andrew	3	2	4		
Jack, Joseph	1				
Brieryhurst, Thomas	1	2	6		
Forbus, John	1				
Rideout, John	1	1	2		
Varnum, John	1				
Jaquish, Isaac	1		1		
Raymond, Samuel	1	2	3		
White, James	1				
Woodard, David	1				
Campbel, David	1	1	2		
Hibbard, Jonathan	1	3	3		
Weekes, James	1		3		
Nutting, Abel	1	1	4		
Davis, Jesse	1	1	4		
Davis, Thomas	1				
Cushing, John	1	2	5		
Gould, Jacob	1				
Seals, William	1				
Higings, Seth	1	1	3		
Simons, Samuel	1	2	3		
Jones, Phinehas	1	1	2		
Jordon, Ephrom	1				
Jordon, Abner	1	1	1		
Sinkler, Adoniram	3	5	1		
Tibbits, Timothy	2		2		
Freeman, Cesor				8	
Hinkly, Isaac	1	3	3		
Hinkly, Reliance			1		
Whitrage, Jacob	1				
Whittimore, Stephen	1		1		
Smullin, John	1				
Combs, Hezekiah	1	2	2		
Donnehue, Joseph	1		3		
Mitcalf, Hugh	1	3	3		
Tibbits, Samuel	1	3	3		
Tibbits, Isaac	1		1		
Hinkly, Samuel	1				
Hinkly, Samuel	1		2		
Ham, Thomas	1	2		1	
White, Hugh	1				
Cowing, Calvin	1	3	3		
Mulloy, Hugh	1	3	3		
Spoldin, Nathl	1				
Berry, Josiah	1	2	4		
White, John	2	1	2		
Tibbits, Thomas	1	5	3		
Staples, Stephen	1		5		
Woodard, John	1	5	5		
White, James	1				
Tibbits, Esther			1		
BOWDOINHAM TOWN.					
Preble, Zebulon	1	4	3		
Blanchard, Theos	2	2	3		
Smith, Herman	1	4	5		
Blanchard, Solomon	1				
Gobart, Nicholas	1	1	8		
Pottle, David	2	1	5		
Perry, James	1	1	3		
Southard, John	2	2	2		
Parks, John	1	5	6		
Chesham, John	1	4	2		
Porter, Frederick	1	3	3		
Weston, Caleb	2	5	3		
Burk, Willm	1	3	3		
BOWDOINHAM TOWN—continued.					
Purnton, Hezekiah	1	1	4		
Hatch, Jethro	1	4	4		
Gitchel, Elihu	1	1	1		1
Purnton, James	1	3	3		
Whitmore, Stephen	4	1	4		
Whitmore, Francis	1	1	1		
Hatch, Ephraim	2		3		
Maxwell, George	2	2	6		
Harwood, Thomas	2	4	6		
McLallen, Nathl	2	2	8		
Gardiner, Charles	2				
Coffin (Widow)		3	5		
Thomas, George	2	1	5		
Takins, Thomas	1	1	2		
Hatch, Clark	1	3	3		
Dinsmore, Thos	1	3	3		
Dinsmore, Thos, Junr	1	1	2		
Preble, Zebulon	1	1	2		
Preble, David			2		
Beel, Zachariah	2				
Beel, Josiah	1		1		
Beel, Joshua	2	1	4		
Hatch, Jethro	3		5		
Adams, John	1	3	4		
Adams, Jer	1	1	1		
Booker, James	2	1	4		
Sedgley, Joseph	2	3	3		
Maxwell, James	2		5		
Gardiner, Benja	2		3		
Preble, Saml	1	2	3		
Preble, Abraham	2	1	3		
Wiggins, Phinehas	1	1	2		
Jellitson, Job	1	3	2		
Sedgley, Robert	2	1	3		
Meloon, Abraham	1	2	1		
Raman, Elaphan	3	2	5		
Preble, Jona	3		3		
Prat, Elisha	1	2	2		
Whitmore, Abraham	2	1	3		
Springer, Thos	2		2		
Prat, John	1	1	2		
Springer, John	1	2	1		
Dunham, Willm	2		2		
Macumber, Ebenezer	1		2		
Jack, Robert	1	4	2		
Macumber, Seth	2	2	2		
Headon, John	1		2		
Mallee, James	2	5	1		
Ross, Joseph	3	2	2		
Macumber, Job	1	3	6		
Adams, Nathan	1	2	2		
Preble, Abraham, Junr	2	2	5		
Cobb, Ablah	1	2	2		
Cooms, Saml C	1	1	1		
Stuart, Isaac	2	2	2		
Ross, Paul	2	1	1		
Staboard, John	1	3	3		
Booker, Willm	1	1	3		
Dinslow, —	1	1	1		
Dinslow, Willm	1		1		
BRISTOL TOWN. (Nobleborough)					
Rollings, John	1	2	4		
moody, Richard	1	1	1		
moody, John	1	1	3		
moody, Cernes	1	4	4		
Grant, Moses			3		
winslow, David	1	1	5		
umbehind, Charles	1		2		
Hussey, Abner	1	3	2		
Smith, Joshua	1	3	2		
Smith, Steven	1	1	3		
Dunbar, Elizer	1	1	3		
Merril, thomas	2	6	3		
hall, James	2	3	5		
hall, Seth	2	3	7		
hussey, Joseph	3		3		
hussey, Joseph, Jun	1	1	3		
hussey, Samuel	1	2	2		
winslow, John	1	3	6		
Zentner, philliss	1	4	3		
wolts, Andrew	1		3		
Sidelinger, George	1	3	3		
kenssil, fredrich	2	2	4		
Sidlinger, peter	1	3	3		
awstin, Ichabod	4	1	2		
clerk, John	2	4	6		
oliver, Jonathan	1	4	3		
Chapman, Jonathan	1	2	5		
knowlton, andrew	1	1	4		
McFadien, Thomas	1	1	5		
turney, Edmond	1				
becker, Silas	1		3		
hatch, fridrik	1	3	4		
hall, levy	1	2	2		
Nobleborough (Bristol Town con.)					
hogekins, David	1	4	5		
winslow, Ezl	1	3	4		
hall, william	1	3	2		
temesson, Joseph	1	1	1		
barslow, John	1		2		
linscutt, John	1				
hopkins, bill	1				
Ross, benjamin	3	3	3		
Juwet, nathan	1	2	4		
Rollings, John	2	2	5		
Plummer, Benj	3	2	8		
Dennis, David	2	1	5		
Gilbert, Daniel	1		2		
tigue, Daniel	3	1	2		
knowlton, Jeremiak	2	3	5		
flint, Thomas	3	2	6		
hisscock, John	2		3		
Rust, Joseph	2	2	6		
flint, Jas	2	5	1		
hogeden, Stephen	4	1	3		
hogeden, benjamin	1	1	1		
kawanagh, James	1	3	2		
chapman, John	1	3	2		
chapman, Isral	1		3		
holland, John	2		1		
Grotten (widow)	3		4		
Palmer, Elnathan	2	3	7		
Rollings, Samuel	3	4	4		
chapman, Nathaniel	1	4	4		
chapman, thomas	1	5	5		
chapman, Joseph	2	3	6		
Gentner, David	1	3	3		
Perkins, James	1	1	3		
chapman, benjamin	1	1	2		
chapman, nathan	1	2	4		
knowlton, nathaniel	1	2	4		
Noble, arthur	5	3	5	1	
linscott, David	1	3	4		
heckelton (widow)	1		1		
clarck, john	1		6		
wethren, arnold	2		2		
Eten, philip	3	2	6		
CANAAN TOWN.					
Wood, Robert	2	1	5		
Steward, William	1	3	3		
Kindal, Biethy	1	3	4		
Castle, Ephrom	1				
Powers, Levi	2	4	4		
Burril, Nathaniel	3	1	3		
Steward, Phinihas	1	1	2		
Steward, Samuel	1	1	5		
Wyman, Seth	1	6	3		
Pratt, Elam	1	2	2		
Hunt, John	1		1		
Stewart, William	2	3	3		
Jewet, Maxie	1	2	3		
Ireland, Abraham	1	3	5		
Brown, Rebekah		2	1		
Okes, Solomon	2		3		
Okes, Levi	2		3		
Fowler, John	1	2	5		
Turner, James	1		2		
Smith, Isaac	1	6	4		
Russ, Luther	1				
Miriek, Andrew	1	2	2		
Okes, John	1	1	3		
Steward, Phinihas	1				
Steward, Abraham	1	2	4		
White, Solomon	1				
Wesson, Samuel	1	3	4		
Howard, Peter, Jn	1	1	2		
Macblin, Brice	1	1	1		
Dartman, Noah	1	1	2		
Clerk, Noah	1		4		
Stewart, Solomon, Jr	2	1	5		
Fletcher, William	1		2		
Webb, James	1	1	1		
Homestead, Daniel	1				
Carson, Adam	1		4		
Russel, Isaac	1	6	3		
Snow, Daniel	1				
Howard, Peter	1		2		
Whitten, Tobias	1	3	2		
Pratt, Michal	2		3		
Savage, Joseph	1	5	2		
Varnum, Samuel	1	1	6		
Castle, William	2	3	2		
Lambart, Daniel	1	6	2		
Kincade, David	1	4	5		
Lewis, George	1		2		
Lambart, Sherebiah	1	5	1		
Lambart, Sherebiah, Jr	1	2	2		
Kindal, Barzeliel	1	3	5		
Maulbone, James	1	5	5		

FIRST CENSUS OF THE UNITED STATES.

LINCOLN COUNTY—Continued.

Name of head of family.	Free white males of 16 years and upward, including heads of families.	Free white males under 16 years.	Free white females, including heads of families.	All other free persons.	Slaves.
CANAAN TOWN—con.					
Ireland, Abraham	1	1	1		
Pishen, Charles	1		1		
Emery, John, Jur	1	1	2		
Robins, Jonathan	1	3	5		
Emery, Levi	1		1		
Lankister, Joseph	1	2	3		
Davis, Jonathan	2		4		
Emery, John	1				
Emery, Samuel	1	2	4		
Ireland, John	1	1	2		
Ireland, John, Ju	1	1	1		
Kindal, David	1				
White, John	1		1		
Wesson, Joseph	1	1	4		
Wesson, Ely	1	2	3		
Piper, Edward	1		2		
Clerk, Solomon	2		4		
Whitiker, Nathaniel	4		3		
Whiteman, Samuel	1	2	3		
Rogers, Darly	1	1	3		
Stewart, Solomon	1		1		
Bigelow, James	1	2	2		
Bigelow, George	1				
Pratt, Micah	1	2	6		
Smith, Daniel	1	5	4		
Webb, Christopher	2	3	4		
Hartwell, Edward	1	7	1		
Wesson, John	1	2	2		
Piper, John	1				
White, John	1		2		
CARRATUNK TOWN.					
Williams, Jacob	1	4	2		
Ball, John	1	1	3		
Foster, Daniel	1		1		
Hale, Ephrom	3				
Wear, Abel	1		2		
Russel, Joseph					
Chace, Rogers	2	2	4		
Chace, Ezekiel	1	2	2		
Gutridg, Joshua	2	3	4		
Wood, Ephrom	1				
Russel, Solomon	1	1	1		
Bosworth, Jonathan	1	3	2		
Chamberlain, Moses	1				
Wilson, John	1	2	2		
Cleavland, Joseph	1	1	1		
Cleavland, Timothy	1				
Trumbul, William	1				
Fletcher, Amos	1	1	1		
Baker, Joseph	2	3	4		
Churchhill, John	1				
Fletcher, William	3	1	4		
Parlin, Silas	1	3	2		
Pattin, Thomas	1	3	2		
Churchhill, Joseph	1	5	2		
Whipple, Elezer	1				
CARRS PLANTATION, OR UNITY.					
Baker, Prince	2	5	5		
Rollings, Benjamin	3	1	4		
Lankister, Ezekiel	1		2		
Meloon, Elizabeth			1		
Rollings, Joseph	1	2	4		
Tibbits, Nathaniel	1	2	5		
Blackston, William	1	3	3		
Welts, Nathaniel	1	1	1		
House, James	1	1	1		
Blackston, William	1		2		
Webber, John	1	1	2		
Russ, Jonathan	1	2	3		
Chambers, Benjamin	1	2	2		
Davis, Simon	1	2	1		
Stover, Timothy	1				
Dutton, Rial	1				
Yongill, Enoch	1	2	4		
Alley, Ephrom	1				
Rollings, Benjamin, Jr	1	1	1		
Boubey, Gideon	3	1	3		
Welts, John	1	2	4		
Fellows, Joseph	1				
Stover, Dependence	2	1	3		
Pilsbury, Edmond	1		2		
Hollis, Stephen	1	2	1		
Whitcum, Stephen	1	1	2		
Porter, Gideon	1				
CHESTER PLANTATION.					
Perry, Samuel	1	1	1		
Judkins, Samuel	4	5	2		
Wyman, Abraham	4	1	2		
Sewall, Dummer	1		2		
Bradbury, William	1		2		
Bradbury, John	1		3		
Devinport, Thomas	1				
Lock, Edward	3	3	4		
Bragdon, Jeremiah	1	1	1		
Wyman, Daniel	1	4	4		
Dunning, William	1		2		
Kinscott, Samuel	1	3	2		
Mitchel, John	1		1		
Sewall, Jonathom	2	1	1		
Devenport, Abraham	1				
CUSHING TOWN.					
Smith, John	1	2	1		
Packard, Micah	1		2		
Packard, Marlborough	2		1		
Vose, Seth	2	5	3		
Vose, Elijah	1		2		
Young, Richard	2		1		
Young, Sarah			3		
Tissaker, John	2		1		
Nutting, Jonathan	2	3	2		
McCarter, John	3	1	5		
Hiler, Simeon	2	1	7		
Hiler, Jacob	3		2		
Hiler, Cornelius	1	2	1		
Thomson, Mary	2	3	2		
Malcom, Andrew	2		3		
Malcom, James	1	1	5		
Robinson, Haunce	5	1	5		
Robinson, Haunce, Junr	1		2		
Annis, Samuel	1	1	1		
Robinson, Joseph	3	2	3		
Brison, John	2		1		
Burton, William	1	2	3		
Hutting, Jonathan	3	1	2		
Benton, Benjamin	1	3	3		
Nehnenhawsen, Henry Frederick	1	3	2		
Lewis, Daniel	2	1	5		
McIntyre, Robert	2	3	5		
Kelleran, Edward	2	4	5		
Parsons, Lawrence	1	2	3		
Parsons, William	2	2	1		
Melony, Walter	3	1	2		
Carnay, Thomas	1		1		
Carney, James	1	3	4		
Wiley, William	4	2	2		
Rivers, Moses	1	2	3		
Robinson, Moses	3		3		
Rivers, Archibald	2	1	4		
Harthorn, Samuel	2	3	4		
Robinson, Archibald	4	1	6		
McLallen, Simon	1	1	1		
Sweetland, Sampson	1	1	5		
Sweetland, James	2	1	3		
Barton, John	1	1	5		
Sweetland, Stephen	2	1	3		
Starling, Josiah	1	2	3		
Higman, Edward	1	1	1		
Graffam, Jacob	1		6		
Graffam, Joseph	1		1		
Adams, Richard	2		2		
Brazier, John	3	2	3		
Brazier, Bathsheba			3		
Carby, James	3	2	2		
Young, George	2	1	2		
Young, William	1		2		
Harthorn, Alexander	2	1	2		
Harthorn, John	1		2		
Henderson, Robert	2	3	2		
Henderson, Dunbar	3		3		
Canary, Dennis	1	1	1		
Young, Henry	1	2	2		
Gay, Elezer	2	2	4		
Robinson, Sarah	5		3		
Kelloch, Moses	3		1		
Kelloch, Matthew	1	2	6		
Kelloch, John	4	2	2		
Nichols, John	1		2		
Hendley, John	2	3	5		
McKellar, John	2	1	2		
Robinson, John	1	1	6		
Robinson, Moses, Junr	1		2		
Robinson, Joseph, Junr	1	2	5		
Robinson, Andrew	1	3	2		
Watt, Samuel	2	5	3		
Gilchrist, Samuel	1	5	1		
Gilchrist, George	1		3		
Rivers, Thomas	3		6		
Fogerty, Dennis	3	2	6		
Long, Alexander	1	2	3		
Long, Michael	1		2		
York, John	1	3	4		
Henderson, Thomas	1	3	2		
Henderson, Jabez	1	2	2		
Harthorn, Alexander, Junr	1	1	5		
Starling, Richard	2		5		
Rawley, Michael	1	1	1		
Murphy, Jeremiah	1	4	2		
Glover, Thomas	1	2	2		
Jameson, Ebenezer	1	2	4		
Howard, Daniel	1	1	4		
Hillwell, Thomas	1	1	4		
Daly, Ellis	3	1	3		
Kiff, Thomas	3	3	4		
Hart, Avery	1	2	4		
Hart, John	1	3	3		
Hart, Jesse	1	1	1		
Maddon, John	1	1	4		
Norwood, Isaac	1	2	3		
Butler, Abraham	1		3		
Ripley, Enoch	1				
Wall, Patrick	2	3	6		
Linniken, Clark	2	1	1		
page, William	1	1	2		
Martin, Richard	1	3	4		
Melzar, John	1		2		
Teel, Adam	2	1	6		
Barter, Pelatiah	2	4	5		
Barter, John	2	5	3		
Allen, Gideon	3		1		
Murray, John	3	1	1		
Covy, David	1	1	2		
Levey, Joseph	1	5	2		
Thorndike, Robert	1	1	1		
Graffam, Pierce	2	2	3		
Rawley, Edward	1	1	1		
Norwood, Solomon	1	3	4		
Simmonds, Aaron	1	2	5		
Simmonds, Nathaniel	1		4		
Wells, John	1	1	2		
Vickery, Stephen	4	1	3		
Davis, John	1	2	5		
Jameson, Martin	1	2	6		
Rogers, Howland	2	2	2		
McCobb, James	1	4	5		
Wiley, Isaac	2	1	5		
Pickard, Nathan	1	2	3		
Thorndike, Joshua	1	1	3		
Ellwell, Andrew	1	4	3		
Roundy, Azor	1	1	2		
Mathews, James	2		3		
Hawes, Robert	1		2		
Rackleff, William	1	1	5		
Gardener, Daniel	1		2		
Wheeler, William	1	3	5		
Linniken, David	2		2		
Willis, Thomas	1	1	3		
Lea, James	1	1	2		
Davis, Mary		1	3		
Linnekon, Daniel	1				
Mathews, Daniel	1	1	3		
Smalley, Joshua	3		5		
Hall, Isaac	2				
Hall, Isaac, Junr	1	3	3		
Hall, Elijah	1		1		
Curtis, John	1		1		
Hall, Caleb	2	5	1		
Hall, Peter	1		1		
Hall, Ephraim	1	1	1		
Hall, Ephraim, Junr	1		1		
Pearson, William	3	3	3		
Dyer, Anthony	1	3	1		
Amory, George	1	1	2		
Crocker, Paul	1	2	2		
Crocker, Timothy	1		1		
McCarty, Thomas	1				
Coombes, Joshua	1	2	5		
Clark, William	1	1	4		
Foster, Ebenezer	2	3	4		
Marshal, Samuel	1	2	2		
Marshal, Samuel, Junr	1	2	2		
Stone, John	1				
EDGECOMB TOWN.					
Clefford, William	2	6	4		
Trask, David	3	5	3		
Davis, Moses	2	2	3		
Patterson, Willm	2	2	5		
Cunningham, John	1	2	3		
Burk, David	1		1		
Patterson, James	1	2	2		
Dodge, Moses	1		2		
Trask, Moses	1				
Trask, Joseph	1	4	5		
Trask, Saml	1		2		
Gove, Enoch	1	1	2		
Hough, Joseph	1	1	2		

HEADS OF FAMILIES—MAINE.

LINCOLN COUNTY—Continued.

NAME OF HEAD OF FAMILY.	Free white males of 16 years and upward, including heads of families.	Free white males under 16 years.	Free white females, including heads of families.	All other free persons.	Slaves.	NAME OF HEAD OF FAMILY.	Free white males of 16 years and upward, including heads of families.	Free white males under 16 years.	Free white females, including heads of families.	All other free persons.	Slaves.	NAME OF HEAD OF FAMILY.	Free white males of 16 years and upward, including heads of families.	Free white males under 16 years.	Free white females, including heads of families.	All other free persons.	Slaves.
EDGECOMB TOWN—con.						**EDGECOMB TOWN—con.**						**FAIRFIELD TOWN—con.**					
Young, Theodore	1		3			Bowland, John	1	3	2			Bowman, Joseph	1	2	1		
Rigs, Goen	1	3	4			Gardiner, John	1		3			Bowman, Zacheus	1	1	1		
Trask, Willm	1	1	2			Whitten, Joseph	1	2	3			Bowman, Benjamin	1				
Hough, Daniel	1		5			Newell, Zebulen	1	2	3			Bowman, Allihu	1	3	2		
Gove, Asa	2	1	6			Neal, David	1	2	4			Davis, John	1				
Riant, John	1	4	2			Wallace, John	1	1	4			Davis, Eber	1				
Chase, John	1	3	4			Hodgdon, Benj^a	1	6	2			Atwood, Nathl	1				
Baker, Amos	1	1	1			Hodgdon, Thomas, Junr	2	2	1			Fuller, Alden	1	1	3		
Moore, Nathl	1	1	4			Hodgdon, Thomas	2		4			Burquis, Josiah	2	2	5		
Moore, Ebenezer	1	1	2			Damerin, Zabiah	1	3	3			Lawrence, James	1	3	2		
Allen, Rachael			1			Webber, Saml	2	4				Toby, Samuel	2	6	3		
Seers, Barnabas	1	1	2			Harrington, Benj^a	1	5	1			Toby, Samuel	1	2	3		
Gove, David, Junr	1	1	1			McCartha, Florence	1	1	1			Blossom, Benjamin	1	1	3		
Chase, James	2	1	2			Hibbard, Daniel	1	1	5			Lovewell, Zelottus	1	2	6		
Horn, Jacob	1	1	2			Duntan, Saml	4	3	7			Jones, John	1	3	3		
Trask, David	1	1	3			Duntan, Daniel	1	1	3			Jones, Ephrom	7	2	5		
Cunningham, Willm	2	7	4			Duntan, Joseph	2	1	7			fuller, Seth	1	2	5		
Hutchins, Jon^a	2	1	2			Duntan, John	2	4	5			Landers, Thomas	3	1	5		
Hutchins, Benj^a	1	2	4			Duntan, Tim^o	1	3	4			Nigh, Samuel	1				
Merril, Stephen	2	2	5			Chadwick, Levi	2		2			Lawrrance, John	1				
Hough, Moses	1	2	1			Knight, Nathl	2	6	1			Holloway, Prince	1				
Cunningham, John, Junr	1	3	2			Thomas, James	1		2			Nigh, Elisha	1	2	5		
Sullivan, John	1	1	1			Thomas, James, Junr	1	1	3			Tosier, John	1		2		
Moore, James	1	3	3			Tarbox, Conellus	2		2			Tosier, Benjamin	1				
Moore, Isaac	1	1	3			Hall, Saml	1	2	4			Pong, Harnis	1	1	6		
Cunningham, John	2		2									Tosier, Jeremiah	2	1	3		
Gove, Nathan	1	2	3			**FAIRFIELD TOWN.**						Pushan, Peter	2	1	1		
Gove, Solomon	3	3	5									Tosier, Amos	1				
Trask, Solomon	2	2	3			Pushan, Peter, Ju	1					fish, Eliab	2	1	3		
Clefford, Isaac	1	5	4			Ausburn, Jonathan	1		1			Tosier, John, Ju^r	1	1	2		
Gove, Ebenezer, Junr	1	1	4			Hutson, Timothy	1	1	3			Tosier, Jonathan	1	4	2		
Gove, Ebenezer	2	2	2			Hustings, James	1	2	3								
Leman, Nathl	1	1	2			Pushan, Abraham	2	2	2			**GEORGETOWN TOWN.**					
Leman, Willm	1	3	3			Kindal, William	1	3	4								
Hodge, Willm	1	1	1			Rose, Jeremiah	1					Oliver, Thomas	1	1	2		
Hodge, Mary		1	1			Wyman, Daniel	2	1	6			Oliver, Jacob	1		2		
Leman, Danl	1	2	4			Hill, James	1					Oliver, Parker	2	2	4		
Berny, Thomas	2	3	6			Emery, Jonathan	2		2			Oliver, Willm	1	3	4		
Fly, Willm	1	3	4			Spensor, Solomon	1		4			Oliver, Benj^a	1	1	2		
Ratclif, Benj^a	1	5	3			Kimbal, Jacob	1	1	2			Oliver, John	3		3		
Tilton, Abraham	3	5	3			Jewit, Pickard	1					Oliver, John, Jn^r	1	4	1		
Merrow, Saml	1		4			Kitridge, Benj^a	1		3			McFadan, James	1	3	3		
Merrow, Joseph	2	1	5			Persons, David	1	1	4			Clary, Jane			1		
Webster, Daniel	2	3	4			Emery, James	1					Campbel, John	1	5	5		
Winslow, Nathl	1	2	4			Goodwin, Daniel	1	1	1			Flitner, Willm	1		2		
Stephens, Hubbard	4	1	3			Jackings, James	1					Trafton, Thos	1	4	3		
Brown, Joseph	2	5	2			Gullison, John	2	5	4			Spinney, Jer^e	2	1	3		
Dodge, Sarah		3	5			White, Joshua	1		2			Grover, Thos	1	1	4		
Webster, David	1	3	5			Sperring, John	1	1	3			Tarr, Benj^a	1	1	5		
Dodge, Winthrop	1	3	4			Emery, Edward	2	2	2			Gahan, John	1	2	2		
Dodge, Malachi	1	4	2			Emery, David	1	3	2			Hinkley, Matthew	1	2	3		
Dodge, Porter	1	3	2			Noble, Benjamin	1	1	1			Stephens, Thos	4	1	3		
Hagget, Benj^a	2	3	4			Mackkee, George	1		2			Brewer, Nathl	2	2	4		
Dodge, Daniel	1	1	2			Darling, Joseph	1	3	3			Powers, Jon^a	1	1	5		
Williams, Henry	2	4	4			Sibley, John	1	1	4			Oliver, Eben^s	3	4	3		
Richards, Jesse	1	3	3			Wheeler, Daniel	1					Rowe, Ebenezer	4	3	2		
Duntan, Willm	1	1	3			Hoxie, Ludwick	1	2	2			Grover, And^w	1	4	3		
Emerson, Edward	2	4	2			Blackwell, Joshua	1	1	1			Mallee, Daniel	1		3		
Peters, John	1		2			Blackwell, Jabez	1	1				McMahan, Daniel	1	1	5		
Cunningham, Tim^o	1	1	2			Burquis, David	1		1			McMahan, Tim^o	2		3		
Lamson, Willm	1	3	3			Blackwell, Thomas	1	2	3			Wyman, Willm	1	3	5		
Deering, John	2	3	3			Jones, Appollo	1		1			Kelley, John	1	3	4		
Cunningham, Willm	1	2	3			Hoxie, David	1	2	1			Gahan, James	1	1	2		
Pinkham, Joseph	1		2			Bowman, Harper	1		1			Duley, Mich^l	1	2	3		
Gove, Nathan	1		2			Bowman, Samuel	1					Coffee, Edward	3	2	2		
Baker, Solomon	3	1	5			Allen, Ebenezer, Jr	1	2	2			Whalen, John	3		3		
White, Nathl	2		3			Shephard, John	1	1	1			Whalen, Thomas	1				
Knight, John	2	2	5			Wing, Phillip	1	2	5			Drummon, Elijah	2	1	1		
Stone, Gabriel	1	1	4			Blackwell, Isreal	1	2	5			Bubler, Thos	1	4	2		
Colbey, James	1	2	2			Mendal, John	1	1	4			Welch, James	1				
Colbey, Saml	1		3			Holloway, Ludwick	1	3	2			Booker, Joseph	1	3	6		
Parsons, Joseph	2	4	6			Allen, Caleb	1	3	5			McCob, Mary	3	2	5	2	
Fowle, Joshua	1	1	1			Jones, Simon	1	1	3			Colyard, Charles	3	2	5	1	
Knight, Westbrook	1	2	6			Hoxie, Gidion	1		4			Sewal, Sarah			3		
Greenleaf, Stephen	1	4	5			Allen, Ebenezer	2	1	2			Parker, Jordan	3	1	9		
Norton, Lemuel	1		1			Hoxie, Barnis	1					Parker, John	4		5	2	
Elby, Benj^a	2	2	5			Holloway, Barnibus	1	1	2			Day, Abra^m	1		3		
Elby, Willm	1	3	2			Copland, Abraham	1		2			Silvester, Nathl	1	1	4		
Colby, Silvester	1	1	3			Holoway, Gideon	1	1	3			Sylvester, Nathl, Junr	1		1		
Mutchmore, Jacob	1	2	3			Cannon, Nathan	1		2			Sprague, William	1		2		
Young, Benaiah	1	2	2			Nigh Bartlett	1	3	2			McIntire, Joseph	1		1		
Greenleaf, Saml	1	1	2			Doe, Joseph	1					Wallace, John	1	1	1		
Greenleaf, Enoch	1	1	5			Davis, Benjamin	1	3	5			Gitchel, Benj^a	1		1		
Cromwel, Joseph	1	2	5			Darling, James	1		1			Morse, David	1	5	3		
Rymes, Joseph	3	3	3			Noble, John	2	3	5			Day, Jacob	3	4	4		
Tyler, Joseph	1	1	2			Bodfish, Nimfis	1	3	4			Manes, James	1	2	1		
Harrington, Elisha	1	4	3			Chace, Mathew	2	3	4			Morse, Jon^a	1	4	1		
Dorril, Thos	1					Townes, Joseph	2		1			Griffen, Ichabod	1		1		
Colbey, Henry	2	2	5			Wyman, Reuben, Jr	2	1	3			Manes, John	1	2	1		
Decker, Spencer	1	1	5			Wheeles, Enos	2					Rogers, Hugh	1				
Nutter, Volentine	1		1			Sturdifent, Lot	1		2			Fisher, John	1		2		
Colbey, Nehemiah	1		1			Mackfarling, Solomon	1		2			Lee, Willm	3	2	4		
Keene, Abel	1	1	3			Bates, Samuel	1	2	4			Rogers, John	3	1	3		
Brooks, Charles S	3		3			Bates, Seth	1					Lee, Willm, Jn^r	2	1	4		
Jewett, James	2	1	5			Shorehead, Daniel	1		2			Burnham, Francis			3		

LINCOLN COUNTY—Continued.

Name of head of family.	Free white males of 16 years and upward, including heads of families.	Free white males under 16 years.	Free white females, including heads of families.	All other free persons.	Slaves.
GEORGETOWN TOWN—continued.					
Turner, Forbs	1		3		
Parsons, John	1	1	2		
Pane, Edward	1	1	3		
Malcom, William	2		7		
Malcom, John	2	2	2		
Lithgow, William	6	1	7	1	
Rogers, Thomas	2	3	5		
Morse, Danl	1	4	4		
Persy, Thos	3	1	4		
Piercy (Widow)	1	1	2		
Stinson, John	4		1		
Stinson, William	1	2	5		
Coolyard, Mary	1	2	3	2	
Hogan, Thomas	4	5	6		
Swanton, Robert	1		2		
Conway, Francis	2		2		
Wallace, William	3		4		
Green, William	1	1	4		
Gushing, Ezekiel	1	2	5		
Rogers, George	5		4		
Butler, William, Jnr	1	1	3		
Butler, William	4	1	4		
Dosey, Jereh	1		2		
Pettey, Benja	3	1	5		
McCobb, Saml	3	2	6	3	
Fisher, John	3	1	6		
Brown, Daniel	1		1		
White, John	1	3	6		
Fisher, Henry	1	1	1		
Swett, Benja	2	4	3		
Sullivan, Danl	1	2	1		
Pettey, Saml	1	2	5		
Pettey, Benja, Jnr	1	1	1		
Pettey, Jane		2	2		
Sewal, James	1	1	6		
McFadan, John	1	4	4		
Potter, William	1	1	4		
Sewall, John	1				
Sewall, John, Jnr	2	1	2		
Sewall, Theodore	2	1	4		
Potter, John	2		4		
Stinson, William	2	2	4		
Emerson, Revd Ezekiel	4	1	4		
Drummon, James	3	3	3		
McFadan, Abigail	2	1	3		
McFredericks, James	3	2	7		
Drummon, Alexander	6	2	5		
McFadan, Danl	4	2	6		
Stinson, James	2	1	2		
Snipe, John	4	1	4		
Preble, Joseph	2	1	3		
Higan, James	1	1	3		
Stinson, John	3	2	4		
McKenny, Robert	1		2		
Preble, Jona	1		3		
Shay, Michl	1	4	4		
Carter, Saml	1	1	3		
Hall, John	2	5	6		
Reardon, John	1	1	4		
Quin, John	2		3		
Welch, Mark	1		1		
Rigs, Benja	1	1	6		
Reardon, Timothy	2	1	3		
McKenny, George	2	2	3		
Tarr, Joseph	1	2	5		
Tarr, Sarah	1	5	3		
Tarr, Seth	2		6		
Mars, William	1	1	1		
Heal, John	2	2	6		
Heal, Gilbart	1		3		
McKenny, Brook	3	2	8		
McFadan, Andw	2		1		
Williams, James	1	1	2		
Hunt, David	2	3	3		
Michaels, George	1	4	3		
Harford, William	2	1	3		
McKenny, Matthew	2	5	1		
Clary, Allen	1	3	2		
Mahony, James	2	4	6		
Poor, Robert	4		7		
Heal, John	1	2	3		
McCarty, Timo	1	4	2		
Higgans, Thomas	1	2	3		
Linnen, Bryant	3	1	5		
McKenny, Thomas	1	1	2		
Trafton, Joseph	2	2	3		
Trafton, Thomas	1		1		
Hinkley, Josiah	2	2	4		
Beal, John	1	2	3		
Oliver, David, 4th	1	1	4		
Oliver, David	3	1	3		
Oliver, David, 3rd	2	1	5		
Linnen, Thomas	1		4		
Lary (Widow)			3		
Grover, James	1	5	5		
GEORGETOWN TOWN—continued.					
Oliver, David, Junr	2	2	6		
Beal, Saml	1	2	3		
Rackley, Saml	1	1	2		
Rackley, Saml, Jnr	1	3	1		
Hunt, Willm	1	2	5		
Hinkley, Edmund	2	2	5		
Green, Richd	1	1	2		
Perkins, Nathl	4	2	4		
Mars, John	1	6	1		
Spinny, Hannah			4		
Spinney, John	1	4	4		
Spinney, Jere	1	1	2		
Oliver, James	1		2		
Neal, John	1	1	1		
Oliver, Ephraim, Jnr	1	3	4		
Oliver, Henry	1	2	3		
Oliver, John	1	2	1		
Morrison, Saml	2	2	5		
Ingerson, George	2		2		
Oliver, Ephraim	1	3	4		
Oliver, Nicholas	1	2	4		
Perry, Ely	1	1	2		
Warry, John	1	1	1		
Bacheldor, Theos	3	1	4		
Snow, Joseph	1	1	2		
Batcheldor, Tims	1	1	4		
Spalding, Ezekiel	4	1	4		
Batcheldor, Elijah	1	2	1		
Morrison, Moses	2	3			
Batcheldor, Josiah	1	1	1		
Marum, John	3	1	1		
Hall, Joseph	3	1	2		
Booker, Joseph	1	2	1		
Walten, John	3	1	1		
Blasdel, Christopher	1	1	3		
Blasdel, Daniel	2	1	2		
Rogers, Robert	1	4	5		
Bisby, Charles	1	1	1		
Lowell, John	1		1		
Lowell, Stephen	1	2	4		
Day, Stephen	1	1	7		
Wallace, Saml	1	2	4		
Totman, Henry	2		3		
Wallace, Willm	1	5	2		
Campbel, Danl	2	1	4		
Wyman, Francis	2	2	3		
Wyman, Martha	1	3	6		
Sprague, Willm	1	2	2		
Whalen, Joseph	1		1		
Hinkley, Hannah	2	1	4		
GREAT POND PLANTATION.					
Davis, James	3		2		
Davis, Charles	1	2	2		
Davis, Joshua	1	2	2		
Davis, William	2	1	2		
Weeks, Shubial	3		3		
Mugridge, Simon	1	1	1		
Waters, Samuel	1		3		
Clay, Daniel	1	2	1		
Silvestor, Ebenesor	2	4	4		
foy, Robert	1	3	4		
Greley, Jacob	1	1	1		
Cresey, Abel	2	2	3		
Sanford, Daniel	1	3	1		
Bolin, William	1	1	1		
Belden, Stephen	1	1	2		
Heselton, Samuel	1	2	2		
Longfelow, Samuel	1	2	4		
Longfellow, Stephen	1	2	3		
Broadstret, John	1	5	4		
Grealey, Jonathan	1		2		
Huckens, Hollis	3	4	3		
Turner, David	1		2		
Erskins, Christopher	1	2	5		
Turner, Benjamen	1	4	5		
Bartlet, Jonathon	2	1	3		
Calley, Aaron	1	3	2		
Bron, Jeremiah	1		1		
Gilpatrick, Thomas	2	1	2		
Gilpatrick, Charles	1		1		
Parkers, Nathan	1	3			
GREENE TOWN.					
Bales, Jabas R	1		2		
Robins, Luther	1	4	2		
Sprags, Jamas	1	3	2		
Sprages, William	1		1		
Tompson, Elick	1	1	1		
Shaw, Elisha	1				
Shaw, Zebulon	1		1		
Astons, Stephen	1		3		
GREENE TOWN—con.					
Sprage, William, Ju	1	2	5		
Lanes, Edman	1	3	5		
Call, Benja	1		1		
harris, Silas	1				
Wilmy, Daniel	1		1		
harris, John	1	2	3		
Cobin, William	3	2	3		
Cobin, Jesse	1		2		
Bings, Elijah	1	1	2		
Sargant, David	1		1		
Cobin, Reuben	1				
herick, Joseph	1	6	2		
Stodard, Phinhas	2		2		
Marill, Benjn	2	2	2		
Marill, John	1	1	1		
Daggett, John	1	4	3		
Ames, Jacob	1	1	3		
Coming, Samuel	3	1	5		
Judkins, Philip	1	2	5		
parham, William	1	1	1		
heredin, William	1	1	7		
Butler, John	1				
Cole, Samuel	1	3	1		
Stevens, Jacob	1		4		
Cole, Benja	1	1	2		
Barker, Uriah	1				
Evens, hannah		1	2		
Barrey, George	1		2		
Smith, thomas	1				
Stephens, Thomas	1	2	4		
Marrill, Benja	1	4	2		
Marrill, Benja, Jn	1	1	2		
larrabb, Stephen	1	3	5		
larrabb, John	1	3	6		
Night, Edman			1		
Brown, abner	1	5	2		
Rackley, Benja	1	3	4		
Astins, Jacob	1	2	7		
Barker, William	1	5	2		
Waterman, Primes	1				
Reed, amesiah	1	2	2		
Bates, Levi	1	1	2		
Bates, Solomon	1	1	1		
Richman, Biethur	1		3		
Allan, John	1	3	4		
Jones, Cuandy	1	1	1		
Rose, Simeon	3		1		
Keen, Elisha	1				
Jones, Nolon	1				
Philips, Gray	2	1	4		
turner, Oliver	1	1	1		
Brigs, abiether	1	1	1		
Rose, asha	3	1	4		
Rose, Zebulon	1				
Rose, Seth	1				
Chamblen, William	1	1	4		
Philip, Ichabod	1		1		
Coshman, Jonm	1	3	3		
hiland, abner	1		1		
Oldon, Benjn	1	2	3		
Sampson, Joseph	1	2	4		
Linsday, thomas	1	2	2		
Saford, andrew	1				
Dean, Seres	1		1		
Mower, Jonm	1	1	3		
Mower, John	1	2	3		
Silvester, Elisha	1				
Bates, Douly	1	1	1		
Bates, Samuel	1				
Brown, Benja	1	1	2		
Brown, Moses	1				
Man, andrew	1				
herrick, Ely	1		2		
herrick, Samuel	1				
lander, Robenson	1				
Mower, William	1	1	2		
Keen, Elezer	1				
Saford, hay	1		1		
petergill, Ephram	1				
quimbey, Benj	1	1	2		
Bates, Lamuel	1				
Bates, Joseph	1				
Drew, Clemant	1	1	1		
HALLOWELL TOWN.					
Perkins, Eliab	1	2	3		
Clark, Uriah	3	1	4		
Clark, Charles	1		1		
Cobb, David	1	2	5		
Smith, Moses	2	1	2		
Bolton, Daniel	1	2	3		
Doin, Saml	1	1	3		
Bisby, Elisha	2		1		
Springer, James	2	1	6		

HEADS OF FAMILIES—MAINE.

LINCOLN COUNTY—Continued.

NAME OF HEAD OF FAMILY.	Free white males of 16 years and upward, including heads of families.	Free white males under 16 years.	Free white females, including heads of families.	All other free persons.	Slaves.
HALLOWELL TOWN—con.					
Dane, Simeon	2	4	2		
Badcock, Henry	1	1	5		
Springer, Edward	1	4	5		
Sprague, William	1	4	3		
Wells, David	2	3	5		
Blackborn, Josiah	1	1	2		
Cowen, Abisha	1	1	5		
Cowen, Jabez	2	2	2		
Ingraham, Beziah	2	2	3		
Woodward, Noah	4	1	3		
Williams, Asa	1	1	4		
Reid, George	1	1	2		
Shaw, John	1	1	2		
Williams, Seth	5	4	4		
Stow, Willm	1		1		
Shaw, John	2	1	4		
Savage, Isaac	1	1	1		
Savage, James	1	1	2		
Brown, Benj^a	1	3	3		
Anderson, John	1				
Bolton, Savage		3	2		
Shaw, Eliab	1	2	4		
Chamberlin, Saml	4	1	3		
Andrews, George	1	4	4		
Sewal, Henry	1	1	3		
Nowland, John	4		2		
Savage, Edward	2	2	6		
Usher, Willm	1				
Pettingale, Benj^a	2		2		
Allen, Phinehas	1	3	4		
Thomas, David	2	1	3	1	
Clark, Isaac	2	3	5		
Carr, James	2				
Foster, Joseph	1	2	1		
Savage, Danl	3	2	4		
Hallowel, Willm	1	4	4		
McKnight, David	1		2		
Cole, Saml	1		1		
Pettingale, Benj^a, Jn^r	1	2	3		
Norcross, Saml, Ju^r	2	3	4		
Couch, John	1	3	3		
Dana, Edmund	1	2	1		
White, Benj^a	1	1	3		
Chase, Ezekiel	3	1	1		
Winkley, Thomas	2	3	4		
Norcross, Saml	4		2		
Norcross, Philip	1	1	4		
Beeman, John	3		4		
Clark, Peter	2	1	2		
Fletcher, David	1	2	1		
Ingraham, Jere^h	3	2	3		
Fletcher, Robert	1		5		
Pierce, Saml	1	3	3		
Pierce, Eliphalet	2	2	4		
Fletcher, Briant	2	1	5		
Gill, John	3	4	6		
Fletcher, Briant	2	1	4		
Badcock, Jer^h	1	1	2		
Huen, Willm	1	1	1		
Badcock, Saml	1	3	4		
Badcock, Saml	1		1		
Badcock, John	1	3	2		
Tolman, Saml	1	3	2		
Dennison, Robert	2	1	2		
Church, Saml	1	2	2		
Stackpole, Joseph	1	5	3		
Cowen, James	2		3		
Clark, Jonas	4	3	4		
Harden, Isaac	1	1	2		
Harden, Isaac, Jn^r	1	2	2		
Page, Enoch	2	1	6	1	
Cass, Moses	1		4		
Hovey, John	1	1	3		
Hewen, Eben^r	1	3	2		
Dutten, Saml	6	2	5	1	
Page, James	6	1	4		
Moore, James	1	1	4		
Cottle, Isaac	1	4	5		
Taylor, Nathl	1	3	5		
Follet, Benj^a	1		1		
Follet, Jesse	1	2	2		
Freeman, John	1	1	2		
Coy, Daniel	1		2		
Gould, Jabez	1		1		
Stevans, Daniel	3	1	9		
Dudley, Saml	1		1		
Floyd, Nathl	1	2	3		
Hall, Oliver	1	3	1		
Benson, Jacob	2	1	3		
Shaw, Nathl	3	1	4		
Snell, Thaddeus	1		2		
Bullen, Saml	3		5		
Jones, Peter	1				
Hatch, David	1	1	1		
HALLOWELL TOWN—con.					
Goodwin, Andrew	1	4	4		
Cox, James	5	1	3		
Huzzy, Mary	2	2	5	1	
Caldwell, Ganham	1			3	
White, Moses	1	5	4		
White, Benj^a	2	1	4		
Jackson, David	5	1	5		
Ward, Benj^a	1	3	6		
Colburn, Margaret	3		6		
Davenport, Jan^a	2	2	3		
Page, Ezekiel	2	1	5		
Page, Abraham	1	2	5		
Coney, Saml	1		3		
Cumming, Solomon	1	1	1		
Coney, Danl	2		5		
Patrige, Amos	1		2		
McMaster, Willm	3	2	3		
Vose, Jesse	1		2		
Church, John	1	2	4	1	
Belcher, Supply	1		2		
Brooks, Willm	4	2	4		
Hersey, Nathl	1	4	3		
Howard, Willm	9		6		
Colman, Saml	5		4		
Parker, Peter	1	2	2	1	
Greely, Enoch	2	3	5		
Burges, Ephraim	1		2		
Gilman, Eliphalet	3	3	5		
Walker, Benj^a	1		2		
Dummer, Nathl	3	1	4		
Sewall, Moses	4	2	3		
Palmer, Willm	2	3	2		
Sherborn, Abiel	1		1		
Swett, Saml		4	4		
Perkins, Ebenezer	1		2	1	
Metcalf, Joseph	5		2		
Daws, Willm	1	4	1		
Fillebrown, Thos	1		2		
Dutten (Widow)	2	1	2		
Goodwin, Lazarus	3	2	3		
Nye, Elisha	3	2	6		
Prescott, Benj^a	1	2	1		
Prescott, Joseph	1	1	3		
Davis, John	1	2	1		
Nye, Elvel	1	1	1		
Hinkley, James	2	5	4		
Smith, Daniel	3	1	4	1	
Switland, Nathl	1	3	3		
Brown, Joseph	1	3	5		
Davis, Benj^a	3	5	6		
Church, Ebenezer	3	5	6		
Harris, Obadiah	1	2	4		
Haynes, John	2	3	5		
Cumming, Saml	2	2	3		
Cumming, Asa	1		1		
Cumming, Saml	2		1		
Curtex, Willm	1				
Brown, John	1	3	2		
Field, Ellas	1		2		
Ballad, Ephraim	3	1	4		
Savage, Isaac, Ju^r	1	4	5		
Pollard, Amos	4	1	3		
Black, James	2		3		
Twing, Nathl	1				
Craige, Elias	3		1	1	
Welch, Saml	1	1	3		
North, Joseph	4	1	6		
Childs, James	2	1	2		
Burten, James	1		1		
Hamlin, Theophilus	1	1	2		
Burges, Joshua	1	2	3		
Wesson, Nathan	3	3	2		
Brigs, Willm	1	2	3		
Taylor, Ebenezer	1		4		
Hodges, Ezra	1	2	3		
Dinsmore, Thomas	1	3	7		
Canada, Robert	1	3	2		
Edson, Elisabeth		2	3		
True, Zebulon	1	1	1		
Livermore, Jason	2	2	5		
Hinkley, Shubal	1	2	5		
HANCOCK TOWN.					
Prat, Asa	3		3		
Prat, James	1	1	2		
Chace, Varnum	1	3	2		
More, Mordica	1	1	4		
Wyman, Dean	1	3	4		
Burril, John, Ju^r	1		1		
Wyman, Reuben	1		1		
Burril, John	1		4		
Burril, Zibe	1	1	4		
Kimbal, David	1		2		
HANCOCK TOWN—con.					
Brown, Ezekiel, Jur	1	3	4		
Brown, Ezekiel	1		4		
Hale, Ebenezer	2	2	4		
Spensor, David	2	2	4		
Richardson, Andrew	1	4	3		
Read, Samuel	1		4		
Burrows, Garrat	1	1	1		
Burton, Nathan	3	1	4		
Leman, John	1				
Gray, John	2	2	5		
Roundly, Job	1	1	1		
Roundly, Micah	1		1		
Sandes, Joseph	1	1	2		
Philbrook, Jonathan	4		1		
Goodwin, Stephen	3	2	2		
Spern, Benjamin	1		3		
Jackings, Fredrick	1	2	3		
Pollard, Barton	1		2		
Flag, Gershom	2	2	2		
Spensor, Isaac	1	2	3		
Read, Samuel, Ju^r	1	1	2		
fuller, Bartholomew	2	1	2		
Costigen, Lawrance	2		2		
Brown, James	1	1	3		
Barnes, Silas	1				
Roundly, Lacet	1		1		
Roundly, Ebenezer	1		1		
Burton, Nathan	1	1	2		
Grave, Paul	1	2	2		
Brown, Charles	3	1	4		
Fitsgerald, George	1	4	4		
Kimbal, David	1		2		
Hartford, John	1				
Cone, Samuel	1	3	2		
Sherring, John	2	1	2	1	
Burril, Belial	1	3	4		
Crosby, Robert	1		2		
Bigsby, Solomon	1		2		
Davis, Samuel	1				
Bigelow, James	1				
Lovejoy, Francis	2	1	2		
fowler, Samuel	1				
Glitton, Reuben	1				
Burgoin, John	1		1		
Mecaheny, Michal	1		3		
Crosby, Jonah, Ju^r	2	3	2		
Shelden, Henry	1	5	1		
Simpson, Simeon	1		3		
Haywood, Nathan	1		2		
Fowler, Thomas	1		2		
Hines, Aushur	1		2		
HUNTS MEADOW TOWN.					
Pearson, Mark	1				
Longfellow, Sewall	1	2	6		
Mason, George	1	2	3		
Tinkham, John	1	2			
Davis, James J	1	5	3		
Lambart, Danl	1	5	2		
Greenleaf, Ebenezer	3		9		
Preble, James	1	4	3		
Prat, Seth	1	1	3		
Cooper, Moses	3		3		
Hunt, Silas	1				
JONES PLANTATION.					
Morton, Michael	3	4	4		
Bragg, Nathl	3	7	3		
Getchell, Elihu	1		2		
Burrel, Abr^m	3	3	5		
Ward, Josiah	2	2	8		
McGlothlin, Geo	2	4	2		
Fairfield, Edwd	1	(*)	(*)		
Evins, Joseph	2	1	2		
Robinson, Geo	1	3	3		
Rose, Seth	1				
Gliddon, Gidion	1	4	2		
Godfry, Prince	2	2	3		
Ward, Mijah	3	3	2		
Langcaster, James	4	1	6		
Brown, Enock	1		3		
McGlothling, Geo., jr	1		2		
Dickey, Elezer Boyad	1		3		
Evens, Nathl	1		7		
Lewis, Jabez	1	3	5		
Wyman, Th^s	1	2	2		
Wiggins, Nathl	1		3		
Williams, Joshua	2	2	2		
Clerk, Jonathan	2		6		
Clerk, Edmond	2	1	6	5	
Fish, George	3		1		

* Illegible.

FIRST CENSUS OF THE UNITED STATES.

LINCOLN COUNTY—Continued.

NAME OF HEAD OF FAMILY.	Free white males of 16 years and upward, including heads of families.	Free white males under 16 years.	Free white females, including heads of families.	All other free persons.	Slaves.
JONES PLANTATION—continued.					
Marithew, William	1	3	2		
Webber, Joseph	1	1	5		
Webber, Lewis	2	2	4		
Clerk, Ephᵐ	2		4		
Goodspeed, Nathˡ	3		3		
Weeks, Abner	1	1	1		
Weeks, Solomon	1				
Weeks, Solomon, Jʳ	1		2		
Chadwick, Job	1	2	2		
Chadwick, Ichᵈ	1		2		
Chadwick, James	1	2	5		
Chadwick, Lot	1				
Chadwick, Judah	1		1		
LEWISTOWN TOWN AND THE GORE ADJOINING.					
Hinkley, Gidion	1	1	3		
Merril, Emly	2		2		
Coal, Samuel	1	3	1		
Pettingill, Sarah		2	4		
Pettingill, Ebenezer	1	2	4		
Coal, Job	2	1	3		
Hacket, Ezekiel	1	1	6		
Right, Timothy	1	3	4		
Thorn, Samuel	3	1	2		
Right, Jesse	1	3	5		
Hacket, Jude	1				
Taylor, Thomas	2	3	2		
Pettingil, Abraham	1	3	3		
Herrick, John	2	2	5		
Barker, Jacob	2		3		
Cutter, Nathan		2	4		
Blasdel, William	1	3	5		
Marshal, John	1	2	2		
Winslow, Kernelm	1	4	4		
Right, Joel	1	7	2		
Rose, unis			2		
Mars, John	1				
Hildrick, Paul	2	2	5		
Herris, Abner	2	1	5		
Grafton, John	2	2	5		
Lamps, Peter	1	4	5		
Pinkhum, Elisha	1				
Morril, Jedediah	1	1	3		
Davis, Daniel	1	2	6		
Thompson, Joel	1	2	4		
Ham, Tobias	1	3	6		
Lake, Elisha	1		1		
Davis, Aaron	1		1		
Wilkins, David	2	2	4		
Golder, William	1	3	2		
Pettingill, David	1		2		
Pinkham, Ebenezer	1		2		
Hacket, Ezekiel, Jʳ	1	1	1		
Hatch, Samuel	1		5		
Hatch, Ellihu	1	1	1		
Landers, Freeman	3		4		
Lake, Joshua	1	2	2		
Randal, Isreal	1	2	1		
Barker, Caleb	1		2		
Barker, Jacob	1		2		
Firck, Samuel	1	3	2		
Davis, Amos	3	2	3		
Far, Seth	1		2		
Herris, Lydia			1		
Blake, John	1	2	4		
Hodgkins, Jonathan	3	1	2		
Carver, Henry	1	2	3		
Ham, Sarah	2		2		
Joslin, James, Jur	1		5		
Joslin, Peter	1	1	2		
Dire, Elhanah	1		2		
Millbank, Phillip	1		4		
Joslin, James	2	1	4		
Joslin, William	1		3		
Joslin, Daniel	1		1		
Proctor, Joseph	1				
Bliffin, John, Jur	1				
Kimbal, Simeon	1	2	2		
Dean, William	1	1	2		
Mores, Nathan	1	2	4		
Green, Daniel	1	2	1		
Mitchel, Josiah	2	4	6		
Merril, Moses	1	3	3		
Purrunton, Ezra	1				
fields, Samuel	1	2	4		
Mitchal, Thomas	3	1	4		
fish, John	1	1	1		
Booby, Andrew	1		2		
Ran, Thomas	1				
Jaeson, James	3		2		
Thompson, Joseph	1	2	2		
Dill, John	2	3	2		
Anderson, Robert	1	3	3		
LEWISTOWN TOWN AND THE GORE ADJOINING—continued.					
Hart, Stephen	2		3		
Davis, Joseph	3	1	3		
Read, Dan	1		2		
Adkins, Williams	1		1		
Davis, Joseph, Juʳ	1	2	1		
Ray, Benjamin	1				
Ray, Hannah	1	1	2		
Dill, Josiah	1	2	3		
Green, William	1	1	4		
Bliffin, John	2	6	4		
Bliffin, James	1	1	1		
Dean, John	1	1	1		
Dean, John, Juʳ	2	3	3		
Sawyer, John	1	1	2		
Fields, Joseph	1	4	4		
Jones, Josiah	1		1		
Carvel, William	1				
Meeder, Tobias	1				
Robertson, Samuel	1	3	3		
Ames, Winslow	1	2	1		
Ames, James	1	2	6		
Higings, Jesse	1		2		
LITTLE RIVER TOWN.					
Fellows, Ebenezer	2		3		
Foster, Stephen	1	1	2		
Tilton, Samuel	1		1		
Right, Ozias	1		1		
Whitney, Abraham	1	3	3		
Moulton, John	1	3	5		
Wilson, Samuel	2	1	3		
Wilson, John	1		1		
Purnton, Allihue	1	1			
Whitney, Benjamin	3	1	6		
Whitney, Jacob	1	1	1		
Southeslin, Alexᵈ	1	3	4		
Crabtree, William	1		1		
LITTLEBOROUGH PLANTATION.					
Gilbert, William	1	1	3		
Bither, Samul	1				
Crocker, Joseph	2	1	4		
Dudson, Jabas	1				
whiting, John	1		2		
Bates, Jacob	1		1		
house, nathaniel	1	2	4		
Samson, michal	1				
Gilbert, henry	1	2	6		
Gilbert, Samuel	1		2		
whitney, John	3	1	6		
Duncat, Prine				3	
wood, Simeon				4	
Barry, amos	3		1		
Choshman, andrew	1	1	1		
Gincing, John	1	2	1		
Gincing, Samuel	1		2		
Treeman, Joseph	2	2	4		
Collard, Isaac	1	2	4		
Shaw, Elisha	1	2	2		
addition, thomas	1	2	2		
Jones, Edward	1		3		
Samson, Bryen	3		2		
Samson, James	1		3		
Shaw, Elisha, juʳ	2				
Dunnam, Joseph	1				
Oties, Oliver	1				
Turner, Gorge		1	3		
Turner, Joseph	1	4	3		
andris, Ephram	2	2	5		
Drake, Oliver	2	6	2		
Millet, Solomon	1	3	6		
Bruster, Morgin	1	1	2		
Curtice, Gasham	1	3	2		
Foster, Stephen	1	2	1		
Tarbble, David	2	2	3		
Lane, Daniel	1		2		
Dunnam, Jonᵃ	1				
otis, thomas	1				
Lane, Daniel, Ju	1	1	3		
lane, James	1				
lane, Giddeon	1		2		
Riols, Adam	1	2	3		
Smith, Zebulon	1				
francis, thomas	1	3	1		
Nap, Joseph	2		2		
linsday, William	2	2	6		
Gorge, Frances	1	1	2		
Paul, Narshfield	1				
West (widow)	2		1		
whitcker, Nanse			1		
Fish, Jicah	2	3	3		
Robins, Daniel	1		2		
LITTLEBOROUGH PLANTATION—continued.					
hicks, Zefeniah	1		4	2	
Stinchfield, Roger	1	4	4		
larnard, hains	1	3	4		
Norcross, Nathaniel	1				
Stinchfield, thomas	2	3	3		
LIVERMORE TOWN, EAST SIDE ANDROSCOGGIN RIVER.					
Dayley, Daniel	2		4		
Dilenow, Jabish	1	1	3		
Wing, Reuben	3	4	3		
Bargish, Seth	1		3		
linsy, William	2	3	4		
George, Frances	1		3		
Learned, Henry	1				
Browner, William (bachlor)	1				
Greay, James	1		1		
Stevens, William	1				
Cobb, Josiah	1				
MEDUNCOOK TOWN.					
Bradford, Carpenter	2		3		
Gay, Jonah	1	1	2		
Gay, Wellington	1	3	6		
Davis, William	3	1	3		
Davis, Ebenezer	2	3	4		
Bickmore, John	4	1	3		
Bickmore, John, Junʳ	1	2	3		
Morton, Ebenezer	1		1		
Morton, James	1	3	4		
Morton, Joshua	1	2	7		
Morton, Ebenezer, Junʳ	4	1	5		
Collamore, Joshua	1				
Bartlet, Nathaniel	1	1	1		
Jameson, Robert	2	2	4		
Jameson, Paul	5		3		
Bradford, Joshua	1	4			
Morton, Cornelius	1		1		
Peckard, Samuel	1	3	3		
Demorse, John	2	1	4		
Cook, Elijah	2	2	7		
Cook, James	1	1	5		
Cook, Hannah		1	3		
Bradford, Joshua, Junʳ	2	3	5		
Thomas, Asa	4	2	4		
Thomas, Jesse	4		1		
Jameson, Alexander	1	1	2		
Laury, Samuel	6		3		
Motte, William	1	2	4		
Conden, Samuel	3		2		
Conden, George	1	1	1		
Wutton, Benjamin	1	5	3		
Geyer, Martin	1	3	3		
Delano, Alpheus	2	2	5		
Trask, Joseph	1				
Newhouse, Christopher	1				
Davis, Robert	2	1	5		
Davis, Samuel	5	1	4		
Demorse, John, Junʳ	1	6	2		
Conner, Charles	1				
Parker, Simon	1		2		
Wingumpaugh, John	1	3	1		
Miller, William	1	4	4		
Wolpgrover, John	1	1	4		
Sage, William	1		2		
Chaples, Richard	1	5	4		
Davis, Jacob	1	1			
Davis, Zechary	1		4		
Davis, Samuel, Jun	1				
Thompson, James	1	3	4		
NEW CASTLE TOWN.					
Tayler, Joseph	2		4		
Trumbal, John	1	1	5		
Brown, James	1	3	3		
Leavitt, Israel	1	2	4		
Hopkins, Christopher	1	1	1		
Hopkins, Willᵐ	1	2	6		
Bester, George	1	1	6		
Winslow, Mary	1		2		
Farley, John	3	1	9		
Kennady, Willᵐ	1		8		
Kennady, Henry	1				
Kennady, Samˡ	1	1	5		
Cook, Orchard	4	1	5		
Morrison, Jonˢ	1				
Carlton, David	1	3	3		
Heath, Moses	1	1	3		
Clough, Daniel	1		1		
Jewett, Moses	1	4	6		

HEADS OF FAMILIES—MAINE.

LINCOLN COUNTY—Continued.

NAME OF HEAD OF FAMILY.	Free white males of 16 years and upward, including heads of families.	Free white males under 16 years.	Free white females, including heads of families.	All other free persons.	Slaves.
NEW CASTLE TOWN—continued.					
Jewett, James	1		1		
Nelson, John	1	3	3		
Herriman, Simon	2				
Sawyer, Wil^m	1		5		
Turner, Nehemiah	2	1	4		
Cook, Mehitable			2		
Carlton, Moses	2	1	3		
Glidden, Benj^a	3	4	5		
Gilman, Peter	2	3	6		
Labree, Peter	1		3		
Hilton, Saml	7	1	3		
Simpson, Saml	1	1	4		
McQuig, Danl	2		4		
Harley, John	2		2		
Cooper, Jesse	1	4	3		
Leighton, Ezekiel	2	4	2		
Cooper, James	1	1	3		
Harley, John, Jn^r	1	2	4		
Greely, Jacob	1	1	4		
Leighton, Richard	2	1	1		
Leighton, Rebecca	1		3		
Waters, Daniel	2	1	2		
Woodbrige, Tho^m	1	1	4		
Woodbridge, Benj^a, Jnr.	1	3	7		
Simpson, James	1	4	5		
Kennedy, Thos	1	4	6		
Murray, David	3	3	5		
Campbel, James	5		2		
Hopkins, Solomon	1	1	7		
Chase, Charles	2	5	5		
Woodbridge, Christopher	1		2		
Perkins, Elias	1	2	2		
Turner, Briggs	3	1	6		
Kennady, Molly			2		
Averal, Ezekiel	2	2	3		
Holmes, Hugh	1	1	1		
McAnen, John	1	3	2		
Woodbridge, Benj^a	1		1		
Glidden, Joseph, J^r	1	3	6		
Tugal, Elkanah	3	4	3		
Cargill, Abanathar	1	1	1		
Cunningham, Thos	2		1		
Kennady (Widow)	3	1	2		
Cunningham, Sarah	2	1	2		
Cunningham, John	2	1	7		
Cargill, James	3	2	2		
Givens, John	1	2	5	1	
Nichols, Saml	6	4	4	1	
Hitchcock, Daniel	2	1	1		
Davidson, Alexander	2	2	3		
Robinson, Robert	1	2	2		
Nichols, Alexander	1	1	1		
Webb, Nathl	1	3	4		
Clap, Enos	3		3		
Gledden, Nathl	1	5	8		
Catland, John	2	2	8		
Speed, Benj^a	2		4		
Bester, Benj^a	1	3	3		
Robertson, Archibald	2	4	3		
Glidden, Tobias	2	2	3		
Perkins, Lemuel	2	1	3		
Perkins, Abizah	3	1	3		
Tufts, Moses	1	2	4		
Nichols, John	1	1	1		
Campbel, Thos	1	1	2		
Somer, David	3	2	5		
Cargill, David	1	3	4		
Trask, John	3	3	10		
Cochran, Robert	1	4	5		
Patterson, Peter	1	3	3		
Malcom, Allen	2		2		
Groves, Saml	1	3	2		
Cochran, John	1	1	2		
Cochran, Adam	1	3	3		
Tufts, Moses	1		4		
Dodge, Paul	3	1	2		
Dodge, David	1	3	1		
Little, James	2	4	6		
Little, Henry	2	3	5		
Day, Tobb	1	2	3		
Perkins, Ebenezer	2		2		
Dodge, John	1	2	4		
Dodge, Zachariah	2	3	4		
Dodge, Daniel	1	1	1		
Dodge, Moses	1	1	2		
Campbel, Thos	4		3		
Givens, James	1	2	5		
Dunbar, Solomon	2		4		
Mirach, Josiah	1		2		
Barker, Hannah			2		
Bryant, Nathl	2	1	2	1	
Jones, Kinsley	4	4	3		
Morgan, Joseph	1		5		
Jones, John, Jn^r	1	3	2		
NEW CASTLE TOWN—continued.					
Hall, Isaac	1	3	3		
Jones, Jon^a	3	1	7		
Jones, John	2	3	2		
Hall, Ebenezer	3	1	4		
Clark, James	3	2	6		
Rollins, Nathl	5		3		
Jones, Jon^a, Jn^r	1	2	3		
Clark, Eben^a	2	4	5		
Lincoln, Benj^a	1	1	4		
Ridlon, Robert	2	3	2		
Rice, John	1	2	3		
Prudent, Willm	1	2	3		
Whitten, John	1	2	1		
Whitten, Ebenezer	1		2		
Jones, Benj^a	2	4	6		
Bester, Isaac	1	2	2		
Huzzy, John	3	1	7		
Glidden, Joseph	4	1	5		
Holmes, John	1		1		
NEW SANDWICH TOWN.					
Wing, Simeon	2		1		
Wing, Alan	1		1		
Wing, Aron	1				
Wing, Simeon, Jr	1		2		
Besse, Ebenezer	1		5		
Adkins, Nathaniel	2	2	5		
Lovjoy, Moses	1	2	4		
Blak, Thomas	1		1		
Norris, Nathan	1	2	2		
Judkins, Jesse	1				
Norris, Ephrim	1	1	4		
Norris, Saml	1				
Norris, Woodin	1	1	1		
Norris, Josiah	1				
Sawell, thomas			1		
Mason, Ebenezer	1	4	2		
Besse, Jabe	1	2	1		
Parrey, David	1	2	2		
Bilenton, Isaac	2		4		
Curtice, David	1	1	1		
Sturdevent, Gamaah	1	1	3		
Smith, John	1	3	3		
Tompson, David	1		1		
Handey, Ebenezer	4	1	2		
Rament, William	1	2	5		
Besse, Jabas, Ju	2	3	4		
Gower, Iaras	1		3		
Perry, Zechriah	2		3		
frost, Saml	4	2	3		
Stevens, Christopher					
Dexter, Isaac	4	4	3		
Besse, Reuben	3		4		
Bilenton, Nathaniel	1	1	3		
Bilenton, Ichabod	3		4		
washburn, hosea	1		6		
Maseam, Nathan	3	4	3		
Wing, Moses	1	2	4		
Bumpas, Zefeniah	1	1	1		
Bumpas, Zefeniah, Ju	1		1		
Reneff, Charly	1		2		
How, Jon^a	1				
Doutey, John	1		1		
Bartlet, Jon^a	1				
fuller, Job	1	1	3		
Lawrance, James	3	1	2		
Parry, Judah	1				
handy, Richard	1	4	2		
Wing, Ebenezer	1	1	2		
Jennis, John	2		4		
Watlon, Abiah	1	1	4		
Walton, William	3	3	3		
Judkins, Jacob	1		3		
ford, Nathaniel	1		4		
ford, James	1				
Cornell, John	1	2	2		
Southword, Constant	1	1	2		
Southword, thomas	1				
ford, Isaac	3	1	3		
Petengall, Mathew	1		2		
Sampson, Jon^a	2	1	2		
Gliten, Jeremiah	1				
handey, Benj^a	1				
ford, henry	1				
Wiket, Abraham	1	2	2		
Waldoborough (NOBLEBOROUGH TOWN).					
hines, Conelis	1	2	4		
heabner, george	1		2		
burghart, John	1	5	2		
welch, Charles	1	1	4		
welch, John, jun	1	3	2		
welch, christopher	1	2	2		
Waldoborough—continued.					
werner, John, jun	1		4		
werner, John	2		1		
werner, andrew	1				
oberlach, John henry	1	2	2		
hofses, mathias	3		5		
ludwig, Jacob	2		1		
Stall, henry	2	1	4		
bornheimer, godfried	2		2		
bornheimer, Jacob	1		4		
weber, george	1	2	3		
wolfgruber, Stofel	2		3		
oberlach, charles	1	2	3		
keler, Jacob	2		1		
miler, peter	2	1	1		
winkenbach, Jacob	1	5	6		
oberlach, frank	1	1	2		
waliser, John	1		2		
gros, peter	3	2	5		
gros, John	1				
gros (widow)	1		1		
huier, conrad	1	2	3		
miller, frank	3		1		
miller, frank, jun	1	1	2		
Sterer, christian	1	2	7		
Sarius, Isaac	1	2	2		
woltz, andrew	4	1	2		
Gentner, andrew	1		2		
hilt (widow)		4	4		
lincoln, Joshua	2	4	5		
brown, benjamin	1	1	3		
beckler, daniel	1	2	3		
wilman, benjamin	1	2	4		
banner, mathias	1	2	5		
Gentner, Jacob	1	3	5		
wickly, bernhard	4	3	5		
hoch, george	1	1	5		
chwartz, Jacob	1		3		
Reed, michel	2	2	8		
keen (widow)			1		
keen, philip	1	1	2		
keen, niclas	1	3	4		
miller, francis	1	3	1		
hofses, anton	1				
hilt (widow)	2	2	6		
Eichorn, Jacob	1		3		
orf, fridrich	1				
wilman, Samuel	1	1	1		
hoch, michel	1				
boseman, Godlieb	1	2	3		
welt, pleosus	2		3		
Cramer, peter	2		1		
cramer, cristoph	1		2		
oberloch, John	1	4	4		
keller, william	2	6	5		
feiler, Stofel	1		5		
Schwartz, peter	1	3	2		
martin, John	2	1	3		
Shmit, christian	2		3		
horn, frederick	1	4	5		
Shuman, philp	1	2	2		
abraham, Susman	1				
levenzeler, adam	3	2	2		
wewer, John	3	3	1		
Shuman, John	3		3		
hoch, martin	1		2		
orf, nicolas	1	1	2		
orf, Stophel	2		2		
Sidenspire (widow)	1	1	4		
Sidenspire, charles	1		1		
keller, Jacob, Jun	1	2	2		
Remly, mathias	1	1	2		
lear, peter	1	2	2		
hossies, christian	1	1	3		
mink, philip	2	3	6		
keiser, francis	1	2	4		
Stall, philp	1		2		
miller, henry	1	4	4		
walk, henry	2	4	4		
kalor, charles	2	2	5		
farnsworth, william, Jun	2	5	6		
farnswort, william	1		2		
farnswort, Robert	1	1	2		
farnswort, Isaac	1	2	15		
morgin, James	2	1	5		
pitcher (widow)			4		
howard, Joshua	3	4	7		
burghart, henry	1	4	4		
ewell, henry	4	5	4		
houpe, Joseph	1	1	4		
heat, John	1	1	5		
Studley, John	1	2	3		
wihal, francis	1		2		
Jones, John	1	2	4		
hevener, mathias	1	3	3		
cumerer, Joseph	1	1	5		

FIRST CENSUS OF THE UNITED STATES.

LINCOLN COUNTY—Continued.

NOBLEBOROUGH TOWN—continued.

NAME OF HEAD OF FAMILY.	Free white males of 16 years and upward, including heads of families.	Free white males under 16 years.	Free white females, including heads of families.	All other free persons.	Slaves.
hossies, godfried	1	1	3		
Mink, valantin	1	1	2		
Payson, John	1	1	2		
warner, george	1	3	3		
oldham, peleg	2		2		
loring, judah	1		2		
pitcher, nath¹	2	2	3		
brow, Joseph	1		3		
turner, alexander	1		3		
drawbridge, John	1	3	1		
From Port Royal				2	
Simons (widow)			1		
haupt, John	1		1		
heisler, martin	1	1	3		
feiler, jaspar	1		1		
fitchgcarald, John	1	3	5		
Sider, cornelius	2	3	6		
cramer, John	1	1	1		
Sidlinger, martin	1		1		
Sidlinger, charles	1	1	2		
Sidlinger, daniel	1	2	1		
kintzel, John	1	1	5		
Sprague, nathan	4		3		
Sprague, michel	1	2	2		
Rota (widow)	1	1	3		
walter, peter	1	2	2		
hunt, John	2	1	3		
fielhauer, daniel	1	1	2		
bradex, John	2		1		
Simons, Stephen	1	2	4		
M°gayer, thomas	2	3	2		
cramer, Jacob	1	1	4		
cramer, charles	1	1	2		
cramer, fridrich	1		1		
turner, cornelius	3	4	4		
leicht, george	1		1		
leicht, peter	2	3	4		
kohn, paul	2	2	2		
winal, david	1	3	6		
keen, abner	2		1		
keller, charles	1	3	3		
Claus, george	1	2	2		
leicht (widow)	1	4	3		
bracht, peter	2	1	1		
bracht, John	1		2		
wagner, william	1		1		
wagner, andrew	1	1	2		
freeman, barnabas	1	2	1		
Eichorn, george	1	1	2		
benner, John	1	1	1		
benner, martin	2		4		
Snaudel, william	3	1	3		
werner, george	2		2		
Eichorn, daniel	1	1	4		
Eichorn, John	1	4	2		
hedwic, Joseph	2	3	6		
lach, asmus	1	3	4		
talheim, george	1		2		
Eichorn, michel	1	1	4		
Reed, Jacob	1		2		
brodman, Charles	1	2	2		
feller, Charles	1	1	3		
benner, John, Jun	1		2		
Snoutelgle, John	1	1	3		
benner, charles	1	2	4		
benner, Jacob	1	1	5		
benner (widow)			1		
ulmer, John	4	3	5		
Razor, charles	1	3	4		
koon, george, jun	1	5	3		
werner, John	1		1		
werner, charles	1				
Schwartz (widow)			3		
Schwartz, friderich	1		2		
demut, george	2	5	5		
demut, henry	1		2		
lish, paul	1		6		
leisner, george	1		2		
chapman (widow)	1	2	2		
chapman, abraham	1		2		
howard, caleb	3	3	7		
cole, Jabish	1		2		
Cole, Isaack	1	2	3		
Isley, michel	1	1	3		
kaastner, ludwig	2	5	3		
nash, Church	2	2	4		
andres, Sthephen	1	2	4	1	
Sides, loring	3	2	4		
newbert, Stophal	2		2		
newbert, John	1	2	2		
filor, John	1		2		
thomas, Joshua	1		1		
walk, peter	3	5	6		
heavener, charles	1		3		
burns, cornelius	1		3		
warner, John, Jun	1		3		
pilcher, abner	1		3		
winchafsaw, henry	1		4		
wade, jacob	2	5	5		
Simons, barnabas	1	2	4		
winal, ezechial	1	1	4		
Swatland, Samuel	2	3	4		
coles, ables	1	4	2		
Russell, Lewis	1	3	3		
prior, John	1	5	4		
fitch, william	3	3	3		
fogler, John	3	3	3		
Sidenspire, John	1	1	2		
andrew, michel	1		2	1	
mink, pacel	1	5	2		
Simons, Zebede	1	2	2		
Simons, Joseph	1	2	2		
lasse, John	1	1	4		
Shenck, Andrew	3		4		
kesler, John	1	1	2		
Shanemar, christian	1				
Shenk (widow)	1	3	3		
Starow, mathias	3	3	6		
Starow, andrew	2	3	3		
Samson, charles	1		2		
Samson, charles, Jun	2	3	5		
Simons, Eckiel (Hungh Island)	1	4	3		
Simons, Joab (Hungh Island)	1				
Simons, Isaac (Hungh Island)	1				
Sidenspire, george	1				
thomas, waterman	5	3	9		
payson, Samuel	1				
Sole (widow)			1		
cole, Josephus	1		3		
morphi (widow)			3		
hofses, george	1	2	3		
maning, Edward	1	2	5		
winchapaw, John	1	4	2		

NORRIDGEWOCK TOWN.

NAME OF HEAD OF FAMILY.	Free white males of 16 years and upward, including heads of families.	Free white males under 16 years.	Free white females, including heads of families.	All other free persons.	Slaves.
Stewart, Daniel	1	3	2		
More, Benjamin	1	2	4		
More, John	2	1	2		
More, Miriham			1		
Parlin, Joseph	1	3	2		
Parlin, Alford	1				
More, Goff	1	2	3		
Richard, Robert	1		3		
Spolden, Elezer, Jur	1	1	3		
Spolden, Elezer	2		2		
Spolden, Seth	1		2		
Wesson, William	1	2	1		
Lankister, David	1	3	4		
Smith, James	1				
Howard, oliver	2		3		
Linsy, Ephrom	1		1		
EsVuire, John	1		2		
Richard, Samuel	1		2		
Fernsworth, Peter	1	3			
Gilman, Zebulon	1		3		
Gilman, Robart	1	1	1		
Hale, Josiah	1	5	1		
Hale, Elizabeth			2		
Varnum, William	1				
Withey, Luke	1	4	1		
Parker, Edmond	1	2	1		
Adams, Amos	2	2	5		
Nutting, Josiah	3	4	2		
Adams, Amos, Ju	1				
Tarble, Joseph	1	1	3		
Withey, Uziel	1				
Layton, Jane		1	3		
Spolden, William	1		2		
Adams, James	1		2		
Wear, Ephrom	1				
Wood, Silas	1	1	2		
Amerson, Ezekiel	1		3		
Hines, Benjamin	1				
Amerson, Calvin	1				
Parlin, Jonathan	1				
Samson, John	1		1		
Martain, Moses	1	1	2		
Brown, George	1	5	3		
Bickford, Moses	1	1	3		
Laplain, James	1		3		
Devinport, John	1		3		
Gould, Meriah	1	1	3		
Thompson, Benjamin	1		1		
Hale, Josiah	1	5	1		
Brown, Ephron	1		3		
Layton, oliver	1				
Spolden, Thomas	1				
Layton, John	1	1	2		
Spolden, William, Ju	1	1	4		
Spolden, Josiah	1		1		
Withey, William	1				
Withey, Nathaniel	1				
Richard, Benjamin	1				
Clerk, John	1	6	5		
Withers, Longly	1				
Withers, Obediah	2	1	3		
Tarble, Joseph	1	1	3		
Longly, Zachry	2	2	3		
Hale, Thomas	1	1	3		
Ward, Ephrom	1	4	3		
Adams, Abraham	1				
Wood, Oliver	1	1	2		
Silvester, William	1		2		
Hale, John	1	5	4		
Parlin, Nathan	1	2	3		
Parlin, John	1	1	1		
Samson, Levi	1				
Keth, Zepheniah	1		3		
Sawyer, Silvinius	2	2	3		
Longly, Zacheriah	1	2	3		
Cook, Anna					
Brown, John	1	1	2		
Whitcum, Thomas	1		3		
Keth, Unite	1	1	3		
Pierce, David	1	1	1		
Peirce, Simon	3		1		
Keth, Alford	1				
Cook, John	2	1	2		

NORRIDGEWOCK TOWN, SETTLEMENT EAST OF.

NAME OF HEAD OF FAMILY.	Free white males of 16 years and upward, including heads of families.	Free white males under 16 years.	Free white females, including heads of families.	All other free persons.	Slaves.
Macfassen, Dagle	1	1	3		
More, Joseph	1	1			
Whitcum, Robart	1				
Russel, Jonathan	1		2		
Russel, Jason	1	1	1		
Nutting, Samuel	1	3	2		
Becker, Magnus	1	2	6		
Russel, Josiah	1				
Warrin, Josiah	1	5	3		
Shade, Amos	1		2		
Shade, William	1				

PITTSTON TOWN.

NAME OF HEAD OF FAMILY.	Free white males of 16 years and upward, including heads of families.	Free white males under 16 years.	Free white females, including heads of families.	All other free persons.	Slaves.
Springer, Thomas	1	3	2		
Andrews, Ely	2	1	2		
Soper, Seth	1	1	1		
Owens, Thomas	1	2	3		
Lapham, Roger	1	2	4		
Colburn, Benjamin	2	4	6		
Jackson, Thomas	1	2	1		
Smith, Henry	7		6		
Law, John	1	1	2	1	
Philbrook, David	1	1	2		
Winslow, Carpenter	1	1	1		
Winslow, Jonª	1		1		
Tarbox, Eleazer	1	4	1		
Currier, James	1				
Barker, John	1	1	1		
Whidden, Mark	1		3		
Mason, Sam¹	1	3	6		
Young, David	2	4	4		
Dudley, James	2	1	3		
Clark, Isaac	1	2	4		
Clark, Burnham	1	1	1		
Dudley, Jeremiah	1	2	3		
Burnes, Joseph	1		1		
Dudley, Samuel	2	3	2		
Blodget, Joseph	2		1		
Hatch, Isaac	1				
Hunt, Benoni	1		3		
Hunt, Benoni, Jur	1		1		
Clark, Timothy	1	1	4		
Prat, Ebenezer	1		3		
Moody, Scribner	1	1	4		
Moody, Jeremiah	1		2		
Pickard, James	2	1	4		
Little, Daniel	1				
Pickard, Thomas	1	2	1		
Palmer, Anna	3	1	2		
Cooper, Leonard	2	2	3		
Bailey, John	1	2	6		
Bln, David	1	1	2		
Glidden, Arnold	1	1	4		
Pulcifer, Joseph	3		3		
Grant, Sam¹	4	1	3	1	
Leasunesse, John	2	4	2		
Lang, Sam¹	2	3	2		

HEADS OF FAMILIES—MAINE.

LINCOLN COUNTY—Continued.

NAME OF HEAD OF FAMILY.	Free white males of 16 years and upward, including heads of families.	Free white males under 16 years.	Free white females, including heads of families.	All other free persons.	Slaves.
PITTSTON TOWN—con.					
Piper, Jonª	1		1		
Doar, James	1		3		
Broadstreet, Andw	3		5		
Towns, Thomas	1		7		
Moore, Reuben	4	3	3		
Goodwin, Simeon	1	3	5		
Wakefield, Dominicus	1	1	1		
McCaslin, Robert	1	2	1		
Berry, Nathl	1	2	3		
Kimbal, Nathl	4	2	2		
Doar, Henry	1	1	2		
Shaw, Benjn	2	3	5		
Pollard, Ezekiel	1	2	1		
Byram, Ebenezer	4		5		
Gay, Seth	2	1	5		
Barker, Willm	2		3		
Jewett, Zedadiah	2	3	5		
Oldham, Jonª	1			4	
Gardiner, Gideon	1	1	3		
McCasslin, Henry, Jur	2	2	2		
McCasslin, Henry	2	1	3		
Nason, Robert E	1	3	2		
Doar, Benaiah	2		3		
Warren, Petten	1	2	4		
Pollard, Elijah	1	1	4		
Doar, Allen	1		2		
Berny, Thos	1	3	1		
Wakefield, Jereh	1	1	2		
Evans, James	1	1	2		
Jewett, Stephen	4		1		
Fitts, Brown Farm	2	1	1		
Lawrence, David	4	2	2		
Eastman, Saml, Jur	1				
Quincy, Henry	2				
Haley (Widow)	4	1	3	5	
Moore, David	1	4	3		
Mason, Abner	5	3	5		
Mason, Abner, Jur	1		1		
Bailey, Nathel	2	4	5		
Dunham, David	1	4	4		
Fuller, Edward	1	3	4		
Bailey (Widow)	1		1		
Davis, Ezra	4		4		
Agry, Thomas	2	1	4		
Agrey (Widow)	4		2		
Colburn, Reuben	7	1	8		
Oakman, Saml	2	1	5		
Springer, Willm	3	1	5		
Blanchard, Jonª	3	1	6		
Easman, Saml	2		4	1	
Shepherd, Levi	1		1		
Robinson, —	1		2		
Pitts, Abel	1				
Flitner, Willm	2	2	3		
Taggot, James	1	2	2		
Walker, Richard	1		1		
Jakens, Christopher	2	3	2		
Dearborn, Henry	3	2	5		
POWNALBOROUGH TOWN.					
Hodge, Henry	6	1	3	2	
Lee, Silas	1	1	3		
Wood, Abiel	31	4	7		
Price, Thomas	3	3	6		
Thaxter, William	1	1	2		
Whittier, Ebenezer	2	1	3		
Cook, Francis	1	3	5		
Payson, David	2		2		
Payson, David, Jnr	2		4		
Bryson, Peter	3		2		
Hughes, John	4	1	3		
Tinkham, Seth	1	2	3		
Crooker, Elijah	2		1		
Arvel, John	2		3		
Colby, Betty	1	2	2		
Carter, Samuel	1		2		
Craft, Foster	1				
Robey, Henry	1				
Sanborn, Bradbury	1				
Cowley, John	2	1	2		
Foster, William	2	1			
Seavey, Michael	1		2		
Stacey, Nimphar	2	3	4		
Place, Annas	1		3		
Place, Samuel	1	1	2		
Ranlet, Charles	1	3	2		
Stephens, Joseph	2	4	2		
Dalton, Jeremiah	3		2		
Blight, Mehitable			1		
Clough, Stephen	1	1	3		
Collins, Lemuel	1	2	4		
Stutson, Zealous	1	3	3		
Haynes, Patty		1	2		
Holmes, John	2		1		
POWNALBOROUGH TOWN—con.					
Light, Robert	6	3	5		
Clark, Nathan	2	1	3		
McAnere, Joseph	1		3		
Parsons, Timothy	9	3	10		
Elbes, Betty		1	4		
Woodman, Thomas	2				
Clark, James	1	2	3		
Langdon, John	3	3	3		
Barker, William	1	1	4		
Bradbury, Anna	1	1	2		
Nute, Paul	1	2	6		
Huntoon, Jonathan	1	3	1		
Blagdon, Rollins	2		2		
Acorn, Jacob	4	1	3		
Young, Reuben	1		2		
Harridon, Ignatious	1	1	1		
Foy, Robert	3		4		
Foy, John	1				
Colby, Susanna	4		4		
Holbrook, Joseph	1	1	1		
Moore, Thomas	1	1	4		
Wilson, John	1	1			
Kincaid, Reuben	1		6		
Ranlet, Henry	2	1	5		
Grandee, Charles	1		2		
Jones, Willm	1	1	3		
Holbrook, Richard	1		2		
Canady, Dennis	1		2		
Moffat, James	3	1	2		
Cunningham, Isaac	1		1		
Harrington, Joseph	1	1	3		
Bridge, John	1		4		
Seavey, John	3	1	3		
Appleton, John	1	2	2		
Flanders, Samuel	1		2		
Silvester, David	2	2	2		
Silvester, Mary	1		2		
Askins, Alexander	4	3	3		
Decker, Joseph	3	3	3		
Langdon, Timothy	1	2	5	1	
Hammon, Frederick	1		2		
Noyes, Thomas		1	4		
Lion, Ezekiel	1	1	4		
Waldo, Benjamin	1	1	2		
Evelet, James	1	2	3		
Hammon, Seth	1		1		
Frizzel, Benjn	4	1	2		
Bennet, Spencer	1	2	2		
Christopher, Joseph	1	2	6		
Woodman, Jacob	1	1	1		
Oaks, Joshua	1	1	3		
Adams, John	1		3		
Merrow, Patrick	1	1	4		
Decker, John	1				
Seavey, William	2	1	3		
Pottle, Hezekiah	2	2	5		
Holbrook, John	2	1	3		
Young, Isaac	4	2	2		
Silvester, Samuel	1	4	4		
Handy, Jonathan	1	2	3		
Sterrey, David	2	2	3		
Williamson, Jonathan	1		3		
Blaire, William	1	1	2		
Duncan, John	1	2	4		
Williamson, Sarah			6		
Kanady, James	1	1	2		
Capen, James	2	2	6		
Quinham, James	2	2	1		
Scott, Daniel	1	1	4		
Smith, Manassa	1	4	5		
Smith, Silas	1		2		
Averel, Samuel	1	6	4		
Averel, Job	2		3		
Fairservice, John	1				
Fairservice, Thomas	2	1	2		
Cheney, Ralph	1	5	3		
Smith, Rogers	2	2	5		
Kincaid, Abigail		2	1		
Forestel, James	1	1	3		
Tucker, John	1	1	2		
Frissel, John	1	1	2		
Clark, William	1	3	3		
Kean, John	1	1	3		
Baker, John	1	5	4		
Dickerson, Abijah	2	4	3		
Dickerson, Samuel	1		2		
Hilton, John	1		3		
Sloman, William	2	2	4		
Honnowel, John	2		4		
Dole, Nathan	1	1	2		
Kenny, Benjamin	1		3		
Gitchel, John	1	1	3		
Hilton, William	1	1	3		
Hilton, Samuel	1	1	4		
Honnowel, Israel	1	1	4		
POWNALBOROUGH TOWN—con.					
Hilton, Joshua	2	1	4		
Dilano, Amasa	1		1		
Chapman, John	2	2	5		
Boynton, Hannah			4		
Taylor, Joseph	3	2	3		
Gray, Alexander					
Boynton, William	1	1	1		
Chovey, John	1		3		
Briggs, John	1	2	1		
Boynton, Joshua	1	1	1		
Blackledge, Jonathan	1	2	2		
Chapman, John, Jr	2		2		
Colman, Jonathan	1	1	1		
Pierce, John	2		1		
Nutter, Anthony	1	2	5		
Young, Joshua	6		5		
White, Jesse	2	3	5		
Nason, Abraham	2		3		
McKenney, David	2	3	2		
Boynton, Joshua, Jnr	1	3	3		
Hilton, Joseph	1	1	5		
Hilton, Morril	1	1	2		
Savage, John	1		3		
Hilton, Moses	1	3	6		
Hamden, Gabriel	1		2		
Mansfield, James	2	3	2		
Baker, Willm C	2		1		
McKenney, John	3	4	6		
McKenney, Danl	1	1	3		
Muncey, David	1	1			
Kincaid, John	1		5		
Muncy, Napthali	1	4	1		
Jackson, James	1				
Blagdon, Paul	1	2	3		
Coffin, Benjª	1	2	3		
Coffin, Benjª, Jnr	1	2	5		
Decker, William	1	1	1		
Pressey, Will	1		1		
Jackson, Samuel	1	4	6		
Jackson, Benjª	1	5	3		
Hersey, Solomon	3	1	5		
Hodge, James			1		
Prince, Isaac	1	1	2		
Mannis, Nathan	3	2	5		
Frost, Ichabod			1		
Brookin, Hannah	1	5	2		
Webber, Nicholas	2	4	4		
Boynton, Oliver	1		3		
Fletcher, Samuel	1	3	3		
Boynton, John	1	2	3		
Bayley, Thaddeus	4		2		
Bailey, Richard	1	2	6		
Plummer, David	1	2	5		
Mason, Stephen	1		1		
Allen, Amos	1	2	3		
Monro, Stephen	1		2		
Gardiner, Willm	3		2		
Brackley, Willm	3	4	4		
McGown, John	1	3	2		
Dunlap, Archibald	3	1	2		
Goodwin, Jeremiah	1	1	2		
Call, James	1				
Clancey, David	3	1	7		
Bickford, Henry	3	4	1		
Bridge, Edmund	1	4	2		
Bickford, Paul	1	2	6		
Barker, Carr	1	4	7		
Barker, Caleb	1	5	5		
Allen, Peter	2	3	4		
Obrien, William	2	5	6		
Page, John	2	1	1		
Call, Obadiah	1	2	3		
McPharlen, Joseph	2	4	3		
Patterson, William	1	5	2		
Pushaw, George	2		2		
King, Moses	2	2	2		
Stiflen, George	2	2	3		
Kendal, Abiathar	1	2	2		
Goud, James	1		2		
Parish, John	1	2	1		
Parish, George	1	5	4		
Southward, Abram	1	6	6		
Holland, Lemuel	1	6	1		
Carlow, Jacob	5	2	5		
Hoodlet, Lewis	2	1	2		
Miers, Philip	2	3	2		
Rittle, Francis	2		3		
Hunt, Steward	2	1	3		
Andrews, Asa	2	3	6		
Ely, Samuel	2	3	4		
Averel, Mary					
Averel, Samuel	2	2	3		
Clark, James	2	3	3		
Clark, William	2	3	3		
Lord, Abraham	1	2	3		

FIRST CENSUS OF THE UNITED STATES.

LINCOLN COUNTY—Continued.

POWNALBOROUGH TOWN—con.

NAME OF HEAD OF FAMILY.	Free white males of 16 years and upward, including heads of families.	Free white males under 16 years.	Free white females, including heads of families.	All other free persons.	Slaves.
Smith, Cheney	4	3	4		
Averal, John	1	3	5		
Gray, Moses	2	1	3		
Hilton, Joseph	2	1	4		
Hoit, Thomas	1		2		
Tobey, Barnabas	1	2	4		
Averel, Willm	2	5	2		
Boynton, Pelatiah	1	3	2		
Meirs, George	1	6	6		
Reid, Jonathan	3	3	2		
Gould, George	1	3	3		
Fisher, Peter	1	2	2		
Kidder, Richard	3	2	3		
Goodwin, Saml	1		1		
Goodwin, Saml, Ju	4	4	4		
Johnson, John	1	5	3		
Fwicross, Lydia	1	2	1		
Hatch, Paul	1	1	5		
Ramsdale, George	2	2	4		
Patten, Willm	1	2	2		
Woodward, Saml	3	3	4		
Tupper, James	1	4	2		
Taylor, Ezra	1		4		
Dinsmore, Asa	1	2	4		
Stilfan, Mich^l	2	2	1		
Brown, Jacob	2	3	5		
Theobald, Philip	1	1	5		
Atkins, James	2		1		
Corteloe, John	1	3	3		
White, Saml	1		4		
Spring, Daniel	2	3	5		
Lamercier, Peter	1	1	5		
D.Pollereski, John	1	1	4		
Rittle, Francis	2	1	5		
Rittle, John	1	2	1		
Pushaw, Peter	2		6		
Lewis, William	1	2	2		
Segar, John	1	1	1		
Call, Stephen	2	4	1		
Hatch, Nathan	1	1	2		
Call, Deliverance	1	2	3		
Call, Philip	1	2	1		
Patterson, Margaret	3		3	1	
Calahan, Rebecca	1		2		
Hatch, Simeon	1	2			
White, John	1	2	4		
Reid, Amos	1	2	3		
Libbey, George	4	3	3		
Hathorn, Nathl	1	3	3		
Gray, Samuel	1	3	2		
Hathorn, James	1	1	3		
Currice, Ephraim	2	1	6		
Doe, Mary	1	3	3		
Nelson, Jacob	2	1	4		
Smith, Asa	3	3	3		
Askins, George	1	3	3		
Ayers, James	2	2	6		
Nelson, Mary	2	1	4		
Carlton, Joseph	2	4	3		
Carlton, Moses	4	1	9		
Adle, Cornelius	1	1	4		
Askins, Christopher	1		2		
Plummer, John	2	5	5		
Rollins, Moses	1	1	2		
Perkins, John	1	1	2		
Seavey, Stephen	2		2		
Seavey, Solomon	1	5	3		
Young, Benj^a	1	1	6		
Pressey, Benj^a	1	2	2		
Lowel, Joseph	2	2	4		
Chatman, Saml	1	1	1		
Burr, Joseph	1		2		
Dwinnel, Moses	1	1	3		
Leman, Henry	1		1		
Lambert, James	1		4		
Pressey, Sarah					
Groves, William	1	1	3		
Greenleaf, Benj^a	1	3	2		
Arnold, Willm	2	1	2		
Foy, Willm	1	4	3		
Stinson, Willm	1		2		
Thompson, Joseph	2	3	4		
Ranlet, Nathl	3	4	2		
Kingsbury, John	2	5	5		
Pressey, Jacob	4	2	1		
Churchill, Susanna			4		
Pressey, Jacob, Ju^r	1	1	2		
Booker, Nicholas	2		1		
Averal, Israel	1	3	4		
Gurrel, John	1	3	2		
Clark, Joseph	1				
Clark, James, Ju^r	1		1		
Clark, John	1	1	3		
Boynton, David	1	3	4		
Booker, Benj^a	1		4		

POWNALBOROUGH TOWN—con.

NAME OF HEAD OF FAMILY.	Free white males of 16 years and upward, including heads of families.	Free white males under 16 years.	Free white females, including heads of families.	All other free persons.	Slaves.
Hamlen, Levi	1	2	2		
Lowel, Jacob	1	3	3		
Sole, Amasa	1	1	2		
Whittier, Joseph	1	2	3		
Farr, Joseph	2		1		
Walker, Abraham	1	4	5		
Gray, Moses, Jn^r	1	3	6		
Bean, Jon^a	1	2	1		
Rowe, John	1		3		
Muncy, Jonathan	3	1	3		
Flanders, Saml	1		2		

PRESCOTTS AND WHITCHERS PLANTATION.

NAME OF HEAD OF FAMILY.					
Thompson, John	1				
Withern, Arnold	1				
Ladd, Josiah	1		3		
Lambart, Abraham				1	
Howland, Elijah	1	2	3		
Gordon, David	1				
Mattock, Richard	1				
Allen, William	1	1	1		
Killsroth, Patrick	1	2	2		
Allen, John	1	1	1		
Whiteher, Moses	1				
Whiteher, Clerk	1	2	1		
Gordon, Jonathan	1				

ROCKMEEKO TOWN, EAST SIDE OF RIVER.

NAME OF HEAD OF FAMILY.					
Addams, John	2		1		
Weston, abraham	3	2	6		
Jackson, Nathaniel	1		4		
fullar, thomas	1	1	1		
fuller, Nathaniel	1	1	2		
Discomb, Thomas	1	2	2		
Mills, Josiah	1		2		
Rogars, John	1		2		
Winter, John	1	1	1		
Cocah, David	1	1	3		
leucrmore, William	1				
black, Garsham	1				
Wright, Oliver	1				
Wiman, thomas	1				
Craft, Moses	1				
fuller, Oliver	1				
fuller, Salham	1				
Craft, henry	1				
Craft, Moses, jr	1				
West, Isaac	1				
west, Obediah	1				
Uslis, William	1				
Bartlet, Solomon	1				
Bartlet, Peter	1				
Massey, Benjn	1				
fuller, Nathan	1				

SANDY RIVER, FIRST TOWNSHIP.

NAME OF HEAD OF FAMILY.					
Sewall, Samuel	1	3	2		
Brainard, Ely	1	2	1		
Knowlton, Samuel	1	2	1		
Wood, John	1	3	5		
Chandler, Samuel	1	3	2		
Gould, Silas	1	3	3		
Butterfield, Ephrom	1				
Nutting, Thomas	1				
Green, Josiah	1				
Hiscock, Thomas	1	1	4		
Gould, Jesse	1				
Gould, William	1		4		
Weathern, Benjamin	1	1	2		
Chandler, Moses	1	3	2		
Kinney, Thomas	1		2		
Mores, Thomas	1		4		
Page, Timothy	1		4		
Butterfield, Samuel	3	3	4		
Turner, Reuben	1		5		
Worit, Josiah	1	1	3		
Powers, Isaac	1		2		
Starling, Moses	3	2	1		
Eaton, Jacob	1	3	5		
Maccardy, James	1				
Surtain, John	1	2	4		
Page, Isaac	1	3	2		
Butler, Benjamin	1	3	4		
Bradford, Joseph	2	1	6		
Handy, Benjamin	1	2	3		
Potter, Ezekiel	1	1	3		
Battle, Joseph	1		3		
Rions, Joseph	1		2		
Smith, Jotham	1	2	2		

SANDY RIVER, FIRST TOWNSHIP—con.

NAME OF HEAD OF FAMILY.	Free white males of 16 years and upward, including heads of families.	Free white males under 16 years.	Free white females, including heads of families.	All other free persons.	Slaves.
Gay, Peter	4	2	7	1	
Pickit, Jonathan	1		2		
Cox, Hugh	1				
Brigs, Samuel	2		2		
How, Lemuel	1	4	3		
Parker, Josiah	2	2	2		
Winslow, James	3		3	1	
Cowing, Ephrom	2	1	2		
Brigs, Adin	1		2		
Cowing, David Baley	1	1	1		
Adams, Moses	2		2		
Russ, Simeon	1	5	3		
Jones, Robart	2		2		
Clayton, John	1	2	1		
Hustings, John	2	5	2		
Brown, Joseph	3		2		
Swift, Turner	1	1	1		
Rise, John	1				
Butterfield, Reuben	1				
Tibbits, Edward	1		4		
Cregg, Enoch	1	1	2		
Cannaday, William	1	1	1		
Silvester, Joseph	4	4	3		
Greeley, Seth	3	4	6		
Keen, Samuel	1		3		
Bullin, Joshua	1				
Brainard, Church	1	2	2		
Blackston, Lydia		2	3		
Gore, Robart	2	3	7		
Tufts, Francis	3	3	3		
Blunt, Lydia	1		1		
Lowell, Reuben	2	2	5		
Knowlton, Jonathan	2	4	5		
Norton, Elijah	2				
Clough, Benjamin	1				
Whiteher, Benjamin	3	1	4		
Baly, Oliver	1	2	2		
Baley, Eliphalet	1	2	2		
Ralph, Joseph	1				
Howland, Joseph	1		2		
Perham, Lemuel	4		2		
Greely, Joseph	3	1	2		
Sweet, Ebenezer	2		1		
Blake, Josiah	1	2	2		
Davis, Nathaniel	1		1		
Page, Amos	2	2	3		
Butterfield, Samuel, Ju^r	1	1	1		
Page, Ezekiel	1		1		
Hartwell, Oliver	1				
Ames, Samuel	1	2	3		
White, William	3	3	1		
Bullin, Samuel	1		1		
Smith, Abraham	2	1	3		
Adams, Solomon	2	1	3		
Corbet, Peter	2	2	2		
Jiteum, Stephen	1	3	5		
Blodget, Nehemiah	1	1	1		
Withers, Zoe	1		2		
Webber, Ezekiel	1	2	4		
Gore, William	1		3		
Lowell, Joshua Bartlet	1				
Butterfield, Jesse	1	2	3		
Luice, Daniel	1	3	4		
Butterfield, Jonas	2	1	3		
Blunt, Ebenezer	1				

SANDY RIVER, FROM ITS MOUTH TO CARRS PLANTATION.

NAME OF HEAD OF FAMILY.					
Mackinney, Daniel	1	2	1		
Boldin, Nahum	1	1	2		
Davis, John	1	1	1		
Grover, John	1	2	2		
porter, Peter	1				
Bickford, Henry	1		2		
Bickford, James	1		1		
Leman, Jacob	1		5		
Leman, David	1	1	3		
Wilson, oliver	1	4	5		
Hitton, Benjamin	2	3	4		
Nichols, George	2	2	5		
Houghton, Thomas, Jr.	1		2		
Whitcum, Thomas	1				
Sawyer, George	1		2		
Dutton, Elijah	1				
Dutton, John	1	2	2		
Waugh, Thomas	1	3	3		
Waugh, James	2	4	3		
Sawyer, Luke	1	1	3		
Wood, Nathan	1	2	3		
Crosby, Jonathan	1				
Greenlief, Joseph	1	1	5		
Skillin, Lewis	1		2		
Sheaf, Samson	1	1	1		

HEADS OF FAMILIES—MAINE.

LINCOLN COUNTY—Continued.

NAME OF HEAD OF FAMILY.	Free white males of 16 years and upward, including heads of families.	Free white males under 16 years.	Free white females, including heads of families.	All other free persons.	Slaves.	NAME OF HEAD OF FAMILY.	Free white males of 16 years and upward, including heads of families.	Free white males under 16 years.	Free white females, including heads of families.	All other free persons.	Slaves.	NAME OF HEAD OF FAMILY.	Free white males of 16 years and upward, including heads of families.	Free white males under 16 years.	Free white females, including heads of families.	All other free persons.	Slaves.
SANDY RIVER, FROM ITS MOUTH TO CARRS PLANTATION—con.						**SEVEN MILE BROOK TOWN—con.**						**SMITHTOWN PLANTATION—continued.**					
Whittum, Caleb	1	2	6			Gray, George	1	1	1			Bary, Jonn	2		3		
Fish, Nathan	1	6	2			Alby, Isaac	1		1			McGunrey, John	1				
Williamson, Samuel	2	3	3			Fling, Morris	1		4			Weber, Stephen	2	1	2		
Green, Joseph	1		2			Yongue, David	2	2	5			Webber, Joseph	1		2		
Crosby, Asa	1		1			Macdanniels, James	1	2	5			Dudley, andrew	3	2	3		
Greenlief, William	1					Forbus, John	1					Baker, Jonn	1	3	1		
Greenlief, Joshua	1					More, John	1	2	1			Baker, Elkrer	1	2	2		
Gray, Amos	1		2			Gitchel, John	1		1			hinkley, Benjn	1	3	4		
Yongue, Joshua	1	1	2			Midcalf, John	2		1			Richardson, abijah	1	4	4		
Williamson, Jonathan	2	2	2			Mackinney, James	1		1			Dunlap, James	1	4	2		
Whittum, Daniel	2	1	1	1		Pain, David	1					Potter, Saml	1	5	2		
Pattin, Nathaniel	1					Pain, Joseph	1					Robinson, Jabez	1	6	5		
Gray, Ebenezer	1					Drummon, Reatherford	1					Potter, Joseph	1		5		
Crosby, Robert	2	3	3			Wade, Charles	1	3	4			Dunlap, Ebereser	1	3	4		
Whittum, Benjamin	1	2	3			Alby, Samuel	1					Dunlap, Robert	1	2	7		
Whittum, Benjamin, Jur	1					Pain, Thomas	1					Goocer, Edward	1	1	1		
Yongue, William	1	3	4			Pain, William	1	2	1			Baker, Barrows	4	1	4		
Parker, James	1		2			Williams, Samuel	1	4	4			Smith, Thomas	3		7		
Pumroy, John	3	3	6			Hunniwell, Thomas	1	2	3			Smith, Benjn	3	3	6		
How, John	1	1	2			Danforth, David	1	2	6			Dunlap, William	1				
Taylor, Robert	1	1	2			Fling, Samuel	1					Shirtlef, James	1	3	1		
Gray, Reuben	1	3	4			Savage, Jacob	1	2	4			Cook, Saul	1	1	4		
Hinkly, Samuel	1	1	1			Mores, Abraham	1					Jackson, Joseph	3	2	5		
Kimbal, Nicholas	1		3			Drummon, Rutherford	1					Brown, John	1	2	1		
Whittum, Ebenezer	1	1										michel, Danbr	1				
Sanders, Rufus	1		3			**SMITHTOWN PLANTATION.**						Brown, William	1				
Arnold, Benjamin	1	3	3									Robinson, David	3		3		
Greenlief, John	1	2	3			Kinmah, James	1	1	3			Smith, Samuel	1				
Greenlief, Ebenezer	1	2	4			Caheel, Thomas	1		2			mograge, Thomas	1	2	3		
Brawn, Jeremiah	1	1	2			Springer, David	1		1			mograge, Charly	1				
Cook, Joseph	1	2	3			Tayler, James	1	1	2			Smith, thomas, Jr	1	2	4		
Brown, Ephrom	1	3	3			Johnson, John	1					Johnson, Adam	1	4	6		
Williamson, Stephen	1	2	1			Salley, William	1					marston, Nathaniel	1	2	1		
Emery, Nathaniel	1	6	1			Hall, Timothy	1	3	3			Baker, abner	4		4		
Taylor, Joseph	2	1	5			Parker, Elisha	3		4			Baker, Smith	1	2	3		
Taylor, Joseph, Ju	1					Springer, David, ju	1		3			Baker, Judah	1	2	3		
Taylor, Nathaniel, Ju	1	1	4			Springer, Andrew	1	1	3			haggat, Isaac	1				
Holbrook, Peter	1	4	1			Jewell, Enoch	1	1	5			huchinson, Nemiah	1				
Taylor, Nathaniel	1	1	3			Morgin, John	2	1	2			Starrde, Edward	1				
Whittum, Benjamin, Ju	1	1	2			Johnson, James	1	3	3			huchinson, Isaac	1				
Pattin, Benjamin	1	1	1			West, Samuel	2	1	3			Bunker, James	1				
Landers, Alvin	1					Priscott, James	1		2			hatch, hapcie			1		
						Loont, Joshson	1		2			Buterfeld, aron	1				
SANDY RIVER, MIDDLE TOWNSHIP.						True, Daniel	1		2			Galowell, Job	2		2		
Withern, Michal	1	2	1			True, John	1										
Read, William	1	2	5			True, aron	1					**STARLING PLANTATION.**					
Eaton, Eliab	1		1			True, abner	1		3			Manter, David	1				
Hiscock, William	2	1	2			Ores, William	1					wing, Benjn	1	1	3		
Bates, Thomas	2	2	3			Palmer, Mulbry	1					wing, Isral	1		3		
Sawyes, Jacob	2		3			Shaw, Isaac	1	1				hubard, frances	1		3		
Dodge, Benjamin	1	1	3			bab, Joshua	1	4	2			Marston, Joseph	1		3		
Humphries, David	1	1	2			bab, Bot (widow)			4			Morse, Isaac	1		3		
Flint, Edward	1		3			Bab, Jonthan, Ju	1		1			Morse, Philip	1	2	6		
McClary, Robert	1					bab, Jonthan						knowly, David	1				
Day, John	1	3	2			Riohiston, Irah	1	2	1			Judkins, Joel	1	3	2		
Humphries, Joseph	1	1	2			Hall, Calvin	1	3	3			Judkins, Joseph	1		2		
Colbey, Abel	1	1	4			Johnson, Adam	1		1			Judkins, Daniel	1				
Morrow, Timothy	1	1	2			Richison, Joshua	1	2	1			lane, Nathan	1				
						Hunttington, John	2					Barry, John	1				
SANDY RIVER, UPPER TOWNSHIP.						huntington, Benjn	1	1	2			Goodin, Elezer	1	1	2		
						Jewell, Henry	1	4	4			wiggens, Asa	1		2		
Humphries, Thomas	1		1			Huchinson, Samuel	2	6	3			Judkins, Benjn	1	2	3		
Dudley, Moses	1	5	3			Borman, Jonas	1	2	1			Page, John	1	1	2		
Thompson, Ebenezer	2	5	3			Potter, John	1	1	2			Rowell, Daniel	1				
Allen, Pirkins	2	2	7			Potter, William	1	4	3			Rusel, Abal	2	3	3		
Church, Charles	2		1			Watson, Daniel	1	1	5			Wolton, Joshua	3	2	3		
Ingham, Daniel	3		2			Watson, Daniel, ju	1		3			anderson, Joseph	1	1	2		
Dudley, Eliphalet	2	1	2			Neall, —*	1	1	3			Walton, Moses	1	2	6		
Spreague, Samuel	1	2	1			Smith, Eliphelat	3		2			Batchelor, Daniel	1		1		
Soul, Joshua	3	2	4			Sawyer, Joseph	1					Batchelor, Moses	1				
Thompson, Isaac	1		1			Sawyer, John	1					French, Moses	1				
						Potter, hugh	1	2	1			Cliford, Benja	1				
SEVEN MILE BROOK TOWN.						Potter, Andrew	1		2			Brown, Isaac	1				
						Colbee, thomas	1	1	1			Brown, Eliphelat	1				
Taylor, John	1					huntington, Timothy	1	1	4			Palmer, Benjn	1				
Taylor, Amos	1					tuckes, abraham	1	2	1			Tuck, Samuel	1				
Hines, Nimrod	1					Peace, James	1	1	1			Tuck, John M	1				
Hilton, Ellihu	1					Heal, John, jur	1		1			Basse, Jabas	1				
Drummon, Rutherford	1					hevemon, Levi	1	1	1			Basse, Solomon	1				
Parker, Josiah	1		2			Loud, James	2	1	3			Sturdevant, andrew	1	1	3		
Richardson, Ebenezer	1		2			Daniel, John	1	2	4			Sturdevent, abisha	1				
Huchings, David	2	4	3			Smith, Thomas	1	2	4			tilton, David	3				
Churchwell, John	1					Brocks, James	1					lane, Ephram	3	1	3		
Huchings, Olive		2	4			Neal, Joseph	1					lane, Ebenezer	1				
Craging, Simon	1		2			neal, George	1					Davies, Joseph	1				
Cleavland, Jonathan	1					noton, Jacob	1					Davies, Philp	1		1		
Cleavland, Joseph	1	3	1			noton, Joab	1		4	1		hilkon, William	1	2	3		
Pain, Isabillah		2	4			Jackson, Benjn	4	2	5			Richard, Jeremiah	1				
Perry, Reuben	1	1	2			Ring, Daniel	1	4	4			Barnfard, James	1				
Alby, Jonathan	1	2	2			Barry, Nathanel	2	1	3			Billings, Oliver	1		1		
						MacCaslin, James	1	2	2			Pitts, Shubal	1				
						MacCaslin, andrew	2	2	5			Wough, Robert	1				
						Piper, John	2		3			Emrson Brown	2		2		

*Illegible.

FIRST CENSUS OF THE UNITED STATES.

LINCOLN COUNTY—Continued.

NAME OF HEAD OF FAMILY.	Free white males of 16 years and upward, including heads of families.	Free white males under 16 years.	Free white females, including heads of families.	All other free persons.	Slaves.
STARLING PLANTATION—continued.					
Emrson, ——					
Elhings, Chase	1	3	2		
knowly, John	1	2	3		
Thomas, Richard	1				
Brocks, Gorge	1	3	3		
Ingham, David	1	1	2		
THOMASTON TOWN.					
Dillaway, John	3	2	4		
Dodge, Ezekiel Goddard	1	1	2		
Fales, Nathaniel	2	1	6		
Fales, Nathaniel, Junr	1	1	4		
Fales, James, Junr	1	1	2		
Fales, John	2	3	3		
Fales, David	5	5	6		
Jenks, David	2	2	4		
Porterfield, Patrick	2		4		
Shibles, Robert	2		1		
Vose, Thomas	4		5		
Vose, Spencer	2	1	2		
Wheaton, Mason	2		1		
Smith, Oliver	1	3	2		
Smith, Ablathar	1	4	3		
Woodcock, Nathaniel	2	2	2		
Stevens, Thomas	2	1	3		
Babbidge, Benjamin	1				
Stevens, Nehemiah	1		1		
Lamson, Jonathan	1	1	6		
McIntosh, William	1	1	1		
Tings, John	1	2	2		
Brown, Samuel	2	1	6		
Brown, James	1	3	3		
Green, William	3	2	6		
Kelloch, Findly	1	3	3		
Loveit, Israel	3	3	3		
Lackay, William	1	1	2		
McLallen, Thomas	2	2	2		
Robbins, Oliver	2	1	3		
Robbins, Otis	1	2	2		
Stackpole, James	2	3	4		
Simonton, John	2	3	5		
Case, Isaac	2	1	3		
Sayward, George	1	4	4		
Weed, James	1	3	5		
Foster, Charles	1		1		
Batchelder, Hezekiah	2		10		
Bridges, John	1	3	6		
Dean, Jonah	1	1	1		
Snow, Ephraim	2	2	3	1	
Rowell, William	2	1	3		
Coombes, Joseph	1	3	5		
Crouch, David	1	3	1		
Covell, Micajah	1		1	1	
Jordan, Israel	3	4	3		
Jordan, Robert	1	3	3		
Kating, Richard	1	4	4		
Webb, William	1	4	1		
Mathews, Anthony	1	2	2		
Mathews, Joseph	1		2		
Orbeton, James	1	1	5		
Orbeton, Jonathan	1	2	6		
Snow, Elisha	3	1	3		
Snow, Ambrose	1	1	2		
Sweetland, David	1		1		
Amory, George	1		1		
Crockit, Nathaniel	1		1		
Crockit, Nathaniel, Junr	2	4	7		
Heard, William	3	4	4		
Haskell, Francis	2	1	4		
Killsa, Hugh	1		4		
Killsa, George	1	3	2		
Packard, Benjamin	1		4		
Pilsbury, Joseph	1	4	4		
Pilsbury, Nathan	1	1	1		
Post, Stephen	1	3	4		
Spaulding, Timothy	1		3	1	
Witham, William		1	2		
Drought, Richard	1		2		
Stetson, William	2	4	2		
Spaulding, Jedidiah	1	1	3		
Gray, Eliphalet	2	3	2		
Brown, John	1				
Brown, Gideon	1				
West, John	2	3	3		
Bartlett, Samuel	1	4	5		
Butler, Phinehas	1	3	3		
Chapman, William	1	2	4		
Godden, John	1	3	4		
Hix, Thomas	1	3	3		
Ingraham, Job	1	6	2		
Ingraham, Joseph	1	2	2		
Ingraham, Josiah	1	2	1		
Lindsey, John	4	2	7		
Lowell, Rosamus	1	2	1		
THOMASTON TOWN—con.					
Perry, Joseph	1	2	1		
Perry, William	2		3		
Rendell, James	1	1	3		
Rendell, Thomas	2		4		
Sherman, Nathan	1	1	3		
Tolman, Jeremiah	1	1	2		
White, John	1	1	1		
Barrows, Ichabod	3		1		
Barrows, Comfort	1	1	3		
Barrows, Benajah	1	1	1		
Brewster, Zadok	2	1	5		
Crockit, Jonathan	2	3	3		
Crockit, John	1		2	1	
Fales, James	1	1	6		
Jameson, Robert	3		1		
Keen, John	1				
Renkins, Constant	2	4	3		
Spear, Jonathan	3	2	4		
Walsh, William	1				
Spear, William	1	2	1		
Spear, Jonathan, Junr	1		1		
Smith, Jonathan	1	2	1		
Tolman, Isaiah	1	4	4		
Ulmer, George	1	3	5		
Ulmer, John	1	1	1		
Watson, David	1	3	6		
Tolman, Samuel	2	2	2		
Tolman, Curtis	2	2	2		
Thomson, William	1	2	5		
Barnard, Isaac	1		3		
Bennett, David Mill	1				
Waterman, Nathaniel	1				
Hewitt, Waterman	1				
Cook, John	1				
Blackington, Benjamin	2	1	4		
Bly, Ebenezer	1		4		
Creighton, David	2	3	4		
Killsa, James	2	1	3		
Lewis, William	1		3		
Morse, Daniel	2	2	4		
Palmer, Daniel	2	3	6		
Robbins, Oliver, Junr	1	3	3		
Stevens, Thomas, Jun	1		2		
Thomson, Ebenezer	2		3		
Bentley, John	4		1		
Emerson, Thomas	1	1	1		
Stevens, Daniel	1				
Kelly, William	1				
Farrow, Peter	1				
Kingman, Loring	1				
Bacon, Michael	1				
Coil, John	1				
McIntyer, James	1				
TITCOMB TOWN.					
Hilton, Ebenezer	1	1	4		
Hilton, John	1	2	3		
Hustings, William	1	2	3		
Hambly, William	1	1	3		
Gray, John	2	1	7		
Mackfaying, James	1	4	7		
Chamberlain, John	1		1		
Chamberlain, Jeremiah	2		3		
Chamberlain, Stephen	1				
Hunniwell, William					
Hilton, William	1	3	3		
Thompson, Benjamin	2	3	3		
Calliborn, John	2	2	5		
Thompson, Aaron	3		5		
Green, Moses	1	3	2		
Thompson, John	1	1	3		
Martain, Nathl	1		5		
Stephens, Jonathan	1		3		
Thompson, Moses	1	2	1		
Airs, Moses	2	2	4		
Pelton, Joel	1				
Colbey, Benjamin	2	4	3		
Dor, Ruel	1				
Pain, Rachal			2		
Hancock, John	1	1			
Campbel, Wm	1				
Pierce, David	1				
Pierce, Calvin	1				
Pierce, Luther	1		1		
TOPSHAM TOWN.					
Graves, Johnson	2		2		
Graves, John	3	1	3		
Graves, Joseph	2	1	3		
Graves, Saml	2		4		
Henry, James	1	4	4		
Small, John	1				
Sanford, John	1	4	5		
TOPSHAM TOWN—con.					
Winchel, John	3	4	5		
Staples, Saml	1	2	6		
Foster, Josiah	1	3	6		
Owens, Gideon	2	5	6		
Rogers, John	3	2	3		
Patten, Thos	2		3		
Burk, Willm	1	6	4		
Berry, Joseph	2	4	2		
Rogers, Alexander	4	2	5		
Purrington, James	2	3	3		
Thompson, Saml	6	3	7		
Dugias (Widow)	1		3		
Whitney, Jon		2	3		
Patten, John1	3	2	4		
Jennison, Saml	3		9		
Sprague, Joseph	1	3	2		
Patten, Robert	2		4		
Sampson, James	2	4	5		
Sampson, Enoch	2		3		
Reid, David	2	4	2		
Fulton, John	4		5		
Stockman, Thos	3	2	5		
Stockman, Jacob	1	2	5		
Ailen, Saml	1	1	2		
Patten, Joseph	1		3		
Perkins, John	1	3	1		
Knowles, Richard	3		3		
Roy, Francis	1	1	4		
Gorden, Robert	1	1	3		
Winchel, Anna			2	1	
Putnam, Caleb	1	1	3		
Perry, Jon	3	1	3		
Merril, John	2	2	2	1	
Patten, Actor	3		3		
Haley, Pelatiah	2		4		
Dunlap, John	3	1	2		
Haley, Joseph, Jnr	3	2	7		
Wilson, Hugh	2	1	4		
Thompson, Alexander	1		2		
Whidden, John	3	2	4		
Alexander, Robert	5	1	2		
Ferren, Ebenezer	1	2	2		
Orr, Robert	1	1	6		
Whidden, John	2		2		
Wilson, Willm	2	5	4		
Mellet, Willm	1	2	3		
Seers, Willard	1		1		
Hinkley, Theos	1	1	3		
Pennel, Stephen	1	2	3		
Hinkley, Elnathan	1	3	3		
Dugan, Thos	2		3		
Lunt, Jobb	1	2	5		
Orr, John	2		4		
Allen, Pelatiah	1	2	5		
Wilson, James	2	5	3		
Blanchard, John	1	1	2		
Walker, Gideon	2	5	2		
Thompson, Benja	5		4		
Purington, James	1				
Hodgkins, Moses			2		
Owens, Moses	1	2	4		
Doughty, Stephen	2		5		
White, Elijah			2		
Jack, Joseph	1	3	4		
Wiman, Nathan	3		3		
Gray, Daniel	1	1	2		
Gray, Alexander	1	1	2		
Thompson, Alexander	1	1	3		
Wilson, Saml	1	1	2		
Wood, Isaac			2		
Ford, Daniel	2		1		
Walker, Jesse	1	1			
Rident, Mark	1		2		
Hewey, James	1	1	4		
Hewey, John	1		2		
Dunlap, John, Jnr	2	1	1		
Haley, Joseph	1	4	2		
Eaton, Benja	1	3	2		
Foster, Steel	1	4	7		
Cleaves, Robert	3	1	2	1	
Dow, Henry	1	5	3		
Hunter, James, Jnr	2	2			
Mustard, James	1		3		
Hunter, Arthur	1	5	4		
Hunter, Robert	3	3	4	1	
Hunter, James	3		4		
Work, Eben	2	2	7		
Hunter, Willm	3		4		
Malcom, Willm	1	2	2		
Randal, Ezra	1	2	2		
Randal, Willm	4	2	3		
Jones, John	1				
Reid, John	2	2	4		
Reid, Willm	4	1	2		
Reid, John, Junr	2	2	6		

HEADS OF FAMILIES—MAINE.
LINCOLN COUNTY—Continued.

NAME OF HEAD OF FAMILY.	Free white males of 16 years and upward, including heads of families.	Free white males under 16 years.	Free white females, including heads of families.	All other free persons.	Slaves.
TOPSHAM TOWN—con.					
Smith, Thomas	1		1		
Holt, Elizabeth	1	2	3		
Wilson, John	1	1	4		
Hunter, Willm	1	1	1		
Stockman, Saml	1	1	3		
Gowel, Charles	1	1	5		
Head, Moses	1		2		
Waid, Calvan	2	2	2		
Howland, Abraham	1		3		
Graves, John, Ju^r	1		3		
Duglas, Francis	1	4	5	6	
Staples, Stephen	3	3	3		
Fulton, James	3	1	3		
Rollins, Saml	1	3	1		
Tufts, Barnabas	2		4		
Thompson, Ezekiel	5	2	4		
TWENTY-FIVE MILE POND TOWN.					
Fowler, Matthew	1		2		
Chace, Stephen	1	2	6		
Runnels, Ephrom	1	3	6		
Brions, Baruch	1				
Dodge, Caleb	1	3	5		
Douglas, William	1	3	4		
Mirick, John	2	2	2		
Bennit, Peter	1		2		
Chace, John	1				
Fly, James	1		2		
Chace, Job	1				
Dody, Nicholas	1	1	1		
Runnels, Robert	1		2		
Bliffin, Increas	1		4		
Wesson, Edmond	1	2	3		
Mitchel, John	4	3	3		
Sewall, Thomas	1	3	3		
Smart, John	1				
Bartlett, Lamuel	1	2	2		
Mitchel, Joseph	1	1	4		
Hinkly, Miller	1	2	2		
Battle, Benjamin	1				
Burton, John	1				
Burton, Jabiz	1				
Brainard, Rachal			1		
Pishen, Charles	1		1		
Foot, John	1				
Whitten, George	1		2		
Whitny, Benjamin	1		1		
Carter, Padius	1				
UNION TOWN.					
Woodcock, David	3	1	5		
Nill, Samuel	1	2	2		
Maxey, Joseph	2		2		
Guild, Joseph	1	2	2		
Hawes, Abijah	1	2	2		
Robbins, Philip	1		4	2	
Robbins, Josiah	2	5	3		
Robbins, David	2	5	3	1	
Robbins, Ebenezer	1		3		
Mero, Amariah	1	1	4		
Hawes, Moses	1	1	4		
Hawes, Matthias	1	1	4		
Adams, Joel	3	3	4		
Robbins, Jesse	1		2		
Cummings, Richard	1	3	4		
Gilmore, Rufus	1	1	2		
Irish, Ichabod	1	3	5		
Butler, John	1	4	4		
Butler, Phinehas	2		2		
Butler, Christopher	1	2	6		
McLintock, Robert	2		3		
Daggett, Thomas	3		2		
Daggett, Samuel	1	4	4		
Daggett, Thomas, Jun	1	1	4		
Jennison, Ebenezer	1				
Luce, Seth	1	4	3		
Morse, Levi	1				
Robbins, Bela	1	1	3		
Ware, Jason	1		4		
Newhall, Jonathan	1	1	1		
Walcott, Spencer	1				
Hart, William	1				
Steward, Timothy	1				
Bowen, Ezra	1	2	4		
Dunnam, Samuel	1	2	2		
Grinnell, Royal	1		4		
Grinnell, Bailey	1	3	1		
Robbins, Philip, Junr	1		1		
Wight, John Morse	1				
UNION TOWN—con.					
Coffin, Uriah	1				
Reed, Josiah	1				
Bennett, Asa	1				
VASSALBOROUGH TOWN.					
Fairwell, Eben^r	4	1	3	2	
Fairwell, Isaac	2		5	4	
Pirkins, Solomon	2	2	5		
Moore, Eben^r	1	5	5		
Horner, Capt	4	1	4		
Haws, Thomas	3	2	3		
Haws, Thomas, jun^r	1		3		
Merchant, John	1	1	3		
Gardiner, Gothro	2		5		
Cowin, William	1	1	5		
Bassett, Saml	1	3	3		
Fought, Jacob	1	2	5		
Brawn, Joseph	1	3	6		
Green, Richard	1	2			
Newcomb, David	1	2	2		
Webber, —*	1	6	5		
Raglin, —*	(*)	(*)	(*)		
Raglin, —*	2	2	5		
Cowin, George	2	5	3		
Mathews, James	1	2	3		
Bacon, James	2	3	2		
Robinson, Winthropt	1	1	3		
Webber, Joseph	4		3	1	
Ballard (Widow)	3		4		
Wing, Gidion	1	1	3		
Bragg, Shuball	1	1	1		
Freeman, Benjamin	1	3	4		
Getchell, Samuel	3	6	3		
Wyman, Francis	1	5	1		
Freeman, Reuben	1	4	2		
Weeks, Phinias	1	1	2		
Fairwell, Bunker	3		4		
Hatch, Sylvanus	1	3	2		
Crowell, Joseph	2		2		
Warren, Richard	2	2	4		
Clark, Jonathan	1	2	4		
Cross, Willm	4	2	3		
Cross, Benj	2	3	5		
Cross, James	1				
Tarbell, —*	1	2	3		
Robins, Herman	2	1	3		
Robins, David	2	1	5		
Wing, Willm	1		2		
Wing, Willm, Junr	2	1	2		
McGlothlin, Gibbins	1		5		
Tillton, John	2		5		
Burges, Jonathan	1	1	4		
Burges, Avery	1		2		
Jackson, David	1		7		
Cross, Cabot	1		2		
Linkley, Saml	1	2	2		
Fairfield, Jeremiah	2	2	3		
Seaward, Giles	1		4		
Robinson, Levi	3	2	2		
Getchell, Neheh	3	6	2		
Redington, Asa	3	2	1		
Getchell, Maj^r	3	1	3		
Childs, Amos	1	1	2		
Low, Jonathan	1	2	4		
Hobbey, Remington	1	4	7	1	
Hussey, Palith^l	1	1	1		
Taber, Jacob	3	1	3		
Jackson, Charles		1	2		
Jackson, John	1		5		
Doe, Nathl	1	5	3		
Pilsbury, Thomas	2	2	5		
McFaden, Daniel	1	2	4		
Doe, James	2		5		
Taylor, John	2	2	4		
Pettee, Elen^r	1	1	11		
Pettee, John	2		10		
Pinkham, Reuben	1	2	2		
Mathews, Edmond	1		3		
Fought, Anthony	1	1	6		
Mathews, Elisher	1	3	4		
Fought, Fredrick	1	3	4		
Runels, Esqr	3		4		
Runels, Nathl	1	2	3		
Runels, David	1				
Runels, Jonathan	1	1	7		
Dyer, Benjamin	1	5	4		
Brach, Benjamin	1	3	3		
Branch, Samuel	1	3	4		
Sherwin, Mr	2	1	3		
Tiffany, Saml	2		3		
Fowler, John	1		1		
VASSALBOROUGH TOWN—continued.					
Thomas, Ichabod	2		2		
Thomas, Joseph	2		4		
Cromit, John	1				
Dudley, Daniel	1	2	2		
Chase, Eben^r	1	2	1		
Tiffany, Daniel	1				
Sawtel, David	1		3		
Sawtel, Moses	3	3	3		
Sawtel, Nathl	1	1	4		
Sawtel, Reuben	1		2		
Swift, John	1	1	2		
Longley, Neh^h	1	2	7		
Sawtel, Jonas	1		1		
Trask, John	1	2	3		
Trask, Eben^r	1	2	3		
Cowin, Isaac	1	1	3		
Jackson, John	2		2		
Jackson, Lem^{ul}	1	2	3		
Jackson, Sam^{el}	1	1	4		
Jackson, John, Ju^r	1		1		
Hutcherson, James	1	4	1		
Branch, Benj	1		2		
Jackson, Joseph	1		1		
Townsen, Daniel	1		3		
Lovejoy, Capt	2	3	5	3	
Lovejoy, Ablel, Jr	1	1	6		
Hastings, Moses	2	3	6		
Marsh, John	1		2		
Hasting, Matthew	1		2		
Towsend, Dodifer	2	2	5		
Clerk, Joseph	1		2		
Doe, Dudley	1	3	6		
Smiley, David	1	1	4		
Balintine, Sam^{el}	1		4		
Fish, David	1	1	1		
Moor, Levi	1	2	3		
Roberts, Willm	1	1	7		
Smiley, Thomas	1	1	5		
Smiley, Hugh	1		2		
Smiley, Alex^r		2	2		
Smiley, Willm	1	2	3		
Moor, Collins	1	2	4		
Bragg, John	1	3	5		
Hoxkey, Hez^h	4		3		
Barton, Flint	2	5	3		
Robinson, Timothy	2		3		
Bacon, Eben^r	4		2		
Davis, Joshua	2	3	5		
Brown, Solomon	2	1	4		
Deleno, Peleg	2	1	3		
Deleno, Benj	1		2		
Brooks, Willm	1	2	7		
Butterfield, Ephrim	3	3	7		
Stedman, James	1	3	5		
Bowman, Thomas	1	2	3		
Butterfield, Samuel	1	1	2		
Dinsmore, Samuel	1		1		
Lincoln, Marthew	1	1	3		
Ward, John	1	1	3		
Wilman, Asa	1		4		
Ward, Samuel	1		2		
Cross, Moses	1		3		
Page, Calob	1	4	4		
Butler, John	1	3	4		
Pullin, Oliver	1	2	2		
Hamblin, Timothy	2	2	3		
Hamblin, Timothy, jr	1		2		
Dow, Jonathan	1	1	2		
Bisby, Stephen	1	3	2		
Butler, Phinius	1	3	2		
Weeks, Benj	3	4	8		
Butler, Jerem^h	1	4	1		
Butler, Obadiah	1		2		
Robinson, Gore^h	4	2	2		
Hammond, Ephrim	1	1	2		
Bolton, James	1		2		
Bolton, George	1	2	2		
Butterfield, Mathew	1	2	3		
Taber, John	4	3	8		
Fry, Joshua	1	1	2		
Sleeper, Moses	1	1	2		
Taber, Jacob	3	2	2		
Balcome, Elijah	1	1	2		
Taber, Bath^w	1		2		
Getchell, John	3	3	3		
Cushing, Willm	1	1	2		
Dow, Benj	1	4	2		
Spratt, George	1		2		
Priest, Jonas	2	2	5		
Priest, Joseph	1		4		
Burges, Benj	3		2		
Gould, Nehemiah	1	5	4		

* Illegible.

FIRST CENSUS OF THE UNITED STATES.

LINCOLN COUNTY—Continued.

VASSALBOROUGH TOWN—continued.

NAME OF HEAD OF FAMILY.	Free white males of 16 years and upward, including heads of families.	Free white males under 16 years.	Free white females, including heads of families.	All other free persons.	Slaves.
Spalding, John	1	1	1		
Dickey, David	2	2	4		
Baxter, John	1	1	3		
Haskell, Willm	1		3		
Ewer, Jonathan	2		1		
Haws, Jacob	1	2	1		
Doe, Samson	1	3	4		
Dow, Benj., Junr	1	3	1		
Getchell, Dominicus	1	3	5		
Getchell, Edmond	1		2		
Blish, Stacy	1	3	6		
Bragg, Matthew	2	2	3		
Blish, John	1		1		
Brackett, James	1		3		
Farfield, Reuben	3	1	10		
Pitts, Ichabod	1	1	1		
Emerson, Phillip	1	1	4		
Fairfield, Jonathan	1	2	2		
Robinson, John	2	4	4		

Bristol TOWN.

NAME OF HEAD OF FAMILY.	Free white males of 16 years and upward, including heads of families.	Free white males under 16 years.	Free white females, including heads of families.	All other free persons.	Slaves.
day, benjamin	2	3	5		
chapman, nathaniel	1	5	1		
church, nathaniel	1	3	4		
hatch, Elizer	3	3	7		
hatch, Jonathan	1		1		
Cortis, Seth	1				
hiscock, Richard	2	1	4		
miller, nickles	2	3	3		
jones, william	3	1	4		
huston, james	5	1	5		
woodard, Sam	4	4	4		
harmond, John	3	1	3		
huston, John	2	2	5		
huston, Robert, jun	3	2	5		
huston, Robert	3		4		
Story (widow)	2		1		
paul, Robert	4	1	5		
patterson, John	2	2	6		
tompson, Robert	2	3	5		
hunter, henry	4	3	3		
Mccluer, thomas	1		2		
wille, James	1	1	2		
askins (widow)			4		
page, william	2	1	2		
hutchons, david	1	1	1		
hutchons, thomas	1	2	2		
askins, ninain	3	1	4		
hersey, Eben	1	2	3		
Mcmical, dowgal	3		7		
fitch, Jonas	1		5		
fitch, tim	1	1	2		
fitch, John	1		1		
howlen, Zeblen	2	4	4		
culbrath, lthen	2	1	3		
kelka (widow)			2		
wintworth (widow)	1	3	3		
little, John	1	3	3		
little, hugh	1	2	1		
fliming, James	1		1		
wintworth, juke	1	2	4		
Clark, Elisha, jun	1	5	1		
Sproul, robert, jun	1	3	2		
jones, Richard	3	2	4		
jones, mical	1		2		
jones, richard, jun	1	2	2		
huston, robert	1	2	3		
kellce, James	1		1		
paul, John	1		1		
paul, mathew	1	1	1		
askins, John	1	1	2		
askins, alexdre	1	3	3		
askins, george	1		2		
Hanley, Rodger	1	2	3		
hanley, pertrik	1	3	3		
crucker, Elijah	4	2	4		
hous, joshua	4	1	2		
askins, william	1	4	3		
Sunders, Sam	1		3		
tompson, natel	1	3	3		
elsworth, Joseph	4	3	3		
nolton, Joseph	3	2	4		
Reed, John	3	3	4		
killse, John	1				
bowly, Epherm	1	4	4		
fitch, John	1	1	1		
askins, david	1				
Stewart, Steven	1				
page, george	1		2		
Clark, Eliza	2		4		
miller, Robert	1	1	4		
Gowday, Emez	1	2	8		
Mcgoyer, pertrick	2	3	3		
bowll, oliver	1	1	3		

Bristol TOWN—continued.

NAME OF HEAD OF FAMILY.	Free white males of 16 years and upward, including heads of families.	Free white males under 16 years.	Free white females, including heads of families.	All other free persons.	Slaves.
Sprouls, william	1	3	2		
Clark, Sam	1	3	8		
cacklin (widow)	1		1		
clark, joseph	1	5	4		
Sprouls, Robert	2	2	5		
young, Edward	3		4	1	
plumer, bedfil	4	2	2		
faster, wilm	1	5	6		
Roberson, alexdr	1	2	4		
connely, John	1		1		
tompson, george	1	4	4		
tompson, thomas	1	3	2		
Stuard, thomas	1	5	4		
fullonton, archibal	1		1		
fullonton, Robert	1	2	4		
dodge, thomas	1	2	4		
gametch, Joshua	2	3	3		
persons, andrew	1	2	1		
Cattlen, daniel	1	4	3		
Story, Sam	1	4	3		
oats, Samuel	2	2	3		
tompson, mils	1	6	2		
Cums, Syl	1	2	2		
oats, Eben	1		3		
faster, nathen	1	1	2		
martin, thomas	1		2		
Mccurdy, dan	2	3	4		
farren, Ezechiel	1	5	2		
bates, calab	1	3	2		
omfry, Eben	1	2	4		
pardridge, John	3	2	2		
tarrow, John, jun	2	1	4		
Rods, John	1		1		
terral, isaac, jun	1	1	4		
terral, isaac	2		1		
stotson, Joseph	1	3	5		
weston, arona	1	2	6		
farow, timt	2	7	2		
farrow, Joseph	1	1	4		
colimer, peter	2	1	2		
keen, Ezak	1				
keen, Robert	2		3		
brow, John	1	4	4		
keen, prince	3		2		
keen, dan (hoge Island)	1	3	3		
osyer, Joseph	1	1	9		
burns, Joseph	1	5	8		
palmer, nat	3		2		
paine, John	1	1	1		
heads, john & joshua	2		1		
hilten, James	4		4		
Rohds, cornelus	1	1	4		
palmer, bazl	1	1	2		
Mcclain, John	1		1		
hilten, William	1	2	2		
martin, John	1		2		
misherver, nath	4	1	5		
palmer, benjm	2		2		
lincoln, Isaac	1	2	7		
cushman, paulus (long Island)	2	4	5		
Studle, sichl (long Island)	1	2	3		
faster, nat, jun	2	4	3		
faster, John	1	2	4		
faster, Sebert	1		2		
tabet, Steven	2	2	3		
tabet, henry	1		2		
Mcfarling, John	5	2	4		
Mcfarling, John, jun	1	1	3		
molton, James	3	3	4		
portefield, Robert	2	2	2		
drumens, James	2	2	4		
Sprouls, william	4		3		
winslow, nicklas	1	2	5		
hatch, philip	1	3	8		
Sproul, James	3	2	2		
nickles, alexander	2	2	5	1	
nickles, william	1	3	2		
Mcintire, william	1	4	3		
nickles, James	2	2	5		
Rodger, patrick	1		2		
Rodger, willm	2	1	2		
Rodger, george	2	2	6		
Mcglathery, alexdr	2	2	9		
Robertson, alexdr	2		1		
Mcfarland, andrew	1		2		
Mcfarland, Robert	1		2		
curtice, daniel	2	3	8		
martin, John	2	3	3		
randal, Robert	1		1		
cox, Israil	3	1	1	1	
gwin, James	1	1	4		
Sproul, James, jun	1		3		
greely, jonathan	1	2	7		

Bristol TOWN—continued.

NAME OF HEAD OF FAMILY.	Free white males of 16 years and upward, including heads of families.	Free white males under 16 years.	Free white females, including heads of families.	All other free persons.	Slaves.
miller, thomas	3				
Russel, william	2	2	6		
tibbets, Jacob	2	1	2		
Greenlew, alexdr	1	1	1		
fossat, alexdr, jun	1	3	3		
child, thomas	2	4	4	1	
doliver, Joseph	1	2	4		
miller, John	2	2	3		
upham, Jablz	2	4	5		
geven, Robert	3		3	5	
fassat, william, jun	1	1	2		
fassat, henry	2	4	7		
fossat, alexdr	2	1	2		
fossat, william	2		3		
Mckown (weidow)			5	1	
Mckown, John	3	3	3	1	
Sproul, william	2	2	6		
boyd, Sam	2	3	7		
boyd, william	2	6	5		
boyd, John	2	3	4		
dwo, lem	2	3	2		
leighton, James	1	2	5		
calderwood, thomas	1	2	3		
Stuard, James	2		2		
fountain, Jacob	1	1	4		
hercy, Eben	1	1	3		
fassat, henry, jun	1	3	6		
blunt, Ebenr	3	2	4		
kent (widow)	2		4		
polline, Ezra	1		4		
lalor, patrik	1	3	3		
bracket (widow)	1		3	1	
Mclen, alexdr	2	3	5		
gates, George	1	4	4		
Richards, Erastus	1	3	6		
bally, Zery	1	2	4		
poland, thomas	1	2	4		
poland, nohemiak	1	1	3		
Smilidge, nathan	2		2		
Elliot, Simon, jun	1	1	2		
fuller, Zenos	1	4	4		
Greenlaw, william	1	1	4		
hanley, malachi	1		1	1	
Elliot, Simon	6		6		
briant, david	2	1	2		
Gates, Samuel	1	4	2		
briant, lemuel	3	6	4		
Richard, william	1				
Richard, william, jun	4	2	4		
Richard, william, 3rd	1	3	1		
Richard, benjamin	2	1	2		
hetcher, thomas	1	3	1		
morton, John	1	1	1		
berms, william	1	5	6		
poland, Stuawrd (mach Island)	1	5	1		
lawd, william (mescongus Island)	1		1		
Salomon, william (mescongus Island)	1	4	5		
Mcmorfey, peter (mescongus Island)	1	1	4		
fountain, barnabas, jun. (mescongus Island)	1	1	2		
fountain, barnabas (mescongus Island)	2	1	4		
fowler, andrew (mescongus Island)	1	2	2		
carter, ephram (mescongus Island)	1	1	5		
morfey, John (mescongus Island)	1				
morfey, peter (mescongus Island)	1	1	1		
Shmit, joseph (mescongus Island)	2		1		
lidge, Sinas (mescongus Island)	1		2		
warren, james	1				
le balister, charles	2	1	3		
hurland, prince	1	3	4		
morton, william	1	3	1		
arnold, thomas	1	3	3		
keen, william	1	2	4		
woodbery, ephram	1	2	5		
tarrow, John	1	1	2		
colimer, Isaac	1		1		
Sier, John	1	2	1		
Studley, dan	3		4		
martin (widow)	1	2	3		
Mcclain, william	2	2	4		
misherve, clemt	1	1	4		
dilinham, leml	1		2		
macher, Richard	2	3	4		
Stevens, alexander	2	1	4		

HEADS OF FAMILIES—MAINE.

LINCOLN COUNTY—Continued.

Bristol (Waldoborough Town—continued)

NAME OF HEAD OF FAMILY.	Free white males of 16 years and upward, including heads of families.	Free white males under 16 years.	Free white females, including heads of families.	All other free persons.	Slaves.
bennet, becheldor	2		6		
dockendorf, Jacob	3	7	6		
mackendorsh, John	1		1		
nash, oliver	1	1	1		
johnson, thom	3	1	3		
poor, james	2	1	2		
Rohds, george	1	2	2		
mats (widow)			2		
mirrit, Jonathan	3	2	2		
Rohds, thomas	1		1		
McClain, Sam	1		2		
wilman, ben	1				
wilman, Joseph	1	1	5		
wilman, Sam	1	1	3		
little, henry	1	1	4		
crucker, trenter	3		2		
turner, calab	2		3		
turner, Robt	2	2	3		
tinkam, elen	1	5	1		
calomer, sickl (long Island.)	1				

WALES PLANTATION.

NAME OF HEAD OF FAMILY.	Free white males of 16 years and upward, including heads of families.	Free white males under 16 years.	Free white females, including heads of families.	All other free persons.	Slaves.
ham, Reuben	1	3	6		
Backer, Young	1		3		
Backer, Eliphelat	1	1	2		
Jacking, David	1	2	2		
niles, Robert	1				
ham, Samuel	1	1	2		
niles, Calab	3	1	2		
ham, Saml	1				
ham, Reuben	1				
ham, John	1	1	2		
Arno, John	2	3	3		
Gray, James	1	3	2		
Ramake, William	1	1	1		
Janking, Philip	4	2	8		
Allen, Joseph	2	1	8		
tompson, Richard	1	2	3		
Andres, John	1	2	4		
labree, James	1	1	4		
labree, Richard	1	2	1		
Astery, Benoney	2	1	4		
Gray, Stephen	1	1	2		
Ramaks, Joseph	1		2		
Cannon, Patrick	1		2		
Cannon, James	1	1	2		
Wamoth, Benjn	1	3	4		
Wamoth, Joseph	1				
Wamoth, Samuel	1	5	1		
tompson, Jonathan	1	3	6		
Gray, Thomas	1	2	3		
Gray, Thomas, ju	1		2		
Kimble, Benjn	1	1	4		
Brown, Josiah	1	2	1		
Deadem, Benjn	1	1	4		
Day, Joseph	1	1	1		
Wite, Timothy	3	4	4		
Gilman, Daniel	2	4	5		
MacCslin, Gardner	1	1	3		
Norris, James	3	3	2		
Norris, Nathl	1				
Titas, Saml	1		6		
titas, William	1	3	5		
Allen, Edman	1	2	2		
Allen, Woodard	1		3		
Allen, Daniel	1		4		
Blake, Phinhas	2	1	3		
Blake, Dearborn	1		2		
Dearborn, Levi	3	2	4		
Baker, Ichabod	2		2		
Wetch, John	1	3	5		
Allen, William	1	3	3		
Chandler, John	1	1	3		
Blake, Ashel	1	4	3		
Blosom, Mathias	1	2	1		
Blosom, James	1	1	2		
Priscott, Suwel	1				
Fogg, Caleb	1	4	1		
Dearborn, Simon. ju	1	2	2		
Sargant, John	1				
Smith, Nathan	1	3	3		
Dearborn, Simon	1		1		
Smart, Robert	2	2	4		
Smart, Eliphelat	1				
Smart, James	1				
Smith, Daniel	1		1		
Blake, John	1	1	1		
Clough, Benjn	1				
Morril, Abraham	1				
Norris, James, ju	1	1	2		
Tompson, Mary		1	4		
tompson, William	1				
Stocking, Thomas	1		3		

WALES PLANTATION—continued.

NAME OF HEAD OF FAMILY.	Free white males of 16 years and upward, including heads of families.	Free white males under 16 years.	Free white females, including heads of families.	All other free persons.	Slaves.
Branard, Nathn	1		1		
Bishop, Zadock	2	4	3		
Witherton, Robert	2	3	1		
Moodey, Gilman	1	5	3		
hopkins, Peter, Ju	1	2	3		
hopkins, Peter	2	1	3		
hopkins, William	1				
Thursten, Jona	1				
Thurston, Peter	1				
Lyon, Peter	1	3	2		
Judkins, Robert	3		1		
Judkins, James	1				
Streter, John	2		1		
Wilson, James	1				
bayweatt, William	1	2	3		
Goadon, Thial	1	1	2		
falls, Joshua	1	1	1		
Parker, Joseph	1	2	5		
Wile, Timothy, Ju	1				
Kimble, thomas	1				
Druce, Climan	1	1	1		

WARREN TOWN.

NAME OF HEAD OF FAMILY.	Free white males of 16 years and upward, including heads of families.	Free white males under 16 years.	Free white females, including heads of families.	All other free persons.	Slaves.
Crawford, John	3		1		
Kirkpatrick, Anne	4	1	3		
Robinson, Thomas	1	2	2		
Boggs, Mary	3	1	4		
Boggs, Samuel	1	1	4		
Boggs, John	2		2		
Boggs, William	3	2	5		
Cobb, Miles	2		1		
Bird, Alexander	1	3	3		
Copeland, Nathaniel	2	2	2		
Crane, Rufus	3	3	3		
Weston, Samuel	1	1	5		
Head, James Walter	2		4		
Morrison, Thomas	1	1	2		
Whiting, Thurston	4	1	2		
Anderson, Archibald	2	3	4		
Anderson, James	2	2	5		
Anderson, Samuel	1	1	3		
Dickey, William	1	3	4		
Dickey, John	2		2		
Alford, Lore	1		2		
Davis, Aaron	1	1	1		
Davis, Jacob	1		1		
Matthews, Robert	1				
Mathews, James	1		2		
Counce, Lemuel	1	3	2		
Fisher, James	1		3		
Crawford, Archibald	1	1	3		
Crawford, James	1				
Copeland, Joseph	2	2	3		
Watt, John	4	1	5		
McCallum, John	2	3	3		
Crawford, John, Junr	2	4	3		
Standish, James	1	2	3		
Paseal, John	1	2	3		
Libbey, John	3	3	2		
Libby, Nathan	1	1	3		
Libbey, Eliakim	1	2	4		
Bosworth, Eli	1	2	4		
Jameson, Joseph	2		3		
Young, Francis		2	2		
Fairbanks, Joel	2	1	2		
Kirkpatrick, William	1	1	2		
Crane, Samuel	1	1	1		
Starret, Thomas	5	1	7		
Starret, Thomas, Junr	1	1	1		
O'Bryan, John	2	1	4		
James, Sarah			3		
Wiley, John	2	3	5		
Lermond, William	3	4	5		
Cox, James	1	1	6		
Lawrence, Amos	1	3	3		
McIntyer, William	1		3		
Spear, John	5	5	5		
Spear, Robert	2		5		
Robinson, William	2	3	2		
Pebbles, Patrick	1	2	2		
McIntyer, John	1	1	2	1	
McIntyer, John, Junr	2	1	2		
Tolman, Reuben	1	2	4		
Sumner, Ezra	1		4		
Hall, Reuben	3	2	2		
Libbey, Hatevil	2	3	4		
Buckland, Nathan	3	3	5		
Creighton, Lucretia	2		2		
Eastman, Sarah			2		
Sumner, Hopestill	1	2	7		
Counce, Samuel	2	1	4		
Copeland, Moses	3	2	4		
Copeland, Rufus	1	3	1		

WARREN TOWN—con.

NAME OF HEAD OF FAMILY.	Free white males of 16 years and upward, including heads of families.	Free white males under 16 years.	Free white females, including heads of families.	All other free persons.	Slaves.
Watson, William	3	2	5		
Crane, Calvin	2		6		
Scheffer, John Martin	3		5		
Secrist, Philip	1	1	3		
Roker, Daniel	2	1	5		
Skinner, Joseph	1	7	4		
Lermond, John	2	2	5		
Farrington, Abner	1	3	4		
Peabody, Stephen	3	1	4		
Peabody, Daniel	2	1	2		
Peabody, Andrew	1		1		
Peabody, Josiah, & Saml Peabody	2				
Andrews, John	3	5	8		
Caravan, James	1	1	2		
Montgomery, Robert	2	2	5		
Kelloch, Alexander	3	3	3		
Kelloch, David	2	2	4		
Cooper, Bolce	1				
Keith, James	1	2	2		
Dunbar, Daniel	3	1	6	1	
Lermond, Alexander	2	2	5		
Payson, Samuel	2	1	2		
Sprague, Nathan	1	2	3		
Hoofles, George	1	2	2		
Isley, Martin	1	1	4		
Rogers, Jesse	1	1	2		
Snell, David	1	2	2		
Fairbanks, John	1	1	1		
Watson, James	1	2	4		
Mink, Peter	1				
Mink, John	1				
Fuller, Isaac	1	1	1		
Otis, William	1				
Leach, Apollos	1				
Prince, Sylvester				5	
peters, Amos				6	

WASHINGTON TOWN.

NAME OF HEAD OF FAMILY.	Free white males of 16 years and upward, including heads of families.	Free white males under 16 years.	Free white females, including heads of families.	All other free persons.	Slaves.
Moors, Timothy	1	1	1		
Tayler, Wilebey	1	1	2		
French, Levi	1		1		
Blake, Robert	1	2	6		
Thomas, Nathan	1	2	4		
French, David	1	2	2		
Tayler, Phinhas	1				
higins, Seth	1		2		
latin, Ephraim	1		2		
Stevens, John	1	1	3		
latin, Moses	1		2		
Roggers, John	1	1	2		
Colbath, lamuel	1		2		
Kilbath, Partrick	1	2	2		
huchings, John	1		3		
Smith, James	1		1		
Paul, Simeon	1		5		
Paul, Silas	1		2		
Blake, Paul	1		2		
Ingham, David	1	1	2		
Boocks, Gorge	1	3	3		
Bishop, Esquire	1	1	2		
Laten, Solomon	1	4	3		
Laton, andrew	1				
Latan, David	1				
latan, John	1				
latan, Benjn	4	1	5		
latan, Ephram	1		2		
Bean, John	1		2		
Bean, Neele	1				
Bean, Josiah	1		2		
Bean, Edward	2		3		
Brown, Nathan	1	1	4		
Keerls, Enoch	2		6		
Weels, Joshua	1				
Weels, James	1	1	2		
Wiggins, Nicholos	1		1		
Robinson, John	1				
Dollor, Richard	2	1	2		
Philbrock, Benjn	1	3	3		
Allan, Nathaniel	1				
Philbrock, Joseph	1	1	3		
Daniles, Reuben	1				
Kane, Reuben	1	1	1		
Killey, William	1				
latan, James	1	1	2		
Brown, Samuel	1				
Philbrock, Stephen	1	1	3		
Scribner, Stephen	1				
Eslman, Benjn	1				
ladd, John	1	2	6		
Rands, Daniel	1				
Ladd, Nathaniel	3	2	7		
Caols, John	1		6		

FIRST CENSUS OF THE UNITED STATES.

LINCOLN COUNTY—Continued.

NAME OF HEAD OF FAMILY.	Free white males of 16 years and upward, including heads of families.	Free white males under 16 years.	Free white females, including heads of families.	All other free persons.	Slaves.	NAME OF HEAD OF FAMILY.	Free white males of 16 years and upward, including heads of families.	Free white males under 16 years.	Free white females, including heads of families.	All other free persons.	Slaves.	NAME OF HEAD OF FAMILY.	Free white males of 16 years and upward, including heads of families.	Free white males under 16 years.	Free white females, including heads of families.	All other free persons.	Slaves.
WASHINGTON TOWN—continued.						**WINSLOW TOWN, WITH ITS ADJACENTS.**						**WINSLOW TOWN, WITH ITS ADJACENTS—con.**					
Kidden, Richard	1					Fairwell, Josiah	1	2	1			Simpson, John	1	1	2		
Emerson, Samuel	1	1	2			Bradford, William	1	2	6			Sturdifent, Lot	1		1		
Row, Stephen	1					Printice, Voluntine	1	4	3			Bates, Thomas	1	3	2		
Philbrock, Nathaniel	1	1	2			Richardson, Joseph	1	3	2			Alles, Micah	1	1	2		
Philbrock, Calab	1					Smith, Manuel	1	3	4			Landers, Abraham	1	4	2		
Gordon, Daniel	2	1	4			Parker, Phinihas	1					Tupper, Peleg	2	2	4		
Gordon, Sam¹	1					Hammon, Fredrick	1	2	3			Rose, John	1		2		
Lyon, Mary			1			Leonard, Abigail			3 1			Fowler, John	1		1		
folsom, Trustom	1	3	1			Dudley, Francis	3	2	3	1		Tosier, Simeon	1	1	2		
folsom, John	1	2	3			Lithgow, Aurthur	1					Mackackeny, Mary	1	2	4		
Bean, Joab	1	1	1			Bounsan, Samuel	1					Lewis, John	1				
Gilman, Nathaniel	1	2	3			Harriss, Winslow		1				Mackackeny, Thomas	1	1	4		
Gilman, Nathaniel, Ju	1					Runnils, Benjamin	4	2	5			Serles, John	1				
Cram, Sam¹	1		1			Turner, Ebenezer	1					Temple, Isaac	1	3	2		
Cram, Sam¹, ju	1	1	2			Brooks, John	1					Leman, Thomas	1	6	4		
Smith, Liddah			1			Carter, Joseph	1	2	5			Pettis, David	1	4	2		
Cram, Timothy	1		2			Wear, David	1	3	1			Pettis, Daniel	1				
Dudley, Nathaniel	1	1	3			Wood, Bennit	1	6	2			Macfarlin, Samuel	1	3	2		
folsom, Nathaniel	1	1	3			Parker, Solomon	2		5			Lewis, Thomas	1				
philbrok, Nathaniel	1		6			Brawn, Charles	2	1	2			Dile, Ralph	1		1		
folsom, Benjᵃ	1		1			Carter, Nathaniel	1		1			Low, Nathaniel	2	3	2		
folsom, Peter	1	2	1			Wood, Jean			1			Crammet, James	1	3	4		
Stair, John	1	1	6			Haden, Josiah	3	1	5			Crowell, Levi	1	3	3		
folsom, Nathaniel, Ju	1	1	3			Haden, Charles	1	1	1			Larree, John	1				
Philbrock, Tites	1	3	5			Lanson, Suttil	1					Green, Timothy	1	2	2		
Philbrock, John	1					Jones, Amos	1	1	2			Killey, Joseph	1				
Stevens, Ebnezer	3	1	2			Pettis, Ezekiel	4	4	4			Wyman, Simon	3	2	1		
Dudley, John	2	3	1			Phillips, Asa	1	2	4			Springer, Job	1	2	3		
Dudley, Daniel	1	3	4			Dingly, Barker	1	2	2			Titton, Cornelius	1	3	3		
Batchelor, William	1		1			Allen, Francis	1					Springer, Stutely	1	2	3		
Hills, John	1	1	2			Warrin, George	1					Springer, Edward	2		1		
Rade, Joshua	1					Whitten, George	1	1	1			Keen, Shibottaish	1	1	1		
Rade, Amos	1					Stagpole, James	1	2	4			Humes, John	2	1	1		
Hills, Joseph	1					Philbrook, John	1					Humes, John, Juʳ	1				
marston, Theoder		1	3			Stagpole, James, Jʳ	1					Amerson, Daniel	1		2		
Ladd, Josses	1	3	3			Stagpole, Samuel	1	2	2			Soul, Jonathan	1	3	3		
Priscott, Jonᵃ	1	2	1			Townes, Ephrom	1	1	5			Shannon, William	3	2	7		
Eaton, Jesse	1		3			Barton, Betty		1	1			Wade, David	2	2	6		
Rade, Joshua	1					Stratton, Hezekiah	1	3	4			Smith, Eliab	1	4	3		
Morse, andrew	1					Collier, James	1	1	4			Toner, Elias	1	4	1		
Smith, Wolden	1					Collier, John	1					Blanchard, Edward	1	4	3		
Smith, Moses	1					Richardson, William	1	2	5			Low, Jonathan	1				
Hills, Robert	1					Macfarling, James	1					Brawn, John	1		1		
Bartlet, Timothy	1	3	5			Fuller, Enoch	1					Crowell, Manoah	1				
Gilman, Samuel	2	4	4			Craging, Joseph	1		3			Wade, Samuel	1	1			
Hall, Josiah	1		2			Shores, Samuel	1		2			Megraw, John	3		2		
Hall, nathan	1		2			Combs, Jonathan	1		2			Crowell, Samuel	2		6		
Hall, allen	1		3			Hallet, Solomon		1	3			Crowell, David	1	3	3		
Page, James, jur	1					Hallet, Elisha	1	1	3			Richardson, Joel	1	3			
Smith, Samuel	1	1	2			Pierce, John	1	1	2			Page, Caleb	1	2	2		
Page, Chase	1	2	2			Lewis, William, Ju	1	1	2			Dullen, oliver	1	2	2		
Page, abraham	1	2	3			Chace, James	1	3	2			Ballard, Betty		1	1		
Williams, Obediah	1	5	3			Cook, Thomas	1		2			Crowell, Joseph	2		1		
Bisbee, Benjᵃ	1	2	3			Amerson, Daniel	1					Taylor, Samuel	1		2		
Mosher, Elisha	1	1	2			Leman, John	1	6	3			Mosier, Elisha	1		2		
Lambord, James	1	1	2			Macathany, Thomas	1	1	2			Howland, William	1	3	4		
Sawtell, hezekiah	1					Goodwin, Caleb	1					Blake, Nathaniel	1		1		
Towle, Francies	2	2	3			Ausburn, Jonathan	1		1			Mosier, Daniel	2	4	4		
Page, John	1					Simpson, Benjamin	1	1	6			Settle, Hezekiah	1				
Else, Robert	1					Copeland, Abraham	1		2			Mosier, Daniel, Juʳ	1	1	2		
Varnam, Stevan	1					Landers, Joseph	1	1	8			Rankins, John	1	2	2		
Snow, Philip	1	5	5			Copeland, Abraham, Jur	1					Whitehouse, Robart	1		1		
Clark, Sherebah	1					Rose, Benjamin		1	2			Whitehouse, John, Jur	1	2	2		
lincell, Lamuel			3			Lankister, John	1	1	3			Whitehouse, John	1		2		
Towsanden, Robert	1		4			Mackim, James	1	4	1			Hamblin, John	1	1	2		
lincell, Joseph	1	3	3			Cool, John	1	1	1			Crowell, ——*rdock	1	2	4		
Right, Asa	1					Amerson, Asa	1		5			Mills, John	2	1	3		
Tilden, Elisha	1					Priest, Jonathan	1	1	2			Branch, Daniel	1		2		
Rowe, Stephen	1					Taylor, Timothy	1					Fall, Aaron	1	1	3		
Crowell, Ezekiel	1	1	2			Taylor, Jonas	1					Richards, Joseph	1	1	3		
Wiman, Jonᵃ	1	2	3			Crosbey, Jonah	2	1	5			Crowell, Ezekiel	1				
Wiman, Simon	3	3	2			Wilson, Ephrom	1	1	4			Mills, Robart	1				
Cane, ——	1					Crosbey, Ezra	1	1	3			Hall, Samuel			2		
Tilton, Cornelias	1	3	4			Chalmor, William	1	4	3			Fall, Samuel, Juʳ	1				
Springer, Job	1	2	3			Hale, Timothy	2	3	6								
Page, Jesse	1	1	2			Haywood, Zimri	4	1	4			**WINTHROP TOWN.**					
Kimball, Andrew	1		4			Hartford, Benjamin	1		2								
Wiman, James	1					Dexter, Nathan	4	2	5			Filer, Ebnezer	1		1		
Lenel, Joseph	1	3	4			Fuller, Jonathan	1	1	2			Tayler, Elias	1	1	4		
Townsand, Robert	1	1	4			Thomas, Richard	1		2			Knowls, Elisha	1		2		
Lenel, Sam¹	2		3			Chace, Benjamin	1		5			Knowls, Simon	1	2	2		
Snow, Philip	1	5	5			Soul, Asa	1	3	1			lyon, Squier	1		2		
Sartwell, Hezekiah	1		2			Coal, John	1		1			lyon, Nathan	1	2	4		
Lombart, James	1	1	2			Wyman, James	1	1	1			Priscott, Elisha	1	1	6		
Mosier, Elisha	1		2			Ausburn, Isaac	1		1			Willman, Abraham	1	2	3		
Hall, Sam¹	2	1	1			Wyman, Moses	2	1	2			Cottle, Isaac	1	1	6		
Hall, Aaron	1		4			Spoldin, John	1	3	4			Knowls, Jonathan	1	1	4		
Ellis, John	2	4	2			Spoldin, Willard	3	3	5			lyon, Eliab	1	3	3		
Blake, Nath¹	1	1	1			Ausburn, Ephrom	2	3	2			Jewet, John	1	2	1		
Hamelton, John	1					Spoldin, John	2	3	5			Shad, John	1				
White, John	1	2	2			Simpson, John	1	1	4			Gilman, David	2	3	5		
Howland, Wmᵐ	1	2	2			Temple, Jacob		3	2			fuller, Francies	1	5	4		
Rankens, John	1	2	2			Guliffin, Thomas	1	4	4			Tayler, Wilebe	1				
Brandt, Daniel	1	1	2			Simpson, Reuben	1		2			hinkley, David	1	1	1		

*Illegible.

HEADS OF FAMILIES—MAINE.

LINCOLN COUNTY—Continued.

NAME OF HEAD OF FAMILY.	Free white males of 16 years and upward, including heads of families.	Free white males under 16 years.	Free white females, including heads of families.	All other free persons.	Slaves.	NAME OF HEAD OF FAMILY.	Free white males of 16 years and upward, including heads of families.	Free white males under 16 years.	Free white females, including heads of families.	All other free persons.	Slaves.	NAME OF HEAD OF FAMILY.	Free white males of 16 years and upward, including heads of families.	Free white males under 16 years.	Free white females, including heads of families.	All other free persons.	Slaves.
WINTHROP TOWN—con.						**WINTHROP TOWN—con.**						**WINTHROP TOWN—con.**					
Reed, Benjn	1	2	1			Morrill, Levi	2	2	1			fairbanks, Elijah	2	2	3		
Sweet, Arnol	2		1			Norton, Daniel	1	1	2			Robins, Daniel	2		2		
Standly, Jacob	4		1			Page, Robert	1	4	6			Robins, Asa	1	1	1		
Standly, Solomon	3	2	5			Wing, Ichabod	1					Blunt, John	1	1	2		
Bakon, Josiah	1					huccosen, henry	1					Priscott, Samuel	1	2	3		
Standley, Reah	1	1	3			Wiman, henry	1		4			white, Benjn	1	2	3		
furenton, Timothy	1	1	4			Waugh, Robert	3	1	2			Priscott, Jediah	1		1		
Smith, Daniel	1		1			Simonons, Ichabod	1	1	3			Priscott, Elijah	1				
Smith, Mrs Eliphelat	2	3	4			Whicher, Moses	1	2	3			Priscott, Jesse	1		4		
Smith, Comford	1	1	2			Whicher, Moses, Ju.	1	3	2			Priscott, Odlin	1	1	3		
Streter, John, ju.	1	1	2			Wing, Daniel, Ju	1		3			Priscott, Benjn	1				
Richman, Nathan	1	2	2			Wing, Reuben	1					Longfelow, Jona	1				
Smith, Benjn	1	4	1			luce, Uriah	1		3			Standley, Adain	1	2	1		
Smith, Jacob	1	1	3			luce, Shuble	1	3	2			Page, Simon	3	3	7		
King, Ebnezer	1	1	1			luce, freeman	1					Blunt, Andrew	1		3		
King, Samuel	1	2	2			Smith, Cyril	1					Priscott, Jedeah, Jun	2	3	6		
fairbanks, Joseph, Jur.	1	4	8			Shurborn, Job	4		3			Mathew, Daniel	1				
Allen, Benjn	1	2	1			Shurborn, Richard	1		2			Bishop, Squire	1		1		
fuller, John	3	3	6			Steper, John	1		1			Bishop, Nathaniel	1				
Allen, Philip	1	4	3			Dudley, Stephen	1		2			Pooling, Stephen	2	3	6		
Tayler, Thomas	2	5	4			Dudley, Eliphelat	1	3	3			fairbanks, Nathaniel	1	3	2		
Sweet, Elias	1					Hoitt, Petralea	2	3	5			midcufs, Joseph	1	1	1		
Turnner, John	1	2	4			Clough, Jabes	1	3	5			Wood, Samuel	1	1	1		
Atkinson, James	2	3	5			Greeley, Joseph	1		1			Wood, Elijah	1				
whrorter, Roling	1					Greeley, Noah	1	3	2			Morton, levy	1	1	1		
Atkinson, thomas	1					Greeley, Joseph, Ju	1	2	2			Morton, Ebnezer	1	1			
Perley, amos	1	3	5			fiacher, Gideon	1					Cilley, William	1				
Devenport, Ebenezer	2		4			Clough, John	1	1	3			Pooling, William	1	2	4		
Devenport, Isaac	1	1	1			Gordon, thiah	2	1	5			Woodcock, David	1	4	5		
harris, Charls	1	2	3			Gordon, Jona	1	2	1			Chandler, John, jur.	1	5	2		
Stevens, William	1	1	6			Gordon, Josiah	1	3	1			herkley, James	1				
Brown, unite	2	1	3			Parram, Samuel	1	2	2			How, Stephan	1				
Brown, Jeremiah	1					hutchison, Joseph	1	2	2			Coal, John	1		2		
Brown, John	1					hutchison, theophas	1		1			Boldon, Jiras	1	1	2		
Stevens, Joseph	1		2			Whicher, Thomas	1	3	4			How, Ichabod	2		6		
Stevens, Jonas	1	3	2			Whicher, Nathaniel	2	4	6			Chandler, John	1	1	2		
Wheler, Moris	1	1	1			Whicher, William	2	2	5			Daxter, Constant	1				
Atkins, David	1	1	2			Judkins, Samuel	1	2	2			Chandler, Joab	1	3	3		
Works, James	1	4	3			Stevens, John	1					Chandler, Joseph	1				
Puling, John	1		4			Evens, John	1	1	1			Chandler, Moses	1		1		
hurlane, Peter	2	4	4			Evens, Daniel	1					Chandler, Jacob	1	1	2		
Gray, John	1	4	4			hubard, John	1		5			lambord, Gideon	1	1	4		
Brown, Steven	1	3	2			Carr, Benjn	1	5	4			lambord, Paul	1	1			
Macfason, Paul	1	1	2			French, Moses	1		1			lambord, Silas	1				
harkerson, John	1		2			Mark, Abijah	1		3			lyford, William	1				
Stephens, Samuel	1	4	6			French, John	1	2	4			Curne, James	1				
Sampson, Noah	2		2			French, John, Jur	1	2	1								
Carwill, John	1	1	3			Gage, John	1	2	3			**WOOLWICH TOWN.**					
hankerson, William	1	2	3			hovey, John	1	1	3								
hankerson, thomas	1		1			Smith, Jesse	1	1	2			Stephenson, Nathl	1	1	3		
Dutten, Joshua	3	3	4			Boyd, Samuel	1		1			Tibbits, Nathl	3	2	4		
Burden, Primes				2		Boyd, Calorn	1					Mitchel, Jonas	1	1	7		
Walton, Moses	1					Cater, lamuel	1	1	1			Burford, Robert	1		1		
Stephens, Amos	2	6	5			freeman, John	1		2			Bailey, John	3	1	2		
Secars, Paul	1	4	3			Talbot, William	1	3	3			Farnham, Saml	2		5		
Boney, hannah (Widdow)		2	2			farthaton, Ithamer	1	4	2			Card, John	1		2		
turner, Christopher	2	5	6			Whiting, Jonathan	1		2			Farnham, Jer.	1		2		
Hains, Dudley	1	1	1			Whiting, Jonathan, Jur	2	1	7			Savage, James	2	2	5		
lane, James	1	2	3			Branard, Timothy	1		3			Sloman, Simon	1	2	6		
Wittiny, Joseph	1		6			Matheys, Joseph	1					Pelson, Joel	1	2	1		
Smith, mathias	3	2	2			White, Joab	1	3	1			Honowell, Rich.	2	1	2		
Smith, mathias, Jur	2	2	1			Estes, Solomon	1	3	7			Abbot, Aaron	1	2	4		
Mayhew, Samuel	1		2			Robins, Daniel	1	2	1			Foster, Nathl	2	2	6		
Norris, Josiah	1	1	3			Richard, William	2	1	3			McMurphy, Archibald	1	3	2		
Kint, Charles	1		5			Cran, Abijah	1	1	2			Shilden, Ephraim	2		5		
Kint, Warrant	1	1	2			Wadworth, John	2	2	1			Lummis, Saml	1	2	2		
thomas, Nathaieh	1	1	2			Branard, Ruth (Widow)			3			Skinner, Henry	2	3	5		
Packad, Joshua	1		2			Branard, Reuben	1		3			Hamlen, Richard	2	2	2		
Packad, Ralf	1		2			Comings, John	3	4	3			Wade, Abner	1	1	4		
Packad, Calab	1		1			Standley, Nathaniel	2	1	2			Sole, John	1	1	4		
ford, Nathaniel	2	1	4			french, Josiah	1	3	6			Snell, Thos	3	1	3		
Crigg, James	1		1			Porter, Benjn	1	3	3			Smith, Israel	3		3		
Crigg, Thomas	1		3			Pond, William	1		1			Savage, Edward	1		3		
Crigg, James, Ju	1	1	1			Keefer, John	1		3			Booker, Josiah	2	6	5		
Crigg, William	1	1				Washbane, Edward	1	1	1			Snell, James	1	1	1		
michals, Josiah	1	3	4			Wardworth, Samuel	1		1			Booker, Josiah, Junr	2		2		
Packad, Joshua Jr	1					Stevens, Ephraim	1	4				Booker, Ebens, Junr	1		2		
Packad, llbary	1		1			foster, Sabel (Widow)			1			Booker, Ebens	2	1	3		
Norton, Stephen	1		2			Rice, Joseph	2					Blin, James	2	4	3		
Norton, Peter	1					foster, Stuard	2	2	2			Dilleno, Ebens	1	1	1		
Norton, Constant	1		3			foster, David	2	4	4			Bailey, Joshua	1	1	1		
wing, Paul	1	3	1			foster, Saml	3	4	3			Blin, Charles	1		3		
Pitts, Seth	2		4			foster, Ebnezer	1					Bailey, Josiah	1		3		
Savage, Benjn	1		3			foster, Richard	1					Leman, Samuel	1		4		
Wing, Daniel	1		4			Wood, Moses	1	1	1			Leman, Saml, Junr	1	2	1		
peterson, abraham	2	3	6			Gay, Moses	1	1	1			Leman, Abigail			2		
peterson, abraham, Ju.	1		1			fairbanks, Joseph	1	2	1			Twing, Nathl	1		2		
peterson, Carnalas	1		1			fairbanks, Benjn	2	2	6			Hathorn, Willm	2	1	4		
Bean, Joshua	2	6	5			foster, Timothy	2	1	4			Eames, Jacob	1	3	2		
Bean, Joel	1	1	1			Dileno, Zebulon	2		1			Reid, Jona	2		2		
Bean, Elijah	1	1	2			Dileno, Seth	1	1	4			Reid, Saml	2	2	1		
Johnson, Joseph	2		5			Cushman, Josiah	1	4	3			Reid, Robert	3	3	3		
Johnson, Joseph, Ju	2		2			Marrow, Daniel	2	2	5			Reid, Joel	3	3	6		
Johnson, Joshua	1		1			Marrow, Daniel, Ju	1	3	3			Frost, Lemuel	2	2	4		
						Morrow, Ebnezer	1					Frost, John	3		2		

FIRST CENSUS OF THE UNITED STATES.

LINCOLN COUNTY—Continued.

NAME OF HEAD OF FAMILY.	Free white males of 16 years and upward, including heads of families.	Free white males under 16 years.	Free white females, including heads of families.	All other free persons.	Slaves.	NAME OF HEAD OF FAMILY.	Free white males of 16 years and upward, including heads of families.	Free white males under 16 years.	Free white females, including heads of families.	All other free persons.	Slaves.	NAME OF HEAD OF FAMILY.	Free white males of 16 years and upward, including heads of families.	Free white males under 16 years.	Free white females, including heads of families.	All other free persons.	Slaves.
WOOLWICH TOWN—con.						**WOOLWICH TOWN—con.**						**WOOLWICH TOWN—con.**					
Blair, John	1	2	2			Otis, Galen	1	1	2			Cushman, Robert	3	3	5		
Baley, Thos	1	3	4			Dilleno, Hopestill	4	1	4			Savage, Ebenr	1	3	4		
Stinson, Thos	1	2	3			Ballard, Thomas	1		3			Blin, James	1	2	2		
Blair, Robert	1	2	4			Stinson, Saml	5	2	4			Hathorn, Seth	1	1	4		
Blair, James	2	1	5			Whitten, Asa	1	2	2			Gould, John	3	1	6		
Blair, James, Junr	1	3	1			Farnham, Joshua	3	1	2			Savage, Abraham					
Dillano, Jona	1	2	4			Trott, Joanna			2								
Manes, Saml	2	3	2			Weymouth, Moses	3		3			**BETWEEN NORRIDGE-WOCK AND SEVEN MILE BROOK.**					
Ford, Francis	3	1	1			Gilmore, Willm	5	1	7								
Grace, Willm	1	1	3			Gilmore, David	1	2	4			Allis, Benjamin	1		2		
Manes, Betsy	1	1	4			Lancaster, Joseph	3	2	4			Dor, Ambrius	1	1	3		
Harnden, Willm	1	1	3			Smith, Ebenezer	1	2	1			Houghton, Thomas	2		1		
White, Robert	4	1	4			Webb (Widow)	1	1	1			Johnson, John	1	2	4		
Motheswill, Thos	2	1	4			Blanchard, James	4	3	5			Piper, John	1	2	2		
Day, Nathl	2	1	5			Carlton, Jane	1	2	3			Gray, Sarah	1	2	4		
Smith, Zebulon	1	2	3			Farnham, Zebedee	1	1	1			Savage, James	1	4	4		
Preble, Saml	1	4	3			Dilleno, Ephraim	1	2	3			Savage, Charles	1	1	5		
Witherby, Jona	1	3	3	1		Trott, Benja	4	4	4			Mores, Joseph	1	1	1		
Harndon, Saml	3	1	4			Wright, John	1	1	1			Fairbroth, Lovewell	1	4	4		
Preble, Jona	4		7			Wright, Joseph	1	1	1			Lovejoy, Thomas	1	2	1		
Ryan, Michl	1	2	3			Wright, Joseph, Junr	1	1	5			Crosby, James	1	1	3		
Curtes, Charles	2	1	5			Blackman, Eliphalet	1	4	6			Forgerson, John	1	3	5		
Stinson, James	1	2	2			Bailey, John, Junr	1		2			Chapman, Nathaniel	1	2	1		
Curtes, John	2	5	5			Cross, John	3	1	2			Wesson, Benjamin	1	1	3		
Card, Thos	1	1	2			Bowen, Jabez	1	1	2			Walker, Stephen	1	4	4		
Card, Danl	1	4	2			Gray, John	1	4	3			Rogers, Robert	1	2	3		
Paine, Moses	1	1	1			Shaw, John	1	1	3			Putnam, John	1	2	3		
Preble, Martha		1	2			Sheldon, Willm	1	1	3			Walker, John	1		3		
Winshop, Josiah	2	1	3			Shaw, Mary			3			Littlefield, Ebenezer	1	2	4		
Stinson, James	3	1	3			Fullerton, James	2	2	4			Barnes, James	2	4	3		
Hathorn, John	2	2	3			Bailey, Benja	1	2	3			Lovewell, Thomas	1		3		
Hathorn, John, Junr	1		1			Gould, Saml	3	2	5			Jones, James	1	3	2		
Perkins, Robert	1	2	3			Walker, Joseph	1	1	2			Ames, Jonathan	1	3	5		
Smith, Mary		1	1			Grant, Elijah	2	1	3			Dean, Ebenezer	1		1		
Curtes, Joseph	1		1			Walker, Andw	3	1	7			Fling, Daniel	1				
Grover, Benja	1		1			Walker, Solomon	2	5	3								
Fuller, Joshua	1	1	1			Williams, Nathl	2		5								
Stinson, Robert	1	2	4			Williams, Timo	1	3	3								

WASHINGTON COUNTY.

NAME OF HEAD OF FAMILY.	Free white males of 16 years and upward, including heads of families.	Free white males under 16 years.	Free white females, including heads of families.	All other free persons.	Slaves.	NAME OF HEAD OF FAMILY.	Free white males of 16 years and upward, including heads of families.	Free white males under 16 years.	Free white females, including heads of families.	All other free persons.	Slaves.	NAME OF HEAD OF FAMILY.	Free white males of 16 years and upward, including heads of families.	Free white males under 16 years.	Free white females, including heads of families.	All other free persons.	Slaves.
BUCKS HARBOR NECK TOWN.						**MACHIAS TOWN—con.**						**MACHIAS TOWN—con.**					
Newcomb, John	1	4	3			Drew, Consider	3	2	1			Hanscom, Aron, junr	1				
Elliot, Simon	1					Dunn, David	1					Hanscom, Nathan	1				
Pettegrow, Benjamin	1	3	4			Dowdele, Michal	1	1	3			Hathaway, Eleazer	1	3	2		
Larrabee, Abner	1					Dowe, Stephen	1					Huntley, Jabez	1		1		
Larrabee, David	1	1				Darby, John	1					Hill, Joseph	1	1	1		
Larrabee, Isaac	3		2			Davis, William	1					Harvey, Seth	1				
Mayhew, Priscilla		1	3			Damons, Garniel	1	3	1			Howe, William	1				
Fogg, Stephen	1	2	4			Dearing, Joseph	1					Hitchings, Josiah	1				
Libbee, Nathan	1		2			Day, John	1					Holmes, Samuel	3	2	2		
Libbee, Josiah	1	3	3			Eden, Samuel	1		3			Innes, Partrick	1				
Coolbroth, Peter	2	3	4			Emmerson, William	1	1	4			Jones, Stephen	3	1	4		
Howard, John	1	1	3			Elsmore, Moses	1	2	2			Johnson, Stephen	2	2	2		
						Eustis, Mrs			1			Kelly, John	1	3	2		
MACHIAS TOWN.						Foster, Benjamin	3	1	3	1		Munson, Joseph	2		1	2	
Avery, James	2	3	2			Foster, Wooden	4	1	3			Munson, Joseph, junr	1	2	1		
Albee, William	1	4	2			Foster, John W	1	3	6			Munson, Stephen	1	4	1		
Aylwood, Partrick	1	2	3			Foster, John	1	1	4			Munson, John	1	1	3		
Averill, Joseph	1	4	3			Foster, Levi	1		3			Meservey, Daniel	3				
Andrews, Israel	1	3	2			Foster, Abijah	1					Mitchel, Noah	1		2		
Ackly, Benajah	1	7	2			Foster, Benjamin, Junr	1	2	4			Moore, Samuel	1				
Berry, Jonathan	2		6			Foster, Moses	1		3			Miller, Francis	1	1	2		
Berry, John	3	2	7			Fenlason, Wallis	1	7	1			McGregor, Alexander	1				
Berry, Benjamin	1	1	3			Foss, Benjamin	1	2	3			Lord, Benjamin	1				
Burnum, Job	2	2	8			Foss, Joseph	1					Libbee, Obed	1	1	1		
Burnum, Samuel	1					Foss, Benjamin, junr	1					Libbee, Daniel	1		1		
Bryant, Barthow	1		4			Flinn, James	2	1	2			Libbee, David	1	2	3		
Boynton, Amos	1	2	6			Hawes, Elizabeth			3			Longfellow, Nathan	3	2	4		
Bowles, Ralph H	1	1	2			Griffiths, Henry	1	1	1	1		Longfellow, Nathan, junr	1	2	5		
Belighter, Jno	1	2	1			Getchell, Joseph	1		1			Longfellow, Jacob	1	1	5		
Belfountain, Rana	1					Getchell, Joseph, Junr	1	4	3			Longfellow, Olive			3		
Brown, Philbrook	1	1	1			Gardner, Ebenr	1	5	3			Libbee, Joseph	2	2	2		
Bryant, William	1					Gillmore, Arthur	1					Lewis, Amasa	1	1	2		
Bryant, Joseph	1					Gooch, Benjamin	1	1	7			Lowry, James	1				
Bryant, John	1					Gooch, James	2	2	5			Lyon, Revd James	2	1	4		
Barns, Ashble	1		3			Gooch, William	1		2			Obrien, Jerimiah	1	3	3	1	
Cary, Edward	1					Gooch, Ebenezer	1		3			Obrien, Gideon	1	3	7		
Crocker, Benjamin	1					Gardner, David	1		2			Obrien, Morris	1		4		
Clark, Parker	4		2			Gardner, David, junr	2	3	4			Elliot, Robert	1				
Chaloner, William	1	5	2			Harris, Josiah	1					Brown, Andrew	1				
Crocker, John	2		3			Howe, Tilly	1	3	3			Phinny, Nathan	1	2	3		
Crocker, James	1	1	2			Hill, Sarah		2	4			Phinny, Nathanl, junr	1				
Clark, Edward	1					Hill, Hannah	1	1	4			Phinny, Josiah	1				
Conners, Partrick	1	1	3			Hill, Samuel	1					Pinco, Jonathan	4	4	3		
Chace, Ephraim	2	2	6			Hollway, Ladwick	1	2	3			Palmer, Jacob	3	2	3		
Chace, William	1		1			Holmes, John	1	3	2			Prescott, David	1				
Cates, Samuel	1	2	4			Hadley, Ephraim	1					Pepper, Anthony	1	2	3		
Crosman, Jacob	1					Hoit, Daniel	2	4	6			Penniman, Jacob	1				
Clefford, Joseph	1	4	4			Harmon, Benjamin	1		4			Parker, Stephen	1		2		
						Hanscom, Aron	3	2	4								

HEADS OF FAMILIES—MAINE.

WASHINGTON COUNTY—Continued.

NAME OF HEAD OF FAMILY.	Free white males of 16 years and upward, including heads of families.	Free white males under 16 years.	Free white females, including heads of families.	All other free persons.	Slaves.	NAME OF HEAD OF FAMILY.	Free white males of 16 years and upward, including heads of families.	Free white males under 16 years.	Free white females, including heads of families.	All other free persons.	Slaves.	NAME OF HEAD OF FAMILY.	Free white males of 16 years and upward, including heads of families.	Free white males under 16 years.	Free white females, including heads of families.	All other free persons.	Slaves.
MACHIAS TOWN—continued.						**PLANTATIONS EAST OF MACHIAS—con.**						**PLANTATIONS EAST OF MACHIAS—con.**					
						No. 2—Continued.						*No. 8—Continued.*					
Richardson, Peter	3	2	6			Lincoln, Joshua	1					Kent, Jonathan	1				
Rich, Samuel	1	6	2			Clark (Widow)	1		3			Sangmeid, Henry	1	2	3		
Smith, Stephen	3	1	5			Dalton, Sipio				5		Coombs, Edward	1	1	3		
Smith, Stephen, jun'	1	2	2			Bender, Christopher	1		2			*No. 9.*					
Smith, Ellis	1					Bridges, John	1		2								
Stillman, George	2	2	4			Morain, Andrew	1					Cook, John	1		2		
Sanborn, Ennoch	2		1			Stoddard, Baley C	1	2	1			Reynolds, Samuel	2	2	2		
Sanborn, John	1	1	2			Gardner, Warren	1					Edwards, Doctor	1	1	1		
Sanborn, Richard	1	1	2			Hersey, Zadock	1	2	5			Layton, Samuel	1	4	3		
Smith, Charles	1	2	1			*No. 4.*						Crew, John	1		2		
Smith, Ebenezer	1		2									Holland, William	2		1		
Sevey, George	2	1	8			Porter, Joseph	5		1			Jourdan, Richard	1		2		
Sevey, Joseph	1		2			Boyden, Jacob	1					*No. 10.*					
Sevey, Sylvanus	1	3	2			Johnson, John	1	1	1								
Sevey, Aron	1					Bugby, William	1	3	2			Hale, James			2		
Sevey, John	1	1	2			Jones, Samuel	1	2	4			Ash, Samuel	1		3		
Singly, Frederick	1	1	1			McDonald, Donald	2	2	5			Hurley, William	1		3		
Scott, Samuel	2		3			Somes, Daniel	1	1	2			Smith, Daniel	2	1	3		
Scott, George	1	3	5			Brewer, John	2		3			Shaw, Benjamin	2	1	3		
Scott, John	1	3	5			Johnson, Job	1	1	1			Ayer, Elijah	1		2		
Scott, Jess	1	1	2			Leshure, Samuel	1	2	3			Ayer, Elijah, jun'	1	1	5		
Scott, Samuel, jun'	1	4	3			Fausett (Widow)		1	3			Hobert, Nath¹	2				
Scott, Daniel	1	1	1			*No. 5.*						Shaw, James	1				
Scott, Mark	1	1	2									Oliver (Widow)	1	2	3		
Stone, Solomon & Son	2	2	6			Sprague, James	1	5	3			Hatch, Hawes	1				
Smith, James	1	1	2			Sprague, Abiel	2	2	3			*No. 11.*					
Sinkler, Nath¹	1					Petigrow, Thomas	4	2	5								
Talbot, Peter	1	4	4			Dyer, Jones	3	2	3			Cates, Robert	1	4	3		
Thompson, George	1	1	5			Dyer, James	1	1	2			Davis, John	1	1	2		
Thaxter, Marshal	1	2	1			Hill, Daniel	3	1	3			Makem, John	1	2	3		
Toby, Matthias	2					Berry, John	1	1	3			Andrews, Jerimiah	1	1	1		
Thompson, Abraham	1					Lane, James	1	3	1			Andrews, Timothy	1	1	4		
Thorp, Thomas		1	3			Jackson, William	1	2	1			Niles, Jonathan	1		4		
Woodruff, Jonathan	1	1	1			Ryen, John	2		3			Andrews, Nathan	2	1	2		
Watts, John	2		1	2		Bohannon, John	2	3	3			*No. 12.*					
Waterhouse, Enoch	2	1	8			Noble, John	1	2	2								
Wescoat, Benjᵃ	1					Bayley, Nath¹ & Son	2		3			Crane, John	3	1	4		
Webb, William	1					Sprague, Eli	1		2			Trescutt, Lemuel	1		2		
Dillaway, James	2	1				*No. 8.*						Peck, George	1	1	4		
Ingly, Moses	1											Harvey, Thomas	1	1	1		
Ingly, Eben	1					Allan, John	3	4	4			Bryant, Davis	2	1	1		
Cooper, John	1					Delesdernier, Lewis Fred	1	2	3			Dowling, John	1	2	4		
Bruce, Phineas	1					Bowman, Andrew	1		4			Huntly, Jabez, jun'	1	2	2		
Jones, Asa	1					Foster, John	4		1			Nickerson, Izachar	1	1	3		
Packard, Cyrus	1					Flagg (Widow)	1	4	2			Huntly, Frederick	2	6	2		
Western, Job	1					Rumney, Dominicus	1					Howe, Sarah			3		
PLANTATIONS EAST OF MACHIAS.						Kent, John	1	2	1			*No. 13.*					
No. 1.						Johnson, James	1										
						Simpson, John	1					Brown, James	1	5	1		
Lincoln, Moses	1		2			Delesdernier, Gideon	1		1			**PLANTATIONS WEST OF MACHIAS.**					
Lincoln, Jacob	1		1			Ramsdell, William	1	2	4			*No. 4.*					
Loring, Peter	1		1			Reynolds, Benjᵃ	2	2	3								
Frost, John	1	3	2			Ramsdell, James	1		1			Small, Joseph	1	1	2		
Frost, Samuel	1					Ramsdell, Isaac	1					Robertson, David	1	1	2		
Patterson, Alex'	1		4			Ramsdell, Ebenezer	1	1	3			Archibald, Thomas	1		3		
Hodges, Alex'	1	2	2			Rumney, William	1	1	4			Gross, Reuben	1		1		
Morrison, William	2	2	4			Clerk, William	3					Campbell, Alex'	4	1	4		
Sweat, Daniel	1	1	2			Jinkins, Thoˢ	3		1			Foster, Robert	4		4		
Tuttle, Samuel	2	4	3			Gooe, Jacob	1		1			Todd, John	1				
Wood, James	2	1	1			Denbow, Nathaniel	3	1	6			Todd, James	1				
Stoddard, Nath¹	1	1	4			Huckings, Samuel	1	2	1			Bracey, Joseph	3	2	5		
Kilbey, William	1	1	1			Kelly, James	1	1	2			Joy, Francis	1		2		
Damons, Abiah	1		3			Burr, Perez	1					Patten (Widow)	2	3	4		
Chubbuck, James	1		2			Bell, William	1	1	2			Stout, Jeremiah	3	2	1		
No. 2.						Simpson, William	1		2			Leighton, Thomas	4	2	3		
						Cockram, James	1	3	5			Leighton, Joseph	1	1	1		
Henderson, Thoˢ	1					Bower, Henry	2	2	2			Clark, James	1	1	3		
Lincoln, Theodore	3	1	3			Hale, Richard	1	1	2			Leighton, Thomas, 3ᵈ	1	1	1		
Preston, Nathan	1	2	3			Shackford, John	1	4	1			West, Thomas	1				
Cushing, Solomon	1					Boynton, Caleb	2		4			Parker, William	1	3	4		
Cushing, Laban	1					Clark, William	3	3	4			Pinkim, Tristram	1	4	5		
Lincoln, Zenas	1		3			Goddard, Nathan¹	2	1				Pinkim, Richard	1	2	3		
Willson, Joshua	1		3			McGuyer, John	1		3			Yeaton, John	4		5		
Ash, Robert	2	1	2			Clark, Joseph	2	1	5			Dyer, Henry	4	4	6		
Lea, Daniel	1	2	2			Dexter, Thomas	1	2	2			Sawyer, Joseph	1		3		
Bridges, Joshᵃ Y Abraᵐ	3	3	1			Hacket, Alexander	1		1			Leighton, Thomas, Jun'	3	5	3		
Blackwood, James	1	2	2			Clark, Nathan¹	2		1			Godfrey, Ichabod	1		3		
Gardiner, Daniel	1		4			Goudy, William	1	1	2			Stevens, Jonathan	2	1	6		
Smith, Richard	1	1	4			Beaman, Thomas	1	1	3			Townsley, Jacob	1	2	3		
Harper, Richard	2		1			Ricker, William	1					Kinsley, Samuel	1	4	3		
Mahaw, Edmund	1	3	4			Maybe, Elias	1					Tracey, Wheeler	1		2		
Laton, Hatewell	2	2	8			Fountain, Stephen			5			Oakes, Atherton	1		2		
Huckings, Clement	1		1			Hammon, William	1	2	3			Guptell, William	1	3	3		
Willson, William	1	1	2			Johnson, Paul	1	2	3			Moore, Robert	2	1	3		
Sprague, Samuel	1	4	1			Boynton, Caleb, jun'	1	1	2			Moore, Josiah	1				
Wilder, Theophilus	1	1	4			Dummer, John	1					Downs, Ebenezer	4	1	1		
Wilder, Theoˢ, jun'	1		2			Carlo, John	1	4	1								
Palmer, John	1		1			Owen, Morgan	1	1	1								
Henry, Isaiah	3	1	5			Carter, James	1		1								
Hatch, Chris	1	2	3	1		Clark, Henry	1		2								
						Maybee, Solomon	1		2								

WASHINGTON COUNTY—Continued.

NAME OF HEAD OF FAMILY.	Free white males of 16 years and upward, including heads of families.	Free white males under 16 years.	Free white females, including heads of families.	All other free persons.	Slaves.	NAME OF HEAD OF FAMILY.	Free white males of 16 years and upward, including heads of families.	Free white males under 16 years.	Free white females, including heads of families.	All other free persons.	Slaves.	NAME OF HEAD OF FAMILY.	Free white males of 16 years and upward, including heads of families.	Free white males under 16 years.	Free white females, including heads of families.	All other free persons.	Slaves.
PLANTATIONS WEST OF MACHIAS—con.						**PLANTATIONS WEST OF MACHIAS—con.**						**PLANTATIONS WEST OF MACHIAS—con.**					
No. 4—Continued.						*No. 6—Continued.*						*No. 13—Continued.*					
Downs, Ebenezer, Jr.	1	1	1			Nash, Samuel	1		1			Dow, Jonathan	2		3		
Wakefield, Samuel	3	2	5			Nash, Isaiah	2	5	2			Hale, Stephen	1	1	5		
Townsley, Gad	1					Norton, Seth	2	1	3			Ingersole, William	1	4	3		
Baker, Lemuel	1	2	4			Nash, Samuel, junr	1					Ingersole, Benjn					
Parrott, Thomas	2	4	3			Nash, Isaac	1	2	3			Ingersol, Benja, Junr	1		1		
Godfrey, Daniel	1					Nash, Joseph	1	3	2			Kelly, Elijah	1	1	3		
No. 5.						Norton, Elias	1		1			Nash, Ebenr	1				
Nash, Reuben	1	1	2			Norton, Abraham	1					McKinsey, Owen	2	3	4		
Cates, Edward	1	2	4			Nash, Isaac, 2d	1					Merritt, Daniel	1	2	2		
Small, Daniel	1	2	3			Plummer, Moses	3	1	5			Merritt, Richard	1		2		
Libbee, Joseph	1	1	4			Plummer, Moses, junr	1					Mansfield, Thomas	1	3	1		
Nash (Widow)		1	2			Reynolds, Eliphalet	1	2	3			McKaslegen, John	1	3	4		
Cole, Ebenezer	2	3	4			Ramsdell, Nathl	1					Nash, John	1	1	5		
Cole, Ebenezer, Jr.	1					Stevens (Widow)		2	4			Nash, Isaac	1	2	3		
Nash, Reuben, 2.	1					Steele, Reuben	1	2	2			Nash, Abraham	1		2		
Campbell, James	1	2	1			Steele (Widow)			4			Reynolds, David	1		2		
Grace, James	2	4	4			Tibbets, Joseph	2	1	2			Tinny, George	1	2	4		
Dorman, Jabez	2	2	6			Tibbets, William	1					Tucker, Samuel	1	3	2		
Jourdain, Ebenr	3		3			Wass, Wilmot	1					Tibbets, Joseph	1	3	2		
Stout, Joseph	2	5	4			Wass, Wilmot, junr	2	5	3			Tinny, John	1				
Denbow, John	2	5	3			Wass, Willmot, 3d	1					Tinny, David	1				
Fichet, Zebulon	1	2	2			Wass, Christor	1					Tinny, George, junr	1				
Nickles, Alexr	1	1	4			White, Tilly	1	3	4			Tinny, Samuel	1				
Collins, Richard	1	1	4			Whitney, Matthias	1	5	4			Whitney, Nathn	2	4	4		
Stout, Benjamin	2		3			Yates, Francis	1	1	5			Willson, Joseph	1		3		
Jones, Joseph		1	4			*No. 11.*						Willson, Joseph, Jr	1	1	2		
Brown, David	1	5	2			Leighton, Theodore	1		7			Willson, Gowen	1				
Sawyer, Josiah	1	1	1			Jordain, John	1		3			Worseter, Moses	3	2	7		
Lovett, Isaac	1	1	5			Willey, Ichabod	3	2	4			Wass, David M.	1	1	3		
Stout, Thomas	3		6			Roff, Moses	2	1	2			Waymouth, James	1				
Wallis, Joseph, Junr	1	1	2			Laurence, John	1		1			*No. 22.*					
Rea, William	1	4	1			Laurence, John, Junr		3	3			Peirpoint, Joseph	3	3	1		
Brown, Jess	2	2	3			Willson, Gawing		4	5			Whitney, Joel	3	5	3		
Wallis, Joseph	2	1	3			Anderson, John	1	1	4			Noyce, Josiah	1	2	3		
Cummings, John	1					Corson, Samuel	1	4	2			Farnsworth, Isaac	2	3	3		
Wallis, Benjamin	2	1	3			Tucker, Josiah	4	2	3			Whitney, Napthm	1		2		
Ward, John	1					Small, John	1					Dunnaven, John	1	1	4		
Wallis, James	1					Small, Elisha	1	1	3			Watts, David	1		2		
Small, John, 3d	1					Corson, Samuel, Jr	1	2	4			Watts, Samuel	1		2		
McCormick, Alexr	1					Corson, John	1		2			Coolidge, Caleb	1		2		
No. 6.						Small, John, Junr	1	3	3			Tupper, William	2	1	1		
Bickford, William	1	3	2			Small, Ebenezer	1	1	3			Tupper, Joseph	1		3		
Batson, William	1	3	2			*No. 12.*						Libbee, Reuben	1	4	4		
Dunbar, Josiah	1					Leighton, Samuel	2	1	2			Bean, Abner	1	1	3		
Coffin, Richard	3		3			Leighton, Isaac	1		1			Randall, Charles	1	1	2		
Coffin, Samuel	1		1			Leighton, Parratt	1					Knight, Jonathan	2	4	5		
Coffin, Barnabas	1		1			*No. 13.*						Knight, Paul	1	3	3		
Cornthwait, Thomas	1					Allan, Obediah	3	2	4			Shappa, Athony	1	3	2		
Drisko, John	2		4			Allan, Gideon	1	2	4			Kellon, Benj	2	1	1		
Drisko, Joseph	2	3	4			Archer, John	1	6	4			Wessen, Josiah	1	1	7		
Hall, John	2	4	6			Buckman, John	1	6	3	2		Roberts, Thomas				1	
Jourdan, James	1	1	2			Black, Sherbone				4		Merret, Samuel	1		5		
Knowles, Francis	1	1	5			Cox, Nathl	2	2	7			Kelly, Thomas	1	3	7		
Look, Daniel	1	1	7			Coffin, Matthew	1	3	2			Sawyer, John	1	2	5		
Look, George	1	3	2			Coffin, Elisha	1	1	2			Sawyer, Nehemiah	1		3		
Look, Moses	1					Calaghan, Wm	1		2			Cumming, Francis	1	2	7		
Merrit, Daniel	1	1	1			Cox, Edward	1					McDonald, Agnes	2	2	2		
Merritt, Wm	1	1	4			Crocker, William	1		1			Buffet, John	1		2		
Merrit, Joseph	1					Drisko, Samuel	1	2	5			Horton, Elihu	2	2	2		
Masten, Samuel	1	1	3			Dunbar, Obed	1	3	4			Beal, Jerimiah	1		4		
Moore, Josiah	1	3	2									Beal, Manwarren	3	2			
Miller, Robert	1		2									Menett, David	1				

YORK COUNTY.

NAME OF HEAD OF FAMILY.	Free white males of 16 years and upward, including heads of families.	Free white males under 16 years.	Free white females, including heads of families.	All other free persons.	Slaves.	NAME OF HEAD OF FAMILY.	Free white males of 16 years and upward, including heads of families.	Free white males under 16 years.	Free white females, including heads of families.	All other free persons.	Slaves.	NAME OF HEAD OF FAMILY.	Free white males of 16 years and upward, including heads of families.	Free white males under 16 years.	Free white females, including heads of families.	All other free persons.	Slaves.
ARUNDEL TOWN.						**ARUNDEL TOWN—con.**						**ARUNDEL TOWN—con.**					
Staples, Willm	1	4	2			Burbank, Asa	2	2	2			Clough Joel	1	1	4		
Bickford, Eliakim	3	2	3			Thompson, Benja	2	2	3			Clough, Joseph	2	3	4		
Tarbox, Lemuel	1	4	3			Watson, Saml	1	2	3			Clough, Noah	1	1	4		
Smith, Jona, Jr.	1	1	2			Burnham, Jane		1	1			Dearing (Widow)			2		
Emery, Jeremiah	1	1	6			Lasdel, Bartholomew	2		2			Dearing, James	2	4	3		
Blaisdel, John	1		3			Lord, Tobias	1	1	1			Hodgdon, Israel	1	1	1		
Perkins, George	3	1	4			Lord, Thos	2		2			Durrel, Thos	1	3	5		
Towns, Danl	2	2	5			Burnham, Seth	2	4	3			Burnham, Isaac	2	1	2		
Hutchins, Josiah, Jr.	1	1	5			Burnham, Grace		2	1			Burnham, Forrest				6	
Hutchins, Saml, jr	1	1	1			Burnham, Jacob	2	1	2			Thompson, Stephen	1	2	4		
Abbot, Silas	1	2	4			Dorman, Jabez	1		2			Thompson, James	1	1	3		
Huff, Danl	2	4	4			Stone, John	1	1	2			Dennico, John	1		4		
Hancom, Timo	3		3			Dorman, John	1	2	6			Hutchens, Ezra	1		2		
Dorman, Jesse	4		3			Miller, John	2	2	2			Ayers, George	1	1	1	2	
Dorman, Israel	1	1	4			Downing, Nicholas	1	1	1			Boston, Shipway	1	2	2		
Patten, John	1	1	7			Miller, Andw			5			Butler, Stephen	1		2		
Lewis, Saml	3	1	2			Fairfield, Saml	1	1	3			Thompson, Benja	1	3	2		
Mitchel, Danl	2	2	4			Huff, Thos	1		4			Towns, Josiah	1	2	2		
Mitchel, Dummer	2	4	3			Benson, Henry	2	4	3			Mitchel, John	1		1		

HEADS OF FAMILIES—MAINE.

YORK COUNTY—Continued.

NAME OF HEAD OF FAMILY.	Free white males of 16 years and upward, including heads of families.	Free white males under 16 years.	Free white females, including heads of families.	All other free persons.	Slaves.	NAME OF HEAD OF FAMILY.	Free white males of 16 years and upward, including heads of families.	Free white males under 16 years.	Free white females, including heads of families.	All other free persons.	Slaves.	NAME OF HEAD OF FAMILY.	Free white males of 16 years and upward, including heads of families.	Free white males under 16 years.	Free white females, including heads of families.	All other free persons.	Slaves.
ARUNDEL TOWN—con.						**ARUNDEL TOWN—con.**						**ARUNDEL TOWN—con.**					
Stone, Jonᵃ	1	3	1			Littlefield, Elijah	1	1	3			Patten, Robert	1	2	5		
Currier, Nathˡ	1		1			Littlefield, Benjᵃ	1	1	2	3		Goodwin (Widow)			2		
Smith, John	1	3	1			Curtes, Joseph	1	2	1			Goodwin, John	1	5	2		
Cleaves, Eaton	2	4	2			Shepherd, Robert	1	1	2			Thompson, Jonᵃ	1	1	2		
Hilton, Abraham	2		3			Chatman, Wilbon	1	1	2			Lord, John	2	1	7		
Cleaves, Stephen	3	2	3			Miller, Jerᵉ	2	1	4			Nason, Joshua	1	1	4		
Cleaves, John	2		2			Fairfield, John, Jr	1	2	2			Patten, James					
Cleaves, John, Jr	1	1	1			Walker, Jonᵃ	1		2			Seavey, Nicholas	1		4		
Smith, Danˡ	1		6			Towns, Amos	2	3	8			Wiles, Samˡ, Jr	1	2	1		
Smith, David	1	2	3			Smith, Willᵐ	2		2			Stone, Jonᵃ, Jr	1		2		
Smith, Jonᵃ	1	2	3			Miller (Widow)		1	2			Whitten, Samˡ	2	2	4		
Burbank, John	1		2			Downing, John	1		3			Cleaves, Benjᵃ	1	1	1		
Lord, Danˡ	1	3	2			Miller, Lemˡ	1	2	3			**BERWICK TOWN.**					
Day, Samˡ	1		4			Downing, Harrison	1	2	2			Chadbourne, Hon. Benjᵃ	2		2		
Hovey, John	1		5			Rhodes, Miles	3	2	3			Goodwin, Hon. Ichabod	3	2	8		
Huff, Ebenezer	1	2	2			Perkins, Abner	3	2	3			Tucker, John	2	1	8		
Davis, Danˡ	1	3	3			Murphy, John	2	3	4			Wood, Danˡ	3	1	2		
Stone (Widow)	1	1	3			Perkins, Thoˢ	1		1			Roberts, Joseph	2	2	2		
Brown, Andʷ	1	2	2			Perkins, Thoˢ	1	1	5			Roberts, Joshua	1		1		
Hutchens, Joseph	3	1	8			Perkins, James	5	2	2			Haggens, John	4	4	7	1	
Brown, Andʷ, Jr	1	1	2			Perkins, Ephraim	3	2	5			Grant, Moses	1	1	2		
Mattocks, Pel. Graves	1	1	3			Wissel, Thoˢ	2	1	2			Jenkins, Jedediah	2				
Wilder, Benjᵃ	1	1	3			Morse, Nathan	1	1	2			Low, Nathˡ	3		2		
Washbourn, Joseph	3	1	1			Walker, John	1	1	3			Kirker, Henery	1	1	2		
Jeffery, John	3		3			Walker, Danˡ	3	1	5			Junkins, Robert	2	2	3	1	
Jeffery, Benjᵃ	4	2	5			Perkins, John	1	1	2			Grant, John	2	2	6		
Hide, Joseph	1	1	3			Perkins, Joseph	1	2	3			Butler, Samˡ	2	2	4		
Avery, Joseph	3	1	2			Gould, James	3	3	3			Butler, Samˡ, Junʳ	1	2	2		
Avery, Shadrack	1	4	2			Gould, John	1	1	2			Butler, Ichabod	1	2	3	1	
Hutchins, David	3		3			Fairfield, Willᵐ	1	2	3			Libbey, Nathan	1		2		
Green, Andʷ	1		2			Stone, Benjᵃ	1		4			Morris, Wᵐ	1	1	2		
Lasdel, Mary	1	2	2			Smith, Jere	1	1	2			Haggens, Edmund	2		4	2	
Perkins, Thoˢ	1	2	3			Ward, Nathˡ	1		3			Hamilton, Jonᵃ	1	1	2		
Wiles, Israel	1		4			Cleaves, James	1	1	3			Hamilton, Millet	1	1	2		
Weeks, Nicholas	1		2			Stone, Nehemiah	1		1			Chadwick, Wᵐ	2	1	5		
Stone, Robert	2	3	6			Walker, Nathˡ	1	1	2			Jordin, John	1		3		
Stone, Dix	3		1			Huff, Samˡ	3	4	4			Smith, Wᵐ	1		2		
Weeks, John	1	2	2			Huff, Israel	1		2			Cutts, Ricᵈ Foxˢᵉ	1	2	4		
Perkins, Thoˢ	2	1	3			Huff, Abner	1		1			Abbot, Benjᵃ	2	4	2		
Chatman, Abraᵐ	1		1			Seavey, Stephen	1	2	5			Lord, Paul	1	1	2		
Perkins, Joseph	1	1	2			Huff, James	1	6	3			Pike, Samˡ	2		3		
Lasdel, Jere	1		1			Mattuck, Thoˢ	1		1			Lord, Mark	5	2	5	1	
Wiles, Jacob	5		2			Barker, —	1	4	1			Gerrish, Clark	2	1	6		
Wiles, Ruth			2			Jackson, Joshua	1	3	3			MᶜGeoch, Allexʳ	2	6	3		
Wiles, Ephraim	1	2	4			Wiles, Samˡ	2	3	2	2		Nason, Nathˡ	1		4		
Emmons, John	2		2			Bukford (Widow)	2		2			Abbot, Thomas	1		3		
Emmons, John, Jr	1	7	2			Huff, Charles	2		3			Abbot, Thomas					
Emmons, Ebenᵃ	1					MᶜCarr, Caleb	1		1			Nason, John	1	1	5		
Emmons, Eliakim	1	2	2			Dishon, Peter	3	4	4			Lord, Nathan	2		4		
Fletcher, John	1		1			Perkins, George	1	3	4			Lord, John	3	3	3	1	
Fletcher, Stephen	3	1	1			Lewis, John	2		3			Marshall, Nahum	1		2		
Fletcher, Pendleton	1		4			Lewis, Benjᵃ	1	4	2			Hovey, Ivory	5	1	6	1	
Fletcher, Jonᵃ	1	1	1			Andrews, John	3	1	2			Furness, Robert	2	1	4		
Goodrigde, Willᵐ	1		3			Hovey, Susana			1			Lee, Martha	1	1	3		
Goodrige, Jere	1		3			Davis, Eliphalet	1	2	2			Chadbourne, Mary			2		
Fletcher, Joseph	1	4	5			Merril, Abel	1	4	3			Chadbourne, Jonᵃ C	2	3	5		
Ferren, Jonᵃ	1		6			Merrill, Gideon	1	1	2			Chadbourne, Benjᵃ	1		2		
Stone, Benjᵃ	1	1	2			Merrill, Jacob	1		2			Chadbourne, Humpʸ	1	2	4	5	
Wiles, Benjᵃ	1	1	2			Emery, Joseph	1	1	1			Emery, Moses	1		2		
Perkins, Thoˢ, 3ᵈ	1	2	3			Whidden, Israel	3	1	5			Sullivan, Ebenezer	2	1	4		
Downing, Benjᵃ	1	1	1			MᶜCullock, Adam	2	1	4			Goodwin, Daniel	1		3	3	
Downing, John	1	2	3			Merril, Obed	3	2	5			Plaisted, James	1	1	1		
Perkins, Danˡ	1	2	3			Downing, Jonᵃ	2	2	2			Gerrish, Allexʳ	3	3	2	3	
Robinson, John	2		4			Downing, Benjᵃ	1	3	2			Hill, John	1	2	3	2	
Robinson, Samˡ	2		3			Curtes (Widow)			4			Frost, James	1	1	3	3	
White, Danˡ	1		3			Perkins, Abner	1		4			Plaisted, John	1	3	5		
Smith, Willᵐ	1	4	1			Perkins, Jotham	2		4			Gᵤrrish, Benjᵃ	1	3	3		
Smith, Charles	1		2			Durrel, Benjᵃ	2	3	5			Hill, Ichabod	1	3	2		
Smith, Samuel	1	2	4			Durrel, Jacob	1	3	3			Goodwin, Dominicus	2	2	4		
Hutchens, Josiah	2	2	4			Cows, Benjᵃ	1	1	3			Thompson, Rev. John	2	3	4	5	
White, Robert	1		2			Durrell, Asa	3	1	3			Lord, Caleb	2	1	5		
Moody, Silas	1	5	4			Thompson, Ephraim	3	3	1			Chadbourne, Thomas	3		4		
Walker, Samˡ	1	4	2			Ham, Joˢ	1	2	1			Brock, Simeon	2	1	4		
Walker, John	3	1	8			Green, Benjᵃ	2	5	3			Ham, Wᵐ			2		
Whidden, Joseph	1	3	3			Lock, Simeon	1	4	1			Verney, Davis	1		2		
MᶜCloud, —	1		1			Rhodes, Jacob	3		5			Lord, Jeremiah	1		3		
Huff, Charles		1	2			Thompson, John	1	1	1			Boyce, Jotham	1		2		
Barter, Mark	1	1	6			Smith (Widow)	1	2	2			Lord, Joseph	4		4		
Towns, Robert	1	1	3			Grant, Willᵐ	1	2	2			Lord, Richard	1	3	3		
Walker, Andʷ	1	1	3			Springer, John	2	2	4			Jones, Vaughn	1		3		
Hutchens, David	1	3	3			Miller, Benjᵃ	1	2	1			Stone, John	1	1	2		
Hutchens, Levi	2		4			Hutchens, Simeon	1	2	3			Young, Stephen	1		2		
Murphy, Joshua	1	4	3			Hutchins, David	1	1	1			Stapole, Lenord	1	1	1		
March, Saul	1	4	7			Wakefield, Nathˡ	1		2			Hearl, Joseph	1		2		
Ridout, Abraham	1		6			MᶜCuen, John	1	1	2			Hubbard, Timothy	1	1	2		
Leach, Nathˡ	1	1	1			Crudiford, Abner	3	1	2			Nason, Danˡ	1		2		
Huff, John	1	3	2			Merrill, Benjᵃ	2	2	3			Lord, Mary			1		
Seavey, Nicholas	1		1			Davis, Nathˡ	2		2			Cushing, John	3	4	4	2	
Dempsey (Widow)			2			Goodwin, Benjᵃ	1	1	2			Hamilton, Jonᵃ	3	5	6	1	
Adams, John	1	1	2			Lord, Benjᵃ	1		2			Chase, Enoch	1	4	6		
Adams, James	1	3	4			Lord, Abraᵐ		1	6			Nason, Joshua			2		
Adams, Benjᵃ	1		2			Lord, Joseph	1	6	3			Nason, Joshua	1	1	7		
Adams, James, Jr	1	1	1			Nason, Edward	1	4	2			Abbot, Theopholus	1		3		
Stone, Dudley	1		3			Nason, Moses	1	2	2			Whitehouse, Abigail					
Stone, Jonᵃ	2		2			Nason Joshua, Jr	1		2								

FIRST CENSUS OF THE UNITED STATES.

YORK COUNTY—Continued.

BERWICK TOWN—con.

NAME OF HEAD OF FAMILY.	Free white males of 16 years and upward, including heads of families.	Free white males under 16 years.	Free white females, including heads of families.	All other free persons.	Slaves.
Abbot, Jonª	2		3		
Abbot, Ricᵈ	1	1	1		
Coopper, John	2	2	4		
Warren, Wᵐ	2		2		
Warren, John	1	1	1		
Warren, Wᵐ	1	1	3		
Abbot, Patience		1	4		
Goodwin, Moses	1		2		
Goodwin, Wᵐ	1	2	3		
Hubbard, Thomas	1		7		
Abbot, John	1	2	7		
Abbot, John, Junʳ	1	2	2		
Grant, Margret			1		
Grant, Nathaniel	1	4	5		
Grant, Peter	1		5		
Grant, Elijah	1	4	5		
Abbot, Samuel	1	1	1		
Abbot, Isaac			2		
Lord, Simeon	3	1	2		
Goodwin, Ebenezer	2	4	4		
Lord, Mercy			1		
Lord, Jedediah	1	1	4		
Emery, Simon	1	1	3		
Hubbard, Phillip	2		2		
Hubbard, John	1	1	3		
Hupper, John	1		1		
Hubbard, Joseph			2		
Hubbard, Samˡ	1		2		
Abbot, Joshua	1		3		
Abbot, Danˡ	1	2	2		
Abbot, Anney			3		
Hodsdon, Hannah	1	2	3		
Lord, Ichabod	1				
Abbot, Amos	1	1	4		
Hodsdon, Wᵐ	1	3	2		
Hodsdon, Samuel	1		1		
Warren, Chadbourne	1	2	4		
Nason, Aaron	1	2	6		
Sharkley, Ricᵈ	1	1	3		
Sharkley, Ricᵈ	2	2	3		
Hodsdon, Ricᵈ	1		5		
Hodsdon, Danˡ	1	1	5		
Hodsdon, Thoˢ	1				
Hodsdon, Jeremiah	2	1	4		
Hodsdon, Benjª	1	4	2	1	
Hodsdon, Stephen	2	2	3		
Emery, Wᵐ	2	6	3		
Emery, Job	2	1	3		
Lord, David	4		3		
Lord, Jeremiah	2	1	4		
Grant, James	1	1	2		
Shorey, Joseph	2	2	5		
Smith, Thomas	1	1	3		
Hearl, Elisha	1	2	3		
Hearl, Wᵐ	1	4	2		
Spencer, Wᵐ	1	1	5		
Spencer, Wᵐ, Junʳ	1		3		
Chadbourne, Sarah			2		
Young, John	1	1	3		
Nason, Meriam			1		
Marss, Ichabod	1	1	1		
Lord, Jabes	2	1	2		
Nason, Mary			2		
Nason, Amos	1	1	3		
Spencer, Thomas	1		1		
Wadley, Moses	1		3		
Goodwin, Jedediah	2	4	3		
Wadley, John	2	1	5		
Wadley, Hannah			5		
Goodwin, Silas	1	1	2		
Whitrow, James	1		1		
Bennet, John	1		1		
Whidden, Ricᵈ	2	3	2		
Marrs, Surplus	3	1	2		
Marrs, Wᵐ	1	1	1		
Cooper, Allexʳ	2	3	6		
Goodwin, James	2	1	2		
Bennet, Moses	2	2	2		
Abbot, Reuben	1		2		
Coopper, Danˡ	2	2	2		
Spencer, Joseph	2	1	3		
Hearl, John	1	1	6		
Hearl, Gilbert	1	1	5		
Wilkison, James	2		2		
Wilkison, George	1	2	3		
Wilkison, Samuel	1		1		
Wilkison, Wᵐ	1		1		
Clark, John	2	1	5		
Hearl, Wᵐ	1	1	4		
Jelison, Margret	1	1	2		
Goodwin, Amos	1	1	2		
Huntrus, Darling	3		4		
Huntrus, Wᵐ	2	2	1		
Lord, Jacob	2		7		
Huntrus, George	2	1	3		
Marrs, Thomas	1		1		
Hearl, Lucia		1	2		
Warren, Gilbert	3	2	4		
Nason, Noah	1	1	3		
Warren, James	2		3		
Thompson, John	1	2	4		
Emery, James	2	2	4		
Emery, Joshua	1	1	2		
Emery, Joshua, Junʳ	1		2		
Emery, John (of York)	3	1	4		
Burdean, Timothy	1		3		
Stevens, Danˡ	1	3	3		
Goodwin, Jeremiah	2		2		
Standley, John	1		3		
Standley, Samˡ	1	2	2		
Standley, James	1		2		
Gray, James	1	1	2		
Gray, James, Junʳ	2	3	4		
Cheek, Isaac	1		2		
Joy, Wᵐ	2	2	6		
Gray, Jonª	1	4	4		
Thurrel, Jacob	3	2	5		
Dennet, Ebenezer	3		2		
Thurrel, Jnᵒ	1	2	3		
Dennet, Ebenezer, Jʳ	1	1	1		
Dow, Moses	1	3	3		
Hunssom, Jerusha		1	4		
Thompson, Jesse	2		3		
Hearl, Mary					
Hearl, John	1	2	4		
Brawn, John	1	2	2		
Walker, Jonª	1	6	3		
Thompson, Amos	2	1	4		
Brawn, George	1	2	4		
Brawn, George	1		4		
Verney, Ricᵈ	1	3	4		
Boyce, James	2	2	4		
Furbush, Abrᵐ	2		3		
Dickson, Ichabod	1	3	1		
Dickson, Mary	1	1	1		
Page, Enoch	2	1	4		
Thurel, Jonª	1	1	5		
Thurrel, John	2	1	3		
Verney, Hezekiah	2		4		
Austin, Andrew	3	1	6		
Hamilton, John	2	1	7		
Stakepole, Aaron	1		1		
Hamilton, Simeon	1	1	6		
Hamilton, Reuben	1	1	3		
Hamilton, Silas	1		2		
Frost, Benjª	1		1		
Brawn, John	2		2		
Thompson, Noah	1				
Goodwin, Wᵐ	1	1	1		
Jallison, Lusia			2		
Walker, Nathˡ	1	2	3		
Knight, John	1		3		
Knight, Benjª	1	2	5		
Welsh, Jonª	2	1	7		
Roberts, Simon	2	1	3		
Meriam, Nathˡ	2	1	1		
Hodsdon, Nathan	1	3	4		
Hodsdon, James	2		3		
Grant, Landers	1	1	1		
Grant, John	2	2	3		
Chadbourne, Joseph	1	1	1		
Chadbourne, Seamon	1	1	3		
Hodsdon, Simon	1		1		
Goodwin, James	2	1	6	1	
Goodwin, James, Jʳ	1		2		
Tuttel, Job	2	1	7		
Pierce, Wᵐ	1	3	2		
Spencer, Frithe	1	2	5		
Smith, Elisabeth			1		
Smith, Danˡ	1	4	3		
Keay, John	1	3	8		
Keay, Love	1	3	4		
Wintworth, Timothy	2	2	7		
Kenney, John	1	2	3		
Goodwin, Charles	2		3		
Clark, Charles	1	1	2		
Nute, Daniel	1	4	4		
Hodsdon, Moses	1	3	4		
Hodsdon, Ebenezer	1	1	1		
Heard, Ebenezer	3		2		
Hodsdon, Benjª	1		3		
Hodsdon, Isreal	2		4		
Worster, Lemuel	2	2	4		
Worster, Lydia			3		
Worster, Samuel	1	2	5		
Lord, Nicholas	1		1		
Bigford, Aaron	1	1	3		
Foye, Elisabeth			1		
Foye, Moses	1	1	3		
Foye, John	1		2		
MᶜCarral, James	3		4		
Downs, Joshua	3	2	3		
Noak, Thomas	2	2	3		
Calley, Samuel	1	1	2		
Hupper, Wᵐ	2	1	1		
Hupper, John	3		5		
Roberts, Joshua	1	1	2		
Roberts, Joshua	1		1		
Lord, Ebenezer	1		4	1	
Lord, Samuel	1	3	3		
Whittier, Jacob	2		2		
Fall, Stephen	3	4	5		
Downs, Nathˡ	3		5		
Wallingford, John	1		1		
Smith, Jemima		1	1		
Worster, Phillip	1	3	3		
Grant, Edward	1	3	2		
Heard, Tristam	1		2		
Heard, Tristam, Jʳ	1	1	3		
Ricker, Moses	2	1	1		
Stanton, Benjª	3	1	3		
Horsum, John	1		2		
Horsum, James	1	2	1		
Tibbets, Ephrim	1	2	2		
Tibbets, Ichabod	1		2		
Tibbets, Ichabod, Jʳ	1	3	4		
Rendal, Danˡ	1	1	1		
Hubbard, Joseph	2		5		
Tibbets, Jedediah	1	2	2		
Wintworth, Ricᵈ	2	2	3		
Hanson, Ebenezer	3		1		
Jones, Eliphelet	1	2	4		
Nock, Zachariah	3		4		
Nock, Jonª	1	1	5		
Sullivan, John	1		2		
Nock, Mary		1	2		
Nock, Joseph	1	1	1		
Ricker, Ephrim	1	2	2		
Clark, Eleazer	1	3	2		
Nock, Wᵐ	1	3	4		
Libbey, Joseph	2	4	5		
Clark, Jonª Denna	2	3	5		
Clark, John	1				
Clark, Stephen	1				
Clark, William		4	3		
Whitehouse, Danˡ	2	2	4		
Nock, Abigail					
Horsum, Wᵐ	1		3		
Lord, Benjª	1	2	3		
Butler, Nehemiah	1	2	1		
Lord, Mary	2	4	7		
Lord, Love					
Nock, Benjª	1	1	2		
Nock, Moses	1	1	2		
Hamilton, Joseph	2		3		
Downs, Aaron	1	2	1		
Downs, Moses	1		3		
Ricker, Dolley			1		
Ricker, Abigal			3		
Abbot, John	1	1	2		
Downs, Daniel	2	1	3		
Hanson, Gersham	1	1	1		
Downs, Jedediah	2	1	3		
Wintworth, Ezekil		5	6		
Fall, Tristam	1	3	3		
Hanson, Elisabeth	1	1			
Yeaton, Jonathan	1		3		
Young, Abner	1		3		
Stanton, George	1	1	2		
Goodrige, Danˡ	3	2	4		
Hodsdon, Benjª	1		2		
Gubtail, Benjª	1	1	5		
Abbot, Joshua	1	2	2		
Gubtail, Moses	1	2	2		
Libbey, Paul	2		2		
Goodrige, John	2	2	2		
Norton, Wintworth	1		2		
Manning, Patrick	1		2		
Pray, Peter	1	3	4	3	
Gerrish, John	1		2	1	
Gerrish, Wᵐ	1	2	4		
Wirthwill, John	1		3		
Hodsdon, Stephen	1	2	3		
Peters, Andrew	1	3	3		
Shorey, Unies			1		
Goodrige, Jedediah	2	1	2		
Norton, Nathˡ	1		5		
Goodrige, John	1	1	2		
Wintworth, Judah	1		1		
Wintworth, Samuel	2	4	4		
Gowel, John	3	2	6		
Welsh, Paul	2	2	4		

HEADS OF FAMILIES—MAINE.

YORK COUNTY—Continued.

NAME OF HEAD OF FAMILY.	Free white males of 16 years and upward, including heads of families.	Free white males under 16 years.	Free white females, including heads of families.	All other free persons.	Slaves.	NAME OF HEAD OF FAMILY.	Free white males of 16 years and upward, including heads of families.	Free white males under 16 years.	Free white females, including heads of families.	All other free persons.	Slaves.	NAME OF HEAD OF FAMILY.	Free white males of 16 years and upward, including heads of families.	Free white males under 16 years.	Free white females, including heads of families.	All other free persons.	Slaves.
BERWICK TOWN—con.						**BERWICK TOWN—con.**						**BERWICK TOWN—con.**					
Nock, Disso	1	1	5			Dennet, John	3	1	4			Robberts, John	2	6	4		
Brown, Paul	2	4	8			Jumkins, Jotham	1	3	5			Brawn, George	1	4	3		
Goodwin, Elijah	1	2	1			Talckut, Jonᵃ	3		3	1		Brawn, Micael	1	2	2		
Pierce, Elisabeth			3			Parington, Benajah	2	1	2			Staple, Ricᵈ	1	4	2		
Worster, George			2			Massey, Woodbuary	1	1	1			Frost, Wm	1	1			
Ricker, Eliphelet	4	4	2			Morrel, Peter	1		1			Lord, Ichabod	1	3	3		
Lord, Jeremiah	2	3	3			Morrel, Peter, Junr	3	1	9			Lord, Elisha	1	5	1		
Furbush, Samˡ	1	2	4			Morrel, Abraham	2	1	1			Estees, John	1	1	2		
Gubtail, James	1	1	1			Morrel, Josiah	1	1	2			Estees, Joseph	1	3	2		
Abbot, Unis		1	2	1		Neal, James	2	3	3			Abbot, Stephen	3	3	4		
Clements, Samuel	3	3	5			Winchel, Job	1		3			Hearl, Benjᵃ	1	2	2		
Spencer, Simeon	1	3	2			Morril, Peaster	1	4	4			Hardison, Stephen	1	3	3		
Hodsdon, Thomas	3	3	5			Hamilton, Abial	1		2			Kean, Jonᵃ	1		3		
Appelby, Halley	3	3	4			Hamilton, Jonᵃ	1		2			Goodwin, Adam	1		1		
Butler, Moses	3	4	3			Tuttel, Ebenezer	2	4	3			Goodwin, Moses	1		1		
Goodwin, Wm	8	3	2			Johnson, Daniel	2	3	3			Furnald, Wm	1	1	3		
Goodwin, Elijah	2	2	2			Warren, Alden	3		4			Clark, Thoˢ	1	1	5		
Lord, Humphrey	1	2	5			Cheek, John	1	2	3			Murry, Samˡ	2	5	3		
Goodwin, Elisha	3	2	3			Wire, John	2		2			Hunssum, Samˡ	2		2		
Lord, William	1	2	3			Morrel, Isaac	2	1	3			Hunssum, Robt	1	2	5		
Seats, John	1		1			Goodwin, Samˡ	2		1			Libbey, Zebulon	1	2	5		
Lord, Elisha	3	1	2			Hubbard, Benjᵃ	1	5	4			Clark, Wm	1		1		
Frost, James	1	2	4			Gowen, Richard	1	2	1			Furnald, Hercelus	2	2	7		
Frost, Stephen	2	1	4			Hobbs, Thomas	5		5			Reed, Lydia	1	1	3		
Spencer, Humpʸ	2	1	5			Hammet, Thomas	1	1	1			Bracket, Miles	1	3	3		
Shorey, Wm	2	1	4			Hammet, Thomas, Jr	1		3			Bracket, John	1		4		
Shorey, Miles	3	3	5			Abbot, Joseph	2	1	3			Bracket, Moses	1		2		
Shorey, John	2		4			Lord, Nicholas	3	2	5			Bracket, John, Junr	1				
Bracket, Samuel	2	2	2	1		Morrel, Thomas	5	1	3			Keay, John	2	2	5		
Bracket, James	2		2			Plummer, Patiance	1	1	3			Tusker, Betty		3	1		
Stone, Paul	1		2			Morrel, David	2	4	6			Heard, Thomas	2	3	4		
Davis, John	1	1	4			Morrel, Wintrop	2	4	6			Hall, Wm	2	3	6		
Nichols, Phebe	2	1	3			Billem, John	2	2				Hall, Silas	1	2	4		
Nichols, David	2	1				Vicker, Ambros	1					Heard, Silas	1	2	3		
Nichols, Samuel	2		3			Whicher, Ricᵈ	1		1			Heard, Benjᵃ	1		1		
Frost, William	4	1	4			Whicher, Foxwell	1	5	1			Stillens, Peter	1	2	6		
Prime, Lydia	5	2	5			Thurston, John	4	2	6			Stillens, Luke	1		1		
Pray, Joseph	4	3	5	2		staple, Joshua	2	1	2			Stillens, Mary			1		
Tibbetts, Ebenezer	3	1	4			Buffum, Caleb	1	2	6			Remmick, Jacob	1	1	2		
Stone, Paul	2	2	3			Rendal, Joanna	2	3	5			Pray, Samˡ	1	1	2		
Clements, Hannah			3			Hussey, Wm	3	3	4			Pray, Samˡ, Junr	1	2	3		
Hutchins, Jeremiah	1	1	3			Twombley, Mercy	2	2	7			Heard, Joseph	2	1	6		
Thompson, Allexʳ	1	3	5			Joy, James	1	3	3			Heard, Benjᵃ	1	6	7		
Brewster, Joseph	2		5			Chadbourne, Humpʸ	3	3	6			Staple, Josiah	2	3	5		
Hamilton, Solomon	2	1	5			Lord, Nathˡ	1	1	2			Rogers, George	2		2		
Hamilton, Jonas	2	3	4			Rendal, Stephen	2	3	3			Furnald, Eleazer	3	1	3		
Goodwin, Shipway	3	2	4			Verney, Timᵒ	1	3	3			Estees, Danˡ	1		1		
Chadboun, Humpʸ, Esqʳ	2		2			Hussey, Stephen	1		4			Estees, Benjᵃ	1		1		
Cheek, Joseph	3		5			Hanson, Nicholas	1		3			Chase, John	1	5	3		
Hobbs, Stephen	2	3	3			Hunsum, Reuben	1	1	2			Bracket, James	2	3	4		
Ricker, Mary			1	1		Hanson, James	1	2	3			Pray, Stephen	1	2	5		
Ricker, Tristam	3	3	6	1		Staple, Stephen	1		1			Estees, Peter	1	3	3		
Stasey, Benjᵃ	1	1	6			Hussey, Stephen, Jr	1	2	4			Pray, Eliphelet	2	2	5		
Ricker, Noah	3	2	3			Jebson, James	1	1	2			Hardison, Samˡ	1	4	3		
Roberts, Aaron	2	2	3			Green, Sarah			1			Hearl, John	1	1	4		
Stone, John	1	4	6			Hill, Joseph	2		3			Hearl, Sarah			3		
Rendal, Eliphelet	1	1	2			Hill, Amos	1		1			Gubtail, Nathˡ	1		1		
Ricker, Richard	1	1	3			Abbot, Thomas	2	1	2			Gubtail, Nat., Junr	2	3	5		
Hussey, Ebenezer	2		3			Abbot, Thoˢ, Jr	2		2			Starpole, Absalom	1	3	3		
Hussey, George	1	3	2			Ford, Robert	4	4	5			Peirce, Stephen	1		4		
Hayes, Ichabod	2	1	6			Hill, Mark	1		4			Libbey, John	2	3	4		
Hayes, Elijah	4	1	6			Libbey, Marthew	1	1	2			Smith, Sarah	1		2		
Rendal, Jeremiah	1	2	3			Abbot, Wm	1	1	2			Furnald, Nathˡ	1	2	3		
Ricker, Reuben	1	1	3			Allen, Jacob	2	2	2			Holmes, Joseph	1	3	5		
Neal, Andrew	2	1	1			Ford, John	4	2	6			Goodwin, Adam	1		1		
Jenkins, Elijah	2	1	3			Estees, John	1	1	2			Gubtail, Wm	1	3	5		
Parington, Moses	3		3			Hunssom, Mark	1	4	1			Stone, Jonathan	3	2	5		
Warren, Gedion	2		3			Grant, James	1		3			Stillens, Samˡ	1	1	6		
Chase, Thomas	1	4	2			Grant, Daniel	1		1			Hodsdon, Joseph	1				
Buffum, Joshua	1		2			Grant, Peter	1	3	3			Goodrige, Joseph	2	2	6		
Buffum, Samˡ	2	1	3			Grant, Thomas	1	1	3			Grant, Joshua	2	7	5		
Buffum, Joshua, Jr	2	7	4			Gerrith, Isaac	1		2	1		Manning, Sarah			1		
Rogers, Paul	3	2	3			Whittom, Andrew	1	3	3			Dunnel, John	1				
Hussey, Simeon	1	2	3			Quint, Wm	1	3	3			Gubtail, Stephen	1	3	3		
Hussey, Elisabeth			3			Quint, John	1		4			Woodman, Mary	1	1	3		
Neal, Johnson	1	1	3			Quint, John, Junr	1	1	4			Holmes, Wm	2		2		
Neal, Wm	1		3			Quint, Joshua	1		2			Murry, Hannah	1		1		
Hussey, Bachelor	3	2	4			Quint, Joshua, Junr	1		4			Murry, Nathan	1	3	3		
Hussey, Joanna	1		2			Quint, Daniel	1	1	5			Frost, John	2	4	3		
Verney, Jonathan	1	3	3			Bowen, Nathaniel	1	2	2			Hupper, Samˡ	4	1	7		
Parker, Samˡ	1	3	4			Heard, John	1		1			Cheek, Aaron	3	2	6		
Waymoth, Francis	1		3			Appelby, Simeon	1	1	3			Cheek, Thomas	3	3	6		
Hubbard, Lydia	1		4			Appelby, Levi	1		1			Cheek, Elizabeth			1		
Nowel, Jonᵃ	2	2	4			Cheek, John	1	1				Gubtail, Samˡ	2				
Waymoth, Moses	1	2	5			Fall, John	1		1			Gubtail, Samˡ, Junr	1		4		
Chadbourne, Frances	1	4	3			Neal, Stephen	1		1			Fogg, James	1	1	1		
Goodwin, Thomas	2	1	1			Staple, Peter	3	1	4			Fogg, Mark	1	2	3		
Adams, Benjᵃ	1		4			Staple, Peter, Junr	1	2	4			Bracket, Mary			1		
Buffum, John	2		3			Frye, Rowlen	2	4	4			Bracket, Samuel	1	1	1		
Nowel, Mark	1	1	5			Staple, Gedion	1	3	4			Andros, Olive			2		
Estees, Henery	3		3			Staple, John	2	2	1			Hardison, Thomas	2	1	1		
Waymoth, Benjᵃ	2		1			Wills, Benajah	2	2	1			Gowen, John	1		3		
Waymoth, Benjᵃ, Jr	1	3	2			Mase, Andrew	2		3			Pike, Jane			1		
Rogers, Levi	3		5			Cheek, Ricᵈ	1	3	4			Pike, Amos	1		2		
						Beel, Anna			2			Libbey, Daniel	2		3		

FIRST CENSUS OF THE UNITED STATES.

YORK COUNTY—Continued.

NAME OF HEAD OF FAMILY.	Free white males of 16 years and upward, including heads of families.	Free white males under 16 years.	Free white females, including heads of families.	All other free persons.	Slaves.
BERWICK TOWN—con.					
Andros, Elisha	1		3		
Andros, Joanna	1	1	2		
Merriam, Rev'd Matthew	1	2	4		
Marther, W'm	1		2		
Shorey, Jacob	2	1	2		
Shorey, John	1	2	2		
Yeaton, Phillip	2	1	2		
Woodsum, John	3		3		
Woodsum, Daniel	1		2		
Andros, John	1	1	1		
Fales, Joshua	1	1	2		
Fogg, Joseph	2	3	2		
Libbey, Nathaniel	3		3		
Morton, Bryant	3	2	5		
Edgerly, Richard	2	2	3		
Hearl, James	1		1		
BIDDEFORD TOWN.					
Jordan, Rishworth, Jr.	1	2	2		
Jordan, Sam'l	1	1	1		
Spring, Seth	2	3	5	1	
Stacey, George	1		2		
Hill, Jeremiah	4	1	8		
Thompson, Paul	2		2		
Porter, Aaron	2	2	6		
Caxey, Elizabeth			1		
Cummins, Donald		1	2		
Chadwick, John	2		2		
Hooper, Benj'a	4	1	3		
Hooper, Daniel	2	1	3		
Cobb, Matthew	3	2	2		
Foss, Lemuel	1	1	4		
Smith, Theo'a	2		1		
Storey, Abra'm	2	3	3		
Gray, Elisha	1	1	3		
Perkins, Stephen	1		2		
Long, Josiah	1		1		
Lee, John	2	1	3		
Dwinnel, Tho'a	1	3	3		
Gray, Aaron	3	2	2		
M'Gra, John	2	3	5		
Cole, Benj'a	2	2	6		
Haley, Will'm	1	2	3		
Long, Josiah	3		3		
Dearborn, Jacob	1	1	1		
Perkins, Nath'l	1	2	1		
Morrill, Reuben	2		2		
Townsend, Tho'a	2	4	5		
Thatcher, George	2	2	4		
Menton, Phinehas	2	3	5		
Tarbox, John	2	3	4		
Staples, And'w	3	3	5		
Tarbox, Jere'a	1	1	1		
Bickford, Pierce	1	2	6		
Bickford, Doddiford	2	4	3		
Cole, Dan'l	1	2	2		
M'Intire, Theodore	2	2	2		
Staples, James	1	1	2		
Gilpatrick, Robert	1	2	4		
Carlisle, James	2	1	3		
Currier, David	1		1		
Bragg, Robert	1	1	2		
Smith, Jere'a	1	2	2		
Hooper, Benj'a, Jr.	3	4	3		
Cole, Elizabeth	2	2	4		
Staples, Benj'a	3	3	4		
Smith, Nicholas	4		3		
Hooper, Noah	2	1	6		
Simpson, Josiah	1	1	4		
Stimpson, Loammi	1	1	2		
Gilpatrick, Will'm	2		4		
Emmery, Hannah		1	2		
Merrill, Joshua	1	1	5		
Rummery, Jon'a	2		2		
Rummery, Tho'a	2	2	2		
Clark, James	2	1	2		
Bradbury, Sam'l	1	2	2		
Bradbury, Moses	3		4		
Mason, Benj'a, Jr.	1	1	3		
Moor (Widow)		3	2		
Gray (Widow)		1	1		
Smith, Theo'a, Jun'r	1		4		
Swett, John	1		2		
Bickford, Pierce, Jr.	2	1	1		
Emery, Obed	2	1	2		
Emery, Ralph	1	1	2		
Rogers, Tho'a	1		2		
Dunham, Joseph	1	3	4		
Perkins, Joseph	1		4		
Morrill, Joseph	1	2	5		
Allen, Elisha	2		2		
Burton, Tho'a	1	1	3		
Nason, Benj'a	1	2	4		
BIDDEFORD TOWN—con.					
Nason, Noah	1		1		
GilPatrick, Tho'a	4	1	5		
Gorden, Amos	4	5	3		
Smith, Ellison	6	2	3		
Harman, John	1	2	1		
Goodwin, Richard	2	4	1		
Smith, Joseph	1		2		
Mason, Benj'a	1		1		
Mason, Amos	1	1	1		
Morril, Tristram	1	1	2		
Dishon, Dan'l	1		2		
Richardson, George	1		2		
Wengate, Simon	1	1	3		
Emery, Ebenezer	1	2	3		
Patten, Robert	2	1	2		
Patten, Lydia			2		
Hill, Joseph	2	2	5		
Beeman, Sam'l	1	1	8		
Moore, Peletiah	1	2	5		
Roff, Sam'l	1	1	2		
Emery, Jon'a	2	3	2		
Proctor, Joseph	1	1	2		
Davis, Josiah	3		3		
Stacey, Ebenezer	4		6		
Hill, Benj'a	2	1	3		
Hill, John	1	3	5		
Proctor, Benj'a	4	2	4		
Benson, John	2	1	3		
Benson, Henry	1		2		
Benson, Robert	1	2	2		
Trueworthy, John	1	2	5		
Webster, Rev'd Nath'l	1	1	4		
GilPatrick, Christopher	1	3	7		
Stockpole, John	1	1	1		
Shepherd, Tho'a	1	1	1		
Tarbox, Elisabeth		1	1		
Haley, Abra'm	1		2		
GilPatrick, Dominicus.	1	1	4		
Stevans, Joseph	1	1	1		
GilPatrick, Sarah			2		
Jones, Stephen	1		2		
Tarbox, Tho'a	2	4	3		
Tarbox, Abijah	1	2	4		
Jordan, Rishworth	1		3		
Jordan, Tristram	1	1	1		
Hill (Widow)	1	2	2		
Lasdel, Israel	1	1	2		
Joy, Stephen	1	4	2		
Harris, Sam'l	1	1	4		
Tarbox, Dan'l	2	4	2		
Davis, John	2	1	5		
Haley, Joseph	1		3		
Tongue, John	1	2	2		
Perkins, Nath'l	1	2	4		
Burnham, Joseph	1	1	1		
Dier, Elizabeth			3		
Dier, John	2	1	7		
Smith, Jon'a	3	1	2		
Tarbox, Ezekiel	3	1	2		
Foy, John	1		1		
Haley, Silvester	2	2	1	5	
Tarbox, Jon'a	1	2	3		
Fletcher, Pendleton	3		4		
Hussey, Paul	1		3		
Wetherby, Elisabeth	1	2	4		
Bettes, Ebe'a	2		6		
Cole, Robert	2		3		
Cole, Ezra	2		3		
Stevenson, Will'm	3	2	4		
Coffin, Elihu	2	2	1		
Bunker, Batcheldor	2	2	3		
Tarbox, Rufus	1	3	2		
Harman, Will'm	1	1	4		
Curtis, Ephraim	4		5		
Thomas, David	5	2	5		
Davis, John	1	5	1		
Stockpole, And'w	2	4	1		
Tarbox, Benj'a	4	1	3		
Shepherd, Tho'a	1		4		
Haley, Joshua	1	8		
Davis, John G.	2	1	5		
Smith, And'w	1	2	4		
M'Kessuk, Matthew	2	2	7		
M'Kessuk, Zebadiah	1	1	2		
Staples, John	1	2	4		
Hill, Joshua	3	2	5		
GilPatrick, Christopher	3		2		
Davis, Robert	1	1	2		
Davis, Sam'l	1		1		
Davis, Joseph	1	1	1		
Beel, Joseph	1		1		
Murch, Will'm	3	4	6		
Smith, Roger	1	4	3		
Smith, Dominicus	1	4	4		
BROWNFIELD TOWNSHIP.					
Brown, Henry Young	3	1	3	1	
Osgood, Joshua Bailey	2	2	3	1	
Ayer, Joseph	1	4	3		
Colby, Sam'l	1	3	1		
Choat, Ammi	1	2	3		
Walker, Supply	1	1	3		
Walker, Joseph	3	3	4		
Osgood, William	1		2		
Emery, Joseph	1		2		
Haley, John	1	1	1		
Long, Daniel	2	1	5		
Boswell, William	2		3		
Kimball, Francis	1	1	3		
Poor, Amos	1	2	3		
Stearns, Dudley	1	1	2		
Miller, John Bolt	1	1	3		
Spring, Josiah	1	1	2		
Howard, James	2	1	1		
Howard, Joseph	2	1	3		
Stickney, John	1	1	3		
Lane, John	3	1	3		
Watson, John	1	2	2		
Neazey, Tho'a	3	1	3		
Burbank, Benj'a	2	1	1		
Burbank, Israel	1	2	4		
Osgood, Asa	1	1	2		
BROWNFIELD TOWNSHIP—IN THE GORE ADJOINING.					
Warren, Ichabod	3		3		
Jellison, Thom'a	1	1	2		
Porter, David	1	3	2		
Stiles, Ezra	1	1	2		
BUXTON TOWN.					
Ayer, Peter	3	1	3		
Ayer, Timothy	2	3	6		
Woods, John	1	1	2		
Ayer, Ebenr	1	1	1		
Ayer, Benj'a	2	1	4		
Moor, Capt. Hugh	4	2	6		
Thompson, Tho'a	1	3	4		
Smith, John	2		3		
Smith, Sam'l	1	3	2		
Lamb, Rich'd	1	1	4		
Irish, Will'm	1	1	2		
Whitney, Steph'a	1	1	4		
Kimball, Dan'l	1	1	1		
Thomes, Tho'a	1		2		
Thomas, Dan'l	1		1		
Hopkinson, Caleb	2	1	3		
Sands, John	1	3	2		
Hopkins, Benj'a	1		2		
Sawyer, Barnabas	1		3		
Emery, John	1	3	4		
Watson, —*	1	4	4		
White, John	2	1	6		
Atkinson, Joseph	1	1	4		
Harmon, Pelatiah	1	4	2		
Kimball, Nathan	1	2	5		
Elwell, Joseph	2		5		
Whitney, Sarah		1	3		
Edward, Steph'a	2		1		
Bab, Peter	2		1		
Smith, John, Jun'r	1	4	3		
Harmon, Josiah	1	2	2		
Davis, W'm	1	3	2		
Smith, W'm	1	4	4		
Thompson, Jn'o	1	2	8		
Edgley, Jn'o	1	3	2		
Whitton, W'm	1	3	2		
Emery, Charles	1	1	2		
Whitton, Rich'd	1	1	2		
Robison, Jn'o	1		4		
Graffam, Uriah	1		2		
Berry, Isaac	1	2	4		
plaisted, Roger	1	2	5		
Berry, Jon'a	2	1	4		
Millican, Joel	1	1	3		
Tole, Phinehas	1	3	3		
Sawyer, Jn'o	2	3	6		
Pennell, Tho'a	2		2		
Hanson, Phineas	2	3	6		
Billings, Enoch	1		1		
Lane, Jn'o	1	2	2		
Beard, Sam'l	1	2	4		
Andrews, W'm	1	2	5		
Woodman, Joshua	1		1		
Cole, Jn'o	1	4	4		
Gould, Isaac	1	1	1		
Dennett, Cadmiel	1		1		
Atkinson, Tho'a	2	2	3		

* Illegible.

HEADS OF FAMILIES—MAINE.

YORK COUNTY—Continued.

NAME OF HEAD OF FAMILY.	Free white males of 16 years and upward, including heads of families.	Free white males under 16 years.	Free white females, including heads of families.	All other free persons.	Slaves.	NAME OF HEAD OF FAMILY.	Free white males of 16 years and upward, including heads of families.	Free white males under 16 years.	Free white females, including heads of families.	All other free persons.	Slaves.	NAME OF HEAD OF FAMILY.	Free white males of 16 years and upward, including heads of families.	Free white males under 16 years.	Free white females, including heads of families.	All other free persons.	Slaves.
BUXTON TOWN—con.						**BUXTON TOWN—con.**						**COXHALL TOWN—con.**					
Whitney, Jonᵃ	1	3	2			Appleton, Jnᵒ	2		2			goodwin, Aaron	1	3	1		
Thompson, Theodore	2	2	1			Bradbury, Samˡ	1	1	1			Dame, Isachar	1	3	1		
Thompson, Samˡ	1	1	3			Woodman, Joshᵇ, 2ⁿᵈ	2	2	8	1		Bracket, Nathaniel	1	3	4		
Jordan, Clemˡ	1	3	2	1		Parker, Chase	2	3	3			Roberts, Jeremiah	3	4	4		
Rounds, Joseph	1	3	4			Bradbury, Benjᵃ	2	5	3			Clarke, John, junʳ	1	2	3		
Rounds, Mark	1	3	2			Bradbury, Thoˢ	1	1	3			Clarke, William	1	1	3		
Lewis, Abijah	3	1	4			Leavitt, Thoˢ	1	1	1			Goodwin, Amaziah	1		3		
Eldridge, Wintrop	1	1	1			Newcomb, Jnᵒ	3	3	4			Chadburn, Paul	3	4	4		
Cresey, John	2	3	6			Dunnell, Joseph	3	3	5			Ricker, George	1	4	3		
Adams, Stephⁿ	1	1	1			Knight, Edmund	2		4			Ricker, Mark	1		3		
McDonald, Jnᵒ	1	2	5			Hill, Nathˡ	3	4	7			Ricker, Phinehas	1	1	2		
McDonald, Robᵗ	3	3	3			Sands, Samˡ	2		7			Nocks, Sylvanus	1	1	2		
Whitney, Isaac	2		3			Norton, James	2	3	4			Nocks, Reuben	1		3		
March, Danˡ	3		8			Newcomb, Joshᵃ	1	2	1			Ford, Paul	2		7		
Sands, Ephᵐ	1	1	1			Trundy, Jnᵒ	1		1			Chadburn, Simeon	1	2	4		
Sands, James	1	3	4			Patten, Hannah			2			tibbets, Joseph	1	3	3		
Harding, Samˡ	1		2			Dearborn, Jacob	1	1	7			Lord, Elias	1		1		
Adams, Willᵐ	2	3	2			Billings, Joshᵃ	1	1	2			Gray, Nehemiah	2	2	5		
Emery, Danˡ	1	2	2			Martin, Robᵗ	1		3			Robberts, Joseph	1	4	4		
Dunn, Nathˡ	1	2	1			Whitney, Amos	1	5	2			Grant, Benjamin	1	1	2		
Libby, Francis	1	2	3			Hancock, Jnᵒ	2	1	2			Roberts, Samuel	1	3	3		
Ward, Danˡ	1	2	1			Cole, Nathˡ	1		3			Grant, Alexander	1	2	1		
Emery, James	2	2	2			Elwell, Benjⁿ	2		1			Goodwin, Jeremiah	1	2	2		
Haines, Benjⁿ	2					Martin, Jonᵃ	1					Grant, Silas	1	4	1		
Jose, John	3	2	5			Bean, Elizabᵗʰ			2			Swanson, Robert	1	2	1		
Elwell, Wᵐ	1		1			Hopkinson, Joses	1	1	7			Straw, Daniel	1	2	6		
Rounds, Samˡ	3	3	3			Gray, Cadwallader	3	1	2			Gould, Samuel	1	1	2		
Murch, James	1	2	2			Woodman, Jnᵒ	2	1	6			Gould, Ezra	2		1		
Edwards, Samˡ	1	2	6			Phinney, Jnᵒ	1		1			Sands, James	2	3	2		
Decker, Joshua	2	5	3			Gutterige, Aaron	1		1			Low, Nathaniel	1		1		
Harmon, Dornˢ	1		2			Roberts, Job	2		4			Low,*———w	1		1		
Davis, Thoˢ	1	2	2			Elden, Jnᵒ	1	1	3			Allen, Joseph	1		1		
Harmon, Joel	1	3	2			Merrill, Samˡ	1		2			Yeaton, Richard	1	4	5		
Clay, Danˡ	1	3	4			Seamman, James	1	1	1			Foster, John	1	1	3		
Robinson, Jnᵒ	1		2			Hobson, Samˡ	1	1	1			Downs, Jershon	1	3	3		
Emery, Benjⁿ	2		3			Atkinson, Joshᵇ, Junʳ	1		2			Lasdale, Caleb	1	1	3		
Libby, Elisha	1	2	4			Taylor, Joseph	1	1	1			Allen, John	1	1	3		
Berry, Jonᵃ, Junʳ	1	3	3			Knights, Samˡ	2	1	7			Lasdale, Asa	1	2	2		
Coolbroth, Jnᵒ	2	2	1			Hancock, Wᵐ	1	1	4			Gutridge, Josiah	2		3		
Harmon, Nathˡ	1	2	4			Hazelton, Timᵒ	3		4			Low, thomas	1	3	3		
Millican, Isaac	1	2	3			Hovey, Samˡ	1		4			Rayment, Samuel	2		2		
Graffam, Increase	2		3			Merrill, Humphy	1	5	5			Low, John, Esqʳ	2		4		
Rice, Nathˡ	2	2	2			Elden, Nathan	2	2	5			Sands, thomas	1	2	4		
Ridley, Ebenʳ	1	2	5			Ridley, David	1	2	2			Downs, John	1		2		
Sawyer, Jabez	4	3	5			Holmes, Samˡ	1	2	3			Gray, Andrew	1	1	1		
Hanson, Moses	3	5	4			Steele, Peter	1	1	2			Rayment, James	1	2	3		
Elden, Jnᵒ, Junʳ	1	2	5			Ridley, Sarah			3			Glass, John	1	2	3		
Billings, Gershom	2	1	4			Coffin, Revᵈ Paul	3	2	7			Emery, Daniel	1	1	3		
Woodman, Jamˢ	2	3	5			Andrews, Elizaᵗʰ		2	2			Quint, William	1	2	5		
Cole, Jnᵒ, Junʳ	1	4	1			Muchemore, Jnᵒ	1	1	3			Gutridge, John	1		2		
Bradbury, Joshᵇ	1	4	3			Leavitt, Danˡ	3	1	8			Roberts, Joseph, junʳ	1	3	2		
McKenny, Jonᵃ	2		1			Palmer, Stephⁿ	4	1	4			Andrews, John	1	3	2		
Woodman, Jerᵇ	1		2			Woodsom, Abiath	2	4	3			Smith, Charles	1	3	2		
Atkinson, Thoˢ, Jʳ	1		3			Brooks, Isaiah	2		2			Barker, John	1	1	3		
Dennett, Jnᵒ	1	1	3			Emery, Thoˢ	2	1	4			Bartlet, Benoni	1		2		
Prescott, Stepⁿ	1		4			Kimball, Jnᵒ	3	1	3			Waymouth (Widʷ)		2	3		
Atkinson, Jnᵒ	2		3			Hill, Samˡ	1	1	3			Jellison, John	1	2	2		
Palmer, Richᵈ	3	4	6			Lord, Nathˡ	2	2	7			Clarke, Daniel	1	3	2		
Hopkinson, Jnᵒ	4	4	1			Brooks, Robᵗ	2		2			Gould, thomas	1	4	2		
Leavitt, Samˡ	3	1	4			Rankin, Joseph	1	2	5			Hambleton, Elijah	1	1	3		
Kimball, Joshua	2	1	9	1		Appleton, Danˡ	2	1	4			Davis, Reuben	2		3		
Woodman, Nathˡ	1	3	1			Bradbury, Jabez	2	1	4			larabee, Tempʳ (Widʷ)		2	3		
Andrews, Abel	1		2			Bradbury, Wᵐ	1	4	7			Wakefield, Israel	1	3	3		
Toworgy, John	1	2	3			Lane, Jabez	2	4	4			Burnham, Benjamin	1	1	1		
Roberts, Joseph	1	2	3			Boothby, Brice	2	2	5			Goodwi-*, Nathaniel	1	(*)	(*)		
Elden, Gibeon	1	3	3			Wentworth, Ebenⁿ	2	4	3			And——*, Stephen	(*)	(*)	(*)		
Merrill, Jnᵒ	1		2			Merrill, Abel	2	2	3			Hill, Volantine	3	2	5		
Merrill, Samˡ, Junʳ	1	2	3			Flood, Henry	1		2			Goodwin, Benjamin	2	3	3		
Hobson, Joseph	1	2	1			Wingate, Snell	2	4	3			Goodwin, Mark	1	2	4		
Boynton, Danˡ	2		1			Boynton, Wᵐ	4	2	4			Hill, John	1	3	1		
Garland, Jnᵒ	1	1	5			Leavitt, Joshᵇ	4	2	3			Day, Abraham	1	1	3		
Lane, Danˡ	1	1	4			Hill, Danˡ	3	1	3			Dallop, Jonathan	3	2	3		
Brooks, Samˡ	2	3	1			Rolf, Jnᵒ	3		3			Drew, Elisha	2		2		
Woodman, Stephᵃ	1		5			Owen, Jnᵒ	1	2	3			Hoof, thomas	2		5		
Haines, Benjⁿ	1	2	4			Newcomb, Solᵐ	3	1	8			bridges, Moses	1	5	1		
Eaton, Jnᵒ	2	4	3			Smith, Solˡ	1		2			Kimball, Daniel	1	3	4		
Hunscomb, Wᵐ	1		8			Harmon, Thoˢ	1	2	3			Burbank, John	1		3		
Rand, Michˡ	1	1	2			Rounds, Lemˡ	1	1	4			Smith, James	1	4	3		
Hunscomb, Jnᵒ	1	3	3			Hutchins, Joshᵇ	1	4	3			Kimball, Ezra	1	4	3		
Steele, Jnᵒ	1	3	4			Elwell, Benjⁿ, Jun	1		2			Kimball, Heber	1	1	3		
Woodman, Ephᵐ	1	2	1			Thomas, Joshᵇ	1	6	6			thomson, Joseph	1	2	3		
Cutts, Samˡ	1	4	5			Smith, Thoˢ	2	5	2			Eldridge, Frances	1	4	1		
Sands, Ephᵐ, Junʳ	2	4	6			Clay, Richᵈ	1		2			Littlefield, Aaron	1	1	1		
Boynton, Jnᵒ	2	3	3			Woodman, Benjᵃ	1	3	4			Boston, Jonathan	1	3	5		
Bradbury, Elijah	1	3	5			Elwell, Jnᵒ	1	2	3			White, Joseph	1	1	1		
Goodwin, Joseph	1	3	2			Hood, Edmᵈ	1		2			Huent (Widʷ)	1	1	2		
Woodsom, Michˡ	2		1									White, Charles	1	2	4		
Bradbury, Jacob, Esqʳ	3	2	3			**COXHALL TOWN.**						Shackley, Joseph	1		1		
Kimball, Joshua, Jun	1	1	1									Currier, Isaac	1	2	2		
Mason, Joseph	1	4	2			Brock, William	1	3	3			Going, Samuel	1		2		
Cole, Wᵐ	1	1	3			Clarke, thomas	2	3	4			Shackford, Paul	1	2	2		
Millican, Nathˡ	2	2	4			goodwin, Jonathan	2	3	4			Harris, Samuel	1	2	5		
Donnell, Benjᵃ	2		2			Clarke, John	1		2			Stimpion, Stephen, junʳ	1	5	1		
Donnell, Benjᵃ, Jun	3	3	3									Evans, Benjamin	2	3	4		

*Illegible.

YORK COUNTY—Continued.

Name of head of family.	Free white males of 16 years and upward, including heads of families.	Free white males under 16 years.	Free white females, including heads of families.	All other free persons.	Slaves.	Name of head of family.	Free white males of 16 years and upward, including heads of families.	Free white males under 16 years.	Free white females, including heads of families.	All other free persons.	Slaves.	Name of head of family.	Free white males of 16 years and upward, including heads of families.	Free white males under 16 years.	Free white females, including heads of families.	All other free persons.	Slaves.
COXHALL TOWN—con.						**FRANCISBOROUGH PLANTATION—con.**						**FRYEBURGH TOWN—con.**					
Kimball, Caleb	1		2			Gray, John	1	2	6			Richardson, Zebulon	2	3	4		
taylor, Joseph	1	3	4			Norton, Benjᵃ	1	2	1			Charles, Abner	3	1	3		
Smith, Elisha	1		1			Harmon, Samuel	1		7			Walker, Joseph	1	1	3		
Smith, Elisha, jun	1	2	4			Jewel, David	1	1	3			Ames, John	1		2		
Littlefield, Elisha	2	3	3			Jewel, John	1					Charles, Samˡ	1	2	6		
Drown, —— *	3	2	4			Barker, Ezra	1					Chandler, Joseph	1	2	2		
Emmons, —— *	1	2	5			Johnson, Simon	1		3			Kilgore, Trueworthy	1	3	3		
Emmons, Obediah	2	3	5			Chadbourn, John	1	3	5			Kilgore, Benjᵃ	1	4	1		
Stimpson, Stephen	1	4	5			Chadbourn, Joshua	2		4			Walker, John	3	1	3		
Burk, Joanna (Widʷ)		1	2			Allen, Joseph	1	1	3			Whiting, John	1		2		
Burk, Joseph	1	2				Barns, Timothy	2	1	3			Pattee, Moses	2	2	4		
Emmons, John	2	1	4			Chadbourn, Wᵐ	1	3	2			Barker, John	4	2	5		
Emmons, Samuel	2	1	4			Storer, Wᵐ	1	2	2			McIntyre, John	2	3	3		
Stephens, Benjamin	1	1	5			Storer, Benjᵃ	1	3	1			Wilham, Morris	1	2	7		
Emmons, Samuel, jun	1	1	1			Thompson, Joseph	2	2	4			Lord, James	2	2	3		
Littlefield, Joel	1	1	2			Thompson, Isaac	1		2			Bemus, Thaddeus	1	1	3		
Straw, William	1	1	4			Hart, Aaron	1	1	4			McKean, James	3	3	3		
Cousins, John	3	3	1			Neal Andrew	1	3	2			Hasetine, Barnes	1	3	3		
Dennit, Ebenezer	1	1	3			Shurban, Andrew	1					Evans, William	1	1	1		
Roberts, Peter	1	2	3			Hubbard, Asa	1		2			Bean, Thomas	1		1		
Murphy, thomas	1	3	3			Hubbard, Heard	1					Eatton, Sarah	1	1	2		
Cousins, Benjamin	1		1			Grant, Daniel	1	1	2								
Hill, Charles	1	4	1			Estes, Ricᵈ	1					**HIRAM TOWN.**					
Gillpatrick, Joseph	1	1	3			Cussens, Joseph	2	2				Burbank, Benjᵃ	1	1	2		
Going, Jane (Widʷ)		1	1									Bucknell, John	1		1		
Waterhouse, John	1	2	5			**FRYEBURGH TOWN.**						Bucknell, Simeon	1	2	3		
taylor, Jerimiah	1	1	3			Osgood, James	2	4	5	1		Ayer, John	2	3	5		
Dennet, Joseph	1	3	2			Page, Phillip	2	1	4			Barker, Thomas	2		2		
Waterhouse, Jacob	1	1	3			Ames, Moses	2		2			Bucknell, John, Jⁿ	1	1	5		
Hanscomb, Gideon	1	1	3			Allen, Wright	1	1	3			* ——oston, Daniel	1	4	2		
Martin, Samuel	1	2	4			Merrill, Nathˡ	3	4	7			Ryan, Curtis	1	3	2		
Wakefield, Gibbins	1	2				Buck, Asa	1	1	2			Dyer, Bickford	1	1	1		
lord, Samuel	2		4			Evans, David	3		2			Goald, Aaron	1	2	4		
Lord (Widʷ)		1	1			Bean, Joseph	1	1	1			Haywood, Lemuel	1				
Martin, William	1	3				Swan, Caleb	1		3			McLucus, John	1	3	3		
Martin, Lewis	1	1	2			Swan, Joseph Frye	2	1	3			Clements, John	1	1	1		
Cousins, Ebenezer	1	2	1			Colby, Asa	1		2			Midget, David	2	3	3		
Cousins, Benjamin	1	1	2			Gammage, Joshua	1	1	4			* ——sman, Solomon	1	3	1		
						Fessenden, Ebenezer	1	3	5			Libby, Jonathan	1	2	2		
FRANCISBOROUGH PLANTATION.						Hutchins, Jonathan	1		1			Libby, Stephen	1	2	2		
						Frye, Simon	2	3	4			Libby, John	2		2		
Clark, Mr. Benjᵃ	3	4	2			Fifield, John	1	1	1								
Barker, Noah	1	3	3			Fessenden, William	1	5	6			**KITTERY TOWN.**					
Barker, Ebenezer	2	3	5			Dresser, Jonathan, Jʳ	1		4			Petegrow, William	2		3		
Chadbourn, Levi	2	3	2			Dresser, Jonathan	3		4			Spotzeswell, Dorothy			4		
Chadbourn, Wᵐ	1	1	2			Frye, Richᵈ	1		3			Parsons, John	1		4		
Perry, James	2	1	9			Frye, Samˡ	3	1	4			Hayley, Joel	2	2	6		
Barker, Nathˡ	1	1	3			Evans, John	2	1	1			Cole, Eli	1	3	4		
Perry, Samˡ	1	1	2			Bragdon, Thomˢ	1		2			Johnston, James	2		3		
Hebbert, Joseph	1	3	3			Abbot, Isaac	1		2			Johnston, James, Jʳ	1	2	2		
Estman, Ezekil	2	1	2			Abbot, Isaac, Junʳ	1	2	1			Lewis, Simon	1	2	6		
Pendexter, Paul	1		1			Abbot, Simeon	1		1			Lewis, Thoˢ H	2	3	3	1	
Eastman, Obediah	1		2			Langdon, Paul	1	1	4			Witham, Tobias	1	2	5		
Sargent, Chase	2	3	3			Walker, Ezekiel	3	4	3			Baker, Joseph	1		1		
Merril, Enoch	1	1	5			Sterling, John	1		3			Lewis, Mary		1	3	1	
Treadwel, Marsters	1	2	2			Chandler, Danˡ	2	1	2			Booker, Jacob	2	1	3		
Waymoth, James	1	1	3			Kimball, William	2	2	2			Muggaridge, Thomˢ	1	2	5		
Holmes, James	2		2			Farington, John	2	2	4			Curtis, Joseph	1		4		
Durgan, John	1	2	5			Gordon, Henry	2		3			Curtis, Phillidelpʰ	1		3		
Pendexter, Henery	3	1	2			Gordon, John	1	1	4			Pope, David	1		2		
Sherburn, Susannah			2			Thoms, William	1	1	3			Rogers, William	2		2		
Lang, John	2	2	2			Parker, James	1	2	3			Pope, Dorcas			2		
Smith, Theophelus	1		1			Bradley, Abraham	1	2	3			Briez, Robert	1	4	3		
Pike, Bennet	1	1	1			Day, Moses	3	2	2			Pickenail, James	1	1	2		
Pike, John	1	1	2			Day, Ebenezer	1	4	5			Frost, Simon	1		2		
Cheek, Isaac	1	1	3			Knight, Stephen	2		1			Furnald, Capⁿ Denes	1		2	1	
Cole, Obediah	2	2	5			Farington, Daniel	1	3	5			Neal, Samuel	1	2	4		
Cole, Robt	1	3	3			Farington, Putnum	2	3	5			Furnald, Colⁿ Andʷ P.	2	2	4		
Hammons, Edmund	2	3	4			Frye, Nathˡ	1	2	2			Libby, Reuben	2	1	4		
Cole, Arzael	1	3	2			Wiley, Benjamin	2	5	4			Paul, Capⁿ Samˡ	1	1	2		
Shurban, Samˡ	1					Wiley, William	2		4			Hunscum, Moses	1	1	1		
Gilpatrick, John	1	2	2			Eastman, Richard	3		4			Tetherly, John	1	1	3		
Grafton, Unite	1		2			Eastman, Daniel	1	1	2			Hunscum, Nathⁿ	1	2	3		
Shute, John	1	1	4			Webster, John	2	2	5			Dame, Joseph	1		3		
Day, Wᵐ	3	3	4			Carter, Hubbard	2		2			Goodwin, Benjᵃ	1		3		
Day, Stephen	1		2			Carter, Ezra	1	3	6			Cato, Colten	1		3		
Davis, Josiah	1	2	4			Shirley, Edward	2	5	3			Staple, Nathan	1	1	4		
Trafton, Charles	1	2	4			Hardy, David	1		4			Ferguson, Eliza			1		
Tynan, Ricᵈ			4			Carlton, Edward	1	3	5			Black, Henry	2		2		
Pendexter, Eliab	1	1	3			Carlton, Woodman	1	3	4			Black, James	1		2		
Estes, Benjᵃ	1		5			Hutchins, Nathaniel	3	1	1			Black, Henry, Juʳ	1	2	3		
Estes, Jonᵃ	1		2			Winslow, Phebe		2	1			Witham, James	1	1	2		
Linscot, Isaac	4	4	6			Farington, Stephen	1	1	3			Furnald, Mary	2		2	2	
Barns, Abrᵐ	1	2	5			Walker, Isaac	3		1			Black, Margery			1		
Gray, George	1		2			Kelley, Edmund	1		1			Laton, Major Samˡ	4	1	2		
Parkins, Daniel	1	2	1			Walker, Samuel	3	2	5			Frost, John, Esqʳ	2	3	4		
McKissek, John	1	2	5			Howard, William	1	1	3			Frost, Joseph	1		3		
McKisseck, Frances	1		2			Wyman, Jonas	1	2	3			Sherbourn, Henry	2	1	2	1	
Morrison, Samuel	1	2	3			Stevens, John	3		3			Roberts, Jack					5
Gubtail, Daniel	1	5	4			Stevens, John, Junʳ	1	1	2			Patch, John	1		2		
Sawyer, Wᵐ	2		4			Gordon, Hugh	1	2	4			Marsh, Amy		1	2		
Cole, Henery	1	1	1			Charles, John	2	5	5			Black Cathrine			2		
Wormwood, James	1	1	4			Walker, Nathˡ	2		4								

*Illegible.

HEADS OF FAMILIES—MAINE.

YORK COUNTY—Continued.

KITTERY TOWN—con.

NAME OF HEAD OF FAMILY.	Free white males of 16 years and upward, including heads of families.	Free white males under 16 years.	Free white females, including heads of families.	All other free persons.	Slaves.
Moral, Patience	1	1	4		
Jordan, Nathⁿ	1		1		
Muggarage, William	1	1	4		
Hutchins, Joseph	1		1		
Wason, Nathⁿ	1	1	4		
Gullison, John	1		1		
Hutchens, John	1		3		
Leavitt, John	1	1	4		
Norton, Temperance	1	1			
Perry, Willᵐ	1		1		
Brier, Nichᵒ	1	1	3		
Norton, Samˡ	1	1	4		
Ingerson, Richᵈ	1	1	7		
Moore, Samˡ	1	1	1		
Gullison, Deacⁿ Jos.	1	1	2		
Gullison, Samˡ	1		1		
Brier, Moses	1	1	3		
Gullison, Wᵐ	1	3	2		
Weeks, Abrahᵐ	1	1	1		
Moore, Edwᵈ	1		2		
Perrey, Eunice	1		2		
Chisom, Hannah		1	2		
Brier, Samˡ	1		2		
Fenix, Abigail	3		2		
Trott, John	2		3		
Weeks, John	2	2	5		
Muggarige, John	1	1	6		
Stevens, John	2	2	3		
Fletcher, Samˡ	2		3		
Billings, Ephᵐ	2	2	3		
Bellamy, John	2		3		
Westcoat, Isaac	1		2		
Billings, Benjⁿ	1	1	2		
Billings, Samˡ	1	1	1		
Mitchel, Mary	1		7		
Mitchel, John	2	2	4		
Mitchel, Lucy		1	2		
Mitchel, Sarah		1	5		
Ryley, Mary	1		1		
Perkins, Magery	1	1	3		
Dearing, Clemᵗ	2		2		
Mitchel, Samˡ	2	2	4		
Mitchel, James	1		3		
Williams, Amos	1	2	2		
Williams, Johanⁿ			3		
Garish, Wᵐ	1		1		
Billings, Jas., Jur.	1	1	6		
Billings, Joseph	2		3		
Cox, Clement	1	1	3		
Page, Edwᵈ	1		4		
Furnald, Thoˢ	1		2		
Fowler, Susanʰ	1	1	2		
Grace, Benjⁿ	1	2	1		
Todd, Wᵐ	2		3		
Davis, Elemuel	2	3	2		
Chancy, Charles, Esqʳ	3	1	4		
Chatman, Mary	1		2		
Welch, David	1	1	3		
Weeks, Lucy		1	1		
Fenix, John	1		4		
Hayley, Ebenˢ	1		2		
Perkins, Thoˢ	1	2	2		
Hutchens, Lydia			2		
Hayley, Joseph	1	2	2		
Hayley, John	1		2		
Hayley, Robᵗ	1	3	3		
Lewis, Dimond	1	4	3		
Lewis, Peter	2		6		
Wilson, Joseph	1	2	3		
Wilson, Thoˢ	1	1	3		
Hutchins, Hannah	2		2		
Weeks, Nick	3		6		
Frunald, Joel	2	4	6		
Cutt, Edwᵈ, Esqʳ	1	3	4		
Cutt, Deacⁿ Thoˢ	1		1		
Cutt, Robᵗ	4	3	4		
Cutt, Capⁿ Thoˢ	3		3		
Leach, Ebenˢ	3		2		
Leach, Nathⁿ	1	1	3		
Harvy, William	1		3		
Weeks, Capⁿ Samˡ	2		2		
Weeks, John	2	1	2		
Ellis, Laurance	2		3		
Grover, Martha	1		2		
Litchfield, Revᵈ Joseph	1	2	4		
Hammond, Edmond	1	1	7		
Chase, Thoˢ	2	1	3		
Leach, Benj	1	2	5		
Lewis, Enoch	1		2		
Cutt, Thoˢ	1	2	3		
Oats, Sarah			2		
Cutt, Noah	1		4		
Pickernail, Wᵐ	1	2	3		

KITTERY TOWN—con.

NAME OF HEAD OF FAMILY.	Free white males of 16 years and upward, including heads of families.	Free white males under 16 years.	Free white females, including heads of families.	All other free persons.	Slaves.
Furnald, Wᵐ	1	1	6		
Hammond, Deacⁿ Samˡ	2	1	3		
Rogers, John, Junʳ	1	1	3		
Nutter, Jacob	1	2	6		
Goodwin, Danˡ	2	6	8		
Kingburg, Joseph	2	1	4		
Emory, Isaac	1	1	1		
Odehorn, Danˡ	3	2	5	1	
Jordan, John	1	1	3		
Rate, Miriam	2	1	4		
Johnson, Rebeck			3		
Johnston, Noah	1	4	5		
Rate, Capⁿ Wᵐ	1	4	4	1	
Frost, Simon, Senʳ	1		4		
Frost, Abigˡ	1		3		
Johnston, Joseph	1	4	3		
Nason, Elizʰ		6	1		
Noulton, John	1	1	1		
Neal, James	3	1	1		
Frizzle, Mary			(*)	2	
Weeks, Joseph	1	1	3		
Weeks, Pellenak	1		3		
Henney, Sarah		1	2		
Smart, Hannah	1		3		
Pratt, John	1	1	1		
Clinton, —*	1		2		
Dearing, Roger	1	1	2		
Landfar, Sam	1	1	2		
Mitchel, Elizʰ			2		
Mitchel, Roger	1	2	5		
Dearing, Capⁿ Wᵐ	1		1		
Odehorn, Samˡ	1		4		
Toby, Joseph	1	1	3		
Webber, Edwᵈ	2	1	2		
Todd, John	1		2		
Stephens, John	1		1		
Hubbard, Phillip	1	3	2		
Moore, Capⁿ Wᵐ	3		3		
Moore, Capⁿ Jnᵒ	1	1	4		
Shackford, Capⁿ Jon	1		2		
Stephens, Moses	1	1	3		
Todd, Elizʰ		1	3		
Underwood, Capⁿ Job			3		
Stephens, Jnᵒ	2	1	3		
Perkins, Sarah		1	2		
Furnald, Joshᵃ	3	2	3		
Welch, David	1	2	3		
Hayley, Samˡ	2	1	3		
Parsons, Richᵈ	1	2	4		
Follet, Mercy		1	3		
Moore, Joshua	1		3		
Moore, Elizʰ	1		3		
Hutchans, Pelthᵃ	1	2	1		
Lampher, Johanᵃ			2		
Dayly, Sarah		1	2		
Wallingford, Abigˡ			4		
Stocker, John	1		2		
Chambers, James	1	1	4		
Sambo (Black)				4	
Smallcorn, Capⁿ Samˡ	2	1	4		
Weeks, Elihu	3		2		
Brier, Josiah	1		2		
Furnald, John	1	4	5		
Stephens, Revᵈ Benjⁿ	2		1		
Parhook, Ebzʰ	1		3	1	
Sessoro (Black)				2	
Mendham, Wᵐ		2	2		
Cutt, Richᵈ, Esqʳ	3	1	5		
Norton, Samˡ	2	1	4		
Garish, Joseph	3	1	8		
Sowards, Richᵈ	2	1	4		
Todd, Willᵐ	1		2		
Billins, Dan	1	2	(*)		
Cutt, Capⁿ Jos.			3		
Lollar, John	2		2		
Garish, Johanna		1	3		
Garish, John	3		2		
Frost, Ellot	2	1	2		
Bartlet, John H	1	1	1	1	
Bartlet, Danˡ	2	2	3		
Bartlet, Jeremʰ	1	5	4		
Tetherly, Willᵐ	1	3	3		
Sympson, Zebediah	1	5	3		
Emory, Danˡ	2	2	3		
Emory, Danˡ, Junʳ	1	2	1		
Emory, Nathⁿ	2	4	4		
Emory, Steven	1		2		
Emory, Samˡ	1		2		
Emory, Samˡ, Junʳ	1		2		
Emory, Simon, Junʳ	1		4		
Nason, Jonathan	1		1		
Davis, Suanna		1	5		
Adams, Danˡ	1	3	3		

KITTERY TOWN—con.

NAME OF HEAD OF FAMILY.	Free white males of 16 years and upward, including heads of families.	Free white males under 16 years.	Free white females, including heads of families.	All other free persons.	Slaves.
Smith, Wᵐ	1	3	3		
Smith, Hozia			2		
Emory, Israel	1		1		
Patch, George	2	2	1		
Furnald, Dennis, Junʳ	1	2	3		
Furnald, Deacⁿ James	1	2	4		
Seavey, Josiah	1		3		
Remick, Joseph	2		4		
Hunskum, Danˡ	2		3		
Varney, Peter	3	2	2		
Stephens, Johanⁿ			2		
Hunscum, Jack				3	
Roberts, James			2		
Hammond, Deacⁿ Jonathⁿ	1	1	3		
Hammond, Jonathⁿ, Juʳ	2		5		
Toby, John	1		4		
Hunscum, Joathⁿ	1		3		
Libby, Seth	1	2	3		
Hammonds, George	1	1	4		
Hammonds, Ebenˢ	1	1	5		
Hanscum, Tobias	1	3			
Cutt, John	1	1	2		
Furnald, Benjⁿ	1	1	2		
Spinny, John	1	3	3		
Spinny, Samson	2	1	4		
Furnald, Wᵐ	2		2		
Furnald, Nathⁿ	1		2		
Wilson, Edmund	3	3	8		
Wilson, Danˡ	2	3	5		
Jones, Dorithy	1	2	2		
Parker, Capⁿ Benjⁿ	2	4	2	1	
Webber, Benjⁿ	1	2	2		
Wilson, Samˡ	1	2	2		
Parker, Molly			2		
Parker, Danˡ	1		3		
Hayley, Noal	2		2		
Wilson, Elihu	3		1		
Wilson, Aaron	1	3	3		
Wilson, Elizʰ	1		3		
Hutchins, Edmund	1	5	4		
Presby, Darias			2		
Toby, Betty	3	1	2		
Amy, Samˡ	1	1	2		
Mitchel, Wᵐ	2	2	3		
Foy, Stephⁿ	1		4		
Phillips, Andʷ	2	2	2		
Phillips (Widow)			2		
Furnald, Margᵗ		1	3		
Furnald, Arcul⁸	1		1		
Treferton, Henry	3	1	3		
Treferten, Danˡ	1	1	1		
Jenkins, Rowland	1		2		
Jenkins, Stephen	3	1	3		
Levey, Capⁿ Stephⁿ	2		1		
Furnald, Tobias	1	5	1		
Furnald, Benjⁿ	3		1		
Phips (Widdow)			2		
Pray, Joshua	3	1	2		
Cane, John	1		2		
Pray, Samˡ	1	1	2		
Hooper, Nathⁿ	3	1	1		
Winkley, John	2		5		
Winkley, Emerson	1		1		
Furnald, Sarah	2	1	2		
Brown, Thoˢ	2	1	1		
Brown, Capⁿ Thoˢ	1	1	5		
Place, John	1	3	5		
Gullison, Benjⁿ	1	1	7		
Furnald, Ebenʳ	2		3		
Brown, Capⁿ James	1	2	4		
Nahaney, Sarah		1	4		
Leach, Samˡ	1		2		
Furnald, David			1		
Furnald, Dorthy			1		
Furnald, Elihu	1	1	3		
Furnald, Benjⁿ	2	5	7		
Furnald, Joseph	1		2		
Tripe, Elizʰ			1		
Witham, Magdalan				5	
Miles, Mary			2		
Peirce, Docᵗ Danˡ	2	3	3		
Hayley, Majʳ Wᵐ	2		1		
Ingram, Edwᵈ	1	1	3		
Shapleigh, Isabel			3		
Pickenail, Nelson	1	2	4		
Pickenail, Esther			3		
Manson, John	1		2		
Fitts, Sarah			4		
Manson, Samˡ	2		3		
Manson, Benjⁿ	1		1		
Rogers, Jnᵒ	1	1	4	1	
Rogers, Elizʰ			9	2	

* Illegible.

FIRST CENSUS OF THE UNITED STATES.

YORK COUNTY—Continued.

NAME OF HEAD OF FAMILY.	Free white males of 16 years and upward, including heads of families.	Free white males under 16 years.	Free white females, including heads of families.	All other free persons.	Slaves.	NAME OF HEAD OF FAMILY.	Free white males of 16 years and upward, including heads of families.	Free white males under 16 years.	Free white females, including heads of families.	All other free persons.	Slaves.	NAME OF HEAD OF FAMILY.	Free white males of 16 years and upward, including heads of families.	Free white males under 16 years.	Free white females, including heads of families.	All other free persons.	Slaves.
KITTERY TOWN—con.						KITTERY TOWN—con.						KITTERY TOWN—con.					
Furnal, John, 3d	1	2	3			Stanley, Mark	1	2	2			Bartlett, Sarah			3		
Furnald, Willm W	2		2			Kinnard, Dimond	2	4	4			Bartlett, James	1	2	4	1	
Toby, Natha	2		5			Kendal, Edwd	1	1	3			Tucker, Jane			2	1	
Johnes, Alixandr	1		1			Spring, Revd Alpheus	1		5	2		Clark, Nathanl	3	1	3		
Manson, Joseph	2	2	2			Starcy, John	1		6			Ferguson, Stephen	1	4	2		
Pettegrow, Joseph	4	1	3			Laton, Wm, Junr	1	1	5			Ferguson, Reuben	1	2	5		
Monson, Thomas	3	5	1			Kinnard, Michl	1		1			Ferguson, Timothy	1	3	3		
Rogers, Thos	1		3			Kinnard, Timoy	1	4	1			Paul, Moses	2	2	5		
Monson, Saml	1	1	5			Nason, James	2	3	3			Clark, Nathanl, Junr	1	2	3		
Kane, Isaac	1		2			Garland, Jacob	2	1	2			Frost, Nathanl	1	2	5		
Kane, Jane	2	1	2			Garland, Wm	1		3			Frost, Capn Charles	1	2	2		
Shepherd, Mark	1		1			Scammond, Umphy	2	2	6			Davis, John	1	4	3		
Keen, Semeon	3	4	2			Layton, Deacn Wm	1		3			Hubard, Josha, Esqr	1	1	2	1	
Shepherd, Mark, Jur	2	1	2			Remick, Benja	1	5	2			Furbush, Danl	2		2		
Jenkins, Lemuel	1	1	2			Spinney, Ebenezr	1	2	2			Emory, Japhet	2	1	3		
Place, Elizh			2			Sowards, Elizh			2			Gould, Daniel	2	1	5		
Keen, Wm	1	2	2			Remick, John	1	1	7			Lord, Danl	1	2	5		
Banks, Sarah		1	2			Coal, John	1	1	2			Lord, Mary			3		
Jenkins, Thos	1	3	2			Coal, Dorithy	1		3			Gowing, Lemuel	1	2	2		
Jenkins, Margery		1	2			Dennet, Jno	1	1	1			Gowing, John	4		3		
Godsoe, —*		4	1			Dennet, Wm	4	3	2			Hodgsdon, Sarah	(*)	(*)	(*)	(*)	
Grover, —*			1			Dennet, Jno, Junr	3		4			Shapleigh, John	(*)	(*)	(*)	(*)	
Grover, Simon	1		3			Furnald, Jno	3		3			Emory, James	1	3	3		
Rogers, —*	1	2	6			Dennet, Sally			3			Gould, Benja		1	3		
Furnald, David	1		1			Furnald, Mark	1	2	5			Gould, Elixandr	1	4	3		
Dame, Abigl			1			Spinny, John	1	2	4			Spinney, Edmund	1	2	1		
Dame, Horsvil	1	3	2			Remick, Steven	2	2	5			Tedderly, Wm	4		1		
Stephens, Nance		1	2			Paul, James	2	2	5			Tedderly, Saml	1	2	5		
Dame, Nathan	1		3			Remick, Samuel	2		5			Peck, Wm	2		2		
Chanlor, Thos	2		1			Dickson, Saml	1	2	4			Spinney, John	2	2	2		
Furnald, Josh W	1	1	2			Paul, John, Junr	1		2			Spinney, John, Jur	1	1	4		
Monson, Josh	2	2	3			Foster, Parker	1	2	3			Spinney, Saml	1	2	2		
Dame, Jonathn	1	1	6			Foster, Simon	1		2			Spinney, Geo	1	2	2		
Tripe, Sarah			2			Field, Capn Joseph	1	3	3			Petegrow, Saml	3	2	2		
Witham, Aaron	1	1	2			Paul, Joseph	1		2			Petegrow, Mary		2	1		
Mendam, Wm	2		2			Brooks, Saml, Jur	1		1			Remick, Isaac	1		1		
Stoutley, Keturah	1		2			Brooks, Saml	2	5	3			Remick, Isaac, Jur	1	1	4		
Kinward, Wm	1		4			Staples, Soloman	3	2	3			Welch, Wm	1	5	5		
Allen, John	1	2	2			Spinney, Willm	3	2	2			Furnald, Moses	1	1	1		
Pray, Wm	1	3	2			Paul, Timy	1		2			Scrigens, John	1	2	4		
Ore, Elle	1		1			Welch, John	1	2	4			Scrigens, John, Jur	1	1	1		
Adams, Mary	1	1	2			Brooks, Josiah	1		2			Scrigens, Winthrop	1	1	1		
Parker, Sarah			1			Knight, George	1	1	6			Scrigens, Thos	1		3		
Rice, Unice		2	2			Brooks, Wm	1	2	4			Rogers, Nathanl	2	3	3		
Rice, Alixr	3	1	4			Lyssen, Wm	1	2	1			Spinney, Timoy	3	1			
Rice, Saml	1		3	2		Paul, Saml	1		3			Remick, Josiah	2		2		
Mendam, Joshua	2	5	7			Knight, Danl	1	3	2			Dixon, Capn Thos	1	2	4		
Spinny, Nicholas	2	2	3			Cole, Johd	2	3	5			Dixon, Thos	1		3		
James, Mary		3	2			Cole, Angnas			1			Staples, Edwd	1	2	4		
Adams, Mark	4		4			Knight, Nathan	1	3	2			Staples, Ruth			3		
Carter, Sarah	3		1			Dixon, Peter	2	3	11			Dixon, Abrhm	1	2	2		
Lydston, Roby	1		3			Featherly, Anna			2			Staples, Mary	3		4		
Lydston, Gedion	1	1	5			Welch, Saml	1	1	4			Remick, Mary		1	2		
Remick, Sarah			2			Paul, Amos	1	3	4			Staples, David	1	2	2		
Remick, Nathan	1		1			Dixon, Steven	1		2			Garish, Timoy	1	1	1		
Remick, Wm	2		1			Petegrow, Steven	2	3	4			Petegrow, Saml, Jur	1	2	2		
—*, Wm	1		4			Cottle, Wm	3		2			Paul, Mary	2	1	4		
Staples, Wm		2	3			Layton, John	1		2			Remick, Dorcas			1		
Floyd, James	1	2	1			Rendal, Willm	1	1	3			Wherren, Wm	1	2	2		
Furnald, Wm	2		4			Scammond, Humphy, Jun		1	3			Brooks, Joseph	1	2	2		
Rogers, James	2		2			Scammond, Ephehm	1	3	1			Paul, Stephen	2		2		
Rogers, John	1		1			Hanscum, Paltiah	1	3	3			Staples, Isaac	1	2	4		
Hammond, Joseph	1		4			Shapley, Saml	1	4	2			Lydston, Waymouth, Jr	1	1	1		
Furnald, Wm, Jur	1		3			Gould, —*	(*)	(*)	(*)			Lydston, Waymouth	1	1	1		
Green, Mary			1			Witham, Abner	2	4	3			Emory, Hannah			2		
Dixon, Hannah			2			Woodman, Benja	1	3	4			Emory, Anna	1		3		
Hanscum, Steven	1	2	1			Staycy, Wm, Junr	2	1	3			Emory, Noah	1	3	4		
Libby, Joel	1	1	4			Stacy, Ellis	1	2	3			Paul, Ebenezr	2		4		
Libby, Isreal	1		4			John, Capn Saml	1	2	3			Gould, Danl, Junr	1	1	2		
Libby, Mary			2			Hanscum, Ebenr	2	3	3			—*, John	2	3	5		
Libby, Sam	1	1	3			Remick, Elemuel	2		4			Emory, Caleb	3	2	2		
Toby, Saml	3	2	4			Staples, Enoch	1	2	1			Ferguson, Wm	1	2	6		
Toby, Stephn	2		3			Remick, Jacob	2		4			Furbush, Joseph, Jr	4	1	5		
Hanscum, Jno		2	2			Richardson, Thimoy, Jur	1	1	1			Furbush, Joseph	2		2		
Hanscum, Nathan	1	3	1			Kinnard, James	1	3	3			Shorey, Jacob	2		1		
Hanscum, James	1		3			Richardson, Timothy	1		2			Furbush, David	1	4	6		
Hanscum, Jothan	1		2			Foster, Abigl	1	1	2			Ferguson, Denis	1	4	4		
Hanscum, Jonathan	2	1	4			Tucker, Stephen	1		2			Gould, Joseph	3		2		
Bartlett, Thos	1	2	4			Rogers, Nathanl	2		5			Gould, John	1	1	2	4	
Libby, David	1	1	1			Tucker, Saml	1		2			Stacy, Ecabod	3	2	5		
Staples, Peter	1		2			Hill, Andrew	1	3	7			Smith, James	2		2		
Hardge, Wm	1		1			Hill, John	1		2			Smith, Wm	1	2	2		
Libby, Nathan	2	3	4			Morrell, Joel	1	3	6			Witham, Moses	1	3	2		
Remick, Mark	1		1			Fry, Tobias	1	1	5			Witham, Kezia	1	1	2		
Staples, Noah	2	1	3			Forrel, Anna			1			Hodgsdon, Benja	2	1	3		
Fogg, John	2	3	4			Jenkins, Renneldes	2	2	3			Kennington, Hugh	1	2	3		
Fogg, Hannah			1			Hill, Isaac	1	3	4			Bartlet, Nathan	3		1		
Hill, Saml	1		2			Greno, Peltiah	1	3	4			Brewer, Jacob			2		
Hill, Sarah		1	1			Shapleigh, Capn Elisha	1		3			Chick, Amos	2	3	3		
Hammond, Christn	1	2	7			Shapleigh, James	2	3	7			Allen, Ephraim			2		
Hammond, Thos	2		2			Shapleigh, Capn Dependo	2	3	6			Allen, Elizh			2		
Johns, Wm	2	2	3			Fry, Ebenezr, Junr	1		5			Allen, Zekiel	1	1	2		
Marriner, Esthr			4									Fry, Susanna			2		
Frost, Caleb	1	2	3									Fry, Silas	1	3	3		

*Illegible.

HEADS OF FAMILIES—MAINE.

YORK COUNTY—Continued.

NAME OF HEAD OF FAMILY.	Free white males of 16 years and upward, including heads of families.	Free white males under 16 years.	Free white females, including heads of families.	All other free persons.	Slaves.	NAME OF HEAD OF FAMILY.	Free white males of 16 years and upward, including heads of families.	Free white males under 16 years.	Free white females, including heads of families.	All other free persons.	Slaves.	NAME OF HEAD OF FAMILY.	Free white males of 16 years and upward, including heads of families.	Free white males under 16 years.	Free white females, including heads of families.	All other free persons.	Slaves.
KITTERY TOWN—con.						**LEBANON TOWN**—con.						**LEBANON TOWN**—con.					
Fry, Ebenezr	2	2	2			Roberts, Samuel	1	2	3			Corson, Aaron	4		3		
Heath, Mary			2			Nock, Zackh	1	2	4			Goodwin, John	1	2	3		
Davis, Anna			2			Yeaton, John	2	1	1			Jones, Wm	1	2	2		
Lewis, Paul	1		1			Fall, Ebenezor	2	4	4			Jones, Nat	1	1	2		
LEBANON TOWN.						Clark, Josiah	1	1	7			Perkins, Mark	1		2		
						Lord, Nathan	1	2	2			Hanson, Daniel	1	3	4		
Farnham, Joseph, Esqr	4	1	3			Sullivan, Benja	1	1	4			Weitherill, Thos	1		1		
Hasey, Revd Isaac	4		5			Pray, Abram	2	1	4			Burrows, Jona	1	3	4		
Hardison, Joseph	3	2	5			Pray, Joshua	3	1	5			Stevens, Samuel	2	3	1		
Kenney, John	1	2	3			Wheelrite, Snell	1		2			Wingate, Saml	1	2	2		
Pray, Joseph	1	3	3			Pray, Experince			2			Burrows, Joseph	1	3	5		
Gowen, Patrick	3	3	5			Pray, Nat	3	3	6			Farnham, David	1	4	2		
Libby, James	1	1	3			Brock, Daniel	3	4	4			Legro, Thomas	1	1	2		
Woodsum, David	1	2	2			Libby, Charles	1	4	3			Legro, John	2	1			
Ross, Hugh	1	5	5			Mills, John	1	1	2			Hill, Jeremiah	1		3		
Libby, Benja	1	4	2			Richardison, Brady	1	2	2			Clark, James	1	1	3		
Brock, Frances	1	1	6			Young, Eliphelet	1	1	2			Bickford, Joseph	1	2	3		
Clark, Jona	2		1			Furbush, Benja	1		2			Davis, John	1	2	1		
Hunssom, Isaac	1	4	2			Furbush, Benja, Junr		8	2			Appelbe, Thomas	1	1	1		
Wintwoth, Amaziah	1	1	1			Rankins, Jona	2	1	5			Legro, Samuel	1		3		
Ricker, Ezekil	1	3	4			Ricker, Ephrim	1	1	2			Legro, David	2		2		
Horsom, Benja	1		3			Stvens, Jona	1	2	3			Goodwin, Mary		2	3		
Pray, Thomas	1	1	2			Door, John	1	1	2			Blasdel, John	1	1	5		
Jones, James	1	2	4			Door, John, Junr	1	1	2			Lord, Elisha	1	2	2		
Ricker, Ebenezer	1		1			Hussey, Ruben	1		3			Garling, Samuel	1	2	2		
Horsom, David	1		4			Hussey, Zackh	1	1	1			Legro, John	1	3	2		
Jones, Ebenezer	1		2			Whitehouse, Nat	1	1	7			Fall, George	1	2	3		
Butler, Thomas			2			Stvens, Thomas			1			Wallingford, Joshua	1	1	3		
Goodwin, Ruben	1		4			Hussey, Patience	1	2	4			Cowel, Ichabod	1	1	1		
Horsom, John	2	3	3			Stvens, Abijah	1	2	4			Cowel, John	2	2	4		
Hart, Robt	1	3	1			Stevens, Wm	1	1	3			Pray, Joseph	1	3	3		
Downs, Ichabod	1	2	2			Door, Jonathan	2		2			Pollock, Thomas	2	2	7		
Keay, Peter	3		5			Wintworth, Benja	1	1	3			Woodman, John	1	6	1		
Pray, Moses	3	2	3			Wintworth, Stimson	1		1			Fox, Daniel					
Lord, Ebenezer	2	3	2			McCreelus, John	3		4			Bracket, Jacob					
Lord, Simon	2	1	3			Garien, Dodifer	1		1			Woodman, David	1	3	4		
Frost, Mark	3	3	2			Verney, Humpy	2	1	2			Loud, Solomon	2	2	1		
Murry, Thomas	1	1	2			Tibbets, Stephen	1	2	3			Wintworth, Gersham	1		2		
Wallingford, Jno	2	1	1			Tibbets, Ephrim	1	1	2			Merrow, James		1	1		
Wallingford, Tobias	1		2			Tuttle, Benja	1		2			Robinson, Samuel	2		1		
Wallingford, Moses	1	1	1			Cook, Daniel	1	1	1			Kimball, Caleb	1		1		
Hanson, Moses	1		4			Cook, Abram	1	2	4			Mason, Nat	1	1	1		
Smith, John	1	1	2			Cook, Daniel	1	1	4								
Roberts, Daniel	3	3	4			Blasdel, Thomas	1	1	2			**LIMERICK TOWN.**					
Holmes, Thomas	1	1	3			Blasdel, Elijah	1	1	1			Gilpatrick, Joseph, Esqr	2	2	4		
Peirce, Ebenr	1		2			Ricker, Moses	3		6			Bradbury, Jacob	3		4		
Peirce, Ebenr, Jr	1	2	5			Ricker, Henery	1	1	1			Felsh, Abijah	5	1	7		
Horn, Ricd	1		1			Harford, Solomon	1	2	5			Furnald, Joshua	1	2	4		
Jones, Ebenr	3	1	3			Libby, Jeremiah	1		3			Libby, Azariah	3	1	4		
Jones, Jno	1	2	1			Shorey, Stephen	1		2			Stone, John	1		2		
Keay, Jno	1	1	4			Stillens, Isaac	1		2			Adams, John	1	3	3		
Ricker, Simeon	1	2	4			Furbush, Ricd	5	2	6			Morrel, John	1	1	4		
Teal, Robert	2	2	4			Wintworth, Thomas M	1	1	2			Wingat, John	2	3	6		
Nock, Stase D	1	2	2			Burrows, Edward	2		1			Gilpatrick, Thomas	2	2	6		
Wintworth, Silas	1	4	2			Burows, Edward	1	2	2			Libby, Nathel	1		3		
Lord, Wm	1	2	1			Foss, Daniel	3	1	3			Perkins, Joseph	3	1	3		
Libby, Saml	1	1	5			Norris, Jona	2		4			Parks, Joseph	1	3	3		
Goodwin, Reuben	1	1	3			Weitherill, James	1	3	5			Durgan, Wm	1	4	3		
Goodwin, Elisha	1	1	1			Chamberlin, Wm	1	2	2			Boothby, Wm	1		5		
Fall, Stephen	1	2	2			Chamberlin, Amos	1	1	2			Kneely, Danl	1	1	2		
Fogg, James	1		1			Blasdel, Eliphelet	2		1			Ricker, Aaron	1		2		
Horsom, Saml	1	1	3			Chamberlin, Nat	1	2	2			Hayes, John	1		3		
Keay, Oles	1		4			Critchet, John	1		2			Favor, Jno	4		3		
Keay, Danl	1	2	1			Corson, Levi	2	2	2			Clark, David	1	3	1		
Smith, Ichabod	1	2	4			Corson, Daniel	1	1	2			Hodsdon, Joseph	3	1	3		
Clements, Aaron	1	2	2			Mills, James	1		2			Derban, Ricd	1	3	3		
Nock, Daniel	3	3	4			Corson, Mary			1			Ricker, Rufus	1	1	1		
Gowel, Benja	1	3	1			Blasdel, Ephrim	3	5	3			Ricker, Ebenezer	1		1		
Downs, Benja	1	1	5			Goodwin, Samuel	1	2	4			Clark, Penewal	2	1	1		
Austen, Nat	2	2	5			Copps, Samuel	4	3	3			Ford, George	2	2	2		
Ricker, Meturen	1	3	2			Copps, Ruben H	1		1			Johnson, Benja	2	4	3		
Ricker, Enoch	1	2	3			Cottel, John	1		4			Hill, Joshua	2	3	2		
Horsom, Jona	1	2	2			White, Silas	1	2	8			Barker, Danl	1	3	2		
Ricker, Joseph	1	2	4			Hayes, John	3	3	3			Hill, Ruben	1	1	2		
Horn, Benja	1	1	3			Hayes, Elihue	1		2			Kean, Benja	1		3		
Lord, Solomon	1	3	4			Wintworth, Jedediah	1	4	5			Beetel, Abial	1	3	3		
Rines, Henery	2	2	7			Wintworth, Caleb	2		2			Mills, James	1	3	4		
Farnham, David	1		2			Hanson, Mary			2			Seve, John	1	2	2		
Downs, Daniel	1	2	2			Lord, Noah	2	3	5			Lord, Thomas	1	2	2	1	
Horn, Ephrim	1		3			Hodsdon, Samson		3	1			Mills, John	1	2	5		
Farnham, Benja	3	3	4			Hodsdon, Joshua	1	2	2			Mills, Jacob	2	1	2		
Moody, John	1		4			Cowel, Edmund	2	2	1			Lord, Ammi R	2	1	5		
Austen, Moses	2	5	2			Warren, George	1	1	2			Durgan, Benja	2	2	4		
Austen, Cathrine			1			Lord, Joseph	1	3	4			Hodsdon, John	1		3		
Pray, John	1	1	2			Gerrish, John	1	3	3			Hodsdon, Jonathan	1	1	2		
Lord, Nicholas	1	2	2			Kenney, Joshua	2	2	6			Hodsdon, John	1		3		
Blasdel, Enoch	1	2	2			Door, Henery	2	3	3			Hodsdon, Wm	1	2	3		
Hanson, Isaac	2	1	4			Grant, Wm	1		2			Hodsdon, Tho	1	3	3		
Hanson, Jona	1		2			Goodwin, Thomas	1	4	3			Fulsom, John					
Jones, Samuel	2	4	5			Furbush, Daniel	2	2	3			Perry, Jesse	2	1	2		
Peirce, Benja	4	4	4			Gerrish, George	3	2	5			Perry, James	1	1	2		
Lord, William W	1		4			Hodsdon, Tho	2	1	8			Perry, George	1		2		
Peirce, Moses	1		2			Nock, John	3	2	2			Perry, John	1	2	3		
						Worster, John	2	1	3								

FIRST CENSUS OF THE UNITED STATES.

YORK COUNTY—Continued.

NAME OF HEAD OF FAMILY.	Free white males of 16 years and upward, including heads of families.	Free white males under 16 years.	Free white females, including heads of families.	All other free persons.	Slaves.	NAME OF HEAD OF FAMILY.	Free white males of 16 years and upward, including heads of families.	Free white males under 16 years.	Free white females, including heads of families.	All other free persons.	Slaves.	NAME OF HEAD OF FAMILY.	Free white males of 16 years and upward, including heads of families.	Free white males under 16 years.	Free white females, including heads of families.	All other free persons.	Slaves.
LIMERICK TOWN—con.						**LITTLE FALLS TOWN—continued.**						**LITTLE OSSIPEE TOWN—continued.**					
Frye, Ebenezer	1					Nason, Joseph	1	2	3			Clark, Ephraim	1	3	1		
Pane, James	1		2			Young, John	1	1	4			Chick, Ephraim	1	1	1		
Bradbury, John	2		1			Berry, James	2	2	3			Brachet, Joshua	1	1	3		
Harper, Samuel	1	3	7			Nason, John	4	1	2			Brachet, Abraham	1	1	4		
Durnel, David	1	3	5			Nason, Robert	1		2			Cobb, Nicholas	1		2		
Foster, Daniel	1	2	3			Davis, James	1	2	3			Foss, Job T	1		4		
Stimson, Jeremiah	1	1	2			Davis, John	2	1	3			Richardson, David	1	4	1		
Gilpatrick, Sarah		3	3			Murphy, Pierce	1	1	1			Rackley (Widow)	1	1	3		
Howard, Amos	1	2	3			Hardy, Abel	3	1	3			Frost, Moses	1		1		
Brown, Amos	1	2	3			Robinson, Isaac	4	2	2			Stout, John	2	1	3		
Bradbury, Daniel	1	2	2			Smith, Elisha	3	3	2			Round, James	1	1	4		
Bradbury, Jabez	1	1	2			Smith, Noah	1		3			Munson, Wm	2	4	3		
Sanbourn, Benja	1	2	2			Tarbox, Carol	1	1	3			Foss, Peletiah	1	2	2		
Durgan, Hannah			3			Tarbox, Benja	1		1			Stout, Prince	1	2	4		
Durgan, Ephrim	1	2	3			Barnes, Joseph	1		2			Hasty, Robert	1		1	1	
Stimson, Joseph	1	4	5			Linscutt, Joseph	1	1	4			Hasty, David	1	2	2		
Staple, Carrel	1	3	3			Staples Joseph	1	1	3			Boody, Robert	3	5	4		
Furlong, Patrick	1	3	3			Simpson, Willm	1		3			Jackson, Robert	1	3	7		
Foster, Isiah	2	1	4			Haley, Sam1	1	3	2			Brachet, Saml	1	3	1		
Peirce, John	1	2	5			Gookins, Joseph	1		2			Rendal, James	1	2	4		
Ricker, Moses	1					Smith, John	1	1	2			Millar, Thomas	1	2	1		
Fitzgearld, Daniel	1	1	1			Banks, Joseph	1	1	2			Frost, Isaac	1	2	5		
						Carl, Joshua	2		5			Molloy, Dennis	1	7	2		
LITTLE FALLS TOWN.						Roff, Saml	1					Gilkey, James	1	3	2		
Gorden, John	1		1			Cole, John	1	4	1			Ridley, Daniel	1	2	4		
Gorden, Zebulen	2	6	2			Jordan, Joseph	1		2			Edgcomb, Nicholas	3		2		
Gorden, Andw	2	1	4			Woodman, Joseph	1	3	3			Libbee, Joseph	1	2	5		
Dow, Jeremiah	2		2			Lane, Isaac	2		1			Rummery, Thos	1	1	4		
Dow, Ebenezer, Jr	1		2			Linscutt, Saml	1		1			Brachet, Reuben	1		1		
Young, Danl	1	3	1			Warren, Joshua	2		1			Mars, Pelatiah	1	1	2		
Dow, Saml	1		2			Warren, Joshua, Jr	1	3	1			McCarty, John	1	3	6		
Dow, Jere, Jr	1	2	2			GilPatrick, Christopher	1	1	2			Clay, Benja	1	1	3		
Dow, Ebenr	2	2	6			Warren, Danl	1		3			Dier, Danl	1	3	4		
Gorden, John, Jr	1	2	2			Simpson, Webster	2	2	2			Richardson, David	1	3	1		
Emery, Benja	1	1	2			Hooper, Jacob	1	3	3			Davis, Ezra	1	4	6		
Young, David	1	1	1			Hooper, Joseph	1	2	2			Johnson, Willm	3	2	4		
Young, Hezekiah	1	1	3			Lord, —	1	1	2			Small, Francis	1	1	1		
Young, Thos	1		1			Goodwin, Danl	1	1	2			Young, David	1	2	2		
Young, Danl, Jr	1	1	1			Hooper, Tristram	1	4	2			Berry, Saml	1				
Townsend, Danl	1	2	4			Clough, Thos	1	2	4			Morton, Willm	1		3		
Dier, Joseph	3	5	2			Hooper, John	3		3			Davis, Nicholas	1	4	3		
Downs, Phinehas	1		4			Hooper, George	1	2	2			Small, Isaac	1	2	3		
Patterson, Joseph	1		6			Linscutt, Saml, Jr	1	1	1			Boothby, Jona	1	2	4		
Leland, Joseph	2		3									Libbee, Jesse	3	2	3		
Chadborn, Joseph	2	2	5			**LITTLE OSSIPEE TOWN.**						Black, Josiah	1	3	3		
Dier, Humphry	1	3	3			Berry, James	1	3	4			Edgcomb, Nicholas, Jr	1		2		
Haley, Willm	2		1			Staples, Robert	2	3	4			Tyler, Joseph	1	2	3		
Hill, Elisha	2	2	1			Hasty, Robert	1	1	1			Edmonds, Asa	1	1	1		
Haley, Robert	1		3			Boody, Ezra	1	1	1			Whitman, Willm	1	2	5		
Cleaves, Ebenezer	1	1	1			Meservey, Nathl	1	2	3			Chase, Amos	1	3	3		
Haley, Joseph	1		2			Cobb, Andw	1	2	2			Sawyer, Joshua	3		5		
Smith, Dominicus	1	1	2			Grindley, —	1	1	1			Sawyer, Nathl	1	4	2		
Lock, Caleb	3	2	3			Small, Danl	1	3	3			Small, Jacob	2	4	2		
Poke, Mary	1		5			Small, Henry	1	3	4			Small, Danl	2	3	4		
Smith, Anna	2		5			Morton, Ebena	1	1	1			Jackson, Bartholomew	1	1	9		
Smith, Nathl	1	2	2			Irish, Ebena	1		3			McKenny, Dominicus	1		1		
Haley, Benja	3	3	2			Irish, Obadiah	1		1			Sparrow, Joseph	1				
Bean, Jona	2		3			Morton, Joseph	1		2			Biter, Peter	1	1	4		
Bean, Jona, Junr	1	1	2			Small, Willm	1		6			Stout, Richard	2	3	4		
Gould, James	1	1	2			Libbee, Philemon	3	2	3			Nason, Jona	3	4	5		
Worth, Saml	1		5			Chick, Nathan	1	3	4			Nason, John	1	1	4		
Parker, Enoch	1	3	6			Richardson, Thaddeus	1	4	2			Strout, Isaac	3	3	3		
Wadley, Moses, jr	2	1	4			Small, Benja	2	2	4			Strout, Gilbart	1		2		
Foss, Obadiah	1		1			Duglass, John	1	1	3			Strout, Willm	1		2		
Hill, John	1	3	3			Wentworth, Willm	1	3	1			Strout, Enoch	1	3	4		
Smith, Jedadlah	3		7			Stone, George	2	1	2			Wing, Nathan	1				
Merry, Willm	1	2	2			McKenny, Humphry	1		1			Small, Joshua	2	1	2		
Smith, Edward	2		4			Stone, John	1	2	2			Small, Joshua, Jr	1	1	3		
Smith, Danl, Jr	1	2	2			Fogg, Charles	1	1	1			Hunscum, Danl	1		2		
Russel, Nathl	2	2	5			Fogg, George	1	1	2								
Cleaves, Israel	1	1	4			Bragdon, Willm	1		4			**NEW PENACOOK TOWN.**					
Whittier, Nathl	1					Higgans, Walter	1		3			Kimball, Moses	1	3	3		
Jellitson, John	1	3	3			Libbee, Robert	1	1	2			Putman, Stephen	1	1	1		
Wadley, Willm	2	3	7			Fogg, Danl	1		2			Mores, Aaron	1	1	3		
Wadley, John	1		2			Boothby, David	1	3	2			Dotloff, Richard	1		2		
Wadley, Moses	1		5			Sawyer, Ebena	1	3	2			Farnum, David	1		2		
Smith, Danl	3	3	6			Sawyer, Saml	1	2	3			Farnum, Benjama	1		2		
Smith, Benja	1	1	1			Andrews, John	2		1			Manuel, James	1		2		
Drew, Zebulon	2		1			Sutten, —	1	2	2			Stone, Moses	1		2		
Drew, Hezekiah	1	1	2			Small, James	2	3	1			Elliot, Benja	1	1	5		
Haley, Joseph	1	3	3			Meservey, Joseph	1	1	2			Capon, Thomas	1	2	2		
Townsend, Abram, Jr	1	3	3			Mars, Isaac	1		2			Keyes, Francis	1		2		
Townsend, Nathan	1	1	2			Clark, Ebena	1	1	3			Lufkin, Benja	1	2	2		
Townsend, Abram	1		2			Latherby, Saml	1		5			Harper, Daniel	3		1		
Townsend, Isaac	1	1	5			Small, Reuben	1	4	1			Seger, Josiah	1		3		
Ridley, Matthias	1		2			Milliken, Phinehas	1	2	2			Abbot, Phillip	1		2		
Ridley, John	1	2	1			Latherby, Isaac	1	2	3			Merrill, Ezekiel	3	2	6		
Field, Danl	1	2	4			Boothby (Widow)	1	2	1			Howard, Phinehas	1		2		
Ridley, Thos	1	1	6			Wiman, John	1	4	5			Howard, Samuel	1	1	2		
Ridley, Abram	1		2			Libbee, Aaron	1	1	4								
Ridley, James	1	3	3			Tyler, Abraham	1		1			**PARSONSFIELD TOWN.**					
Bryant, John	2	3	3			Humprys, Danl	1										
Kimbal, Rufus	1		3			Frost, Wingate	1		1			Kinsman, Jona, Esqr	2	3	4		
Cousins, Ichabod	1	1	3			Richardson, Elisha	1	1	1			Parsons, Thomas, Esqr	1	2	7		
Rummery, Moses	1		3			Stout, Saml	1	2	1			Sanborn, John	1	1	1		
Rummery, Jona	1		4			Stout, Simon	1	2	3			Marsten, Daniel	1		1		

HEADS OF FAMILIES—MAINE.

YORK COUNTY—Continued.

NAME OF HEAD OF FAMILY.	Free white males of 16 years and upward, including heads of families.	Free white males under 16 years.	Free white females, including heads of families.	All other free persons.	Slaves.	NAME OF HEAD OF FAMILY.	Free white males of 16 years and upward, including heads of families.	Free white males under 16 years.	Free white females, including heads of families.	All other free persons.	Slaves.	NAME OF HEAD OF FAMILY.	Free white males of 16 years and upward, including heads of families.	Free white males under 16 years.	Free white females, including heads of families.	All other free persons.	Slaves.
PARSONSFIELD TOWN—continued.						**PARSONSFIELD TOWN—continued.**						**PEPPERELLBOROUGH TOWN—con.**					
Hobbs, Samuel	1		5			Divorux, Ricd	1		3			Dearben, Thomas	2	2	4		
Doe, John	3		6			Floyd, Michael	2	1	3			Dearben, Jacob	1	1	1		
Morss, Benja	1	1	5			Pain, Wm	1		1			Dearben, Ebenezer	1	2	4		
Sanbourn, Benja	1					Libby, Enoch	1	2	6			Deshon, Chase	1	2	4		
Doe, Levi	2		1			Blaso, Joseph	1					Durill, Benja	3		2		
Doe, Samuel	1		1			Wedgwood, Lot	1	5	2			Dorman, Charles	1		2		
Marsten, David	1	1	4			Smith, Benja	1	1	3			Drinkworter, Thos	2	1	7		
Marsten, Caleb	1	2	1			Mighill, Josiah	1	2	3			Dearing, John	1		1		
Cobbet, Nat	1	1	3			Gilman, James	1	1	2			Dearing, Thos	2	2	7		
Ames, John	3	2	3			Scnegel, Jacob	1	3	2			Dearing, Joseph	2	3	3		
Page, Saml	1	2	3			Schegel, George	2					Dearing, John, Jur	1	4	1		
Brown, Robt	1		1			Wiggen, Bradstreet	1		3			Dearing, James	1		1		
Holland, Elisabeth			2			Fox, Edward	1	1	2			Davis, John	1	5	4		
Brown, Benja	2		1			Fox, John	3	1	2			Edgcomb, Saml	2	1	5		
Marsten, James	1	2	2			Remmick, James	1		2			Edgcomb, Ebenezer	1	2	2		
Kent, Josiah	1	1	3			Lowge, John	1	3	1			Edgcomb, Thos	1	3	3		
Avery, Jeremiah	1	1	2			Stacy, Benja	1		2			Edgcomb, Saml, Jur	1	1	1		
Avery, Walter	1					Lowge, Joanna		1	3			Emery, Job	1	2	4		
Doe, Gedion	3	2	4			Miles, Wm	1	5	1			Elwell, James	1	1	1		
Doe, Jona	1	2	6			Berry, James	1	2	2			Elwell, Mehitable			2		
Pees, Asa	1					Lowge, Samul	2	1	2			Fairfield, Revd John	2	1	4		
Peas, Josiah	1		1			Kezer, George	3		3			Foss, James	2	3	5		
Ames, Nathal	2	1	6			Kezer, George	1					Foss, John	2	1	7		
Bacheler, Benja	1		1			Kezer, Josiah	1		1			Foss, Benjamin	1	5	3		
Sanborn, Wm	1		2			Abbot, David	1		3			Foss, Wm	2	3	3		
Sanborn, Wm	1	1	2			Parsons, Stephen	1	1	2			Foss, Daniel	1	2	2		
Tole, Levi	2		2			Blaso, John	1					Foss, James, Jur	2	3	6		
Tole, Stephen D	1		1			Blaso, Joseph	1		1			Foss, James, 3d	1	1	1		
Wiggen, Nathan	1	2	2			Weeks, Samuel	5	4	3			Foss, Walter	2	1	2		
Fulsom, John	1	3	2			Mason, Jane	1	1	1			Foss, Walter, Jur	1		4		
Wedgwood, Noah	1	2	1			Ellot, Wm	1		2			Foss, Walter, 3d	1		1		
Moulton, Samuel	1	3	4			Fox, Elijah	2					Fernald, Nathl	1	2	1		
Wedgwood, Jesse	1		4			Muget, James	1	1	1			Fendarson, John	1	3	6		
Hilton, Dudley	2		3									Flood, Nathan	1	1	3		
Sargent, Robt	1	2	1			**PEPPERELLBOROUGH TOWN.**						Fairfield, Josiah	1	1			
Peas, Zebulon	1	2	2									Fowler, Ebenezer	1	1	2		
Bickford, George	2	5	4			Abbot, Samuel	1	1	2			Foss, Joseph	3	5	5		
Benson, James	1	2	3			Ellis, John	1	1	3			Gray, James	4	1	4		
Quint, Joseph	1	2	1			Abbot, Moses	1	1	5			Googins, John	3		2		
Quint, John	1					Ayers, Moses	1	1	3			Googins, Wm	3		3		
Quint, Martha			1			Brady, Joseph	3	1	6			Gould, Samuel	3	3	4		
Piper, Elisha	3	3	5			Bryant, Stephen	1	2	4			Gogens, David	1		2		
Morrison, James	1	3	3			Bryant, Jerathwell	2	2	4			Gould, Joseph	2	2	2		
Pees, Joseph	1	3	6			Bryant, Ephraim	2	3	3			Googins, Joseph	2		4		
Norris, Joseph	1		1			Bryant, Stephen, Jur	2	2	6			Guttridge, Benjamin	3		2		
Norris, Jeremiah	1	3	4			Bryant, David	1	1	4			Guttridge, Benja, Jur	1		4		
Chase, Lydia		1	1			Bryant, Ephraim, Jur	1		3			Gilford, Joseph	1	2	3		
Mighill, Moses	1	1	1			Berry, Richard	3	1	5			Goulthrite, Philip	1				
Mighill, Joseph	1		2			Berry, Nicholas	1	5	7			Guttridge, Hannah		3			
Pees, Samuel	1		1			Bradby, Edward	1	1	2			Honycomb, Benaiah	2		1		
Pees, Samuel	1	1	4			Bachelor, David	1	1	1			Hase, Zephemiah	1	3	2		
Moore, Ebenezer	1	4	4			Bachelor, Jonathan	1		1			Harmon, Pettcah	1	2	2		
Moore, John	2	3	2			Barker, David	1	1	2			Hopkins, Solomon	1		3		
Furbacks, Joshua	3	4	3			Bailey, Thos	1	1	2			Heins, Samuel	2	2	3		
Wiggen, Nathel	1		1			Bryant, Daniel	1	2	2			Hill, Benjamin	1		2		
Burnham, Paul	1	2	3			Banks, John	1	1	3			Jordan, Tristram, Esqr	3	2	2		
Hutchins, Enoch	2	1	2			Banks, Pheby	2	1	6			Jordan, Saml, Esqr	2		2		
Bickford, John	1	3	2			Banks, Joseph	1	2	2			Jordan, Tristram, Jur	1		1		
Pearl, Joseph	1	1	3			Boothby, Saml	1	3	2			Junkins, Sarah	3	1	6		
Dockum, James	1	2	1			Boothby, Josiah	3	2	2			Jameson, Wm	1		1		
Wintworth, Wm	1	2	1			Boothby, John	2	2	3			Jameson, Robert	1		2		
Morrel, Stephen	1	2	4			Bond, Robert	1	2	5			Jewett, George	2				
Moulton, Cuting	2	3	3			Bond, Robert, Jur	1	1	2			Johnson, James	2	5	5		
Page, Taylor	1	3	3			Barry, Saml	1	3	5			Keindrick, John	1		4		
Brown, Robert	1	1	2			Bangs, John	2	1	1			Keindrick, Joseph	1	1	3		
Brown, John	3	1	5			Branan, Thos	1	2	1			Keelly, Phinehas	3	2	3		
Parsons, Abigail		1	1			Barry, Richard, Junr	1	1	1			King, Josiah	1		1		
Bickford, Wm	1					Brown, Jonathan	1	4	3			Libbey, Joseph	3		3		
Palmer, Wm	2	2	2			Chase, Dr. Amos	3		3			Lumbard, Solomon	1	5	2		
Neal, Walter	1		4			Cutts, Thos, Esqr	11	2	5			Libbey, Thomas	2		2		
Neal, Enoch	1		2			Chase, Saml	3	1	4			Libbey, Solomon	2	2			
Parsons, Joseph	2		4			Coffin, James	3	2	6			Libbey, Philip	1		1		
Hobbs, David	1	1	4			Cole, Willm	2	1	4			Libbey, Elijah	1	3	1		
Hobbs, James	1	1	2			Chandler, John	1	2	3			Lowel, Saml	1	1	3		
Granvill, Josiah	2	2	5			Carll, Benjamin	2		2			Loyns, Willm	1	1	1		
Cluff, John	1	1	1			Carll, Robert	2		1			Moody, Elizabeth	2	4	4		
Colkut, Josiah	2	1	4			Carll, John	2	2	2			Means, Thomas	2	1	4		
Kennison, John	2	4	4			Carll, Wm	2		4			Means, George	1	3	2		
Champen, James	1	4	2			Carll, Elias	1		2			McKinney, John	1	1	3		
Chase, Edmund	3	2	3			Chamberlain, Thomas	1	3	4			McKinney, Jeremiah	1	2	2		
Gilman, Abijah	1	2	2			Chamberlain, Wm	1		2			Moody, George	1		2		
Gilman, Samuel	1					Chamberlain, John	1	3	4			Hason, Benja, Jur	2	1	3		
Hart, James	1	2	3			Cutts, Foxl	1	1	2			Merrill, Joseph	1	4	4		
Kennison, Abram	1	1	1			Chase, Amos, Jur	1		2			Newbegin, George	1		2		
Dalton, Samuel	2	1	2			Chase, Daniel	1		1			Pike, Humphrey	4	1	4		
Ranckens, James	1		2			Cleaves, Jonathan	2	2	5			Pike, Israel	3	3	2		
Muget, John	2		2			Coit, Hannah		1	3			Patterson, Robert	1		1		
Muget, Jeremiah	1	2	2			Cleaves, John	2	1	5			Patterson, Robert, Jur	1	4	3		
Muget, Joseph	1		4			Cleaves, Robert	1	2	2			Patterson, Samuel	1	3	5		
Colkut, Job	1	2	2			Chase, John	2	1	2			Patterson, Andrew	1	4	4		
Chase, Moses	2	3	3			Dennet, Saml	2		3			Patterson, Benja	1		1		
Tole, Jonathan	1	2	2			Dennett, Nicholas	2	5	5			Patterson, David	1	1	1		
Blaso, Amos	2	3	1			Dennet, Saml, Jur	4	2	3			Patterson, Elisha	1		2		
Peirce, Frances	1		4			Dennet, Ebenezer	3	2	3			Patterson, John	4		6		
Pain, Phillip	3	4	6														

YORK COUNTY—Continued.

NAME OF HEAD OF FAMILY.	Free white males of 16 years and upward, including heads of families.	Free white males under 16 years.	Free white females, including heads of families.	All other free persons.	Slaves.	NAME OF HEAD OF FAMILY.	Free white males of 16 years and upward, including heads of families.	Free white males under 16 years.	Free white females, including heads of families.	All other free persons.	Slaves.	NAME OF HEAD OF FAMILY.	Free white males of 16 years and upward, including heads of families.	Free white males under 16 years.	Free white females, including heads of families.	All other free persons.	Slaves.
PEPPERELLBOROUGH TOWN—con.						**SANFORD TOWN.**						**SANFORD TOWN—con.**					
Patterson, Abraham	1	1	4			tripe, Samuel	2		5			Bean, Joshua	1	1	3		
Patterson, Daniel	1	3	3			parsons, Olive (Wid.)	1	3	5			hanson, Caleb	1	3	4		
Pritham, John	1	3	3			Bragdon, Aaron	1	3	3			Low, Jonathan	1	4	3		
Paul, Willm	1	2	2			taylor, Noah	1	3	2			Beal, Zebilon	1	3	3		
Phillips, John	1	3	2			Stanyan, John	1	1	1			hanson, Joshua	3	2	3		
Phillips, Wm	1		1			Bragdon, Amous	1	1	1			Withum, Jonathan	1	2	4		
Phillips, John, Junr	1	1	1			Tompson, John	2		2			ChadBourn, Ebenezer	1	4	2		
Page, Dan	2	2	5			Thompson, Ruben	1	2	3			Withum, Mouses	1	1	1		
Page, Peter	2		1			Emeary, Caleb, Esq	3	1	2			Withum, Jacob	1	1	1		
Parcher, George	1	1	2			Emeary, William	1	2	3			gouen, Ezekel	2	5	2		
Parcher, Elias	2	2	5			Young, Daniel	2	3	3			Wodley, Daniel	1	3	3		
Rollings, James	1		2			Johnson, Samuel	1	2	3			Batchellor, Joshua	1	4	3		
Richards, Nathl	1	4	4			Standley, Edward	2		4			Webber, Daniel	1		2		
Ridlin, Mathias	1	2	3			Standley, John	1		2			Gouen, Stephen	1	4	4		
Rose, Solomon	1		1			Johnson, Jonthan	4		3			Gouen (Widow)			2		
Rose, Solomon, Junr	2	1	3			tibbls, Moses	1		1			Low, Ephraim, Junr	2	1	5		
Ridlen, Daniel	2	2	1			huzey, Daniel	1		2			Low, David	1		3		
Ridlen, Ephraim	1	2	3			Lord, mary (Wid.)		1	2			Bostone, Timothy	1	2	3		
Runnels, John	1		1			Gray, James	3		5			Shaw, Samuel	1	3	2		
Ridlen, Lewis	1	1	1			Bennet, Nathinel	1	5	1			Withum, Jeremiah	1		3		
Ridlen, Jeremiah	3	2	4			Bennet, William	3		2			tripe, William	1	2	5		
Rumary, Edward	1	1	2			Bennet, David		1	5			thompson, Ezra	1	1	2		
Rumery, John	1		2			powers, John	1	2	2			powers, William	2	1	4		
Rumery, Edward, Jur	1	1	1			Molton, Joel	1	2	4			powers, Nathan	1		3		
Sawyer, David	1		1			hanelton, heneary	1	3	3			harmon, Napthalum, Jun	1	1	1		
Sawyer, David, Jur	2	1	2			Swet, Moses	1	1	3			harmon, Napthalum	2	1	3		
Sawyer, David, 3d	1		1			paul, Josieah	2	3	5			thompson, Ebenezer	2	1	3		
Sawyer, Joel	2	1	6			hale, Enoch	1	1	1			thompson, Solomon	1		5		
Sawyer, John	1	1	3			thompson, phiness	1	3	3			Gray, James, the 3	2		2		
Sawyer, Abner	2	3	4			Johnson, Jonathan, Jur	1	1	1			true, Obdiah	1		5		
Sawyer, Willm	1	4	5			tripe, Robt	1	1	1			peare, James	1		2		
Staples, Elisha	1	3	6			Crain, John	1	1	5			Norton, Josiah	1	1	4		
Sinnot, Thos	1	5	2			Jacobs, John	1	3	1			haskel, thomas	2	2	4		
Sillea, Nathan	1	1	2			Bostone, Thomas	2		5			Wilkeson, Joseph	1	3	1		
Sillea, John	1	1	1			peary, Stephen	1	1	2			Beane, David, Senr	2	1	3		
Scamman, Elizabeth	1	2	1			morel, Samuel	3	1	4			Beane, David	1		2		
Scamman, Samuel	2	1	5			morel, Stephen	1					Beane, Joseph	1		2		
Scamman, Dominicus	2	2	7			Low, Ephraim	2		1			penney, Stephen	1		2		
Scamman, James	2		1			Low, Obdiah	1	2	3			penney, Thomas	1		2		
Scamman, Nathaniel	3	4	3			more, William	1					morroson, Francis		1	1		
Scamman, Isaac	3	5	2			tibbits, Jonathan	3	5	3			Welch, Edmend, Jur	1	2	3		
Scamman, Freman	1	3	5			Nason, Samuel, Esq	7	2	8			annies, Nehemiah	1		2		
Scamman, John	1	4	4			Withum, Ganzbury	1		1			annies, Charles	1	1	1		
Scamman, Benjamin	1	2	3			Withum, John	1	1	2			Welch, Solomon	1	2	3		
Scamman, Daniel	2		2			Withum, Edmond	1	1	4			Staple, William	1		2		
Scamman, Nathl, Jur	1	2	1			Adams, John	1		2			meldrom, John	1	1	2		
Storer, Seth	2	3	7			Adams, Jonathan	1		2			Gray, Diminaus	1		2		
Simpson, Benjamin	1	2	2			Frost, William	2	1	3			more, Ebenezer	1	2	1		
Tucker, John	1	1	2			Adams, Jonathan, Sen	1		2			Estes, Benjamin	3	1	4		
Tucker, Catharine			2			Welch, Joseph	1	2	5			parkins, David	2		2		
Tucker, Francis	1	1	1			Kicker, Dodford	1	1	3			Cram, Joseph	1	1	2		
Tapley, Job	2	1	4			Morroson, David	3	4	2			Warmwood, Amous	2	1	2		
Tapley, John	1		1			Cheaney, Elifalet	1	3	4			more, William	2		2		
Tappen, Wiglesworth	3	3	3			Jelleson, Joseph	1	1	1			Noble, John	1	1	2		
Tiler, James	1	1	6			morroson, Ebenezer	1	2	3			Nutter (Widow)		3	2		
Tiler, Humphrey	1	2	3			Morroson, Daniel	1		1			Gatchel, Seith	1	4	1		
Tarbox, Loring	1		2			Welch, David	2	5	2			hastey, James	2		1		
Thomas, John	1	2	2			Welch, Edmand	1		2			annies, John	1	1	4		
Tibbets, Stephen	2		3			morroson, Abraham	1		3			Litchfield, Joseph	3	4	5		
Tibbets, Saml	2	3	3			morroson, Bradbury	1	1	1			Spears, Isrul	1	1	2		
Tibbets, Timothy	1		3			Chaney, Joseph	1	1	3			Spears, Ebenezer	3	4	2		
Tibbets, Obidiah	1	1	1			Gatchel, Ephraim	1	1	3			Hill, Joseph	1	3			
Warren, Samuel	1		3			Beatie, John	1		2			Butler, Nathaniel	1		1		
Warren, David	1		5			heartwell, James	1		1			Butler, Thomas	2	1	8		
Webster, Joseph	1	2	3			Bandwell, Nathaniel	1	2	2			penney, Settathel	1	1	2		
Woodsom, Samuel	1	2	3			hatch, Jacob	1		2			Grant, Ephrain	2	4	3		
Woodsom, John	1	2	3			Firbush, William	1		2			plumer, Moses	1	5	2		
Whitney, Jesse	1		4			Chatman, Isaac	1	2	1			Frost, Elht	1	4	4		
Woodsom, Benja	1	3	1			Spener, Ichabod	1	2	3			hatch, Samuel	2		4		
Withain, Robert	1		3			Jenkins, Jabis	1					Wise, Jeremlah	3	6	2		
Patterson, Loin	1		1			Coleords, Jesse	2		2			heard, James	2	2	4		
Underwood, John	1	2	3			More, John	2	1	3			farbush, Isaac	2	3	4		
Underhand, ——	1	2	2			pugeley, Franes	2	2	7			Cole, John	3		2		
Witham, Mary			2			Dearing, Gideon	1		2			Allen, Solomon	3	2	4		
Swain, Elizabeth			3			Morefield, hipsebath (Wid.)	2	1	5			Allen, Jerediah	1	1	1		
Pierce, Abigall		3	1			Dennet, Samuel	2	3	6			frost, Moses	1		1		
POTTERFIELD TOWN.						Kicker, William	1	3	5			Brooks, Joshua	2		2		
Libby, Meshech	2		4			Kicker, Simeon	1		4			Allen, Franes	2	3	5		
Rankines, Moses	2		2			Woster, William	1		2			Cole, Tobias	1	3	5		
Elenwood, Benjamin	2	3	4			Woster, Thomas	1		3			tripe, Jonthan	1		2		
Lamson, Samuel	1	2	1			Kicker, Samuel	1	3	5			pirkins, Josiah	1	1	1		
Allod, David	2	2	2			hobbos, Stephen	2		3			Davies, James	1	3	2		
Clark, Joseph	1	1	3			Dearing, John	2	1	2			Galahel, Daniel	1	2	7		
Bickford, Benjamin Jun	1		1			Carl, Joseph	1	3	3			perkins, Jabes	1	5	2		
Bickford, Benjamin	2		3			hall, Nellson	1	1	5			haston, John, Jurer	2	2	3		
Bickford, Samuel	1	2	3			Quint, John	1					huston, John	1		2		
Briges, Paul	1	1	1			Quint, Joseph	2	1	3			Willard, anna (Widow)			3		
Rankins, Moses, junr	2		1			Quint, David	1	2	2			Willard, Samuel	2	2	2		
Clemons, Jonathan	2	1	2			hatch, Nathan	1		3			Willard, John	2	2	2		
Haywood, Lemuel	1	1	2			Garey, Frost	1		2			hatch, David	1		1		
Dyer, Bickford	1	1	3			paul, Josiah	1		3			hatch, Stephen	1	3	1		
Goald, Aaron	1		5			ChadBourn, James	1	3	3			Littelfield, Ithamor, Jun	2	3	6		
Towl, Josiah	1					husey, Ruben	1	3	3			Withum, Zeblion	1	3	3		
						Bean, Daniel	1		3			Day, Aaron	1	3	4		

HEADS OF FAMILIES—MAINE.

YORK COUNTY—Continued.

NAME OF HEAD OF FAMILY.	Free white males of 16 years and upward, including heads of families.	Free white males under 16 years.	Free white females, including heads of families.	All other free persons.	Slaves.	NAME OF HEAD OF FAMILY.	Free white males of 16 years and upward, including heads of families.	Free white males under 16 years.	Free white females, including heads of families.	All other free persons.	Slaves.	NAME OF HEAD OF FAMILY.	Free white males of 16 years and upward, including heads of families.	Free white males under 16 years.	Free white females, including heads of families.	All other free persons.	Slaves.
SANFORD TOWN—con.						**SANFORD TOWN—con.**						**SHAPLEIGH TOWN—con.**					
Day, hilkem	1		2			Rich, Barnbus	1	1	2			Grant, Charles	2	2	4		
Day, Dependence	1	1	2			hatch, Ezekel	1		2			Willey, Saml	3		8		
Littelfeild, Ithamor	1	1	1			Emeary, Joshua	2	1	1			Gilman, Zebulon	2	2	2		
Bridges, Thomas	1	4	4			Barnes, Benjmin	1	1	5			Gilman, Dudley	2		1		
Littelfeild, Stephen	1	1	1			Barnes, David	1		6			Marsh, Isaah	1		1		
Wakefield, hazakiah	3		2			Cotten, Elizebeth (Wid.)			3			Marsh, Stephen	1		2		
Wormwood, John	2	1	3			Walley, John	1	1	4			Merrow, Joseph	3	1	3		
Gatchel, Joshua	2	2	2			fillpact, James	2		2			Corson, Moses	1	7	3		
Russall, John	1	3	1			Stone, Joseph	3					Gubtail, Benja	1		1		
Linskit, Nathaniel	1	1	3			Kicker, Jason	1		1			Corson, Lemuel	1	3	5		
Day, hiltten	1	1	2			hall, Ebenezer	1	2	2			Nason, Moses	1	3	3		
Goodwin, Joshua	2	2	7			hill, James, Junr	1	2	5			Bean, Willm	1	2	3		
Jonnes, Bartholimu	1	2	7			—*—						Corson, Isaac	1	1	1		
Jonnes, Elisha	2	2	2			Withum, Ichabod	2	1	2			Bracket, Danl	1	1	1		
Shakford, John	1	2	3			Kobards, Samuel	2	2	6			Magoon, Edward	1	1	3		
knight, Joseph	1	2	4			Kobards, Ebenezer	2	1	3			Remmick, Joseph	1	1	2		
martin, John	1		2			Juett, Benjmin	1	1	1			Row, John	3	1	2		
Linskiet, John	1		4			Gastrige, Joshua	4	2	2			Merrll, Levi	1	4	2		
Linskiet, Jacob	1	2	1			moodey, Samuel	1	1	2			Row, John	1	2	2		
horn, Joseph	1	1	3			yourk, Nathan	2	1	4			Hussey, Ruben	1	2	1		
Day, heneary	2	2	2			tweed, Samuel	1	1	1			Door, James	2	4	4		
horn, Samuel	1		1			Davies, Daniel	1		2			Tibbets, Ebenezer	1		3		
Norton, Nathaniel	1	2	1			Davies, David	1		4			Wintworth, Grant	1		2		
Jellison, Samuel	2	3	4			Stanton, paul	1	1	4			Bracket, Benja	1		2		
taylor, Joshua	2	1	2			Bean, mary (Wid.)		2	2			Downs, Gersham					
Gray, William	1	2	5			Stanton, Benjmin	1		3			Tibbets, Danl	1	2	2		
Gray, Daniel	1	3	4			Bean, Jeremiah	1	3	5			Merrow, Samuel	1	4	5		
pugsley, John	1		1			Bean, John	1		4			Merrow, Edmund	1		2		
taylor, Elifilate	1	1	2			Stone, Gidon	1	2	5			Bracket, Joshua	1		3		
pugsely, Benjemin	1		3			marshall, William	2	3	5			Copps, Jona	1		1		
Coule, Samuel	1		2			Scribner, John	1		2			Copps, Peter	1		2		
Gouen, John, Junor	1		3			Leavil, William	1	1	1			Tibbets, Wm	1	4	1		
Cleark, David	1		1			Gile, Daniel	3	1	2			James, John	1	4	5		
Going, John	1	2	4			Guile, Stephen	1	3	1			Quemby, John	1	1	2		
Jellison, Jeddoh	2		2			Coffen, Eliphalet	1	3	2			Door, Joseph	2	2	5		
powers, Jonathan	1	3	1									Fox, Joseph	1				
White, John	2		2			**SHAPLEIGH TOWN.**						Runnels, Saml	1	2	4		
White, John, Junor	1	3	1			Rogers, Wm, Esqr	5	3	5			Farnham, Paul	1	1	2		
Kicker, Solomon	3	2	2			Gilman, Jeremiah	2					Horne, Benja	3	1	3		
White, Charles	1		1			Ricker, Gersham	1	2	2			Goodhue, Josiah	2		3		
White, Samuel	1	2	1			Gilman, Jona	1	3	2			Dodge, Benja	1	1	5		
avery, Joseph	1		1			Cook, Daniel	1	1	3			Rogers, David	1	2	1		
friend, John	2	1	1			Gilman, Benja	1					Horne, Danl	1	2	1		
Swett, Moses, Junr	3	3	3			Hussey, Benja	1	5	6			Levet, Joseph	1	1	5	7	
Cozont, Nathaniel	5	1	2			Door, Phillip	1	2	2			Allen, Jude	1	3	2		
Whitten, Umpery	3	6	3			Wintworth, Paul	1	1	2			Thing, Wintrop	1	2	3		
killam, John	1	3	3			Farnham, Ralf	1	2	2			Wilson, Humpy	1	1	3		
Whitten, Samuel	1	2	2			Stvens, Henery		2	3			Bragdon, Saml	1				
Whitten, James	1	1	2			Farnham, Paul	1		2			Remmick, Timothy	1	1	1		
Vitterin, Benjemin	2	1	5			Farnham, Dummer	1		1			Hammon, Elisha	2	1	4		
Webber, Paul	1		1			Prescot, Jona	1	2	2			Sanborn, Saml	1	2	4		
Cluff, Samuel	2	3	4			Roberts, Love	2	3	4			Sanborn, Joseph	1	3	2		
Willson, Jonathan	1	1	4			Hilton, Ricd	2	2	4			Gilman, Danl	1				
hutchings, Levy	1	1	2			Downs, Paul	1	2	3			Quembe, Jona	2	1	2		
hutchings, Edmand	1					Drew, Benja	1	4	4			Lord, Josher	3	4	4		
plumer, John			2			Hussey, Robt	1	3	3			Tibbets, Phillip	1	3	4		
tripe, Benjemin	4	3	4			Hussey, John	1	2	3			Magoon, Benja	1	4	3		
kimbull, Thomas	2	2	5			Door, Ricd	1		1			Steel, Clement	2		4		
Alley, Olais	1	1	3			Bodwell, Jno	1	1	2			Kimmens, Benja	2	1	1		
parsins, William	2	5	4			Cook, Jno	1	2	2			York, Nicholas	2	4	6		
—*—, John	(*)	(*)	(*)	(*)	(*)	Heard, Abigail	1	1				Merrow, David	2	4	4		
Emson, Joseph	2	3	3			Hanson, Abram	1		5			York, Edward	1				
Luies, Saray (Wid.)	2	1	4			Door, Peter	1	1	3			Waldron, Ebenezer	1	4	2		
Gray, Joseph	3	1	2			Door, Silas	1	2	2			Magoon, Josiah	1	4	1		
Gray, James, the 3	1	1	5			Kennikum, Aurther	2	2	1			Marsten, James	1		4		
Linsent, Joseph	1		1			Blasdel, Ralf	2	2	2			Nason, Jacob	1	3	4		
Linsent, William	1	3	4			Thompson, Miles	1	2	5			Abbot, Jona	1	5	3		
haley, Richard	3	2	5			Door, Ricd	2		2			Weeds, Jona	1	4	6		
manentier, Ebenezer	2	5	1			Shorey, Benja	2	5				Goodwin, Joseph	1	1	3		
williams, Simien	1	2	1			Felsh, Jona	1	2	3			Hubbard, Danl	1	3	2		
trafen, Jeremiah	1	2	1			Felsh, Hannah			1			Goodwin, Nathan	1	1	4		
trafen, Benjamln	1	1	1			Tibbets, Ichabod	1	1	2			Hubbard, James	1	1	2		
Linscot, theodah	1	2	2			Goodwin, Ephrim	1	1	1			Bragdon, Aurther	1	1	1		
Lord, Ambrose	2	2	3			Shorey, Samuel	1	2	4			Trafton, Josiah	1	3	2		
Newell, Jonathan	2	2	7			Shorey, Saml, Junr	1	2	2			Patch, Jona	2	1	3		
harden, Joshua	1	1	1			Clark, Hanson	2	3	3			Patch, Paul	2		2		
Alley, Samuel	1	2	4			Libby, Stephen	2	3	4			Patch, Jno	2		1		
Sayards, John	2	4	4			Libby, Stephen, Junr	1	3	1			Patch, Saml	1	3	4		
Conant, Joshua	1	1	2			Hersom, Jacob	5	1	3			Saward, James	1		4		
allen, Told	4	2	3			Grant, James	2	1	5			Coffen, Nat	3	1	4		
Sayards, Ebenezer	1		2			Wintworth, Ruben	2	1	6			Bartlet, John	1		1		
Nble, abbigale (Wid.)	1	2	3			Bracket, Joshua	4		3			Coffen, Nathan	1	3	4		
Williams, Thomas	1	3	3			Grant, Joshua	1	2	3			Grant, Peter	3	1	3		
Emeary, Stephen	1	3	3			Nock, Eleazer	1		2			Huntrus, Ichabod	1	1	3		
Luies, Jeremiah	1	1	4			Bracket, Nathan	1	4	3			Huntrus, Darling	3	2	3		
Whiton, Aaron	1	1	10			Heard, Jethro	3	2	6			Hastyes, Saml	3		4		
Stevens, David	2	3	5			James, Jno	2		1			Tynan, Joseph	2	2	4		
Stevens, hubbard	2	1	3			James, Elisha	2	2	5			Tynan, Ricd	2		4		
Stevens, Aaron	3		4			Dudley, Trueworth	2		3			Davis, James	2	3	2		
Smith, heneary	2	2	4			Hubbard, Aaron	2	1	5			Morrel, David	1	1	1		
freeman, Nathan	2	2	6			Hubbard, Ricd	2					Abbot, Moses	2		3		
Writne, Josiah	1	3	3			Nock, Zackh	1	2	3			Abbot, Moses, Junr	2	1	4		
Brown, Samuel	3		4			Nock, Nicholas	1	3	4			Trafton, Lemuel	1	3	1		
Godard, Samuel	1		1									Trafton, Joshua	1	3	3		

* Illegible.

FIRST CENSUS OF THE UNITED STATES.

YORK COUNTY—Continued.

Name of head of family.	Free white males of 16 years and upward, including heads of families.	Free white males under 16 years.	Free white females, including heads of families.	All other free persons.	Slaves.
SHAPLEIGH TOWN—con.					
Tynan, Mary		1	1		
Low, Bazaliel	1	3	2		
Low, Saml	1		1		
Moody, Joseph	1	2	2		
Davis, John	1	2	2		
Thing, Nathaniel	2		3		
Philpot, Moses	1	3	1		
Giles, Dan	1	2	3		
Giles, Joseph	1	1	3		
Giles, Saml	1	2	2		
Giles, John	1		1		
Kent, Nathl	1	3	4		
Wood, Stephen	1	4	5		
Poland, Nat	1	1	2		
Pray, Joseph	1	1	2		
Wodley, John	1	1	3		
Warren, Aaron	1		4		
Warren, Gilbert	1	2	3		
Thompson, Wm	5	1	5		
Welsh, Jona	1	1	2		
Haysles, Jno	1		5		
Neal, Edmund	2	2	5		
Hodsdon, Solomon	1		1		
Goodwin, Danl	1		2		
Goodwin, Thos	1	3	3		
Davis, Nehemiah	1	3	4		
Stone, Wm	3	4	3		
Stone, Judah			1		
Pilsbury, Stephen	2	4	4		
Crocket, Benja	1	1	3		
Ham, George	2		2		
Trafton, Zachariah	1	1	2		
Wilson, Danl	2	2	3		
Cheek, Abram	1	3	4		
Ross, Jona	1	5	3		
Perkins, Nat	1	1	3		
Goodwin, Benja	1	1	7		
Shackley, Thomas	1	3	7		
Standley, Wm	2	5	3		
Emery, Charles	2		3		
Lord, Ichabod	1	2	3		
Ham, Saml	2	3	3		
Morrison, Edward	1		2		
Ham, George	6	1	6		
Webber, Benja	1		7		
Ricker, Simon	1	3	6		
Low, Jeddah	2	2	3		
Patch, Andrew	1		1		
Standley, John	1		1		
Goodwin, John	1		2		
Standly, Mary			2		
Jallison, Joseph	2	3	4		
Abbot, Samuel	1	2	3		
Horn, Jona	1		5		
Pugsley, Abram	1		1		
Pugsley, Abram	1	3	3		
Murry, Wm	1		4		
Murry, John	2	3	2		
Gowen, David	1	2	2		
Thompson, John	1	1	2		
Pugsley, Andrew	1		2		
Nason, Ham	1	1	6		
Emery, Jeremiah	1	4	2	1	
Fulsom, Moses	1	3	4		
Grant, Elisha	1	1	4		
Nason, Caleb	1	2	2		
Hearl, Moses	1		1		
Welsh, John	1	1	5		
Goodwin, David	1	3	3		
Emery, Simon	2	1	1		
Emery, Jotham	1				
Hupper, John	1		1		
Kent, Sarah			2		
Jones, Isreal	1	2	1		
Evely, Sarah		3	3	1	
Poland, Asa			4		
Bickford, Abner	1	2	4		
SUDBURY-CANADA TOWN.					
Duston, Jesse	2	2	4		
Swan, James	1		1		
Swan, Joseph G	4	3	4		
Russel, Abraham	1		7		
Russel, Benjamin	2	1	2		
Russell, Theodore	1		2		
Bean, Jonathan	1		1		
Bean, Daniel	3	3	3		
Kilgore, John, Junr	1	1	1		
Russel, Jacob	1		1		
Kilgore, Joseph	1	1	3		
Hastings, Amos	1	3	4		
Bartlett, Enoch	4		4		
Easters, Stephen	1		1		
SUDBURY-CANADA TOWN—con.					
Frost, Matthias	1	2	1		
Kilgore, John	1	1	3		
Russel, Benja, Junr	1	2	2		
Holt, Zela	2		3		
Swan, James, Junr		2			
Holt, John	1	1	1		
York, Isaac	1	1	3		
York, John	2	1	4		
Bean, Josiah	1	5	3		
Ingalls, Saml	1	4	3		
Bartlett, Thaddeus	2		6		
Bartlett, Jonathan	3	1	2		
Powers, Amos	2	2	3		
Goss, Saml	1		5		
Andrews, Jeremiah	1	3	2		
Seger, Nathl	2	1	2		
Seger, Josiah	1		2		
Powers, Gideon	1	3	4		
Powers, Silas	1		2		
Bartlett, Stephen	1	2	1		
Bartlett, Moses	2	1	2		
Abbott, John	1		1		
Abbott, John, Junr	1	1	2		
Bean, Jonathan, Junr	1	2	3		
Harvey, William	1	5	2		
Smith, Thial	1				
Smith, Thial, Junr	1				
Frost, Thomas	1				
Twitchel, Eli	1	1	2		
Twitchel, Ezra	1	4	3		
Stearns, Thomas	1				
Twitchel, Eleazar	2	4	4		
Chatman, Eliphaz	2	4	4		
Grover, Jedidiah	1		3		
Grover, John	1	2	4		
Mason, Walter	1				
Abbot, Jonathan	2	2	3		
Mason, John	1	1	1		
Mills, Deborah		2	3		
Asten, Peter	2	4	5		
Grover, James	2		3		
Gage, Amos	1	2	1		
Gage, Daniel	1		2		
Fannon, Oliver	1	2	3		
Clark, Benjan	2	2	3		
Clark, Jonathan	2	1	5		
SUDBURY-CANADA TOWN, SETTLEMENTS ADJOINING.					
Foster, Asa	1	1	1		
Foster, Abner	2	2	3		
Littleale, John	3		2		
Spafford, Nathl	1				
Jackson, Joseph	1	3	3		
Barker, Jonathan	1	1	1		
Barker, Jesse	1		3		
Swan, Elijah	1	2	2		
Barker, Benjamin	2	2	1		
Larey, Joseph	2	2	3		
Blake, David	1	2	1		
Messer, John	1	2	1		
SUNCOOK TOWN.					
Stearns, John	3	1	1		
Dresser, Levi	1	1	2		
Dresser, Stephen	1	2	2		
Kilgore, Joseph	2		4		
Kilgore, James	1		5		
Butters, Abel	1	2	2		
Andrews, Abraham	2	2	4		
Patch, Timothy	1	5	2		
Whiting, Oliver	1	2	2		
McAllaster, Danl	1	1	3		
McAllaster, Ananias	2	3	2		
McAllaster, Joseph	1	2	2		
Hale, Josiah	1	3	4		
Whiting, Joshua	1		1		
Stearns, Benja	2				
McKean, James	1	1	2		
WASHINGTON PLANTATION.					
Adams, Revd John	4	2	4		
Nelson, Joseph	1	3	5		
McClannen, James	1	1	2		
Smith, Jethro	1	3	2		
Ayers, Elisha	2	2	6		
Piper, Stephen	1	2	3		
Chelles, Wm	1	1	3		
Chelles, Mary			4		
Symes, Ebenezer			4		
WASHINGTON PLANTATION—continued.					
Campernel, John	1		1		
Dunnel, John	1				
Symes, Wm	1	1	2		
Adams, John	1				
Berry, Samuel	1		3		
Drew, Elisabeth	2	1	1		
Staple, David	2	1	4		
Doe, Brodstreet	3	1	4		
Davis, Thomas	1	3	3		
Balch, Nat	1	1	6		
Balch, Nat	1				
Turner, Stabert	1	1	4		
Cromwel, James	1		2		
Doe, Eliphelet	1		2		
Day, Thomas	1	2	2		
Nelson, Daniel	1		2		
Nelson, Leder	1		2		
Waymoth, Joshua	1		2		
Doe, Nathl	1		2		
Campernel, Wm	1		2		
Campernel, Wm	2		2		
Dam, Joseph	1	2			
Doe, Henery	1		3		
Doe, Simon	1		3		
Doe, John	1				
Hayes, Peter	1	2	2		
Berry, James	1				
Berry, James	2	1	4		
Thompson, George	1	3	4		
Boothby, Ebenezer	1		3		
Hobbs, Josiah	1	1			
Atterd, Daniel	1		2		
Moulton, Simeon	1		2		
Moulton, Levi	1	1	1		
Moulton, Ephrim	1	1	2		
Moulton, Stephen	1				
Moulton, David	1	1	3		
Libby, Wm	1	3	3		
Staple, Benja	1		2		
Stone, Levi	1		2		
Libby, Zebulon	3	1	5		
McDannels, Paul	2		2		
Whitten, Thomas	1	3	3		
Thompson, Robt	1	3	1		
Clark, James	1	1	2		
Kennison, Nicholas	1		3		
Smith, Thos	1	1	3		
Durgan, David	2	2	3		
Richardson, Resolved	1		1		
WATERBOROUGH TOWN.					
Russull, Joseph	1		2		
Russull, Joseph, Junr	1	4	3		
Wotson (Widw)	1		2		
Lord, Nason	1	4	2		
heselton, Jonathan	1		3		
Leuet, Daniel	3	2	6		
Giles, John	1	2	2		
Pits, John	2	2	5		
Scribner, Daniel	2	2	4		
Scribner, Samuel	3	1	5		
burley, Andrew	1		5		
Scribner, Edword	1	1	1		
thing, Coffin	1				
Scribner, Joseph	1	2	4		
taylor, Daniel	1		4		
harvey, James	2	1	2		
Dame, Samuel	2	2	3		
Kimball, David	4	4	4		
Colcord, Phineas	1	1	2		
Smith, John	3		2		
Smith, thomas, Junr	1				
Smith, Jacob	1				
kinsmon, Ebenezer			1		
Smith, Jonathan	1		2		
Coffin, Benjamin	1	3	2		
Coffin, Napthalim	1		2		
Coffin, Daniel	2	2	4		
Coffin, Daniel, junr	1	2	2		
haines, Simeon	1		4		
Haines, Nathaniel	1	2	4		
bean, Richard	3	2	4		
Robbirson, James	1				
Robbirson, Daniel	1	1	2		
Bean, William	1		2		
Bean, William, junr	4	2	3		
thing, Catharine (Widw)		2	2		
Pike, Joseph	2	2	4		
Smith, John	1	3	4		
Moody, Clament	2		4		
Smith, Israil	1	1	2		
Scribner, Edward, junr	1		1		
barners, James		3	1		
Smith, Israil, junr	1	4	3		

HEADS OF FAMILIES—MAINE.

YORK COUNTY—Continued.

NAME OF HEAD OF FAMILY.	Free white males of 16 years and upward, including heads of families.	Free white males under 16 years.	Free white females, including heads of families.	All other free persons.	Slaves.
WATERBOROUGH TOWN—continued.					
kimball, Joseph	1	3	1		
Smith, Nehemiah	1		5		
Pearey, Joseph	2		3		
Dudley, Peter	1		4		
pike, Joseph	1	1	1		
kimball, Levy	1	4	4		
Ricker, Noah	1	1	4		
Hill, David	1	4	2		
Jones, Stephen	1	2	2		
Bouden, Michal	1	1	1		
Mirick, John	1	2	3		
Penny, Frances	2	2	4		
folsom, Peter	1	2	5		
Hibbord, Israil	1	4	3		
henderson, Samuel	1	2	6		
Sambourn, Joseph	1	1	1		
Sanbon, Joseph, junr	1	1	2		
Sanbon, Paul	1	1	3		
Coak, John	2	1	6		
Shores, Joseph	1		2		
Night, Jonathan	1		2		
Ricker, timothy	1	1	4		
Emery, Jacob	1	1	5		
Hobbs, Moril	1	2	4		
Hobbs, Henery	1		1		
Hobbs, Goarge	1	1	2		
Androse, Samuel	1	1	3		
Parcher, timothy	2	1	3		
Farl (Widw)		3	2		
emery, Zachariah	1	3	2		
Bagley, John	1	4	4		
Stuart, Josiah	1	1	3		
Buzell, Ebenezer	1	1	1		
Hill, Joseph	1	1	2		
Scribner, Samuel, junr	1	6	1		
Foy, James	1	1	5		
Scribner, John	2		1		
Smith, John, junr	1	2	2		
Smith, thomas	7	3	1		
Hill, John	1	3	1		
Henderson, Joseph	1	2	1		
Henderson, John	2		1		
Webster, Joshua	1	1	1		
Perry, Benjamin	3	1	1		
Carpinder, Nocholas	1		1		
Carpinder, Nathaniel	1		1		
Carpinder, John	1	1	3		
Carpinder, thomas	1	2	3		
Gerlin, Nathaneal	1		1		
dudley, Truworthy	1	2	4		
Sinkler, Benjamin	1	1	2		
Cammat, Samuel	1	1	3		
Gelpatrick, William	2	1	3		
Webster, Waldren	1	1	3		
dudley, Stephen	1	2	3		
Tinglen, Paletiah	1	1	4		
Mills, Eligood	2	3	2		
Deshaun, Moses, junr	1	2	4		
Deshaun, James	1		1		
Hutchings, thomas	2	1	2		
Cortle, Stephen	1	1	1		
Carlile, James	1		2		
Smith, John	1	1	2		
Straw, Valintine	2	3	4		
Smith, Aaron	1		2		
laton, tobias	1	2	4		
Butler, John	2		2		
Leuer, William	1	3	2		
Brown, Jeremiah	4		4		
Brown, Jacob	1		3		
Night, Zebulon	1	2	2		
Page, Benjamin	1	2	4		
Carle, John	1	4	3		
Carle, Elizabeth (Widw)			2		
Carle, Anna (Wid)		1	1		
Gabtale, thomas	2	2	2		
Gubtale, Stephen	2	2	3		
ford, Mils	1		2		
hanson, William	1	3	4		
Gubtale, thomas, Jun	1	1	3		
tibits, William	1		1		
tibits, Mary (Widw)		2	4		
tibits, James	1		4		
Bilford, thomas	2		3		
Dearing, William	1	2	2		
Hodgdan, timothy	2	3	2		
Mattoks, Henory	1	2	1		
Harford, John	2		2		
tibits, Simeon	1	1	4		
tibits, Joshua	2		2		
Roods, Jacob	1		2		
Jeleson, George	1	5	2		
Jeleson, David	1	1	2		
fillpot, William	4	1	5		
Vrine, James	1		1		
WATERBOROUGH TOWN—continued.					
Ricker, Levy	2	5	3		
Woodword, William	2	1	2		
Welch, thomas	1	5	5		
Gutterage, Anna (Widw)			2		
Goodwin, Amaziah	2	3	3		
Wodword, Sarah (Widw)			2		
Bogse, Elisha	1		2		
Sagiley, Daniel	1	2	1		
Moulton, William	1		2		
Sedgley, John	1	5	2		
Gray, Samuel	1	3	1		
Haeley, John	1	1	1		
Junkins, William	1	1	1		
luis, Joseph	1	4	3		
Rankins, Andrew	1	1	5		
Gous, Moses	1	2	2		
Jahnson, James	1	1	1		
Bridges, Samuel	1	2	3		
Bridges, Josiah	1	2	2		
Beedeen, Robert	2	4	2		
Goue, John	1		1		
harmon, Edward	2	1	6		
Night, John	1	3	4		
Worrim, Benjamin	3	4	5		
Bicker, Joseph	2	2	4		
Downs, Umphry	1	3	4		
Downs, Richard	2		1		
knock, Ebenezer	2	2	5		
Roberch, Ichabod	1	3	5		
Bunker, Elijah	1		1		
Walker, Gedeon	1	1	3		
Hamelton, Abel	1	3	3		
Hamelton, James	1	1	4		
Hamelton, Richard	1	1	4		
Hamelton, John	1	2	1		
Hamelton, Benjamin	1	2	6		
WATERFORD TOWN.					
Sanderson, Stephen	1	2	3		
Barker, Joseph	1	2			
Holton, Jonathan	2	2	2		
Jewel, John	1	2	1		
Brown, Asaph	1	1	4		
Bryant, Richard	1	1	1		
Robbins, Jonathan	1	1	1		
Jewet, Stephen	4	1	5		
Green, Thoms	3	1	5		
Gates, William	1	1	3		
Johnson, Asa	1		3		
Hor, Phillip	4		2		
Sampson, Phinehas	1		3		
Langley, Eli	2	1	3		
Brown, Silas	1	2	2		
Brown, Thaddeus	1	1	2		
Chamberlain, Ephraim	1		3		
Nurse, John	1		2		
Homan, James	3	2	1		
McWane, David	1		1		
Langley, Jonathan	1	2	2		
Atherington, John	1		3		
Hamlin, Africa	1	1	2		
Hamlin, America	1	2	3		
Jewel, Ezra	1		2		
Hale, Oliver	1	1	2		
Hale, Israel	1		4		
Hapgood, Oliver	1	3	3		
Whitney, Joshua	1		2		
Whitney, Phinehas	1	2	3		
Chamberlain, Nathl	2		1		
WELLS TOWN.					
Wakefield, Ezekiel	1	1	4		
Colburn, Ebenezer	2	1	3		
Littlefield, Jotham	1	2	3		
Littlefield, Reuben	1	3	4		
Cousens, Saml	1	1	1		
Thompson, Richd, Jr	1	1	1		
Thompson, Caleb	1	4	2		
Bussel, Jonathan	1	2	4		
Treadwell, Saml	1	1	2		
Bussel, Isaac	2	1	2		
Thompson, David	5	2	4		
Gil Patrick, John	5		4		
Littlefield, Lydia	1	1	3		
Noble, Stephen	1		2		
Littlefield, Jacob	1	1	3		
Shackley, Richd	1	4	1		
Cousins, Joseph	3		4		
Gil Patrick, Joseph	1	1	2		
Jones, Thos	1		5		
Treadwell, Nathl	1	4	3		
Day, Ebenezer	1		2		
Titcomb, Benja	1	3	4		
WELLS TOWN—con.					
Ross, John	1	2	4		
Hubbard, Moses	1	1	4		
Hubbard, James	1	1	3		
Taylor, John	2	2	2		
Lord, Benja	1	2	2		
Burnham, Abram	1	1	2		
Burnham, Saml	3		4		
Walker, Elephalet	3	5	4		
Kimbal, Saml	2	2	6		
Kimbal, Isaac	1	4	4		
Waterhouse, Saml	2		2		
Waterhouse, Saml, Jr	1	2	4		
Day, Benja	1		3		
Day, Benja, Jr	1	1	2		
Smith, James	4	1	2		
Littlefield, Moses	2		3		
Latherby, Stephen	2	1	3		
Taylor, John	5	2	3		
Thompson, Richd	1		2		
Maddix, John	1	2	2		
Maddix, John	1	3	3		
Littlefield, Anthony	1	1	2		
Littlefield, Edmond	1	2	2		
Littlefield, Abram	1	4	3		
Ross, Adam	1		1		
Hatch, Leml	2		1		
Storer, Isaac	2	3	1		
Kimbal, Baruch	1	3	3		
Hatch, Elisha	1	3	3		
Clark, Aaron	1	1	3		
Wells, Robert	2	4	3		
Storer, Jere	3	1	4		
Storer, Nathl	1		2		
Storer, Willm	2		3		
Borton, Willm	1				
Hatch, David	1	3	2		
Hilton, Joshua	1	2	3		
Williams, Saml	1	4	5		
Little, Revd Danl	1		2		
Storer, Jere	1		1		
Hatch, Gideon, Jr	1	1	4		
Sawyer, Willm	1	2	1		
Littlefield, Anthony	1	1	2		
Littlefield, Pelatiah	1	2	1		
Winn, Nathan	3	2	2		
Whittam, John	1				
Clark, John	2		3		
Going, Nicholas	2	1	4		
Wormwood, Ebena	1	1	4		
Wormwood, Joseph	1		1		
Cole, Remick	1	1	4		
Annis, Abram	3	3	6		
Annis, Stephen	2	3	5		
Hill, Jona	4	2	3		
Littlefield, Joseph	1	4	4		
Hatch, Benja	1	1	1		
Storer, Isaac	2	3	2		
Hatch, Noah	1		2		
Hatch, Ebena	1		1		
Hatch, Leml	2	1	1		
Hill, Saml	1		2		
Littlefield, Nehemiah	2	2	5		
Moffat, John	2	2	4		
Hatch, Jere	2	1	2		
Hatch, Jesse	3		2		
Eaton, Joshua	2	3	3		
Annis, Nehemiah	1	1	6		
Hatch, Benja, Jr	2	1	2		
Pease, Richd	1		1		
Eaton, Joseph	1	1	5		
Chadbourn, Saml	1	3	4		
Hatch, Elias	1	1	2		
Littlefield, David	1	2	4		
Penny, George	1		2		
Littlefield, Stephen	1	2	2		
Penny, Danl	1		2		
Penny, John	2		1		
Storer, Amos	4		3		
Hatch, Jona, Jr	1	4	2		
Hatch, Elijah	1		1		
Gitchel, George	1	4	3		
Williams, Joseph	2	4	3		
Penny, Benja	2	1	4		
Staples, John	2	1	7	4	
Littlefield, Jona	4		2		
Littlefield, Willm	1	3	5		
Emery, Saml	1	1	2		
Bicknal, Tabitha			4		
Whitehouse, Saml	1		4		
Littlefield, Noah	5		2		
Aldrige, Amos	1	2	6		
Wheelright, Aaron	1	5	4		
Treadwell, James	2	3	3		
Stephens, Jere	1		1		
Winn, Saml	1	1	3		

YORK COUNTY—Continued.

NAME OF HEAD OF FAMILY.	Free white males of 16 years and upward, including heads of families.	Free white males under 16 years.	Free white females, including heads of families.	All other free persons.	Slaves.	NAME OF HEAD OF FAMILY.	Free white males of 16 years and upward, including heads of families.	Free white males under 16 years.	Free white females, including heads of families.	All other free persons.	Slaves.	NAME OF HEAD OF FAMILY.	Free white males of 16 years and upward, including heads of families.	Free white males under 16 years.	Free white females, including heads of families.	All other free persons.	Slaves.
WELLS TOWN—con.						**WELLS TOWN—con.**						**WELLS TOWN—con.**					
Davis, James	4	2	2			Winn, John	2	1	5			Jeffreys, Wilˡᵐ	5	4	4		
Furbush, Catharine	1	3	2			Littlefield, Danˡ	2		5			Lord, Dominicus	1		3		
Hubbard, John H	2		2			Littlefield, Joseph	4		2			Wilson, Benjᵃ	2	1	3		
Wheelright, Joseph	1	1	2			West, Nicholas, Jʳ	1		2			Blasdel, Moses	1	2	6		
Wheelright, Benjᵃ	1	1				West, James	1	1	2			Wells, Wilˡᵐ	2	1	4		
Winn, Josiah	1		6	2		Stuart, Reuben	1		2			Hart, Henry	4	1	2		
Hubbard, Joseph	1	4	3			Littlefield, Isaac	2	3	6			Blaisdel, Jacob	1	3	5		
Jones, John	3	4	1			Littlefield, Jesse	1	3	4			Cousins, Nathˡ, Jʳ	3	2	7		
Patten, Hance	1	2	2			Littlefield, James	2	4	2			Wormwood, Thoˢ	2	2	2		
Bourne, Isaac	1	2	6			Gitchel, Joseph	2		2			Chauncey, Joseph	3	1	3		
Bourne, Joseph	2	3	3			West, Nicholas	1	1	2	1		Boston, Gershom	1		4		
Cousins, Enoch	2		2			Gitchel, Jonathan	1	5	2			Curtes, Charles	1	5	4		
Ross, Danˡ	2		2			Gitchel, Joshua	4	1	1			Goodwin, Danˡ	1	1	1		
Smith, Stephen	1		2			Morrison, Josiah	1	1	3			Webber, Edmond	2		4		
Hatch, Reuben	1	1	3			Morrison, Wilˡᵐ	1	3	2			Webber, Edmond, Jʳ	1		2		
Gil Patrick, Samˡ	3		4			Morrison, Benjᵃ	1	4	2			Webber, Samˡ	1		2		
Kimbal, Israel	2	3	5			Cain, Joshua	1		5			Webber, John	3	3	3		
Kimbal (Widow)			2			Piercey, James	2		3			Allen, Elijah	2	2	2		
Eaton, Joshua	1		2			Wadley, Thoˢ	2		1			Allen, James	1		4		
Hatch, Eliab	1	3	4			Cruddiford, Wilˡᵐ	3	1	3			Allen, Jotham	1	2	1		
Davis, Sarah	1	1	3			Cruddiford, John	2	1	2			Boston, James	1	4	4		
Kimbal, Richᵈ	2		2			Hatch, Samˡ	1	1	2			Allen, James, Jʳ	1		5		
Ross (Widow)		2	1			Hatch, Jonᵃ	4		2			Chadborn, James	1	1			
Shackley, John, Jʳ	2	4	2			Hubbard, Warwick	3		1			Brooks, Joshua	1		2		
Shackley, John	1	1	3			Herd, Danˡ	4	2	3			Hasty, James	2	1	4		
Latherby, Joel	2	3	5			Lowe, Job	1	3	3			Brawn, Robert	1	2	3		
Kimbal, Nathˡ	2	2	3			Lowe, Asa	1	5	3			Littlefield, Jacob	2	1	5		
Wormwood, Abner	1		1			Littlefield, Abraᵐ	3		3			Jones, Lazarus	2	4	1		
Kimbal, James	4	3	3			Chauncey, Reuben	3	3	5			Gitchel, Zachariah	1	1	7		
Taylor, Wilˡᵐ	2	3	2			Curtes, Samˡ	1	5	2			Hilton, Joseph	1	4	2		
Currier, Abraᵐ	1	2	2			Wheelright, Joseph, Jʳ	1	4	3			Hilton, Wilˡᵐ	1		2		
Wakefield, James	1	2	2			Furbush, Samˡ	2	1	3			Hilton, Ebeneʳ	1	1	3		
Nason, Benjᵃ	1	1	3			Wheelright, Joseph	1	1	2			Boston, Shubal	1		2		
Barnard, Joseph	3	4	3			Wheelwright, Benjᵃ	1	1	2			Wilton, Edmond	1	2	2		
Hill, Samˡ	1	1	6			Merrifield, John	2	3	6			Boston, John	1	1	1		
Storer, Joseph	4	1	2			Goodale, John	3	1	6			Boston, Elijah	3	2	2		
Osborn, James	1	2	2			Winn, Stephen	1		9			Boston, Elijah, Jʳ	1	1	3		
Lord, Tobias	2	2	6	4		Aldrige (Widow)			2			Boston, Wilˡᵐ	2		4		
Littlefield, Moses	2	1	2			Kimball, Joseph	1		2			Boston, Abraham	2	4	4		
Condy, Thoˢ H	1	1	2			Kimball, Joshua	1	3	2			Littlefield, Josiah	2		1		
Howard, Pomper N	3					Morse, Joseph	1	3	6			Stevens, Solomon	1	1	4		
Brown, Benjᵃ	1	1	3			Mitchel, John	1	1	3			Littlefield, Merriam			4		
Silby, Benjᵃ	2	2	3			Dwinnel, Joseph	3	1	4			Littlefield, Anna		3	2		
Jewett, Joseph	1					Tibbets, John	1	4	4			Merrifield, John	3	3	4		
Tucker, Stephen	1					Winn, John	1		1			Allen, Elijah	1		2		1
Clark, Jonas L	1		3			Winn, Danˡ	1	4	5			Stuart, Elijah	1	1	6		
Fisher, Jacob	1	1	2			Winn, Joseph	1		2			Kimbal, Benjᵃ	1	2	2		
Wakefield, John	2		2			Winn, Benjᵃ	1	1	2			Stuart, Elijah, 3ᵈ	1	1	5		
Wakefield, John, Jʳ	1		4			Maxwel, Gershorn	1	3	6			Stuart, Danˡ	1	4	2		
Trickey, Wilˡᵐ	1	1	1			Littlefield, Timothy	1	1	3			Brock, Joshua	1	1	1		
Hubbard, Diamond	1		3			Littlefield, Jotham	1	3	5			Goodale, Zachariah	3		4		
Wise, Danˡ	1	1	3			Maxwell, Alexander	1	1	6			Stuart, David	1	1	1		
Little, David	3	1	1			Maxwell, Baruch	6	4	4			Stuart, Samˡ	3	2	5		
Little, Nathˡ	1		1			Maxwell, David	1		1			Elwell, Joseph	1	2	2		
Keating, Oliver	3	1	4			Maxwell, Gershorn	1		1			Gray, Joshua	2	2	3		
Jellitson, Wilˡᵐ	1	3	3			Perkins, Jacob	2	3	3			Stuart, Elijah, Jʳ	1	3	2		
Littlefield, Elijah	1	3	4			Jacobs, Elias	2	2	6			Brozzel, Ezekiel	1	3	7		
Goddard, Thatcher	1	1	4			Titcomb, Stephen	1		2			Littlefield, Samˡ	1				
Bowen, John	2	2	2			Fisk, Mark	1		1			Parsons, Alice			3		
Hill, Abraᵐ	2	4	4			Fisk, John	1	1	4			Hatch, Seth	1	1			
Webster, Nathˡ	2	4	3			Towns, Jacob	1	2	2			Boston, Shubal	3		4		
Elwel, —	1					Mitchel, Jotham	1	2	2			Hatch, Francis	3		2		
Murphy, Michˡ	1	1	3			Emery, Isaac	1	1	4			Goodale, Zachariah, Jʳ	1	2	3		
Emery, Jabez	1	1	5			Emery, Job	1	3	2			Littlefield, James	1	1	3		
Bicknal, William	1	1	6			Towns, Samˡ	2		1			Hubbart, Moses	1		2		
Penny, Joseph	1	3	4			Webber, Stephen	1	2	4			Laban, Richᵈ	1				
Hatch, John	1	3	5			Kimbal, Benjᵃ	4		2			Banks (Widow)					
Littlefield, Samˡ	3	5	5			Mitchel, John	2	1	2			Rines, John	1	1	3		
Hatch, Wilˡᵐ	1		6			Brown, Samˡ	2		3			Peasley, Enoch	1	1			
Maxwell, John	2		3			English, Edward	1	1	1			Gipson, Wilˡᵐ	1		3		
Varney, Jonᵃ	3		4			Harden (Widow)		2	1			Gipson, Wilˡᵐ, Jʳ	1	3	4		
Robertson, Danˡ	2		4			Wells, Edward	1		1			Gipson, Zedediah	1	2	4		
Merryfield, Simeon	2	2	2			Varney, Francis	1	1	3			Jacobs, George	1	3	3		
Kinard, John	2	2	7			Gouch, Samˡ	1	2	5			Jacobs, Jonᵃ	1	2	2		
Maxwell, John, Jʳ	2	2	4			Boothby, Thoˢ	1	3	4			Jacobs, Josiah	1	1	2		
Grant, Ebenezer	1	3	4			Webber, George	1	2	3			Littlefield, Johnson	1		2		
Sargeant, Wilˡᵐ	1	3	3			Spinney, Nathˡ	1	4	4			Littlefield, Levi	2	4	4		
Littlefield, Dependance	2	1	2			Oaks, Jacob	1	2	1			Littlefield, Abraᵐ	1	1	3		
Bragdon, Thoˢ	2		2			Meeder, Danˡ	1		3			Littlefield, David	2		3		
Littlefield, Joshua	2		1			Drown, Moses	1	1	3			Littlefield, Eliab	5		3		
Perkins, Elisha	3		2			Gouch, Jedediah	1	1	3			Littlefield, Jerᵃ	3		4		
Brooks, Joshua	1	2	3			Gouch, Joseph	1	2	3			Littlefield, Danˡ	2	4	2		
Perkins, Josiah	2	1	2			Bucknal, John	2		3			Stevens, Jonᵃ	2	2	4		
Perkins, Nusman	1	1	3			Bucknal, Rebecca		1	2			Dutten, Richᵈ	1		3		
Lord, John	2		5			Wormwood, Benjᵃ	1	3	2			Taylor, Jonᵃ	4	1	2		
Perkins, Wilˡᵐ	2		6			Drown, Stephen	1	2	2			Hatch (Widow)			2		
Perkins, Jonᵃ	1	1	2			Latherby, Jessa	3	2	5			Littlefield, Moses	1	5	2		
Littlefield, Susanna	3		2			Latherby, Stephen	1		1			Mitchel, Samˡ	4	2	2		
Perkins, Jacob	1	1	2			Wakefield, Josiah	1	3	1			Stevens, Benjᵃ	3	2	4		
Littlefield, Francis	1	1	2			Emmons, Samˡ	1		3			Day, John	2	4	4		
Bennet, Joel	2	1	3			Bragdon, John	1	2	2			Littlefield, Nathan	2		6		
Goodale, Nehemiah	1		1			Howard, Samˡ	1	1	3			Dennick, John	2	1	2		
Bennett, George	4	3	4			Wormwood, Wilˡᵐ	2	2	4			Webber, John	2	2	6		
Hatch, Eliakim	1	2	2			English (Widow)			3			Day, Benjᵃ	2	2	6		
Maxwell, Samˡ	1	4	2			Gil Patrick, Richᵈ	4	3	3			Stevens, Samˡ	4	3	2		

HEADS OF FAMILIES—MAINE.

YORK COUNTY—Continued.

NAME OF HEAD OF FAMILY.	Free white males of 16 years and upward, including heads of families.	Free white males under 16 years.	Free white females, including heads of families.	All other free persons.	Slaves.
WELLS TOWN—con.					
Cousens, John	3	1	3		
Stevans, Moses	3	3	5		
Stevans, Joel	1	4	4		
Hatch, Danˡ	1	2	7		
Hatch, Obadiah	1	1	4		
Littlefield, Seth	1	2	3		
Littlefield, Roger	1	3	3		
Littlefield, Ebenʳ	2	1	3		
Goodwin, Joshua	1	1	2		
Littlefield, Ebeneʳ, Jʳ	1	1	1		
Littlefield, Danˡ	1	1	2		
Chick, Thoˢ	1	1	2		
Chick, Joshua	2	1	6		
Hatch, Solomon	1		2		
Hobbs, Willᵐ	1	1	3		
Hobbs, Joseph	1		4		
Edes, Willᵐ	2	1	4		
Clark, Solomon	2	1	4		
Wakefield, Benjᵃ	1		3		
Cousins, Samˡ	2	5	3		
Clark (Widow)	2		4		
Meldrom, Samˡ	1	2	2		
Clark, Eleazer	4		1		
Littlefield, Noah	1	2	1		
Day, Joseph	1	1	6		
Day, Moses	1	1	2		
Littlefield, Elisha	2	1	1		
Hubbard, Jerᵉ	1	3	3		
Sherman (Widow)	2		3		
Hobbs, Joseph	1	1	2	1	
Goodwin, Joseph	3	2	5		
Storer, John	2	1	4		
Hobbs, Thoˢ	1		2		
Day, Robert	1		5		
Hatch, Gideon	1		1		
Chick, Moses	2	3	7		
Lord, Richᵈ	3		4		
Clark, Nathan	1		3		
Storer, John	2		6		
Wheelright, John	5	1	3	1	
Bourn, Samˡ	2		4		
Wheelright, Ralph	2		3		
Gouch, Samˡ	3	2	4		
Kean, John	1	3	1		
Bourn (Widow)	1		3		
Norman, John	2	2	2		
Bouden (Widow)		1	1		
Harvey, John	1	1	1		
Clark, Knowles	1	1	1		
Clark, Sarah	2		1		
Wells, John N	1	3	3		
Wells, Nathˡ	5	1	5		
Clark, Ebenˢ	1		1		
Cole, John	1	5	4		
Clark, Lydia	1	1	2		
Boothby, Henry	1		1		
Bankins, James	1	5	7		
Snow, James	1	1	4		
Eaton, Joseph	2	1	3		
Boothby, Benjᵃ	2	1	5		
Wells, Danˡ	4	2	3		
Wells, Dependence	2	3	3		
Clark, Adam	4		4		
Wells, Nathan	1	2	5		
Gould, Nathˡ	2	1	2		
Goodwin John	3	1	4		
Wells (Widow)	2	1	3		
Goodwin, Thoˢ	3	1	5		
Jeffreys, Simon	3		6		
Fisk, Abner	1	2	3		
GilFatrick, James	1	1	2		
Storer, Abrᵐ	3		1		
Goodwin, Paul	1		7		
Wells, Joshᵃ	1	1	2		
Goodwin, Caleb	1	2	4		
Goodwin, John Jʳ	1		1		
Ricker, Stephen	1	2	3		
Taylor, Nathˡ	2	2	4		
Jeffers, Samˡ	1	2	1		
Eaton, Jerᵉ M	2	2	1		
Gates, John	2		4		
Bartlet, John	4		3		
Hemmingway, Revᵈ Moses	3	1	3		
Hill, Benjᵃ	2	3	4		
Littlefield, David	2		5		
Littlefield, Seth	1	4	3		
Morrill, Nahum	2		4		
Bragdon, Joshua	3	1	3		
Patten (Widow)	1		1		
Hatch, Amos	2		1		
Sawyer, Danˡ	3	3	4		
Pope, Isaac	3	4	6		
Hill, Mary	2		1	1	
Young, Solomon	1	1	3		
WELLS TOWN—con.					
Hatch, Joshua	3	1	4		
Jacobs, Samˡ	1		2		
Bucknal, Jessa	1	1	3		
Buzzel, Isaac	3		2		
Eaton, Willᵐ	1	2	2		
Bucknal, Francis	1		5		
Hatch, Simeon	3	1	3		
Littlefield, Benjᵃ	3	1	6		
YORK TOWN.					
Wilson, Miles	1		1		
Moody, Ebenˢ	1	2	3		
Kimbal, Joshua	1	2	3		
Kimbal, Joseph	1		9		
Winn, Stephen	1		9		
Winn, Joseph	1	2	2		
Winn, Jonᵃ	1	2	1		
Kimbal, Nathan	1		3		
Kean, David	1	1	3		
Kean, John	1	1	1		
Boston, John	1		3		
Norton, Joseph	2	3	5		
Dixon, Samˡ	1	1	1		
Littlefield, Elisha	1	3	3		
Sloman, John	3		3		
Staples, Willᵐ	1	1	1		
Staples, Francis	1		3		
Perkins, John	1		1		
Perkins, Joseph	1	2	2		
Perkins, Jere	1	3	2		
Hutchens, Jere	1	2	1		
Hutchens, Enoch, Jr	1		6		
Hutchens, Enoch	3	1	3		
Parsons, Elihu	1		1		
Parsons, Joseph	3	4	3		
Philips, Henry	3		3		
Philips, Norton	1	2	4		
Littlefield, Jerᵃ	3	2	5		
Avery, Samˡ	2	3	5		
Perkins, Pelatiah	1	3	3		
Weare, Jerᵉ	3	1	5	3	
Weare, Jerᵉ, Jʳ	1	3	4	1	
Seavey, Eliakim	1		1		
Seavey, Thoˢ	1	2	4		
Webber, Nathˡ	4	1	3		
Webber, Theodore	1		2		
Storer, Willᵐ	1	1	1		
Bradbury, Danˡ	1	2	1		
Clark, Anna		2	3		
Clark, Jerᵉ	2		3		
Weare, John	3	1	3		
Adams, Ezekiel	1	2	4		
Webber, Matthias	2		3		
Weare, Joseph, Jʳ	2	1	3		
Weare. Joseph	1		2		
Weare, Danˡ	2	4	3	2	
Averall, Job	3		5		
Littlefield, Ephraim	1	2	3		
Madden, James	1	2	3		
Freeman, John	3	2	5		
Wilson, Jonᵃ	1	2	6		
Welch, Willᵐ	1				
Welch, Joseph	1				
Ramsdale, Danˡ, Jʳ	2		3		
Ramsdale, Timᵒ	1		1		
Wilson, Noah	1	1	3		
Wilson, Joseph	1	2	3		
Wilson, Michael	1		2		
Woodbridge, Norton	1		2		
Trafton, Abiah	2	1	3		
Card, Joseph	1	1	2		
Cole, James	1	1	2		
Littlefield, Peter	2	2	5		
Molton, Nathˡ	2	2	4		
Swett, Nathˡ	1	4	4		
Beel, Richᵈ	3		2		
Trafton, Thaddeus	2		1		
Ramsdale, Nathˡ	2		3		
Ramsdale, Danˡ	3	1	3		
Chase, Josiah	4	3	6		
Carlisle, John	1	1	3		
Preble, Edward	4		2		
Preble, Joseph	2		2		
Beetle, Ithumer	3		4		
Pearsons, Nathˡ	1	2	3		
Sedgley, Joseph	1	2	2		
Sedgley, John	1		3		
Preble, Samˡ	2	1	4		
Simpson, Thoˢ	2		2		
Bradbury, John	2	1	4		
Simpson, Joseph	1	1	2		
Sewall, Henry	2		2		
Bridges, Joshua	1	3	3		
Tolpy, Henry	3	4	7		
YORK TOWN—con.					
Welch, Tabitha	1	1	2		
Simpson, George	4	1	2		
Hutchens, Job	1		4		
Clark, Danˡ	1	1	4		
Tolpy, Thoˢ	1	3	4		
Leach, John	1		2		
Bowden, David	1	1	2		
Lord, Jere	1	1	2		
Stover, Samˡ	3		4		
Stover, George	1	5	2		
Norton, John	3		4		
Robinson, Sarah		2	3		
Gunnison, Willᵐ	2	1	4		
Bouden, Danˡ	3		1		
Stover, Huldah	1	1	4	3	
Sewall, Moses	1	1	4		
Stover, Mary	2		2		
Mathews, Elijah	1		2		
Beal, Elisabeth		1	2		
Avery, Hannah	1		2		
Kinsley, James	1	1	1		
Bridges, Mary	1	1	4		
MᶜCauley, Susanna			4	4	
Moody, Joseph	4	2	3		
Tinney, John	2	3	7		
King, Richᵈ	1		2		
Whittam, Bartholomew	1		2		
Whittem, Elisabeth	1		2		
Dwinnels, Samˡ	1		2		
Dwinnels, Samˡ, Jʳ	1	2	2		
Freeman, Nathˡ	1	4	4		
Avery, David	1	2	4		
Verrill (Widow)	1		4		
Dwinnel, Jotham	1	2	4		
Stone, Josiah	2		2		
Stone, Samˡ	1		1		
Bradbury, James	1	2	4		
Banks, Peletiah	1	1	5		
Rose, Robert	2		2		
Preble, Abigail	1	3	5		
Grove, Olive	1		3		
Grove, Dorcas		1	4		
Dwinnel, Timothy	1		3		
Emerson, Edward	4	1	7		
Sewall, David	1	2	2		
Sargeant, Nathˡ	1	2	3		
Low, Thoˢ	2	2	7		
Emerson, Edward, Jʳ	1	2	4		
Woodbridge, Paul D	1	3	3		
Young, John, Jʳ	1		2		
Young, John	1	1	3		
Young, Rowland	2	3	3		
Sewall, John	1				
Low, Edward	1	2	6		
Emerson, Eunice	1		1		
Safford, Moses	1	2	3		
Grove, Willᵐ, Jʳ	2	2	4		
Kimbal, Abigail			5		
Sewall, Danˡ	1		2		
Horn, Joseph	1		2		
Sawyer, Abrᵐ	1	1	2		
Nowel, Paul	2		5		
Trivet, Samˡ	1	3	3	1	
Andrews, Solomon	2		2		
Andrews, Henry	2		1		
Sewal, Nicholas	3		3	1	
Black, ——	1		2		
Fletcher, John	1	1	2		
Soward, Willᵐ	1	4	3		
Scott, Giles				6	
Dwinnel (Widow)	3	1	1		
Matman (Widow)			2		
Verril, Solomon	1	2	4		
Holman, John	4	2	2		
Philbrick (Widow)	2	1	6		
Dwinnel, Nathˡ	3		3		
Lewis, Hannah		1	2		
Verrill (Widow)		2	2		
Goodale, Timᵒ	1	3	3		
Milbory, Samˡ	4	2	2		
Norward (Widow)	1	5	7		
Avery, David	1	2	2		
Bridge, Arthur	1	1	3		
Sayward, Jonᵃ	2		5	1	
Trevitt, Richᵈ	1		1		
Bowdy, Edward	1	4	3		
Sayward (Widow)			4		
Keaton (Widow)	2		2		
Farn, John	2		1		
Derby, Samˡ	3		2		
Stover, John	3	1	6		
Stover, John, Jʳ	1	1	3		
Grove, Willᵐ	2		1		
Tricet, John	1	3	3		

FIRST CENSUS OF THE UNITED STATES.

YORK COUNTY—Continued.

NAME OF HEAD OF FAMILY.	Free white males of 16 years and upward, including heads of families.	Free white males under 16 years.	Free white females, including heads of families.	All other free persons.	Slaves.	NAME OF HEAD OF FAMILY.	Free white males of 16 years and upward, including heads of families.	Free white males under 16 years.	Free white females, including heads of families.	All other free persons.	Slaves.	NAME OF HEAD OF FAMILY.	Free white males of 16 years and upward, including heads of families.	Free white males under 16 years.	Free white females, including heads of families.	All other free persons.	Slaves.
YORK TOWN—con.						**YORK TOWN—con.**						**YORK TOWN—con.**					
Harris (Widow)			1			Bean, Lewis	1	1	1			Linscutt, Jere	4		1		
Dwinnel, Obadiah	1	2	3			Swett, Sarah			6	1		Linscutt, Danˡ	3	2	5		
Harman, Zebadiah	2		2			Bean, Mary			3			Linscutt, Samˡ	1		5		
Harman, Thoˢ	2	1	7			Simpson, Tabitha	1		3			Simpson, Ebenˢ	2		4	1	
Rendal (Widow)		2	3			Molton, Johnson	2		3			Kingsbury, John	2		2		
Moor, Willᵐ	1	1	1			Going, Hannah			2			Emery, Danˡ	1	2	5		
Bennett, John	1		3			Grant, Jasper	1	1	3			Kean, Arthur	3	3	4		
Cheswell, Peletiah	2	1	4			Carlisle, John	1	1	1			McIntire, Ebeˢ	3	1	3		
Perkins (Widow)			2			Bean, James	1	4	1			Paul, Samˡ	2	2	4		
Stimpson, Joseph	1	1	2			Preble, Benjᵃ	2	1	3			Rogers, Benjᵃ	1	1	3		
Crocher (Widow)	2	1	2			Woodward, Lemˡ	3		3			Rogers, Joseph	1		2		
Currier (Widow)		1	1			Bank, Richᵈ	2	3	2			Harvey, Willᵐ	1	1	2		
Bragdon, Danˡ	2		1			Nason, Sarah	2		2			Kingsbury, Samˡ	2		5		
Bouden, Isaac	1	2	6			Austins, Woodward	1	3	2			Thompson, Jonᵃ	1	3	4		
Beal, Joseph	1	1	3			Grant, Joseph	2	2	2			Thompson, Dodiford C	2		1		
Derby, Jere	1		2			Bragdon, Warren	1		2			Bridges, Edmond	2		3		
Harman, John	2		2			Perkins, Isaac	1	1	2			Linscutt, Isaiah	1	2	1		
Harman, John, Jr	1	1	1			Young, Jonᵃ	3	1	3			Kingsbury, John	1		1		
Jacobs, Joseph	1	1	5			Whittem, Reuben	3	2	4			Kingsbury, Benjᵃ	1		2		
Liman, Job	4	1	8			Whittem, John S	1		1			McIntire, Joseph	3	4	4		
Simpson, Joshua	2		2			FitsGerald, Patrick	1	1	4			McIntire, Joseph, Jr	1	2	3		
Sellars, Willᵐ	1	2	3			FitsGerald, James	2	3	2			McIntire, Samˡ	1	4	3		
Stacey, Willᵐ	1	2	3			FitsGerald, David	1	1	4			Grover, Danˡ	2	1	4		
Tucker, Susanna			2			Lewis, Willᵐ	2	1	4			Grover, Simon	1	2	3		
Sheaf, Samˡ	1					Welch, Paul	1	1	4			Sargeant, Daniel	1		4		
Wheeler, John	1	2	6			Welch, Benjᵃ	2		4			McIntire, Micum	3	2	2		
Woodbridge, John	1	1	2			Welch, David	2	1	2			Lewis, Nathˡ	5		3		
Tucker, Joseph	2		4			Young, Joseph	1	2	2			Blaisdel, Ebenˢ	3		3		
Lindsey (Widow)	2	1	2			Moulton, Thoˢ	3	3	1			Thompson, Benjᵃ	1				
Downs, Robert	1	1	1			Austins, Benjᵃ	1	1	2			Sargeant, Jonᵃ	1	2	2		
Adams, Nathˡ	1		1			Grant, Nathˡ	1	1	2			Berry, Joseph	1		4		
Adams, Betsey		3	4			Lunt, Samˡ	2	1	4			Sargeant, Danˡ	1		4		
Currier, Joseph	1		1			Lunt, Henry	1		3			Blaisdel, David	1	2	2		
Lowe, Edward	1	2	5			Moulton, Abel	1	1	3			Welch, Moses	3		2		
Nowel, Paul	2		6			Grant, David	3	2	5			Welch, Sarah			2		
Simpson, Joseph	3	3	3			Grant (Widow)	1		2			Barrell, Nathˡ	2	3	7		
Hatch, Samˡ	1	1	2			Grant, Joshua	1	3	4			Trafton, Jotham	2	1	3		
Sayward, Willᵐ	1	4	3			Grant, Stephen	1	2	1			Crosby (Widow)	2		2		
Allenwood, Theodore	1	2	3			Plaisted, John	5		2			Allen, Eleanor			2		
Down, Solomon	1		3			Molton, John	1	4	3			Trafton (Widow)		1	2		
Keswell, Amos	1	2	5			Molton, Danˡ	1	4	3			Trafton, James	1	2	2		
Keswell, Willᵐ	1		1			Molton, Samˡ	1	1	1			Gorden, Nathˡ	1	2	4		
Perkins, Edward	2	1	1			Molton, Ebenˢ	1		5			Crawley, Hannah			2		
Moore, John	2	2	3			Young, Marstinson	3		3			Trafton, Samˡ	1		2		
Moore, Thoˢ	1		2			Young, Joel	1	2	1			Maines, Elias	1	1	2		
Hilton, Ellakim	1	1	6			Young, Samˡ	4	4	4			Main, John	2		3	2	
Shaw, Merriam			1			Grant, Dorothy	2		5			Moulton, Samˡ	3		7		
Goodwin, Danˡ	1		2			Frether, Samˡ	1	1	5			Bragdon, Matthias	1	1	4		
Young, Matthias	1		2			Nowel, John	1	5	5			Varnham, Jonᵃ	2	1	2		
Cawd, Joseph	1	3	2			Bragdon, Thoˢ	4	3	2			Blaisdel, Elijah	2	3	5		
Cawd, John	1	2	6			Bragdon, Danˡ	2	1	4			Baker, Issacar	1		3		
Babb, Samˡ	1		1			Barnard, Jonᵃ	1	1	7			Baker, Joseph	1	1	3		
Babb, Willᵐ	1		4			Laneton, Revᵈ Samˡ	1		4			Smith, Edward	3	1	2		
Haines, Thoˢ	2		2			Junkins, Eunice	1	2	4			Bragdon, Joseph	2		5		
Bradbury, Cotten	3		3			Junkins, Alexander	2	2	6			Bragdon, Mary	1		3		
Carlisle, Alexander	2		3			Moody, Thomas	2	2	2			Bragdon (Widow)			1	1	
Molton, Joseph	2	2	3			McIntire Samˡ	4		3			Bragdon, Samˡ	2	1	2		
Teel, Thoˢ	1	1	2			Grant, Sarah	2	1	3			Baker, Samˡ	1	3	4		
Soward, Joseph	1		2			Junkins, Hepsibath	2		2			Baker, Thoˢ	1		1		
Lyman, Revᵈ Isaac	2		6			Haley, John	2	1	2			Hill, Theodore	1	1	2		
Preble, Caleb	2	1	2			Nowel, Joseph	3	3	3			Allen, Bassum	3	1	5		
Preble, Esaias	1	3	10			Nowel, Thoˢ	1	1	4			Pell, John	2		2		
Preble, John	1	2	4			Nowel, John	2	1	3			Sewall, Samˡ	2		3		
Frost, Willᵐ	1	2	6			Shaw, John	3		4			Parsons, Samˡ	2	3	7		
Bean, Mary			1			Shaw, Joseph	1		3			McIntire, Danˡ	1	2	4		
Hunt, Willᵐ	1		2			Junkins, James	2	3	4			McIntire, Jedediah	1	2	2		
Sewall, Samˡ	2		6			Junkins, Joseph	1		1			Bragdon, Hepsibah			2		
Sewall, Story	1		3			Junkins, Danˡ	1		2			Young, Joshua	1	1	4		
Banks (Widow)			1			Junkins, Danˡ, Jr	2	1	6			Sewall, John	2	1	3		
Moulton, Willᵐ	1	3	2			Junkins, Jonᵃ	1	1	2			Crawley, Rachael			3		
Preble, David	1		4			Junkins, Eliphalet	1	1	6			Holt, Ebenˢ	3		1		
Todd, Joseph	1	3	1			Jellitson, Ichabod	1		3			Baker, John	1	3	5		
Abbot, Thoˢ	1		6			Jellitson, Joel	1	1	2			Beel, Josiah	1		4		
Molton, Theodore	1	2	4			Shaw, Samˡ	1		3			Booker, Aaron	1	3	3		
Lunt, Danˡ	1	2	4			Shaw, Abraᵐ	1	2	4			Hanes, John	1	3	1		
Savage, John	3	5	3			Shaw, Willᵐ	1	1	2			Harriss, Timothy	1	1	5		
Simpson, Joseph	1	1	2			Gary, John	1		3			Harriss, Samˡ	2	1	5		
Sewall, Henry	1		2			Gary, Danˡ	1	2	1			Molton, Danˡ	1		6		
Bridges, Joshua	1	3	2			Gary, Abel	1	3	2			Moore, Joshua	4	2	3		
Bradbury, John	2	1	4			Nowel, Danˡ	1	4	4			Perkins, Jonᵃ	2	3	2		
Simpson, Thoˢ	2		3			Nowel, Shadrach	2		6			Johnston, Danˡ	3		4		
Holman, John	3	3	2			Nowel, Sarah	2		3			Narman, John	1		1		
Harman, Nathˡ	1	2	4			Emery, Simon	1	2	1			Norman, Thoˢ	1	1	1		
Varnum, Jonᵃ	1	2	2			Furrel, Nicholas	1	2	2			Harrison (Widow)			3		
Parsons, Isaac	1		1			Smith, Danˡ	1	3	2			Swett, Samˡ		2	3		
Simpson, Danˡ	1	1	4			Leavitt, Jer	2	1	6			Swett, John	2		3		
Simpson, Nathˡ	1	1	2			Thompson, Danˡ	4	1	4			Bridge, Benjˢ	1		4		
Miller (Widow)			3			Bragdon, Solomon	1	2	4			Booker, Jacob	1		1		
Bragdon, Lydia	1		2			Smith, Ebenezer	1	5	3			Reins, Nathˡ	3	1	4		
Currier, Anna		2	2			Smith, John	1		1			Reins, Robert, Jr	1	2	4		
Simpson, Joseph	3	2	2			Thompson, Ebenezer	2	2	6			Reins, Francis	1		2		
Simpson, Pelatiah	2		4			Preble, Joseph	2	1	2			Reins, Danˡ		2	2		
Simpson, Timothy	1		2			Preble, David	2		3			Reins, Nathˡ, Jr	2	2	4		
Bean, Nehemiah	1	1	2			Thompson, Joseph		1	3		1	Paine (Widow)	3	1	6		

HEADS OF FAMILIES—MAINE.

YORK COUNTY—Continued.

NAME OF HEAD OF FAMILY.	Free white males of 16 years and upward, including heads of families.	Free white males under 16 years.	Free white females, including heads of families.	All other free persons.	Slaves.	NAME OF HEAD OF FAMILY.	Free white males of 16 years and upward, including heads of families.	Free white males under 16 years.	Free white females, including heads of families.	All other free persons.	Slaves.	NAME OF HEAD OF FAMILY.	Free white males of 16 years and upward, including heads of families.	Free white males under 16 years.	Free white females, including heads of families.	All other free persons.	Slaves.
YORK TOWN—con.						YORK TOWN—con.						YORK TOWN—con.					
Reins, Robert	2		4			Oliver, Jotham	1		1			Warren, Moses	3	2	5		
Welch (Widow)			1			Oliver (Widow)	1		4			Joy, Samˡ	2	2	5		
Moore, Joshua, Jr	1	1	2			Bracey, James	2	1	2			Blaisdel, Elijah	1	2	1		
Moore, Samˡ	2	1	3			Bracey, Danˡ	1	2	3			Gray, Jonᵃ	1	3	4		
Moore, George	2	1	4			Adams, Willᵐ	1	1	2			Abbott, Aaron	2	1	5		
Moore, Willᵐ	1		4			Beal, John	2	2	3			Abbot, Aaron, Jr	1	3	1		
Reins (Widow)	3		4			Allen, Samˡ	1	1	2			Blaisdel, Danˡ	2	1	5		
Thompson, Alexander	1	2	3			Blaisdel, Zedediah	1	1	4	1		Emery, John	3	1	3		
Sargeant, Charles	1	1	4			Bussel, James	1	1	5			Joy, Ephraim	1	1	2		
Varnham, Jonᵃ	3		4			Bragdon, James	1	3	1			Allen, Bassam	1	1	4		
Bragdon, Benjᵃ	3	4	7			Beetle, Eleazer	1	1	1			Stevans, John	2	1	4		
Bragdon, Jethro	1		7			Allen, Samˡ	1	1	2			Walker, Edward	1	1	3		
Bragdon, Zachariah	1		2			Beetle, Henry	1	1	3			Stevans, John	1	1	1		
Cook, Danˡ	2	2	5			Stephens, Pelatiah	1	1	1			Stevans, Jonᵃ	1	1	1		
Oliver, James	1		4			Jellitson, James	1	3	2								

INDEX.[1]

Abbot, Aaron, 51.
Abbot, Aaron, Jr, 73.
Abbot, Amos, 56.
Abbot, Anney, 56.
Abbot, Benj^a, 55.
Abbot, Danl, 56.
Abbot, David, 65.
Abbot, George, 15.
Abbot, Henry, 34.
Abbot, Isaac, 56.
Abbot, Isaac, 60.
Abbot, Isaac, Junr, 60.
Abbot, James, 13.
Abbot, John, 34.
Abbot, John, 56.
Abbot, John, 56.
Abbot, John, Junr, 56.
Abbot, Jon^a, 56.
Abbot, Jon^a, 67.
Abbot, Jonathan, 68.
Abbot, Joseph, 57.
Abbot, Joshua, 56.
Abbot, Joshua, 56.
Abbot, Moses, 65.
Abbot, Moses, 67.
Abbot, Moses, Junr, 67.
Abbot, Nathaniel, 14.
Abbot, Patience, 56.
Abbot, Phillip, 64.
Abbot, Reuben, 56.
Abbot, Ric^d, 56.
Abbot, Samuel, 56.
Abbot, Samuel, 65.
Abbot, Samuel, 68.
Abbot, Silas, 54.
Abbot, Simeon, 60.
Abbot, Stephen, 57.
Abbot, Theopholus, 55.
Abbot, Thomas, 55.
Abbot, Thomas, 55.
Abbot, Thomas, 57.
Abbot, Thos, 72.
Abbot, Thos, Jr, 57.
Abbot, Unis, 57.
Abbot, W^m, 57.
Abbott, Aaron, 73.
Abbott, James, 30.
Abbott, James, 31.
Abbott, John, 31.
Abbott, John, Junr, 68.
Abbott, Moses, 31.
Abbott, Reuben, 31.
Abbott, Reuben, jun^r, 31.
abraham, Susman, 41.
Abram, Paddy, 31.
Ackly, Benajah, 52.
Acorn, Jacob, 43.
Adam, John, 28.
Adam, John, jun^r, 28.
Adams, Abraham, 42.
Adams, Amos, 42.
Adams, Amos, Ju., 42.
Adams, And^w, 13.
Adams, Benjⁿ, 16.
Adams, Benj^a, 55.
Adams, Benj^a, 57.
Adams, Barney, 72.
Adams, Danl, 61.
Adams, David, 27.
Adams, Ezekiel, 71.
Adams, Francis, 30.
Adams, Isaac, 32.
Adams, Jacob, 14.
Adams, James, 42.
Adams, James, 55.
Adams, James, J^r, 55.
Adams, Jer^e, 35.
Adams, Joel, 47.
Adams, John, 35.
Adams, John, 35.
Adams, John, 43.
Adams, John, 55.
Adams, John, 63.
Adams, John, 66.
Adams, John, 68.
Adams, Revd John, 68.
Adams, Jonathan, 15.
Adams, Jonathan, 66.
Adams, Jonathan, Senr, 66.
Adams, Joshua, 16.
Adams, Joshua, 28.

Adams, Joshua, Jr., 16.
Adams, Mark, 62.
Adams, Mary, 62.
Adams, Moses, 15.
Adams, Moses, 44.
Adams, Nathan, 35.
Adams, Nathl, 72.
Adams, Richard, 36.
Adams, Saml, 34.
Adams, Samuel, 35.
Adams, Saml, Junr, 34.
Adams, Solomon, 44.
Adams, Stephⁿ, 59.
Adams, Thomas, 29.
Adams, Willm, 59.
Adams, Willm, 73.
Addams, John, 44.
addition, thomas, 40.
Adkins, Nathaniel, 41.
Adkins, Williams, 40.
Adle, Cornelius, 44.
Adridge, Nathl, 16.
Agrey (Widow), 43.
Agry, Thomas, 43.
Airs, Moses, 46.
Akers, John, 16.
Akers, Moses, 16.
Albee, William, 52.
Alby, Isaac, 45.
Alby, Jonathan, 45.
Alby, Obadah, 34.
Alby, Samuel, 45.
Alden, Abiather, 16.
Alden, Austin, 16.
Alden, Elisabeth, 13.
Alden, Josiah, 16.
Alden, Nathl, 16.
Aldrige, Amos, 69.
Aldrige (Widow), 70.
Alexander, David, 20.
Alexander, James, 34.
Alexander, James, 34.
Alexander, John, 26.
Alexander, John, 34.
Alexander, Robert, 46.
Alexander, Saml, 34.
Alexander, Willm, 20.
Alexander, William, 34.
Alexander, William, 34.
Alford, Lore, 49.
All, James, 34.
Allan, Gideon, 54.
Allan, John, 38.
Allan, John, 53.
Allan, Nathaniel, 49.
Allan, Obediah, 54.
Allen, Abel, 11.
Allen, Abraham, 27.
Allen, Amos, 43.
Allen, Bassam, 73.
Allen, Bassum, 72.
Allen, Benjⁿ, 51.
Allen, Caleb, 37.
Allen, Daniel, 34.
Allen, Daniel, 49.
Allen, David, 13.
Allen, Ebenezer, 21.
Allen, Ebenezer, 37.
Allen, Ebenezer, Jr, 37.
Allen, Edman, 49.
Allen, Elanor, 72.
Allen, Elijah, 20.
Allen, Elijah, 20.
Allen, Elijah, 70.
Allen, Elijah, 70.
Allen, Elisabeth, 20.
Allen, Elisha, 20.
Allen, Elisha, 58.
Allen, Eliz^h, 62.
Allen, Ephraim, 20.
Allen, Ephraim, 62.
Allen, Francis, 50.
Allen, Franes, 66.
Allen, Gideon, 36.
Allen, Hannah, 15.
Allen, Isaac, 11.
Allen, Isaac, 14.
Allen, Isaac, 15.
Allen, Isaac, 20.
Allen, Jacob, 21.
Allen, Jacob, 57.

Allen, James, 20.
Allen, James, 70.
Allen, James, J^r, 70.
Allen, Jerediah, 66.
Allen, Joanna, 31.
Allen, Job, 22.
Allen, John, 11.
Allen, John, 44.
Allen, John, 59.
Allen, Jchn, 62.
Allen, Jonathan, 32.
Allen, Joseph, 20.
Allen, Joseph, 25.
Allen, Joseph, 49.
Allen, Joseph, 59.
Allen, Joseph, 60.
Allen, Joshua, 11.
Allen, Jotham, 70.
Allen, Jude, 67.
Allen, Nathaniel, 29.
Allen, Nathaniel C., 20.
Allen, Nehemiah, 20.
Allen, Nehemiah, 21.
Allen, Nehemiah, 31.
Allen, Pelatiah, 26.
Allen, Pelatiah, 46.
Allen, Peter, 30.
Allen, Peter, 43.
Allen, Phillp, 51.
Allen, Phinehas, 39.
Allen, Pirkins, 45.
Allen, Rachael, 37.
Allen, Saml, 46.
Allen, Saml, 73.
Allen, Saml, 73.
Allen, Asa, 43.
Allen, Seth, 13.
Allen, Solomon, 66.
Allen, Thos, 12.
Allen, Tobias, 29.
allen, Told, 67.
Allen, Willm, 11.
Allen, William, 44.
Allen, William, 49.
Allen, Woodard, 49.
Allen, Wright, 60.
Allen, Zacheus, 15.
Allen, Zekiel, 34.
Allenwood, Theodore, 72.
Alles, Micah, 50.
Allexander, Hugh, 20.
Allexander, Jane, 20.
Allexander, John, 34.
Allexander, Robart, 34.
Alley, Ephrom, 36.
Alley, John, 34.
Alley, John, Jn^r, 34.
Alley, Joshua, 34.
Alley, Olais, 67.
Alley, Saml, 34.
Alley, Stephⁿ, 29.
Alley, Samuel, 67.
Alline, Benj^a, 29.
Allis, Benjamin, 52.
Allod, David, 66.
Amerson, Asa, 50.
Amerson, Calvin, 42.
Amerson, Daniel, 50.
Amerson, Daniel, 50.
Amerson, Ezekiel, 42.
Ames, Jabez, 29.
Ames, Jacob, 26.
Ames, Jacob, 26.
Ames, Jacob, 38.
Ames, James, 40.
Ames, John, 28.
Ames, John, 60.
Ames, John, 65.
Ames, Jonathan, 33.
Ames, Jonathan, 52.
Ames, Josiah, 29.
Ames, Justus, 32.
Ames, Margaret, 32.
Ames, Mark, 32.
Ames, Moses, 60.
Ames, Nath^{ls}, 65.
Ames, Saml, 24.
Ames, Samuel, 44.
Ames, Thomas, 29.
Ames, Winslow, 40.
Amory, George, 36.
Amory, George, 46.

Amory, John, 13.
Amy, Saml, 61.
And——, Stephen, 59.
Anderson, Abraham, 25.
Anderson, Ann, 25.
Anderson, Archibald, 49.
Anderson, Daniel, 20.
Anderson, Edward, 25.
Anderson, Jacob, 12.
Anderson, Jacob, 16.
Anderson, James, 16.
Anderson, James, 49.
Anderson, Job, 31.
Anderson, John, 15.
Anderson, John, 16.
Anderson, John, 16.
Anderson, John, 16.
Anderson, John, 39.
Anderson, John, 54.
Anderson, Joseph, 16.
Anderson, Nancy, 25.
Anderson, Robert, 16.
Anderson, Robert, 24.
Anderson, Robert, 40.
Anderson, Samuel, 49.
Andres, John, 49.
andres, Sthephen, 42.
andrew, michel, 42.
Andrews, Abel, 59.
Andrews, Abraham, 68.
Andrews, Amos, 16.
Andrews, Amos, 32.
Andrews, Asa, 43.
Andrews, David, 22.
Andrews, Elizath, 59.
Andrews, Ely, 42.
Andrews, George, 39.
Andrews, Henry, 71.
Andrews, Israel, 52.
Andrews, Jeremiah, 68.
Andrews, Jerimiah, 53.
Andrews, John, 12.
Andrews, John, 26.
Andrews, John, 33.
Andrews, John, 49.
Andrews, John, 55.
Andrews, John, 59.
Andrews, John, 64.
Andrews, Jon^a, 16.
Andrews, Jon^a, Jr., 16.
Andrews, Mark, 25.
Andrews, Nathan, 53.
Andrews, Perez, 11.
Andrews, Robert, 11.
Andrews, Samuel, 15.
Andrews, Saml, 25.
Andrews, Solomon, 71.
Andrews, Stephⁿ, 16.
Andrews, Timothy, 53.
Andrews, W^m, 58.
andris, Ephram, 40.
Andros, Elisha, 58.
Andros, Joanna, 58.
Andros, John, 58.
Andros, Olive, 57.
Androse, Samuel, 69.
annies, Charles, 66.
annies, John, 66.
annies, Nehemiah, 66.
Annis, Abra^m, 69.
Annis, Benjamin, 32.
Annis, Nehemiah, 69.
Annis, Ralph, 31.
Annis, Samuel, 36.
Annis, Stephen, 69.
Anthine, Nicholis, 25.
Appelbe, Thomas, 63.
Appelby, Halley, 57.
Appelby, Levi, 57.
Appelby, Simeon, 57.
Appleby, John, 32.
Appleton, Danl, 59.
Appleton, Francis, 29.
Appleton, John, 43.
Appleton, Jno, 59.
Archer, John, 54.
Archibald, Thomas, 53.
Arey, Ebenezer, 32.
Arey, Isaac, 32.

Armstrong, John, 13.
Armstrong, Jonathan, 15.
Armstrong, Richard, 32.
Arno, John, 49.
Arnold, Benjamin, 45.
Arnold, Bildad, 20.
arnold, thomas, 48.
Arnold, Willm, 44.
Arvel, John, 43.
Ash, Benjamin, 29.
Ash, Robert, 29.
Ash, Robert, 53.
Ash, Samuel, 53.
Ash, Thomas, 31.
Ashley, Abner, 16.
Askins, Alexander, 43.
askins, alex^{dm}, 48.
Askins, Christopher, 44.
Askins, David, 48.
Askins, George, 44.
askins, george, 48.
askins, John, 48.
askins, ninain, 48.
askins, thomas, 51.
askins (widow), 48.
askins, william, 48.
Aspinwall, Caleb, 24.
Asten, Peter, 68.
Astery, Benoney, 49.
Astins, Jacob, 38.
Astons, Stephen, 38.
Athenton, Benj^a, 29.
Atherington, John, 69.
Atherton, Jona, 20.
Atkins, Cornelius, 27.
Atkins, David, 51.
Atkins, James, 44.
Atkins, Nathaniel, 23.
Atkins, Nathaniel, 30.
Atkinson, James, 51.
Atkinson, Jno, 59.
Atkinson, Joseph, 58.
Atkinson, Jos^h, Junr, 59.
Atkinson, Moses, 16.
Atkinson, thomas, 51.
Atkinson, Thos, 58.
Atkinson, Thos, Jr, 59.
Atterd, Daniel, 68.
Atwood, Jesse, 30.
Atwood, Nathan, 32.
Atwood, Nathl, 37.
Atwood, Solomon, 20.
Atwood, Stephen, 13.
Ausburn, Ephrom, 50.
Ausburn, Isaac, 50.
Ausburn, Jonathan, 37.
Ausburn, Jonathan, 50.
Austen, Cathrine, 63.
Austen, Moses, 63.
Austen Nat., 63.
Austin, Andrew, 56.
Austin, Benjamin, 15.
Austin, George, 11.
Austin, Jonas, 25.
Austin, Ruth, 16.
Austia, Stephen, 19.
Austins, Benj^a, 72.
Austins, Woodward, 72.
Averal, Ezekiel, 41.
Averal, Israel, 44.
Averal, John, 44.
Averall, Job, 71.
Averel, Job, 43.
Averel, Mary, 43.
Averel, Samuel, 43.
Averel, Samuel, 43.
Averel, Willm, 44.
Averill, Joseph, 52.
Avery, David, 71.
Avery, David, 71.
Avery, Hannah, 71.
Avery, James, 52.
Avery, Jane, 13.
Avery, Jeremiah, 65.
Avery, Joseph, 55.
avery, Joseph, 67.
Avery, Saml, 71.
Avery, Shadrack, 55.
Avery, Thatcher, 30.
Avery, Walter, 65.
Avrill, Samuel, 33.
awstin, Ichabod, 35.

[1] No attempt has been made in this publication to correct mistakes in spelling made by the deputy marshals, but the names have been reproduced as they appear upon the census schedules.

76 INDEX.

Ayer, Benjn, 58.
Ayer, Ebenr, 58.
Ayer, Elijah, 53.
Ayer, Elijah, junr, 53.
Ayer, John, 60.
Ayer, Joseph, 58.
Ayer, Peter, 58.
Ayer, Timothy, 58.
Ayers, Ebens, 14.
Ayers, Elisha, 68.
Ayers, George, 54.
Ayers, James, 44.
Ayers, Jemime, 23.
Ayers, Moses, 65.
Ayers, Thomas, 20.
Aylwood, Patrick, 52.

bab, Bot (widow), 45.
bab, Jonthan, 45.
Bab, Jonthan, Ju., 45.
bab, Joshua, 45.
Bab, Peter, 58.
Babb, James, 13.
Babb, Rhoda, 15.
Babb, Saml, 72.
Babb, Thos, 19.
Babb, William, 15.
Babb, Willm, 72.
Babbidge, Benjamin, 46.
Babbige, Courtney, 27.
Babbige, Stephen, 27.
Babbige, William, 27.
Babrick, John, 32.
Babson, Joseph, 31.
Bacheldor, Joseph, 15.
Bacheldor, Theos, 38.
Bacheler, Benja, 65.
Bachelor, David, 65.
Bachelor, Ephraim, 16.
Bachelor, Jonathan, 65.
Bachelor, Saml, 16.
Backer, Eliphelat, 49.
Backer, Young, 49.
Bacon, Ebenr, 47.
Bacon, James, 47.
Bacon, Josiah, 17.
Bacon, Michael, 46.
Bacon, Nathl, Junr, 17.
Bacon, Nathl, Senr, 17.
Bacon, Thomas, 29.
Bacon, Timy, 17.
Badcock, Henry, 39.
Badcock, Jerh, 39.
Badcock, John, 39.
Badcock, Saml, 39.
Badcock, Saml, 39.
Bagley, Enoch, 14.
Bagley, Israel, 14.
Bagley, John, 69.
Bagly, John, 23.
Bailey, Benja, 52.
Bailey, Christopher, 33.
Bailey, Edmund, 11.
Bailey, Hudson, 23.
Bailey, Jacob, 20.
Bailey, John, 23.
Bailey, John, 42.
Bailey, John, 51.
Bailey, John, Junr, 52.
Bailey, Joseph, 24.
Bailey, Joseph, 26.
Bailey, Joshua, 51.
Bailey, Josiah, 51.
Bailey, Nathaniel, 23.
Bailey, Nathel, 43.
Bailey. Richard, 43.
Bailey, Samuel, 11.
Bailey, Seth, 16.
Bailey, Thos, 11.
Bailey, Thos, 65.
Bailey, Timothy, 14.
Bailey (Widow), 43.
baily, Zery, 48.
Bakeman, John, 30.
Bakeman, John, junr, 30.
Baker, Abner, 45.
Baker, Amos, 37.
Baker, Barnard, 34.
Baker, Barraws, 45.
Baker, Edmund, 24.
Baker, Elisha, 12.
Baker, Elkrer, 45.
Baker, Ichabod, 49.
Baker, Issacar, 72.
Baker, James, 22.
Baker, John, 23.
Baker, John, 24.
Baker, John, 43.
Baker, John, 72.
Baker, Jonah, 15.
Baker, Jona, 45.
Baker, Joseph, 30.
Baker, Joseph, 36.
Baker, Joseph, 60.
Baker, Joseph, 72.
Baker, Josiah, 23.
Baker, Josiah, 25.
Baker, Judah, 34.
Baker, Judah, 45.
Baker, Lemuel, 54.
Baker, Moses, 28.
Baker, Prince, 36.
Baker, Saml, 22.
Baker, Saml, 22.
Baker, Samuel, 24.
Baker, Saml, 72.
Baker, Saml, Junr, 22.
Baker, Smith, 34.
Baker, Smith, 45.
Baker, Solomon, 37.
Baker, Thos, 72.
Baker, William, 14.
Baker, William, 29.
Baker, Willm C., 43.
Bakon, Josiah, 51.
Balch, Nat., 68.
Balch, Nat., 68.
Balcome, Elijah, 47.
Bales, Jabas R., 38.
Baley, Benjamin, 14.
Balcy, Benjamin, 14.
Baley, Daniel, 14.
Baley, David, 15.
Baley, Eilphalet, 44.
Baley, James, 14.
Baley, John, 20.
Baley, Joseph, 14.
Baley, Josiah, 14.
Baley, Robert, 20.
Baley, Thos, 52.
Baley, William, 13.
Balintine, Samel, 47.
Ball, John, 36.
Ball, Levi, 34.
Ball, Saml, 34.
Ballad, Ephraim, 39.
Ballard, Baze, 32.
Ballard, Betty, 50.
Ballard, Thomas, 52.
Ballard (Widow), 47.
Balley, Joseph, 33.
Balley, Nathan, 33.
Baly, Oliver, 44.
Bancroft, John, 24.
Bandford, Willm, 15.
Bandwell, Nathaniel, 66.
Bangs, Barns, 17.
Bangs, Barns, Junr, 17.
Bangs, Ebenr, 17.
Bangs, Herman, 17.
Bangs, James, 17.
Bangs, John, 65.
Bangs, Joshua, 15.
Bangs, Thos, 17.
Bank, Richd, 72.
Bankins, James, 71.
Bankins, John, 20.
Banks, Aaron, 30.
Banks, Bracy, 19.
Banks, John, 27.
Banks, John, 65.
Banks, Joseph, 64.
Banks, Joseph, 65.
Banks, Moses, 19.
Banks, Peletiah, 71.
Banks, Pheby, 65.
Banks, Sarah, 62.
Banks (Widow), 70.
Banks (Widow), 72.
Barber, Adam, 15.
Barber, John, 14.
Barber, Joseph, 23.
Barber, Lucy, 19.
Barber, Robert, 16.
Barber, Solomon, 23.
Bargish, Seth, 40.
Bark, Joseph, 31.
Barker, ——, 55.
Barker, Benjamin, 68.
Barker, Caleb, 40.
Barker, Caleb, 43.
Barker, Carr, 43.
Barker, Daniel, 25.
Barker, Danl, 63.
Barker, David, 26.
Barker, David, 65.
Barker, Ebenezer, 60.
Barker, Ezra, 60.
Barker, Hannah, 41.
Barker, Jacob, 40.
Barker, Jacob, 40.
Barker, Jeremiah, 14.
Barker, Jesse, 68.
Barker, John, 42.
Barker, John, 59.
Barker, John, 60.
Barker, Jonathan, 68.
Barker, Joseph, 69.
Barker, Nathel, 60.
Barker, Noah, 60.
Barker, Thomas, 25.
Barker, Thomas, 60.
Barker, Uriah, 38.
Barker, William, 38.
Barker, Willm, 43.
Barker, William, 43.
Barnam, Simeon, 11.
Barnard, Isaac, 46.
Barnard, Jona, 72.
Barnard, Joseph, 70.
barners, James, 68.
Barnes, Benjamin, 34.
Barnes, Benjmin, 67.
Barnes, David, 67.
Barnes, James, 52.
Barnes, Joseph, 64.
Barnes, Silas, 39.
Barnfard, James, 45.
Barns, Abram, 60.
Barns, Ashble, 52.
Barns, Jotham, 27.
Barns, Timothy, 60.
Barnsbotom, James, 13.
Barnwell, Edward, 22.
Barr, Alexander, 23.
Barrat, Benjamin, 34.
Barrell, Nathl, 72.
Barret, James, 23.
Barret, Simeon, 13.
Barrett, Daniel, 26.
Barrett, Nathan, 26.
Barrett, Simon, 26.
Barrett, Timothy, 26.
Barrey, George, 38.
Barrick, William, 32.
Barronock, John, 31.
Barrows, Asa, 22.
Barrows, Benajah, 46.
Barrows, Benjn, 24.
Barrows, Benjn, Jur, 24.
Barrows, Comfort, 46.
Barrows, Ephraim, 24.
Barrows, Ichabod, 46.
Barrows, Joseph, 24.
Barrows, Malaga, 22.
Barrows, Willm, 24.
Barry, amos, 40.
Barry, John, 45.
Barry, Nathan, 45.
Barry, Richard, Junr, 65.
Barry, Saml, 65.
barslow, John, 35.
Barter, John, 34.
Barter, John, 36.
Barter, Joseph, 34.
Barter, Mark, 55.
Barter, Pelatiah, 36.
Barter, Saml, 34.
Barter, Saml, Jur., 34.
Bartlet, Asa, 24.
Bartlet, Benoni, 59.
Bartlet, Caleb, 33.
Bartlet, Danl, 24.
Bartlet, Danl, 61.
Bartlet, Jeremh., 61.
Bartlet, John, 16.
Bartlet, John, 67.
Bartlet, John H., 61.
Bartlet, Jonathan, 33.
Bartlet, Jonathon, 38.
Bartlet, Jonn, 41.
Bartlet, Joseph, 33.
Bartlet, Nathan, 62.
Bartlet, Nathaniel, 40.
Bartlet, Peter, 44.
Bartlet, Saml, 71.
Bartlet, Solomon, 44.
Bartlet, Timothy, 50.
Bartlet, Willm, 16.
Bartlett, Caleb, 14.
Bartlett, Christopher, 29.
Bartlett, Christopher, jun., 29.
Bartlett, Daniel, 26.
Bartlett, David, 29.
Bartlett, Eleazer, 22.
Bartlett, Elias, 29.
Bartlett, Enoch, 68.
Bartlett, George, 16.
Bartlett, Isaac, 26.
Bartlett, Israel, 29.
Bartlett, James, 62.
Bartlett, Jonathan, 68.
Bartlett, Josiah, 21.
Bartlett, Lamuel, 47.
Bartlett, Malchi, 21.
Bartlett, Moses, 68.
Bartlett, Noah, 26.
Bartlett, Samuel, 26.
Bartlett, Samuel, 30.
Bartlett, Samuel, 46.
Bartlett, Sarah, 62.
Bartlett, Stephen, 68.
Bartlett, Thaddeus, 68.
Bartlett, Thomas, 15.
Bartlett, Thos, 62.
Barton, Ammy, 22.
Barton, Betty, 50.
Barton, Flint, 47.
Barton, Isaac, 24.
Barton, James, 23.
Barton, James, 29.
Barton, John, 36.
Barton, Robert, 23.
Barton, Wm, 17.
Barton, Winthrop, 22.
Bartrick, Dolly, 31.
Bary, Jonn, 45.
Basse, Jabas, 45.
Basse, Solomon, 45.
Bassett, Ebenezer, 32.
Bassett, Saml, 47.
Bassick, George, 28.
Basteen, Joseph, 30.
Batchelder, Hezekiah, 46.
Batcheldor, Elijah, 38.
Batcheldor, Josiah, 38.
Batcheldor, Peter, 21.
Batcheldor, Tima, 38.
Batchellor, Joshua, 66.
Batchelor, Daniel, 45.
Batchelor, Moses, 45.
Batchelor, William, 50.
bates, calab, 48.
Bates, Douly, 38.
Bates, Edsel, 22.
Bates, Hozea, 12.
Bates, Jacob, 11.
Bates, Jacob, 40.
Bates, Joseph, 38.
Bates, Lamuel, 38.
Bates, Levi, 38.
Bates, Mercy, 12.
Bates, Samuel, 37.
Bates, Samuel, 38.
Bates, Seth, 37.
Bates, Solomon, 38.
Bates, Thomas, 45.
Bates, Thomas, 50.
Batson, William, 54.
Battle, Benjamin, 47.
Battle, Joseph, 44.
Baty, John, 28.
Bavage, James, 14.
Baxter, John, 48.
Bayley, Samuel, 27.
Bayley, Nathl & Son, 53.
Bayley, Thaddeus, 43.
bayweatt, William, 49.
Beal, Ebenezer, 13.
Beal, Elisabeth, 71.
Beal, Jerimiah, 54.
Beal, Joanna, 31.
Beal, John, 38.
Beal, John, 73.
Beal, Jona, 14.
Beal, Joseph, 72.
Beal, Manwarren, 54.
Beal, Saml, 38.
Beal, Simeon, 19.
Beal, Zebilon, 66.
Beals, Benjamin, 11.
Beals, Isaiah, 17.
Beaman, Aaron, 12.
Beaman, Noah, 25.
Beaman, Thomas, 53.
Bean, Abner, 54.
Bean, Daniel, 66.
Bean, Daniel, 68.
Bean, Edward, 49.
Bean, Elijah, 51.
Bean, Elizabth, 59.
Bean, James, 31.
Bean, James, 72.
Bean, Jeremiah, 67.
Bean, Joab, 50.
Bean, Joel, 51.
Bean, John, 31.
Bean, John, 49.
Bean, John, 67.
Bean, John, junr, 31.
Bean, Jona, 44.
Bean, Jona, 64.
Bean, Jonathan, 68.
Bean, Jona, Junr, 64.
Bean, Jonathan, Junr, 68.
Bean, Joseph, 60.
Bean, Joshua, 51.
Bean, Joshua, 66.
Bean, Josiah, 49.
Bean, Josiah, 68.
Bean, Lewis, 72.
Bean, Mary, 72.
Bean, Mary, 72.
Bean, mary (Wid.), 67.
Bean, Neele, 49.
Bean, Nehemiah, 72.
bean, Richard, 68.
Bean, Samuel, 31.
Bean, Saml, 33.
Bean, Thomas, 60.
Bean, Willim, 67.
Bean, William, 68.
Bean, William, junr, 68.
Beane, David, 66.
Beane, David, Senr, 66.
Beane, Joseph, 66.
Bearce, Asa, 24.
Bearce, Asa, Jur, 24.
Bearce, Gideon, 24.
Beard, Saml, 58.
Beasse, Wllm, 13.
Beath, Jere, 34.
Beath, John, 34.
Beath, Joseph, 34.
Beatle, John, 66.
Beck, Thomas, 23.
Becker, Magnus, 42.
becker, Silas, 35.
beckler, daniel, 41.
Beedeen, Robert, 69.
Beel, Anna, 57.
Beel, Joseph, 58.
Beel, Joshua, 35.
Beel, Josiah, 35.
Beel, Josiah, 72.
Beel, Richd, 71.
Beel, Zachariah, 35.
Beeman, Abraham, 23.
Beeman, John 39.
Beeman, Saml, 58.
Beetel, Abial, 63.
Beetle, Eleazer, 73.
Beetle, Henry, 73.
Beetle, Ithumer, 71.
Belcher, Supply, 39.
Belden, Stephen, 38.
Belfountain, Rana, 52.
Belighter, Jno, 52.
Bell, William, 53.
Bellamy, John, 61.
Beman, Joseph, 14.
Bemus, Thaddeus, 60.
Bender, Christopher, 53.
benner, charles, 42.
benner, Jacob, 42.
benner, John, 42.
benner, John, Jun., 42.
benner, martin, 42.
benner, mathias, 41.
benner (widow), 42.
bennet, becheldor, 49.
Bennet, David, 66.
Bennet, Francis, 20.
Bennet, Isaac, 20.
Bennet, Job, 16.
Bennet, Joel, 70.
Bennet, John, 56.
Bennet, Jonathan, 20.
Bennet, Moses, 56.
Bennet, Nathaniel, 20.
Bennet, Nathaniel, 21.
Bennet, Nathinel, 66.
Bennet, Phineas, 15.
Bennet, Spencer, 43.
Bennet, William, 66.
Bennett, Asa, 47.
Bennett, Benja, 31.
Bennett, David Mill, 46.
Bennett, George, 70.
Bennett, John, 72.
Bennett, Nathl, 22.
Bennit, Peter, 47.
Benson, Caleb, 11.
Benson, Elnathan, 24.
Benson, Henry, 54.
Benson, Henry, 58.
Benson, Jacob, 39.
Benson, James, 65.
Benson, Jepthah, 24.
Benson, John, 58.
Benson, Robert, 58.
Bentley, John, 46.
Benton, Benjamin, 36.
berms, william, 48.
Bernard, Danl, 11.
Berny, Thomas, 37.
Berny, Thos., 43.
Berry, Benjn, 19.
Berry, Benjamin, 52.
Berry, David, 19.
Berry, Edward, 31.
Berry, Elisha, Jr., 19.
Berry, Enoch, 19.
Berry, Ephm, 19.
Berry, George, 15.
Berry, Isaac, 58.
Berry, James, 33.
Berry, James, 64.
Berry, James, 64.
Berry, James, 65.
Berry, James, 68.
Berry, James, 68.
Berry, Jeremiah, 23.
Berry, Jno, 19.
Berry, John, 33.
Berry, John, 52.
Berry, John, 53.
Berry, Jona, 19.
Berry, Jonathan, 52.
Berry, Jona, 58.
Berry, Jona, Junr, 59.
Berry, Joseph, 46.
Berry, Joseph, 72.
Berry, Joshua, 23.
Berry, Josiah, 14.
Berry, Josiah, 19.
Berry, Josiah, 35.
Berry, Nathl, 43.
Berry, Nicholas, 65.
Berry, Obediah, 14.
Berry, Pellatiah, 20.
Berry, Richard, 19.
Berry, Richard, 65.
Berry, Saml, 33.
Berry, Saml, 64.
Berry, Samuel, 68.
Berry, Solo, 19.
Berry, Thomas, 23.
Berry, Timy, 19.
Berry, Timothy, 24.
Berry, Wllm, 12.
Berry, Willm, 19.
Berry, Zebulon, 19.
Besse, Ebenezer, 41.
Besse, Jabas, Ju., 41.
Besse, Jabe, 41.
Besse, Reuben, 41.
Bessee, John, 22.
Bessee, Thos, 22.
Bester, Benja, 41.
Bester, George, 40.
Bester, Isaac, 41.
Bester, Timothy, 23.
Besto, Joseph, 22.
Bettes, Jere, 58.

INDEX.

Beverege, Thomas, 32.
Beverly, David, 24.
Beverly, Farnham, 17.
Bibber, James, 20.
Bibber, Lemuel, 20.
Bicker, Joseph, 69.
Bickford, Abner, 68.
Bickford, Benjamin, 66.
Bickford, Benjamin, Jun., 66.
Bickford, Doddiford, 58.
Bickford, Eliakim, 54.
Bickford, George, 65.
Bickford, Henry, 43.
Bickford, Henry, 44.
Bickford, James, 44.
Bickford, John, 65.
Bickford, Joseph, 31.
Bickford, Joseph, 63.
Bickford, Joshua, 31.
Bickford, Moses, 42.
Bickford, Paul, 43.
Bickford, Pierce, 58.
Bickford, Pierce, J^r, 58.
Bickford, Samuel, 66.
Bickford, William, 54.
Bickford, W^m, 65.
Bickmore, John, 40.
Bickmore, John, Junr, 40.
Bicknal, Tabitha, 69.
Bicknal, Thos, 16.
Bicknal, William, 70.
Bigelow, George, 36.
Bigelow, James, 36.
Bigelow, James, 39.
Bigford, Aaron, 56.
Bigford, Joshua, 13.
Biggs, Josiah, 23.
Bignal, John, 24.
Bigsby, John, 15.
Bigsby, Solomon, 39.
Bilenton, Ichabod, 41.
Bilenton, Isaac, 41.
Bilenton, Nathaniel, 41.
Biles, Charles, 22.
Bilford, thomas, 69.
Billem, John, 57.
Billing, Oliver, 45.
Billings, Abel, 31.
Billings, Benj^a, 31.
Billings, Benj^a, 61.
Billings, Enoch, 58.
Billings, Epha^m, 61.
Billings, Gershom, 59.
Billings, Jas., Jur^r, 61.
Billings, John, 22.
Billings, John, 31.
Billings, Joseph, 61.
Billings, Jos^h, 59.
Billings, Mary, 14.
Billings, Saml, 61.
Billings, Solomon, 31.
Billings, Timothy, 27.
Billington, John, 28.
Billins, Dan., 61.
Bings, Elijah, 38.
Binney, Joseph, 30.
Bird, Alexander, 49.
Bird, Edward, 34.
Birthright, Peter, 20.
Bisbee, Benj^a, 50.
Bisby, Charles, 13.
Bisby, Charles, 38.
Bisby, Elisha, 13.
Bisby, Elisha, 38.
Bisby, Moses, 13.
Bisby, Ruben, 29.
Bisby, Stephen, 47.
Bishop, Abner, 20.
Bishop, Enos, 17.
Bishop, Esquire, 49.
Bishop, Hudson, 30.
Bishop, James, 20.
Bishop, Luke, 20.
Bishop, Mary, 14.
Bishop, Nathaniel, 51.
Bishop, Squire, 51.
Bishop, William, 34.
Bishop, Zadock, 49.
Biter, Peter, 64.
Bither, Samul, 40.
Black, ——, 71.
Black, Anna, 31.
Black, Boston, 20.
Black, Catbrine, 60.
Black, Daniel, 31.
Black, Edmund, 31.
black, Garsham, 44.
Black, Henry, 28.
Black, Henry, 60.
Black, Henry, jun^r, 29.
Black, Henry, Ju^n, 60.
Black, James, 39.
Black, James, 60.
Black, Joab, 21.
Black, John, 31.
Black, John, jun^r, 31.
Black, Josiah, 64.
Black, Margery, 60.
Black, Moses, 31.
Black, Sally, 31.
Black, Samuel, 31.
Black, Samuel, 32.
Black, Sherbone, 54.

Blackborn, Josiah, 39.
Blackington, Benjamin, 46.
Blackledge, Jonathan, 43.
Blackman, Eleazer, 28.
Blackman, Eliphalet, 52.
Blackmore, Joseph, 12.
Blackston, Lydia, 44.
Blackston, William, 36.
Blackston, William, 36.
Blackstone, Benjamin, 15.
Blackwell, Isreal, 37.
Blackwell, Jabez, 37.
Blackwell, Joshua, 37.
Blackwell, Thomas, 37.
Blackwood, James, 53.
Blagden, Charles, 27.
Blagdon, Paul, 43.
Blagdon, Rollins, 43.
Blair, James, 52.
Blair, James, Junr, 52.
Blair, John, 52.
Blair, Robert, 52.
Blaire, William, 43.
Blaisdel, Danl, 73.
Blaisdel, David, 72.
Blaisdel, Eben^s, 72.
Blaisdel, Elijah, 72.
Blaisdel, Elijah, 73.
Blaisdel, Jacob, 70.
Blaisdel, Jeremiah, 21.
Blaisdel, John, 54.
Blaisdel, Zedediah, 73.
Blak, Thomas, 41.
Blake, Andrew, 30.
Blake, Ashel, 49.
Blake, Benj^a, 17.
Blake, Benj^a, Junr, 17.
Blake, Caleb, 25.
Blake, Daniel, 31.
Blake, David, 68.
Blake, Dearborn, 49.
Blake, Ephraim, 30.
Blake, Ithiel, 17.
Blake, Jacob, 20.
Blake, James, 14.
Blake, James, 20.
Blake, John, 13.
Blake, John, 14.
Blake, John, 14.
Blake, Jno, 17.
Blake, John, 30.
Blake, John, 40.
Blake, John, 49.
Blake, John, Junr, 20.
Blake, Jonathan, 30.
Blake, Josiah, 44.
Blake, Moses, 30.
Blake, Nathl, 17.
Blake, Nathl, 50.
Blake, Nathaniel, 50.
Blake, Paul, 49.
Blake, Phinhas, 49.
Blake, Robert, 49.
Blake, Samuel, 25.
Blake, Solomon, 30.
Blake, Will, 14.
Blanchard, Bezaiah, 21.
Blanchard, Ebenezer, 21.
Blanchard, Edward, 50.
Blanchard, Hozea, 21.
Blanchard, James, 52.
Blanchard, Jno, 17.
Blanchard, John, 22.
Blanchard, John, 46.
Blanchard, Jon^a, 43.
Blanchard, Joshua, 22.
Blanchard, Nathl, 21.
Blanchard, Nathl, 21.
Blanchard, Nathl, 22.
Blanchard, Seth, 22.
Blanchard, Solomon, 35.
Blanchard, Theo^s, 35.
Blasdel, Christopher, 38.
Blasdel, Daniel, 38.
Blasdel, Elijah, 63.
Blasdel, Eliphelet, 63.
Blasdel, Enoch, 63.
Blasdel, Ephrim, 63.
Blasdel, John, 63.
Blasdel, Moses, 70.
Blasdel, Ralf, 67.
Blasdel, Thomas, 63.
Blasdel, William, 40.
Blasdell, Abner, 6.
Blasdell, Ebenezer, 28.
Blasdell, Enoch, 31.
Blasdell, James, 28.
Blasdell, Sanburn, 27.
Blasdell, Moses, 29.
Blasdell, Moses, jun^r, 28.
Blasdell, Susanna, 24.
Blaso, Amos, 65.
Blaso, John, 65.
Blaso, Joseph, 65.
Blastow, Noah, 27.
Bliffen, James, 14.
Bliffen, Job, 14.
Bliffin, Increas, 47.
Bliffin, James, 40.
Bliffin, John, 40.
Bliffin, John, Jur., 40.

Blight, Mehitable, 43.
Blin, Charles, 51.
Blin, David, 42.
Blin, James, 51.
Blin, James, 52.
Blish, John, 48.
Blish, Stacy, 48.
Blodget, Joseph, 42.
Blodget, Nehemiah, 44.
Blodgett, David, 26.
Blodgett, Seth, 30.
Blosom, James, 49.
Blosom, Mathias, 49.
Blossom, Benjamin, 37.
Blunt, Andrew, 71.
Blunt, Ebenezer, 44.
blunt, Eben^r, 48.
Blunt, John, 51.
Blunt, Lydia, 44.
Bly, Ebenezer, 46.
Boah, Alexander, 35.
Bodfish, Nimfis, 37.
Bodge, John, 26.
Bodwell, Jno, 67.
Boggs, John, 49.
Boggs, Mary, 49.
Boggs, Samuel, 49.
Boggs, William, 49.
Bogse, Elisha, 69.
Bohannon, John, 53.
Boldin, Nahum, 44.
Boldon, Jiras, 51.
Bolen, John, 28.
Bolin, William, 38.
Bolter, Benj^a, 24.
Bolter, Nathl, 24.
Bolter, Nathl, Jn^r, 24.
Bolton, Daniel, 38.
Bolton, Elisha, 28.
Bolton, George, 47.
Bolton, James, 47.
Bolton, Rachel, 25.
Bolton, Savage, 39.
Bolton, Thos, 17.
Bolton, W^m, 17.
Bond, David, 32.
Bond, Robert, 65.
Bond, Robert, Junr, 65.
Bond, William, 24.
Boney, hannah (Widdow), 51.
Bonney, Ichabod, 25.
Bonney, Ichabod, Jur^r, 25.
Bonney, Isaac, 13.
Bonney, Isaiah, 25.
Bonney, John, 25.
Boober, Benj^a, 27.
Booby, Andrew, 40.
Booby, Christopher, 34.
Booby, Joseph, 34.
Booby, William, 34.
Boocks, Gorge, 49.
Boody, Ezra, 64.
Boody, Robert, 64.
Booker, Aaron, 72.
Booker, Benj^a, 44.
Booker, David, 34.
Booker, Eben^s, 51.
Booker, Eben^s, Junr, 51.
Booker, Jacob, 60.
Booker, Jacob, 72.
Booker, James, 20.
Booker, James, 35.
Booker, John, 34.
Booker, John, Junr, 34.
Booker, Joseph, 20.
Booker, Joseph, 34.
Booker, Joseph, 37.
Booker, Joseph, 38.
Booker, Josiah, 20.
Booker, Josiah, 51.
Booker, Josiah, Junr, 51.
Booker, Nicholas, 44.
Booker, Willm, 35.
Booker, Zacheus, 34.
Boothby, Benj^a, 71.
Boothby, Brice, 59.
Boothby, David, 64.
Boothby, Ebenezer, 68.
Boothby, Henry, 71.
Boothby, James, 17.
Boothby, John, 65.
Boothby, Jon^a, 64.
Boothby, Joseph, 17.
Boothby, Josiah, 65.
Boothby, Nathl, 17.
Boothby, Rich^d, 17.
Boothby, Saml, 65.
Boothby, Thos, 70.
Boothby (Widow), 64.
Boothby, W^m, 63.
Bootman, Broadstreet, 23.
Bordman, Joseph, 29.
Borman, Jonas, 45.
bornheimer, godfried, 41.
bornheimer, Jacob, 41.
Borton, Willm, 69.
boseman, Godlieb, 41.
Boston, Abraham, 70.
Boston, Elijah, 70.
Boston, Elijah, J^r, 70.
Boston, Gershom, 70.
Boston, James, 70.
Boston John, 70.

Boston, John, 71.
Boston, Jonathan, 59.
Boston, Shipway, 54.
Boston, Shubal, 70.
Boston, Shubal, 70.
Boston, Willm, 70.
Bostone, Thomas, 66.
Bostone, Timothy, 66.
Boswell, William, 58.
Bosworth, Eli, 49.
Bosworth, Jonathan, 36.
Bosworth, Noah, 13.
Botster, Isaac, 22.
Boubey, Gideon, 36.
Bouden, Danl, 71.
Bouden, Isaac, 72.
Bouden, Michal, 69.
Bouden (Widow), 71.
Bounsan, Samuel, 50.
Bourn, Saml, 71.
Bourn (Widow), 71.
Bourne, Isaac, 70.
Bourne, Joseph, 70.
Bowa, George, 13.
Bowden, Abraham, 30.
Bowden, Caleb, 30.
Bowden, David, 71.
Bowden, Ebenezer, 30.
Bowden, Ebenezer, 30.
Bowden, Jacob, 30.
Bowden, Lucy, 30.
Bowden, Paul, 30.
Bowden, Paul, jun^r, 28.
Bowden, Samuel, 29.
Bowden, Samuel, 30.
Bowden, Thomas, 30.
Bowden, William, 30.
Bowdy, Edward, 71.
Bowen, Ezra, 47.
Bowen, Jabez, 52.
Bowen, John, 70.
Bowen, Michael, 32.
Bowen, Nathaniel, 57.
Bowen, Saml, 11.
Bower, Henry, 53.
Bowland, John, 34.
Bowland, John, 37.
Bowles, Ralph H., 52.
bowli, oliver, 48.
bowly, Epher^m, 48.
Bowman, Allihu, 37.
Bowman, Andrew, 53.
Bowman, Benjamin, 37.
Bowman, Harper, 37.
Bowman, Joseph, 37.
Bowman, Nathl, 17.
Bowman, Samuel, 37.
Bowman, Thomas, 47.
Bowman, Zacheus, 37.
Boyce, James, 56.
Boyce, Jotham, 55.
Boyd, Calorn, 51.
Boyd, George, 34.
boyd, John, 48.
Boyd, Joseph, 28.
boyd, Sam., 48.
Boyd, Samuel, 51.
Boyd, Thomas, 34.
Boyd, Thomas, Junr, 34.
boyd, william, 48.
Boyden, Jacob, 53.
Boynton, Amos, 52.
Boynton, Caleb, 53.
Boynton, Caleb, jun^r, 53.
Boynton, Danl, 59.
Boynton, David, 44.
Boynton, Hannah, 43.
Boynton, Isaac, 27.
Boynton, John, 33.
Boynton, John, 43.
Boynton, Jno., 59.
Boynton, John, Junr, 33.
Boynton, Joshua, 43.
Boynton, Joshua, Jn^r, 43.
Boynton, Oliver, 43.
Boynton, Pelatiah, 44.
Boynton, Theophilus, 23.
Boynton, William, 28.
Boynton, William, 43.
Boynton, W^m, 59.
Bracey, Danl, 73.
Bracey, James, 73.
Bracey, Joseph, 53.
Brach, Benjamin, 47.
Brachet, Abraham, 64.
Brachet, Joshua, 64.
Brachet, Reuben, 64.
Brachet, Saml, 64.
bracht, John, 42.
bracht, peter, 42.
Bracket, Abraham, 15.
Bracket, Anthony, 14.
Bracket, Benj^a, 67.
Bracket, Danl, 67.
Bracket, Jacob, 63.
Bracket, James, 14.
Bracket, James, 17.
Bracket, James, 33.
Bracket, James, 57.
Bracket, James, 57.
Bracket, Jeremiah, 21.
Bracket, John, 14.
Bracket, John, 15.

Bracket, John, 57.
Bracket, John, Junr, 57.
Bracket, John S., 14.
Bracket, Joshua, 23.
Bracket, Joshua, 23.
Bracket, Joshua, 67.
Bracket, Joshua, 67.
Bracket, Mary, 57.
Bracket, Miles, 57.
Bracket, Moses, 57.
Bracket, Nathan, 67.
Bracket, Nathaniel, 59.
Bracket, Peter, 14.
Bracket, Samuel, 57.
Bracket, Samuel, 57.
Bracket, Thomas, 14.
Bracket, William, 14.
bracket (widow), 48.
Brackett, Daniel, 24.
Brackett, James, 48.
Brackett, John, 23.
Brackett, Thomas, 23.
Brackley, Willm, 43.
Bradberry, Abigail, 23.
Bradberry, Benjamin, 20.
Bradberry, Jabes, 20.
Bradberry, Moses, 20.
Bradberry, Samuel, 20.
Bradberry, William, 21.
Bradbury, Anna, 43.
Bradbury, Benj^l, 11.
Bradbury, Benj^a, 59.
Bradbury, Cotten, 72.
Bradbury, Daniel, 64.
Bradbury, Danl, 71.
Bradby, Edward, 65.
Bradbury, Elijah, 59.
Bradbury, Jabez, 59.
Bradbury, Jabez, 64.
Bradbury, Jacob, 22.
Bradbury, Jacob, 63.
Bradbury, Jacob, Esqr, 59.
Bradbury, James, 71.
Bradbury, John, 36.
Bradbury, John, 64.
Bradbury, John, 71.
Bradbury, John, 72.
Bradbury, Joseph, 11.
Bradbury, Jos^h, 59.
Bradby, Joseph, 65.
Bradbury, Moses, 11.
Bradbury, Moses, 58.
Bradbury, Samuel, 22.
Bradbury, Saml, 58.
Bradbury, Saml, 59.
Bradbury, Thomas, 22.
Bradbury, Thos, 59.
Bradbury, William, 36.
Bradbury, W^m, 59.
Bradbury, Wyman, 23.
bradex, John, 42.
Bradford, Carpenter, 40.
Bradford, Chandler, 25.
Bradford, Elijah, 26.
Bradford, Ephraim, 20.
Bradford, Ezekiel, 25.
Bradford, Ezekiel, Jur., 25.
Bradford, Isaac, 33.
Bradford, Jesse, 25.
Bradford, Jonathan, 11.
Bradford, Joseph, 44.
Bradford, Joshua, 40.
Bradford, Joshua, Junr, 40.
Bradford, Martin, 21.
Bradford, Peabody, 11.
Bradford, Willm, 25.
Bradford, William, 50.
Bradish, David, 23.
Bradley, Abraham, 60.
Bradley, Bryant, 30.
Bradley, Levi, 30.
Brady, John, 33.
Bragden, Ebenezer, 31.
Bragden, Jeremiah, 31.
Bragden, Jeremiah, jun., 31.
Bragden, John, 31.
Bragden, Joseph, 31.
Bragdon, Aaron, 66.
Bragdon, Amous, 66.
Bragdon, Aurther, 67.
Bragdon, Benj^a, 73.
Bragdon, Danl, 72.
Bragdon, Danl, 72.
Bragdon, Ebenezer, 14.
Bragdon, Gideon, 17.
Bragdon, Hepsibah, 72.
Bragdon, James, 73.
Bragdon, Jeremiah, 36.
Bragdon, Jethro, 73.
Bragdon, Jno, 17.
Bragdon, John, 70.
Bragdon, Jon^a, 17.
Bragdon, Joseph, 72.
Bragdon, Joshua, 71.
Bragdon, Lydia, 72.
Bragdon, Mary, 72.
Bragdon, Matthias, 72.
Bragdon, Saml, 17.
Bragdon, Saml, 72.
Bragdon, Sol^o, 17.
Bragdon, Solomon, 72.
Bragdon, Thom^s, 60.
Bragdon, Thos, 70.

INDEX.

Bragdon, Thos, 72.
Bragdon, Warren, 72.
Bragdon (Widow), 17.
Bragdon (Widow), 72.
Bragdon, Willm, 64.
Bragdon, Zachariah, 73.
Bragg, John, 47.
Bragg, Matthew, 48.
Bragg, Nathl, 39.
Bragg, Robert, 58.
Bragg, Shuball, 47.
Brainard, Church, 44.
Brainard, Ely, 44.
Brainard, Rachal, 47.
Bramhall, Cornelius, 32.
Bramijon, Thomas, 34.
Bran, Ebenezer, 16.
Branan, Thos, 65.
Branard, Natha, 49.
Branard, Reuben, 51.
Branard, Ruth (Widow), 51.
Branard, Timothy, 51.
Branch, Benj., 47.
Branch, Daniel, 50.
Branch, Samuel, 47.
Brand, Isac, 33.
Brandt, Daniel, 50.
Brastow, Billings, 30.
Brastow, Thomas, 30.
Brawn, Charles, 50.
Brawn, George, 56.
Brawn, George, 56.
Brawn, George, 57.
Brawn, Jeremiah, 45.
Brawn, John, 50.
Brawn, John, 56.
Brawn, John, 56.
Brawn, Joseph, 47.
Brawn, Micael, 57.
Brawn, Robert, 70.
Bray, Ebenezer, 11.
Bray, Ezekiel, 22.
Bray, Henry, 11.
Bray, Israel, 11.
Bray, John, 30.
Bray, Nathaniel, 27.
Bray, Nicholas, 11.
Bray, William, 27.
Brazier, Bathsheba, 36.
Brazier, Daniel, 24.
Brazier, Enoch, 23.
Brazier, John, 36.
Brazier, Moses, 23.
Brazier, Sarah, 23.
Bremhall, Sylva, 17.
Brewer, Danl, 18.
Brewer, Edward, 16.
Brewer, Jacob, 62.
Brewer, John, 30.
Brewer, John, 34.
Brewer, John, 53.
Brewer, Joseph, 16.
Brewer, Josiah, 30.
Brewer, Nathl, 37.
Brewster, Joseph, 57.
Brewster, William, 23.
Brewster, Zadok, 46.
briant, david, 48.
briant, lemuel, 48.
Brickett, Moses, 27.
Bride, John, 22.
Bridge, Arthur, 71.
Bridge, Benja, 72.
Bridge, Edmund, 43.
Bridge, John, 43.
Bridges, Daniel, 31.
Bridges, Daniel, junr, 31.
Bridges, Edmond, 72.
Bridges, Edmund, 30.
Bridges, Henry, 30.
Bridges, Isaac, 33.
Bridges, Job, 31.
Bridges, John, 46.
Bridges, John, 53.
Bridges, Jonathan, 31.
Bridges, Joshua, 71.
Bridges, Joshua, 72.
Bridges, Josha Y. Abra, 53.
Bridges, Josiah, 69.
Bridges, Mary, 71.
bridges, Moses, 59.
Bridges, Samuel, 69.
Bridges, Thomas, 67.
Bridgham, William, 20.
Brier, Josiah, 61.
Brier, Moses, 61.
Brier, Nichos, 61.
Brier, Saml, 34.
Brier, Saml, 61.
Brieryhurst, Thomas, 35.
Briez, Robert, 60.
Briges, Paul, 66.
Briggs, Barnabas, 11.
Briggs, Danl, 11.
Briggs, Daniel, 25.
Briggs, Ephraim, 11.
Briggs, John, 13.
Briggs, John, 43.
Briggs, Jotham, 25.
Briggs, Jotham, Jnr, 25.
Briggs, Rufus, 11.
Briggs, Seth, 22.
Brigham, Daniel, 11.

Brigham, John, 11.
Brigham, John, Jr., 11.
Brigham, Joseph, 11.
Brigham, Saml, 24.
Brigham, Willard, 11.
Brigs, abiether, 38.
Brigs, Adin, 44.
Brigs, Samuel, 44.
Brigs, Willm, 39.
Brimhall, Corna, 17.
Brions, Baruch, 47.
Brison John, 36.
Brition, Jonathan, 22.
Broad, Ephraim, 24.
Broad, Thaddeus, 15.
Broadstreet, Andw, 43.
Broadstreet, David, 11.
Broadstreet, Dudley, 23.
Broadstret, John, 38.
Broch, John, 12.
Brock, Frances, 63.
Brock, John, 63.
Brock, Joshua, 70.
Brock, Mary, 11.
Brock, Simeon, 55.
Brock, William, 59.
Brockelbank, Joseph, 11.
Brocks, Gorge, 46.
Brocks, James, 45.
brodman, Charles, 42.
Bron, Jeremiah, 38.
Brookin, Hannah, 43.
Brooks, ——, 12.
Brooks, Charles S., 37.
Brooks, Daniel, 14.
Brooks, George, 30.
Brooks, Isaiah, 59.
Brooks, John, 14.
Brooks, John, 50.
Brooks, Joseph, 62.
Brooks, Joshua, 66.
Brooks, Joshua, 70.
Brooks, Joshua, 70.
Brooks, Josiah, 62.
Brooks, Martin, 28.
Brooks, Peter, 22.
Brooks, Robt, 59.
Brooks, Saml, 59.
Brooks, Saml, 62.
Brooks, Saml, Jur, 62.
Brooks, Silas, 26.
Brooks, Willm, 39.
Brooks, Willm, 47.
Brooks, Wm, 62.
brow, John, 48.
brow, Joseph, 42.
Brown, abner, 38.
Brown, Amos, 12.
Brown, Amos, 64.
Brown, Andrew, 24.
Brown, Andrew, 52.
Brown, Andw, 55.
Brown, Andw, Jr, 55.
Brown, Asaph, 25.
Brown, Asaph, 69.
Brown, Benja, 17.
Brown, Benja, 33.
Brown, Benja, 33.
Brown, Benja, 38.
Brown, Benja, 39.
brown, benjamin, 41.
Brown, Benja, 65.
Brown, Benja, 70.
Brown, Charles, 39.
Brown, Cyrel, 32.
Brown, Daniel, 20.
Brown, Danl, 22.
Brown, Daniel, 38.
Brown, David, 16.
Brown, David, 54.
Brown, Eliphelat, 45.
Brown, Ellison, 19.
Brown, Enock, 39.
Brown, Ephraim, 21.
Brown, Ephrom, 45.
Brown, Ephron, 42.
Brown, Ezekiel, 12.
Brown, Ezekiel, 39.
Brown, Ezekiel, Jur, 39.
Brown, Ezra, 25.
Brown, Francis, 16.
Brown, George, 42.
Brown, Gideon, 46.
Brown, Henry Young, 58.
Brown, Isaac, 45.
Brown, Jacob, 13.
Brown, Jacob, 21.
Brown, Jacob, 44.
Brown, Jacob, 69.
Brown, Jacob, Junr, 21.
Brown, James, 33.
Brown, James, 39.
Brown, James, 40.
Brown, James, 46.
Brown, James, 53.
Brown, Capn James, 61.
Brown, Jeremiah, 51.
Brown, Jeremiah, 69.
Brown, Jess, 54.
Brown, John, 12.
Brown, John, 20.
Brown, John, 21.
Brown, John, 25.

Brown, John, 25.
Brown, John, 26.
Brown, John, 33.
Brown, John, 39.
Brown, John, 42.
Brown, John, 45.
Brown, John, 46.
Brown, John, 51.
Brown, John, 65.
Brown, Hon. Jno Josha, 17.
Brown, Jonathan, 29.
Brown, Jonathan, 34.
Brown, Jonathan, 65.
Brown, Joseph, 21.
Brown, Joseph, 21.
Brown, Joseph, 24.
Brown, Joseph, 37.
Brown, Joseph, 39.
Brown, Joseph, 44.
Brown, Joshua, 24.
Brown, Josiah, 49.
Brown, Luthur, 17.
Brown, Margaret, 33.
Brown, Mary, 11.
Brown, Moses, 24.
Brown, Moses, 38.
Brown, Nathan, 49.
Brown, Paul, 57.
Brown, Peter, 16.
Brown, Philbrook, 52.
Brown, Rebekah, 35.
Brown, Reuben, 16.
Brown, Robt, 65.
Brown, Robert, 65.
Brown, Saml, 14.
Brown, Samuel, 46.
Brown, Samuel, 49.
Brown, Samuel, 67.
Brown, Saml, 70.
Brown, Silas, 25.
Brown, Silas, 69.
Brown, Simeon, 17.
Brown, Solomon, 47.
Brown, Steven, 51.
Brown, Thaddeus, 25.
Brown, Theophilus, 32.
Brown, Thomas, 15.
Brown, Thomas, 32.
Brown, Thos, 61.
Brown, Capn Thos, 61.
Brown, unite, 51.
Brown, William, 24.
Brown, Willm, 33.
Brown, William, 45.
Browner, John, 20.
Browner, William (bachlor), 40.
Brozzel, Ezekiel, 70.
Bruce, Phineas, 53.
Bruer, Curried, 16.
Bruster, Morgin, 40.
Bryant, Abraham, 13.
Bryant, Balden, 20.
Bryant, Baldwin, 11.
Bryant, Bartho, 52.
Bryant, Daniel, 65.
Bryant, David, 65.
Bryant, Davis, 53.
Bryant, Eleazer, 19.
Bryant, Ephraim, 65.
Bryant, Ephraim, Jur., 65.
Bryant, Hezekiah, 25.
Bryant, Jerathwell, 65.
Bryant, Jno, 19.
Bryant, John, 52.
Bryant, John, 64.
Bryant, Jonathan, 23.
Bryant, Joseph, 52.
Bryant, Nathl, 41.
Bryant, Richard, 25.
Bryant, Richard, 69.
Bryant, Samuel, 23.
Bryant, Soloman, 22.
Bryant, Stephen, 25.
Bryant, Stephen, 65.
Bryant, Stephen, Jur, 65.
Bryant, William, 23.
Bryant, William, 52.
Bryer, Elihu, 34.
Bryson, Peter, 43.
Bubler, Thos, 37.
Buck, Abijah, 12.
Buck, Asa, 60.
Buck, Benjamin, 32.
Buck, Daniel, 32.
Buck, Ebenezer, 32.
Buck, John, 12.
Buck, John, Jur, 12.
Buck, Jonathan, 32.
Buck, Jonathan, junr, 32.
Buck, Moses, 12.
Buck, Nathl, 12.
Buck, Peter, 22.
Buckland, Nathan, 49.
Buckley, Daniel, 30.
Buckley, James, 29.
Buckley, John, 31.
Buckling, Barrack, 26.
Buckman, Danl, 11.
Buckman, Danl, 24.
Buckman, Jeremiah, 15.
Buckman, John, 54.
Buckman, Nathan, 15.

Buckman, Samuel, 15.
Buckman, Willm, 22.
Bucknal, Francis, 71.
Bucknal, Jessa, 71.
Bucknal, John, 70.
Bucknal, Rebecca, 70.
Bucknell, John, 60.
Bucknell, John, Jn, 60.
Bucknell, Simeon, 60.
Bucks, Abraham, 13.
Budge, James, 27.
Buffet, John, 54.
Buffum, Caleb, 57.
Buffum, John, 57.
Buffum, Joshua, 57.
Buffum, Joshua, Jr, 57.
Buffum, Saml, 57.
Bugby, William, 53.
Buker, Daniel, 20.
Buker, Dimmick, 35.
Buker, Israel H., 19.
Buker, Job, 34.
Buker, Joseph, 35.
Bukford (Widow), 55.
Bullen, Saml, 39.
Bullin, Joshua, 44.
Bullin, Samuel, 44.
Bullings, Danl, 24.
Bumpas, Zefeniah, 41.
Bumpas, Zefeniah, Ju., 41.
Bumpus, John, 24.
Bumpus, Morris, 24.
Bumpus, Shubael, 24.
Bumpus, Willm, 24.
Bunker, Aaron, 29.
Bunker, Batcheldor, 58.
Bunker, Benja, 29.
Bunker, Elijah, 69.
Bunker, Isaac, 29.
Bunker, James, 45.
Bunker, John, 29.
Bunker, Joseph, 29.
Bunker, Mark, 29.
Bunker, Silas, 31.
Burbank, Asa, 54.
Burbank, Benja, 58.
Burbank, Benja, 60.
Burbank, David, 17.
Burbank, Eleazer, 17.
Burbank, Israel, 58.
Burbank, John, 16.
Burbank, John, 55.
Burbank, John, 59.
Burbank, Silas, 17.
Burdean, Timothy, 56.
Burden, Primes, 51.
Burford, Robert, 51.
Burges, Avery, 47.
Burges, Benja, 47.
Burges, Ephraim, 39.
Burges, John, 32.
Burges, John, junr, 30.
Burges, Jonathan, 47.
Burges, Joshua, 39.
Burges, Peter, 27.
burghart, henry, 41.
burghart, John, 41.
Burgoin, John, 39.
Burk, David, 36.
Burk, Joanna (Wldw), 60.
Burk, Joseph, 60.
Burk, Willm, 35.
Burk, Willm, 46.
Burkmar, Thomas, 27.
burley, Andrew, 68.
Burnal, John, 16.
Burnal, John, Jr., 16.
Burnam, Aaron, 17.
Burnam, Danl, Jr (Wldw), 19.
Burnam, Jeremiah, 11.
Burnel, Jno, Jr., 17.
Burnes, Joseph, 42.
Burnham, Abra, 69.
Burnham, Benjamin, 59.
Burnham, Ephraim, 33.
Burnham, Forrest, 54.
Burnham, Francis, 37.
Burnham, Grace, 54.
Burnham, Isaac, 54.
Burnham, Jacob, 54.
Burnham, Jane, 54.
Burnham, John, 23.
Burnham, Joseph, 58.
Burnham, Paul, 65.
Burnham, Saml, 69.
Burnham, Seth, 54.
Burnham, Solomon, 33.
Burnham, Solomon, 34.
Burnham, Solomon, 34.
burns, cornelius, 42.
Burns, George, 23.
Burns, John, 15.
burns, Joseph, 48.
Burns, William, 29.
Burnum, Danl, 17.
Burnum, Job, 52.
Burnum, Jona, 19.
Burnum, Robt, 17.
Burnum, Samuel, 52.
Burnum, Solo, 17.
Burnum, Thos (Widow), 17.
Burows, Edward, 63.
Burquis, David, 37.

Burquis, Josiah, 37.
Burr, Joseph, 44.
Burr, Perez, 53.
Burrel, Abra, 39.
Burrel, Humphry, 12.
Burril, Belial, 39.
Burril, John, 39.
Burril, John, Jur, 39.
Burril, Nathaniel, 35.
Burril, Zibe, 39.
Burrill, Phillip, 27.
Burrows, Edward, 63.
Burrows, Garrat, 39.
Burrows, Jona, 63.
Burrows, Joseph, 63.
Burten, James, 39.
Burton, Jabiz, 47.
Burton, John, 47.
Burton, Nathan, 39.
Burton, Nathan, 39.
Burton, Thos, 58.
Burton, William, 36.
Bussel, Isaac, 69.
Bussel, James, 73.
Bussel, Jonathan, 69.
Bussell, Isaac, 27.
Bussell, Jacob, 27.
Bussell, Stephen, 28.
Buterfield, Aron, 45.
Butlar, Willm, 38.
Butlar, Willm, Jr, 38.
Butler, Abraham, 36.
Butler, Benjamin, 44.
Butler, Christopher, 47.
Butler, George, 31.
Butler, Ichabod, 55.
Butler, James, 20.
Butler, James, 30.
Butler, Jeremh, 47.
Butler, John, 17.
Butler, John, 38.
Butler, John, 47.
Butler, John, 47.
Butler, John, 69.
Butler, Moses, 31.
Butler, Moses, 57.
Butler, Moses, junr, 31.
Butler, Nathaniel, 31.
Butler, Nehemiah, 56.
Butler, Obadiah, 47.
Butler, Peter, 31.
Butler, Phinehas, 46.
Butler, Phinehas, 47.
Butler, Phinius, 47.
Butler, Saml, 55.
Butler, Saml, Junr, 55.
Butler, Stephen, 54.
Butler, Thomas, 63.
Butlor, Nathaniel, 66.
Butlor, Thomas, 66.
Butterfield, Ephrim, 47.
Butterfield, Ephrom, 44.
Butterfield, Jesse, 44.
Butterfield, Jonas, 44.
Butterfield, Joseph, 24.
Butterfield, Mathew, 47.
Butterfield, Reuben, 44.
Butterfield, Samuel, 44.
Butterfield, Samuel, 47.
Butterfield, Samuel, Jur, 44.
Butters, Abel, 68.
Butts, Samuel, 23.
Buxton, Benja, 21.
Buxton, James, 15.
Buxton, Samuel, 21.
Buxton, William, 15.
Buxton, William, 15.
Buxton, Willm, 21.
Buzell, Ebenezer, 69.
Buzzel, Isaac, 71.
Buzzel, Noah, 11.
Byard, Robert, 31.
Byram, David, 16.
Byram, Ebenezer, 43.
Byram, Jona, 16.
Byram, Melcher, 16.
Byram, Theo, 22.
Bysom, Oliver, 21.

cacklin (widow), 48.
Caheel, Thomas, 45.
Cain, John, 32.
Cain, Joshua, 70.
Cain, Samuel, 31.
Calaghan, Wm., 54.
Calahan, Rebecca, 44.
Calderwood, James, 32.
Calderwood, John, 32.
Calderwood, John, jun., 32.
Calderwood, Samuel, 32.
calderwood, thomas, 48.
Caldwell, Ganham, 39.
Calef, Allen, 28.
Calef, Joseph, 30.
Calif, Samuel, 13.
Call, Benja, 38.
Call, Deliverance, 44.
Call, James, 43.
Call, Obadiah, 43.
Call, Philip, 44.
Call, Stephen, 44.
Calley, Aaron, 38.
Calley, Samuel, 56.

INDEX.

Calliborn, John, 46.
calomer, sickl (long Island), 49.
Cambol, James, 32.
Camel, Alexander, 11.
Camel, Phillp, 24.
Cammat, Samuel, 69.
Cammet, Dudley, 22.
Cammet, Paul, 24.
Cammet, Thomas, 23.
Campbel, Dan¹, 38.
Campbel, David, 35.
Campbel, James, 41.
Campbel, John, 33.
Campbel, John, 34.
Campbel, John, 37.
Campbel, Thoˢ, 41.
Campbel, Thoˢ, 41.
Campbel, William, 34.
Campbel, Wᵐ, 46.
Campbell, Alex³, 53.
Campbell, Andrew, 20.
Campbell, Daniel, 27.
Campbell, Elisabeth, 25.
Campbell, James, 54.
Campbell, John, 27.
Campbell, Thomas, 30.
Campbell, Thomas, junʳ, 30.
Campbell, William, 23.
Campernel, John, 68.
Campernel, Wᵐ, 68.
Campernel, Wᵐ, 68.
Canada, Robert, 39.
Canady, Dennis, 43.
Canary, Dennis, 36.
Candish, James, 26.
Candish, John, 26.
Candish, Joseph, 26.
Cane, ——, 50.
Cane, James, 13.
Cane, John, 13.
Cane, John, 61.
Cane, Joshua, Juʳ, 24.
Cane, Lemuel, 13.
Cane, Mesheck, 13.
Canfield, Ebenezer, 28.
Cannaday, William, 44.
Cannon, James, 49.
Cannon, Nathan, 37.
Cannon, Partrick, 49.
Caols, John, 49.
Capen, James, 43.
Capers, John, 27.
Capon, Theoˢ, 33.
Capon, Thomas, 64.
Caravan, James, 49.
Carby, James, 36.
Card, Dan¹, 52.
Card, John, 51.
Card, Joseph, 31.
Card, Joseph, 71.
Card, Stephen, 31.
Card, Thoˢ, 52.
Cargill, Abanathar, 41.
Cargill, David, 41.
Cargill, James, 41.
Carl, Ebenʳ, 17.
Carl, Ebenʳ, 17.
Carl, Joseph, 66.
Carl, Joshua, 64.
Carl, Sam¹, 17.
Carle, Anna (Widʷ), 69.
Carle, Elizabeth (Widʷ), 69.
Carle, John, 69.
Carless, Willᵐ, 16.
Carlile, James, 69.
Carlisle, Alexander, 72.
Carlisle, Dan¹, 71.
Carlisle, James, 58.
Carlisle, John, 72.
Carlisle, Joseph, 34.
Carll, Benjamin, 65.
Carll, Elias, 65.
Carll, John, 65.
Carll, Nathaniel, 15.
Carll, Robert, 65.
Carll, Wᵐ, 65.
Carlo, John, 53.
Carlow, Jacob, 43.
Carlow, Martin, 33.
Carlton, David, 31.
Carlton, David, 40.
Carlton, Edward, 26.
Carlton, Edward, 60.
Carlton, Jane, 52.
Carlton, John, 28.
Carlton, Jonathan, 27.
Carlton, Joseph, 44.
Carlton, Moses, 26.
Carlton, Moses, 41.
Carlton, Moses, 44.
Carlton, Stephen, 34.
Carlton, Woodman, 60.
Carman, Francis, 22.
Carman, Levi, 27.
Carnay, Thomas, 36.
Carney, James, 36.
Carpenter, William, 27.
Carpinder, John, 69.
Carpinder, Nathaniel, 69.
Carpinder, Nocholas, 69.
Carpinder, thomas, 69.
Carr, Benjᵃ, 32.
Carr, Benjᵃ, 51.

Carr, James, 39.
Carr, John B., 32.
Carr, Joseph, 20.
Carr, Josiah, 33.
Carr, Silvanus, 32.
Carr, William, 28.
Carsley, Jnᵒ, 17.
Carsley, Jnᵒ, Jʳ, 17.
Carson, Adam, 35.
Carter, Allen, 31.
Carter, Benjᵃ, 17.
Carter, Benjᵃ, Jr., 17.
Carter, Dan¹, 16.
Carter, Dan¹, Junʳ, 16.
Carter, Edward, 28.
carter, ephram (mescongus Island), 48.
Carter, Ezra, 60.
Carter, Henry, 26.
Carter, Hubbard, 60.
Carter, James, 26.
Carter, James, 31.
Carter, James, 53.
Carter, James, jun., 26.
Carter, John, 31.
Carter, John, junʳ, 31.
Carter, Joseph, 50.
Carter, Nathaniel, 50.
Carter, Padius, 47.
Carter, Richᵈ, 17.
Carter, Sam¹, 38.
Carter, Samuel, 43.
Carter, Sarah, 62.
Cartton, Samuel, 33.
Carvar, Reuben, 16.
Carvel, William, 40.
Carver, Amos, 16.
Carver, Benjᵃ, 29.
Carver, Caleb, 32.
Carver, Calvan, 16.
Carver, Henry, 40.
Carver, Israel, 32.
Carver, Seth, 16.
Carver, Stephen, 32.
Carver, Thadeus, 32.
Carwill, John, 51.
Cary, Dan¹, 24.
Cary, Edward, 52.
Cary, James, 12.
Cary, Richard, 27.
Cary, Samuel, 27.
Case, Isaac, 46.
Casey, William, 27.
Cash, John, 24.
Cash, Nathaniel, 13.
Cash, Samuel, 13.
Cass, Moses, 39.
Casten, Thomas, 33.
Castle, Ephrom, 35.
Castle, Job, 11.
Castle, Simeon, 11.
Castle, Squire, 11.
Castle, Wilᵐ, 11.
Castle, William, 35.
Cater, lamuel, 51.
Cates, Andrew, 17.
Cates, Benjᵃ, 17.
Cates, Ebenʳ, 17.
Cates, Edward, 54.
Cates, Joseph, 17.
Cates, Joseph, 22.
Cates, Robert, 53.
Cates, Samuel, 52.
Catland, John, 41.
Cato, Colten, 60.
Cattien, daniel, 48.
Caverno, Charles, 17.
Cawd, John, 72.
Cawd, Joseph, 72.
Caxey, Elizabeth, 58.
Chace, Benjamin, 50.
Chace, Ephraim, 52.
Chace, Ezekiel, 36.
Chace, Isaac, 34.
Chace, James, 50.
Chace, Job, 47.
Chace, John, 47.
Chace, Mathew, 37.
Chace, Rogers, 36.
Chace, Stephen, 47.
Chace, Varnum, 39.
Chace, William, 52.
Chadborn, James, 70.
Chadborn, Joseph, 64.
Chadboun, Humpʳ, Esqʳ, 57.
ChadBourn, Ebenezer, 66.
ChadBourn, James, 66.
Chadbourn, John, 60.
Chadbourn, Joshua, 60.
Chadbourn, Levi, 60.
Chadbourn, Sam¹, 69.
Chadbourn, Wᵐ, 60.
Chadbourn, Wᵐ, 60.
Chadbourne, Benjᵃ, 55.
Chadbourne, Hon. Benjᵃ, 55.
Chadbourne, Frances, 57.
Chadbourne, Humpʸ, 55.
Chadbourne, Humpʸ, 57.
Chadbourne, Jonᵃ C., 55.
Chadbourne, Joseph, 56.
Chadbourne, Mary, 55.
Chadbourne, Sarah, 56.
Chadbourne, Seamon, 56.

Chadbourne, Thomas, 55.
Chadburn, James, 17.
Chadburn, Paul, 59.
Chadburn, Silas, 17.
Chadburn, Simeon, 59.
Chadwick, Benjᵃ, 17.
Chadwick, Ichᵈ, 40.
Chadwick, James, 40.
Chadwick, Job, 40.
Chadwick, John, 58.
Chadwick, Judah, 40.
Chadwick, Levi, 37.
Chadwick, Lot, 40.
Chadwick, William, 15.
Chadwick, Wᵐ, 55.
Chalmor, William, 50.
Chaloner, William, 52.
Chamberlain, Aaron, 23.
Chamberlain, Benjᵃ, 17.
Chamberlain, Ephraim, 25.
Chamberlain, Ephraim, 69.
Chamberlain, Jeremiah, 46.
Chamberlain, John, 25.
Chamberlain, John, 46.
Chamberlain, John, 65.
Chamberlain, Moses, 36.
Chamberlain, Nath¹, 25.
Chamberlain, Nath¹, 69.
Chamberlain, Stephen, 46.
Chamberlain, Thomas, 65.
Chamberlain, Wᵐ, 65.
Chamberlin, Amos, 63.
Chamberlin, Nat., 63.
Chamberlin, Sam¹, 39.
Chamberlin, Wᵐ, 63.
Chambers, Benjamin, 36.
Chambers, James, 61.
Chamblen, William, 38.
Champen, James, 65.
Chancy, Charles, Esqʳ, 61.
Chandler, Dan'l, 60.
Chandler, David, 22.
Chandler, David, 22.
Chandler, Edmond, 16.
Chandler, Edmund, 12.
Chandler, Elisabeth, 22.
Chandler. Ichabod, 11.
Chandler, Jacob, 51.
Chandler, Joab, 51.
Chandler, John, 11.
Chandler, John, 49.
Chandler, John, 51.
Chandler, John, 65.
Chandler, John, Jr., 11.
Chandler, John, jur., 51.
Chandler, Jonᵃ, 21.
Chandler, Joseph, 11.
Chandler, Joseph, 60.
Chandler, Joshua, 21.
Chandler, Moses, 44.
Chandler, Moses, 51.
Chandler, Nath¹, 11.
Chandler, Peleg, 20.
Chandler, Philip, 20.
Chandler, Reuben, 11.
Chandler, Rufus, 22.
Chandler, Rufus, 22.
Chandler, Samuel, 44.
Chaney, Joseph, 66.
Chanlor, Thoˢ, 62.
Chaples, Richard, 40.
Chaplin. John, 11.
chapman, abraham, 42.
chapman, benjamin, 35.
chapman, Isral, 35.
chapman, John, 35.
Chapman, John, 43.
Chapman, John, Jʳ, 43.
Chapman, Jonathan, 35.
chapman, Joseph, 35.
Chapman, Mary, 16.
chapman, nathan, 35.
chapman, nathaniel, 35.
Chapman, Nathaniel, 48.
Chapman, Nathaniel, 52.
Chapman, Shadrack, 14.
chapman, thomas, 35.
chapman (widow), 42.
Chapman, William, 46.
Charles, Abner, 60.
Charles, John, 60.
Charles, Sam¹, 60.
Chase, Amos, 64.
Chase, Amos, Juʳ, 65.
Chase, Dr. Amos, 65.
Chase, Benjᵃ, 12.
Chase, Charles, 41.
Chase, Daniel, 65.
Chase, Ebenʳ, 47.
Chase, Edmund, 65.
Chase, Enoch, 55.
Chase, Ezekiel, 39.
Chase, Francis, 41.
Chase, Humphry, 22.
Chase, Isaac, 25.
Chase, James, 12.
Chase, James, 37.
Chase, John, 12.
Chase, John, 26.
Chase, John, 37.
Chase, John, 57.
Chase, John, 65.
Chase, Joseph, 13.

Chase, Joseph, 24.
Chase, Josiah, 71.
Chase, Judah, 12.
Chase, Lydia, 65.
Chase, Moses, 65.
Chase, Nath¹, 13.
Chase, Sam¹, 65.
Chase, Thomas, 57.
Chase, Thoˢ, 61.
Chase, William, 15.
Chase, Willᵐ, 22.
Chatman, Abraᵐ, 55.
Chatman, Eliphaz, 68.
Chatman, Isaac, 66.
Chatman, Mary, 61.
Chatman, Samˡ, 44.
Chatman, Wilbon, 55.
Chauncey, Joseph, 70.
Chauncey, Reuben, 70.
Cheaney, Elifalet, 66.
Check, Nathan, 15.
Check, Peeter, 15.
Cheek, Aaron, 57.
Cheek, Abraᵐ, 68.
Cheek, Elizabeth, 57.
Cheek, Isaac, 56.
Cheek, Isaac, 60.
Cheek, John, 57.
Cheek, John, 57.
Cheek, Joseph, 57.
Cheek, Ricᵈ, 57.
Cheek, Thomas, 57.
Chelles, Mary, 68.
Chelles, Wᵐ, 68.
Chellis, Joseph, 24.
Cheney, Ralph, 43.
Chenneston, Benjamen, 33.
Chesham, John, 35.
Chesley, David, 22.
Chesley, Joseph, 25.
Cheswell, Peletiah, 72.
Chick, Amos, 62.
Chick, Ephraim, 64.
Chick, Joshua, 71.
Chick, Moses, 71.
Chick, Nathan, 64.
Chick, Thoˢ, 71.
Chickering, Zechariah, 11.
child, thomas, 48.
Childs, Amos, 47.
Childs, Daniel, 25.
Childs, James, 39.
Childs, John, 20.
Childs, Mary, 23.
Childs, Rebecca, 23.
Chipar, John, 29.
Chipman, Benjᵃ, 11.
Chipman, Daniel, 11.
Chipman, Wilᵐ, 11.
Chisom, Hannah, 61.
Choat, Aaron, Juner, 33.
Choat, Abraham, 33.
Choat, Abraham, 33.
Choat, Ammi, 58.
Choat, frances, 33.
Choshman, Andrew, 40.
Chovey, John, 43.
Christopher, Joseph, 43.
Chubb, Jabez, 11.
Chubbuck, James, 53.
Church, Charles, 45.
Church, Ebenezer, 39.
Church, John, 39.
Church, Nathan, 11.
church, nathaniel, 48.
Church, Sam¹, 39.
Churchhill, John, 36.
Churchhill, Joseph, 36.
Churchill, Jabez, 24.
Churchill, Joseph, 24.
Churchill, Josiah, 24.
Churchill, Susanna, 44.
Churchill, Wᵐ, 24.
Churchwell, John, 45.
Churchwell, Seth, 24.
Chute, John, 26.
Chute, Josiah, 26.
Chute, Thomas, 26.
chwartz, Jacob, 41.
Cilley, William, 51.
Clambo, Willᵐ, 34.
Clancey, David, 43.
Clap, Asa, 23.
Clap, Enos, 41.
clarck, john, 35.
Clark, Aaron, 69.
Clark, Abraham, 26.
Clark, Adam, 71.
Clark, Alexander, 26.
Clark, Anna, 71.
Clark, Archibald, 12.
Clark, Benjᵃ, 31.
Clark, Benjamᵐ, 68.
Clark, Mr. Benjᵃ, 60.
Clark, Burnham, 42.
Clark, Charles, 38.
Clark, Charles, 56.
Clark, Dan¹, 71.
Clark, David, 11.
Clark, David, 12.
Clark, David, 63.
Clark, Ebenʳ, 41.
Clark, Ebenʳ, 64.

Clark, Ebenˢ, 71.
Clark, Edward, 52.
Clark, Eleazer, 56.
Clark, Eleazer, 71.
Clark, Elisabeth, 23.
Clark, Elisha, 26.
Clark, Elisha, 31.
Clark, Elisha, 33.
Clark, Elisha, jun., 48.
clark, Eliza, 48.
Clark, Ephraim, 64.
Clark, Gershom, 25.
Clark, Hanson, 67.
Clark, Henry, 53.
Clark, Ichabod, 11.
Clark, Ichabod, 26.
Clark, Isaac, 26.
Clark, Isaac, 28.
Clark, Isaac, 39.
Clark, Isaac, 42.
Clark, Jacob, 17.
Clark, James, 28.
Clark, James, 32.
Clark, James, 41.
Clark, James, 43.
Clark, James, 43.
Clark, James, 53.
Clark, James, 58.
Clark, James, 63.
Clark, James, 68.
Clark, James, Juʳ, 44.
Clark, Jerˢ, 71.
Clark, John, 20.
Clark, John, 28.
Clark, John, 33.
Clark, John, 44.
Clark, John, 56.
Clark, John, 56.
Clark, John, 69.
Clark, Jonas, 39.
Clark, Jonas L., 70.
Clark, Jonathan, 28.
Clark, Jonathan, 28.
Clark, Jonathan, 47.
Clark, Jonˢ, 63.
Clark, Jonathan, 68.
Clark, Jonᵃ Denna, 56.
Clark, Joseph, 27.
Clark, Joseph, 44.
clark, joseph, 48.
Clark, Joseph, 53.
Clark, Joseph, 66.
Clark, Josiah, 20.
Clark, Josiah, 63.
Clark, Knowles, 71.
Clark, Lemuel, 28.
Clark, Lydia, 71.
Clark, Morris, 15.
Clark, Nathan, 12.
Clark, Nathan, 43.
Clark, Nathan, 71.
Clark, Nathaniel, 28.
Clark, Nathan¹, 53.
Clark, Nathan¹, 62.
Clark, Nathan¹, Junʳ, 62.
Clark, Parker, 52.
Clark, Penewal, 63.
Clark, Peter, 39.
Clark, Richard, 31.
Clark, Robert, 13.
Clark, Sam, 48.
Clark, Sarah, 71.
Clark, Sherebah, 50.
Clark, Solomon, 71.
Clark, Stephen, 31.
Clark, Stephen, 56.
Clark, Thoˢ, 57.
Clark, Timothy, 42.
Clark, Uriah, 38.
Clark (Widow), 53.
Clark (Widow), 71.
Clark, William, 33.
Clark, William, 43.
Clark, William, 43.
Clark, William, 53.
Clark, William, 56.
Clark, Wᵐ, 57.
Clarke, Daniel, 59.
Clarke, Ephraim, 13.
Clarke, John, 59.
Clarke, John, junʳ, 59.
Clarke, thomas, 59.
Clarke, William, 59.
Clarkes, John R., 13.
Clary, Allen, 38.
Clary, Daniel, 28.
Clary, Jane, 37.
Claus, george, 42.
Clay, Benjᵃ, 64.
Clay, Daniel, 38.
Clay, Dan¹, 59.
Clay, John, 12.
Clay, Jonathan, 26.
Clay, Richᵈ, 59.
Clayton, John, 44.
Cleark, David, 67.
Cleaver, Willᵐ, 42.
Cleaves, Benjᵃ, 55.
Cleaves, Eaton, 55.
Cleaves, Ebenezer, 21.
Cleaves, Ebenezer, 21.
Cleaves, Ebenezer, 64.

INDEX.

Cleaves, Edmund, 21.
Cleaves, Israel, 64.
Cleaves, James, 55.
Cleaves, John, 55.
Cleaves, John, 65.
Cleaves, John, Jr, 55.
Cleaves, Jonathan, 65.
Cleaves, Robert, 46.
Cleaves, Robert, 65.
Cleaves, Stephen, 55.
Cleavland, Jonathan, 45.
Cleavland, Joseph, 36.
Cleavland, Joseph, 45.
Cleavland, Timothy, 36.
Clefford, Benjamin, 11.
Clefford, Benj^a, 33.
Clefford, Isaac, 37.
Clefford, Joseph, 52.
Clefford, William, 36.
Clements, Aaron, 63.
Clements, Hannah, 57.
Clements, James, 32.
Clements, John, 60.
Clements, Samuel, 57.
Clemmons, Joseph, 24.
Clemmons, Ruth, 33.
Clemons, ——, 17.
Clemons, Jeremiah, 17.
Clemons, Jonathan, 66.
Clerk, Edmond, 39.
Clerk, Eph^{rm}, 40.
clerk, John, 35.
Clerk, John, 42.
Clerk, Jonathan, 39.
Clerk, Joseph, 47.
Clerk, Noah, 35.
Clerk, Solomon, 36.
Clerk, William, 53.
Clever, Harrison, 20.
Clifford, David, 33.
Clifford, Jacob, 28.
Clifford, John, 28.
Clifford, Nathaniel, 28.
Cliford, Benjn, 45.
Clinton, ——, 61.
Closson, John, 27.
Closson, Josiah, 27.
Clough, Amos, 21.
Clough, Benj^a, 26.
Clough, Benjamin, 44.
Clough, Benjn, 49.
Clough, Daniel, 40.
Clough, Jabes, 51.
Clough, Joel, 54.
Clough, John, 23.
Clough, John, 51.
Clough, Joseph, 54.
Clough, Josiah, 11.
Clough, Noah, 54.
Clough, Saml, 14.
Clough, Stephen, 43.
Clough, Thos, 64.
Cloutman, Tim^y, 17.
Cluff, John, 65.
Cluff, Samuel, 67.
Cluley, Isaac, 28.
Cluley, Isaac, 30.
Cluston, Alexander, 23.
Coak, John, 69.
Coal, Dorithy, 62.
Coal, Job, 40.
Coal, John, 50.
Coal, John, 51.
Coal, John, 62.
Coal, Samuel, 40.
Coates, Charles, 31.
Cobb, Ablah, 35.
Cobb, Andrew, 17.
Cobb, And^w, 64.
Cobb, Benjamin, 15.
Cobb, Chitman, 14.
Cobb, Chitman, 17.
Cobb, Daniel, 22.
Cobb, David, 38.
Cobb, Ebenezer, 23.
Cobb, Elisha, 16.
Cobb, Elisha, Jr, 17.
Cobb, Enoch, 23.
Cobb, Ephraim, 15.
Cobb, Ezekiel, 28.
Cobb, Isaac, 25.
Cobb, James, 14.
Cobb, Jedediah, 17.
Cobb, Jedediah, 20.
Cobb, Jonathan, 14.
Cobb, Joseph, 13.
Cobb, Joseph, 14.
Cobb, Joseph, 20.
Cobb, Josiah, 40.
Cobb, Matthew, 58.
Cobb, Miles, 49.
Cobb, Nicholas, 64.
Cobb, Olive, 15.
Cobb, Peeter, 14.
Cobb, Peeter, 14.
Cobb, Pelatiah, 24.
Cobb, Silvenus, 21.
Cobb, Smith, 23.
Cobb, Thos, 16.
Cobb, Thomas, 26.
Cobb, William, 22.
Cobbet, Nat, 65.

Cobby, John, 15.
Cobham, Sarah, 23.
Cobin, Jesse, 38.
Cobin, Reuben, 38.
Cobin, William, 38.
Coburn, Jonas, 12.
Coburns, Thos, 12.
Cocah, David, 44.
Cockram, James, 53.
Cochran, Adam, 41.
Cochran, John, 26.
Cochran, John, 41.
Cochran, Robert, 41.
Codman, Richard, 23.
Codman, Richard, 23.
Coffee, Edward, 37.
Coffen, Eliphalet, 67.
Coffen, Nat, 67.
Coffen, Nathan, 67.
Coffin, Barnabas, 54.
Coffin, Benj^a, 43.
Coffin, Benjamin, 68.
Coffin, Benj^a, Jn^r, 43.
Coffin, Daniel, 68.
Coffin, Daniel, jun^r, 68.
Coffin, Elihu, 58.
Coffin, Elisha, 54.
Coffin, Isaac, 17.
Coffin, James, 65.
Coffin, Matthew, 54.
Coffin, Napthalim, 68.
Coffin, Nathaniel, 23.
Coffin, Rev^d, Paul, 59.
Coffin, Richard, 54.
Coffin, Samuel, 54.
Coffin, Stephen, 16.
Coffin, Uriah, 47.
Coffin (Widow), 35.
Coffran, John, 26.
Coggins, Hezekiah, 32.
Coggins, Josiah, 32.
Coggins, Samuel, 26.
Coggins, Thomas, 26.
Cogswell, Sarah, 30.
Cohon, John, 16.
Cohoon, Daniel, 23.
Coit, Hannah, 65.
Colbath, lamuel, 49.
Colbee, thomas, 45.
Colbey, Abel, 35.
Colbey, Benjamin, 46.
Colbey, Henry, 37.
Colbey, James, 37.
Colbey, Nehemiah, 37.
Colbey, Saml, 37.
Colburn, Benjamin, 42.
Colburn, Ebenezer, 69.
Colburn, Jeremiah, 27.
Colburn, Margaret, 39.
Colburn, Reuben, 43.
Colburn, William, 27.
Colby, Ambrose, 27.
Colby, Asa, 60.
Colby, Betty, 43.
Colby, Joseph, 27.
Colby, Joseph, jun^r, 27.
Colby, Saml, 58.
Colby, Samuel, 27.
Colby, Silvester, 37.
Colby, Susanna, 43.
Colcord, Phineas, 68.
Cole, Abijah, 29.
Cole, Angnas, 62.
Cole, Arzael, 60.
Cole, Benjamin, 27.
Cole, Benjn, 38.
Cole, Benj^a, 58.
Cole, Benjamin, jun^r, 27.
Cole, Danl, 58.
Cole, Ebenezer, 54.
Cole, Ebenezer, Jr., 54.
Cole, Eleazer, 22.
Cole, Eli, 60.
Cole, Elizabeth, 58.
Cole, Ezra, 58.
Cole, Henery, 60.
Cole, Henry, 30.
Cole, Icabod, 62.
Cole, Isaack, 42.
cole, Jabish, 42.
Cole, James, 71.
Cole, John, 22.
Cole, John, 24.
Cole, Jno, 58.
Cole, John, 64.
Cole, John, 66.
Cole, John, 71.
Cole, Jno, Junr, 59.
Cole, Joseph, 32.
cole, Josephus, 42.
Cole, Nathl, 59.
Cole, Obediah, 60.
Cole, Pheobe, 28.
Cole, Remick, 69.
Cole, Robert, 58.
Cole, Robt, 60.
Cole, Samuel, 58.
Cole, Saml, 39.
Cole, Thomas, 31.
Cole, Tobias, 66.
Cole, W^m, 59.
Cole, Willm, 65.
Colebroth, Danl, 17.
Colebroth, George, 17.

Colebroth, Jo^s, 17.
Colebroth, Saml, 17.
Coleords, Jesse, 66.
coles, ables, 42.
Coley, James, 19.
Coley, Noah, 23.
colimer, Isaac, 48.
colimer, peter, 48.
Colkut, Job, 65.
Colkut, Josiah, 65.
Coll, John, 46.
Collamore, Elisha, 26.
Collamore, Isaac, 26.
Collamore, Joseph, 28.
Collamore, Joshua, 40.
Collamore, Joshua, jun^r, 26.
Collard, Isaac, 40.
Colley, John, 15.
Colley, William, 15.
Collier, James, 50.
Collier, John, 50.
Collins, Ebenezer, 20.
Collins, Jon^a, 17.
Collins, Lemuel, 43.
Collins, Philemon, 20.
Collins, Richard, 54.
Collins, Saml, 14.
Collins, Syrenus, 29.
Collson, Ebenezer, 32.
Collson, Hateevil, 28.
Collson, James, 28.
Collson, Josiah, 32.
Colman, Jonathan, 43.
Colman, Saml, 39.
Colson, David, 33.
Colyard, Charles, 37.
Colyer, Joshua, 2.
Combs, Hezekiah, 35.
Combs, John, 34.
Combs, Jonathan, 50.
Combs, Leonard, 34.
Coming, Samuel, 38.
Comings, John, 51.
Conant, Bartholomew, 15.
Conant, Joseph, 15.
Conant, Joshua, 23.
Conant, Samuel, 15.
Conant, William, 15.
Conden, George, 40.
Conden, Samuel, 40.
Condon, John, 30.
Condy, Thos H., 70.
Cone, Samuel, 39.
Coney, Danl, 39.
Coney, Saml, 39.
Conklin, Samuel, 26.
connely, John, 48.
Conner, Charles, 40.
Conners, Patrick, 52.
Connor, Alice, 30.
Conry, Thomas, 27.
Constable, James, 23.
Conway, Francis, 38.
Cook, Abra^m, 63.
Cook, Anna, 42.
Cook, Betty, 31.
Cook, Croell, 27.
Cook, Daniel, 25.
Cook, Daniel, 63.
Cook, Daniel, 63.
Cook, Daniel, 67.
Cook, Danl, 73.
Cook, Elijah, 40.
Cook, Elisabeth, 33.
Cook, Ephraim, 30.
Cook, Francis, 40.
Cook, Hannah, 40.
Cook, Isaiah, 33.
Cook, James, 40.
Cook, John, 15.
Cook, John, 23.
Cook, John, 42.
Cook, John, 46.
Cook, John, 53.
Cook, Jno, 67.
Cook, Joseph, 45.
Cook, Mehitable, 41.
Cook, Orchard, 40.
Cook, Paul, 26.
Cook, Samuel, 45.
Cook, Stephen, 12.
Cook, Thomas, 50.
Cooker, Isaiah, 33.
Cookson, Elizabeth, 25.
Cookson, Reuben, 24.
Cool, John, 50.
Coolbroth, Jno, 50.
Coolbroth, Peter, 52.
Cooley, Richard, 19.
Coolidge, Caleb, 54.
Coolidge, Silas, 31.
Coolier, Francis, 28.
Coolier, James, 28.
Coolyard, Mary, 38.
Coombes, Joseph, 46.
Coombes, Joshua, 36.
Coombs, Anthony, 29.
Coombs, Anthony, 32.
Coombs, Anthony, Junr, 29.
Coombs, Benjn, 11.
Coombs, Edward, 53.
Coombs, Fields, 29.
Coombs, Hosea, 29.

Coombs, Peter, 29.
Coombs, Robert, 29.
Cooms, Anthony, 20.
Cooms, Asa, 12.
Cooms, Caleb, 12.
Cooms, George, 33.
Cooms, John, 20.
Cooms, Joseph, 12.
Cooms, Joseph, 20.
Cooms, Joshua, 33.
Cooms, Nathan, 12.
Cooms, Peter, 12.
Cooms, Saml C., 35.
Cooms, Stephen, 33.
Cooms, Stephen, 33.
Cooms, Thomas, 12.
Cooms, Willm, 20.
Cooper, Allex^r, 56.
Cooper, Boice, 49.
Cooper, James, 32.
Cooper, James, 41.
Cooper, James, jun., 32.
Cooper, Jesse, 41.
Cooper, John, 53.
Cooper, Leonard, 42.
Cooper, Moses, 39.
Cooper, Philip, 34.
Cooper, Thomas, 32.
Cooper, William, 32.
Coopper, Danl, 56.
Coopper, John, 56.
Cootman, Stephen, 23.
Copeland, Abraham, 50.
Copeland, Abraham, Junr, 50.
Copeland, Joseph, 49.
Copeland, Moses, 49.
Copeland, Nathaniel, 49.
Copeland, Rufus, 49.
Copelin, Joseph, 25.
Copland, Abraham, 37.
Copps, Jon^a, 67.
Copps, Peter, 67.
Copps, Ruben H., 63.
Copps, Samuel, 63.
Corbet, Peter, 44.
Cordwell, John, 24.
Cordwell, Willm, 11.
Corless, Ebenezer, 21.
Cornell, John, 41.
Cornish, John, 12.
Cornish, Sipperon, 35.
Cornthwait, Thomas, 54.
Correy, James, 23.
Corson, Aaron, 63.
Corson, Daniel, 63.
Corson, Isaac, 67.
Corson, John, 54.
Corson, Lemuel, 67.
Corson, Levi, 63.
Corson, Mary, 63.
Corson, Moses, 67.
Corson, Samuel, 54.
Corson, Samuel, Jr, 54.
Corsson, Ichabod, 29.
Corsson, John, 30.
Corsson, John, 31.
Corsson, Nathaniel, 31.
Corteloe, John, 44.
Corthall, Peletiah, 26.
Cortis, Seth, 48.
Cortle, Stephen, 69.
Coshman, Jon^m, 38.
Costigen, Lawrance, 39.
Costin, Daniel, 30.
Cottel, John, 63.
Cotten, Elizebeth (Wid.), 67.
Cottle, Isaac, 39.
Cottle, Isaac, 50.
Cottle, W^m, 62.
Cotton, Adam, 20.
Cotton, Adam, 21.
Cotton, Eben^r, 17.
Cotton, John, 17.
Cotton, Thomas, 11.
Cotton, Thomas, 12.
Cotton, Willm, 12.
Cottrell, Ezra, 32.
Cottrell, Silvester, 29.
Couch, John, 39.
Coule, Samuel, 67.
Coullard, Joshua, 32.
Counce, Lemuel, 49.
Counce, Samuel, 49.
Cousens, John, 71.
Cousens, Saml, 69.
Cousins, Benjamin, 60.
Cousins, Benjamin, 60.
Cousins, Ebenezer, 60.
Cousins, Enoch, 70.
Cousins, Ichabod, 64.
Cousins, John, 60.
Cousins, Joseph, 69.
Cousins, Nathl, Jr, 70.
Cousins, Saml, 71.
Covell, Micajah, 46.
Covy, David, 36.
Cowel, Edmund, 63.
Cowel, Ichabod, 63.
Cowel, John, 63.
Cowel, Samuel, 63.
Cowen, Abisha, 39.
Cowen, Betsy, 12.
Cowen, Charles, 12.

Cowen, Jabez, 39.
Cowen, James, 39.
Cowen, Thos, 24.
Cowin, George, 47.
Cowin, Isaac, 47.
Cowin, William, 47.
Cowing, Calvin, 35.
Cowing, David Baley, 44.
Cowing, Ephrom, 44.
Cowley, John, 43.
Cows, Benj^a, 55.
Cox, Artemas, 12.
Cox, Benjn, 24.
Cox, Clement, 61.
Cox, Ebenezer, 32.
Cox, Edward, 54.
Cox, Ely, 12.
Cox, Hugh, 44.
Cox, Israll, 48.
Cox, James, 23.
Cox, James, 39.
Cox, James, 49.
Cox, Josiah, 14.
Cox, Lemuel, 23.
Cox, Nathl, 54.
Cox, Sarah, 24.
Cox, William, 23.
Coy, Daniel, 39.
Coy, John, 11.
Cozens, Elisha, 29.
Cozens, John, 29.
Cozens, Nathaniel, 28.
Cozens, Samuel, 31.
Cozens, Samuel, jun^r, 31.
Cozens, Thomas, 31.
Cozont, Nathaniel, 67.
Crabb, Jonathan, 26.
Crabtree, Agreen, 31.
Crabtree, Eleazer, 32.
Crabtree, William, 31.
Crabtree, William, 40.
Crafford, James, 12.
Crafford, John, 33.
Crafford, Mary, 33.
Crafford, Thos, 33.
Craft, Foster, 43.
Craft, henry, 44.
Craft, Moses, 44.
Craft, Moses, jr., 44.
Craft, Saml, 24.
Crage, Andrew, 28.
Crage, John, 28.
Crage, Moses, 28.
Crage, Samuel, 28.
Crage, Samuel, jun^r, 28.
Craging, Joseph, 50.
Craging, Simon, 45.
Craige, Elias, 39.
Craige, Eveleth, 25.
Craige, Thomas, 25.
Crain, John, 66.
Cram, Danl, 24.
Cram, Danl, Jn^r, 24.
Cram, Joseph, 66.
Cram, Saml, 50.
Cram, Saml, ju., 50.
Cram, Timothy, 50.
cramer, charles, 42.
cramer, cristoph, 41.
cramer, fridrich, 42.
cramer, Jacob, 42.
cramer, John, 42.
cramer, peter, 41.
Crammet, James, 50.
Cran, abijah, 51.
Crandall, Philip, 14.
Crandall, Philip, 24.
Crane, Calvin, 49.
Crane, John, 53.
Crane, Rufus, 49.
Crane, Samuel, 49.
Crary, Joseph, 29.
Crawford, Archibald, 49.
Crawford, James, 30.
Crawford, James, 49.
Crawford, John, 49.
Crawford, John, Junr, 49.
Crawley, Hannah, 72.
Crawley, Rachael, 72.
Creamer, Edward, 34.
Creasey, Joseph, 17.
Cree, John, 32.
Creesy, Benjamin, 14.
Cregg, Enoch, 44.
Creighton, David, 46.
Creighton, Lucretia, 49.
Cresey, Abel, 33.
Cresey, Abel, 38.
Cresey, John, 59.
Crew, John, 53.
Crigg, James, 51.
Crigg, James, Ju., 51.
Crigg, Thomas, 51.
Crigg, Willm, 51.
Crips, John, 12.
Crisp, Thomas, 24.
Critchet, John, 63.
Crocke, John, 13.
Crocher (Widow), 72.
Crocker, Benjamin, 52.
Crocker, James, 16.
Crocker, James, 52.
Crocker, John, 30.

INDEX.   81

Crocker, John, 52.
Crocker, Joseph, 40.
Crocker, Paul, 36.
Crocker, Timothy, 36.
Crocker, William, 54.
Crocket, Benja, 68.
Crocket, Danl, 13.
Crocket, Eph{m}, 17.
Crocket, James, 17.
Crocket, Jon{a}, 17.
Crocket, Josh{a}, Junr, 17.
Crocket, Joshua, Jr, 17.
Crocket, Joshua, Senr, 17
Crocket, Palatiah, 17.
Crocket, Peter, 17.
Crocket, Richard, 13.
Crocket, Saml, 17.
Crocket, Saml, Jr, 17.
Crocket, Simon, 15.
Crockett, Daniel, 25.
Crockett, George, 26.
Crockett, Isaac, 32.
Crockett, Josiah, 27.
Crockett, Robinson, 27.
Crockett, Samuel, 13.
Crockit, John, 46.
Crockit, Jonathan, 46.
Crockit, Nathaniel, 46.
Crockit, Nathaniel, Junr, 46.
Cromett, Jere{h}, 34.
Cromett, John, 34.
Cromlt, John, 47.
Cromwel, James, 68.
Cromwel, Joseph, 37.
Cromwell, Joshua, 16.
Crooker, Elijah, 43.
Crooker, Francis, 26.
Crooker, Isaac, 11.
Crooker, Joshua, 11.
Crooker, Lemuel, 12.
Crooks, William, 26.
Crosbey, Ezra, 50.
Crosbey, Jonah, 50.
Crosby, Abner, 27.
Crosby, Asa, 45.
Crosby, James, 52.
Crosby, John, 27.
Crosby, Jonah, Jur, 39.
Crosby, Jonathan, 44.
Crosby, Lydia, 22.
Crosby, Robert, 39.
Crosby, Robert, 45.
Crosby, Simon, 27.
Crosby (Widow), 72.
Crosman, Jacob, 52.
Cross, Benj., 47.
Cross, Cabot, 47.
Cross, James, 47.
Cross, John, 52.
Cross, Joshua, 34.
Cross, Moses, 47.
Cross, Nathaniel, 23.
Cross, Ralf, 24.
Cross, Willm, 47.
Crossman, David, 14.
Crossman, Solomon, 14.
Crouch, David, 46.
Crowel, Thomas, 12.
Crowell, ——rdock, 50.
Crowell, David, 50.
Crowell, Ezekiel, 50.
Crowell, Ezekiel, 50.
Crowell, Joseph, 47.
Crowell, Joseph, 50.
Crowell, Levi, 50.
Crowell, Manoah, 50.
Crowell, Samuel, 50.
Crowley, Jeremiah, 13.
Croxford, John, 24.
crucker, Elijah, 48.
crucker, trenter, 49.
Cruddiford, John, 70.
Cruddiford, Willm, 70.
Crudlford, Abner, 55.
Crumell, Thomas, 33.
culbrath, lithen, 48.
cumerer, Joseph, 41.
Cumings, Josiah, 16.
Cumings, Thomas, 22.
Cumming, Asa, 39.
Cumming, Francis, 54.
Cumming, Saml, 39.
Cumming, Saml, 39.
Cumming, Solomon, 39.
Cummings, Daniel, 19.
Cummings, Isaac, 19.
Cummings, John 54.
Cummings, Joseph, 19.
Cummings, Richard, 47.
Cummings, Thomas, 13.
Cummins, Abra{m}, 16.
Cummins, Donald, 58.
Cummins, Elisha, 22.
Cummins, John, 24.
Cummins, Oliver, 13.
Cummins, Thos, 24.
Cummins, Thomas, 30.
Cummins, Willm, 24.
Cums, Syl{l}, 48.
Cunengham, Isaac, 33.
Cuningham, David, 33.
Cunlngham, John, 33.
Cuningham, Samuel, 33.

Cuningham, William, 33.
Cunningham, Isaac, 43.
Cunningham, James, 29.
Cunningham, James, 32.
Cunningham, John, 36.
Cunningham, John, 37.
Cunningham, John, 41.
Cunningham, John, Junr, 37.
Cunningham, Ruggles, 34.
Cunningham, Sarah, 41.
Cunningham, Thomas, 31.
Cunningham, Thos, 41.
Cunningham, Tim{o}, 37.
Cunningham, Willm, 37.
Cunningham, Willm, 37.
Curne, James, 51.
Currey, Mehitable, 21.
Currice, Ephraim, 44.
Currier, Abra{m}, 70.
Currier, Anna, 72.
Currier, David, 58.
Currier, Isaac, 59.
Currier, James, 42.
Currier, Joseph, 72.
Currier, Nathl, 55.
Currier, Sarah, 14.
Currier (Widow), 72.
Curtes, Ambros, 20.
Curtes, Benja, 20.
Curtes, Charles, 52.
Curtes, Charles, 70.
Curtes, Ezekiel, 20.
Curtes, Jacob, 20.
Curtes, James, 12.
Curtes, James, 16.
Curtes, John, 52.
Curtes, Joseph, 52.
Curtes, Joseph, 55.
Curtes, Mercy, 20.
Curtes, Mich{l}, 20.
Curtes, Nehemiah, 20.
Curtes, Paul, 20.
Curtes, Saml, 70.
Curtes, Thomas, Junr, 16.
Curtes (Widow), 55.
Curtex, Willm, 39.
curtice, daniel, 48.
Curtice, David, 41.
Curtice, Gasham, 40.
Curtls, Abel, 32.
Curtis, Ashley, 24.
Curtis, Benja, 16.
Curtis, Benja, 30.
Curtis Benja, junr, 30.
Curtis, Caleb, 20.
Curtis, Charles, 30.
Curtis, Danl, 16.
Curtis, David, 16.
Curtis, Ephraim, 58.
Curtis, Ezra, 16.
Curtis, John, 24.
Curtis, John, 36.
Curtis, Joseph, 30.
Curtis, Joseph, 60.
Curtis, Joshua, 16.
Curtis, Noah, 6.
Curtis, Obadiah, 16.
Curtis, Philldelp{h}, 60.
Curtis, Stephen, 16.
Curtis, Thomas, 16.
Cushing, Abigail, 13.
Cushing, Apolos, 23.
Cushing, Charles, Junr, 14.
Cushing, Christopher, 33.
Cushing, Ezekiel, 24.
Cushing, Jeremiah, 24.
Cushing, John, 13.
Cushing, John, 14.
Cushing, John, 16.
Cushing, John, 35.
Cushing, John, 55.
Cushing, Laban, 53.
Cushing, Loring, 15.
Cushing, Mehitable, 24.
Cushing, Solomon, 53.
Cushing, Willm, 47.
Cushman, Caleb, 22.
Cushman, Caleb, 24.
Cushman, Gideon, 24.
Cushman, Isaac, 24.
Cushman, Isaiah, 22.
Cushman, Jabes, 20.
Cushman, Job, 24.
Cushman, Joseph, 24.
Cushman, Josiah, 51.
cushman, paulus (long Island), 48.?
Cushman, Robert, 52.
Cushman, Sarah, 24.
Cushman, Zebadiah, 24.
Cussens, Joseph, 60.
Cutler, John, 22.
Cutler, Tim{o}, 17.
Cutt, Edwd, Esqr, 61.
Cutt, John, 61.
Cutt, Cap{a} Jos., 61.
Cutt, Noah, 61.
Cutt, Richd, Esqr, 61.
Cutt, Robt, 61.
Cutt, Thos, 61.
Cutt, Cap{a} Thos, 61.
Cutt, Deac{n} Thos, 61.
Cutter, Ebenezer, 15.

Cutter, Nathan, 40.
Cutter, Saml, 21.
Cutts, Fox{l}, 65.
Cutts, Richd Fox{se}, 55.
Cutts, Saml, 59.
Cutts, Thos, Esqr, 65.

Daggett, Benja, 32.
Daggett, Benja, jun., 32.
Daggett, John, 38.
Daggett, Samuel, 47.
Daggett, Thomas, 47.
Daggett, Thomas, Jun., 47.
Daily, Emour, 24.
Dallop, Jonathan, 59.
Dalton, Jeremiah, 43.
Dalton, Samuel, 65.
Dalton, Sipio, 53.
Daly, Ellis, 36.
Dam, Joseph, 68.
Dame, Abig{l}, 62.
Dame, Horsvil, 62.
Dame, Isachar, 59.
Dame, Jonath{n}, 62.
Dame, Joseph, 60.
Dame, Nathan, 62.
Dame, Samuel, 68.
Damerin, Zabiah, 37.
Damon, Jon{a}, 12.
Damons, Abiah, 53.
Damons, Gamiel, 52.
Dan, Nathl, 17.
Dana, Edmund, 39.
Dana, Gardiner, 12.
Dane, Simeon, 39.
Danford, Phillip, 28.
Danforth, Abner, 12.
Danforth, David, 45.
Danforth, Willm, 12.
Daniel, John, 45.
Daniels, John, 22.
Daniles, Reuben, 49.
Darby, John, 52.
Darby, Sarah, 70.
Darling, Eliakim, 28.
Darling, James, 37.
Darling, Jonathan, 26.
Darling, Joseph, 37.
Darrow, George, 30.
Dartman, Noah, 35.
Davenport, Abner, 12.
Davenport, Jan{a}, 39.
Davenport, John, 12.
Davidson, Alexander, 41.
Davies, Daniel, 67.
Davies, David, 67.
Davies, James, 66.
Davies, Joseph, 45.
Davies, Philip, 45.
Davin, Danl, 55.
Davis, Aaron, 11.
Davis, Aaron, 40.
Davis, Aaron, 49.
Davis, Abel, 20.
Davis, Allen, 11.
Davis, Amos, 40.
Davis, Anna, 63.
Davis, Benja, 39.
Davis, Benjamin, 37.
Davis, Charles, 38.
Davis, Christopher, 13.
Davis, Daniel, 13.
Davis, Daniel, 23.
Davis, Daniel, 40.
Davis, David, 17.
Davis, Ebenr, 17.
Davis, Ebenezer, 20.
Davis, Ebenezer, 23.
Davis, Ebenezer, 40.
Davis, Eber, 37.
Davis, Elemuel, 61.
Davis, Elias, 11.
Davis, Eliphalet, 55.
Davis, Ezra, 27.
Davis, Ezra, 64.
Davis, Gershom, 12.
Davis, Gideon, 24.
Davis, Isaac, 14.
Davis, Israel, 31.
Davis, Jacob, 25.
Davis, Jacob, 40.
Davis, Jacob, 49.
Davis, James, 24.
Davis, James, 32.
Davis, James, 38.
Davis, James, 67.
Davis, James, 70.
Davis, James J., 39.
Davis, Jesse, 28.
Davis, Jesse, 35.
Davis, John, 17.
Davis, John, 21.
Davis, John, 24.
Davis, John, 24.
Davis, John, 26.
Davis, John, 36.
Davis, John, 37.
Davis, John, 39.
Davis, John, 44.
Davis, John, 53.
Davis, John, 57.

Davis, John, 58.
Davis, John, 58.
Davis, John, 62.
Davis, John, 63.
Davis, John, 64.
Davis, John, 65.
Davis, John, 68.
Davis, John G., 58.
Davis, Jon{a}, 33.
Davis, Jonathan, 36.
Davis, Joseph, 14.
Davis, Joseph, 40.
Davis, Joseph, 58.
Davis, Joseph, Jur, 40.
Davis, Joshua, 12.
Davis, Joshua, 47.
Davis, Josiah, 17.
Davis, Josiah, 58.
Davis, Josiah, 60.
Davis, Mary, 36.
Davis, Micah, 28.
Davis, Moses, 11.
Davis, Moses, 36.
Davis, Nathaniel, 44.
Davis, Nathl, 55.
Davis, Nehemiah, 68.
Davis, Nicholas, 64.
Davis, prince, 17.
Davis, prince, Junr, 17.
Davis, Reuben, 59.
Davis, Robert, 40.
Davis, Robert, 58.
Davis, Roland, 15.
Davis, Roland, 15.
Davis, Saml, 17.
Davis, Samuel, 32.
Davis, Samuel, 39.
Davis, Samuel, 40.
Davis, Saml, 58.
Davis, Samuel, Jun., 40.
Davis, Sarah, 21.
Davis, Sarah, 70.
Davis, Simeon, 13.
Davis, Simon, 36.
Davis, Suanna, 61.
Davis, Sylv{s}, 17.
Davis, Thomas, 21.
Davis, Thomas, 30.
Davis, Thomas, 35.
Davis, Thos, 59.
Davis, Thomas, 68.
Davis, Timothy, 21.
Davis, Willm, 11.
Davis, William, 19.
Davis, William, 27.
Davis, William, 38.
Davis, William, 40.
Davis, William, 52.
Davis, Wm, 58.
Davis, Zebulon, 11.
Davis, Zebulon, Jr, 11.
Davis, Zechary, 40.
Dawes, John, 34.
Dawes, Jon{a}, 34.
Daws, Willm, 39.
Daxter, Constant, 51.
Day, Aaron, 66.
Day, Abra{a}, 37.
Day, Abraham, 59.
day, benjamin, 48.
Day, Benja, 69.
Day, Benja, 70.
Day, Benja, Jr, 69.
Day, Catherine, 10.
Day, Dependence, 67.
Day, Ebenezer, 60.
Day, Ebenezer, 69.
Day, George, 23.
Day, heneary, 67.
Day, hitkem, 67.
Day, bitten, 67.
Day, Jacob, 37.
Day, James, 17.
Day, James, 26.
Day, James, 34.
Day, John, 29.
Day, John, 32.
Day, John, 45.
Day, John, 59.
Day, John, 70.
Day, Jonathan, 26.
Day, Joseph, 49.
Day, Joseph, 71.
Day, Josiah, 14.
Day, Mehitable, 16.
Day, Moses, 60.
Day, Moses, 71.
Day, Nathl, 52.
Day, Robert, 71.
Day, Saml, 55.
Day, Stephen, 38.
Day, Stephen, 60.
Day, Thomas, 33.
Day, Thomas, 68.
Day, Tobb, 41.
Day, Wm, 60.
Day, Zebedee, 20.
Dayley, Daniel, 40.
Dayly, Sarah, 61.
Deadem, Benja, 49.
Deakes, George, 13.
Dean, Abraham, 24.

Dean, Ebenezer, 52.
Dean, Edmund, 22.
Dean, Eliphalet, 23.
Dean, Jacob, 22.
Dean, John, 23.
Dean, John, 24.
Dean, John, 40.
Dean, John, Jur, 40.
Dean, Jonah, 46.
Dean, Joseph, 27.
Dean, Samuel, 22.
Dean, Seres, 38.
Dean, Thomas, 30.
Dean, Thomas, junr, 30.
Dean, William, 40.
Dean, Zadock, 24.
Dearben, Ebenezer, 65.
Dearben, Jacob, 65.
Dearben, Thomas, 65.
Dearborn, Henry, 43.
Dearborn, Jacob, 58.
Dearborn, Jacob, 59.
Dearborn, Levi, 49.
Dearborn, Simon, 49.
Dearborn, Simon, ju., 49.
Dearing, Clem{t}, 61.
Dearing, Gideon, 66.
Dearing, Isaac, 17.
Dearing, James, 54.
Dearing, James, 65.
Dearing, John, 65.
Dearing, John, 66.
Dearing, John, Jur, 65.
Dearing, Joseph, 52.
Dearing, Joseph, 65.
Dearing, Roger, 61.
Dearing, Thos, 65.
Dearing (Widow), 54.
Dearing, William, 69.
Dearing, Cap{n} Wm, 61.
Debeck, Samuel, 31.
Decker, Abraham, 34.
Decker, David, 34.
Decker, John, 24.
Decker, John, 33.
Decker, John, 43.
Decker, Joseph, 43.
Decker, Joshua, 55.
Decker, Spencer, 37.
Decker, Thomas, 34.
Decker, Willm, 34.
Decker, William, 43.
Deering, Ellot, 23.
Deering, Eunice, 23.
Deering, James, 23.
Deering, John, 37.
Deering, Nathaniel, 22.
Delano, Alpheus, 40.
Delano, Ameziah, 19.
Delano, Bezilla, 13.
Delano, Thomas, 15.
Deleno, Benj., 47.
Deleno, Peleg, 47.
Delesdernier, Gideon. 53.
Delesdernier, Lewis Fred, 53.
Dellingham, Jeremiah, 25.
Dellingham, John, 25.
Demorse, Charles, 26.
Demorse, John, 40.
Demorse, John, Junr, 40.
Dempsey (Widow), 55.
demut, george, 42.
demut, henry, 42.
Denbow, John, 54.
Denbow, Nathaniel, 53.
Dennet, Ebenezer, 56.
Dennet, Ebenezer, 65.
Dennet, Ebenezer, J{r}, 56.
Dennet, John, 57.
Dennet, J{no}, 62.
Dennet, J{no}, Junr, 62.
Dennet, Joseph, 60.
Dennet, Sally, 62.
Dennet, Saml, 65.
Dennet, Samuel, 66.
Dennet, Saml, Jur, 65.
Dennet, Wm, 62.
Dennett, Cadmiel, 58.
Dennett, Jacob, 27.
Dennett, J{no}, 59.
Dennett, Nicholas, 65.
Dennick, John, 70.
Dennico, John, 54.
Denning, James, 27.
Denning, Jane, 27.
Denning, Samuel, 11.
Dennis, Andrew, 25.
Dennis, David, 35.
Dennison, Abner, 16.
Dennison, Ame, 16.
Dennison, David, 16.
Dennison, David, J{r}, 16.
Dennison, George, 16.
Dennison, Gideon, 16.
Dennison, Robert, 39.
Dennit, Ebenezer, 60.
Densmore, David, 11.
D{e}Pollereski, John, 44.
Derban, R{lcd}, 63.
Derby, Jere, 72.
Derby, Saml, 71.
Derry, Lewis, 26.
Deshaun, James, 69.

INDEX.

Deshaun, Moses, junr, 69.
Deshon, Chase, 65.
Devenport, Abraham, 36.
Devenport, Ebenezer, 51.
Devenport, Isaac, 51.
Devereaux, Ralph, 30.
Devinport, John, 42.
Devinport, Thomas, 36.
Dexter, Isaac, 41.
Dexter, Nathan, 50.
Dexter, Thomas, 53.
Dexter, William P., 27.
Dicker, Willm, 24.
Dickerson, Abijah, 43.
Dickerson, Samuel, 43.
Dickey, David, 48.
Dickey, Elezer Boyad, 39.
Dickey, John, 49.
Dickey, William, 28.
Dickey, William, 49.
Dickrow, Daniel, 28.
Dickrow, Peleg, 28.
Dickrow, Zepheniah, 28.
Dickson, Ichabod, 56.
Dickson, Mary, 56.
Dickson, Saml, 62.
Dier, Danl, 64.
Dier, Elizabeth, 58.
Dier, Humphry, 64.
Dier, John, 58.
Dier, Joseph, 64.
Dilano, Amasa, 43.
Dile, Ralph, 50.
Dileno, Seth, 51.
Dileno, Zebulon, 51.
Dilenow, Jabish, 40.
dilinham, leml, 48.
Dill, John, 40.
Dill, Josiah, 40.
Dillano, Jona, 52.
Dillaway, James, 53.
Dillaway, John, 46.
Dillenham, Melatiah 16.
Dillenham, Saml, 16.
Dilleno, Ebena, 51.
Dilleno, Ephraim, 52.
Dilleno, Ezekiel, 22.
Dilleno, Hopestill, 52.
Dillingham, Jeremiah, 11.
Dillingham, John, 11.
Dillingham, Joshua, 26.
Dillingham, Lemuel, 27.
Dingley, Joseph, 24.
Dingley, Levi, 20.
Dingly, Barker, 50.
Dingly, Samuel, 24.
Dingly, William, 13.
Dinsdell, Henry, 23.
Dinslow, ——, 35.
Dinslow, Benja, 20.
Dinslow, Joseph, 35.
Dinslow, Willm, 35.
Dinsmore, Asa, 44.
Dinsmore, John, 21.
Dinsmore, Samuel, 47.
Dinsmore, Thos, 35.
Dinsmore, Thomas, 39.
Dinsmore, Thos, Junr, 35.
Dire, Elhanah, 40.
Discomb, Thomas, 44.
Dishon, Danl, 58.
Dishon, Peter, 55.
Divorux, Ricd, 65.
Dixon, Abrhm, 62.
Dixon, Hannah, 62.
Dixon, Peter, 62.
Dixon, Saml, 71.
Dixon, Steven, 62.
Dixon, Thos, 62.
Dixon, Capn Thos, 62.
Doan, Amos, 28.
Doane, Ebenezer, 13.
Doane, Ebenezer, 13.
Doane, Edward, 13.
Doane, Oliver, 30.
Doane, Seth, 29.
Doar, Allen, 43.
Doar, Benajah, 43.
Doar, Henry, 43.
Doar, James, 43.
Dobbie, John, 30.
Doble, Willm, 12.
dockendorf, Jacob, 49.
Dockum, James, 65.
Dodd, Stephen, 15.
Dodd, Thomas, 15.
Dodge, Abner, 31.
Dodge, Abraham, 31.
Dodge, Amaziah, 31.
Dodge, Benjamin, 45.
Dodge, Benja, 67.
Dodge, Caleb, 47.
Dodge, Daniel, 37.
Dodge, Daniel, 41.
Dodge, David, 41.
Dodge, Jabez, 26.
Dodge, Ezekiel Goddard, 46.
Dodge, Ezra H., 29.
Dodge, John, 41.
Dodge, Jonah, 31.
Dodge, Malachi, 37.
Dodge, Moses, 36.
Dodge, Moses, 41.

Dodge, Noah, 29.
Dodge, Paul, 41.
Dodge, Porter, 37.
Dodge, Rathburn, 29.
Dodge, Sarah, 26.
Dodge, Sarah, 37.
Dodge, Simon, 29.
Dodge, Simon, junr, 29.
dodge, thomas, 48.
Dodge, Winthrop, 37.
Dodge, Zachariah, 41.
Dody, Nicholas, 47.
Doe, Brodstreet, 68.
Doe, Dudley, 47.
Doe, Eliphelet, 68.
Doe, Gedion, 65.
Doe, Henery, 68.
Doe, James, 47.
Doe, John, 65.
Doe, John, 68.
Doe, Jona, 65.
Doe, Joseph, 37.
Doe, Levi, 65.
Doe, Mary, 44.
Doe, Nathl, 47.
Doe, Nathel, 68.
Doe, Samson, 48.
Doe, Samuel, 65.
Doe, Simon, 68.
Doll, James, 20.
Dolle, Elijah, 20.
Dolle, Elisha, 20.
Doln, Saml, 38.
Dole, Amos, 27.
Dole, Daniel, 14.
Dole, John, 23.
Dole, Nathan, 43.
Dole, Richard, 26.
doliver, Joseph, 48.
Dolley, John, 19.
Dolley, John, 25.
Dolley, Samuel, 25.
Dolliff, Daniel, 26.
Dolliff, John, 26.
Dolliver, William, 30.
Dollor, Richard, 49.
Dones, Bangs, 32.
Donnehue, Joseph, 35.
Donnell, Abraham, 31.
Donnell, Benja, 59.
Donnell, Benja, Jun., 59.
Door, Benja, 31.
Door, Henery, 63.
Door, James, 67.
Door, John, 31.
Door, John, 63.
Door, John, Junr, 63.
Door, Jonathan, 63.
Door, Joseph, 67.
Door, Peter, 67.
Door, Philip, 67.
Door, Ricd, 67.
Door, Ricd, 67.
Door, Silas, 67.
Dor, Ambrius, 52.
Dor, Ruel, 46.
Dorman, Charles, 65.
Dorman, Israel, 54.
Dorman, Jabez, 54.
Dorman, Jabez, 54.
Dorman, Jesse, 54.
Dorman, John, 54.
Dorothy, David, 31.
Dorothy, Robert, 31.
Dorrey, David, 25.
Dorrey, Elijah, 25.
Dorrey, Jonathan, 25.
Dorrey, Timothy, 25.
Dorril, Thos, 37.
Dorset, Jereh, 17.
Dosey, Jereh, 38.
Dotloff, Richard, 64.
Doubty, George, 19.
Doubty, James, 15.
Doubty, Joseph, 19.
Doubty, Thomas, 15.
Doughty, Daniel, 12.
Doughty, David, 16.
Doughty, James, 20.
Doughty, Stephen, 46.
Doughty, Willm, 12.
Douglas, James, 30.
Douglas, James, 31.
Douglas, John, 31.
Douglas, Robert, 32.
Douglas, Robert, jun, 32.
Douglas, William, 47.
Douglis, Archbald, 13.
Doutey, John, 41.
Dow, Abner, 24.
Dow, Benj., 47.
Dow, Benj., Junr, 48.
Dow, Ebena, 64.
Dow, Ebenezer, Jr, 64.
Dow, Henry, 46.
Dow, Jabez, 64.
Dow, Jeremiah, 64.
Dow, Jer, Jr, 64.
Dow, John, 31.
Dow, Jonathan, 47.
Dow, Jonathan, 54.
Dow, Joseph, 24.
Dow, Moses, 56.

Dow, Nathan, 27.
Dow, Nathan, junr, 27.
Dow, Peter, 33.
Dow, Peter, Juner, 33.
Dow, Saml, 64.
Dowdele, Michal, 52.
Dowe, Stephen, 52.
Dowling, John, 53.
Down, Solomon, 72.
Downing, Benja, 55.
Downing, Benja, 55.
Downing, Dennit, 17.
Downing, Harrison, 55.
Downing, John, 11.
Downing, John, 55.
Downing, John, 55.
Downing, Jona, 55.
Downing, Nicholas, 54.
Downing, Richard, 31.
Downing, Saml, 11.
Downs, Aaron, 56.
Downs, Asa, 28.
Downs, Benja, 63.
Downs, Daniel, 56.
Downs, Ebenezer, 53.
Downs, Ebenezer, Jr., 54.
Downs, Ephraim, 28.
Downs, Gersham, 67.
Downs, Ichabod, 63.
Downs, Jedediah, 56.
Downs, Jershon, 59.
Downs, John, 59.
Downs, Joshua, 56.
Downs, Moses, 56.
Downs, Nathel, 56.
Downs, Noah, 28.
Downs, Paul, 28.
Downs, Paul, 67.
Downs, Phinehas, 64.
Downs, Richard, 69.
Downs, Robert, 72.
Downs, Thomas, 28.
Downs, Umphry, 69.
Doyle, Thomas, 31.
Drake, Ebenezer, 24.
Drake, John, 24.
Drake, Oliver, 40.
Drake, Robert, 23.
drawbridge, John, 42.
Dresser, John, 17.
Dresser, Jonathan, 60.
Dresser, Jonathan, Jr 60.
Dresser, Levi, 68.
Dresser, Mark, 17.
Dresser, Mindwell, 17.
Dresser, Stephen, 68.
Dresser, Wentworth, 17.
Drew, Benja, 67.
Drew, Clemant, 38.
Drew, Consider, 52.
Drew, Elisabeth, 68.
Drew, Elisha, 59.
Drew, Hezekiah, 64.
Drew, Zebulon, 64.
Drinkwater, Dan1, 22.
Drinkwater, David, 21.
Drinkwater, John, 22.
Drinkwater, John, 22.
Drinkwater, Joseph, 22.
Drinkwater, Micajah, 28.
Drinkwater, Perris, 22.
Drinkwater, Saml, 21.
Drinkwater, Silvanus, 21.
Drinkwater, Zenas, 28.
Drinkworter, Thos, 65.
Drisko, John, 54.
Drisko, Joseph, 54.
Drisko, Samuel, 54.
Drought, Richard, 46.
Drown, ——, 60.
Drown, Moses, 70.
Drown, Stephen, 70.
Druce, Climan, 49.
drumens, James, 48.
Drummon, Alexander, 38.
Drummon, Elijah, 37.
Drummon, James, 38.
Drummon, Reatherford, 45.
Drummon, Rutherford, 45.
Drummon, Rutherford, 45.
Dudley, andrew, 45.
Dudley, Daniel, 47.
Dudley, Daniel, 50.
Dudley, Eliphalet, 45.
Dudley, Eliphelat, 51.
Dudley, Francis, 50.
Dudley, James, 42.
Dudley, Jeremiah, 42.
Dudley, John, 50.
Dudley, Micajah, 14.
Dudley, Moses, 45.
Dudley, Nathaniel, 50.
Dudley, Peter, 69.
Dudley, Saml, 39.
Dudley, Samuel, 42.
Dudley, Stephen, 51.
dudley, Stephen, 69.
Dudley, Trueworth, 67.
dudley, Truworthy, 69.
Dudly, Nathan, 24.
Dudson, Jabas, 40.
Dugan, Thos, 46.

Dugen, William, 27.
Duggins, Mrs, 17.
Duglas, Cornelius, 14
Duglas, Daniel, 20.
Duglas, Elijah, 14.
Duglas, Elijah, 20.
Duglas, Francis, 47
Duglas, Job, 16.
Duglas, John, 14.
Duglas, Joseph, 14.
Duglas (Widow), 46
Duglass, John, 64.
Duley, Michl, 37.
Dullen, oliver, 50.
Dummer, John, 43.
Dummer, Nathl, 39.
Dun, Christopr, 17.
Dunbar, Daniel, 49.
Dunbar, Elizer, 35.
Dunbar, Hannah, 26.
Dunbar, Josiah, 54.
Dunbar, Moses, 28.
Dunbar, Obed, 54.
Dunbar, Solomon, 41.
Duncan, John, 43.
Duncan, Robart, 34.
Duncat, Prine, 40.
Dunham, Amaziah, 16.
Dunham, Asa, 22.
Dunham, Dan1, 16.
Dunham, David, 43.
Dunham, Elijah, 27.
Dunham, James, 24.
Dunham, James, 32.
Dunham, John, 16.
Dunham, Joseph, 58.
Dunham, Willm, 35.
Duning, John, 16.
Dunlap, Archibald, 43.
Dunlap, Ebereser, 45.
Dunlap, Hugh, 12.
Dunlap, James, 45.
Dunlap, John, 12.
Dunlap, John, 12.
Dunlap, John, 46.
Dunlap, John, Jnr, 46.
Dunlap, Robert, 45.
Dunlap, Saml, 12.
Dunlap, William, 45.
Dunn, David, 52.
Dunn, Enoch, 13.
Dunn, Joshua, 11.
Dunn, Josiah, 11.
Dunn, Nathl, 59.
Dunnam, Jona, 40.
Dunnam, Joseph, 40.
Dunnam, Samuel, 47.
Dunnaven, John, 54.
Dunnel, John, 57.
Dunnel, John, 68.
Dunnell, Joseph, 59.
Dunning, Andw, 12.
Dunning, Andrew, 12.
Dunning, Andw, 20.
Dunning, Benja, 20.
Dunning, David, 12.
Dunning, David, 12.
Dunning, John, 12.
Dunning, Robert, 12.
Dunning, Willm, 12.
Dunning, William, 36.
Duntan, Daniel, 37.
Duntan, John, 37.
Duntan, Joseph, 37.
Duntan, Saml, 37.
Duntan, Timo, 37.
Duntan, Willm, 37.
Dunton, John, 27.
Dupee, Elias, 30.
Duran, Matthew, 14.
Dureld, Saml, 23.
Durgan, Benja, 63.
Durgan, David, 68.
Durgan, Ephrim, 64.
Durgan, Hannah, 64.
Durgan, John, 60.
Durgan, Wm, 63.
Durham, John, 26.
Durham, Talford, 26.
Durill, Benja, 65.
durley, John, 33.
Durnel, David, 64.
Durnton, John, 33.
Durrel, Benjl, 55.
Durrel, Jacob, 55.
Durrel, Thos, 54.
Durrell, Asa, 55.
Duston, Jesse, 68.
Dutten, Joshua, 51.
Dutten, Richd, 70.
Dutten, Saml, 39.
Dutten (Widow), 39.
Dutton, Elijah, 44.
Dutton, Jesse, 31.
Dutton, John, 44.
Dutton, Rial, 36.
Dutton, Sarah, 19.
Duval, Peter, 22.
Dwella, Allen, 22.
Dwelly, John, 28.
Dwinell, Aaron, 11.
Dwinell, Amos, 11.
Dwinell, Jacob, 11.

Dwinell, Joseph, 70.
Dwinell, Jotham, 71.
Dwinnel, Moses, 44.
Dwinnel, Nathl, 71.
Dwinnel, Obadiah, 72.
Dwinnel, Thos, 58.
Dwinnel, Timothy, 71.
Dwinnel (Widow), 71.
Dwinnels, John, 12.
Dwinnels, Saml, 71.
Dwinnels, Saml, Jr, 71.
dwo, lem, 48.
Dyer, Abigail, 13.
Dyer, Anthony, 32.
Dyer, Anthony, 36.
Dyer, Benjamin, 13.
Dyer, Benjamin, 32.
Dyer, Benjamin, 47.
Dyer, Bickford, 60.
Dyer, Bickford, 66.
Dyer, Caleb, 13.
Dyer, David, 14.
Dyer, Ephraim, 13.
Dyer, Ephraim, 31.
Dyer, Ezekiel, 24.
Dyer, Hannah, 13.
Dyer, Henry, 13.
Dyer, Henry, 53.
Dyer, Isaac, 13.
Dyer, Isaac, 13.
Dyer, Jabes, 13.
Dyer, James, 13.
Dyer, James, 20.
Dyer, James, 53.
Dyer, Jedediah, 19.
Dyer, John, 17.
Dyer, John, Jr., 17.
Dyer, Jones, 53.
Dyer, Joshua, 13.
Dyer, Josiah, 14.
Dyer, Lemuel, 20.
Dyer, Levi, 17.
Dyer, Micael, 13.
Dyer, Michael, 14.
Dyer, Michael, 30.
Dyer, Nathaniel, 13.
Dyer, Paul, 13.
Dyer, Robert, 13.
Dyer, Samuel, 13.
Dyer, Samuel, 13.
Dyer, Sarah, 31.
Dyer, William, 13.
Dyer, Wm, 17.
Dyer, William, 32.

Eames, Jacob, 51.
Eams, Phinas, 33.
Easinsy, Henry, 26.
Easman, Kingsbury, 20.
Easman, Nathl, 20.
Easman, Saml, 43.
Easters, John, 20.
Easters, Stephen, 68.
Eastman, Daniel, 60.
Eastman, Job, 24.
Eastman, Obediah, 60.
Eastman, Richard, 60.
Eastman, Saml, Jur, 43.
Eastman, Sarah, 49.
Eaton, Abel, 33.
Eaton, Benja, 46.
Eaton, Daniel, 37.
Eaton, Daniel, 12.
Eaton, David, 29.
Eaton, Ebenezer, 31.
Eaton, Eliab, 45.
Eaton, Eliakim, 27.
Eaton, Israel, 25.
Eaton, Jacob, 44.
Eaton, Jeremiah, 27.
Eaton, Jerm M., 71.
Eaton, Jesse, 50.
Eaton, Jno, 59.
Eaton, Jonathan, 27.
Eaton, Jonathan, 31.
Eaton, Joseph, 26.
Eaton, Joseph, 69.
Eaton, Joseph, 71.
Eaton, Joshua, 69.
Eaton, Joshua, 70.
Eaton, Moses, 12.
Eaton, Moses, 31.
Eaton, Obadiah, 22.
Eaton, Saml, 12.
Eaton, Saml, 20.
Eaton, Theophilus, 27.
Eaton, Thirza, 30.
Eaton, William, 27.
Eaton, Willm, 71.
Eaton, Ziba, 11.
Eatton, Sarah, 60.
Eayr's, Joshua, 27.
Eddy, Elias, 28.
Eddy, Ibrook, 28.
Eddy, Jonathan, 28.
Eden, Samuel, 52.
Edes, Gideon, 16.
Edes, Joseph, 16.
Edes, Thomas, 24.
Edes, Willm, 71.
Edgcomb, Gideon, 17.
Edgcomb, James, 65.
Edgcomb, Nicholas, 64.

INDEX.

Edgcomb, Nicholas, Jr, 64.
Edgcomb, Robert, 17.
Edgcomb, Saml, 65.
Edgcomb, Saml, Jur, 65.
Edgcomb, Thos, 65.
Edgerly, Richard, 58.
Edgley, Jno, 58.
Edmonds, Asa, 64.
Edson, Elisabeth, 39.
Edward, Nathaniel, 22.
Edward, Stephn, 58.
Edwards, Doctor, 53.
Edwards, Joshua, 17.
Edwards, Nathl, 17.
Edwards, Nathl, Jr., 17.
Edwards, Richd, 17.
Edwards, Saml, 59.
Eichorn, daniel, 42.
Eichorn, george, 42.
Eichorn, Jacob, 41.
Eichorn, John, 42.
Eichorn, michel, 42.
Elbes, Betty, 43.
Elby, Benja, 37.
Elby, Willm, 37.
Elden, Gibeon, 59.
Elden, Jno, 59.
Elden, Jno, Junr, 59.
Elden, Nathan, 59.
Elder, Ellis, 13.
Elder, George, 13.
Elder, Isaac, 17.
Elder, John, 13.
Elder, John, 14.
Elder, Joseph, 25.
Elder, Joshua, 13.
Elder, Reuben, 17.
Elder, Saml, 17.
Elder, William, 25.
Eldridge, Danl, 17.
Eldridge, Frances, 59.
Eldridge, James, 32.
Eldridge, Wintrop, 59.
Elenwood, Benjamin, 66.
Elhings, Chase, 46.
Elkins, William, 25.
Ellingwood, Richard, 28.
Elliot, Andrew, 25.
Elliot, Benjn, 64.
Elliot, Jacob, 25.
Elliot, Jacob, 25.
Elliot, James, 12.
Elliot, John, 12.
Elliot, Robert, 52.
Elliot, Simon, 48.
Elliot, Simon, 52.
Elliot, Simon, jun., 48.
Ellis, Berrick, 59.
Ellis, John, 50.
Ellis, John, 65.
Ellis, Laurance, 61.
Ellis, Levi, 25.
Ellis, Manoah, 28.
Ellis, Sarah, 28.
Ellot, Wm, 65.
Ellwell, Andrew, 36.
Ellwill, William, 29.
Elly, Saml, 11.
Else, Robert, 50.
Elsmore, Moses, 52.
elsworth, Joseph, 48.
Elwel, ——, 70.
Elwel, Henry, 21.
Elwel, Jona, 17.
Elwel, Pain, 21.
Elwel, Pain, Junr, 21.
Elwell, Benjn, 59.
Elwell, Benjn, Jun., 59.
Elwell, James, 65.
Elwell, Jno, 59.
Elwell, Joseph, 58.
Elwell, Joseph, 70.
Elwell, Mehitable, 65.
Elwell, Willm, 11.
Elwell, Wm, 59.
Ely, Samuel, 43.
Emeary, Caleb, Esq., 66.
Emeary, Joshua, 67.
Emeary, Stephen, 67.
Emeary, William, 66.
Ementon, Joseph, 31.
Emerson, Edward, 37.
Emerson, Edward, 71.
Emerson, Edward, Jr, 71.
Emerson, Eunice, 71.
Emerson, Revd Ezekiel, 38.
Emerson, John, 34.
Emerson, Joshua, 27.
Emerson, Phillip, 48.
Emerson, Samuel, 29.
Emerson, Saml, 33.
Emerson, Samuel, 50.
Emerson, Theodore, 11.
Emerson, Thomas, 46.
Emerson, Willm, 11.
Emery, Benjn, 59.
Emery, Benja, 64.
Emery, Charles, 58.
Emery, Charles, 68.
Emery, Danl, 59.
Emery, Daniel, 59.
Emery, Danl, 72.
Emery, David, 34.

Emery, David, 37.
Emery, Ebenezer, 58.
Emery, Edward, 37.
Emery, Isaac, 70.
Emery, Jabez, 70.
Emery, Jacob, 09.
Emery, James, 27.
Emery, James, 37.
Emery, James, 56.
Emery, James, 59.
Emery, Jeremiah, 54.
Emery, Jeremiah, 68.
Emery, Job, 56.
Emery, Job, 65.
Emery, Job, 70.
Emery, John, 30.
Emery, John, 36.
Emery, John, 58.
Emery, John, 73.
Emery, John, junr, 27.
Emery, John, Jur, 36.
Emery, John (of York), 56.
Emery, Jonathan, 37.
Emery, Jona, 58.
Emery, Joseph, 34.
Emery, Joseph, 55.
Emery, Joseph, 58.
Emery, Joshua, 56.
Emery, Joshua, Junr, 56.
Emery, Jotham, 68.
Emery, Levi, 36.
Emery, Moses, 55.
Emery, Nahum, 27.
Emery, Nathaniel, 45.
Emory, Obed, 58.
Emory, Ralph, 58.
Emery, Samuel, 36.
Emery, Saml, 69.
Emery, Simon, 56.
Emery, Simon, 68.
Emery, Simon, 72.
Emery, Thos, 59.
Emery, Wm, 56.
emery, Zachariah, 69.
Emes, Phineas, 32.
Emmerson, Jos., 17.
Emmerson, Saml, 11.
Emmerson, William, 52.
Emmery, Hannah, 58.
Emmons, ——, 60.
Emmons, Eben, 55.
Emmons, Eleakim, 55.
Emmons, John, 23.
Emmons, John, 55.
Emmons, John, 60.
Emmons, John, Jr, 55.
Emmons, Obediah, 60.
Emmons, Samuel, 60.
Emmons, Saml, 70.
Emmons, Samuel, jun., 60.
Emmory, Mark, 21.
Emmory, Moses, 11.
Emmory, William, 20.
Emory, Anna, 62.
Emory, Caleb, 62.
Emory, Danl, 61.
Emory, Danl, Junr, 61.
Emory, Hannah, 62.
Emory, Isaac, 61.
Emory, Israel, 61.
Emory, James, 17.
Emory, James, 62.
Emory, Japhet, 62.
Emory, Nathn, 61.
Emory, Noah, 62.
Emory, Saml, 61.
Emory, Saml, Junr, 61.
Emory, Simon, Junr, 61.
Emory, Steven, 61.
Emrson, ——, 46.
Emrson, Brown, 45.
Emson, Joseph, 67.
English, Edward, 70.
English (Widow), 70.
Epes, Daniel, 15.
Erskins, Christopher, 38.
Erving, Shirley, 23.
Erykins, George, 33.
Esiman, Benja, 49.
Estees, Benja, 57.
Estees, Danl, 57.
Estees, Henery, 57.
Estees, John, 57.
Estees, John, 57.
Estees, Joseph, 57.
Estees, Peter, 57.
Estes, Benja, 60.
Estes, Benjamin, 66.
Estes, Jona, 60.
Estes, Ricd, 60.
Estes, Solomon, 51.
Esthers, Caleb, 14.
Esthers, Edward, 14.
Esthers, Joseph, 14.
Estis, Samuel, 25.
Estis, Simeon, 25.
Estman, Ezekil, 60.
EsVuire, John, 42.
Eten, philip, 35.
Eustis, Jacob, 28.
Eustis, Mrs., 52.
Evani, Benjamin, 59.
Evans, David, 60.

Evans, James, 43.
Evans, John, 28.
Evans, John, 60.
Evans, Willm, 16.
Evans, William, 60.
Evelet, James, 43.
Evelith, Isaac, 21.
Evelith, Nathaniel, 20.
Evelith, Nathaniel, 21.
Evely, Sarah, 68.
Evens, Daniel, 51.
Evens, hannah, 38.
Evens, John, 51.
Evens, Nathl, 39.
Everett, Henry, 31.
Everton, Thomas, 26.
Evins, Joseph, 39.
ewell, henry, 41.
Ewer, Jonathan, 48.
Ewers, John, 33.
Ewing, Alexander, 20.
Ewing, James, 20.
Ewing, Joseph, 20.
Ewing, Joseph, Junr, 20.

Fabin, John, 17.
Fabin, Joshua, 17.
Fabree, Peeter, 24.
fairbanks, Benja, 51.
fairbanks, Elijah, 51.
Fairbanks, Joel, 49.
Fairbanks, John, 49.
fairbanks, Joseph, 51.
fairbanks, Joseph, Jur., 51.
fairbanks, Nathaniel, 51.
Fairbroth, Lovewell, 52.
Fairfeld, Edwd, 39.
Fairfield, Jeremiah, 47.
Fairfield, John, Jr, 55.
Fairfield, Revd John, 65.
Fairfield, Jonathan, 48.
Fairfield, Josiah, 65.
Fairfield, Saml, 54.
Fairfield, Willm, 55.
Fairservice, John, 43.
Fairservice, Thomas, 43.
Fairwell, Bunker, 47.
Fairwell, Ebenr, 47.
Fairwell, Isaac, 47.
Fairwell, Josiah, 50.
Fales, David, 46.
Fales, James, 46.
Fales, James, Junr, 46.
Fales, John, 46.
Fales, Joshua, 58.
Fales, Nathaniel, 46.
Fales, Nathaniel, Junr, 46.
Fall, Aaron, 50.
Fall, Ebenezer, 63.
Fall, George, 63.
Fall, John, 57.
Fall, Samuel, Jur, 50.
Fall, Stephen, 56.
Fall, Stephen, 63.
Fall, Tristam, 56.
falls, Joshua, 49.
fanders, Enoch, 33.
Fannon, Oliver, 68.
Far, Seth, 40.
farbush, Isaac, 66.
Farfield, Reuben, 48.
Farington, Daniel, 60.
Farington, John, 60.
Farington, Putnum, 60.
Farington, Stephen, 60.
Farl (Widw), 69.
Farley, John, 40.
Farley, William, 28.
Farn, John, 71.
Farnall, John, 11.
farnan, Daniel, 33.
Farnham, Ansel, 34.
Farnham, Benja, 63.
Farnham, Chapen, 34.
Farnham, David, 63.
Farnham, David, 63.
Farnham, Dummer, 67.
Farnham, Jerr, 51.
Farnham, Jona, 34.
Farnham, Joseph, 34.
Farnham, Joseph, Esqr, 63.
Farnham, Joshua, 52.
Farnham, Paul, 63.
Farnham, Paul, 67.
Farnham, Ralf, 67.
Farnham, Saml, 51.
Farnham, Simeon, 17.
Farnham, Zebedee, 52.
farnsworth, Isaac, 41.
farnswort, Robert, 41.
farnswort, William, 41.
farnswort, William, Jun., 41.
Farnsworth, Isaac, 54.
Farnsworth, Jonas, 31.
Farnsworth, Saml, 11.
Farnum, Benjam, 64.
Farnum, David, 64.
farow, timt., 48.
Farr, Joseph, 44.
Farr, Thos, 20.
Farrell, Farrington, 31.
Farrell, Peggy, 27.
farren, Ezechiel, 48.

Farrington, Abner, 49.
Farrington, John, 30.
Farrington, William, 23.
Farron, David, 12.
Farrow, John, 14.
Farrow, John, 22.
farrow, Joseph, 48.
Farrow, Josiah, 29.
Farrow, Nathan, 22.
Farrow, Peter, 46.
farthaton, Ithamer, 51.
Farthingham, John, 14.
fassat, henry, 48.
fassat, henry, jun., 48.
fassat, william, jun., 48.
Fasset, Richd, 14.
faster, John, 48.
faster, nathen, 48.
faster, nat., jun., 48.
faster, Sebert, 48.
faster, wilm, 48.
Faulkner, Daniel, 26.
Fausett (Widow), 53.
Favor, Jno, 63.
Featherly, Anna, 62.
feiler, jaspar, 42.
feiler, Stofel, 41.
feiler, Charles, 42.
Fellows, Ebenezer, 40.
Fellows, Joseph, 36.
Fellows, Saml, 21.
Felsh, Abijah, 63.
Felsh, Hannah, 67.
Felsh, Jona, 67.
Fendarson, John, 65.
Fenderson, Nathl, 17.
Fenderson, Nathl, Jr., 17.
Fenderson, Pelatiah, 17.
Fenix, Abigail, 61.
Fenix, John, 61.
Fenlason, Wallis, 52.
Ferguson, Reuben, 62.
Ferguson, Stephen, 62.
Ferguson, Timothy, 62.
Ferguson, Wm, 62.
Fernald, Nathl, 65.
Fernald, Peltiah, 23.
Fernalld, Clement, 29.
Fernalld, Nathaniel, 32.
Fernsworth, Peter, 42.
Ferren, Ebenezer, 46.
Ferren, John, 12.
Ferren, John, Junr, 12.
Ferren, Jona, 55.
Ferren, Richd, 12.
ferrin, Timothy, 33.
Fessenden, Ebenezer, 60.
Fessenden, William, 60.
Fewell, John, 22.
Fichet, Zebulon, 54.
Ficket, Vincent, 17.
Field, Danl, 64.
Field, Ebenr, 17.
Field, Elias, 30.
Field, James, 21.
Field, Capa Joseph, 62.
Field, Stephen, 15.
Field, Zachariah, 14.
Field, Zachariah, 21.
Fields, Benjamin, 15.
Fields, Joseph, 15.
Fields, Joseph, 40.
fields, Samuel, 40.
Fields, Thomas, 30.
Fields, William, 25.
Fields, Zachariah, 15.
fielhauer, daniel, 42.
Fifield, Edward, 14.
Fifield, John, 60.
Filbrick, Jonathan, 12.
File, Ebenr, 17.
File, George, 17.
File, Saml, 17.
File, Wm, 17.
File, Wm, Jr, 17.
Filer, Ebenezer, 50.
Fillebrown, Thos, 39.
fillpact, James, 67.
fillpot, William, 69.
filor, John, 42.
Finney, Seth, 20.
Firbush, William, 66.
Firck, Samuel, 40.
Fish, David, 47.
fish, Ellab, 37.
Fish, George, 39.
Fish, Jicah, 40.
fish, John, 40.
fish, Jonathan, 32.
Fish, Nathan, 45.
Fisher, Elijah, 11.
Fisher, Henry, 38.
Fisher, Jacob, 70.
Fisher, James, 49.
Fisher, John, 37.
Fisher, John, 38.
Fisher, Joseph, 22.
Fisher, Onesiphorus, 22.
Fisher, Peter, 44.
Fisher, Thomas, 14.
Fisk, Abner, 71.
Fisk, John, 70.
Fisk, Mark, 70.

fitch, John, 48.
fitch, John, 48.
fitch, Jonas, 48.
Fitch, Richard, 16.
fitch, tim, 48.
Fitch, Wilm, 16.
fitch, william, 42.
fitchgearald, John, 42.
FitsGerald, David, 72.
Fitsgerald, George, 39.
FitsGerald, James, 72.
FitsGerald, Patrick, 72.
Fitts, Brown Farm, 43.
Fitts, Ephraim, 33.
Fitts, John, 16.
Fitts, Sarah, 61.
Fitz, Obadiah, 17.
Fitz, Saml, 17.
Fitz, Simeon, 17.
Fitzgearild, Daniel, 64.
flacher, Gideon, 51.
Flag, Gershom, 39.
Flag, John, 34.
Flagg (Widow), 53.
Flahartha, Daniel O., 12.
Flanders, Samuel, 43.
Flanders, Saml, 44.
Fletcher, Amos, 36.
Fletcher, Briant, 39.
Fletcher, Briant, 39.
Fletcher, David, 39.
Fletcher, Ephraim, 27.
Fletcher, John, 13.
Fletcher, John, 55.
Fletcher, John, 71.
Fletcher, Jonathan, 27.
Fletcher, Jona, 55.
Fletcher, Joseph, 55.
Fletcher, Pendleton, 55.
Fletcher, Pendleton, 58.
Fletcher, Robert, 39.
Fletcher, Samuel, 43.
Fletcher, Saml, 61.
Fletcher, Stephen, 55.
Fletcher, Thos, 13.
Fletcher, Thomas, 28.
Fletcher, William, 31.
Fletcher, William, 35.
Fletcher, William, 36.
Fletcher, Zachariah, 20.
fliming, James, 48.
Fling, Daniel, 52.
Fling, Morris, 45.
Fling, Samuel, 45.
Flinn, James, 52.
Flinn, Thomas, 29.
Flint, Cummins, 16.
Flint, Edward, 45.
Flint, Eleazer, 16.
Flint, James, 11.
flint, Jas., 35.
Flint, Thomas, 13.
flint, Thomas, 35.
Flitner, Willm, 37.
Flitner, Willm, 43.
Flood, Andrew, 32.
Flood, Bartholomew, 32.
Flood, Dominicus, 32.
Flood, Henry, 59.
Flood, Nathan, 65.
Floyd, Ebenezer, 26.
Floyd, James, 62.
Floyd, Michael, 65.
Floyd, Nathl, 39.
Fly, Isaac, 16.
Fly, James, 16.
Fly, James, 31.
Fly, James, 47.
Fly, William, 32.
Fly, Willm, 37.
Fogerty, Dennis, 36.
Fogg, Aaron, 17.
Fogg, Benaiah, 16.
Fogg, Benja, 16.
Fogg, Caleb, 49.
Fogg, Charles, 64.
Fogg, Danl, 64.
Fogg, Edmund, 21.
Fogg, Enoch, 20.
Fogg, George, 64.
Fogg, Hannah, 62.
Fogg, Hannah (Ww), 17.
Fogg, James, 17.
Fogg, James, 57.
Fogg, James, 63.
Fogg, Jereh, 17.
Fogg, John, 13.
Fogg, John, 62.
Fogg, Jona, 17.
Fogg, Joseph, 17.
Fogg, Joseph, 58.
Fogg, Mark, 57.
Fogg, Moses, 17.
Fogg, Moses, 17.
Fogg, Nelson, 17.
Fogg, Reuben, 17.
Fogg, Reuben, Jr., 17.
Fogg, Saml, 16.
Fogg, Samuel, 21.
Fogg, Seth, 17.
Fogg, Seth, 17.
Fogg, Stephen, 52.
Fogg, Timothy, 19.

INDEX.

Fogg, Wm, 17.
Fogginson, George, 14.
fogler, John, 42.
Follet, Benja, 39.
Follet, Jesse, 39.
Follet, Mercy, 61.
folsom, Benja, 50.
folsom, John, 50.
folsom, Nathaniel, 50.
folsom, Nathaniel, Ju., 50.
folsom, Peter, 50.
folsom, Peter, 69.
folsom, Trustom, 50.
Foot, John, 33.
Foot, John, 47.
Foot, Thos, 33.
Foot, Thos, Junr, 33.
Forbes, Jonah, 12.
Forbus, John, 35.
Forbus, John, 45.
Forbush, John, 21.
Forbush, Robert, 20.
Forbush, Samuel, 21.
ford, Abner, 33.
ford, Abner, Juner, 33.
Ford, Charles, 13.
Ford, Daniel, 46.
Ford, Francis, 52.
Ford, George, 63.
ford, henry, 41.
ford, Isaac, 41.
ford, James, 41.
Ford, John, 31.
Ford, John, 47.
Ford, Joshua, 13.
ford, Mils, 69.
Ford, Nathaniel, 19.
ford, Nathaniel, 41.
ford, Nathaniel, 51.
Ford, Paul, 59.
Ford, Robert, 57.
Forestel, James, 43.
Forgerson, John, 52.
Forguson, Denis, 62.
Forguson, Eliza, 60.
Forrel, Anna, 62.
Fosdick, James, 24.
Fosdick, Nathaniel, 23.
Fosdick, Thomas, 23.
Foss, Abner, 17.
Foss, Benjamin, 52.
Foss, Benjamin, 65.
Foss, Benjamin, junr, 52.
Foss, Danl, 17.
Foss, Daniel, 63.
Foss, Daniel, 65.
Foss, James, 65.
Foss, James, Jur, 65.
Foss, James, 3d, 65.
Foss, Job, 15.
Foss, Job T., 64.
Foss, John, 65.
Foss, Joseph, 17.
Foss, Joseph, 52.
Foss, Joseph, 65.
Foss, Lemuel, 58.
Foss, Obadiah, 64.
Foss, Peletiah, 64.
Foss, Peter, 17.
Foss, Saml, Junr, 17.
Foss, Saml, Senr, 17.
Foss, Thomas, 31.
Foss, Uriah, 17.
Foss, Walter, 65.
Foss, Walter, Jur, 65.
Foss, Walter, 3d, 65.
Foss, Wm, 17.
Foss, Wm, 65.
Foss, Wm, Jr, 17.
Foss, Zech, 17.
fossat, alexdr, 48.
fossat, alexdr, jun., 48.
fossat, william, 48.
Foster, Abigl, 62.
Foster, Abijah, 52.
Foster, Abner, 68.
Foster, Asa, 8.
Foster, Asael, 11.
Foster, Benjamin, 52.
Foster, Benjamin, Junr, 52.
Foster, Charles, 15.
Foster, Charles, 46.
Foster, Daniel, 36.
Foster, Daniel, 64.
foster, David, 51.
Foster, Ebenezer, 36.
foster, Ebenezer, 51.
Foster, Isaac, 12.
Foster, Isaac, 19.
Foster, Isiah, 64.
Foster, Jacob, 31.
Foster, Joel, 12.
Foster, John, 52.
Foster, John, 53.
Foster, John, 59.
Foster, John W., 52.
Foster, Jonathan, 32.
Foster, Joseph, 39.
Foster, Josiah, 46.
Foster, Levi, 52.
Foster, Mary, 33.
Foster, Moses, 52.
Foster, Nathl, 21.

Foster, Nathl, 51.
Foster, Parker, 62.
foster, Richard, 51.
Foster, Robert, 53.
Foster, William, 27.
foster, Sabel (Widow), 51.
foster, Saml, 51.
Foster, Simon, 62.
Foster, Steel, 46.
Foster, Stephen, 40.
Foster, Stephen, 40.
foster, Stuard, 51.
foster, Timothy, 51.
Foster, Wooden, 52.
Foster, William, 27.
Foster, William, 43.
Fought, Anthony, 47.
Fought, Fredrick, 47.
Fought, Jacob, 47.
fountain, barnabas (mescongus Island), 48.
fountain, barnabas, jun. (mescongus Island), 48.
fountain, Jacob, 48.
Fountain, Stephen, 53.
Fowle, Joshua, 37.
fowler, andrew (mescongus Island), 48.
Fowler, Ebenezer, 65.
Fowler, John, 19.
Fowler, John, 35.
Fowler, John, 47.
Fowler, John, 50.
Fowler, Levi, 32.
Fowler, Matthew, 47.
Fowler, Moses, 24.
fowler, Samuel, 39.
Fowler, Simeon, 30.
Fowler, Susanh, 61.
Fowler, Thomas, 39.
fowls, Samuel, 33.
fowls, William, 33.
Fox, Daniel, 63.
Fox, Edward, 65.
Fox, Elijah, 65.
Fox, John, 22.
Fox, John, 65.
Fox, Joseph, 67.
Foxcroft, Samuel, 20.
Foy, James, 69.
Foy, John, 43.
Foy, John, 58.
Foy, Robert, 43.
foy, Robert, 38.
Foy, Steph, 61.
Foy, Willm, 44.
Foye, Elisabeth, 56.
Foye, John, 56.
Foye, Moses, 56.
francis, thomas, 40.
Frank, James, 19.
Frank, Thomas, 14.
Frank, Thomas, 19.
Frazer, Thomas, 29.
Frazier, Alexander, 23.
Freathey, Joseph, junr, 31.
Freathy, Joseph, 31.
freeman, barnabas, 42.
Freeman, Benja, 17.
Freeman, Benjamin, 47.
Freeman, Cesor, 35.
Freeman, Chandler, 11.
Freeman, Enoch, 15.
Freeman, George, 24.
Freeman, James, 30.
Freeman, John, 39.
freeman, John, 51.
Freeman, John, 71.
Freeman, Jona, 17.
Freeman, Joseph, 11.
freeman, Nathan, 67.
Freeman, Nathl, 17.
Freeman, Nathl, 71.
Freeman, Nathl, Jr., 17.
Freeman, Peletiah, 30.
Freeman, Reuben, 29.
Freeman, Reuben, 47.
Freeman, Samson, 34.
Freeman, Samuel, 23.
Freeman, Samuel, 30.
Freeman, Timothy, 30.
Frees, Abraham, 27.
Frees, George, 27.
Frees, Isaac, 27.
Frees, Isaac, 27.
Frees, John, 27.
Freman, Joshua, 24.
French, Daniel, 25.
French, David, 49.
French, Dearborn, 28.
French, John, 51.
French, John, Jur, 51.
french, Josiah, 51.
French, Levi, 49.
French, Moses, 45.
French, Moses, 51.
French, Nathaniel, 26.
French, Willm, 12.
French, Zetham, 28.
Frether, Saml, 72.
Friend, Benja, 31.
Friend, John, 12.
friend, John, 67.

Friket, Benjamin, 13.
Friket, John, 13.
Friket, Nathaniel, 13.
Friket, William, 13.
Frikit, John, 13.
Frissel, Saml, 51.
Frissel, John, 43.
Frizzel, Benja, 43.
Frizzle, Mary, 61.
Frost, Abigl, 61.
Frost, Abm, 17.
Frost, Benja, 17.
Frost, Benja, 56.
Frost, Caleb, 62.
Frost, Cato, 15.
Frost, Charles, 15.
Frost, Capn Charles, 62.
Frost, David, 17.
Frost, Elht., 66.
Frost, Ellot, 61.
Frost, Enoch, 17.
Frost, Ichabod, 43.
Frost, Isaac, 64.
Frost, James, 15.
Frost, James, 55.
Frost, James, 57.
Frost, Johanna, 14.
Frost, John, 51.
Frost, John, 53.
Frost, John, 57.
Frost, John, Esqr, 60.
Frost, Joseph, 60.
Frost, Lemuel, 51.
Frost, Mark, 63.
Frost, Matthias, 68.
Frost, Moses, 64.
frost, Moses, 66.
Frost, Nathl, 17.
Frost, Nathanl, 62.
Frost, Pepperell, 15.
Frost, Peter (Widow), 17.
Frost, Phinehas, 16.
frost, Saml, 41.
Frost, Samuel, 53.
Frost, Simon, 60.
Frost, Simon, Senr, 61.
Frost, Stephen, 67.
Frost, Thomas, 68.
Frost, William, 57.
Frost, William, 66.
Frost, Willm, 72.
Frost, Wingate, 64.
Frothingham, John, 23.
Frunald, Joel, 61.
Fry, Benjamin, 14.
Fry, Ebenezr, 63.
Fry, Ebenezr, Junr, 62.
Fry, Joshua, 47.
Fry, Silas, 62.
Fry, Susanna, 62.
Fry, Tobias, 62.
Frye, Ebenezer, 64.
Frye, Nathl, 60.
Frye, Richd, 60.
Frye, Rowlen, 57.
Frye, Saml, 60.
Frye, Simon, 60.
fullar, thomas, 44.
Fuller, Aaron, 22.
Fuller, Alden, 37.
fuller, Bartholomew, 39.
Fuller, Barzilla, 24.
Fuller, Edward, 43.
Fuller, Enoch, 50.
fuller, Francies, 50.
Fuller, Isaac, 49.
Fuller, Jesse, 11.
Fuller, Jesse, 24.
fuller, Job, 41.
fuller, John, 51.
Fuller, Jonathan, 50.
Fuller, Joshua, 52.
fuller, Nathan, 44.
Fuller, Nathl, 24.
fuller, Nathaniel, 44.
fuller, Oliver, 44.
fuller, Salham, 44.
fuller, Seth, 37.
fuller, Zenos, 48.
Fullerton, Ebenezer, 34.
Fullerton, James, 52.
Fullerton, William, 27.
fullonton, archibal, 48.
fullonton, Robert, 48.
Fulman, George, 30.
Fulsom, John, 63.
Fulsom, John, 65.
Fulsom, Moses, 68.
Fulton, James, 47.
Fulton, John, 46.
Furbacks, Joshua, 65.
Furbush, Abm, 56.
Furbush, Benja, 63.
Furbush, Benja, Junr, 63.
Furbush, Catharine, 70.
Furbush, Danl, 62.
Furbush, Daniel, 63.
Furbush, Joseph, 62.
Furbush, Joseph, Jr, 62.
Furbush, Richd, 63.
Furbush, Saml, 57.
Furbush, Saml, 70.

furenton, Timothy, 51.
Furlong, Patrick, 64.
Furnal, John, 3d, 62.
Furnald, Coln Andw P., 60.
Furnald, Arculs, 61.
Furnald, Benja, 61.
Furnald, Benja, 61.
Furnald, Benja, 61.
Furnald, David, 61.
Furnald, David, 61.
Furnald, David, 62.
Furnald, Capn Denes, 60.
Furnald, Dennis, Junr, 61.
Furnald, Dorthy, 61.
Furnald, Ebnezr, 61.
Furnald, Eleazer, 57.
Furnald, Elihu, 61.
Furnald, Hercelus, 57.
Furnald, Deacn James, 61.
Furnald, John, 61.
Furnald, Jno, 62.
Furnald, Joseph, 61.
Furnald, Josha, 61.
Furnald, Joshua, 63.
Furnald, Josh W., 62.
Furnald, Margt, 61.
Furnald, Mark, 62.
Furnald, Mary, 60.
Furnald, Moses, 62.
Furnald, Nathl, 61.
Furnald, Nathel, 57.
Furnald, Sarah, 61.
Furnald, Tobias, 61.
Furnald, Thos, 61.
Furnald, Wm, 57.
Furnald, Wm, 61.
Furnald, Wm, 61.
Furnald, Wm, 62.
Furnald, Wm, Jur, 62.
Furnald, Nathaniel, 61.
Furnald, Willm W., 62.
Furness, Robert, 55.
Furrel, Nicholas, 72.
Fwicross, Lydia, 44.

Gabtale, thomas, 69.
Gage, Amos, 68.
Gage, Daniel, 68.
Gage, John, 51.
Gage, Isaac, 15.
Gahan, James, 37.
Gahan, John, 37.
Galahel, Daniel, 66.
Galloway, Job, 34.
Galowell, Job, 45.
gametch, Joshua, 48.
Gammage, Joshua, 60.
Gammon, Benja, 17.
Gammon, Danl, Jr., 17.
Gammon, David, 22.
Gammon, James, 28.
Gammon, Jona, 17.
Gammon, Jos., 17.
Gammon, Jos., Jr., 17.
Gammon, Moses, 17.
Gammon, Nathl, 12.
Gammon, Philip, 17.
Gammon, Pilip, 25.
Gammon, Samuel, 22.
Gammon, William, 13.
Gammon, William, 22.
Gardener, Daniel, 36.
Gardiner, —, 16.
Gardiner, Benja, 35.
Gardiner, Charles, 35.
Gardiner, Daniel, 53.
Gardiner, George, 30.
Gardiner, Gideon, 43.
Gardiner, Gothro, 47.
Gardiner, James, 20.
Gardiner, John, 11.
Gardiner, John, 37.
Gardiner, Joshua, 32.
Gardiner, Luther, 20.
Gardiner, Nathl, 22.
Gardiner, Saml, 22.
Gardiner, Seth, 20.
Gardiner, Wllm, 22.
Gardiner, Willm, 43.
Gardner, David, 52.
Gardner, David, junr, 52.
Gardner, Ebenr, 52.
Gardner, Elisha, 22.
Gardner, Warren, 53.
Garey, Frost, 66.
Garish, Johanna, 61.
Garish, John, 61.
Garish, Joseph, 61.
Garish, Timoy, 62.
Garish, Wm, 61.
Garland, Ebenezer, 28.
Garland, Jacob, 62.
Garland, Jno, 59.
Garland, Josiah, 32.
Garland, Wm, 62.
Garlen, Dodifer, 63.
Garling, Samuel, 63.
Garrish, Jack, 27.
Gary, Abel, 72.
Gary, Danl, 72.
Gary, John, 72.
Gastrige, Joshua, 67.
Gatchall, Nathaniel, 29.
Gatchel, Ephraim, 66.

Gatchel, Joshua, 67.
Gatchel, Seith, 66.
Gatchell, James, 28.
Gatcomb, William, 31.
Gates, George, 48.
Gates, John, 71.
Gates, Samuel, 48.
Gates, Stephen, 11.
Gates, Wllm, 25.
Gates, William, 69.
Gay, David, 28.
Gay, Elezer, 36.
Gay, Ephraim, 26.
Gay, Jonah, 40.
Gay, Moses, 30.
Gay, Moses, 51.
Gay, Peter, 44.
Gay, Seth, 43.
Gay, Wellington, 40.
Gelpatrick, William, 69.
Gent, Ephraim, 13.
Gentner, andrew, 41.
Gentner, David, 35.
Gentner, Jacob, 41.
George, Daniel, 23.
George, Francies, 40.
George, William, 28.
Gerlin, Nathaneal, 69.
Gerrish, Allexr, 55.
Gerrish, Benja, 55.
Gerrish, Charles, 14.
Gerrish, Clark, 55.
Gerrish, George, 14.
Gerrish, George, 63.
Gerrish, John, 56.
Gerrish, John, 63.
Gerrish, Joseph, 20.
Gerrish, Nathl, 14.
Gerrish, Nathaniel, 14.
Gerrish, Willm, 14.
Gerrish, Wm, 56.
Gerrith, Isaac, 57.
Getchell, Dominicus, 48.
Getchell, Edmond, 48.
Getchell, Elihu, 39.
Getchell, John, 47.
Getchell, Joseph, 52.
Getchell, Joseph, Junr, 52.
Getchell, Majr, 47.
Getchell, Neheh, 47.
Getchell, Samuel, 47.
geven, Robert, 48.
Geyer, Martin, 40.
Gibbs, Alpheus, 11.
Gibbs, Elisha, 26.
Gibbs, Ezra, 11.
Gibbs, Sally, 28.
Gibbs, William, 15.
Gibson, Jacob, 25.
Gibson, James, 28.
Giddings, Joseph, 34.
Gilbert, Daniel, 35.
Gilbert, Elijah, 25.
Gilbert, henry, 40.
Gilbert, Nathl, 25.
Gilbert, Samuel, 40.
Gilbert, William, 40.
Gilchrist, George, 36.
Gilchrist, Samuel, 36.
Gile, Daniel, 67.
Giles, Danl, 68.
Giles, John, 68.
Giles, John, 68.
Giles, Joseph, 34.
Giles, Joseph, 68.
Giles, Joseph, Junr, 34.
Giles, Saml, 68.
Gifford, Jno, 17.
Gilford, Jno, Jr., 17.
Gilford, Joseph, 65.
Gilkey, Isaac, 17.
Gilkey, James, 17.
Gilkey, James, 64.
Gilkey, Jno, 17.
Gilkey, John, 29.
Gilkey, Jos., 17.
Gill, John, 39.
Gillcott, George, 29.
Gilley, William, 29.
Gillmore, Arthur, 52.
Gillpatrick, Joseph, 60.
Gilman, Abijah, 65.
Gilman, Benja, 67.
Gilman, Daniel, 49.
Gilman, Danl, 67.
Gilman, David, 50.
Gilman, Dudley, 67.
Gilman, Eliphalet, 39.
Gilman, James, 65.
Gilman, Jeremiah, 67.
Gilman, Jona, 67.
Gilman, Nathaniel, 50.
Gilman, Nathaniel, Ju., 50.
Gilman, Peter, 28.
Gilman, Peter, 41.
Gilman, Robart, 42.
Gilman, Samuel, 33.
Gilman, Samuel, 50.
Gilman, Samuel, 65.
Gilman, Revd Tristram, 21.
Gilman, Zebulon, 42.
Gilman, Zebulon, 67.
Gilmore, David, 52.

INDEX.   85

Gilmore, James, 26.
Gilmore, John, 26.
Gilmore, Rufus, 47.
Gilmore, Samuel, 30.
Gilmore, William, 30.
Gilmore, Willm, 52.
Gilpatrick, Charles, 38.
GilPatrick, Christopher, 58.
GilPatrick, Christopher, 64.
GilPatrick, Christopher, 58.
GilPatrick, Dominicus, 58.
GilPatrick, James, 71.
Gilpatrick, John, 60.
GilPatrick, John, 69.
GilPatrick, Joseph, 69.
Gilpatrick, Joseph, Esqr, 63.
Gilpatrick, Nathaniel, 34.
GilPatrick, Rich^d, 70.
Gilpatrick, Robert, 58.
GilPatrick, Saml, 70.
GilPatrick, Sarah, 58.
Gilpatrick, Sarah, 64.
Gilpatrick, Thomas, 38.
GilPatrick, Thos, 58.
Gilpatrick, Thomas, 63.
Gilpatrick, Willm, 58.
Gincing, John, 40.
Gincing, Samuel, 40.
Ginn, James, 30.
Ginn, Thomas, 32.
Gipson, Thos, 22.
Gipson, Willm, 70.
Gipson, Willm, Jr, 70.
Gipson, Zedediah, 70.
Gitchel, Benj^a, 37.
Gitchel, Elihu, 35.
Gitchel, George, 69.
Gitchel, Hugh, 14.
Gitchel, John, 12.
Gitchel, John, 14.
Gitchel, John, 43.
Gitchel, John, 45.
Gitchel, Jonathan, 70.
Gitchel, Joseph, 14.
Gitchel, Joseph, 35.
Gitchel, Joshua, 70.
Gitchel, Nathl, 14.
Gitchel, Robert, 14.
Gitchel, Saml, 12.
Gitchel, Stephen, 12.
Gitchel, Stephen, Junr, 12.
Gitchel, Willm, 12.
Gitchel, Willm, Junr, 12.
Gitchel, Zachariah, 70.
Givens, Daniel, 12.
Givens, James, 41.
Givens, John, 12.
Givens, John, 41.
Givens, John, Junr, 12.
Givens, Robert, 12.
Glass, Ezekiel, 20.
Glass, John, 59.
Gledden, Nathl, 41.
Gledden, Tobias, 41.
Glidden, Arnold, 42.
Glidden, Benj^a, 41.
Glidden, Joseph, 41.
Glidden, Joseph, Jr, 41.
Gliddon, Gidion, 39.
Gliden, Anddrew, 33.
Gliden, Charles, 33.
Glidon, Charles, 33.
Gliten, Jeremiah, 41.
Glitton, Reuben, 39.
Glover, James, 32.
Glover, John, 21.
Glover, Robert, 24.
Glover, Thomas, 36.
Goadon, Thial, 49.
Goald, Aaron, 60.
Goald, Aaron, 66.
Gobart, Nicholas, 35.
Godard, Robert, 16.
Godard, Samuel, 67.
Godard, Silas, 16.
Goddard, Nathan^l, 53.
Goddard, Thatcher, 70.
Godden, John, 46.
Godfrey, Benj^a, 29.
Godfrey, Daniel, 54.
Godfrey, Ichabod, 53.
Godfrey, Thomas, 12.
Godfry, Prince, 39.
Godsoe, ——, 62.
Goff, James, 11.
Gogens, David, 65.
Going, Hannah, 72.
Going, Jane (Wid^w), 60.
Going, John, 67.
Going, Nicholas, 69.
Going, Samuel, 59.
Golder, William, 40.
Goocer, Edward, 45.
Gooch, Benj^a, 22.
Gooch, Benjamin, 52.
Gooch, Ebenezer, 52.
Gooch, James, 52.
Gooch, John, 62.
Gooch, Nathl, 22.
Gooch, William, 52.
Goodale, Daniel, 28.
Goodale, John, 70.
Goodale, Nehemiah, 70.

Goodale, Tim^o, 71.
Goodale, Zachariah, 70.
Goodale, Zachariah, Jr, 70.
Goodhue, Josiah, 67.
Goodin, Elezer, 45.
Gooding, Luxford, 30.
Goodridge, Jewett, 20.
Goodrigde, Willm, 55.
Goodrige, Danl, 56.
Goodrige, Jedediah, 56.
Goodrige, Jere., 55.
Goodrige, John, 56.
Goodrige, John, 56.
Goodrige, Joseph, 57.
Goodspeed, Nathl, 40.
goodwin, Aaron, 59.
Goodwin, Adam, 57.
Goodwin, Adam, 57.
Goodwin, Amaziah, 59.
Goodwin, Amaziah, 69.
Goodwin, Amos, 56.
Goodwin, Andrew, 39.
Goodwin, Benj^a, 55.
Goodwin, Benjamin, 59.
Goodwin, Benjn, 60.
Goodwin, Benj^a, 68.
Goodwin, Caleb, 50.
Goodwin, Caleb, 71.
Goodwin, Charles, 56.
Goodwin, Daniel, 37.
Goodwin, Daniel, 55.
Goodwin, Danl, 61.
Goodwin, Danl, 64.
Goodwin, Danl, 68.
Goodwin, Danl, 70.
Goodwin, Danl, 71.
Goodwin, David, 68.
Goodwin, Dominicus, 55.
Goodwin, Ebenezer, 56.
Goodwin, Elijah, 57.
Goodwin, Elijah, 57.
Goodwin, Elisha, 57.
Goodwin, Elisha, 63.
Goodwin, Ephrim, 67.
Goodwin, George, 14.
Goodwin, Hon. Ichabod, 55.
Goodwin, James, 56.
Goodwin, James, 56.
Goodwin, James, Jr, 56.
Goodwin, Jedediah, 56.
Goodwin, Jeremiah, 43.
Goodwin, Jeremiah, 56.
Goodwin, Jeremiah, 59.
Goodwin, John, 21.
Goodwin, John, 23.
Goodwin, John, 55.
Goodwin, John, 63.
Goodwin, John, 68.
Goodwin, John, 71.
Goodwin, John, Jr, 71.
goodwin, Jonathan, 59.
Goodwin, Joseph, 59.
Goodwin, Joseph, 67.
Goodwin, Joseph, 71.
Goodwin, Joshua, 67.
Goodwin, Joshua, 71.
Goodwin, Lazarus, 39.
Goodwin, Mark, 59.
Goodwin, Mary, 63.
Goodwin, Moses, 56.
Goodwin, Moses, 57.
Goodwin, Nathan, 67.
Goodwi—, Nathaniel, 59.
Goodwin, Paul, 71.
Goodwin, Reuben, 63.
Goodwin, Richard, 24.
Goodwin, Richard, 58.
Goodwin, Ruben, 63.
Goodwin, Saml, 13.
Goodwin, Samuel, 23.
Goodwin, Saml, 44.
Goodwin, Saml, 57.
Goodwin, Samuel, 63.
Goodwin, Saml, Ju., 44.
Goodwin, Shipway, 57.
Goodwin, Silas, 56.
Goodwin, Simeon, 43.
Goodwin, Stephen, 39.
Goodwin, Thomas, 57.
Goodwin, Thomas, 63.
Goodwin, Thos, 68.
Goodwin, Thos, 71.
Goodwin (Widow), 55.
Goodwin, W^m, 56.
Goodwin, W^m, 56.
Goodwin, W^m, 57.
Gooe, Jacob, 53.
Googin, Simon, 14.
Googings, Samuel, 23.
Googins, John, 65.
Googins, Joseph, 65.
Googins, Rogers, 31.
Googins, Thomas, 32.
Googins, W^m, 65.
Gookins, Joseph, 64.
Gookins, Rich^d, 16.
Gorden, Amos, 58.
Gorden, And^w, 64.
Gorden, James, 12.
Gorden, John, 64.
Gorden, John, Jr, 64.
Gorden, Nathl, 21.
Gorden, Nathl, 72.

Gorden, Robert, 46.
Gorden (Widow), 16.
Gorden, Zebulen, 64.
Gordon, Caleb, 50.
Gordon, David, 44.
Gordon, Henry, 60.
Gordon, Hugh, 60.
Gordon, John, 26.
Gordon, John, 31.
Gordon, John, 60.
Gordon, John, jun^r, 26.
Gordon, Jonathan, 44.
Gordon, Jon^a, 51.
Gordon, Josiah, 51.
Gordon, Saml, 50.
Gordon, thiah, 51.
Gore, Joshua, 20.
Gore, William, 44.
Gore, Robart, 44.
Gorge, Franices, 40.
Gorham, David, 22.
Gorham, Samuel, 25.
Gorham, W^m, 17.
Gorton, Simeon, 27.
Goss, Ebenezer H., 12.
Goss, Saml, 68.
Gott, Daniel, 29.
Gott, Daniel, jun^r, 29.
Gott, Joseph, 29.
Gott, Nathaniel, 29.
Gott, Peter, 29.
Gott, Stephen, 29.
Gouch, Jedediah, 70.
Gouch, Joseph, 70.
Gouch, Saml, 70.
Gouch, Saml, 71.
Goud, James, 43.
Goudy, William, 53.
Goue, John, 69.
gouen, Ezekel, 66.
Gouen, John, Junor, 67.
Gouen, Stephen, 66.
Gouen (Widow), 66.
Gould, ——, 62.
Gould, Benjamin, 25.
Gould, Benjn, 62.
Gould, Daniel, 62.
Gould, Danl, Junr, 62.
Gould, Elixand^r, 62.
Gould, Ezra, 59.
Gould, Gardner, 15.
Gould, George, 44.
Gould, Isaac, 58.
Gould, Jabez, 39.
Gould, James, 55.
Gould, James, 64.
Gould, Jesse, 44.
Gould, John, 15.
Gould, John, 52.
Gould, John, 55.
Gould, John, 62.
Gould, Joseph, 23.
Gould, Joseph, 33.
Gould, Joseph, 62.
Gould, Joseph, 65.
Gould, Miriah, 42.
Gould, Nathaniel, 30.
Gould, Nathl, 71.
Gould, Nehemiah, 47.
Gould, Saml, 52.
Gould, Samuel, 59.
Gould, Samuel, 65.
Gould, Silas, 44.
Gould, thomas, 59.
Gould, William, 44.
Goulthrite, Philip, 65.
Gous, Moses, 69.
Gove, Asa, 37.
Gove, David, Junr, 37.
Gove, Ebenezer, 37.
Gove, Ebenezer, Junr, 37.
Gove, Enoch, 36.
Gove, Nathan, 37.
Gove, Nathan, 37.
Gove, Solomon, 37.
Gowday, Emez, 48.
Gowel, Benj^a, 63.
Gowel, Charles, 47.
Gowel, John, 56.
Gowel, William, 34.
Gowan, David, 68.
Gowan, John, 57.
Gowen, Patrick, 63.
Gowen, Richard, 57.
Gower, Iaras, 41.
Gowing, John, 62.
Gowing, Lemuel, 62.
Gra, Andrew, 31.
Gra, Christopher, 27.
Gra, James, 31.
Gra, Joshua, 31.
Gra, Joshua, jun^r, 31.
Gra, Nathaniel, 31.
Gra, Reuben, 31.
Gra, Reuben, jun^r, 26.
Gra, Samuel, 31.
Gra, Samuel, jun^r, 37.
Grace, Benj^o, 61.
Grace, James, 54.
Grace, Jane, 33.
Grace, Jno, 17.
Grace, Patrick, 33.

Grace, W^m, 17.
Grace, Willm, 52.
Grace, W^m, Jr., 17.
Graffam, Caleb, 25.
Graffam, Enoch, 25.
Graffam, Increase, 59.
Graffam, Jacob, 36.
Graffam, Joseph, 36.
Graffam, Josiah, 17.
Graffam, Mary, 20.
Graffam, Pierce, 36.
Graffam, Uriah, 58.
Grafton, Ephraim, 12.
Grafton, John, 40.
Grafton, Unite, 60.
Gran. Willm, 33.
Grandee, Charles, 43.
Grant, Abram, 16.
Grant, Adam, 28.
Grant, Alexander, 28.
Grant, Alexander, 31.
Grant, Alexander, 59.
Grant, Andrew, 28.
Grant, Benjamin, 59.
Grant, Charles, 67.
Grant, Daniel, 57.
Grant, Daniel, 60.
Grant, David, 72.
Grant, Dorothy, 72.
Grant, Ebenezer, 70.
Grant, Edward, 56.
Grant, Elijah, 52.
Grant, Elijah, 56.
Grant, Elisha, 68.
Grant, Ephraim, 28.
Grant, Ephraim, 66.
Grant, Francis, 31.
Grant, Gooding, 28.
Grant, James, 14.
Grant, James, 28.
Grant, James, 56.
Grant, James, 57.
Grant, James, 67.
Grant, Jasper, 72.
Grant, John, 16.
Grant, John, 55.
Grant, John, 56.
Grant, Joseph, 72.
Grant, Joshua, 57.
Grant, Joshua, 67.
Grant, Joshua, 72.
Grant, Landers, 56.
Grant, Margret, 56.
Grant, Moses, 35.
Grant, Moses, 55.
Grant, Nathaniel, 56.
Grant, Nathl, 72.
Grant, Peter, 56.
Grant, Peter, 57.
Grant, Peter, 67.
Grant, Richard, 16.
Grant, Saml, 16.
Grant, Samuel, 28.
Grant, Saml, 42.
Grant, Sarah, 72.
Grant, Silas, 50.
Grant, Stephen, 28.
Grant, Stephen, 72.
Grant, Thomas, 57.
Grant (Widow), 72.
Grant, William, 15.
Grant, William, 28.
Grant, Willm, 55.
Grant, W^m, 63.
Granvill, Josiah, 65.
Grave, Paul, 39.
Graves, Crispus, 14.
Graves, John, 46.
Graves, John, Jr, 47.
Graves, Johnson, 46.
Graves, Joseph, 46.
Graves, Moses, 27.
Graves, Saml, 46.
Gray, Aaron, 59.
Gray, Alexander, 34.
Gray, Alexander, 43.
Gray, Alexander, 46.
Gray, Amos, 45.
Gray, Andrew, 22.
Gray, Andrew, 59.
Gray, Cadwallader, 59.
Gray, Daniel, 46.
Gray, Daniel, 67.
Gray, Diminaus, 66.
Gray, Ebenezer, 45.
Gray, Ellphalet, 46.
Gray, Elisha, 58.
Gray, George, 45.
Gray, George, 60.
Gray, Grace, 12.
Gray, Jablah, 22.
Gray, James, 49.
Gray, James, 56.
Gray, James, 65.
Gray, James, Junr, 56.
Gray, James, the 3^d, 66.
Gray, James, the 3^d, 67.
Gray, John, 22.
Gray, John, 39.
Gray, John, 46.

Gray, John, 51.
Gray, John, 52.
Gray, John, 60.
Gray, Jon^a, 56.
Gray, Jon^a, 73.
Gray, Joseph, 22.
Gray, Joseph, 67.
Gray, Joshua, 70.
Gray, Levi, 27.
Gray, Lewis, 24.
Gray, Mary, 28.
Gray, Moses, 44.
Gray, Moses, Jn^r, 44.
Gray, Nehemiah, 59.
Gray, Reuben, 45.
Gray, Samuel, 44.
Gray, Samuel, 69.
Gray, Sarah, 52.
Gray, Stephen, 49.
Gray, Tabitha, 17.
Gray, Thomas, 49.
Gray, Thomas, ju., 49.
Gray (Widow), 58.
Gray, William, 67.
Grealey, Jonathan, 38.
Greay, James, 40.
Greeley, Elisaboth, 23.
Greeley, John, 24.
Greeley, Joseph, 51.
Greeley, Joseph, Ju., 51.
Greeley, Noah, 51.
Greeley, Seth, 44.
Greely, Eliphalet, 22.
Greely, Enoch, 39.
Greely, Jacob, 41.
greely, Jonathan, 48.
Greely, Joseph, 44.
Greely, Stephen, 22.
Greely, William, 19.
Green, And^w, 55.
Green, Anna, 31.
Green, Benjamin, 22.
Green, Benj^a, 55.
Green, Casiah, 23.
Green, Daniel, 23.
Green, Daniel, 40.
Green, Henry, 23.
Green, Isaac, 32.
Green, John, 17.
Green, John, 31.
Green, Jon^a, 17.
Green, Joseph, 32.
Green, Joseph, 45.
Green, Josiah, 17.
Green, Josiah, 44.
Green, Mary, 62.
Green, Moses, 46.
Green, Rich^d, 38.
Green, Richard, 47.
Green, Sarah, 57.
Green, Thos, 17.
Green, Thos, 25.
Green, Thomas, 28.
Green, Thom^s, 69.
Green, Timothy, 50.
Green, William, 23.
Green, Willm, 38.
Green, William, 40.
Green, William, 46.
Greenlaw, John, 17.
Greenlaw, William, 27.
Greenlaw, william, 48.
Greenleaf, Amos, 23.
Greenleaf, Benj^a, 44.
Greenleaf, Ebenezer, 39.
Greenleaf, Enoch, 37.
Greenleaf, Joseph, 23.
Greenleaf, Saml, 37.
Greenleaf, Stephen, 37.
Greenlew, alex^dr, 48.
Greenlief, Ebenezer, 45.
Greenlief, John, 45.
Greenlief, Joseph, 44.
Greenlief, Joshua, 45.
Greenlief, William, 45.
Greenough, Jon^a, 34.
Greenwood, John, 24.
Greffen, Ephraim, 16.
Gregory, William, 26.
Gregory, William, jun^r, 26.
Greley, Jacob, 38.
Greno, Peltiah, 62.
Griffen, Ephraim, 16.
Griffen, Ichabod, 37.
Griffen, Jon^a, 16.
Griffen, Saml, 16.
Griffen, Seth, 16.
Griffin, Jacob, 27.
Griffin, John, 11.
Griffin, Nathan, 28.
Griffin, Samuel, 28.
Griffin, William, 28.
Griffin, William, 29.
Griffiths, Henry, 52.
Grindall, Daniel, 31.
Grindall, Ichabod, 30.
Grindall, John, 30.
Grindall, John, jun^r, 30.
Grindall, Joshua, 31.
Grindall, Reuben, 31.
Grindall, William, 31.
Grindley, ——, 64.
Grinnall, William, 29.

INDEX.

Grinnell, Bailey, 47.
Grinnell, Royal, 47.
Groce, Isaac, 21.
Groo, Joseph, 29.
Groo, Joseph, jun'r, 29.
gros John, 41.
gros, peter, 41.
gros (widow), 41.
Gross, Ebenezer, 28.
Gross, Ebenezer, jun'r, 28.
Gross, George, 12.
Gross, Jacob, 12.
Gross, John, 26.
Gross, John, 28.
Gross, Joseph, 28.
Gross, Joseph, jun'r, 28.
Gross, Michael, 12.
Gross, Mich'l, Jun'r, 12.
Gross, Moses, 27.
Gross, Reuben, 53.
Gross, Sam'l, 12.
Gross, Zachary, 28.
Grotten (widow), 35.
Grout, William, 30.
Grove, Dorcas, 71.
Grove, Olive, 71.
Grove, Will'm, 71.
Grove, Will'm, Jr, 71.
Grover, ——, 62.
Grover, Andrew, 15.
Grover, Andrew, 34.
Grover, And'w, 37.
Grover, Benj'a, 52.
Grover, Dan'l, 72.
Grover, Ebenezer, 33.
Grover, James, 34.
Grover, James, 38.
Grover, James, 68.
Grover, Jedidiah, 58.
Grover, John, 44.
Grover, John, 68.
Grover, Martha, 61.
Grover, Simon, 62.
Grover, Simon, 72.
Grover, Tho'␣, 37.
Grover, William, 20.
Groves, Sam'l, 41.
Groves, William, 44.
Gubtail, Abijah, 29.
Gubtail, Benj'a, 56.
Gubtail, Benj'a, 67.
Gubtail, Daniel, 60.
Gubtail, James, 57.
Gubtail, John, 29.
Gubtail, John, jun'r, 29.
Gubtail, Moses, 56.
Gubtail, Nath'el, 57.
Gubtail, Nat., Jun'r, 57.
Gubtail, Sam'l, 57.
Gubtail, Sam'l, Jun'r, 57.
Gubtail, Stephen, 57.
Gubtail, Thomas, 29.
Gubtail, W'm, 57.
Gubtale, Stephen, 69.
Gubtale, thomas, Jun., 69.
Guerney, Lemuel, 21.
Guild, Joseph, 47.
Guile, Stephen, 67.
Gullifin, Thomas 50.
Gullison, Benj'a, 61.
Gullison, Deac'n Jos., 61.
Gullison, Sam'l, 61.
Gullison, John, 37.
Gullison, John, 61.
Gullison, W'm, 61.
Gunnison Will'm, 71.
Guptell, William, 53.
Gurney, Ellab, 16.
Gurney, Jon'a, 11.
Gurney, Lemuel, Jun'r, 21.
Gurney, Thos., 11.
Gurrel, John, 44.
Gushing, Ezekiel, 38.
Gustin, Ebenezer, 23.
Gustin, Tho'␣, 17.
Gutridg, Joshua, 36.
Gutridge, John, 59.
Gutridge, Josiah, 59.
Gutterage, Anna (Wid'w), 69.
Gutterige, Aaron, 59.
Guttridge, Benjamin, 65.
Guttridge, Benj'a, Jr, 65.
Guttridge, Hannah, 65.
Gwin, James, 48.

Hacker, Jere'h, 12.
Hacker, Jere'h, Jun., 12.
Hacket, Alexander 53.
Hacket, Ezekiel, 40.
Hacket, Ezekiel, Ju'r, 40.
Hacket, Jude, 40.
Haden, Charles, 50.
Haden, Josiah, 50.
Hadley, Ephraim, 52.
Hadley, Simeon, 29.
Hadlock, Samuel, 29.
Haeley, John, 69.
Hagerty, Jane, 14.
haggat, Isaac, 45.
Haggens, Edmund, 55.
Haggens, John, 55.
Hagget, Benj'a, 37.

Hagget, Elijah, 11.
Hagget, Moses, 11.
Hagget, William, 23.
Haines, Benj'a, 59.
Haines, Benj'a, 59.
Haines, Ephraim, 31.
Haines, Frederick, 30.
Haines, Peter, 31.
Haines, Nathaniel, 68.
Haines, Parley, 31.
haines, Simeon, 68.
Haines, Tho'␣, 72.
Haines, Tim'y, 17.
Hains, Dan'l, 17.
Hains, Dudley, 51.
Haite, John, 23.
Haldershaw, John, 28.
Haldershaw, John, jun'r, 28.
Hale, Benj'n, 13.
Hale, Benj'n, 25.
Hale, David, 11.
Hale, Ebenezer, 39.
Hale, Elizabeth, 42.
hale, Enoch, 66.
Hale, Ephrom, 36.
Hale, Israel, 25.
Hale, Israel, 69.
Hale, James, 53.
Hale, John, 42.
Hale, Josiah, 42.
Hale, Josiah, 42.
Hale, Josiah, 68.
Hale, Nath'l, 11.
Hale Nathaniel, 15.
Hale, Oliver, 25.
Hale, Oliver, 69.
Hale, Richard, 53.
Hale, Samuel, 31.
Hale, Stephen, 54.
Hale, Thomas, 42.
Hale, Timothy, 50.
Haley, Abra'm, 58.
Haley, Benj'a, 64.
Haley, John, 58.
Haley, Joseph, 46.
Haley, Joseph, 58.
Haley, Joseph, 64.
Haley, Joseph, 64.
Haley, Joseph, Jn'r, 46.
Haley, Joshua, 58.
Haley, Pelatiah, 46.
Haley, Robert, 64.
haley, Richard, 67.
Haley, Sam'l, 64.
Haley, Silvester, 58.
Haley (Widow), 43.
Haley, Will'm, 58.
Haley, Will'm, 64.
Hall, Aaron, 50.
Hall, Abijah, 22.
Hall, Ab'm, 17.
Hall, allen, 50.
Hall, Andrew, 14.
Hall, Caleb, 36.
Hall, Calvin, 45.
Hall, Charles, 24.
Hall, Eben'r, 17.
Hall, Ebenezer, 32.
Hall, Ebenezer, 41.
hall, Ebenezer, 67.
Hall, Elijah, 36.
Hall, Enoch, 12.
Hall, Enoch, 13.
Hall, Ephraim, 36.
Hall, Ephraim, Jun'r, 36.
Hall, Hatevil, 14.
Hall, Hatevil, 25.
Hall, Hezekiah, 11.
Hall, Isaac, 36.
Hall, Isaac, 41.
Hall, Isaac, Jun'r, 36.
Hall, Isac. 33.
Hall, James, 33.
hall, James, 35.
Hall, Jedediah, 14.
Hall, Job, 11.
Hall, John, 20.
Hall, John, 24.
Hall, John, 33.
Hall, John, 38.
Hall, John, 54.
Hall, Jon'a, 22.
Hall, Joseph, 20.
Hall, Joseph, 38.
Hall, Josiah, 50.
Hall, Lemuel, 34.
hall, levy, 35.
Hall, Luther, 34.
Hall, Moses, 22.
Hall, nathan, 50.
Hall, Nath'l, 20.
hall, Neilson, 66.
Hall, Nicholis, 14.
Hall, Oliver, 39.
Hall, Peter, 36.
Hall, Reuben, 49.
Hall, Sam'l, 37.
Hall, Sam'l, 50.
Hall, Samuel, 50.
hall, Seth, 35.
Hall, Silas, 57.
Hall, Stephen, 23.

Hall, Stephen, 25.
Hall, Timothy, 45.
Hall, William, 15.
Hall, William, 21.
Hall, Will'm, 24.
Hall, William, 25.
hall, william, 35.
Hall, W'm, 57.
Hall, Winslow, 25.
Hallet, Elisha, 50.
Hallet, Solomon, 50.
Halliburton, George, 30.
Hallowel, Will'm, 39.
Ham, Benjamin, 25.
Ham, Benj'a, 33.
Ham, George, 68.
Ham, George, 68.
Ham, John, 33.
ham, John, 49.
Ham, Joseph, 12.
Ham, Jos'a, 55.
ham, Reuben, 49.
ham, Reuben, 49.
ham, Samuel, 49.
ham, Sam'l, 49.
Ham, Sam'l, 68.
Ham, Sarah, 40.
Ham, Thomas, 35.
Ham, Tobias, 12.
Ham, Tobias, 40.
Ham, W'm, 55.
Hamar, David, 29.
Hamblen, Africa, 25.
Hamblen, America, 25.
Hambleton, Elijah, 59.
Hamblin, Dan'l, 17.
Hamblin, Eben'r, 17.
Hamblin, George, 17.
Hamblin, Gershom, 17.
Hamblin, Jacob, 17.
Hamblin, John, 50.
Hamblin, Jos'., 17.
Hamblin, Nathan, 17.
Hamblin, Nathaniel, 27.
Hamblin, Perez, 28.
Hamblin, Prince, 17.
Hamblin, Sam'l, Jr., 17.
Hamblin, Seth, 17.
Hamblin, Tim'y, 17.
Hamblin, Timothy, 47.
Hamblin, Timothy, jr., 47.
Hambly, William, 46.
Hamden, Gabriel, 43.
Hamelton, Abel, 69.
Hamelton, Benjamin, 69.
Hamelton, James, 69.
Hamelton, John, 50.
Hamelton, John, 69.
Hamelton, Richard, 69.
Hamer, John, 29.
Hamilton, Abial, 67.
Hamilton, Ambros, 22.
Hamilton, John, 22.
Hamilton, John, 22.
Hamilton, John, 34.
Hamilton, John, 56.
Hamilton, Jonas, 57.
Hamilton, Jon'a, 55.
Hamilton, Jon'a, 57.
Hamilton, Joseph, 56.
Hamilton, Millet, 56.
Hamilton, Reuben, 56.
Hamilton, Roland, 22.
Hamilton, Silas, 56.
Hamilton, Simeon, 56.
Hamilton, Solomon, 57.
Hamilton, Will'm, 22.
Hamilton, William, 28.
Hamlen, Levi, 44.
Hamlen, Richard, 51.
Hamlin, Africa, 69.
Hamlin, America, 69.
Hamlin, Theophilus, 39.
Hammet, Thomas, 57.
Hammet, Thomas, Jr., 57.
Hammon, Bebla, 11.
Hammon, Elisha, 67.
Hammon, Frederick, 43.
Hammon, Fredrick, 50.
Hammon, Samuel, 21.
Hammon, Seth, 43.
Hammon, William, 53.
Hammond, Benj'a, Jn'r, 22.
Hammond, Christ'a, 62.
Hammond, Edmond, 61.
Hammond, Ephraim, 47.
Hammond, John, 22.
Hammond, John, 31.
Hammond, John, 31.
Hammond, Jonath'n, Jur, 61.
Hammond, Deac'n Jonath'a, 61.
Hammond, Joseph, 22.
Hammond, Moses, 32.
Hammond, Nathaniel, 32.
Hammond, Peter, 22.
Hammond, Sam'l, 22.
Hammond, Deac'n Sam'l, 61.
Hammond, Tho'␣, 62.
Hammonds, Eben'␣, 61.
Hammonds, George, 61.
Hammons, Edmund, 60.
Hana, John, 23.

Hance, John, 23.
Hancock, John, 28.
Hancock, John, 46.
Hancock, Jn'o, 59.
Hancock, Joseph, 22.
Hancock, Nathan, 28.
Hancock, W'm, 59.
Hancom, Tim'o, 54.
Henderson, Benjamin, 34.
handey, Benj'a, 41.
Handey, Ebenezer, 41.
Handy, Benjamin, 44.
Handy, Jonathan, 43.
handy, Richard, 41.
hanelton, heneary, 66.
Hanes, John, 72.
Haney, Daniel, 19.
hankerson, William, 51.
hankerson, thomas, 51.
hanley, malachi, 48.
hanley, pertrik, 48.
Hanley, Rodger, 48.
Hanscom, Aron, 52.
Hanscom, Aron, jun'r, 52.
Hanscom, Nathan, 52.
Hanscomb, Elisha, 17.
Hanscomb, George, 17.
Hanscomb, Geo., Jr, 17.
Hanscomb, Gideon, 60.
Hanscomb, Humpy, 17.
Hanscomb, Ketarah, 17.
Hanscomb, Moses, 17.
Hanscomb, Nathan, 17.
Hanscum, Eben'␣, 62.
Hanscum, James, 62.
Hanscum, Jno., 62.
Hanscum, Jonathan, 62.
Hanscum, Nathan, 62.
Hanscum, Paltiah, 62.
Hanscum, Steven, 62.
Hanscum, Tobias, 61.
Hanson, Abra'm, 67.
hanson, Caleb, 66.
Hanson, Daniel, 63.
Hanson, Ebenezer, 56.
Hanson, Elijah, 25.
Hanson, Elisabeth, 56.
Hanson, Ezra, 25.
Hanson, Gersham, 56.
Hanson, Ichabod, 25.
Hanson, Ichabod, 25.
Hanson, Isaac, 63.
Hanson, James, 57.
Hanson, Jonathan, 25.
Hanson, Jon'a, 63.
hanson, Joshua, 66.
Hanson, Mary, 63.
Hanson, Moses, 59.
Hanson, Moses, 63.
Hanson, Nicholas, 57.
Hanson, Phineas, 58.
Hanson, Ruth, 15.
Hanson, Samuel, 25.
Hanson, William, 25.
hanson, William, 69.
Hapa, Amos, 11.
Hapgood, Oliver, 25.
Hapgood, Oliver, 69.
Hapworth, Thomas, 31.
Harden, Hezekiah, 12.
Harden, Isaac, 39.
Harden, Isaac, Jn'r, 39.
harden, Joshua, 67.
Harden, Sam'l, 12.
Harden, Stephen, 23.
Harden (Widow), 70.
Harden, Stephen, 70.
Hardge, W'm, 62.
Hardin, William, 23.
Harding, Archibald, 28.
Harding, David, 17.
Harding, David, Jr, 17.
Harding, David, Sen'r, 17.
Harding, Elkanah, 17.
Harding, Ezekiel, 32.
Harding, Jesse, 28.
Harding, Jn'o, 17.
Harding, John, 31.
Harding, Jn'o, Jr., 17.
Harding, Josiah, 28.
Harding, Josiah, 31.
Harding, Martha, 17.
Harding, Nich'l, 17.
Harding, Sam'l, 59.
Harding, Seth, 17.
Harding, Simon, 16.
Harding, Zeph'a, 17.
Hardison, Joseph, 63.
Hardison, Nathaniel, 31.
Hardison, Sam'l, 57.
Hardison, Stephen, 31.
Hardison, Stephen, 57.
Hardison, Thomas, 57.
Hardy, Abel, 64.
Hardy, David, 60.
Hardy, Isaac, 25.
Hardy, Joseph, 29.
Hardy, Peter, 27.
Harford, John, 69.
Harford, Sole, 17.
Harford, Solomon, 63.
Harford, William, 38.
harkerson, John, 51.

Harkness, John, 26.
Harley, John, 41.
Harley, John, Jn'r, 41.
Harley, Ralph, 28.
Harlon, Andrew, 12.
Harlow, Ebenezer, 11.
Harlow, Nathaniel, 27.
Harman, Abner, 17.
Harman, Benj'a, 17.
Harman, Dan'l, 17.
Harman, Elias, 17.
Harman, Eliz'a, 17.
Harman, George, 17.
Harman, Ja'␣, 17.
Harman, James, Jr., 17.
Harman, Jn'o, 17.
Harman, John, 58.
Harman, John, 72.
Harman, John, Jr, 72.
Harman, Jon'a, 17.
Harman, Joseph, 17.
Harman, Moses, 17.
Harman, Nath'l, 72.
Harman, Sam'l, 17.
Harman, Tho'␣, 72.
Harman, W'm, 17.
Harman, Will'm, 58.
Harman, Zebadiah, 72.
Harman, Zech'r, 17.
Harmon, Benjamin, 52.
Harmon, Dan'l, 24.
Harmon, Dorn'␣, 59.
harmon, Edward, 69.
Harmon, Elliot, 24.
Harmon, Joel, 59.
Harmon, John, 25.
Harmon, Josiah, 58.
harmon, Napthalum, 66.
harmon, Napthalum, Jun, 66.
Harmon, Nath'l, 59.
Harmon, Pelatiah, 58.
Harmon, Pettcah, 65.
Harmon, Samuel, 60.
Harmon, Tho'␣, 59.
Harmon, W'lm, 59.
harmond, John, 48.
Harn. Shadrick, 24.
Harnden, Will'm, 52.
Harndon, Sam'l, 52.
Harnock, Elias, 22.
Harper, Daniel, 64.
Harper, Richard, 53.
Harper, Samuel, 64.
Harper, William, 15.
Harper, William, 31.
Harridon, Ignatious, 43.
Harrington, Benj'a, 37.
Harrington, David, 26.
Harrington, Elisha, 37.
Harrington, Isaac, 26.
Harrington, Joseph, 43.
Harris, Amos, 11.
Harris, Amos, 21.
Harris, Amos, 21.
harris, Charls, 51.
Harris, John, 20.
harris, John, 38.
Harris, Joseph, 27.
Harris, Josiah, 52.
Harris, Obadiah, 39.
Harris, Sam'l, 34.
Harris, Sam'l, 58.
Harris, Samuel, 59.
harris, Silas, 38.
Harris, Simeon, 20.
Harris, Step'n, 17.
Harris, Stephen, 22.
Harris (Widow), 72.
Harris, Will'm, 11.
Harris, William, 20.
Harrison (Widow), 72.
Harriss, Sam'l, 72.
Harriss, Timothy, 72.
Harriss, Winslow, 50.
Hart, Aaron, 60.
Hart, Avery, 36.
Hart, Henry, 70.
Hart, James, 65.
Hart, Jesse, 36.
Hart, John, 28.
Hart, John, 36.
Hart, Rob't, 63.
Hart, Stephen, 40.
Hart, William, 47.
Hartford, Benjamin, 50.
Hartford, John, 39.
Harthaway, Seth, 21.
Harthorn, Alexander, 36.
Harthorn, Alexander, Jun'r, 36.
Harthorn, Ashbell, 27.
Harthorn, David, 27.
Harthorn, John, 36.
Harthorn, Samuel, 36.
Harthorn, Silas, 27.
Harthorn, Solomon, 30.
Harthorn, Thomas, 29.
Hartwell, Edward, 36.
Hartwell, Oliver, 44.
Harup, Thomas, 26.
Harves, Joseph, 11.
Harvey, David, 16.
Harvey, Enoch, 16.
harvey, James, 68.

INDEX.

Harvey, John, 25.
Harvey, John, 28.
Harvey, John, 71.
Harvey, Seth. 52.
Harvey, Thomas, 53.
Harvey, William, 68.
Harvey, Wm, 72.
Harvy, William, 61.
Harwood, Thomas, 35.
Hase, Zephemiah, 65.
Hasetine, Barnes, 60.
Hasoy, Revd Isaac, 63.
Hasey, William, 27.
Haskel, Benjamin, 21.
Haskel, Benjn, 24.
Haskel, Israel, 11.
Haskel, Israel, 25.
Haskel, Jacob, 17.
Haskel, Jcb, 20.
Haskel, John, 17.
Haskel, Jona, 24.
Haskel, Jonathan L., 20.
Haskel, Josiah, 23.
Haskel, Moses, 21.
Haskel, Nathl, 22.
Haskel, Ruth, 20.
Haskel, Solomon, 15.
haskel, thomas, 66.
Haskel, Ward, 20.
Haskel, Willcbe, 20.
Haskel, Willm, 11.
Haskel, William, 15.
Haskel, Willm, 20.
Haskell, Abijah, 27.
Haskell, Caleb, 27.
Haskell, Catharine, 22.
Haskell, Eliphalet, 21.
Haskell, Francis, 27.
Haskell, Francis, 46.
Haskell, Gideon, 21.
Haskell, Ignatius, 27.
Haskell, Jacob, 20.
Haskell, Joel, 21.
Haskell, John, 20.
Haskell, John, 21.
Haskell, John, 25.
Haskell, Jonathan, 27.
Haskell, Joshua, 27.
Haskell, Mark, 27.
Haskell, Mary, 20.
Haskell, Moses, 21.
Haskell, Nathan, 21.
Haskell, Nathan, 27.
Haskell, Nathaniel, 20.
Haskell, Thomas, 14.
Haskell, Thomas, 27.
Haskell, Willm, 11.
Haskell, William, 21.
Haskell, Willm, 48.
Haslem, George, 32.
Hason, Benja, Jur, 65.
Hassa, James, 11.
Hassa, Noah, 11.
Hassack, Charles, 23.
Hassan, William, 28.
hastey, James, 66.
Hasting, Marthew, 47.
Hastings, Amos, 68.
Hastings, Moses, 47.
haston, John, Jurr, 66.
Hasty, Danl, 24.
Hasty, David, 64.
Hasty, James, 24.
Hasty, James, 70.
Hasty, Nathl, 17.
Hasty, Robt, 17.
Hasty, Robert, 64.
Hasty, Robert, 64.
Hasty, Wm, 17.
Hastyes, Saml, 67.
Hatch, Abijah, 21.
Hatch, Amos, 71.
Hatch, Asa, 17.
Hatch, Benja, 69.
Hatch, Benja, Jr, 69.
Hatch, Chris., 53.
Hatch, Clark, 35.
Hatch, Danl, 71.
Hatch, David, 39.
hatch, David, 66.
Hatch, David, 69.
Hatch, Ebenr, 17.
Hatch, Ebena, 69.
Hatch, Eliab, 70.
Hatch, Eliakim, 70.
Hatch, Elias, 69.
Hatch, Elijah, 69.
Hatch, Elisha, 69.
hatch, Elizer, 21.
Hatch, Ellihu, 40.
Hatch, Ephraim, 35.
hatch, Ezekel, 65.
Hatch, Ezekiel, 13.
Hatch, Fisher, 21.
Hatch, Francis, 70.
hatch, fridrik, 35.
Hatch, Gideon, 71.
Hatch, Gideon, Jr, 69.
hatch, hapcle, 45.
Hatch, Hawes, 53.
Hatch, Isaac, 42.
hatch, Jacob, 66.
Hatch, Jeremiah, 29.

Hatch, Jera, 69.
Hatch, Jesse, 69.
Hatch, Jethro, 35.
Hatch, Jethro, 35.
Hatch, John, 13.
Hatch, John, 70.
hatch, Jonathan, 48.
Hatch, Jona, 70.
Hatch, Jona, Jr, 69.
Hatch, Joseph, 28.
Hatch, Joshua, 71.
Hatch, Leml, 69.
Hatch, Leml, 69.
Hatch, Mark, 30.
Hatch, Nathan, 44.
hatch, Nathan, 66.
Hatch, Nathl, 17.
Hatch, Noah, 69.
Hatch, Obadiah, 71.
Hatch, Paul, 44.
hatch, philip, 48.
Hatch, Reuben, 70.
Hatch, Samuel, 40.
hatch, Samuel, 66.
Hatch, Saml, 70.
Hatch, Saml, 72.
Hatch, Seth, 27.
Hatch, Seth, 70.
Hatch, Simeon, 44.
Hatch, Simeon, 71.
Hatch, Solomon, 71.
hatch Stephen. 66.
Hatch, Sylvanus, 47.
Hatch (Widow), 70.
Hatch, Willm, 70.
Hatch, Zach., 33.
Hathaway, Eleazer, 52.
Hathorn, James, 44.
Hathorn, John, 52.
Hathorn, John, Junr, 52.
Hathorn Nathl, 44.
Hathorn, Seth, 52.
Hathorn, Willm, 51.
Hathway, Ichabod, 12.
haupt, John, 42.
Hawes, Abijah, 47.
Hawes, David, 30.
Hawes, Elizabeth, 52.
Hawes, Matthias, 47.
Hawes, Moses, 47.
Hawes, Robert, 36.
Hawk, Edward, 11.
Hawkes, Amos, 25.
Hawkes, Amos, 26.
Hawkes, Amos, 26.
Hawkes, Ebenezer, 25.
Hawkes, James, 25.
Hawkes, Nathaniel, 25.
Haws, Jacob, 48.
Haws, Thomas, 47.
Haws, Thomas, junr, 47.
Hayden, Jeremiah, 19.
Hayden, John, 30.
Hayes, Elihue, 63.
Hayes, Elijah, 57.
Hayes, George, 13.
Hayes, Ichabod, 57.
Hayes, John, 15.
Hayes, John, 21.
Hayes, John, 63.
Hayes, John, 63.
Hayes, Peter, 68.
Hayley, Ebena, 61.
Hayley, Joel, 60.
Hayley, John, 61.
Hayley, Joseph, 61.
Hayley, Noal, 61.
Hayley, Robt, 61.
Hayley, Saml, 61.
Hayley, Majr Wm, 61.
Haynes, David, 20.
Haynes, John, 39.
Haynes, Matthias, 22.
Haynes, Patty, 43.
Haysles, Jno, 68.
Haywood, Lemuel, 60.
Haywood, Lemuel, 66.
Haywood, Nathan, 39.
Haywood, Ziniri, 50.
Haze, Amos, 22.
Haze, Jacob, 22.
Haze, John, 22.
Hazelton, Timo, 59.
heabner, george, 41.
Head, James Walter, 49.
Head, Moses, 47.
Headon, John, 35.
heads, john & joshua, 48.
heads, joshua. *See* heads, john & joshua, 48.
Heal, Chesley, 27.
Heal, Gilbart, 38.
Heal, Isaac, 27.
Heal, John, 38.
Heal, John. 38.
Heal, John, jurr, 45.
Heard, Abigail, 67.
Heard, Benja, 57.
Heard, Benja, 57.
Heard, Ebenezer, 56.
Heard, James, 32.
heard, James, 66.
Heard, Jethro, 67.

Heard, John, 57.
Heard, Joseph, 57.
Heard, Silas, 57.
Heard, Thomas, 57.
Heard, Tristam, 56.
Heard, Tristam, Jr, 56.
Heard, William, 46.
Hearl, Benja, 57.
Hearl, Elisha, 56.
Hearl, Gilbert, 56.
Hearl, James, 58.
Hearl, John, 56.
Hearl, John, 56.
Hearl, John, 57.
Hearl, Joseph, 55.
Hearl, Lucia, 56.
Hearl, Mary, 56.
Hearl, Moses, 68.
Hearl, Sarah, 57.
Hearl, Wm, 55.
Hearl, Wm, 56.
Hearne, Nicha, 17.
Hearsy, Elisabeth, 20.
Hearsy, Elisabeth, 21.
Hearsy, Peleg, 29.
heartwell, James, 66.
heat, John, 41.
Heath, Abraham, 33.
Heath, Asa, 33.
Heath, Eldad, 30.
Heath, Isaac, 33.
Heath, Jonathan, 33.
Heath, Mary, 63.
Heath, Moses, 40.
Heath, Richard, 29.
Heath, William, 29.
Heath, William, 34.
Heaton, Elijah, 24.
Heaton, Richard, 24.
heavener, charles, 42.
Hebbert, Joseph, 60.
heckelton (widow), 35.
hedwic, Joseph, 42.
Heffords, Wm, 13.
Heffords. Wm, 25.
Heins, Samuel, 65.
heisler, martin, 42.
Hemmingway, Revd Moses, 71.
Henderson, Dunbar, 36.
Henderson, Jabez, 36.
Henderson, John, 69.
Henderson, Joseph, 69.
Henderson, Robert, 36.
henderson, Samuel, 69.
Henderson, Thomas, 36.
Henderson, Thos, 53.
Hendley, John, 36.
Henney, Sarah, 61.
Henry, Archibald, 30.
Henry, Isaiah, 53.
Henry, James, 46.
Henry, Robert, 32.
hercy, Eben, 48.
Herd, Danl, 70.
heredin, William, 38.
herick, Joseph, 38.
herkley, James, 51.
Hern, Daniel, 34.
Hern, Patrick, 34.
Herrick, Andrew, 30.
Herrick, Daniel, 14.
Herrick, Ebenezer, 31.
herrick, Ely, 38.
Herrick, John, 11.
Herrick, John, 31.
Herrick, John, 40.
Herrick, Joseph, 30.
Herrick, Joseph, 31.
Herrick, Joshua, 31.
Herrick, Samuel, 31.
herrick, Samuel, 38.
Herrick, Shadrach, 31.
Herriman, Simon, 41.
Herrin, Robert, 21.
Herring, Benjr, 24.
Herris, Abner, 40.
Herris, Lydia, 40.
Herryman, Ahasael, 32.
Herryman, Asa, 28.
Herryman, Asa, junr, 28.
Herryman, Benja, 32.
Herryman, Daniel, 32.
Herryman, Ezekiel, 28.
Herryman, John, 32.
Herryman, Joshua, 28.
Herryman, Peter, 28.
hersey, Eben, 48.
Hersey, Nathl, 39.
Hersey, Solomon, 43.
Hersey, Willm, 20.
Hersey, Zadock, 53.
Hersom, Jacob, 67.
heselton, Jonathan, 68.
Heselton. Samuel, 38.
hetcher, thomas, 48.
hevemon, Levi, 45.
hevener, mathias, 41.
Hewoll, Henry, 27.
Hewen, Ebenr, 39.
Hewes, Eliu, 27.
Hewes, Paoli, 29.
Hewey, James, 34.
Hewey, James, 46.

Hewey, John, 34.
Hewey, John, 46.
Hewey, John, Jur, 34.
Hewey, Robert, 34.
Hewit, William, 26.
Hewitt, Waterman, 46.
Heyden, George, 12.
Hibbard, Daniel, 37.
Hibbard, Jonathan, 35.
Hibbart, James, 14.
Hibbart, John, 14.
Hibbert, Joseph, 30.
Hibbert, Joseph, junr, 30.
Hibbord, Israll, 69.
Hichborn, Robert, junr, 27.
Hichborn, William, 28.
Hicks, James, 14.
Hicks, Leml, 17.
Hicks, Samuel, 14.
Hicks, prout Timy, 17.
hicks, Zefeniah, 40.
Hide, Joseph, 55.
Higan, James, 38.
Higgam, Philip, 33.
Higgam, Simeon, 33.
Higgans, Thomas, 38.
Higgans, Walter, 64.
Higgin, Edmd, 17.
Higgin, Jos. 17.
Higgins, Abisha, 28.
Higgins, Barnabas, 30.
Higgins, Benja, 28.
Higgins, Benja, 33.
Higgins, David, 29.
Higgins, Ebenezer, 24.
Higgins, Edmd, 18.
Higgins, Elisha, 15.
Higgins, Elkanah, 25.
Higgins, Elkanah, 29.
Higgins, Israel, 29.
Higgins, James, 32.
Higgins, Jesse, 29.
Higgins, Jerusha, 29.
Higgins, Jethro, 32.
Higgins, John, 28.
Higgins, Josiah, 32.
Higgins, Levi, 29.
Higgins, Massy, 13.
Higgins, Philip, 33.
Higgins, Reuben, 33.
Higgins, Robert, 24.
Higgins, Samuel, 23.
Higgins, Simeon, 33.
Higgins, Solomon, 29.
Higgins, Stephen, 29.
Higgins, Timothy, 24.
Higgins, Willm, 12.
Higgins, Willm, 24.
Highser, Adam, 28.
Higings, Jesse, 40.
Higings, Seth, 35.
Higings, Timothy, 34.
higins, Seth, 49.
Higman, Edward, 36.
hiland, abner, 38.
Hildrick, Paul, 40.
Hiler, Cornelius, 36.
Hiler, Jacob, 36.
Hiler, Simeon, 34.
hilkon, William, 45.
Hill, Abram, 70.
Hill, Amos, 57.
Hill, Andrew, 62.
Hill, Benja, 58.
Hill, Benjamin, 65.
Hill, Benja, 71.
Hill, Charles, 60.
Hill, Daniel, 53.
Hill, Danl, 59.
Hill, David, 69.
Hill, Eleazer, 22.
Hill, Elisha, 64.
Hill, Geofry, 31.
Hill, Hannah, 52.
Hill, Ichabod, 55.
Hill, Isaac, 62.
Hill, James, 11.
Hill, James, 37.
hill, James, Junr, 67.
Hill, Jeremiah, 55.
Hill, Jeremiah, 63.
Hill, John, 29.
Hill, John, 55.
Hill, John, 59.
Hill, John, 62.
Hill, John, 64.
Hill, John, 69.
Hill, Jona, 69.
Hill, Joseph, 52.
Hill, Joseph, 57.
Hill, Joseph, 58.
Hill, Joseph, 66.
Hill, Joseph, 69.
Hill, Joshua, 63.
Hill, Josiah, 58.
Hill, Kiah, 22.
Hill, Mark, 57.
Hill, Mary, 71.
Hill, Nathl, 59.
Hill, Ruben, 63.
Hill, Samuel, 52.
Hill, Saml, 59.

Hill, Saml, 62.
Hill, Saml, 69.
Hill, Saml, 70.
Hill, Sarah, 52.
Hill, Sarah, 62.
Hill, Theodore, 72.
Hill, Thomas, 21.
Hill, Thos, 24.
Hill, Thomas, 29.
Hill, Volantine, 59.
Hill (Widow), 58.
Hills, John, 50.
Hills, Joseph, 50.
Hills, Robert, 50.
Hillwell, Thomas, 36.
Hilt, John, 26.
Hilt, Margaret, 26.
hilt (widow), 41.
hilt (widow), 41.
hilten, James, 48.
hilten, William, 48.
Hilton, Abraham, 55.
Hilton, Daniel, 30.
Hilton, Dudley, 65.
Hilton, Ebenezer, 46.
Hilton, Ebena, 70.
Hilton, Eliakim, 72.
Hilton, Elihu, 45.
Hilton, Emma, 14.
Hilton, Isaac, 23.
Hilton, Isaac, 33.
Hilton, John, 33.
Hilton, John, 43.
Hilton, John, 46.
Hilton, Joseph, 43.
Hilton, Joseph, 44.
Hilton, Joseph, 70.
Hilton, Joshua, 43.
Hilton, Joshua, 69.
Hilton, Morril, 43.
Hilton, Moses, 43.
Hilton, Nathaniel, 27.
Hilton, Ricd, 67.
Hilton, Saml, 41.
Hilton, Samuel, 43.
Hilton, William, 43.
Hilton, William, 46.
Hilton, Willm, 70.
Hines, Aushur, 39.
Hines, Benjamin, 42.
hines, Conelis, 41.
Hines, Nimrod, 45.
Hines, Richd, 17.
Hinkley, Aaron, 12.
hinkley, Benja, 45.
hinkley, David, 50.
Hinkley, Ebenezer, 26.
Hinkley, Edmund, 12.
Hinkley, Edmund, 38.
Hinkley, Elnathan, 46.
Hinkley, Gidion, 40.
Hinkley, Hannah, 38.
Hinkley, Isaiah, 26.
Hinkley, James, 39.
Hinkley, Josiah, 58.
Hinkley, Matthew, 37.
Hinkley, Nehemiah, 26.
Hinkley, Ruth, 12.
Hinkley, Seth, 29.
Hinkley, Shubal, 39.
Hinkley, Susannah, 26.
Hinkley, Theo*, 46.
Hinkly, Aaron, 34.
Hinkly, Isaac, 35.
Hinkly, Miller, 47.
Hinkly, Reliance, 35.
Hinkly, Samuel, 35.
Hinkly, Samuel, 35.
Hinkly, Samuel, 45.
Hinshaw, Sarah, 15.
hiscock, Richard, 48.
Hiscock, Thomas, 44.
Hiscock, William, 45.
hisscock. John, 35.
Hitchcock, Daniel, 41.
Hitchings, Josiah. 52.
Hitton, Benjamin, 44.
Hix, Joseph, 21.
Hix, Thomas, 46.
Hobbey, Remington, 47.
hobbos, Stephen, 66.
Hobbs, Amos, 24.
Hobbs, David, 65.
Hobbs, Goarge, 69.
Hobbs, Henery, 60.
Hobbs, James, 65.
Hobbs, Jeremiah, 24.
Hobbs, Jonathan, 14.
Hobbs, Joseph, 71.
Hobbs, Joseph, 71.
Hobbs, Josiah, 21.
Hobbs, Josiah, 68.
Hobbs, Moril, 69.
Hobbs, Obed, 12.
Hobbs, Samuel, 65.
Hobbs, Stephen, 57.
Hobbs, Thomas, 57.
Hobbs, Thos, 71.
Hobbs, Willm, 21.
Hobbs, Willm, 71.
Hobby, John, 23.
Hobby, William, 23.
Hobert, Nathl, 53.

INDEX.

Hobson, Joseph, 59.
Hobson, Samˡ, 59.
hoch, george, 41.
hoch, martin, 41.
hoch, michel, 41.
Hodgan, timothy, 69.
Hodgdon, Benjᵃ, 37.
Hodgdon, Israel, 25.
Hodgdon, Israel, 54.
Hodgdon, Jeremiah, 12.
Hodgdon, Joseph, 29.
Hodgdon, Moses, 11.
Hodgdon, Thomas, 37.
Hodgdon, Thomas, Junʳ, 37.
Hodge, James, 43.
Hodge, John, 11.
Hodge, Henry, 43.
Hodge, Mary, 37.
Hodge, Willᵐ, 37.
Hodges, Alexʳ, 53.
Hodges, Ezra, 39.
Hodgkins, Ebenezer, 11.
Hodgkins, Edward, 31.
Hodgkins, Francis, 33.
Hodgkins, James, 11.
Hodgkins, James, Juʳ, 11.
Hodgkins, Jonathan, 40.
Hodgkins, Joseph, 11.
Hodgkins, Joseph, 29.
Hodgkins, Moses, 31.
Hodgkins, Moses, 46.
Hodgkins, Phillip, 31.
Hodgkins, Shemuell, 31.
Hodgkins, William, 29.
Hodgkins, Willᵐ, 33.
Hodgman, John, 34.
Hodgsdon, John, 17.
Hodgsdon, Jos., 17.
Hodgsdon, Benjⁿ, 62.
Hodgsdon, Sarah, 62.
Hodgsdon (Widow), 17.
Hodsdon, Benjᵃ, 56.
Hodsdon, Benjⁿ, 56.
Hodsdon, Benjᵃ, 56.
Hodsdon, Danˡ, 56.
Hodsdon, Ebenezer, 56.
Hodsdon, Hannah, 56.
Hodsdon, Isreal, 56.
Hodsdon, James, 56.
Hodsdon, Jeremiah, 56.
Hodsdon, John, 63.
Hodsdon, John, 63.
Hodsdon, Jonathan, 63.
Hodsdon, Joseph, 57.
Hodsdon, Joseph, 63.
Hodsdon, Joshua, 63.
Hodsdon, Moses, 56.
Hodsdon, Nathan, 56.
Hodsdon, Riᶜᵈ, 56.
Hodsdon, Samuel, 56.
Hodsdon, Samson, 63.
Hodsdon, Simon, 56.
Hodsdon, Solomon, 68.
Hodsdon, Stephen, 56.
Hodsdon, Stephen, 56.
Hodsdon, Thᵒˢ, 56.
Hodsdon, Thomas, 57.
Hodsdon, Thᵒˢ, 63.
Hodsdon, Wᵐ, 56.
Hodsdon, Wᵐ, 63.
hofses, anton, 41.
hofses, george, 42.
hofses, mathias, 41.
Hogan, Michˡ, 12.
Hogan, Thomas, 38.
hogeden, benjamin, 35.
hogeden, Stephen, 35.
hogekins, David, 35.
Hogeman, Job, 26.
Hogings, William, 34.
Hoit, Daniel, 52.
Hoit, Elizabeth, 47.
Hoit, George, 17.
Hoit, John, 14.
Hoit, Thomas, 44.
Hoitt, Petralea, 51.
Holbrook, Abizah, 33.
Holbrook, Jesse, 30.
Holbrook, John, 20.
Holbrook, John, 28.
Holbrook, John, 43.
Holbrook, Jonˢ, 20.
Holbrook, Joseph, 43.
Holbrook, Peter, 45.
Holbrook, Prince, 29.
Holbrook, Richard, 43.
Holbrook, Silas, 16.
Holland, Elisabeth, 65.
Holland, John, 25.
holland, John, 35.
Holland, Lemuel, 43.
Holland, William, 53.
Holbrook, Calvin, 30.
Hollis, Stephen, 36.
Holloway, Barnibus, 37.
Holloway, Ludwick, 37.
Holloway, Prince, 37.
Hollway, Ladwick, 52.
Holly, Joanna, 31.
Holman, John, 71.
Holman, John, 72.
Holmes, ——, 17.
Holmes, Ephᵐ, 17.

Holmes, Gershom, 11.
Holmes, Greshom, 11.
Holmes, Hugh, 41.
Holmes, James, 24.
Holmes, James, 60.
Holmes, Job, 24.
Holmes, Jnᵒ, 17.
Holmes, John, 41.
Holmes, John, 43.
Holmes, John, 52.
Holmes, Jonˢ, 24.
Holmes, Joseph, 57.
Holmes, Josiah, 11.
Holmes, Samuel, 52.
Holmes, Samˡ, 59.
Holmes, Simeon, 11.
Holmes, Thomas, 63.
Holmes, Wᵐ, 57.
Holms, Wᵐ, 17.
Holoway, Gideon, 37.
Holt, Ebenᵃ, 72.
Holt, Humphry, 28.
Holt, Jedediah, 26.
Holt, John. 68.
Holt, Nickolas, 26.
Holt, Nickolas, junʳ, 26.
Holt, Zela, 68.
Holton, John, 34.
Holton, Jonathan, 60.
Holyoak, John, 30.
Homan, James, 69.
Homan, Jonas, 25.
Homer, William, 32.
Homes, Jeremiah, 30.
Homes, Samuel, 28.
Homes, Tilden. 29.
Honeyford, Robert, 20.
Honeyford, Robert B., 21.
Honeyford, Thomas, 15.
Honeywell, Elijah, 25.
Honnowel, Israel, 43.
Honnowel, John, 43.
Honowell, Richᵈ., 51.
Honycomb, Benalah, 65.
Hood, David, 15.
Hood, Edmᵈ, 59.
Hood, James, 23.
Hoodlet, Lewis, 43.
Hoof, thomas, 59.
Hooffes, George, 49.
Hoole, William, 13.
Hooper, Abigail, 25.
Hooper, Benjᵃ, 58.
Hooper, Benjᵃ, Jr, 58.
Hooper, Daniel, 58.
Hooper, David, 16.
Hooper, David, 31.
Hooper, George, 64.
Hooper, Jacob, 64.
Hooper, John, 27.
Hooper, John, 31.
Hooper, John, 64.
Hooper, Joseph, 25.
Hooper, Joseph, 64.
Hooper, Nathᵃ, 61.
Hooper, Noah, 58.
Hooper, Robert, 25.
Hooper, Tristram, 64.
Hooper, William, 7.
Hopkins, Allen, 32.
Hopkins, Bazilah, 29.
Hopkins, Benjⁿ, 58.
hopkins, bill, 35.
Hopkins, Christopher, 40.
Hopkins, Elisha, 30.
Hopkins, Elisha, 35.
Hopkins, Isaac, 28.
Hopkins, James, 31.
Hopkins, Joseph, 29.
Hopkins, Nathan, 28.
hopkins, Peter, 49.
hopkins, Peter, Ju. 49.
Hopkins, Simeon, 29.
Hopkins, Smith, 29.
Hopkins, Solomon, 32.
Hopkins, Solomon, 41.
Hopkins, Solomon, 65.
Hopkins, Theodore, 24.
Hopkins, Thomas, 24.
Hopkins, William, 31.
Hopkins, William, 32.
Hopkins, Willᵐ, 40.
hopkins, William, 49.
Hopkins, William, Junʳ, 32.
Hopkinson, Caleb, 58.
Hopkinson, Jnᵒ, 59.
Hopkinson, Joses, 59.
Hopson, Wᵐ, 17.
Hor, Phillip, 69.
Hore, Philip, 23.
Horks, Joseph, 33.
Horn, Benjᵃ, 63.
Horn, Cornelius, 34.
Horn, Ephrim, 63.
horn, frederich, 41.
Horn, Jacob, 37.
Horn, Jonˢ, 68.
horn, Joseph, 67.
Horn, Joseph, 71.
Horn, Ricᵈ, 63.
horn, Samuel, 67.
Horn, Thoˢ, 34.
Horn (Widow), 34.

Horne, Benjᵃ, 67.
Horne, Danˡ, 67.
Horner, Captˢ, 47.
Hornestead, Daniel, 35.
Horsom, Benjᵃ, 63.
Horsom, David, 63.
Horsom, John, 63.
Horsom, Jonᵃ, 63.
Horsom, Samˡ, 63.
Horsum, James, 56.
Horsum, John, 56.
Horsum, Wᵐ, 56.
Horton, Elihu, 54.
Horton, Joshua, 26.
Hosmer, Abel, 30.
Hosmer, Asa, 26.
Hosmer, Nathaniel, 26.
Hosmer, Nathaniel, junʳ, 26.
hossies, christian, 41.
hossies, godfried, 42.
Hough, Daniel, 37.
Hough, Joseph, 36.
Hough, Moses, 37.
Houghton, Jonᵃ, 25.
Houghton, Thomas, 52.
Houghton, Thomas, Jr, 44.
houpe, Joseph, 41.
hous, joshua, 48.
House, Caleb, 25.
House, Gershom, 12.
House, James, 36.
House, Moses, 11.
House, Moses, 24.
house, nathaniel, 40.
Houston, Robert, 26.
Houston, Samuel, 26.
Houston, Samuel, junʳ, 26.
Hovey, Ivory, 55.
Hovey, John, 39.
hovey, John, 51.
Hovey, John, 55.
Hovey, Samˡ, 59.
Hovey, Susanna, 55.
How, Danˡ, 24.
How, Ichabod, 51.
How, John, 45.
How, Jonᵃ, 41.
How, Lemuel, 44.
How, Stephan, 51.
Howard, Amos, 64.
Howard, Andrew, 33.
Howard, Benjᵃ, 30.
Howard, Benjᵃ, junʳ, 30.
howard, caleb, 42.
Howard, Daniel, 36.
Howard, Edward, 30.
Howard, Ezra, 27.
Howard, James, 58.
Howard, John, 27.
Howard, John, 52.
Howard, Joseph, 58.
howard, Joshua, 41.
Howard, oliver, 42.
Howard, Peter, 35.
Howard, Peter, Jᵘ, 35.
Howard, Phinehas, 64.
Howard, Pomper N., 70.
Howard, Samuel, 27.
Howard, Samuel, 64.
Howard, Samˡ, 70.
Howard, Thomas, 27.
Howard, Willᵐ, 39.
Howard, Willliam, 60.
Howe, Danˡ, 11.
Howe, David, 30.
Howe, Jacob, 16.
Howe, Moses, 11.
Howe, Sarah, 53.
Howe, Tilly, 52.
Howe, William, 52.
Howell, Silas, 14.
Howland, Abraham, 47.
Howland, Arthur, 33.
Howland, Elijah, 44.
Howland, Joseph, 44.
Howland, Wilᵐ, 50.
Howland, William, 50.
howlen, Zebien, 48.
Hoxie, Barnis, 37.
Hoxie, David, 37.
Hoxie, Gidion, 37.
Hoxie, Ludwick, 37.
Hoxkey, Hezʰ, 47.
Hoyt, Richard, 29.
Hoyt, Solomon A., 29.
hubard, franices, 45.
hubard, John, 51.
Hubard, Joshᵃ, Esqʳ, 62.
Hubbard, Aaron, 67.
Hubbard, Asa, 60.
Hubbard, Benjᵃ, 57.
Hubbard, Danˡ, 67.
Hubbard, Diamond, 70.
Hubbard, Heard, 60.
Hubbard, James, 67.
Hubbard, James, 69.
Hubbard, Jerⁿ, 71.
Hubbard, John H., 70.
Hubbard, Joseph, 56.
Hubbard, Joseph, 56.
Hubbard, Joseph, 70.
Hubbard, Levi, 22.

Hubbard, Lydia, 57.
Hubbard, Moses, 69.
Hubbard, Phillip, 56.
Hubbard, Phillip, 61.
Hubbard, Reuben, 22.
Hubbard, Ricᵈ, 67.
Hubbard, Samˡ, 56.
Hubbard, Thomas, 56.
Hubbard, Timothy, 55.
Hubbard, Warwick, 70.
Hubbart, Moses, 70.
huccosen, henry, 51.
Huchings, David, 45.
huchings, John, 49.
Huchings, Olive, 45.
Huckens, Holis, 38.
Huckings, Clement, 53.
Huckings, Samuel, 53.
Huen, Willᵐ, 39.
Huent (Widʷ), 59.
Huff, Abner, 55.
Huff, Charles, 55.
Huff, Charles, 55.
Huff, Danˡ, 41.
Huff, Ebenezer, 55.
Huff, Israel, 55.
Huff, James, 55.
Huff, John, 55.
Huff, Moses, 35.
Huff, Samˡ, 55.
Huff, Thoˢ, 54.
Hugh, Samˡ, 12.
Hughes, John, 43.
huler, conrad, 41.
Humes, John, 50.
Humes, John, Juʳ, 50.
Humphrey, Oliver, 19.
Humphreys, James, 19.
Humphries, David, 45.
Humphries, Joseph, 45.
Humphries, Thomas, 45.
Humphry, Benjᵃ, 21.
Humphry, Ebenᵉ, 21.
Humphrys, Joseph, 21.
Humprys, Danˡ, 64.
Hunewell, Richard, 30.
Hunniford, David, 12.
Hunniwel, Benjᵃ, 17.
Hunniwel, Richᵈ, 17.
Hunniwel, Roger, 17.
Hunniwel, Sarah, 17.
Hunniwel, Zorubbael, 18.
Hunniwell, Thomas, 45.
Hunniwell, William, 46.
Hunscom, Moses, 13.
Hunscomb, Jnᵒ, 59.
Hunscomb, Wᵐ, 59.
Hunscum, Danˡ, 64.
Hunscum, Jack, 61.
Hunscum, Joathᵃ, 61.
Hunscum, Moses, 60.
Hunscum, Nathᵃ, 60.
Hunskum, Danˡ, 61.
Hunssom, Isaac, 63.
Hunssom, Jerusha, 56.
Hunssom, Mark, 57.
Hunssum, Robˡ, 57.
Hunssum, Samˡ, 57.
Hunsum, Reuben, 57.
Hunt, Benoni, 42.
Hunt, Benoni, Juʳ, 42.
Hunt, Daniel, 12.
Hunt, David, 19.
Hunt, David, 38.
Hunt, Ephraim, 12.
Hunt, Ephᵐ, 17.
Hunt, Ichabod, 17.
Hunt, John, 35.
hunt, John, 42.
Hunt, Laban, 30.
Hunt, Mary, 12.
Hunt, Samˡ, 12.
Hunt, Silas, 39.
Hunt, Steward, 43.
Hunt, Willᵐ, 38.
Hunt, Willᵐ, 72.
Hunter, Arthur, 46.
hunter, henry, 48.
Hunter, James, 46.
Hunter, James, Jnʳ, 46.
Hunter, Robert, 46.
Hunter, Willᵐ, 46.
Hunter, Willᵐ, 47.
huntington, Benjⁿ, 45.
huntington, Timothy, 45.
Huntley, Jabez, 52.
Huntly, Jabez, junʳ, 53.
Huntly, Frederick, 53.
Huntoon, Jonathan, 43.
Huntriss, Pearson, 14.
Huntrus, Darling, 56.
Huntrus, Darling, 67.
Huntrus, George, 56.
Huntrus, Ichabod, 67.
Huntrus, Wᵐ, 56.
Hunttington, John, 45.
Hupper, John, 56.
Hupper, John, 68.
Hupper, Samˡ, 57.

Hupper, Wᵐ, 56.
hurland, prince, 48.
hurlane, Peter, 51.
Hurley, William, 53.
husoy, Ruben, 66.
Hussey, Abner, 35.
Hussey, Bachelor, 57.
Hussey, Benjᵃ, 57.
Hussey, Ebenezer, 57.
Hussey, Elisabeth, 57.
Hussey, George, 57.
Hussey, Joanna, 57.
Hussey, John, 12.
Hussey, John, 67.
hussey, Joseph, 35.
Hussey, Joseph, Juⁿ, 35.
Hussey, Palithˡ, 47.
Hussey, Patience, 63.
Hussey, Paul, 58.
Hussey, Robᵗ, 67.
Hussey, Ruben, 63.
Hussey, Ruben, 67.
hussey, Samuel, 35.
Hussey, Simeon, 57.
Hussey, Stephen, 57.
Hussey, Stephen, Jr, 57.
Hussey, Wᵐ, 57.
Hussey, Zackʰ, 63.
Hussay, Samuel, 23.
Hustead, Robert, 15.
Hustin, Stephen, 15.
Hustin, Mary, 23.
Hustings, James, 37.
Hustings, John, 44.
Hustings, William, 46.
huston, james, 48.
huston, John. 48.
huston, John, 66.
huston, Robert, 48.
huston, robert, 48.
huston, Robert, jun., 48.
Huston, Simon, 17.
Hutchans, Peltʰ, 61.
Hutchens, David, 55.
Hutchens, Elisha, 33.
Hutchens, Enoch, 71.
Hutchens, Enoch, Jr., 71.
Hutchens, Ezra, 54.
Hutchens, Jere, 71.
Hutchens, Job, 71.
Hutchens, John, 61.
Hutchens, Joseph, 55.
Hutchens, Josiah, 55.
Hutchens, Levi, 55.
Hutchens, Lydia, 61.
Hutchens, Simeon, 55.
Hutcherson, James, 47.
Hutcherson, William, 21.
hutchings, Edmand, 67.
hutchings, Levy, 67.
Hutchings, thomas, 69.
Hutchins, Benjᵃ, 37.
Hutchins, David, 55.
Hutchins, David, 55.
Hutchins, Edmund, 61.
Hutchins, Enoch, 65.
Hutchins, Hannah, 61.
Hutchins, Jeremiah, 57.
Hutchins, John, 30.
Hutchins, Jonˢ, 37.
Hutchins, Jonathan, 60.
Hutchins, Joseph, 15.
Hutchins, Joseph, 61.
Hutchins, Joshᵃ, 59.
Hutchins, Josiah, Jʳ, 54.
Hutchins, Nathaniel, 60.
Hutchins, Samˡ, jr, 60.
Hutchins, William, 36.
Hutchinson, Ann, 25.
Hutchinson, John, 31.
Hutchinson, Joseph, 25.
Hutchinson, Joseph, 31.
Hutchinson, Samuel, 25.
Hutchinson, Stephen, 25.
hutchison, Joseph, 51.
hutchison, theophas, 51.
hutchons, david, 48.
hutchons, thomas, 48.
Hutson, Timothy, 37.
Hutting, Jonathan, 36.
huzey, Daniel, 66.
Huzzy, John, 41.
Huzzy, Mary, 30.
Hyde, Ezra, 28.

Ilsley, Hosea, 23.
Ilsley, Jonathan, 14.
Ilsly, Daniel, 23.
Ilsly, Enoch, 22.
Ilsly, Joshua, 23.
Ingalls, Asa, 11.
Ingalls, Benjᵃ, 16.
Ingalls, Ephraim, 23.
Ingalls, Francis, 11.
Ingalls, Isah, 11.
Ingalls, Nathan, 11.
Ingalls, Phineas, 11.
Ingalls, Samuel, 31.
Ingalls, Samˡ, 68.
Ingalls, William, 31.
Ingersol, Benjᵃ, Junʳ, 54.
Ingersol, Nathaniel, 21.
Ingersole, Benjᵃ, 54.

INDEX. 89

Ingersole, William, 54.
Ingersoll, John, 25.
Ingerson, George, 38.
Ingerson, Rich^d, 61.
Ingham, Daniel, 45.
Ingham, David, 46.
Ingham, David, 49.
Ingly, Eben, 53.
Ingly, Moses, 53.
Ingraham, Beziah, 39.
Ingraham, Jere^h, 39.
Ingraham, Job, 46.
Ingraham, Joseph, 23.
Ingraham, Joseph, 46.
Ingraham, Josiah, 46.
Ingraham, William, 23.
Ingram, Edwd, 61.
Inman, Joseph, 27.
Innes, Partrick, 52.
Ireish, John, 15.
Ireland, Abraham, 35.
Ireland, Abraham, 36.
Ireland, John, 36.
Ireland, John, Ju., 36.
Irish, Ebenezer, 12.
Irish, Eben^r, 64.
Irish, Ichabod, 47.
Irish, Isaac, 18.
Irish, James, 18.
Irish, James, J^r, 18.
Irish, John, 12.
Irish, John, Jur, 12.
Irish, Joseph, 12.
Irish, Obadiah, 64.
Irish, Partrick, 13.
Irish, Step^n, 18.
Irish, Thos, 12.
Irish, Thos, 18.
Irish, William, 20.
Irish, Willm, 58.
Isley, Martin, 49.
Isley, michel, 42.

Jack, Andrew, 35.
Jack, Joseph, 46.
Jack, Joseph, 35.
Jack, Robert, 35.
Jacking, David, 49.
Jackings, Fredrick, 39.
Jackings, James, 37.
Jackman, Anna, 15.
Jackson, Barnabas, 22.
Jackson, Bartholomew, 64.
Jackson, Benj^a, 43.
Jackson, Benj^a, 45.
Jackson, Charles, 47.
Jackson, Danl, 11.
Jackson, David, 39.
Jackson, David, 47.
Jackson, Francis, 19.
Jackson, Henry, 11.
Jackson, Henry, 24.
Jackson, Isaac, 22.
Jackson, James, 43.
Jackson, John, 47.
Jackson, John, 47.
Jackson, John, Jur, 47.
Jackson, Joseph, 32.
Jackson, Joseph, 45.
Jackson, Joseph, 47.
Jackson, Joseph, 68.
Jackson, Joshua, 55.
Jackson, Lemuel, 22.
Jackson, Lemu^l., 47.
Jackson, Lemuel, Jn^r, 22.
Jackson, Levi, 22.
Jackson, Nathaniel, 44.
Jackson, Reuben, 18.
Jackson, Robt, 18.
Jackson, Robert, 64.
Jackson, Samuel, 33.
Jackson, Samuel, 43.
Jackson, Saml, 47.
Jackson, Thomas, 13.
Jackson, Thomas, 42.
Jackson, William, 53.
Jacobs, Andrew, 26.
Jacobs, Elias, 70.
Jacobs, George, 70.
Jacobs, John, 66.
Jacobs, Joseph, 72.
Jacobs, Jon^a, 70.
Jacobs, Josiah, 70.
Jacobs, Samuel, 26.
Jacobs, Saml, 71.
Jaeson, James, 40.
Jahnson, James, 69.
Jakens, Christopher, 43.
Jallison, Joseph, 68.
Jallison, Lusia, 56.
Jamerson, James, 16.
James, Elisha, 67.
James, Jno, 67.
James, John, 67.
James, Mary, 62.
James, Sarah, 49.
Jameson, Alexander, 40.
Jameson, Ebenezer, 36.
Jameson, Joseph, 49.
Jameson, Martin, 36.
Jameson, Paul, 40.
Jameson, Robert, 40.
Jameson, Robert, 46.

Jameson, Robert, 65.
Jameson, W^m, 65.
Janking, Philip, 49.
Jaquish, Benjamin, 34.
Jaquish, Isaac, 35.
Jaquish, Richard, 34.
Jealoson, Nathaniel, 31.
Jealouson, John, 31.
Jealouson, W^m, 31.
Jebson, James, 57.
Jeffers, Saml, 71.
Jeffery, Benj^a, 55.
Jeffery, John, 55.
Jeffreys, Simon, 71.
Jeffreys, Willm, 70.
Jeleson, David, 69.
Jeleson, George, 69.
Jeleson, Nathaniel, 34.
Jelison, Margret, 56.
Jelleson, John, 25.
Jelleson, Joseph, 66.
Jellison, Jeddoh, 67.
Jellison, John, 59.
Jellison, Samuel, 67.
Jellison, Thom^s, 58.
Jellitson, Ichabod, 72.
Jellitson, James, 73.
Jellitson, Job, 35.
Jellitson, Joel, 72.
Jellitson, John, 64.
Jellitson, Willm, 70.
Jeminson, Alexander, 26.
Jeminson, Daniel, 30.
Jenks, David, 46.
Jenks, William, 23.
Jenkins, David, 31.
Jenkins, Elijah, 57.
Jenkins, Jabis, 66.
Jenkins, Jedediah, 55.
Jenkins, Josiah, 18.
Jenkins, Lemuel, 62.
Jenkins, Margery, 62.
Jenkins, Renneldes, 62.
Jenkins, Rowland, 61.
Jenkins, Saml, 18.
Jenkins, Stephen, 61.
Jenkins, Thos, 62.
Jennings, Benj^a, 13.
Jennings, Eliphalet, 13.
Jennis, John, 41.
Jennison, Ebenezer, 47.
Jennison, Saml, 46.
Jewel, David, 60.
Jewel, Ezra, 25.
Jewel, Ezra, 69.
Jewel, John, 25.
Jewel, John, 60.
Jewel, John, 69.
Jewell, Enoch, 45.
Jewell, Henry, 45.
Jewell, James, 32.
Jewell, James, junr, 32.
Jewet, Ephraim, 11.
Jewet, John, 50.
Jewet, Maxie, 35.
Jewet, Stephen, 25.
Jewet, Stephen, 69.
Jewett, Caleb, 18.
Jewett, George, 65.
Jewett, James, 23.
Jewett, James, 37.
Jewett, James, 41.
Jewett, Joseph, 23.
Jewett, Joseph, 70.
Jewett, Moses, 40.
Jewett, Stephen, 43.
Jewett, Zedadiah, 43.
Jewit, Pickard, 37.
Jiluce, Joseph, 34.
Jinkins, Thos, 53.
Jiteum, Stephen, 44.
John, Cap^n Saml, 62.
Johnes, Allxand^r, 62.
Johns, W^m, 62.
Johnson, Adam, 45.
Johnson, Adam, 45.
Johnson, Revd Alfred, 16.
Johnson, Asa, 25.
Johnson, Asa, 69.
Johnson, Benj^a, 63.
Johnson, Daniel, 57.
Johnson, David, 20.
Johnson, David, 21.
Johnson, Dorcas, 31.
Johnson, Eph^m, 18.
Johnson, Giles, 31.
Johnson, Isaac, 11.
Johnson, Jacob, 20.
Johnson, James, 20.
Johnson, James, 22.
Johnson, James, 45.
Johnson, James, 53.
Johnson, James, 65.
Johnson, Jesper, 16.
Johnson, Job, 53.
Johnson, Jno, 18.
Johnson, John, 31.
Johnson, John, 33.
Johnson, John, 44.
Johnson, John, 45.
Johnson, John, 52.
Johnson, John, 53.
Johnson, Jon^a, 20.

Johnson, Jonathan, Jur, 66.
Johnson, Jonthan, 66.
Johnson, Joseph, 51.
Johnson, Joseph, Ju., 51.
Johnson, Joshua, 51.
Johnson, Matthew, 18.
Johnson, Miller, 28.
Johnson, Nathan, 22.
Johnson, Nathan, 27.
Johnson, Obed, 26.
Johnson, Paul, 53.
Johnson, Repock, 61.
Johnson, Robt, 18.
Johnson, Samuel, 33.
Johnson, Samuel, 56.
Johnson, Simeon, 30.
Johnson, Simon, 60.
Johnson, Step^n, 18.
Johnson, Stephen, 52.
Johnson, Thos, 21.
johnson, thom., 49.
Johnson, Willm, 64.
Johnston, Danl, 72.
Johnston, George, 15.
Johnston, James, 15.
Johnston, James, 60.
Johnston, James, Jur, 60.
Johnston, John, 15.
Johnston, Joseph, 15.
Johnston, Joseph, 61.
Johntson, Noah, 61.
Johnston, Rishworth, 15.
Johnston, Rishworth, Jr, 58.
Johnston, Samuel, 13.
Johonnot, Gabriel, 30.
Joice, James, 27.
Jones, Abraham, 26.
Jones, Amos, 50.
Jones, Appollo, 37.
Jones, Asa, 53.
Jones, Benjamin, 25.
Jones, Benj^a, 41.
Jones, Caleb, 12.
Jones, Cuandy, 38.
Jones, David, 21.
Jones, Dorithy, 61.
Jones, Eben^r, 63.
Jones, Ebenezer, 63.
Jones, Edward, 12.
Jones, Edward, 15.
Jones, Edward, 40.
Jones, Elijah, 39.
Jones, Eliphelet, 56.
Jones, Ephraim, 24.
Jones, Ephraim, Jur., 24.
Jones, Ephrom, 37.
Jones, Ezekiel, 14.
Jones, Francis, 15.
Jones, Henry, 18.
Jones, Henry, 25.
Jones, Isaac, 34.
Jones, Isreal, 68.
Jones, James, 18.
Jones, James, 26.
Jones, James, 52.
Jones, James, 63.
Jones, Jeremiah, 30.
Jones, John, 23.
Jones, John, 32.
Jones, John, 37.
Jones, John, 41.
Jones, John, 46.
Jones, Jno, 63.
Jones, John, 70.
Jones, John, Jn^r, 41.
Jones, John Stephen, 20.
Jones, Jon^a, 41.
Jones, Jon^a, Jn^r, 41.
Jones, Joseph, 18.
Jones, Joseph, 29.
Jones, Joseph, 33.
Jones, Joseph, 54.
Jones, J^s, Jr., 18.
Jones, Joshua, 14.
Jones, Josiah, 40.
Jones, Kinsley, 41.
Jones, Lazarus, 70.
Jones, Lemuel, 12.
Jones, luke, 41.
jones, mical, 48.
Jones, Morgan, 31.
Jones, Nat, 63.
Jones, Nathan, 29.
Jones, Noah, 14.
Jones, Nolon, 38.
Jones, Peter, 39.
Jones, Phinehas, 35.
Jones, Richard, 48.
jones, richard, jun., 48.
Jones, Robart, 44.
Jones, Saml, 18.
Jones, Samuel, 25.
Jones, Samuel, 30.
Jones, Samuel, 53.
Jones, Samuel, 63.
Jones, Simon, 37.
Jones, Step^n, 18.
Jones, Stephen, 52.
Jones, Stephen, 58.
Jones, Stephen, 69.
Jones, Theodore, 31.
Jones, Thos, 69.

Jones, Vaughn, 55.
Jones, W^m, 18.
Jones, Wll^m, 24.
Jones, Willm, 43.
jones, william, 48.
Jones, W^m, 63.
Jones, W^m, Junr, 18.
Jones, W^m, 3^d, 18.
Jones, Windsor, 26.
Jonnes, Bartholimu, 67.
Jonnes, Elisha, 67.
Jordain, John, 54.
Jordan, Benj^a, 7.
Jordan, Benjn, 18.
Jordan, Clem^t, 59.
Jordan, Ebenezer, 31.
Jordan, Hezekiah, 24.
Jordan, Israel, 46.
Jordan, James, 12.
Jordan, James, 24.
Jordan, James, 27.
Jordan, John, 20.
Jordan, John, 20.
Jordan, John, 61.
Jordan, Joseph, 64.
Jordan, Lem^l, 18.
Jordan, Meletiah, 32.
Jordan, Moses, 18.
Jordan, Nath^n, 61.
Jordan, Nathaniel, 32.
Jordan, Peter, 12.
Jordan, Rishworth, 58.
Jordan, Rishworth, Jr, 58.
Jordan, Robert, 12.
Jordan, Robert, 40.
Jordan, Saml, 11.
Jordan, Saml, 58.
Jordan, Saml, Esqr, 65.
Jordan, Secomb, 14.
Jordan, Solomon, 31.
Jordan, Tristram, 58.
Jordan, Tristram, Esqr, 65.
Jordan, Tristram, Jur, 65.
Jorden, Abraham, 13.
Jorden, Benjamin, 13.
Jorden, Cezar, 15.
Jorden, David, 19.
Jorden, Dominicus, 13.
Jorden, Dominicus, 24.
Jorden, Elijah, 19.
Jorden, Elisha, 13.
Jorden, Elisha, 13.
Jorden, Ezekiel, 13.
Jorden, Isaac, 13.
Jorden, James, 22.
Jorden, James, 24.
Jorden, Jeremiah, 13.
Jorden, Jeremiah, 13.
Jorden, Jeremiah, 25.
Jorden, John, 13.
Jorden, John, 13.
Jorden, Jonathan, 13.
Jorden, Jonathan, 24.
Jorden, Joseph, 15.
Jorden, Joshua, 13.
Jorden, Nathaniel, 13.
Jorden, Nathaniel, 13.
Jorden, Nathaniel, 13.
Jorden, Nathaniel, 26.
Jorden, Noah, 13.
Jorden, Noah, 13.
Jorden, Rachel, 13.
Jorden, Richard, 13.
Jorden, Roger, 24.
Jorden, Samuel, 13.
Jorden, Samuel, 13.
Jorden, Samuel, 13.
Jorden, Samuel, 24.
Jorden, Secomb, 13.
Jorden, Solomon, 13.
Jorden, Stephen, 13.
Jorden, Thomas, 13.
Jorden, Timothy, 13.
Jorden, Timothy, 24.
Jorden, Trustim, 13.
Jordin, John, 55.
Jordon, Abner, 35.
Jordon, Ephrom, 35.
Jose, John, 59.
Jose, Nathl, 18.
Jose, W^m, 18.
Joslin, Daniel, 40.
Joslin, James, 40.
Joslin, James, Jur., 40.
Joslin, Peter, 40.
Joslin, William, 40.
Josselin, Thos, 12.
Jourdain, Eben^r, 54.
Jourdan, James, 54.
Jourdan, Richard, 53.
Joy, Benjamin, 32.
Joy, Ephraim, 73.
Joy, Francis, 53.
Joy, John, 29.
Joy, John, 52.
Joy, John, 57.
Joy, Samuel, 29.
Joy, Samuel, 32.
Joy, Saml, 73.
Joy, Stephen, 58.
Joy, W^m, 56.
Judkins, Benj^a, 45.
Judkins, Daniel, 45.
Judkins, Jacob, 41.

Judkins, James, 49.
Judkins, Jesse, 41.
Judkins, Joel, 45.
Judkins, Joseph, 45.
Judkins, Philip, 38.
Judkins, Robert, 49.
Judkins, Samuel, 36.
Judkins, Samuel, 51.
Juett, Benjamin, 67.
Junkins, Jotham, 57.
Jumper, Danl, 11.
Jumper, Edward, 11.
Junin, Joseph, 30.
Junkins, Alexander, 72.
Junkins, Danl, 72.
Junkins, Danl, J^r, 72.
Junkins, Eliphalet, 72.
Junkins, Eunice, 72.
Junkins, Hepsibath, 72.
Junkins, James, 72.
Junkins, Jon^a, 72.
Junkins, Joseph, 72.
Junkins, Robert, 55.
Junkins, Sarah, 65.
Junkins, William, 69.
Juwet, nathan, 35.

kaastner, ludwig, 42.
Kain, John, 33.
kalor, charles, 41.
Kanadey, Thomas, 33.
Kanady, James, 43.
Kane, Isaac, 62.
Kane, Jane, 62.
Kane, Rouben, 49.
Kating, Richard, 46.
Katon, William, 26.
kawanagh, James, 35.
Kean, Arthur, 72.
Kean, Benj^a, 63.
Kean, David, 71.
Kean, John, 43.
Kean, John, 71.
Kean, John, 71.
Kean, Jon^a, 57.
Keating, Oliver, 70.
Keaton (Widow), 71.
Keay, Danl, 63.
Keay, John, 56.
Keay, John, 57.
Keay, Jno, 63.
Keay, Love, 56.
Keay, Oles, 63.
Keay, Peter, 63.
Keefer, John, 51.
Keelly, Phinehas, 65.
keen, abner, 42.
keen, dan. (hoge Island), 48.
Keen, Elezer, 38.
Keen, Elisha, 38.
keen, Ezak, 48.
Keen, John, 46.
keen, niclas, 41.
keen, philip, 41.
keen, prince, 48.
keen, Robt., 48.
Keen, Samuel, 44.
Keen, Semeon, 62.
Keen, Shibottaish, 50.
keen (widow), 41.
keen, william, 48.
Keon, W^m, 62.
Keene, Abel, 37.
Keene, John, 25.
Keene, Joshua, 24.
Keene, Snow, 24.
Keeris, Enoch, 49.
Keindrick, John, 65.
Keindrick, Joseph, 65.
keiser, francis, 41.
Keith, Cornelius, 12.
Keith, James, 49.
keler, Jacob, 41.
kelka (widow), 48.
kellce, James, 48.
keller, charles, 42.
keller, Jacob, Jun., 41.
keller, william, 41.
Kelleran, Edward, 36.
Kelley, Benj^a, 34.
Kelley, Edmund, 60.
Kelley, John, 37.
Kelley, Mary, 23.
Kelloch, Alexander, 49.
Kelloch, David, 49.
Kelloch, Findly, 46.
Kelloch, John, 36.
Kelloch, Matthew, 36.
Kelloch, Moses, 36.
Kellon, Benj^a, 54.
Kelly, Chris^r, 18.
Kelly, Elijah, 54.
Kelly, James, 53.
Kelly, John, 52.
Kelly, Peter, 18.
Kelly, Thomas, 54.
Kelly, William, 46.
Kemp, Eben^r, 18.
Kempton, John, 28.
Kempton, Zacheus, 28.
Kench, Thomas, 30.
Kendal, Ablathar, 43.
Kendal, Benj^a, 16.

INDEX.

Kendal, Edwd, 62.
Kendall, Chever, 26.
Keniard, Thos, 18.
Kennady, Henry, 40.
Kennady, James, 34.
Kennady, Molly, 41.
Kennady, Patrick, 12.
Kennady, Saml, 40.
Kennady, Thos, 41.
Kennady (Widow), 41.
Kennady, Willm, 34.
Kennady, Willm, 40.
Kennard, Samuel, 25.
Kenney, John, 56.
Kenney, John, 63.
Kenney, Joshua, 63.
Kenney, Thomas, 23.
Kennikum, Aurther, 67.
Kenningston, Hugh, 62.
Kennison, Abram, 65.
Kennison, John, 65.
Kennison, Nicholas, 68.
Kenny, Abijah, 34.
Kenny, Benja, 34.
Kenny, Benjamin, 43.
Kenny, Henry, 30.
Kenny, Henry, 34.
Kenny, Paul, 28.
Kenny, Saml, 34.
Kenny, Stephen, 32.
Kenny, Thos, 34.
kensall, fredrich, 35.
Kent, Benjamin, 32.
Kent, Benja, 34.
Kent, John, 23.
Kent, John, 53.
Kent, Jonathan, 53.
Kent, Josiah, 65.
Kent, Nathl, 68.
Kent, Sarah, 68.
Kent, Susanah, 32.
kent (widow), 48.
Kent, William, 32.
Keresland, Abraham, 11.
kesler, John, 42.
Keswell, Amos, 72.
Keswell, Willm, 72.
Keth, Alford, 42.
Keth, Unite, 42.
Keth, Zepheniah, 42.
Keyes, Francis, 64.
Keyes, Samuel, 28.
Kezer, George, 65.
Kezer, George, 65.
Kezer, Josiah, 65.
Kibbon, John, 11.
Kicker, Dodford, 66.
Kicker, Samuel, 66.
Kicker, Samuel, 67.
Kicker, Simeon, 66.
Kicker, Solomon, 67.
Kicker, William, 66.
Kidden, Richard, 50.
Kidder, Richard, 44.
Kiff, Thomas, 36.
Kilbath, Partrick, 49.
Kilbey, William, 53.
Kilby, Richd, 16.
Kilgore, Benja, 60.
Kilgore, James, 68.
Kilgore, John, 68.
Kilgore, John, Junr, 68.
Kilgore, Joseph, 68.
Kilgore, Joseph, 68.
Kilgore, Trueworthy, 60.
killam, John, 67.
Killey, Joseph, 50.
Killey, William, 49.
Killpatrick, Marten, 31.
Killpatrick, Robert, 31.
Killpatrick, Samuel, 31.
Killsa, George, 46.
Killsa, Hugh, 46.
Killsa, James, 46.
killse, John, 48.
Killsroth, Patrick, 44.
Killum, Ivory, 18.
Kilpartrick, Daniel, 15.
Kilpartrick, Iland, 15.
Kimbal, Abigail, 71.
Kimbal, Baruch, 69.
Kimbal, Benja, 70.
Kimbal, Benja, 70.
Kimbal, David, 39.
Kimbal, David, 39.
Kimbal, Isaac, 69.
Kimbal, Israel, 70.
Kimbal, Jacob, 37.
Kimbal, James, 70.
Kimbal, Jeremiah, 24.
Kimbal, Joseph, 71.
Kimbal, Joshua, 71.
Kimbal, Nathan, 71.
Kimbal, Nathl, 22.
Kimbal, Nathl, 43.
Kimbal, Nathl, 70.
Kimbal, Nicholas, 45.
Kimbal, Peter S., 16.
Kimbal, Ruben, 70.
Kimbal, Rufus, 64.
Kimbal, Saml, 69.
Kimbal, Simeon, 40.
Kimbal (Widow), 70.

Kimball, Andrew, 50.
Kimball, Asa, 11.
Kimball, Asa, Jnr. 12.
Kimball, Benja, 12.
Kimball, Benja, Jur, 11.
Kimball, Caleb, 60.
Kimball, Caleb, 63.
Kimball, Danl, 58.
Kimball, Daniel, 59.
Kimball, David, 68.
Kimball, Ezra, 59.
Kimball, Francis, 58.
Kimball, Heber, 59.
Kimball, John, 15.
Kimball, Jno, 59.
kimball, Joseph, 69.
Kimball, Joseph, 70.
Kimball, Joshua, 59.
Kimball, Joshua, 70.
Kimball, Joshua, Jun., 50.
kimball, Levy, 69.
Kimball, Moses, 64.
Kimball, Nathan, 58.
Kimball, Richard, 11.
Kimball, Richard, 33.
Kimball, Saml, 11.
Kimball, Solomon, 27.
Kimball, William, 29.
Kimball, William, 60.
Kimble, Benjn, 49.
Kimble, thomas, 49.
kimbull, Thomas, 67.
Kimmens, Benjn, 67.
Kinard, John, 70.
Kincade, David, 35.
Kincaid, Abigail, 43.
Kincaid, John, 43.
Kincaid, Peter, 12.
Kincaid, Reuben, 43.
Kindal, Barzeliel, 35.
Kindal, Biethy, 35.
Kindal, David, 36.
Kindal, William, 37.
King, Benjamen, 33.
King, Ebenezer, 51.
King, Eliab, 21.
King, Ichabod, 11.
King, Josiah, 65.
King, Mary, 18.
King, Moses, 43.
King, Richard, 18.
King, Richd, 71.
King, Samuel, 51.
King, Willm, 18.
Kingburg, Joseph, 61.
Kingbury, Phineas, 28.
Kingman, Loring, 46.
Kingsbury, Benja, 72.
Kingsbury, Enoch, 28.
Kingsbury, John, 44.
Kingsbury, John, 72.
Kingsbury, John, 72.
Kingsbury, Saml, 72.
Kinkad, Samuel, Juner, 33.
Kinkado, Samuel, Junr, 33.
Kinmah, James, 45.
Kinnard, Dimond, 62.
Kinnard, James, 62.
Kinnard, Michl, 62.
Kinnard, Timov, 62.
Kinney, Thomas, 44.
Kinnicum, Daniel, 34.
Kinnicum, Edward, 34.
Kinscott, Samuel, 36.
Kinsley, James, 71.
Kinsley, Samuel, 53.
Kinsman, Jona, Esqr, 64.
kinsmon, Ebenezer, 68.
Kint, Charles, 51.
Kint, Warrant, 51.
kintzel, John, 42.
Kinward, Wm, 62.
Kirker, Henery, 55.
Kirkpatrick, Anne, 49.
Kirkpatrick, William, 49.
Kirkwood, Alexr, 18.
Kitridge, Benja, 37.
Knap, Jesse, 11.
Knap, Samuel, 30.
Kneeland, David, 22.
Kneely, Danl, 63.
Knight, Benja, 56.
Knight, Daniel, 22.
Knight, Daniel, 34.
Knight, Danl, 62.
Knight, Edmund, 59.
Knight, Enoch, 21.
Knight, George, 62.
Knight, Jeremiah, 16.
Knight, John, 37.
Knight, John, 56.
Knight, Jonathan, 22.
Knight, Jonathan, 54.
knight, Joseph, 67.
Knight, Joshua, 15.
Knight, Mark, 22.
Knight, Nathl, 37.
Knight, Nathan, 62.
Knight, Paul, 14.
Knight, Pettishal, 34.
Knight, Robert, 23.
Knight, Benja, 32.
Knight, Stephen, 60.
Knight, Westbrook, 37.

Knight, William, 15.
Knight, Zebulon, 22.
Knights, Amos, 14.
Knights, Benjamin, 14.
Knights, Benjamin, 23.
Knights, George, 14.
Knights, George, 15.
Knights, George, 26.
Knights, Henry, 14.
Knights, Jacob, 14.
Knights, John, 23.
Knights, John, 23.
Knights, John, 25.
Knights, John, 25.
Knights, Joseph, 18.
Knights, Mark, 14.
Knights, Merrell, 14.
Knights, Moses, 15.
Knights, Nathan, 27.
Knights, Nathaniel, 15.
Knights, Nathl, 18.
Knights, Samuel, 24.
Knights, Saml, 59.
Knights, Thomas, 28.
knock, Ebenezer, 69.
Knowles, Francis, 54.
Knowles, Freeman, 28.
Knowles, Henry, 29.
Knowles, Mary, 28.
Knowles, Richard, 46.
Knowles, Samuel, 31.
Knowls, Elisha, 50.
Knowls, Jonathan, 50.
Knowls, Simon, 50.
knowlton, andrew, 35.
knowlton, Jeremiah, 35.
Knowlton, Jonathan, 44.
Knowlton, Reuben, 27.
Knowlton, Samuel, 44.
Knowlton, Thomas, 28.
Knowlton, William, 27.
knowly, David, 45.
Knowly, John, 46.
Kobards, Ebenezer, 67.
Kobards, Samuel, 67.
kohn, paul, 42.
koon, george, jun., 42.
Korah, Stephen, 16.

Laban, Richd, 70.
Labree, James, 33.
labree, James, 49.
Labree, Peter, 41.
labree, Richard, 49.
lach, asmus, 42.
Lackay, William, 46.
ladd, John, 49.
Ladd, Josiah, 44.
Ladd, Josses, 50.
Ladd, Nathaniel, 49.
Laiken, Joseph, 16.
Lake, Benja, 16.
Lake, Elisha, 40.
Lake, Joshua, 40.
Lake, Lydia, 16.
Lakeman, Josiah, 18.
Lakeman, Wm, 18.
lalor, patrik, 48.
Lamb, John, 18.
Lamb, Joshua, 27.
Lamb, Richd, 58.
Lamb, William, 15.
Lambart, Abraham, 44.
Lambart, Daniel, 35.
Lambart, Danl, 35.
Lambart, Isaac, 16.
Lambart, Shereblah, 35.
Lambart, Shereblah, Jr, 35.
Lambert, James, 44.
Lambert, Joseph, 33.
Lambert, Luke, 33.
lambord, Gideon, 51.
Lambord, James, 50.
lambord, Paul, 51.
lambord, Silas, 51.
Lampher, Johana, 61.
Lamps, Peter, 40.
Lamson, James, 34.
Lamson, Jonathan, 46.
Lamson, Saml, 34.
Lamson, Samuel, 66.
Lamson, Willm, 37.
Lancaster, Daniel, 28.
Lancaster, Joseph, 31.
Lancaster, Joseph, 52.
Lancaster, Revd, 18.
Lancaster, William, 30.
Lander, Edmund, 11.
lander, Robenson, 38.
Landers, Abraham, 50.
Landers, Alvin, 45.
Landers, Freeman, 40.
Landers, Joseph, 50.
Landers, Stephen, 24.
Landers Thomas, 37.
Landfar, Sam, 61.
Lane, Benjamin, 11.
Lane, Benjamin, 21.
Lane, Daniel, 28.
Lane, Daniel, 40.

Lane, Danl, 59.
Lane, Daniel, Ju., 40.
Lane, Ebenezer, 21.
Lane, Ebenezer, 21.
Lane, Ebenezer, 21.
lane, Ebenezer, 45.
lane, Ephram 45.
lane, Giddeon, 40.
Lane, Gideon, 16.
Lane, Hezeklah, 27.
Lane, Isaac, 64.
Lane, Isachar, 32.
Lane, Jabez, 59.
lane, James, 40.
lane, James, 51.
Lane, James, 53.
Lane, John, 58.
Lane, Jno, 58.
Lane, Joseph, 32.
lane, Nathan, 45.
Lane, Oliver, 27.
Lanes, Edman, 38.
Laneton, Revd Saml, 72.
Lang, John, 60.
Lang, Saml, 42.
Langcaster, James, 39.
Langdon, John, 43.
Langdon, Joseph, 34.
Langdon, Paul, 60.
Langdon, Timothy, 43.
Langley, Eli, 69.
Langley, Jonathan, 69.
Langley, Phillip, 29.
Lankister, David, 42.
Lankister, Ezekiel, 36.
Lankister, John, 50.
Lankister, Joseph, 36.
Lanpher, Anson, 32.
Lanpher, Langworthy, 28.
Lanpher, Stephen, 32.
Lanson, Suttil, 50.
Lapham, Roger, 42.
Laplain, James, 42.
Laraba, Benja, 12.
Laraba, Nathl, 12.
larabee, Tempr (Widw), 59.
Larey, Joseph, 68.
larnard, hains, 40.
Laroch, Thomas, 23.
larrabb, John, 38.
larrabb, Stephen, 38.
Larrabee, Abner, 52.
Larrabee, Benja, 18.
Larrabee, David, 52.
Larrabee, Isaac, 52.
Larrabee, Nathl, 18.
Larrabee, Philip, 18.
Larrabee, Stepn, 18.
Larrabee, Thos, 18.
Larrabee, Wm, 18.
Larrabee, Wm, Junr, 18.
Larree, John, 50.
Larribee, Zebulon, 15.
Larry, Michael, 31.
Larry, Step, 18.
Lary (Widow), 38.
Lasdale, Asa, 59.
Lasdale, Caleb, 59.
Lasdel, Bartholomew, 54.
Lasdel, Israel, 58.
Lasdel, Jere, 55.
Lasdel, Mary, 55.
Lasdell, Ellison, 29.
Lasdell, Ellison, junr, 29.
Lasly, George, 24.
lasse, John, 42.
latan, Benja, 49.
Latan, David, 49.
latan, Ephram, 49.
latan, James, 49.
latan, John, 49.
Laten, George, 15.
Laten, Jedediah, 14.
Laten, Joseph, 14.
Laten, Peltiah, 14.
Laten, Robert, 14.
Laten, Solomon, 49.
Latham, Eliab, 19.
Latham, George, 19.
Latherby, Isaac, 64.
Latherby, Jessa, 70.
Latherby, Joel, 42.
Latherby, Saml, 21.
Latherby, Saml, 64.
Latherby, Stephen, 12.
Latherby, Stephen, 69.
Latherby, Stephen, 70.
latin, Ephraim, 49.
Latin, Hatevil, 15.
latin, Moses, 49.
Laton, andrew, 49.
Laton, Hatewell, 53.
Laton, Major Saml, 60.
laton, toblas, 69.
Laton, Wm, Junr, 62.
Laurence, John, 54.
Laurence, John, Junr, 54.
Laury, Samuel, 40.
Law, John, 42.
lawd, william (mescongus Island), 48.
Lawrance, James, 41.
Lawrance, Willm, 16.

Lawrence, Abel, 28.
Lawrence, Amos, 49.
Lawrence, David, 43.
Lawrence, James, 37.
Lawrence, John, 21.
Lawrence, Rogers, 30.
Lawrence, Saml, 22.
Lawrence, William, 32.
Lawrence, Zachariah, 28.
Lawrrance, John, 37.
Layton, Jane, 42.
Layton, John, 42.
Layton, John, 62.
Layton, oliver, 42.
Layton, Samuel, 53.
Layton, Deacn Wm, 62.
Lea, Daniel, 53.
Lea, James, 36.
Leach, Apollos, 49.
Leach, Benj., 61.
Leach, Eben, 61.
Leach, James, 13.
Leach, James, 30.
Leach, John, 11.
Leach, John, 71.
Leach, Joseph, 11.
Leach, Mark, 24.
Leach, Nathl, 55.
Leach, Nathn, 61.
Leach, Peletiah, 30.
Leach, Saml, 61.
Leadbotter, Increase, 32.
Leadbetter, Increase, jun., 32.
Leadbetter, John, 32.
Leadbotter, Luther, 32.
lear, peter, 41.
Learned, Henry, 40.
Leasunesse, John, 42.
Leatherby, Benjamin, 23.
Leatherby, John, 24.
Leatherby, Jonathan, 13.
Leathers, Enoch, 12.
Leavensellers, Jacob, 26.
Leavil, William, 67.
Leavit, Jacob, 11.
Leavit, Jacob, 25.
Leavit, Joseph, 25.
Leavitt, Danl, 59.
Leavitt, Israel, 40.
Leavitt, Jer., 72.
Leavitt, John, 61.
Leavitt, Josh, 59.
Leavitt, Naphthali, 20.
Leavitt, Saml, 59.
Leavitt, Thos, 59.
le balister, charles, 48.
Lebarran, James, 24.
LeBroke, James, 24.
Lecraw, Susannah, 26.
Lee, John, 30.
Lee, John, 58.
Lee, Martha, 55.
Lee, Silas, 43.
Lee, Willm, 37.
Lee, Willm, Jur, 37.
Leechfield, Nathl, 16.
Leechfield, Noah, 16.
Leechfield, Saml, 16.
Leechfield, Willm, 16.
Legro, David, 63.
Legro, Elias, 25.
Legro, John, 63.
Legro, Samuel, 63.
Legro, Thomas, 63.
leicht, george, 42.
leicht, peter, 42.
leicht (widow), 42.
Leighton, Andw, 21.
Leighton, Ezekiel, 41.
Leighton, Isaac, 54.
leighton, James, 48.
Leighton, Joseph, 53.
Leighton, Parratt, 54.
Leighton, Rebecca, 41.
Leighton, Richard, 41.
Leighton, Samuel, 54.
Leighton, Theodore, 54.
Leighton, Thomas, 53.
Leighton, Thomas, Junr, 53.
Leighton, Thomas, 3d, 53.
leisner, george, 42.
Leland, Ebenezer, 29.
Leland, Ezra, 29.
Leland, James, 31.
Leland, Joseph, 64.
Leman, Abigail, 51.
Leman, Danl, 37.
Leman, David, 44.
Leman, Henry, 44.
Leman, Jacob, 44.
Leman, John, 39.
Leman, John, 50.
Leman, Nathl, 37.
Leman, Samuel, 51.
Leman, Sam'l, Junr, 51.
Leman, Thomas, 51.
Leman, Willm, 37.
Lemont, Adam, 33.
Lemont, David, 33.
Lemont, James, 33.
Lemont, John, 33.
Lemont, Samuel, 33.

INDEX.

Lemont, Thomas, 33.
Lenel, Joseph, 50.
Lenel, Sam¹, 50.
Leonard, Abigail, 50.
Lermond, Alexander, 49.
Lermond, John, 49.
Lermond, William, 49.
Leshure, Samuel, 53.
Letherbe, Tom, 18.
leucrmore, William, 44.
Leuer, William, 69.
Leuet, Daniel, 68.
levenzeler, adam, 41.
Levet, Joseph, 67.
Levey, Joseph, 36.
Levey, Capⁿ Stephⁿ, 61.
Lewis, Abijah, 59.
Lewis, Amasa, 52.
Lewis, Archelas, 14.
Lewis, Asa, 21.
Lewis, Benjⁿ, 55.
Lewis, Daniel, 36.
Lewis, Dimond, 61.
Lewis, Enoch, 61.
Lewis, George, 18.
Lewis, George, 35.
Lewis, Hannah, 71.
Lewis, Jabez, 39.
Lewis, John, 21.
Lewis, John, 32.
Lewis, John, 34.
Lewis, John, 50.
Lewis, John, 55.
Lewis, Joseph, 34.
Lewis, Joseph, Junr, 34.
Lewis, Lathley, 32.
Lewis, Mary, 60.
Lewis, Nathan, 14.
Lewis, Nathⁱ, 72.
Lewis, Paul, 63.
Lewis, Peter, 61.
Lewis, Samˡ, 54.
Lewis, Simon, 60.
Lewis, Stephen, 34.
Lewis, Thoˢ, 12.
Lewis, Thomas, 50.
Lewis, Thoˢ H., 60.
Lewis, Willᵐ, 34.
Lewis, William, 44.
Lewis, William, 46.
Lewis, Willᵐ, 72.
Lewis, William, Jr, 50.
Libbee, Aaron, 64.
Libbee, Daniel, 52
Libbee, David, 52.
Libbee, Jesse, 64.
Libbee, Joseph, 52.
Libbee, Joseph, 54.
Libbee, Joseph, 64.
Libbee, Josiah, 52.
Libbee, Nathan, 52.
Libbee, Obed, 52
Libbee, Philemon, 64.
Libbee, Reuben, 54.
Libbee, Robert, 64.
Libbey, Daniel, 52
Libbey, Eliakim, 49.
Libbey, Elijah, 65.
Libbey, George, 44.
Libbey, Hatevil, 49.
Libbey, John, 49.
Libbey, John, 57.
Libbey, John, 65.
Libbey, Joseph, 56.
Libbey, Joseph, 65.
Libbey, Paul, 56.
Libbey, Philip, 65.
Libbey, Marthew, 57.
Libbey, Nathan, 55.
Libbey, Nathaniel, 58.
Libbey, Reuben, 22.
Libbey, Samuel, 29.
Libbey, Solomon, 65.
Libbey, Thomas, 65.
Libbey, Zebulon, 57.
Libby, Abner, 18.
Libby, Allison, 18.
Libby, Allison, 18.
Libby, Amos, 18.
Libby, Andrew, 19.
Libby, Andrew, 20.
Libby, Anthʸ, 18.
Libby, Arther, 19.
Libby, Asa, 19.
Libby, Asa, 19.
Libby, Azariah, 63.
Libby, Benjⁿ, 18.
Libby, Benjamin, 19.
Libby, Benjⁿ, 63.
Libby, Cpᵗ, 18.
Libby, Charles, 63.
Libby, Danˡ, 18.
Libby, Daniel, 19.
Libby, David, 18.
Libby, David, 62.
Libby, Dominicus, 18.
Libby, Ebenʳ, 18.
Libby, Edmᵈ, 18.
Libby, Edwᵈ, 18.
Libby, Edwᵈ, 18.
Libby, Eliakim, 18.
Libby, Elisha, 18.
Libby, Elisha, 59.

Libby, Enoch, 18.
Libby, Enoch, 65.
Libby, Franois, 59.
Libby, H. Richᵈ, 18.
Libby, Hanson, 18.
Libby, Hezekiah, 18.
Libby, Ichabod, 18.
Libby, Isaac, 18.
Libby, Isaac, 24.
Libby, Isreal, 62.
Libby, James, 11.
Libby, James, 18.
Libby, James, 63.
Libby, Jereʰ, 18.
Libby, Jeremiah, 63.
Libby, Jethro, 18.
Libby, Jethro, 18.
Libby, Joel, 19.
Libby, Joel, 62.
Libby, Jnᵒ, 18.
Libby, John, 18.
Libby, John, 60.
Libby, Jonᵃ, 18.
Libby, Jonathan, 60.
Libby, Joseph, 18.
Libby, Joseph, 19.
Libby, Joshua, 18.
Libby, Josiah, 18.
Libby, Josiah, 18.
Libby, Lemˡ, 18.
Libby, Mark, 18.
Libby, Mark, 18.
Libby, Mary, 62.
Libby, Matthew, 18.
Libby, Matthias, 18.
Libby, Meshech, 66.
Libby, Moses, 19.
Libby, Nathan, 18.
Libby, Nathan, 49.
Libby, Nathan, 62.
Libby, Nathⁱ, 18.
Libby, Natheˡ, 63.
Libby, Neheʰ, 18.
Libby, Peter, 18.
Libby, Phinᵃ, 18.
Libby, R. Hubᵈ, 18.
Libby, Reuben, 18.
Libby, Reuben, 60.
Libby, Reuben, Jr, 18.
Libby, Richᵈ, 18.
Libby, Richᵈ, 18.
Libby, Robᵗ, 18.
Libby, Roger, 18.
Libby, Samˡ, 18.
Libby, Sam., 62.
Libby, Samˡ, 63.
Libby, Seth, 18.
Libby, Seth, 61.
Libby, Simeon, 18.
Libby, Simon, 18.
Libby, Skilling Jnᵒ, 18.
Libby, Stepⁿ, 18.
Libby, Stephen, 60.
Libby, Stephen, 67.
Libby, Stephen, Junr, 67.
Libby, Theoˢ, 18.
Libby, Theoˢ, Junr, 18.
Libby, Thoˢ, 18.
Libby, Wᵐ, 18.
Libby, William, 19.
Libby, Wᵐ, 68.
Libby, Zebulon, 18.
Libby, Zebulon, 68.
lidge, Sinas (mescongus Island), 48.
Light, Robert, 43.
Lillie, Benjᵃ, 80.
Liman, Job, 72.
lincell, Joseph, 50.
lincell, Lamuel, 50.
Lincoln, Benjᵃ, 41.
lincoln, Isaac, 48.
Lincoln, Jacob, 53.
Lincoln, John, 14.
lincoln, Joshua, 41.
Lincoln, Joshua, 53.
Lincoln, Marthew, 47.
Lincoln, Moses, 53.
Lincoln, Theodore, 53.
Lincoln, Thomas, 15.
Lincoln, Zadoc, 33.
Lincoln, Zenas, 53.
Lindsay, James, 32.
Lindsey, John, 46.
Lindsey (Widow), 72.
Linkley, Samˡ, 47.
Linn, Robert, 27.
Linnecon, Benjᵃ, 34.
Linnekon, Daniel, 36.
Linnel, Enoch, 24.
Linnel, Samˡ, 24.
Linnen, Bryant, 38.
Linnen, Thomas, 38.
Linniken, Clark, 36.
Linniken, David, 36.
Linscot, Isaac, 80.
Linscot, theodah, 67.
Iinscott, David, 35.
Linscott, John, 20.
Linscut, David, 12.
Linscutt, Danˡ, 72.
Linscutt, Isaiah, 72.

Linscutt, Jere., 72.
linscutt, John, 35.
Linscutt, Joseph, 64.
Linscutt, Samˡ, 64.
Linscutt, Samˡ, 72.
Linscutt, Samˡ, Jr, 64.
Linsday, thomas, 38.
linsday, William, 40.
Linscnt, Joseph, 67.
Linsent, William, 67.
Linskiet, Jacob, 67.
Linskiet, John, 67.
Linskit, Nathaniel, 67.
Linsuit, John, 33.
Linsuit, Joshua, 33.
Linsy, Ephrom, 42.
linsy, William, 40.
Lion, Ezekiel, 43.
lish, paul, 42.
Lishman, John, 34.
Litchfield, Joseph, 66.
Litchfield, Revᵈ Joseph, 61.
Lithgow, Aurthur, 50.
Lithgow, Willᵐ, 38.
Littelfeield, Ithamor, 67.
Littelfield, Ithamor, Juⁿ, 66.
Littlefeild, Stephen, 67.
Little, Daniel, 42.
Little, Revᵈ Danˡ, 69.
Little, David, 70.
Little, Henry, 41.
little, henry, 49.
little, hugh, 48.
Little, James, 41.
little, John, 48.
Little, Joshua, 18.
Little, Nathˡ, 70.
Little, Paul, 25.
Little, Sarah, 15.
Littleale, John, 68.
Littlefield, Aaron, 59.
Littlefield, Abraᵐ, 69.
Littlefield, Abraᵐ, 70.
Littlefield, Abraᵐ, 70.
Littlefield, Anna, 70.
Littlefield, Anthony, 69.
Littlefield, Anthony, 69.
Littlefield, Benjᵃ, 55.
Littlefield, Benjˡ, 71.
Littlefield, Danˡ, 70.
Littlefield, Danˡ, 70.
Littlefield, Danˡ, 71.
Littlefield, David, 69.
Littlefield, David, 70.
Littlefield, David, 71.
Littlefield, Dependance, 70.
Littlefield, Ebenezer, 52.
Littlefield, Ebenˢ, 71.
Littlefield, Ebeneˢ, Jr, 71.
Littlefield, Edmond, 69.
Littlefield, Eliab, 70.
Littlefield, Elijah, 30.
Littlefield, Elijah, 55.
Littlefield, Elijah, 70.
littlefield, Elisha, 60.
Littlefield, Elisha, 71.
Littlefield, Elisha, 71.
Littlefield, Ephraim, 71.
Littlefield, Francis, 70.
Littlefield, Isaac, 70.
Littlefield, Jacob, 69.
Littlefield, Jacob, 70.
Littlefield, James, 28.
Littlefield, James, 70.
Littlefield, James, 70.
Littlefield, Jerᵉ, 70.
Littlefield, Jerᵉ, 71.
Littlefield, Jesse, 70.
Littlefield, Joel, 60.
Littlefield, Johnson, 70.
Littlefield, Jonᵃ, 69.
Littlefield, Joseph, 30.
Littlefield, Joseph, 69.
Littlefield, Joseph, 70.
Littlefield, Joshua, 70.
Littlefield, Josiah, 70.
Littlefield, Jotham, 69.
Littlefield, Jotham, 70.
Littlefield, Levi, 70.
Littlefield, Lydia, 69.
Littlefield, Merriam, 70.
Littlefield, Moses, 28.
Littlefield, Moses, 69.
Littlefield, Moses, 70.
Littlefield, Moses, 70.
Littlefield, Nathan, 70.
Littlefield, Nehemiah, 69.
Littlefield, Noah, 69.
Littlefield, Noah, 71.
Littlefield, Pelatiah, 69.
Littlefield, Peter, 71.
Littlefield, Reuben, 69.
Littlefield, Roger, 71.
Littlefield, Samuel, 28.
Littlefield, Samˡ, 70.
Littlefield, Seth, 71.
Littlefield, Seth, 71.
Littlefield, Stephen, 28.
Littlefield, Stephen, 69.
Littlefield, Susanna, 70.
Littlefield, Timothy, 70.
Littlefield, Willᵐ, 69.

Livermore, Jason, 39.
Look, Abijah, 15.
Lock, Caleb, 64.
Lock, Edward, 36.
Lock, John, 15.
Lock, Jonathan, 15.
Lock, Josiah, 15.
Lock, Simeon, 55.
Lollar, John, 61.
Lombard, Butler, 18.
Lombard, Calvin, 18.
Lombard, Jedadiah, 25.
Lombard, Jnᵒ, 18.
Lombard, Jnᵒ, Jr, 18.
Lombard, Joseph, 18.
Lombard, Nathˡ, 18.
Lombard, Richᵈ, 18.
Lombard, Solᵒ, 18.
Lombard, Thoˢ, 18.
Lombard, Thoˢ, 25.
Lomberde, John, 24.
Lombart, James, 50.
Long, Alexander, 36.
Long, Daniel, 58.
Long, Josiah, 58.
Long, Josiah, 58.
Long, Michael, 36.
Longfellow, Jacob, 52.
Longfellow, Nathan, 52.
Longfellow, Nathan, junr, 52.
Longfellow, Olive, 52.
Longfellow, Sewall, 39.
Longfellow, Stepⁿ, 18.
Longfellow, Stephen, 38.
Longfelow, Jonˢ, 51.
Longfelow, Nathan, 33.
Longfelow, Samuel, 38.
Longley, Ely, 25.
Longley, Jonᵃ, 25.
Longley, Nehʰ, 47.
Longly, Zacheriah, 42.
Longly, Zachry, 42.
Look, Daniel, 54.
Look, George, 54.
Look, Moses, 54.
Loont, Joshson, 45.
Lord, ——, 64.
Lord, Abraham, 43.
Lord, Abraᵐ, 55.
Lord, Ambrose, 67.
Lord, Ammi R., 63.
Lord, Benjamin, 52.
Lord, Benjᵃ, 55.
Lord, Benjˢ, 56.
Lord, Benjᵃ, 69.
Lord, Caleb, 55.
Lord, Charles, 25.
Lord, Danˡ, 55.
Lord, Danˡ, 62.
Lord, David, 56.
Lord, Dominicus, 70.
Lord, Ebenezer, 56.
Lord, Ebenezer, 63.
Lord, Elias, 59.
Lord, Elisha, 57.
Lord, Elisha, 57.
Lord, George, 32.
Lord, Humphrey, 57.
Lord, Ichabod, 56.
Lord, Ichabod, 57.
Lord, Ichabod, 68.
Lord, Isaac, 31.
Lord, Jabes, 56.
Lord, Jacob, 32.
Lord, Jacob, 56.
Lord, James, 14.
Lord, James, 31.
Lord, James, 60.
Lord, Jedediah, 56.
Lord, Jere, 71.
Lord, Jeremiah, 30.
Lord, Jeremiah, 55.
Lord, Jeremiah, 56.
Lord, Jeremiah, 57.
Lord, John, 55.
Lord, John, 55.
Lord, John, 70.
Lord, Joseph, 55.
Lord, Joseph, 55.
Lord, Joseph, 63.
Lord, Josher, 67.
Lord, Love, 56.
Lord, Mark, 55.
Lord, Mary, 55.
Lord, Mary, 56.
Lord, Mary, 62.
Lord, mary (Wid.), 66.
Lord, Mercy, 56.
Lord, Nason, 68.
Lord, Nathan, 15.
Lord, Nathan, 55.
Lord, Nathan, 63.
Lord, Nathˡ, 59.
Lord, Nicholas, 56.
Lord, Nicholas, 57.
Lord, Nicholas, 63.
Lord, Noah, 63.
Lord, Paul, 55.
Lord, Richard, 55.
Lord, Richᵈ, 71.
Lord, Samuel, 25.

Lord, Samuel, 56.
lord, Samuel, 60.
Lord, Simeon, 25.
Lord, Simeon, 56.
Lord, Simon, 63.
Lord, Solomon, 63.
Lord, Thoˢ, 54.
Lord, Thomas, 63.
Lord, Tobias, 54.
Lord, Tobias, 70.
Lord (Widʷ), 60.
Lord, William, 57.
Lord, Wᵐ, 63.
Lord, William W., 63.
Lords, Henry, 29.
Loring, Ance, 21.
Loring, Asa, 21.
Loring, Bezeliel, 21.
Loring, Ezekiel, 21.
Loring, Jeromy, 33.
Loring, John, 22.
loring, Judah, 42.
Loring, Levi, 22.
Loring, Mary, 22.
Loring, Peter, 53.
Loring, Richmond, 21.
Loring, Richmond, 22.
Loring, Samˡ, 21.
Loring, Solomon, 22.
Lotter, Robert, 16.
Loud, James, 45.
Loud, Solomon, 63.
Loushon, Anthony, 27.
Lovett, Israel, 46.
Lovejoy, Abiel, Jr, 47.
Lovejoy, Capᵗ, 47.
Lovejoy, Francis, 39.
Lovejoy, Phillip, 27.
Lovejoy, Thomas, 52.
Lovell, Josiah, 16.
Lovet, Abᵐ, 18.
Lovet, Joseph, 18.
Lovet, Richᵈ, 18.
Lovett, Francis, 27.
Lovett, Isaac, 54.
Lovett, James, 13.
Lovett, Jonathan, 25.
Lovewell, Thomas, 52.
Lovewell, Zelottus, 37.
Lovjoy, Moses, 41.
Low, ——w, 59.
Low, Bazalial, 68.
Low, Benniah, 23.
Low, David, 66.
Low, Edward, 71.
Low, Ephraim, 66.
Low, Ephraim, Junr, 66.
Low, Esther, 14.
Low, Jacob, 33.
Low, Jeddiah, 68.
Low, John, Esqʳ, 59.
Low, Jonathan, 47.
Low, Jonathan, 50.
Low, Jonathan, 68.
Low, Nathaniel, 50.
Low, Nathˡ, 55.
Low, Nathaniel, 59.
Low, Nicholls, 21.
Low, Obdiah, 66.
Low, Samˡ, 68.
Low, thomas, 59.
Low, Thoˢ, 71.
Lowder, Jonathan, 30.
Lowe, Asa, 70.
Lowe, Charles, 27.
Lowe, Daniel, 30.
Lowe, Edward, 72.
Lowe, Job, 70.
Lowe, Solomon, 21.
Lowe, Thomas, 27.
Lowe, Willᵐ, 12.
Lowe, Willᵐ, 16.
Lowel, Danˡ, 44.
Lowel, Jacob, 44.
Lowel, John, 33.
Lowel, Jonᵃ, 16.
Lowel, Jonᵃ, 24.
Lowel, Joseph, 44.
Lowel, Lydia, 18.
Lowel, Martha, 33.
Lowel, Moses, 16.
Lowel, Paul, 12.
Lowel, Samˡ, 65.
Lowel, Stephen, 12.
Lowel, Stephen, 21.
Lowel, Thoˢ, 11.
Lowel, Thoˢ, 12.
Lowel, Willᵐ, 12.
Lowell, Abner, 23.
Lowell, Abner, 32.
Lowell, Benjˢ, 32.
Lowell, Dancy, 24.
Lowell, Eliphalet, 30.
Lowell, John, 23.
Lowell, John, 38.
Lowell, Joseph, 30.
Lowell, Joshua, 26.
Lowell, Joshua Bartlet, 44.
Lowell, Mary, 15.
Lowell, Mary, 23.
Lowell, Nathaniel, 32.
Lowell, Reuben, 44.
Lowell, Rosamus, 46.

INDEX.

Lowell, Stephen, 38.
Lowge, Joanna, 65.
Lowge, John, 65.
Lowge, Samul, 65.
Lowing, Thos, 22.
Lowry, James, 52.
Lowther, John, 23.
Loyns, Wilm, 65.
Luce, Bethuel, 32.
luce, freeman, 51.
Luce, Seth, 47.
luce, Shuble, 51.
luce, Uriah, 51.
Lucus, Elkanah, 24.
Lucus, Elnathan, 24.
Lucus, Warren, 24.
Ludon, Joseph, 21.
ludwig, Jacob, 41.
Lufkin, Aaron, 16.
Lufkin, Benja, 64.
Lufkin, Nathl, 22.
Luice, Daniel, 44.
Luies, Jeremiah, 67.
Luies, Saray (Wid.), 67.
Luis, George, 34.
luis, Joseph, 69.
Lukes, Ebenezer, 21.
Lukes, Elkany, 21.
Lumbard, Solomon, 65.
Lumber, Samuel, 33.
Lumber, Thos, 33.
Lummis, Saml, 51.
Lunt, Abner, 29.
Lunt, Amos, 12.
Lunt, Benjamin, 14.
Lunt, Benjamin, 15.
Lunt, Benja, 30.
Lunt, Daniel, 15.
Lunt, Daniel, 15.
Lunt, Danl, 72.
Lunt, Ephraim, 15.
Lunt, Henry, 72.
Lunt, James, 23.
Lunt, Job, 23.
Lunt, Jobb, 46.
Lunt, John, 19.
Lunt, Joseph, 14.
Lunt, Joseph, 31.
Lunt, Micael, 23.
Lunt, Michael, 27.
Lunt, Moses, 23.
Lunt, Nathan, 15.
Lunt, Saml, 72.
Lunt, William, 15.
Lydston, Gedion, 62.
Lydston, Roby, 62.
Lydston, Waymouth, 62.
Lydston, Waymouth, Jr, 62.
lyford, William, 51.
Lyman, Revd Isaac, 72.
Lymburner, Cunningham, 30.
Lymburner, John, 31.
Lynam, William, 29.
lyon, Eliab, 50.
Lyon, Revd James, 52.
Lyon, Mary, 50.
lyon, Nathan, 50.
Lyon, Peter, 49.
lyon, Squier, 50.
Lyssen, Wm, 62.

McAllaster, Ananias, 68.
McAllaster, Danl, 68.
McAllaster, Joseph, 68.
McAnen, John, 41.
McAnere, Joseph, 43.
Macathany, Thomas, 50.
Macblin, Brice, 35.
McCallum, John, 49.
McCaning, Elisabeth, 13.
Maccardy, James, 44.
McCarr, Caleb, 55.
McCarral, James, 56.
McCarter, John, 36.
McCartha, Florence, 37.
McCarty, John, 64.
McCarty, Thomas, 36.
McCarty, Timo, 38.
McCaslin, Alexander, 31.
MacCaslin, andrew, 45.
MacCaslin, James, 45.
McCaslin, Robert, 43.
McCasslin, Henry, 43.
McCasslin, Henry, Ju., 43.
McCauley, Susanna, 71.
Mcclain, John, 48.
Mcclain, Sam., 49.
Mcclain, william, 48.
McClane, Fergus, 26.
McClannen, James, 68.
mcClary, Robert, 33.
McClary, Robert, 45.
McCloud, —, 55.
Mccluer, thomas, 48.
McCob, Mary, 37.
McCobb, David, 34.
McCobb, James, 36.
McCobb, John, 34.
McCobb, Saml, 34.
McCobb, Saml, 38.
McCobb, Saml, Jur, 34.
McCobb, Willm, 34.
McCollistor, Archable, 32.

McCollistor, Richard, 32.
McCormal, James, 16.
McCormick, Alexr, 54.
McCown, Margara, 34.
McCreat, William, 13.
McCreelus, John, 63.
MacCslin, Gardner, 49.
M'Cuen, John, 55.
McCullister, Js, 18.
McCullock, Adam, 55.
mcCurdey, Samuel, 33.
Mccurdy, dan., 48.
McCurdy, Robert, 30.
McDaniel, James, 32.
McDaniel, John, 29.
McDaniels, Betsy, 33.
McDannels, Paul, 68.
Macdanuiels, James, 45.
McDermot, John, 28.
McDonald, Abner, 18.
McDonald, Agnes, 54.
McDonald, Donald, 53.
McDonald, John, 14.
McDonald, John, 29.
McDonald, Jno, 29.
McDonald, Jos., 18.
McDonald, Lauchlan, 32.
McDonald, Pelatiah, 18.
McDonald, Robt, 59.
McDonald, Roderick, 32.
McDonald, Timo, Jr, 18.
McDonald, Timo, Sr., 18.
McDusle, David, 18.
Mace, Thomas, 26.
Mace, William, 29.
McFadan, Abigail, 38.
McFadan, Andrw, 38.
McFadan, Danl, 38.
McFadan, James, 37.
McFaden, Daniel, 47.
Mcfadien, Thomas, 35.
Mcfarland, andrew, 48.
Mcfarland, Robert, 48.
McFarlen, John, 33.
McFarlin, James, 32.
Macfarlin, Samuel, 50.
McFarlin, Thomas, 32.
McFarlin, William, 27.
Macfarling, James, 50.
Mcfarling, John, 48.
Mcfarling, John, jun., 48.
Macfason, Paul, 51.
Macfasson, Dagle, 42.
McFredericks, James, 38.
Mcgayer, thomas, 42.
McGeoch, Allexr, 55.
McGill, John, 24.
McGill, William, 14.
Mcglathery, Alexdr, 48.
McGlathry, William, 26.
McGlothlin, Geo., 39.
McGlothlin, Gibbins, 47.
McGlothling, Geo., Jr, 39.
McGown, John, 43.
Mcgoyer, pertrick, 48.
McGra, John, 58.
McGra, Will. 14.
McGreger, Alexander, 52.
McGuilly, Jno, 18.
McGuire, John, 21.
McGunrey, John, 45.
McGuyer, John, 53.
macher, Richard, 48.
McHonnen, James, 33.
McIntire, Benjamin, 15.
McIntire, Danl, 72.
McIntire, David, 20.
McIntire, Ebec, 72.
McIntire, Jedediah, 72.
McIntire, Joseph, 37.
McIntire, Joseph, 72.
McIntire, Joseph, Jr, 72.
McIntire, Micum, 72.
McIntire, Saml, 72.
McIntire, Saml, 72.
McIntire, Theodore, 58.
McIntire, william, 48.
McIntosh, John, 14.
McIntosh, William, 19.
McIntosh, William, 46.
McIntyer, Angus, 28.
McIntyer, James, 46.
McIntyer, John, 28.
McIntyer, John, 49.
McIntyer, John, Junr, 49.
McIntyer, Robert, 36.
McIntyer, William, 49.
McIntyre, John, 60.
Mackackeny, Mary, 50.
Mackackeny, Thomas, 50.
McKaslegen, John, 54.
McKean, Ephraim, 26.
McKean, James, 60.
McKean, James, 68.
McKean, Samuel, 26.
McKellar, John, 36.
mackendorsb, John, 49.
McKenney, Danl, 43.
McKenney, David, 43.
McKenney, John, 43.
McKenny, Abner, 18.
McKenny, Brook, 38.

McKenny, Dominicus, 64.
McKenny, Eleazer, 13.
McKenny, Eliza, 18.
McKenny, George, 38.
McKenny, Humphry, 64.
McKenny, James, 18.
McKenny, Jonathan, 13.
McKenny, Jona, 59.
McKenny, Margt, 18.
McKenny, Matthew, 38.
McKenny, Moses, 18.
McKenny, Robt, 18.
McKenny, Robert, 38.
McKenny, Robt, Jr., 18.
McKenny, Saml, 18.
McKenny, Thomas, 38.
McKensle, Mary, 23.
McKenzie, John, 29.
McKenzie, Konneth, 27.
McKessuk, Matthew, 58.
McKessuk, Zobadiah, 58.
Mackfarling, Solomon, 37.
Mackfaying, James, 46.
Mackini, James, 50.
Mackinney, Daniel, 44.
Mackinney, James, 45.
McKinncy, Jeremiah, 65.
McKinney, John, 65.
McKinsey, Owen, 54.
McKissock, Frances, 60.
McKissek, John, 60.
Mackkee, George, 37.
McKnight, David, 39.
Mckown, John, 48.
Mckown (weidow), 48.
McLallen, Nathl, 35.
McLallen, Simon, 36.
McLallen, Thomas, 46.
McLaughlin, Samuel, 26.
McLaughlin, Wm, 23.
McLaulan, Robt, 18.
McLaulan, Wm, 18.
McLellan, Arthur, 23.
McLellan, Cary, 18.
McLellan, Hugh, 23.
McLellan, Jno, 18.
McLellan, Js, 18.
McLellan, Joseph, 23.
McLellan, Joseph, 23.
McLellan (old Mrs.), 18.
McLellan, Stephen, 18.
McLellan, Thos, 18.
McLellan, Wm, 18.
McLellan, William, 24.
McLellan, Wm, Jr, 18.
Mclen, Alexdr, 48.
McLintock, Robert, 47.
McLucus, John, 60.
McMahan, Daniel, 12.
McMahan, Daniel, 37.
McMahan, Timo, 37.
McMann, Joseph, 28.
McMann, Thankful, 28.
Macmanners, John, 34.
McMaster, Willm, 39.
Mcmical, dowgal, 48.
Mcmorfey, peter (mescongus Island), 48.
McMullen, Alexander, 26.
McMullen, Archibald, 32.
McMurphy, Archibald, 51.
McMurphy, William, 26.
McPharlen, Andw, 34.
McPharlen, Benja, 34.
McPharlen, Elizabeth, 34.
McPharlen, Joseph, 43.
McPhetres, Archibald, 27.
McPhetres, Archibald, junr, 27.
McQuig, Danl, 41.
McQuin, Edmund, 21.
Macumber, Ebenezer, 35.
Macumber, Job, 35.
Macumber, Seth, 35.
McWane, David, 25.
McWane, David, 35.
Madden, James, 71.
Madden, Owen, 27.
Maddix, John, 69.
Maddix, John, 69.
Maddocks, Ichabod, 26.
Maddon, John, 36.
Maddox, Caleb, 30.
Maddox, Caleb, 32.
Maddox, Henry, 31.
Maddox, Ichabod, 32.
Maddox, John, 32.
Maddox, Joshua, 32.
Maddox, Samuel, 32.
Magee, Nell, 30.
Magee, Robert, 30.
Magoon, Benja, 67.
Magoon, Edward, 67.
Magoon, Josiah, 67.
Mahany, Patrick, 28.
Mahaw, Edmund, 53.
Mahoney, James, 31.
Mahony, James, 38.
Mailen, John, 23.
Main, John, 72.
Maines, Elias, 72.
Mains, David, 18.
Mains, Nichs, 18.
Mains, Thos, 18.

Majory, John, 23.
Makom, John, 53.
Maker, Joseph, 31.
Malcom, Allen, 41.
Malcom, Andrew, 36.
Malcom, James, 36.
Malcom, John, 38.
Malcom, Joseph, 15.
Malcom, Willm, 38.
Malcom, Willm, 46.
Mallee, Daniel, 37.
Mallee, James, 35.
Mallet, John, 12.
Mallet, John, 34.
Man, andrew, 38.
Manchester, Gershom, 25.
Manchester, John, 29.
Manchester, John, junr, 29.
Manchester, Stephen, 25.
manentier, Ebenezer, 67.
Manes, Betsy, 52.
Manes, James, 37.
Manes, John, 37.
Manes, Saml, 52.
maning, Edward, 42.
Mann, Amos, 27.
Mann, Daniel, 18.
Mann, Daniel, 28.
Mann, David, 30.
Mann, Hannah, 30.
Mann, John, Jr, 16.
Mann, Joseph, 16.
Mann, Obediah, 24.
Mann, Oliver, 30.
Manning, Patrick, 56.
Manning, Sarah, 57.
Mannis, Nathan, 43.
Mans, John, 16.
Mans, Thos, 16.
Mansfield, Daniel, 26.
Mansfield, Jacob, 26.
Mansfield, James, 43.
Mansfield, Thomas, 54.
Manson, Benja, 61.
Manson, John, 61.
Manson, Joseph, 62.
Manson, Saml, 61.
Manssell, John, 30.
Manssell, Joseph, 30.
Manter, David, 45.
Manuel, James, 64.
Manwell, Samuel, 11.
Marble, Ebenezer, 11.
Marble, Nancy, 23.
March, Danl, 59.
March, Edmund, 15.
March, Peltiah, 15.
March, Samuel, 15.
March, Saml, 18.
March, Saul, 55.
Marchant, Anthony, 27.
Marill, Benja, 38.
Marill, John, 38.
Mariner, John, 13.
Mariner, Jona N., 33.
Mariner, Joseph, 13.
Mariner, Moses, 13.
Mariner, Willm, 12.
Marithew, William, 40.
Mark, Abijah, 51.
Marr, Danl, 18.
Marr, James, 18.
Marr, Lydia, 18.
Marrill, Benja, 38.
Marrill, Benja, Ju., 38.
Marriner, Esthr, 62.
Marriner, John, 12.
Marriner, Saml, 12.
Marrow, Daniel, 51.
Marrow, Daniel, Ju., 51.
Marrs, John, 13.
Marrs, Surplus, 56.
Marrs, Thomas, 56.
Marrs, Wm, 56.
Mars, Isaac, 64.
Mars, John, 38.
Mars, John, 40.
Mars, Pelatiah, 64.
Mars, Willm, 38.
Marsh, Amy, 60.
Marsh, Caleb, 33.
Marsh, Isaah, 67.
Marsh, John, 27.
Marsh, John, 47.
Marsh, Stephen, 67.
Marshal, John, 40.
Marshal, Samuel, 36.
Marshal, Samuel, Junr, 36.
Marshal, Willm, 33.
Marshall, Benja, 29.
Marshall, Ephraim, 27.
Marshall, Ezekiel, 27.
Marshall, Isaac, 18.
Marshall, Joshua, 27.
Marshall, Nahum, 55.
Marshall, Wm, 18.
marshall, William, 67.
Marshall, Zachariah, 29.
Marss, Ichabod, 56.
Marsten, Caleb, 65.
Marsten, Daniel, 64.
Marsten, David, 65.
Marsten, James, 65.

Marsten, James, 67.
Marston, Danl, 16.
Marston, Jesper, 22.
Marston, John, 22.
Marston, Joseph, 45.
Marston, Joshua, 22.
Marston, Leml, 18.
Marston, Levi, 21.
Marston, Nathaniel, 34.
marston, Nathaniel, 45.
Marston, Simeon, 21.
marston, Theoder, 50.
Martain, Moses, 42.
Martain, Nathl, 46.
Marten, Joseph, 28.
Marten, Phillip, 31.
Marten, Thomas, 12.
Marther, Wm, 58.
Martin, Bryan, 24.
Martin, Ezekiol, 11.
martin, John, 41.
martin, John, 48.
martin, John, 48.
martin, John, 67.
Martin, Jona, 59.
Martin, Lewis, 60.
Martin, Matthias, 20.
Martin, Richard, 36.
Martin, Robt, 59.
Martin, Samuel, 26.
Martin, Samuel, 60.
martin, thomas, 48.
martin (widow), 48.
Martin, Willm, 37.
Martin, William, 60.
Marum, John, 38.
Marwick, Hugh, 23.
Mase, Andrew, 57.
Maseam, Nathan, 41.
Mason, Abner, 43.
Mason, Abner, Jur, 43.
Mason, Amos, 58.
Mason, Benja, 58.
Mason, Benja, Jr, 58.
Mason, Broadstreet, 24.
Mason, Ebenezer, 21.
Mason, Ebenezer, 41.
Mason, George, 39.
Mason, Jane, 65.
Mason, John, 15.
Mason, John, 68.
Mason, Joseph, 59.
Mason, Nat., 63.
Mason, Saml, 22.
Mason, Saml, 42.
Mason, Stephen, 43.
Mason, Walter, 68.
Mason, William, 29.
Massey, Benja, 44.
Massey, Woodbuary, 57.
Massy, Nathaniel, 29.
Massy, Robert, 31.
Masten, Samuel, 54.
Mastin, Benjamin, 14.
Mastin, Ephraim, 14.
Mastin, Robert, 21.
Maston, Daniel, 23.
Mathow, Daniel, 51.
Mathows, Abigail, 30.
Mathews, Anthony, 46.
Mathews, Daniel, 36.
Mathews, Edmond, 47.
Mathews, Elijah, 71.
Mathews, Flisher, 47.
Mathews, James, 36.
Mathews, James, 47.
Mathews, John, 12.
Mathews, Joseph, 46.
Mathews, Samuel, 31.
Matheys, Joseph, 51.
Matman (Widow), 71.
mats (widow), 49.
Matthews, Jabez, 19.
Matthews, James, 49.
Matthews, Jno, 18.
Matthews, John, 18.
Matthews, John, 20.
Matthews, John, 47.
Matthews, Robert, 49.
Matthews, Volatiah, 12.
Mattock, Richard, 44.
Mattocks, Pel. Graves, 55.
Mattoks, Henory, 69.
Mattuck, Thos, 15.
Maugridge, Benja, 22.
Maulbone, James, 35.
Maxey Joseph, 67.
Maxwel, Gershorn, 70.
Maxwell, Alexander, 70.
Maxwell, Baruch, 70.
Maxwell, David, 70.
Maxwell, George, 35.
Maxwell, Gershorn, 70.
Maxwell, James, 13.
Maxwell, James, 13.
Maxwell, James, 35.
Maxwell, John, 70.
Maxwell, John, Jr, 70.
Maxwell, Joseph, 13.
Maxwell, Patrick, 13.
Maxwell, Robert, 13.
Maxwell, Saml, 70.
Maxwell, Thomas, 13.

INDEX.

Maxwell, William, 13.
Maxwell, William, 14.
Maxwell, Willm, 18.
Maybe, Elias, 53.
Maybee, Solomon, 53.
Mayberry, David, 22.
Mayberry, James, 25.
Mayberry, John, 25.
Mayberry, John, 25.
Mayberry, John, 25.
Mayberry, Richard, 24.
Mayberry, Richard, 25.
Mayberry, Thomas, 22.
Mayberry, William, 25.
Mayberry, William, 25.
Mayberry, William, 26.
Mayew, Andrew, 30.
Mayew, Reuben, 30.
Mayew, Whitewood 13.
Mayhew, James, 12.
Mayhew, Priscilla, 52.
Mayhew, Samuel, 51.
Mayo, Ebenezer, 28.
Mayo, Israel, 28.
Mayo, James, 27.
Mayo, James, 28.
Mayo, Joseph, 29.
Mayo, Joshua, 29.
Mayo, Nathaniel, 27.
Mayo, Nathaniel, 28.
Mead, George, 11.
Means, George, 65.
Means, James, 14.
Means, Robert, 32.
Means, Thomas, 65.
Mecaheny, Michal, 39.
Meeder, Danl, 70.
Meeder, Tobias, 40.
Megraw, John, 50.
Meirs, George, 44.
Melcher, Anum, 21.
Melcher, Joseph, 12.
Melcher, Noah, 12.
Melcher, Saml, 12.
meldrom, John, 66.
Meldrom, Saml, 71.
Mellet, Willm, 46.
Melony, Walter, 36.
Meloon, Abraham, 35.
Meloon, Elizabeth, 36.
Melvil, Jno, 18.
Melzar, John, 36.
Mendal, John, 37.
Mendam, Joshua, 62.
Mendham, W^m, 61.
Mendom, W^m, 62.
Menett, David, 54.
Menton, Phinehas, 58.
Merchant, John, 47.
Meriam, Nathl, 56.
Merithue, Roger, 28.
Mero, Amariah, 47.
Merrel, Abel, 20.
Merrel, Edmund, 14.
Merrel, Edmund, 15.
Merrel, Enoch, 15.
Merrel, Humphrey, 15.
Merrel, Jacob, 15.
Merrel, James, 14.
Merrel, John, 19.
Merrel, John, 20.
Merrel, Joseph, 15.
Merrel, Joseph, 19.
Merrel, Moses, 15.
Merrel, Nathan, 19.
Merrel, Peeter, 21.
Merrel, Silas, 15.
Merrel, Stephen, 15.
Merrell, Adam, 14.
Merrell, Adam, 15.
Merrell, Amos, 15.
Merrell, Daniel, 15.
Merrell, Ebenezer, 25.
Merrell, Elias, 14.
Merrell, Elias, 15.
Merrell, Ezekiel, 21.
Merrell, Humphrey, 15.
Merrell, Jacob, 15.
Merrell, James, 14.
Merrell, James, 14.
Merrell, James, 14.
Merrell, John, 21.
Merrell, Joseph, 14.
Merrell, Joshua, 15.
Merrell, Joshua, 20.
Merrell, Moses, 21.
Merrell, Samuel, 15.
Merrot, Samuel, 54.
Merriam, Revd Marthew, 58.
Merrifield, John, 70.
Merrifield, John, 70.
Merril, Abel, 55.
Merril, Bradley, 18.
Merril, Daniel, 18.
Merril, Danl, 18.
Merril, Emly, 40.
Merril, Enoch, 60.
Merril, Henry, 20.
Merril, John, 46.
Merril, Levi, 18.
Merril, Levi, 67.
Merril, Moses, 40.
Merril, Nathan, 21.
Merril, Obed, 55.
Merril, Roger, 14.
Merril, Samuel, 34.
Merril, Sarah, 21.
Merril, Stephen, 37.
Merril, Susanna, 16.
Merril, thomas, 35.
Merrill, Abel, 59.
Merrill, Caleb, 30.
Merrill, Danl, 25.
Merrill, Danl, 55.
Merrill, Edmund, 11.
Merrill, Ezekiel, 64.
Merrill, Gideon, 55.
Merrill, Giles, 11.
Merrill, Humphy, 59.
Merrill, Jabesh, 24.
Merrill, Jabesh, 25.
Merrill, Jacob, 16.
Merrill, Jacob, 55.
Merrill, James, 11.
Merrill, John, 16.
Merrill, Jno, 59.
Merrill, Joseph, 65.
Merrill, Joshua, 58.
Merrill, Levi, 25.
Merrill, Nathan, 11.
Merrill, Nathl, 22.
Merrill, Nathl, 60.
Merrill, Saml, 22.
Merrill, Saml, 50.
Merrill, Saml, Junr, 22.
Merrill, Saml, Junr, 59.
Merriman, Hugh, 20.
Merriman, James, 20.
Merriman, Mich^l, 20.
Merriman, Thomas, 12.
Merriman, Thomas, 20.
Merriman, Tim^o, 20.
Merriman, Walter, 20.
Merriman, Walter, 20.
Merriner, John, Jur., 12.
Merrit, Daniel, 54.
Merrit, Joseph, 54.
Merritt, Daniel, 54.
Merritt, Richard, 54.
Merritt, W^m, 54.
Merrow, David, 67.
Merrow, Edmund, 67.
Merrow, James, 63.
Merrow, Joseph, 37.
Merrow, Joseph, 67.
Merrow, Patrick, 43.
Merrow, Saml, 37.
Merrow, Samuel, 67.
Merry, Willm, 64.
Merryfield, Simeon, 70.
Meserve, Danl, Senr, 18.
Meserve, Elisha, 18.
Meserve, Elisha, Jr., 18.
Meserve, Eliz^a, 18.
Meserve, George, 18.
Meserve, Gideon, 18.
Meserve, John, 18.
Meserve, Sol^o, 18.
Meserve, Thos, 18.
Meserve, W^m, 18.
Meservee, Bazaliel, 52.
Meservey, Joseph, 64.
Meservey, Nathl, 64.
Meservy, Clement, 18.
Messer, John, 68.
Messerve, Benj^a, 26.
Messerve, Joseph, 26.
Metcalf, Joseph, 39.
Metcalf, Leonard, 26.
Metguin, John, 20.
Metguin, William, 20.
Michaels, George, 38.
Michaels, James, 12.
Michals, Josiah, 51.
michel, Danbr., 45.
Midcalf, John, 45.
midcufs, Joseph, 51.
Midgot, David, 60.
Miers, Philip, 43.
Mighill, Joseph, 65.
Mighill, Josiah, 65.
Mighill, Moses, 65.
Milbory, Saml, 71.
Milekin, John, 22.
miler, peter, 41.
Miles, Mary, 61.
Miles, Nathan, 26.
Miles, W^m, 65.
Milikin, John, 33.
Millar, Thomas, 64.
Millbank, Phillip, 40.
Millens, Robert, 25.
Millens, Thomas, 25.
Miller, And^w, 55.
Miller, Benj^a, 55.
Miller, David, 13.
Miller, David, 27.
miller, francis, 41.
Miller, Francis, 52.
miller, frank, 41.
miller, frank, jun., 41.
miller, henry, 41.
Miller, Hugh, 13.
Miller, James, 13.
Miller, James, 26.
Miller, James, 31.
Miller, Jer^e, 55.
Miller, Jno, 18.
Miller, John, 32.
miller, John, 48.
Miller, John, 54.
Miller, John Bolt, 58.
Miller, Joshua, 13.
Miller, Lem^l, 55.
Miller, Margaret, 12.
Miller, Mary, 22.
miller, nickles, 48.
Miller, Noah, 27.
Miller, Robert, 32.
miller, Robert, 48.
Miller, Robert, 54.
miller, thomas, 48.
Miller (Widow), 55.
Miller (Widow), 72.
Miller, William, 40.
Millet, David, 11.
Millet, Elisha, 13.
Millet, John, 11.
Millet, John, 24.
Millet, Solomon, 40.
Millet, Thos, 16.
Millican, Isaac, 59.
Millican, Joel, 58.
Millican, Nathl, 59.
Millikan, Benj^a, 18.
Millikan, Edwd, 18.
Millikan, Isaih, 18.
Millikan, John, 18.
Millikan, Jon^a, 18.
Millikan, Jo^s, 18.
Millikan, Joshua, 18.
Millikan, Lem^l, 18.
Millikan, M. John, 18.
Millikan, Polly, 18.
Millikan, Saml, 18.
Millikan, Thos, 18.
Millikan, W^m, 18.
Milliken, Phinehas, 64.
Millikin, Abner, 27.
Millikin, Benjamin, 15.
Millikin, Elias, 25.
Millikin, Robert, 31.
Millikin, Samuel, 29.
Mills, Alexander, 22.
Mills, Deborah, 68.
Mills, Eligood, 69.
Mills, Jacob, 63.
Mills, James, 63.
Mills, James, 63.
Mills, John, 50.
Mills, John, 63.
Mills, John, 64.
Mills, Josiah, 44.
Mills, Robart, 50.
Mink, John, 49.
mink, pacel, 42.
Mink, Peter, 49.
mink, philip, 41.
Mink, valantin, 42.
Minot, John, 12.
Minot, Thomas, 14.
Mirach, Josiah, 41.
Mirach, Willm, 22.
Mireck, Bazaliel, 24.
Mirick, John, 47.
Mirick, John, 69.
Miriek, Andrew, 35.
Mirrick, Nathaniel, 28.
mirrit, Jonathan, 49.
misherve, clemt., 48.
misherver, nath., 48.
Mitcalf, Hugh, 35.
Mitchal, Thomas, 40.
Mitchel, Abraham, 16.
Mitchel, Abra^m, 16.
Mitchel, Benj^a, 21.
Mitchel, Danl, 16.
Mitchel, Daniel, 21.
Mitchel, Danl, 54.
Mitchel, David, 21.
Mitchel, Dominicus, 24.
Mitchel, Dummer, 54.
Mitchel, Eliz^h, 61.
Mitchel, Horton, 21.
Mitchel, Jacob, Jr, 22.
Mitchel, James, 61.
Mitchel, James M., 21.
Mitchel, Jeremiah, 14.
Mitchel, Jere^h, 18.
Mitchel, Job, 18.
Mitchel, John, 16.
Mitchel, John, 36.
Mitchel, John, 47.
Mitchel, John, 54.
Mitchel, John, 61.
Mitchel, John, 70.
Mitchel, John, 70.
Mitchel, Jonas, 51.
Mitchel, Jon^a, 21.
Mitchel, Jon^a, 21.
Mitchel, Jon^s, 48.
Mitchel, Jonathan, J^r, 22.
Mitchel, Joseph, 47.
Mitchel, Joseph, Junr, 16.
Mitchel, Joshua, 16.
Mitchel, Josiah, 40.
Mitchel, Jotham, 70.
Mitchel, Loring, 21.
Mitchel, Lucy, 61.
Mitchel, Mary, 61.
Mitchel, Mehitable, 21.
Mitchel, Noah, 52.
Mitchel, Rich^d, 14.
Mitchel, Roger, 61.
Mitchel, Saml, 21.
Mitchel, Saml, 61.
Mitchel, Saml, 70.
Mitchel, Sarah, 61.
Mitchel, Seth, 21.
Mitchel, Solomon, 21.
Mitchel, Thomas, 14.
Mitchel, Willm, 12.
Mitchel, Willm, 16.
Mitchel, W^m, 18.
Mitchel, Willm, 21.
Mitchel, W^m, 61.
Mitchell, Benjamin, 26.
Mitchell, John, 24.
Mitchell, Jonathan, 13.
Mitchell, Robert, 23.
Mitchell, Robert, 26.
Moffat, James, 43.
Moffat, John, 69.
mograge, Charly, 45.
mograge, Thomas, 45.
Molloy, Dennis, 64.
Molton, Danl, 72.
Molton, Danl, 72.
Molton, Eben^r, 72.
Molton, Elizabeth, 22.
molton, James, 48.
Molton, Joel, 66.
Molton, John, 72.
Molton, Johnson, 72.
Molton, Joseph, 72.
Molton, Nathl, 71.
Molton, Saml, 72.
Molton, Theodore, 72.
Molton, William, 23.
Monro, Stephen, 43.
Monson, Jos^h, 62.
Monson, Saml, 62.
Monson, Thomas, 62.
Montgomery, Lydia, 34.
Montgomery, Robert, 49.
Montgomery, Saml, 34.
Moodey, Gilman, 49.
moodey, Samuel, 67.
Moody, Benjamin, 15.
Moody, Benjamin, 23.
moody, Cernes, 35.
Moody, Clament, 68.
Moody, Daniel, 19.
Moody, Dorcas, 14.
Moody, Elizabeth, 65.
Moody, George, 65.
Moody, James, 24.
Moody, Jeremiah, 42.
moody, John, 35.
Moody, John, 63.
Moody, Joseph, 18.
Moody, Joseph, 68.
Moody, Joseph, 71.
Moody, Joshua, 24.
Moody, Josiah, 14.
Moody, Mary, 18.
Moody, Moses, 27.
Moody, Nathaniel, 23.
moody, Richard, 35.
Moody, Robt, 18.
Moody, Saml, 33.
Moody, Scribner, 42.
Moody, Silas, 55.
Moody, Thomas, 72.
Moody, William, 23.
Moody, William, 27.
Moody (Widow), 18.
Moon, Joseph, 31.
Moon, Thomas, 31.
Moor, Collins, 47.
Moor, Capt. Hugh, 58.
Moor, Levi, 47.
Moor (Widow), 58.
Moor, Willm, 72.
Moore, David, 43.
Moore, Ebenezer 37.
Moore, Eben^r, 61.
Moore, Ebenezer, 65.
Moore, Edmond, 22.
Moore, Edwd, 61.
Moore, Eliz^h, 61.
Moore, Elkins, 16.
Moore, George, 73.
Moore, Isaac, 37.
Moore, James, 37.
Moore, James, 39.
Moore, Joanna, 21.
Moore, John, 23.
Moore, John, 65.
Moore, John, 72.
Moore, Cap^n Jno, 61.
Moore, Joshua, 61.
Moore, Joshua, 72.
Moore, Joshua, J^r, 73.
Moore, Josiah, 53.
Moore, Josiah, 54.
Moore, Nathl, 37.
Moore, Peletiah, 58.
Moore, Reuben, 43.
Moore, Robert, 53.
Moore, Samuel, 52.
Moore, Saml, 61.
Moore, Saml, 73.
Moore, Thomas, 43.
Moore, Thos, 72.
Moore, Willm, 73.
Moore, Cap^n W^m, 61.
Moors, Timothy, 49.
Morain, Andrew, 53.
Moral, Patience, 61.
Morean, John, 24.
More, Benj^a, 32.
More, Benjamin, 42.
More, David, 30.
more, Ebenezer, 66.
More, Edward, 32.
More, Goff, 42.
More, James, 30.
More, Jeremiah, 29.
More, Joel, 29.
More, John, 30.
More, John, 42.
More, John, 45.
More, John, 66.
More, John, jun^r, 30.
More, Joseph, 31.
More, Joseph, 42.
More, Miriham, 42.
More, Mordica, 39.
More, William, 28.
More, William, 30.
more, William, 66.
more, William, 66.
More, Wyat, 32.
Morefield, hipsebath (Wld.), 60.
morel, Samuel, 66.
morel, Stephen, 66.
Mores, Aaron, 64.
Mores, Abraham, 45.
Mores, Jonathan, 22.
Mores, Joseph, 52.
Mores, Nathan, 40.
Mores, Thomas, 44.
Mores, William, 11.
Morey, Elias, 27.
Morey, Ezekiel, 27.
Morey, Ezekiel, 32.
Morey, Phillip, 34.
morfey, John (mescongus Island), 48.
morfey, peter (mescongus Island), 48.
Morgan, Benj^a, 32.
Morgan, John, 21.
Morgan, Joseph, 41.
Morgan, Luke, 21.
Morgan, Saml, 11.
morgin, James, 41.
Morgin, John, 45.
Morgrage, Peter, 30.
morphi (widow), 42.
Morrel, Abraham, 57.
Morrel, David, 57.
Morrel, David, 67.
Morrel, Isaac, 57.
Morrel, John, 63.
Morrel, Josiah, 57.
Morrel, Peter, 57.
Morrel, Peter, Junr, 57.
Morrel, Stephen, 15.
Morrel, Stephen, 65.
Morrel, Thomas, 57.
Morrel, William, 15.
Morrel, Wintrop, 57.
Morrell, Benjamin, 25.
Morrell, Benjamin, 25.
Morrell, Jedediah, 26.
Morrell, Joel, 62.
Morrell, John, 15.
Morrell, Peeter, 26.
Morril, Abraham, 49.
Morril, Jedediah, 40.
Morril, Peaster, 57.
Morril, Tristram, 58.
Morrill, Benj^a, 25.
Morrill, Joseph, 58.
Morrill, Levi, 51.
Morrill, Nahum, 71.
Morrill, Reuben, 58.
Morris, Ch^s, 18.
Morris, Charles, 18.
Morris, Dennis, 18.
Morris, W^m, 55.
Morrison, Benj^a, 70.
Morrison, Edward, 68.
Morrison, James, 65.
Morrison, Jon^a, 67.
Morrison, Joseph, 31.
Morrison, Josiah, 70.
Morrison, Moses, 38.
Morrison, Nathl L., 33.
Morrison, Robert, 15.
Morrison, Saml, 38.
Morrison, Samuel, 60.
Morrison, Thomas, 49.
Morrison, Willm, 11.
Morrison, William, 53.
Morrison, Willm, 70.
morroson, Abraham, 66.
morroson, Bradbury, 66.
Morroson, Daniel, 66.
Morroson, David, 66.
morroson, Ebenezer, 66.

INDEX.

morroson, Francis, 66.
Morrow, Ebnezer, 51.
Morrow, Timothy, 45.
Morse, —— (Clothier), 18.
Morse, andrew, 50.
Morse, Anthony, 12.
Morse, Dan¹, 38.
Morse, Daniel, 46.
Morse, David, 37.
Morse, Isaac, 45.
Morse, James, 22.
Morse, Jon⁰, 37.
Morse, Joseph, 12.
Morse, Joseph, 70.
Morse, Levi, 47.
Morse, Mary, 20.
Morse, Nathan, 55.
Morse, Paul, 12.
Morse, Philip, 45.
Morse, Seth, 22.
Morse, Stephen, 33.
Morss, Benj⁴, 65.
Morton, Bryant, 18.
Morton, Bryant, 58.
Morton, Cornellus, 40.
Morton, David, 18.
Morton, Ebenezer, 40.
Morton, Ebenezer, 51.
Morton, Ebenᵉ, 64.
Morton, Ebenʳ, Jrᵉ, 18.
Morton, Ebenezer, Junʳ, 40.
Morton, Isaac, 18.
Morton, Jabez, 18.
Morton, James, 18.
Morton, James, 40.
morton, John, 48.
Morton, Joseph, 64.
Morton, Joshua, 40.
Morton, levy, 51.
Morton, Michael, 39.
Morton, Reuben, 18.
Morton, Thoˢ, 18.
morton, william, 48.
Morton, Willᵐ, 64.
Moseley, Willᵐ, 12.
Moses, Dan¹, 18.
Moses, George, 18.
Moses, George, 18.
Moses, Josiah, 25.
Moses, Nath¹, 18.
Mosher, Elisha, 50.
Mosher, Jʳ, 18.
Mosher, Jaˢ, Jr, 18.
Mosier, Daniel, 50.
Mosier, Daniel, Juʳ, 50.
Mosier, Elisha, 50.
Mosier, Elisha, 50.
Moss, Anthony, 15.
Moss, Eliphalet, 23.
Moss, Eliphalet, 23.
Moss, Jethniel, 15.
Moss, John, 19.
Moss, Jonathan, 23.
Moss, Joseph, 22.
Moss, Levi, 19.
Moss, Mark, 19.
Moss, Nathan, 19.
Moss, Nathaniel, 23.
Motheswill, Thoˢ, 52.
Motley, Alexander, 23.
Motley, Thomas, 24.
Motley, William, 23.
Motte, William, 40.
Moulton, Abel, 72.
Moulton, Charles, 18.
Moulton, Cuting, 65.
Moulton, Dan¹, 18.
Moulton, Dan¹, Jr., 18.
Moulton, David, 68.
Moulton, Ephrim, 68.
Moulton, Jnᵒ, 18.
Moulton, John, 40.
Moulton, Jonˢ, 18.
Moulton, Jonˢ, Jr., 18.
Moulton, Jonˢ, 3ᵈ, 18.
Moulton, Jos., 18.
Moulton, Jos., 18.
Moulton, Levi, 68.
Moulton, Peter, 24.
Moulton, Samuel, 65.
Moulton, Samˡ, 72.
Moulton, Simeon, 68.
Moulton, Stephen, 68.
Moulton, Thoˢ, 72.
Moulton, William, 69.
Moulton, Willᵐ, 72.
Mower, John, 38.
Mower, Jonˢ, 38.
Mower, William, 38.
Moxy, Mercy, 21.
Muchemore, Jnᵉ, 59.
Mudgett, Abraham, 28.
Mudgett, John, 26.
Muget, James, 65.
Muget, Jeremiah, 65.
Muget, Joseph, 65.
Mugford, John, 25.
Mugford, Nathaniel, 25.
Mugford, Robert, 25.
Muggarage, William, 61.
Muggaridge, Thomˢ, 60.
Muggarige, John, 61.
Mugget, John, 65.

Mugridge, Simon, 38.
Mullikin, Josiah, 15.
Mulloy, Hugh, 35.
Mumford, Daniel, 24.
Mumford, Edmund, 14.
Mumford, Samuel, 14.
Mumford, Samuel, 22.
Muncey, David, 43.
Muncy, Jonathan, 44.
Muncy, Napthali, 43.
Munson, John, 52.
Munson, Joseph, 52.
Munson, Joseph, junʳ, 52.
Munson, Stephen, 52.
Munson, Wᵐ, 64.
Murch, Benjamin, 28.
Murch, Ebenʳ, 18.
Murch, Ebenʳ, Jr, 18.
Murch, Isaac, 18.
Murch, James, 18.
Murch, James, 59.
Murch, Jeremiah, 18.
Murch, John, 18.
Murch, John, 31.
Murch, John, junʳ, 31.
Murch, Joseph, 18.
Murch, Joseph, 32.
Murch, Matthias, 18.
Murch, Samˡ, 18.
Murch, Walter, 18.
Murch, William, 28.
Murch, Willᵐ, 58.
murphy, James, 33.
Murphy, Jeremiah, 36.
Murphy, John, 55.
Murphy, Joshua, 55.
Murphy, Michˡ, 70.
Murphy, Pierce, 64.
Murphy, Thomas, 32.
Murphy, thomas, 60.
Murray, Anthʸ, 18.
Murray, Anthʸ, Jr., 18.
Murray, David, 41.
Murray, John, 34.
Murray, John, 36.
Murrey, James, 14.
Murry, Hannah, 57.
Murry, John, 68.
Murry, Nathan, 57.
Murry, Samˡ, 57.
Murry, Thomas, 63.
Murry, Wᵐ, 68.
Mussey, Theodore, 24.
Mussy, Daniel, 23.
Mussy, Daniel, 23.
Mussy, John, 24.
Mustard, James, 46.
Mutchmore, Jacob, 37.
Myreen, John, 34.
Myrick, Isaac, 18.

Nahaney, Sarah, 61.
Nap, Joseph, 40.
Narman, John, 72.
Nash, Abraham, 54.
nash, Church, 42.
Nash, David, 20.
Nash, Ebenʳ, 54.
Nash, Isaac, 54.
Nash, Isaac, 54.
Nash, Isaac, 2ᵈ, 54.
Nash, Isaiah, 54.
Nash, John, 19.
Nash, John, 54.
Nash, Jonˢ, 11.
Nash, Joseph, 54.
nash, olivor, 49.
Nash, Reuben, 54.
Nash, Reuben, 2ᵈ, 54.
Nash, Samuel, 19.
Nash, Samuel, 54.
Nash, Samuel, junʳ, 54.
Nash (Widow), 54.
Nason, Aaron, 56.
Nason, Abᵐ, 18.
Nason, Abraham, 43.
Nason, Amos, 56.
Nason, Benjˢ, 58.
Nason, Benjˢ, 70.
Nason, Caleb, 68.
Nason, Danˡ, 55.
Nason, Edward, 55.
Nason, Elizʰ, 61.
Nason, Ephᵐ, 18.
Nason, Ham, 68.
Nason, Isaac, 20.
Nason, Jacob, 67.
Nason, James, 62.
Nason, Jeremiah, 16.
Nason, John, 11.
Nason, John, 27.
Nason, John, 55.
Nason, John, 64.
Nason, John, 64.
Nason, Jonathan, 61.
Nason, Jonˢ, 64.
Nason, Joseph, 64.
Nason, Joshua, 55.
Nason, Joshua, 55.
Nason, Joshua, Jrᵉ, 55.
Nason, Mary, 56.
Nason, Meriam, 56.
Nason, Moses, 55.

Nason, Moses, 67.
Nason, Nathˡ, 55.
Nason, Noah, 56.
Nason, Noah, 58.
Nason, Robert, 64.
Nason, Robert E., 43.
Nason, Samuel, Esq., 66.
Nason, Sarah, 72.
Nason, Uriah, 13.
Nason, Uriah, 18.
Nason, Wᵐ, 18.
Nason, Wᵐ, 55.
Nble, abbigale (Wid.), 67.
Neal, Andrew, 57.
Neal, Andrew, 60.
Neal, David, 37.
Neal, Edmund, 68.
Neal, Enoch, 65.
neal, George, 45.
Neal, James, 57.
Neal, James, 61.
Neal, John, 38.
Neal, Johnson, 57.
Neal, Joseph, 45.
Neal, Samuel, 60.
Neal, Stephen, 57.
Neal, Walter, 65.
Neal (Widow), 14.
Neal, Wᵐ, 57.
Neall, ——, 45.
Neazcy, Thos., 58.
Nehnenhawsen, Henry Frederick, 36.
Neil, John, 18.
Nellson, David, 21.
Nelson, Daniel, 68.
Nelson, David, 54.
Nelson, Jacob, 44.
Nelson, John, 41.
Nelson, Joseph, 68.
Nelson, Mary, 44.
Nelson, Leder, 68.
Nelson, Nathan, 22.
Nelson, Thoˢ, 20.
Neptune, Junior, 29.
Nesmith, Benjˢ, 26.
Nevers, Elisha, 27.
Nevins, John, 11.
Nevus, Samuel, 20.
Newal, Ebenezer, 14.
Newal, Ebenˢ, Junʳ, 14.
Newbegin, George, 65.
Newbegin, Jnᵒ, 18.
Newberry, John, 32.
newberrt, John, 42.
newbert, Stophal, 42.
Newbet, John, 26.
Newcomb, David, 47.
Newcomb, Enos, 18.
Newcomb, Jnᵒ, 52.
Newcomb, Jnᵒ, 59.
Newcomb, Jonathan, 28.
Newcomb, Joshˢ, 59.
Newcomb, Reuben, 28.
Newcomb, Samˡ, 18.
Newcomb, Simeon, 28.
Newcomb, Solᵐ, 59.
Newell, Jonathan, 67.
Newell, Zachariah, 23.
Newell, Zebulen, 37.
Newhall, Jonathan, 47.
Newhouse, Christopher, 40.
Newman, Joseph, 29.
Newman, Thomas, 23.
Newman, Thomas, 23.
Nichols, Alexander, 41.
Nichols, David, 57.
Nichols, Elisabeth, 23.
Nichols, George, 44.
Nichols, John, 23.
Nichols, John, 36.
Nichols, John, 41.
Nichols, Phebe, 57.
Nichols, Samˡ, 14.
Nichols, Samˡ, 41.
Nichols, Samuel, 57.
Nickerson, Aaron, 29.
Nickerson, Daniel, 30.
Nickerson, Eliphalet, 30.
Nickerson, Eliphalet, junʳ, 30.
Nickerson, Izachar, 30.
Nickerson, Paul, 30.
Nickerson, Reuben, 29.
Nickerson, Warren, 30.
Nickerson, William, 29.
nickles, alexander, 48.
Nickles, Alexʳ, 54.
nickles, James, 48.
nickles, william, 48.
Nickols, Alexander, 32.
Nickolls, James, 28.
Nickolls, James, 29.
Nickolls, James, junʳ, 29.
Nigh, Bartlett, 37.
Nigh, Elisha, 37.
Nigh, Samuel, 37.
Night, Amos, 15.
Night, Edman, 38.
Night, George, 15.
Night, Job, 15.
Night, John, 69.
Night, Jonathan, 15.
Night, Jonathan, 69.

Night, Joseph, 14.
Night, Joseph, 15.
Night, Peeter, 15.
Night, Richard, 15.
Night, Samuel, 15.
Night, Stephen, 15.
Night, Thomas, 14.
Night, Zebulon, 69.
Nights, Josiah, 19.
Nights, Phebe, 20.
Niles, Beniah, 25.
niles, Caleb, 49.
Niles, Jonathan, 53.
Niles, Nathan, 25.
niles, Robert, 49.
Nill, Samuel, 47.
Noak, Thomas, 56.
Noble, arthur, 35.
Noble, Benjamin, 37.
Noble, Christopher, 16.
Noble, Christopher, Ju., 16.
Noble, John, 37.
Noble, John, 53.
Noble, John, 68.
Noble, Nathan, 24.
Noble, Reuben, 29.
Noble, Seth, 27.
Noble, Stephen, 69.
Nock, Abigail, 56.
Nock, Benjˢ, 56.
Nock, Daniel, 83.
Nock, Disso, 57.
Nock, Eleazer, 67.
Nock, John, 63.
Nock, Jonˢ, 56.
Nock, Joseph, 56.
Nock, Mary, 56.
Nock, Moses, 56.
Nock, Nicholas, 67.
Nock, Stase D., 63.
Nock, Wᵐ, 56.
Nock, Zachariah, 56.
Nock, Zackʰ, 63.
Nock, Zackʰ, 67.
Nocks, Reuben, 59.
Nocks, Sylvanus, 59.
nolton, Joseph, 48.
Noonan, Abigail, 29.
Norcross, Nathaniel, 40.
Norcross, Philip, 39.
Norcross, Samˡ, 39.
Norcross, Samˡ, Jur, 39.
Noris, Benjamen, 33.
Norman, John, 71.
Norman, Thoˢ, 72.
Norris, Ephrim, 41.
Norris, James, 49.
Norris, James, ju., 49.
Norris, Jeremiah, 65.
Norris, Jonˢ, 63.
Norris, Joseph, 65.
Norris, Josiah, 41.
Norris, Josiah, 51.
Norris, Nathan, 41.
Norris, Nathˡ, 49.
Norris, Samˡ, 41.
Norris, William, 31.
Norris, Woodin, 41.
North, Joseph, 39.
Norton, Abraham, 54.
Norton, Benjˢ, 60.
Norton, Constant, 51.
Norton, Daniel, 51.
Norton, Elias, 54.
Norton, Elijah, 44.
Norton, James, 59.
Norton, John, 27.
Norton, John, 71.
Norton, Joseph, 71.
Norton, Josiah, 66.
Norton, Lemuel, 37.
Norton, Nathˡ, 56.
Norton, Nathaniel, 67.
Norton, Noah, 30.
Norton, Peter, 51.
Norton, Pheobe, 32.
Norton, Samuel, 32.
Norton, Samˡ, 61.
Norton, Samˡ, 61.
Norton, Sarah, 32.
Norton, Seth, 54.
Norton, Stephen, 51.
Norton, Temperence, 61.
Norton, Uriah, 32.
Norton, Wintworth, 56.
Norward (Widow), 71.
Norwood, Isaac, 36.
Norwood, Joshua, 29.
Norwood, Solomon, 36.
Norwood, Stephen, 29.
noton, Jacob, 45.
noton, Joab, 45.
Noulton, John, 61.
Nowel, Danˡ, 72.
Nowel, John, 72.
Nowel, John, 72.
Nowel, Jonˢ, 72.
Nowel, Joseph, 72.
Nowel, Mark, 57.
Nowel, Paul, 71.
Nowel, Paul, 72.
Nowel, Sarah, 72.
Nowel, Shadrach, 72.

Nowel, Thoˢ, 72.
Nowland, John, 39.
Noyce, Josiah, 54.
Noyes, Amos, 14.
Noyes, Bella, 11.
Noyes, David, 23.
Noyes, James, 15.
Noyes, Joseph, 15.
Noyes, Moses, 21.
Noyes, Moses, 23.
Noyes, Nathan, 15.
Noyes, Nathˡ, 21.
Noyes, Nicholas, 11.
Noyes, Noah, 14.
Noyes, Peeter, 14.
Noyes, Samuel, 15.
Noyes, Samuel, 15.
Noyes, Simeon, 21.
Noyes, Thomas, 43.
Noyes, Willᵐ, 21.
Noyes, Zebulon, 21.
Noys, Jonathan, 33.
Nunan, John, 12.
Nurse, John, 69.
Nute, Daniel, 56.
Nute, Paul, 43.
Nutt, David, 26.
Nutt, John, 26.
Nutter, Anthony, 43.
Nutter, Jacob, 61.
Nutter, Thomas, 30.
Nutter, Volentine, 37.
Nutter (Widow), 66.
Nutter, William, 30.
Nutting, Abel, 35.
Nutting, Jonathan, 36.
Nutting, Josiah, 42.
Nutting, Samuel, 42.
Nutting, Thomas, 44.
Nye, Elisha, 39.
Nye, Elvel, 39.

Oakes, Atherton, 53.
Oakman, Samˡ, 43.
Oaks, Jacob, 70.
Oaks, John, 22.
Oaks, Joshua, 43.
Oaksman, Tobias, 28.
oats, Eben, 48.
oats, Samuel, 48.
Oats, Sarah, 61.
oberlach, charles, 41.
oberlach, frank, 41.
oberlach, John henry, 41.
oberloch, John, 41.
Obins, Philip, 20.
Obrien, Gideon, 52.
Obrien, Jerimiah, 52.
Obrien, Morris, 52.
Obrien, William, 43.
O'Bryan, John, 49.
Odehorn, Danˡ, 61.
Odehorn, Samˡ, 61.
Ogier, Abraham, 26.
Ogier, Lewis, 27.
Okes, John, 35.
Okes, Levi, 35.
Okes, Solomon, 35.
Oldham, Danˡ, 13.
Oldham, Jonˢ, 43.
oldham, peleg, 42.
Oldon, Benjˢ, 38.
Oliver, Benjˢ, 37.
Oliver, David, 38.
Oliver, David, Junʳ, 38.
Oliver, David, 3ʳᵈ, 38.
Oliver, David, 4ᵗʰ, 38.
Oliver, Ebenˢ, 37.
Oliver, Ephraim, 38.
Oliver, Ephraim, Jnʳ, 38.
Oliver, Henry, 38.
Oliver, Jacob, 37.
Oliver, Jacob, 37.
Oliver, James, 38.
Oliver, James, 73.
Oliver, John, 37.
Oliver, John, 38.
Oliver, John, Jnʳ, 37.
oliver, Jonathan, 35.
Oliver, Jotham, 73.
Oliver, Nicholas, 38.
Oliver, Parker, 37.
Oliver, Thomas, 37.
Oliver (Widow), 53.
Oliver (Widow), 73.
Oliver, Wᵐ, 11.
Oliver, Willᵐ, 37.
omfry, Eben, 48.
Oneal, John, 24.
Orbeton, James, 46.
Orbeton, Jonathan, 46.
Orcutt, Emerson, 30.
Orcutt, Jacob, 30.
Orcutt, John, 32.
Orcutt, Malachi, 30.
Ore, Elle, 62.
Ores, William, 45.
orf, fridrich, 41.
orf, nicolas, 41.
orf, Stophel, 41.
Orr, Clement, 20.
Orr, Debby, 30.
Orr, John, 20.

INDEX.

Orr, John, 46.
Orr, Phillip, 25.
Orr, Richard, 12.
Orr, Robert, 46.
Orr, William, 31.
Osborn, James, 70.
Osgood, Aaron, 14.
Osgood, Abraham, 25.
Osgood, Asa, 58.
Osgood, Christopher, 26.
Osgood, Daniel, 26.
Osgood, Ezekiel, 26.
Osgood, James, 60.
Osgood, John, 26.
Osgood, Jon^a, 33.
Osgood, Joshua Bailey, 58.
Osgood, Nathan, 26.
Osgood, Nathl, 14.
Osgood, Phineas, 26.
Osgood, William, 58.
osyer, Joseph, 48.
Oties, Oliver, 40.
Otis, Galen, 52.
Otis, Saml, 20.
otis, thomas, 40.
Otis, William, 49.
Ott, Peter, 26.
Ott, Peter, jun^r, 26.
Over, William, 31.
Over, William, jun^r, 31.
Owen, Jno, 59.
Owen, Morgan, 52.
Owens, Ebenezer, 23.
Owens, Gideon, 46.
Owens, James, 23.
Owens, Moses, 46.
Owens, Philip, 12.
Owens, Thomas, 42.
Owens, Willm, 12.
Oxnerd, Edward, 24.
Oxnord, Thomas, 23.

Packad, Caleb, 51.
Packad, Joshua, 51.
Packad, Joshua, Jr., 51.
Packad, libary, 51.
Packad, Ralf, 51.
Packard, Benjamin, 46.
Packard, Cyrus, 53.
Packard, Marlborough, 36.
Packard, Micah, 36.
Packer, Danl, 12.
Packer, Edward, 46.
Packer, Ichabod, 24.
Packer, Job, 12.
Packer, Reuben, 24.
Page, Abraham, 39.
Page, abraham, 50.
Page, Amos, 44.
Page, Benj^a, 32.
Page, Benjamin, 69.
Page, Caleb, 50.
Page, Caleb, 47.
Page, Chase, 50.
Page, Dan^s, 66.
Page, Edwd, 61.
Page, Edward H., 33.
Page, Enoch, 39.
Page, Enoch, 56.
Page, Ezekiel, 39.
Page, Ezekiel, 44.
page, george, 48.
Page, Isaac, 27.
Page, Isaac, 44.
Page, James, 27.
Page, James, 39.
Page, James, jur., 50.
Page, Jesse, 50.
Page, John, 43.
Page, John, 45.
Page, John, 50.
Page, Joseph, 27.
Page, Joseph, jun^r, 27.
Page, Moses, 32.
Page, Peter, 66.
Page, Phillip, 60.
Page, Robert, 51.
Page, Saml, 65.
Page, Simon, 29.
Page, Simon, 51.
Page, Taylor, 65.
Page, Timothy, 44.
Page, William, 28.
page, William, 36.
page, william, 48.
Pain, David, 45.
Pain, Isabllilah, 45.
Pain, Jno, 18.
Pain, Joseph, 45.
Pain, Joshua, 33.
Pain, Phillip, 65.
Pain, Rachal, 46.
Pain, Rich^d, 18.
Pain, Thos, 18.
Pain, Thomas, 45.
Pain, Timothy, 34.
Pain, W^m, 18.
Pain, William, 45.
Pain, W^m, 65.
paine, John, 48.
Paine, Jonathan, 23.
Paine, Joseph, 25.

Paine, Joseph, 32.
Paine, Thos, 25.
Paine, Thomas, 29.
Paine, Moses, 52.
Paine (Widow), 72.
Pall, Joseph, 14.
Palmer, Anna, 42.
palmer, bazl., 48.
Palmer, Benj^a, 27.
Palmer, Benj^a, 45.
palmer, benjm. 48.
Palmer, Daniel, 46.
Palmer, Elnathan, 35.
Palmer, Jacob, 52.
Palmer, John, 53.
Palmer, Joshua, 27.
Palmer, Mulbry, 45.
Palmer, Nathaniel, 27.
palmer, nat., 48.
Palmer, Rich^d, 59.
Palmer, Simon, 33.
Palmer, Steph^a, 59.
Palmer, Willm, 39.
Palmer, W^m, 65.
Pane, Edward, 38.
Pane, James, 64.
Parcher, Elias, 66.
Parcher, George, 66.
Parcher, timothy, 69.
pardridge, John, 48.
parham, William, 38.
Parhook, Ebza^b, 61.
Parington, Benajah, 57.
Parington, Moses, 57.
Parish, George, 43.
Parish. John, 43.
Parish, Samuel, 24.
Park, John, 28.
Parker, Aaron, 25.
Parker, Benj^a, 16.
Parker, Benj^a, 22.
Parker, Cap^n Benj^a, 61.
Parker, Chase, 59.
Parker, Danl, 61.
Parker, Ebenezer, 13.
Parker, Edmond, 42.
Parker, Eliphalet, 25.
Parker, Elisha, 45.
Parker, Enoch, 64.
Parker, Ezra, 26.
Parker, Hannah (Wid^w), 18.
Parker, James, 11.
Parker, James, 14.
Parker, James, 22.
Parker, James, 45.
Parker, James, 60.
Parker, John, 14.
Parker, John, 37.
Parker, Johns (Widow), 18.
Parker, Jordan, 37.
Parker, Joseph, 21.
Parker, Joseph, 26.
Parker, Joseph, 33.
Parker, Joseph, 49.
Parker, Josiah, 44.
Parker, Josiah, 45.
Parker, Mighill, 30.
Parker, Molly, 61.
Parker, Moses, 25.
Parker, Nathan, 26.
Parker, Oliver, 28.
Parker, Oliver, 30.
Parker, Oliver, jun^r, 31.
Parker, Peter, 26.
Parker, Peter, 39.
Parker, Phinihas, 50.
Parker, Robert, 26.
Parker, Saml, 21.
Parker, Saml, 57.
Parker, Sarah, 62.
Parker, Simeon, 31.
Parker, Simon, 40.
Parker, Solomon, 50.
Parker, Stephen, 52.
Parker, William, 53.
Parkers, Nathan, 38.
Parkes, Anna, 15.
Parkins, Daniel, 60.
parkins, David, 66.
Parks, John, 35.
Parks, Joseph, 63.
Parlin, Alford, 42.
Parlin, John, 42.
Parlin, Jonathan, 42.
Parlin, Joseph, 42.
Parlin, Nathan, 42.
Parlin, Saml, 13.
Parlin, Silas, 36.
Parram, Samuel, 51.
Parrey, David, 41.
Parrott, Thomas, 54.
Parry, Judah, 41.
Parry, William, 32.
parsins, William, 67.
Parsons, Abigail, 65.
Parsons, Alice, 9.
Parsons, Edward, 11.
Parsons, Edward, 21.
Parsons, Eleazer, 11.
Parsons, Elihu, 71.
Parsons, Isaac, 21.
Parsons, Isaac, 72.

Parsons, John, 24.
Parsons, John, 60.
Parsons, Jon^a, 18.
Parsons, Joseph, 37.
Parsons, Joseph, 71.
Parsons, Lawrence, 36.
Parsons, Moses, 21.
parsons, Olive (Wid.), 66.
Parsons, Phillemon, 12.
Parsons, Rich^d, 61.
Parsons, Saml, 72.
Parsons, Stephen, 65.
Parsons, Thomas, Esqr, 64.
Parsons, Timothy, 43.
Parsons, W^m, 24.
Parsons, William, 20.
Parsons, William, 21.
Parsons, William, 36.
Partrick, William, 14.
Partridge, Anna, 15.
Partridge, David, 14.
Partridge, Jesse, 14.
Partridge, Jotham, 15.
Partrige, Clark, 28.
Partrige, Daniel, 28.
Partrige, David, 28.
Partrige, John, 28.
Partrige, Samuel, 28.
Partrige, Thomas, 28.
Paseal, John, 49.
Patch, Andrew, 68.
Patch, Benjamin, 22.
Patch, George, 61.
Patch, John, 60.
Patch, Jno, 67.
Patch, Paul, 67.
Patch, Saml, 67.
Patch, Timothy, 68.
Patrick, Benj^a, 18.
Patrick, Charles, 18.
Patrige, Amos, 39.
Pattee, Moses, 60.
Patten, Actor, 46.
Patten, Hance, 70.
Patten, Hannah, 59.
Patten, James, 32.
Patten, James, 55.
Patten, John, 27.
Patten, John, 32.
Patten, John, 46.
Patten, John, 54.
Patten, Joseph, 46.
Patten, Lydia, 58.
Patten, Robert, 46.
Patten, Robert, 55.
Patten, Robert, 58.
Patten, Susannah, 32.
Patten, Thos, 46.
Patten (Widow), 53.
Patten (Widow), 71.
Patten, William, 27.
Patten, Willm, 44.
Patterson, Abraham, 66.
Patterson, Adam, 28.
Patterson, Alex^r, 53.
Patterson, Andrew, 27.
Patterson, Andrew, 65.
Patterson, Benj^a, 65.
Patterson, Daniel, 66.
Patterson, David, 65.
Patterson, Elisha, 65.
Patterson, James, 26.
Patterson, James, 36.
Patterson, John, 24.
Patterson, John, 29.
patterson, John, 48.
Patterson, John, 65.
Patterson, Joseph, 64.
Patterson, Loin, 66.
Patterson, Margaret, 44.
Patterson, Nat^l, 26.
Patterson, Peter, 41.
Patterson, Robert, 26.
Patterson, Robert, 65.
Patterson, Robert, Jur, 65.
Patterson, Samuel, 65.
Patterson, W^m, 26.
Patterson, Matthew, 26.
Patterson, William, 26.
Patterson, Willm, 36.
Patterson, William, 43.
Pattin, Benjamin, 45.
Pattin, Nathaniel, 45.
Pattin, Thomas, 36.
Pattinger, Arthur, 22.
Paul, Amos, 62.
Paul, David, 20.
Paul, Benj^a, 69.
Paul, Ebenez^r, 62.
Paul, James, 62.
paul, John, 48.
Paul, Joseph, 62.
Paul, Joseph, Junr, 62.
paul, Josiah, 66.
paul, Josieah, 66.
Paul, Mary, 62.
paul, mathew, 48.
Paul, Moses, 62.
Paul, Narshfield, 40.
paul, Robert, 48.
Paul, Saml, 62.

Paul, Saml, 72.
Paul, Cap^n Saml, 60.
Paul, Silas, 49.
Paul, Simeon, 49.
Paul, Stephen, 62.
Paul, Tim^y, 62.
Paul, Willm, 66.
Payson, David, 43.
Payson, David, Jn^r, 43.
Payson, Ephraim, 26.
Payson, John, 42.
payson, Samuel, 42.
Payson, Samuel, 49.
Peabody, Andrew, 49.
Peabody, Daniel, 49.
Peabody, John, 11.
Peabody, Josiah & Saml Peabody, 49.
Peabody, Saml, 18.
Peabody, Saml. See Peabody, Josiah, & Saml Peabody, 49.
Peabody, Stephen, 49.
Peace, James, 45.
Peache, John, 29.
pcare, James, 66.
Pearey, Joseph, 69.
Pearl, Joseph, 65.
Pearly, Samuel, 19.
Pearson, Mark, 39.
Pearson, Thomas, 14.
Pearson, William, 36.
Pearsons, Nathl, 71.
peary, Stephen, 66.
Peas, Josiah, 65.
Peas, Zebulon, 65.
Pease, Aaron, 26.
Pease, James, 26.
Pease, Prince, 26.
Pease, Prince, jun^r, 26.
Pease, Rich^d, 69.
Pease, Shubael, 26.
Peasley, Daniel, 33.
Peasley, Enoch, 70.
Peasley, Jonathan, 33.
Peasley, Nathan, 33.
Pebples, Patrick, 49.
Peck, George, 53.
Peck, W^m, 62.
Peckard, Samuel, 40.
Pecker, Nehemiah, 11.
Peckman, Bettey, 16.
Pees, Asa, 65.
Pees, Joseph, 65.
Pees, Samuel, 65.
Pees, Samuel, 65.
Peirce, Benj^a, 63.
Peirce, Doct Danl, 61.
Peirce, Eben^r, 63.
Peirce, Eben^r, Jr, 63.
Peirce, Frances, 65.
Peirce, John, 64.
Peirce, Moses, 63.
Peirce, Simon, 42.
Peirce, Stephen, 27.
Peirpoint, Joseph, 54.
Pell, John, 72.
Pelson, Joel, 51.
Pelton, Joel, 46.
Pendelton, Gideon, 29.
Pendelton, Henry, 29.
Pendelton, Job, 29.
Pendelton, John, 29.
Pendelton, Joshua, 29.
Pendelton, Nat^l, 29.
Pendelton, Oliver, 29.
Pendelton, Thomas, 29.
Pendciton, Thomas, jun^r, 29.
Pendelton, W^m, 29.
Pendoxter, Paul, 60.
Pendextor, Eliab, 60.
Pendextor, Henery, 60.
Pendleton, Jonathan, 29.
Pendleton, Peleg, 29.
Pendleton, Samuel, 29.
Pendleton, William, 28.
Penley, Joseph, 16.
Pennel, Clemuel, 19.
Pennel, John, 12.
Pennel, Joseph, 20.
Pennel, Matthew, 23.
Pennel, Stephen, 46.
Pennel, Thos, 12.
Pennel, Thomas, 15.
Ponnell, Thos, 58.
penney, Setthathol, 66.
penney, Stephen, 66.
penney, Thomas, 66.
Penniman, Jacob, 52.
Penny, Benj^a, 69.
Penny, Danl, 69.
Penny, Frances, 69.
Penny, George, 69.
Penny, John, 69.
Penny, Joseph, 70.
Penny, Thomas, 20.
Penny, Thomas, 21.
Pepper, Anthony, 52.
Pepper, Mercy, 30.
Perham, Lemuel, 44.
Perham, Rias, 33.
Perkins, Abizah, 41.
Perkins, Abner, 55.

Perkins, Abner, 55.
Perkins, Abraham, 30.
Perkins, Benj^a, 30.
Perkins, Daniel, 30.
Perkins, Danl, 55.
Perkins, Ebenezer, 24.
Perkins, Ebenezer, 39.
Perkins, Ebenezer, 41.
Perkins, Edward, 72.
Perkins, Eliab, 38.
Perkins, Elias, 41.
Perkins, Eliphalet, 30.
Perkins, Elisha, 70.
Perkins, Ephraim, 55.
Perkins, George, 54.
Perkins, George, 55.
Perkins, Isaac, 30.
Perkins, Isaac, 72.
perkins, Jabes, 66.
Perkins, Jacob, 70.
Perkins, Jacob, 70.
Perkins, James, 35.
Perkins, James, 55.
Perkins, Jere, 71.
Perkins, John, 18.
Perkins, John, 18.
Perkins, John, 30.
Perkins, John, 44.
Perkins, John, 46.
Perkins, John, 55.
Perkins, John, 71.
Perkins, Jon^a, 70.
Perkins, Jon^a, 72.
Perkins, Joseph, 24.
Perkins, Joseph, 30.
Perkins, Joseph, 34.
Perkins, Joseph, 55.
Perkins, Joseph, 55.
Perkins, Joseph, 58.
Perkins, Joseph, 63.
Perkins, Joseph, 71.
Perkins, Josiah, 70.
Perkins, Jotham, 55.
Perkins, Lemuel, 41.
Perkins, Magory, 61.
Perkins, Mark, 63.
Perkins, Mary, 30.
Perkins, Nathaniel, 30.
Perkins, Nathl, 38.
Perkins, Nathl, 58.
Perkins, Nathl, 58.
Perkins, Nat, 68.
Perkins, Nusman, 70.
Perkins, Pelatiah, 71.
Perkins, Robert, 52.
Perkins, Saml, 24.
Perkins, Saml, 34.
Perkins, Sarah, 61.
Perkins, Sparks, 30.
Perkins, Stephen, 58.
Perkins, Stover, 30.
Perkins, Thos, 55.
Perkins, Thos, 55.
Perkins, Thos, 55.
Perkins, Thos, 55.
Perkins, Thos, 55.
Perkins, Thos, 34, 55.
Perkins (Widow), 72.
Perkins, Willm, 70.
Perley, Amos, 51.
Perley, Danl, 11.
Perley, Enoch, 11.
Perrey, Eunice, 61.
Perroy, Willm, 61.
Perry, Benjamin, 69.
Perry, Corn^s, 19.
Perry, David, 34.
Perry, Dimon, 11.
Perry, Ely, 38.
Perry, Ezra, 21.
Perry, George, 63.
Perry, James, 35.
Perry, James, 60.
Perry, James, 63.
Perry, Jesse, 29.
Perry, Jesse, 63.
Perry, John, 32.
Perry, John, 63.
Perry, Jon^a, 46.
Perry, Joseph, 22.
Perry, Joseph, 46.
Perry, Reuben, 45.
Perry, Samuel, 36.
Perry, Saml, 60.
Perry, William, 46.
Perry, Zechriah, 41.
persons, andrew, 48.
Persons, David, 37.
Persy, Thos, 38.
Pervish, Adam, 23.
Pesley, Ezekiel, 33.
Pesley, Oliver, 33.
Petegrow, Mary, 62.
Petegrow, Saml, 62.
Petegrow, Saml, Jur, 62.
Petegrow, Steven, 62.
Petegrow, William, 60.
Petengall, Mathew, 41.
petergill, Ephram, 38.
peters, Amos, 49.
Peters, Andrew, 56.
Peters, John, 26.

INDEX.

Peters, John, 37.
peterson, abraham, 51.
peterson, abraham, Juⁿ, 51.
peterson, Carnalas, 51.
Peterson, John, 12.
Petigrow, Thomas, 53.
Pettee, Elenʳ, 47.
Pettee, James, 22.
Pettee, John, 47.
Pettegrow, Benjamin, 52.
Pettegrow, Joseph, 62.
Pettengill, Benjamin, 15.
Pettengill, Daniel, 23.
Pettey, Benjᵃ, 38.
Pettey, Benjᵃ, Jnʳ, 38.
Pettey, Jane, 38.
Pettey, Samˡ, 38.
Pettingale, Benjᵃ, 39.
Pettingale, Benjᵃ, Jnʳ, 39.
Pettingale, Edward, 33.
Pettingale, Summon, 33.
Pettingall, Edward, 31.
Pettingall, Eliphalet, 24.
Pettingall, Samˡ, 11.
Pettingil, Abraham, 40.
Pettingill, Daniel, 25.
Pettingill, David, 40.
Pettingill, Ebenezer, 40.
Pettingill, Moses, 25.
Pettingill, Sarah, 40.
Pettis, Daniel, 50.
Pettis, David, 50.
Pettis, Ezekiel, 50.
Petty, Oliver, 19.
Pharis, James, 24.
Philbrick, George, 12.
Philbrick, Gideon, 25.
Philbrick, Jonᵃ, 25.
Philbrick, Joshua, 33.
Philbrick, Michael, 16.
Philbrick, Michael, 25.
Philbrick (Widow), 71.
Philbrick, Wᵐ, 25.
Philbrook, Benjᵃ, 49.
Philbrook, Caleb, 50.
Philbrook, John, 50.
Philbrook, Joseph, 49.
Philbrook, Nathaniel, 50.
Philbrook, Stephen, 49.
Philbrook, Tites, 50.
philbrok, Nathaniel, 50.
Philbrook, David, 42.
Philbrook, John, 50.
Philbrook, Jonathan, 39.
Philbrooks, Ebenezer, 33.
Philbrooks, Ebenezor, 33.
Philbrooks, John, 33.
Philip, Eliphus, 20.
Philip, Ichabod, 38.
Philips, Gray, 38.
Philips, Henry, 71.
Phillips, Norton, 71.
Phllbrook, Jeremiah, 32.
Phillbrook, Job, 32.
Phillbrook, Joel, 32.
Phillbrook, Jonathan, 28.
Phillbrook, Joseph, 29.
Phillbrook, Wᵐ, 29.
Phillbrook, Wᵐ, junʳ, 29.
Phillbrooks, James, 27.
Phillips, Abner, 25.
Phillips, Andʷ, 61.
Phillips, Asa, 50.
Phillips, John, 23.
Phillips, John, 28.
Phillips, John, 66.
Phillips, John, Juʳ, 66.
Phillips, Mary, 25.
Phillips, Richard, 25.
Phillips, Richard, Jr., 25.
Phillips (Widow), 61.
Phillips, Wᵐ, 66.
Philpot, Moses, 68.
Phinney, Jnᵒ, 59.
Phinney, Stephen, 25.
Phinny, Decker, 18.
Phinny, Ebenʳ, 18.
Phinny, Edmᵈ, 18.
Phinny, Edmᵈ, Junʳ, 18.
Phinny, Jaˢ, 18.
Phinny, Jnᵒ, 18.
Phinny, Jnᵒ, Jʳ, 18.
Phinny, Joˢ, 18.
Phinny, Joˢ, Jʳ, 18.
Phinny, Josiah, 52.
Phinny, Nathan, 52.
Phinny, Nathanˡ, junʳ, 52.
Phinny, Stepᵃ, 18.
Phips (Widdow), 61.
Pickard, James, 42.
Pickard, Jonathan, 27.
Pickard, Nathan, 36.
Pickard, Thomas, 42.
Pickenall, Esther, 61.
Pickenall, James, 60.
Pickenall, Nelson, 61.
Pickering, Daniel, 31.
Pickering, Samuel, 31.
Pickernall, Wᵐ, 61.
Pickit, Jonathan, 44.
Pierce, 12.
Pierce, Abigail, 66.
Pierce, Abraham, 21.

Pierce, Calvin, 46.
Pierce, David, 42.
Pierce, David, 46.
Pierce, Eliphalet, 39.
Pierce, Elisabeth, 57.
Pierce, Ezekiel, 34.
Pierce, George, 22.
Pierce, John, 25.
Pierce, John, 28.
Pierce, John, 43.
Pierce, John, 50.
Pierce, Joseph, 20.
Pierce, Joseph, 20.
Pierce, Joseph, 20.
Pierce, Joseph, 34.
Pierce, Josiah, 16.
Pierce, Lettice, 27.
Pierce, Luther, 46.
Pierce, Nathaniel, 30.
Pierce, Richard, 25.
Pierce, Samuel, 20.
Pierce, Samˡ, 34.
Pierce, Samˡ, 39.
Pierce, Silvester, 34.
Pierce, Thomas, 14.
Pierce, Wᵐ, 56.
Piercey, James, 70.
Piercy (Widow), 38.
Pierson, Samuel, 21.
Pierson, Samuel, 23.
Pike, Amos, 57.
Pike, Bonnet, 60.
Pike, Dudley, 24.
Pike, Humphrey, 65.
Pike, Israel, 65.
Pike, Jane, 57.
Pike, John, 24.
Pike, John, 60.
Pike, Joseph, 68.
pike, Joseph, 69.
Pike, Samˡ, 55.
Pike, Timothy, 15.
pitcher, abner, 42.
Pilley, John, 11.
Pilsberry, Hannah, 13.
Pilsberry, Jonᵃ, 19.
Pilsberry, Joˢ, 19.
Pilsbury, Edmond, 36.
Pilsbury, Joseph, 46.
Pilsbury, Nathan, 46.
Pilsbury, Phineas, 26.
Pilsbury, Stephen, 68.
Pilsbury, Thomas, 47.
Pinco, Jonathan, 52.
Pinkham, Andʷ, 14.
Pinkham, Calvin, 34.
Pinkham, Daniel, 23.
Pinkham, Ebenᵃ, 20.
Pinkham, Ebenezer, 40.
Pinkham, Elijah, 16.
Pinkham, Ichabod, 34.
Pinkham, James, 28.
Pinkham, Joseph, 37.
Pinkham, Nathˡ, 20.
Pinkham, Nathˡ, 34.
Pinkham, Reuben, 47.
Pinkham, Solomon, 34.
Pinkham, Stephen, 16.
Pinkham, Tristani, 29.
Pinkum, Elisha, 40.
Pinkim, Richard, 53.
Pinkim, Tristram, 53.
Piper, Edward, 36.
Piper, Elisha, 65.
Piper, John, 36.
Piper, John, 45.
Piper, John, 52.
Piper, Jonᵃ, 43.
Piper, Stephen, 68.
pirkins, Josiah, 66.
Pirkins, Solomon, 47.
Pishen, Charles, 36.
Pishen, Charles, 47.
Pitcher, Lewis, 28.
pitcher, nathˡ, 42.
pitcher (widow), 41.
Pits, John, 68.
Pitts, Abel, 43.
Pitts, Ichabod, 48.
Pitts, Seth, 51.
Pitts, Shubal, 45.
Place, Annas, 43.
Place, Elizᵃ, 62.
Place, John, 61.
Place, Samuel, 43.
Plaisted, Andrew, 19.
Plaisted, James, 55.
Plaisted, John, 25.
Plaisted, John, 55.
Plaisted, John, 72.
plaisted, Roger, 58.
plumar, Moses, 66.
plumer, bedfil, 48.
Plumer, Benjemen, 33.
Plumer, Daniel, 33.
plumer, John, 67.
Plumer, Joseph, 33.
Plumer, Timithy, 33.
Plummer, Aaron, 18.
Plummer, Asa, 52.
Plummer, Benjˡ, 35.
Plummer, Chrisʳ, 18.
Plummer, David, 43.

Plummer, Isaac, 18.
Plummer, Jereᵃ, 19.
Plummer, Jesse, 13.
Plummer, Jesse, 19.
Plummer, John, 44.
Plummer, Moses, 18.
Plummer, Moses, 22.
Plummer, Moses, 54.
Plummer, Moses, junʳ, 54.
Plummer, Patiance, 57.
Plummer, Robert, 13.
Plummer, Robert, 14.
Plummer, Samˡ, 19.
Plummer, Samˡ, Jr., 19.
Plympton, Joseph, 27.
Plympton, William, 27.
Poge, Robert, 23.
Poke, Mary, 64.
Poland, Asa, 58.
Poland, Benjamin, 23.
Poland, Moses, 18.
Poland, Natᵗ, 68.
poland, nohemiak, 48.
poland, Stuawrd (mach Island), 48.
poland, thomas, 48.
Pollard, Amos, 39.
Pollard, Avis, 30.
Pollard, Barton, 39.
Pollard, Elijah, 43.
Pollard, Ezekiah, 43.
Pollard, Hezekiah, 23.
Polley, Samuel, 34.
pollina, Ezra, 48.
Pollock, Deliverance, 13.
Pollock, Thomas, 43.
Pomeroy, Joseph, 15.
Pomroy, John, 28.
Pomroy, Joseph, 27.
Pomroy, William, 30.
Pond, William, 51.
Pong, Harris, 37.
Pool, Abijah, 23.
Pool, James, 23.
Pool, Thomas, 23.
Poole, Joshua, 61.
Poole, Samuel, 11.
Pooling, Moses, 51.
Pooling, William, 51.
Poor, Amos, 58.
poor, james, 49.
Poor, John, 34.
Poor, Richard, 33.
Poor, Robert, 38.
Poor, Samuel, 24.
Poor, Willᵐ, 34.
Poores, Richard, 34.
Pope, David, 60.
Pope, Dorcas, 60.
Pope, Elijah, 15.
Pope, Isaac, 71.
porteñeld, Robert, 48.
Porter, Aaron, 53.
Porter, Benjᵃ, 16.
Porter, Benjᵃ, 51.
Porter, Benjamin J., 14.
Porter, David, 11.
Porter, David, 11.
Porter, David, 58.
Porter, Frederick, 35.
Porter, Gideon, 36.
Porter, Joseph, 53.
Porter, Nehemiah, 22.
Porter, Nehemiah, 22.
porter, Peter, 44.
Porter, Robert, 29.
Porter Seward, 16.
Porterfield, Elisabeth, 15.
Porterfield, Patrick, 46.
Porterfield, William, 15.
Porterfield, Wᵐ, 26.
Port Royal, From, 42.
Post, Stephen, 46.
Pote, Gamaliel, 15.
Pote, Green, 16.
Pote, Greenfield, 15.
Pote, Increase, 15.
Pote, Jeremiah, 15.
Pote, Samˡ, 11.
Pote, Samuel, 15.
Pote, Thoˢ, 11.
Pote, William, 15.
Potte, John, 33.
Potter, Alexander, 34.
Potter, Alexander, 34.
Potter, Andrew, 45.
Potter, David, 34.
Potter, Ezekiel, 44.
Potter, hugh, 45.
Potter, James, 34.
Potter, James, 34.
Potter, John, 38.
Potter, John, 45.
Potter, Joseph, 45.
Potter, John, 3ᵈ, 27.
Potter, Samˡ, 45.
Potter, Solomon, 33.
Potter, Willᵐ, 38.
Potter, William, 45.
Pottle, Daniel, 27.
Pottle, David, 35.
Pottle, Hezekiah, 43.
Pounder, William, 23.
Powars, Battry, 30.

Powars, Peter, 27.
Powers, Amos, 68.
Powers, Gideon, 68.
Powers, Isaac, 44.
powers, John, 66.
Powers, Jonᵃ, 37.
powers, Jonathan, 67.
Powers, Levi, 35.
powers, Nathan, 66.
Powers, Silas, 68.
powers, William, 66.
Prat, Asa, 39.
Prat, Ebenezer, 42.
Prat, Elisha, 35.
Prat, James, 39.
Prat, John, 35.
Prat, Noah, 16.
Prat, Seth, 39.
Prat, Sherebiah, 21.
Prat, Thomas, 21.
Pratt, David, 16.
Pratt, Elam, 35.
Pratt John, 61.
Pratt, Jonᵃ, 25.
Pratt, Luther, 22.
Pratt, Micah, 36.
Pratt, Michal, 35.
Pratt, Nathˡ, 22.
Pratt, Seth, 28.
Pratt, Thaddeus, 24.
Pratt, Zenas, 13.
Pray, Abraᵐ, 63.
Pray, David, 22.
Pray, Ebenezer, 63.
Pray, Eliphelet, 57.
Pray, Ephraim, 29.
Pray, Ephraim, junʳ, 29.
Pray, Experince, 63.
Pray, James, 26.
Pray, James, 32.
Pray, John, 63.
Pray, Joseph, 57.
Pray, Joseph, 63.
Pray, Joseph, 63.
Pray, Joseph, 68.
Pray, Joshua, 61.
Pray, Joshua, 63.
Pray, Moses, 63.
Pray, Nat, 63.
Pray, Peter, 56.
Pray, Samˡ, 57.
Pray, Samˡ, 61.
Pray, Samˡ, Junʳ, 57.
Pray, Stephen, 57.
Pray, Thomas, 63.
Pray, Wᵐ, 62.
Prebble, John, 31.
Prebble, Nathaniel, 31.
Prebble, Nathaniel, 31.
Prebble, Samuel, 31.
Preble, Abigail, 71.
Preble, Abraham, 35.
Preble, Abraham, Junʳ, 35.
Preble, Benjᵃ, 72.
Preble, Caleb, 72.
Preble, David, 35.
Preble, David, 72.
Preble, David, 72.
Preble, Ebenezer, 23.
Preble, Ebenezer, 34.
Preble, Edward, 71.
Preble, Esaias, 72.
Preble, James, 39.
Preble, John, 72.
Preble, Jonᵃ, 35.
Preble, Jonᵃ, 38.
Preble, Jonᵃ, 52.
Preble, Joseph, 38.
Preble, Joseph, 71.
Preble, Joseph, 72.
Preble, Martha, 52.
Preble, Mehitable, 23.
Preble, Samˡ, 35.
Preble, Samˡ, 52.
Preble, Samˡ, 71.
Preble, Zebulon, 35.
Preble, Zebulon, 35.
Prentiss, Samˡ, 18.
Prescot, Jonᵃ, 67.
Prescott, Benjᵃ, 39.
Prescott, David, 61.
Prescott, Joseph, 39.
Prescott, Stepᵃ, 59.
Presscott, Samuel, 27.
Pressey, Benjᵃ, 44.
Pressey, Jacob, 44.
Pressey, Jacob, Jnʳ, 44.
Pressey, Sarah, 44.
Pressey, Will, 43.
Pressy, Chace, 27.
Pressy, John, 27.
Pressy, John, junʳ, 27.
Pressy, John, 3ᵈ, 27.
Preston, Nathan, 53.
Prible, Jedediah, 33.
Price, Elisabeth, 23.
Price, Thomas, 43.
Pride, Benjamin, 15.
Pride, Henry, 15.
Pride, Isaac, 14.
Pride, Joseph, 15.
Pride, Joseph, 15.

Pride, William, 15.
Priest, Jonas, 47.
Priest, Jonathan, 50.
Priest, Joseph, 47.
Primo, Lydia, 57.
Prince, Ammi, 22.
Prince, Amos, 15.
Prince, Benjamin, 15.
Prince, Cushing, 22.
Prince, David, 21.
Prince, Elizabeth, 22.
Prince, Isaac, 43.
Prince, James, 21.
Prince, John, 11.
Prince, John, 21.
Prince, John, 22.
Prince, John, 31.
Prince, Joseph, 31.
Prince, Paul, 21.
Prince, Paul, 22.
Prince, Pyan, 22.
Prince, Stephen, 22.
Prince, Sylvester, 49.
Prince, Thomas, 21.
Prince, Thoˢ, 22.
Printice, Voluntine, 50.
Prior, James, 24.
prior, John, 42.
Priscott, Benjᵃ, 51.
Priscott, Elijah, 51.
Priscott, Elisha, 50.
Priscott, James, 45.
Priscott, Jedeah, Jun., 51.
Priscott, Jediah, 51.
Priscott, Jesse, 51.
Priscott, Jonᵃ, 50.
Priscott, Odlin, 51.
Priscott, Samuel, 51.
Priscott, Suwel, 49.
Pritham, John, 66.
Procter, John, 14.
Procter, Nathaniel, 14.
Procter, Samˡ, 14.
Procter, Samuel, 23.
Procter, William, 25.
Proctor, Benjᵃ, 58.
Proctor, Joseph, 40.
Proctor, Joseph, 58.
Proctor, Wᵐ, 11.
Prout, James, 16.
Prout, John, 19.
Prout, Joseph, 19.
Prudent, Willᵐ, 41.
pugeley, Franes, 66.
pugsely, Benjamin, 67.
Pugsley, Abram, 68.
Pugsley, Abram, 68.
Pugsley, Andrew, 68.
pugsley, John, 67.
Pulcifer, Joseph, 42.
Puling, John, 51.
Pullin, Oliver, 47.
Pumroy, John, 45.
Punington, Sarah, 25.
Purington, Abraham, 15.
Purington, David, 25.
Purington, Elisha, 15.
Purington, James, 46.
Purington, Joshua, 33.
Purington, William, 23.
Purnton, Allihue, 40.
Purnton, Hezekiah, 35.
Purnton, Humphry, 33.
Purnton, James, 35.
Purnton, Joshua, 20.
Purnton, Joshua, Jurᵃ, 20.
Purnton, Robert, 20.
Purnton, Stephen, 20.
Purrington, James, 46.
Purrinton, Humphry, 34.
Purrinton, Nathˡ, 35.
Purrunton, Ezra, 40.
Pushan, Abraham, 37.
Pushan, Peter, 37.
Pushan, Peter, Juᵃ, 37.
Pushaw, George, 43.
Pushaw, Peter, 44.
Putman, Stephen, 64.
Putnam, Caleb, 46.
Putnam, John, 52.
Putney, Jonathan, 32.

Quembe, Jonᵃ, 67.
Quembey, John, 67.
quimbey, Benjˡ, 38.
Quimby, Benjamin, 15.
Quimby, John, 14.
Quimby, Joseph, 15.
Quimby, Nathan, 15.
Quin, James, 27.
Quin, John, 38.
Quincy, Henry, 43.
Quinham, James, 43.
Quint, Daniel, 66.
Quint, David, 66.
Quint, John, 57.
Quint, John, 65.
Quint, John, 66.
Quint, John, Junʳ, 57.
Quint, Joseph, 65.
Quint, Joseph, 66.
Quint, Joshua, 57.
Quint, Joshua, Junʳ, 57.

INDEX. 97

Quint, Martha, 65.
Quint, Wm, 57.
Quint, William, 59.

Race, George, 34.
Rackleff, William, 36.
Rackley, Benja, 38.
Rackley, Saml, 38.
Rackley, Saml, Jnr, 38.
Rackley (Widow), 64.
Rade, Amos, 50.
Rade, Joshua, 50.
Rade, Joshua, 50.
Radman, Benjn, 30.
Radman, Israel, 30.
Radman, John, 30.
Rafanel, Augustus, 29.
Raglin, ——, 47.
Rains, Joseph, 20.
Ralph, Joseph, 44.
Ramake, William, 49.
Ramaks, Joseph, 49.
Raman, Elaphan, 35.
Rament, William, 41.
Ramsdale, Danl, 71.
Ramsdale, Danl, Jr, 71.
Ramsdale, George, 44.
Ramsdale, Nathl, 71.
Ramsdale, Timo, 71.
Ramsdel, Gideon, 19.
Ramsdel, Kimball, 21.
Ramsdell, Ebenezer, 53.
Ramsdell, Isaac, 53.
Ramsdell, James, 53.
Ramsdell, Nathl, 54.
Ramsdell, William, 53.
Ramsy, John, 22.
Ran, Thomas, 40.
Ranckens, James, 65.
Rand, Benjamin, 14.
Rand, Christopher, 19.
Rand, James, 15.
Rand, Jereh, 19.
Rand, John, 25.
Rand, John, 34.
Rand, Lazarus, 14.
Rand, Michl, 59.
Rand, Philemon, 19.
Randal, Daniel, 20.
Randal, Ezra, 46.
Randal, Isreal, 40.
Randal, John, 14.
Randal, Joseph, 35.
Randal, Paul, 20.
randal, Robert, 48.
Randal, Stephen, 13.
Randal, Willm, 46.
Randall, Charles, 54.
Randall, Isaac, 23.
Randall, Rebecca, 16.
Randall, Seth, 24.
Rands, Daniel, 49.
Ranos, Joshua, 33.
Rankens, John, 50.
Rankin, Joseph, 59.
Rankines, Moses, 66.
Rankins, Andrew, 69.
Rankins, John, 50.
Rankins, Jona, 63.
Rankins, Moses, junr, 66.
Rankins, Robert, 28.
Ranlet, Charles, 43.
Ranlet, Henry, 43.
Ranlet, Nathl, 44.
Raredan, David, 27.
Ratclif, Benja, 37.
Ratclif, John, 34.
Rate, Miriam, 61.
Rate, Cap. Wm, 61.
Rawley, Edward, 36.
Rawley, Michael, 36.
Rawlins, Benja, 30.
Rawson, Ebenezer, 22.
Ray, Benjamin, 40.
Ray, Hannah, 40.
Ray, Mathew, 32.
Ray, William, 13.
Rayment, James, 59.
Rayment, Samuel, 59.
Raymon, Samuel, 35.
Raymond, Lemuel, 21.
Raymond, Samuel, 35.
Raynes, Anna, 27.
Raynes, John, 27.
Raynes, Martha, 27.
Raynes, William, 27.
Razor, charles, 42.
Rea, Benja, 30.
Rea, Caleb, 26.
Rea, William, 54.
Read, Dan., 40.
Read, John, 16.
Read, Josiah, 16.
Read, Samuel, 39.
Read, Samuel, Jur, 39.
Read, William, 45.
Readhead, William, 30.
Reardon, John, 38.
Reardon, Timothy, 38.
Rearson, Luke, 21.
Reaves, James, 33.
Records, David, 12.
Records, Dominicus, 12.
Records, Jona, 12.
Records, Simon, 12.
Redington, Asa, 47.
Redock, John, 20.
Reed, Abraham, 31.
Reed, amesiah, 38.
Reed, Benjn, 51.
Reed, Frederick, 26.
Reed, Ichabod, 15.
Reed, Jacob, 29.
Reed, Jacob, 42.
Reed, John, 48.
Reed, Jonathan, 14.
Reed, Josiah, 47.
Reed, Lydia, 57.
Reed, Mary, 22.
Reed, michel, 41.
Reed, Samuel, 29.
Reed, William, 31.
Reed, Zebulon, 21.
Reid, Abram, 16.
Reid, Amos, 44.
Reid, Andw, 34.
Reid, Andw, Junr, 34.
Reid, Andw, 3rd, 34.
Reid, Bartholomew, 16.
Reid, David, 34.
Reid, David, 46.
Reid, David, Junr, 34.
Reid, David, 3rd, 34.
Reid, George, 39.
Reid, James, 34.
Reid, Joel, 51.
Reid, John, 20.
Reid, John, 34.
Reid, John, 46.
Reid, John, Junr, 46.
Reid, Jonathan, 44.
Reid, Jons, 51.
Reid, Joseph, 34.
Reid, Mary, 34.
Reid, Paul, 34.
Reid, Robert, 34.
Reid, Robert, 51.
Reid, Saml, 51.
Reid, Stephen, 16.
Reid, Willm, 21.
Reid, Willm, 34.
Reid, Willm, 46.
Reins, Danl, 72.
Reins, Francis, 72.
Reins, Nathl, 72.
Reins, Nathl, Jr, 72.
Reins, Robert, 73.
Reins, Robert, Jr, 72.
Reins (Widow), 73.
Remick, Benjn, 62.
Remick, Dorcas, 62.
Remick, Elemuel, 62.
Remick, Isaac, 62.
Remick, Isaac, Jur, 62.
Remick, Jacob, 62.
Remick, John, 62.
Remick, Joseph, 61.
Remick, Josiah, 62.
Remick, Mark, 62.
Remick, Mary, 62.
Remick, Nathan, 62.
Remick, Samuel, 62.
Remick, Sarah, 62.
Remick, Steven, 62.
Remick, Wm, 62.
Remly, mathias, 41.
Remmick, Jacob, 57.
Remmick, James, 65.
Remmick, Joseph, 67.
Remmick, Timothy, 67.
Rendal, Danl, 56.
Rendal, Eliphelet, 57.
Rendal, James, 64.
Rendal, Jeremiah, 57.
Rendal, Joanna, 57.
Rendal, Stephen, 57.
Rendal (Widow), 72.
Rendal, Willm, 62.
Rendell, James, 46.
Rendell, Thomas, 46.
Reneff, Charly, 41.
Renkins, Constant, 46.
Rerce, Nathan, 22.
Reynolds, Benja, 53.
Reynolds, David, 54.
Reynolds, Eliphalet, 54.
Reynolds, Samuel, 53.
Rhodes, Esther, 30.
Rhodes, Jacob, 55.
Rhodes, Miles, 55.
Riant, John, 37.
Rice, Alixr, 62.
Rice, Gideon, 19.
Rice, James, 19.
Rice, John, 32.
Rice, John, 41.
Rice, John, Junier, 32.
Rice, Joseph, 51.
Rice, Leml, 19.
Rice, Lettice, 22.
Rice, Matthias, 19.
Rice, Mehitable, 19.
Rice, Nathl, 59.
Rice, Richd, 19.
Rice, Saml, 19.
Rice, Saml, 62.
Rice, Unice, 62.
Rich, Amos, 19.
Rich, Barnbus, 67.
Rich, Ezekiel, 24.
Rich, James, 25.
Rich, Joel, 12.
Rich, John, 29.
Rich, Jonathan, 29.
Rich, Lemuel, 25.
Rich, Samuel, 53.
Rich, Zephaniah, 23.
Richard, Benjamin, 42.
Richard, benjamin, 48.
Richard, Jeremiah, 45.
Richard, Robert, 42.
Richard, Samuel, 42.
Richard, william, 48.
Richard, William, 51.
Richard, william, jun., 48.
Richard, william, 3rd, 48.
Richardison, Brady, 63.
Richards, Bezilla, 13.
Richards, Dodefer, 26.
Richards, Erastus, 48.
Richards, Humphrey, 13.
Richards, James, 26.
Richards, Jesse, 37.
Richards, John, 13.
Richards, Jonathan, 26.
Richards, Joseph, 19.
Richards, Joseph, 26.
Richards, Joseph, 28.
Richards, Joseph, 50.
Richards, Jos., Jr., 19.
Richards, Jos. (Dumb), 19.
Richards, Nathl, 66.
Richards, Saml, 19.
Richards, Samuel, 30.
Richards, William, 27.
Richardson, Abather, 33.
Richardson, abijah, 45.
Richardson, Andrew, 39.
Richardson, Benjn, 11.
Richardson, Benja, 16.
Richardson, Daniel, 29.
Richardson, David, 25.
Richardson, David, 64.
Richardson, David, 64.
Richardson, Ebenezer, 45.
Richardson, Edward, 23.
Richardson, Elijah, 11.
Richardson, Elisha, 64.
Richardson, George, 29.
Richardson, George, 58.
Richardson, James, 29.
Richardson, James, junr, 29.
Richardson, Joel, 50.
Richardson, John, 34.
Richardson, John, 34.
Richardson, John G., 29.
Richardson, Jona, 25.
Richardson, Joseph, 16.
Richardson, Joseph, 34.
Richardson, Joseph, 50.
Richardson, Moses, 25.
Richardson, Peter, 53.
Richardson, Resolved, 68.
Richardson, Stephen, 29.
Richardson, Thaddeus, 64.
Richardson, Thimoy, Jur, 62.
Richardson, Thomas, 29.
Richardson, Thomas, junr, 29.
Richardson, Timothy, 62.
Richardson, William, 15.
Richardson, William, 50.
Richardson, Zebulon, 60.
Richey, Mathew, 30.
Richison, Joshua, 45.
Richiston, Irah, 45.
Richman, Biethur, 38.
Richman, Nathan, 51.
Richmond, Eliab, 24.
Ricker, Aaron, 63.
Ricker, Abias, 12.
Ricker, Abigal, 56.
Ricker, Dolley, 56.
Ricker, Ebenezer, 63.
Ricker, Ebenezer, 63.
Ricker, Eliphelet, 57.
Ricker, Enoch, 63.
Ricker, Ephrim, 56.
Ricker, Ephrim, 63.
Ricker, Ezekil, 63.
Ricker, George, 59.
Ricker, Gersham, 67.
Ricker, Henery, 63.
Ricker, Joseph, 63.
Ricker, Levy, 69.
Ricker, Mark, 59.
Ricker, Mary, 57.
Ricker, Meturen, 63.
Ricker, Moses, 56.
Ricker, Moses, 63.
Ricker, Moses, 64.
Ricker, Noah, 57.
Ricker, Noah, 69.
Ricker, Phinehas, 59.
Ricker, Reuben, 57.
Ricker, Richard, 57.
Ricker, Rufus, 63.
Ricker, Simeon, 63.
Ricker, Simon, 68.
Ricker, Stephen, 71.
Ricker, timothy, 69.
Ricker, Tristam, 57.
Ricker, William, 53.
Ricker, Wintworth, 22.
Ricket, Isaac, 22.
Ricket, John, 22.
Rident, Mark, 46.
Rideout, Benjamin, 34.
Rideout, John, 35.
Rideout, Stephen, 34.
Rider, James, 21.
Ridlen, Daniel, 66.
Ridlen, Ephraim, 66.
Ridlen, Jeremiah, 66.
Ridlen, Lewis, 66.
Ridley, Abram, 64.
Ridley, Daniel, 64.
Ridley, David, 59.
Ridley, Ebenr, 59.
Ridley, James, 20.
Ridley, James, 64.
Ridley, John, 64.
Ridley, Mark, 20.
Ridley, Mark, 20.
Ridley, Matthias, 64.
Ridley, Sarah, 59.
Ridley, Thos, 64.
Ridlin, Mathias, 66.
Ridlon, Robert, 41.
Ridly, Daniel, 35.
Ridly, George, 35.
Ridly, James, 35.
Ridout, Abraham, 55.
Ridout, Nicholas, 21.
Ridout, Willm, 21.
Riggs, Daniel, 24.
Riggs, Enoch, 14.
Riggs, James, 15.
Riggs, Jeremiah, 14.
Riggs, Joseph, 14.
Riggs, Joseph, 23.
Riggs, Rebecca, 23.
Riggs, Stephen, 15.
Riggs, Stephen, 15.
Right, Asa, 50.
Right, Jesse, 40.
Right, Joel, 40.
Right, Ozias, 40.
Right, Timothy, 40.
Rigs, Benja, 38.
Rigs, Goen, 37.
Rindse, Jotham, 19.
Rines, Ambrose, 11.
Rines, Henery, 63.
Rines, John, 70.
Ring, Andw, 22.
Ring, Batcheldor, 14.
Ring, Daniel, 45.
Ring, David, 33.
Ring, Eleazer, 22.
Ring, Eliphus, 11.
Ring, Jacob, 28.
Ring, Josiah, 24.
Riols, Adam, 40.
Rions, Joseph, 44.
Ripley, Abraham, 26.
Ripley, Enoch, 36.
Ripley, Josiah, 33.
Rise, John, 44.
Rittie, Francis, 43.
Rittle, Francis, 44.
Rittle, John, 44.
Rivers, Archibald, 36.
Rivers, Moses, 36.
Rivers, Thomas, 36.
Roak, Martin, 14.
Robarts, James, 16.
Robberts, John, 57.
Robberts, Joseph, 59.
Robbins, Bela, 47.
Robbins, Benjamin, 32.
Robbins, David, 47.
Robbins, Ebenezer, 47.
Robbins, Isaac, 30.
Robbins, Jacob, 26.
Robbins, Jesse, 47.
Robbins, Jona, 25.
Robbins, Jonathan, 69.
Robbins, Josiah, 47.
Robbins, Nathaniel, 27.
Robbins, Oliver, 46.
Robbins, Oliver, Junr, 46.
Robbins, Otis, 46.
Robbins, Philip, 47.
Robbins, Philip, Junr, 47.
Robbins, Thomas, 27.
Robbins, Thomas, jun., 27.
Robbirson, Daniel, 68.
Robbirson, James, 68.
Roberch, Ichabod, 69.
Roberson, alexdr, 48.
Roberts, ——, 19.
Roberts, Aaron, 57.
Roberts, Benjn, 19.
Roberts, Daniel, 63.
Roberts, Ebenezer, 14.
Roberts, Ephraim, 13.
Roberts, George, 16.
Roberts, Hannah, 13.
Roberts, Jack, 60.
Roberts, James, 61.
Roberts, Jeremiah, 59.
Roberts, Job, 59.
Roberts, Jonathan, 12.
Roberts, Jonathan, 26.
Roberts, Joseph, 12.
Roberts, Joseph, 13.
Roberts, Jos., 19.
Roberts, Joseph, 55.
Roberts, Joseph, 59.
Roberts, Joseph, Jur, 12.
Roberts, Jos., Jr., 19.
Roberts, Joseph, junr, 59.
Roberts, Joshua, 55.
Roberts, Joshua, 56.
Roberts, Joshua, 56.
Roberts, Love, 67.
Roberts, Mary, 13.
Roberts, Peter, 60.
Roberts, Samuel, 59.
Roberts, Samuel, 63.
Roberts, Simon, 56.
Roberts, Thomas, 14.
Roberts, Thomas, 54.
Roberts, Vincent, 14.
Roberts, Willm, 14.
Roberts, Willm, 47.
Robertson, Alexander, 33.
Robertson, alexdr, 48.
Robertson, Archibald, 41.
Robertson, Danl, 70.
Robertson, David, 53.
Robertson, John, 13.
Robertson, John, 33.
Robertson, Joshua, 13.
Robertson, Joshua, 13.
Robertson, Samuel, 13.
Robertson, Samuel, 40.
Robertson, Solomon, 21.
Robertson, William, 34.
Robey, Henry, 43.
Robin, Thaddeus, 22.
Robins, Asa, 51.
Robins, Daniel, 40.
Robins, Daniel, 51.
Robins, Daniel, 51.
Robins, David, 47.
Robins, Herman, 47.
Robins, Jonathan, 36.
Robins, Luther, 38.
Robinson, ——, 43.
Robinson, Andrew, 36.
Robinson, Archibald, 36.
Robinson, Asa, 13.
Robinson, Daniel, 31.
Robinson, David, 45.
Robinson, Elijah, 24.
Robinson, Geo., 39.
Robinson, Goreh, 47.
Robinson, Haunce, 36.
Robinson, Haunce, Junr, 36.
Robinson, Increase, 13.
Robinson, Isaac, 64.
Robinson, Israel, 26.
Robinson, Jabez, 45.
Robinson, John, 25.
Robinson, John, 25.
Robinson, John, 26.
Robinson, John, 29.
Robinson, John, 36.
Robinson, John, 48.
Robinson, John, 49.
Robinson, John, 55.
Robinson, Jno, 59.
Robinson, John, junr, 29.
Robinson, Joseph, 13.
Robinson, Joseph, 36.
Robinson, Joseph, Junr, 36.
Robinson, Joshua, 23.
Robinson, Levi, 47.
Robinson, Moses, 36.
Robinson, Moses, Junr, 36.
Robinson, Robert, 41.
Robinson, Samuel, 13.
Robinson, Saml, 55.
Robinson, Samuel, 63.
Robinson, Sarah, 36.
Robinson, Sarah, 71.
Robinson, Stephen, 22.
Robinson, Stephen, 25.
Robinson, Thomas, 23.
Robinson, Thomas, 49.
Robinson, Timothy, 47.
Robinson, William, 49.
Robinson, Winthropt, 47.
Robison, Jas, 19.
Robison, Jno, 58.
Robshaw, Peter, 30.
Rockley, Chandler, 25.
Rodger, george, 48.
Rodger, patrick, 48.
Rodger, willm, 48.
Rodick, Daniel, 29.
Rods, John, 48.
Roe, Benjn, 11.
Roe, Benjn, 16.
Roe, John, 11.
Roe, Lazarus, 16.
Roe, Noah, 16.
Roe, Webber, 16.
Roff, Benjamin, 23.
Roff, James, 28.
Roff, Moses, 54.
Roff, Saml, 58.
Roff, Saml, 64.
Roff (Widow), 19.

INDEX.

Rogars, John, 44.
Rogers, ——, 62.
Rogers, Alexander, 46.
Rogers, Benj^a, 72.
Rogers, Darly, 36.
Rogers, David, 67.
Rogers, Eliz^h, 61.
Rogers, George, 16.
Rogers, George, 38.
Rogers, George, 57.
Rogers, Gershom, 26.
Rogers, Howland, 36.
Rogers, Hugh, 37.
Rogers, James, 16.
Rogers, James, 35.
Rogers, James, 62.
Rogers, Jesse, 30.
Rogers, Jesse, 49.
Rogers, John, 30.
Rogers, John, 37.
Rogers, John, 46.
Rogers, Jno, 61.
Rogers, John, 62.
Rogers, John, Junr, 61.
Rogers, Joseph, 33.
Rogers, Joseph, 72.
Rogers, Joshua, 23.
Rogers, Josiah, 12.
Rogers, Levi, 57.
Rogers, Mark, 16.
Rogers, Moses, 30.
Rogers, Nathaniel, 25.
Rogers, Nathan^l, 62.
Rogers, Nathan^l, 62.
Rogers, Paul, 57.
Rogers, Prince, 33.
Rogers, Robert, 38.
Rogers, Robert, 52.
Rogers, Samuel, 30.
Rogers, Thos, 38.
Rogers, Thos, 58.
Rogers, Thos, 62.
Rogers, Willm, 16.
Rogers, William, 60.
Rogers, W^m, Esqr, 67.
Roggers, John, 49.
Rohds, cornelus, 48.
Rohds, george, 49.
Rohds, thomas, 49.
Roker, Daniel, 49.
Rolf, Jno, 59.
Rollings, Benjamin, 36.
Rollings, Benjamin, Jr., 36.
Rollings, James, 66.
Rollings, John, 35.
Rollings, John, 35.
Rollings, Joseph, 36.
Rollings, Samuel, 35.
Rollins, Bethoah, 23.
Rollins, Eliphlot, 33.
Rollins, John, 33.
Rollins, Moses, 44.
Rollins, Nathaniel, 33.
Rollins, Nathl, 41.
Rollins, Saml, 47.
Rollins, Stephen, 11.
Rollins, Stephen, 34.
Roo, Zaccheus, 24.
Roods, Jacob, 69.
Rooks, Benj^a, 28.
Rooks, Joseph, 28.
Rose, asha, 38.
Rose, Benjamin, 50.
Rose, George Pottar, 34.
Rose, Jeremiah, 37.
Rose, John, 50.
Rose, Prince, 34.
Rose, Robert, 71.
Rose, Seth, 38.
Rose, Seth, 39.
Rose, Simeon, 38.
Rose, Solomon, 56.
Rose, Solomon, Jur, 56.
Rose, unis, 40.
Rose, Zebulon, 38.
Ross, Adam, 69.
Ross, Alex^r, 19.
Ross, benjamin, 35.
Ross, Daniel, 32.
Ross, Danl., 70.
Ross, David, 23.
Ross, Eliphalet, 12.
Ross, Hugh, 63.
Ross, Isaac, 21.
Ross, James, 19.
Ross, John, 69.
Ross, Jon^a, 68.
Ross, Joseph, 12.
Ross, Joseph, 35.
Ross, Paul, 35.
Ross, Peter, 21.
Ross, Robert, 34.
Ross, Thos, 20.
Ross (Widow), 70.
Ross, Willm, 12.
Ross, Willm, 33.
Rota (widow), 42.
Roughf, Sarah, 15.
Roulstone, Benj^a, 32.
Round, James, 64.
Rounday, John, 26.
Roundly, Ebenezer, 39.
Roundly, Job, 39.

Roundly, Lacet, 39.
Roundly, Micah, 39.
Rounds, Joseph, 59.
Rounds, Lem^l, 59.
Rounds, Mark, 59.
Rounds, Saml, 59.
Roundy, Azor, 36.
Row, Caleb, 25.
Row, Ephraim, 25.
Row, John, 67.
Row, John, 67.
Row, Jonathan, 21.
Row, Robert, 25.
Row, Stephen, 50.
Row, William, 21.
Row, Zebedee, 21.
Rowall, Jacob, 33.
Rowe, Ebenezer, 37.
Rowe, John, 44.
Rowe, Stephen, 50.
Rowe, Zebulon, 30.
Rowell, Daniel, 45.
Rowell, Patience, 28.
Rowell, William, 46.
Roy, Francis, 46.
Royal, Eli, 20.
Rumary, Edward, 66.
Rumery, Edward, Ju^r, 66.
Rumery, John, 66.
Rummery, Jon^a, 58.
Rummery, Jon^a, 64.
Rummery, Moses, 64.
Rummery, Thos, 58.
Rummery, Thos, 64.
Rumney, Dominicus, 53.
Rumney, William, 53.
Runels, David, 47.
Runels, Esqr, 47.
Runels, Jonathan, 47.
Runels, Nathl, 47.
Runnel, Nathl, 33.
Runnels, Ch^s, 19.
Runnels, Ephrom, 47.
Runnels, John, 66.
Runnels, Robert, 47.
Runnels, Saml, 67.
Runnils, Benjamin, 50.
Rusel, Abal, 5.
Russ, John, 25.
Russ, Jonathan, 36.
Russ, Luther, 35.
Russ, Simeon, 44.
Russall, John, 67.
Russel, Abraham, 68.
Russel, Benjamin, 68.
Russel, Benj^a, Junr, 68.
Russel, Hannah, 21.
Russel, Isaac, 35.
Russel, Jacob, 68.
Russel, James, 19.
Russel, Jason, 42.
Russel, Jonathan, 42.
Russel, Joseph, 36.
Russel, Josiah, 42.
Russel, Nathl, 64.
Russel, Solomon, 36.
Russel, Thos Chandler, 22.
Russel, william, 48.
Russell, Lewis, 42.
Russell, Samuel, 31.
Russell, Theodore, 68.
Russey, David, 33.
Russull, Joseph, 68.
Russull, Joseph Junr, 68.
Rust, Joseph, 35.
Rutburgh, John, 23.
Ryal, Winthrop, 21.
Ryall, Eli, 20.
Ryals, Danl, 24.
Ryan, Charles, 12.
Ryan, Curtis, 60.
Ryan, James, 21.
Ryder, Amos, 28.
Ryder, James, 21.
Ryder, John, 30.
Ryen, John, 53.
Ryley, Mary, 61.
Rymes, Joseph, 37.
Ryon, John, 13.

Sabine, Lewis, 16.
Safford, Moses, 11.
Safford, Moses, 71.
Safford, Nathan, 22.
Safford, Stephen, 11.
Saford, andrew, 38.
Saford, hay, 38.
Sage, William, 40.
Sagiley, Daniel, 69.
Salisbury, Ebenezer, 29.
Salisbury, Jabez, 29.
Salisbury, Reuben, 29.
Salley, William, 45.
Saloan, Adam, 15.
Salomon, william (mescongus Island), 48.
Salter, Francis, 31.
Sambo (Black), 61.
Sambourn, Joseph, 69.
Sampson, Caleb, 33.
Sampson, Enoch, 46.
Sampson, James, 46.
Sampson, Jon^a, 41.

Sampson, Joseph, 38.
Sampson, Micael, 15.
Sampson, Noah, 51.
Sampson, Phineas, 25.
Sampson, Phinehas, 69.
Sampson, Seth, 11.
Samson, Bryen, 40.
Samson, charles, 42.
Samson, charles, Jun., 42.
Samson, James, 40.
Samson, John, 42.
Samson, Levi, 42.
Samson, michal, 40.
Sanbon, Joseph, jun^r, 60.
Sanbon, Paul, 69.
Sanborn, Benj^a, 21.
Sanborn, Bradbury, 43.
Sanborn, Ennoch, 53.
Sanborn, Jethrow, 34.
Sanborn, John, 53.
Sanborn, John, 64.
Sanborn, Joseph, 67.
Sanborn, Mrs., 19.
Sanborn, Paul, Junr, 21.
Sanborn, Richard, 53.
Sanborn, Saml, 67.
Sanborn, Simeon, 14.
Sanborn, W^m, 65.
Sanborn, W^m, 65.
Sanbourn, Benj^a, 64.
Sanbourn, Benj^a, 65.
Sandbourn, David, 16.
Sandbourn, David, 25.
Sandbourn, Jeremiah, 25.
Sandbourn, John, 11.
Sandbourn, John, 25.
Sandbourn, John, Jur, 25.
Sandbourn, Jon^a, 16.
Sandbourn, Mary, 25.
Sandbourn, Simeon, 25.
Sanders, James, 27.
Sanders, Moses, 29.
Sanders, Rufus, 45.
Sanders, Timothy, 27.
Sanders, William, 28.
Sanderson, Stephen, 69.
Sandes, Joseph, 39.
Sands, Eph^m, 59.
Sands, Eph^m, Junr, 59.
Sands, James, 59.
Sands, James, 59.
Sands, John, 58.
Sands, Saml, 59.
Sands, thomas, 59.
Sanford, Daniel, 38.
Sanford, John, 46.
Sanford, Thomas, 22.
Sangmeid, Henry, 53.
Sargant, David, 38.
Sargant, John, 49.
Sargeant, Charles, 73.
Sargeant, Daniel, 72.
Sargeant, Danl, 72.
Sargeant, Jon^a, 33.
Sargeant, Jon^a, 33.
Sargeant, Jon^a, 72.
Sargeant, Joseph, 33.
Sargeant, Nathl, 71.
Sargeant, Willm, 21.
Sargeant, Willm, 70.
Sargent, Benj^a, 29.
Sargent, Chase, 60.
Sargent, Diamond, 29.
Sargent, Paul Dudley, 31.
Sargent, Robt, 65.
Sargent, Stephen, 29.
Sargent, William, 29.
Sargent, W^m, jun^r, 29.
Sarius, Isaac, 41.
Sark, Polly, 21.
Sartwell, Hezekiah, 50.
Saunders, Jon^a, 11.
Saunderson, Stephen, 29.
Savage, Abraham, 52.
Savage, Benjn, 51.
Savage, Charles, 52.
Savage, Danl, 39.
Savage, Eben^r, 52.
Savage, Edward, 39.
Savage, Edward, 51.
Savage, Isaac, 39.
Savage, Isaac, Jur, 39.
Savage, Jacob, 39.
Savage, James, 39.
Savage, James, 51.
Savage, James, 52.
Savage, John, 43.
Savage, John, 72.
Savage, Joseph, 35.
Saward, James, 67.
Sawell, thomas, 41.
Sawtel, David, 47.
Sawtel, Jonas, 47.
Sawtel, Moses, 47.
Sawtel, Nathl, 47.
Sawtel, Reuben, 47.
Sawtell, hezekiah, 50.
Sawyer, Aaron, 34.
Sawyer, Abner, 66.
Sawyer, Abra^m, 71.
Sawyer, Anthony, 14.
Sawyer, Barnabas, 58.
Sawyer, Benjamin, 14.

Sawyer, Benj^a, 16.
Sawyer, Benj^a, 21.
Sawyer, Benj^a, 34.
Sawyer, Daniel, 13.
Sawyer, Danl, 71.
Sawyer, David, 19.
Sawyer, David, 66.
Sawyer, David, Ju^r, 66.
Sawyer, David, 34, 66.
Sawyer, Ebenezer, 13.
Sawyer, Ebenezer, 34.
Sawyer, Eben^a, 64.
Sawyer, Elisha, 15.
Sawyer, Ezekiel, 23.
Sawyer, George, 44.
Sawyer, Isaac, 14.
Sawyer, Jabez, 59.
Sawyer, Jacob, 13.
Sawyer, Jacob, 34.
Sawyer, James, 16.
Sawyer, James, 23.
Sawyer, Jeremiah, 13.
Sawyer, Joel, 19.
Sawyer, Joel, 66.
Sawyer, Jno, 19.
Sawyer, John, 21.
Sawyer, John, 21.
Sawyer, John, 25.
Sawyer, John, 40.
Sawyer, John, 45.
Sawyer, John, 54.
Sawyer, Jno, 58.
Sawyer, John, 66.
Sawyer, Jonathan, 13.
Sawyer, Jonathan, 15.
Sawyer, Jonathan, 24.
Sawyer, Jon^a, 34.
Sawyer, Joseph, 13.
Sawyer, Joseph, 45.
Sawyer, Joseph, 53.
Sawyer, Joshua, 64.
Sawyer, Josiah, 54.
Sawyer, Luke, 44.
Sawyer, Mary, 13.
Sawyer, Merrel, 14.
Sawyer, Nathl, 64.
Sawyer, Nehemiah, 54.
Sawyer, Obediah, 14.
Sawyer, Parker, 21.
Sawyer, Peeter, 13.
Sawyer, Philip, 23.
Sawyer, Reubin, 13.
Sawyer, Samuel, 23.
Sawyer, Saml, 64.
Sawyer, Silvinius, 42.
Sawyer, Solomon, 22.
Sawyer, Solomon, Ju^r, 22.
Sawyer, Step^n, 19.
Sawyer, Thomas, 14.
Sawyer, Unis, 15.
Sawyer, Willm, 41.
Sawyer, W^m, 60.
Sawyer, Willm, 66.
Sawyer, Willm, 69.
Sawyer, Zachariah, 14.
Sawyer, Zech^r, 19.
Sawyes, Jacob, 45.
Sayards, Ebenezer, 67.
Sayards, John, 67.
Sayward, George, 46.
Sayward, Jon^a, 71.
Sayward (Widow), 71.
Sayward, Willm, 72.
Scales, Henry, 16.
Scales, Samuel, 16.
Scamman, Benjamin, 66.
Scamman, Daniel, 66.
Scamman, Dominicus, 66.
Scamman, Elizabeth, 56.
Scamman, Freman, 66.
Scamman, Isaac, 66.
Scamman, James, 66.
Scamman, John, 66.
Scamman, Nathaniel, 66.
Scamman, Nathl, Ju^r, 66.
Scamman, Samuel, 66.
Scammond, Eph^m, 62.
Scammond, Humph^y, Jun., 62.
Scammond, Umph^y, 62.
Scammons, Daniel, 31.
Scevy, James, 32.
Scheffer, John Martin, 49.
Schegel, George, 65.
Schegel, Jacob, 65.
Schwartz, friderich, 42.
Schwartz, peter, 41.
Schwartz (widow), 42.
Scofield, Clement, 20.
Scofield, Joseph, 12.
Scofield, Stephen, 20.
Scofield, Thomas, 12.
Scott, Daniel, 43.
Scott, Daniel, 53.
Scott, George, 53.
Scott, Giles, 71.
Scott, James, 29.
Scott, Jess, 53.
Scott, John, 23.
Scott, John, 53.
Scott, Mark, 53.
Scott, Nathaniel, 27.
Scott, Samuel, 53.
Scott, Samuel, jun^r, 53.

Scott, William, 29.
Scribner, Daniel, 68.
Scribner, Edward, jun^r, 68.
Scribner, Edward, 68.
Scribner, John, 67.
Scribner, John, 69.
Scribner, Joseph, 68.
Scribner, Samuel, 68.
Scribner, Samuel, jun^r, 69.
Scribner, Stephen, 40.
Scrigens, John, 62.
Scrigens, John, Jur, 62.
Scrigens, Thos, 62.
Scrigens, Winthrop, 62.
Seabury, Paul, 11.
Seales, Elizabeth, 22.
Seals, William, 35.
Seamman, James, 59.
Seargeant, Benj^a, 34.
Sears, Paul, 32.
Seats, John, 57.
Seavey, Eliakim, 71.
Seavey, John, 43.
Seavey, Josiah, 61.
Seavey, Michael, 43.
Seavey, Nicholas, 55.
Seavey, Nicholas, 55.
Seavey, Solomon, 44.
Seavey, Stephen, 44.
Seavey, Stephen, 55.
Seavey, Thos, 71.
Seavey, William, 43.
Seaward, Giles, 47.
Seborey, Saml, 21.
Sebry, Elizabeth, 21.
Secars, Paul, 51.
Secrist, Philip, 49.
Sedgley, John, 69.
Sedgley, John, 71.
Sedgley, Joseph, 35.
Sedgley, Joseph, 71.
Sedgley, Robert, 35.
Seers, Barnabas, 37.
Seers, Willard, 46.
Segar, John, 44.
Seger, Josiah, 64.
Seger, Josiah, 68.
Seger, Nathl, 68.
Sele, Jessa, 22.
Sellars, Willm, 72.
Sellers, Charles, 27.
Sellers, Joseph, 27.
Separd, Samuel, Juner, 33.
Sergeant, Daniel, 29.
Serles, John, 50.
Sessoro (Black), 61.
Settle, Hezekiah, 50.
Seve, John, 63.
Sever, William, 32.
Severance, Caleb, 30.
Severance, Joshua, 30.
Sevey, Aron, 53.
Sevey, George, 52.
Sevey, John, 53.
Sevey, Joseph, 53.
Sevey, Sylvanus, 53.
Sevy, David, 19.
Sevy, Eben^r, Jr., 19.
Sevy, Eben^r, 19.
Sevy, Nathl, 19.
Sevy, Reuben, 19.
Sevy, Thos, 19.
Sevy, Thos, Jr., 19.
Sewal, Henry, 39.
Sewal, James, 38.
Sewal, Nicholas, 71.
Sewal, Sarah, 37.
Sewall, Danl, 71.
Sewall, David, 71.
Sewall, Dummer, 33.
Sewall, Dummer, 36.
Sowall, Henry, 33.
Sewall, Henry, 71.
Sewall, John, 38.
Sewall, John, 71.
Sewall, John, 72.
Sewall, John, Jn^r, 38.
Sewall, Jonachom, 36.
Sewall, Moses, 39.
Sewall, Moses, 71.
Sewall, Samuel, 44.
Sewall, Saml, 72.
Sewall, Saml, 72.
Sewall, Stephen, 33.
Sewall, Story, 72.
Sewall, Theodore, 38.
Sewall, Thomas, 47.
Seymour, John, 24.
Shackford, John, 53.
Shackford, Cap^n Jon., 61.
Shackford, Paul, 50.
Shackley, John, 70.
Shackley, John, Jr, 70.
Shackley, Joseph, 59.
Shackley, Ric^d, 56.
Shackley, Ric^d, 56.
Shackley, Rich^d, 69.
Shackley, Thomas, 68.
Shad, John, 50.
Shaddock, Moses, 14.
Shade, Amos, 42.
Shade, William, 42.

INDEX.

Shakford, John, 67.
Shane, Richard, 25.
Shanemar, christian, 42.
Shannon, William, 50.
Shapleigh, Cap^n Depend^e, 62.
Shapleigh, Cap^n Elisha, 62.
Shapleigh, Isabel, 61.
Shapleigh, James, 62.
Shapleigh, John, 62.
Shapley, Saml, 62.
Shappa, Athony, 54.
Shattuck, Moses, 23.
Shattuck, Summers, 23.
Shaw, Abra^m, 72.
Shaw, Benjamin, 21.
Shaw, Benj^a, 22.
Shaw, Benj^a, 43.
Shaw, Benjamin, 53.
Shaw, Daniel, 21.
Shaw, David, 33.
Shaw, Ebenezer, 25.
Shaw, Eliab, 39.
Shaw, Elisha, 38.
Shaw, Elisha, 40.
Shaw, Elisha, jur, 40.
Shaw, Hannah, 29.
Shaw, Isaac, 45.
Shaw, James, 53.
Shaw, John, 39.
Shaw, John, 39.
Shaw, John, 52.
Shaw, John, 72.
Shaw, Joseph, 21.
Shaw, Joseph, 25.
Shaw, Joseph, 72.
Shaw, Joshua, 33.
Shaw, Josiah, 24.
Shaw, Josiah, 25.
Shaw, Jotham, 12.
Shaw, Levi, 11.
Shaw, Mary, 52.
Shaw, Merriam, 72.
Shaw, Nathaniel, 23.
Shaw, Nathl, 39.
Shaw, Saml, 11.
Shaw, Samuel, 23.
Shaw, Samuel, 66.
Shaw, Saml, 72.
Shaw, Serjant, 25.
Shaw, Thos, 25.
Shaw, William, 29.
Shaw, Willm, 72.
Shaw, Zebulon, 38.
Shay, Mich^l, 38.
Shays, Michael, 20.
Sheaf, Samson, 44.
Sheaf, Saml, 72.
Sheen, Jonathan, 34.
Shelden, Ephraim, 27.
Shelden, Henry, 39.
Sheldon, Nathaniel, 27.
Sheldon, Willm, 52.
Shenck, Andrew, 42.
Shenk (widow), 42.
Shepard, James, 33.
Shepard, William, 33.
Shephard, John, 34.
Shephard, John, 37.
Shepherd, Levi, 43.
Shepherd, Lewis, 19.
Shepherd, Mark, 62.
Shepherd, Mark, Ju^r, 62.
Shepherd, Robert, 55.
Shepherd, Thos, 58.
Shepherd, Thos, 58.
Sherborn, Abiel, 39.
Sherbourn, Henry, 60.
Sherburn, Susannah, 60.
Sherburne, Jacob, 28.
Sherburne, Samuel, 28.
Sherman, Barnabas, 23.
Sherman, Eleazer, 34.
Sherman, Joseph, 27.
Sherman, Margaret, 16.
Sherman, Nathan, 46.
Sherman, Valentine, 29.
Sherman (Widow), 71.
Sherring, John, 39.
Sherwin, Mr., 47.
Shibles, Robert, 46.
Shilden, Ephraim, 51.
Shillings, Daniel, 11.
Shillings, John, 13.
Shillings, Joseph, 13.
Shillings, Josiah, 13.
Shillings, Nehemiah, 13.
Shillings, Samuel, 13.
Shillings, Samuel, 13.
Shillings, Simeon, 13.
Shirley, Edward, 60.
Shirtlef, James, 45.
Shirtliff, Jon^a, 22.
Shirtliff, Jon^a, Jr., 22.
Shmit, christian, 41.
Shmit, joseph (mescongus Island), 48.
Shorehead, Daniel, 37.
Shores, Joseph, 69.
Shores, Samuel, 50.
Shorey, Benj^a, 67.
Shorey, Jacob, 58.
Shorey, Jacob, 62.
Shorey, John, 57.

Shorey, John, 58.
Shorey, Joseph, 56.
Shorey, Miles, 57.
Shorey, Samuel, 67.
Shorey, Saml, Junr, 67.
Shorey, Stephen, 63.
Shorey, Unles, 56.
Shorey, W^m, 57.
Shuman, John, 41.
Shuman, philip, 41.
Shurban, Andrew, 60.
Shurban, Saml, 60.
Shurborn, Job, 51.
Shurborn, Richard, 51.
Shute, Benj^a, 28.
Shute, Benjamin, jun^r, 28.
Shute, George, 19.
Shute, Hannah, 19.
Shute, John, 60.
Shute, J^s, 19.
Shute, W^m, 19.
Sibley, John, 37.
Sidelinger, George, 35.
Sidenspire, charles, 41.
Sidenspire, george, 42.
Sidenspire, John, 42.
Sidenspire (widow), 41.
Sider, cornelius, 42.
Sides, loring, 42.
Sidlinger, charles, 42.
Sidlinger, daniel, 42.
Sidlinger, martin, 42.
Sidlinger, peter, 35.
Sier, John 48.
Silby, Benj^a. 70.
Sillea, John, 66.
Sillea, Nathan, 66.
Silvester, Abner, 16.
Silvester, Abner, Ju^r, 16.
Silvester, Amos, 16.
Silvester, Bester, 16.
Silvester, Caleb, 16.
Silvester, David, 43.
Silvester, Edmund, 27.
Silvester, Elisha, 38.
Silvester, Hinhman, 16.
Silvester, John, 16.
Silvester, Joseph, 16.
Silvester, Joseph, 44.
Silvester, Mary, 43.
Silvester, Nathl, 37.
Silvester, Nathl, Junr, 37.
Silvester, Samuel, 43.
Silvester, Thos, 16.
Silvester, Willm, 20.
Silvester, William, 42.
Silvester, Zachariah, 24.
Silvestor, Ebenesor, 38.
Simmonds, Aaron, 36.
Simmonds, Nathaniel, 36.
Simmons, Joel, 11.
Simon, Francis, 11.
Simonons, Ichabod, 51.
Simons, barnabas, 42.
Simons, Eckiel (Hungh Island), 42.
Simons, Isaac (Hungh Island), 42.
Simons, Joab (Hungh Island), 42.
Simons, John, 12.
Simons, Joseph, 42.
Simons, Samuel, 35.
Simons, Stephen, 42.
Simons, Thos, 11.
Simons (widow), 42.
Simons, Zebede, 42.
Simonton, Andrew, 13.
Simonton, Ebenezer, 13.
Simonton, James, 26.
Simonton, James, jun., 26.
Simonton, John, 46.
Simonton, Jonathan, 24.
Simonton, London, 13.
Simonton, Mary, 13.
Simonton, Matthew, 13.
Simonton, Thomas, 13.
Simonton, Thomas, 13.
Simonton, William, 26.
Simonton, William, 29.
Simpson, Benjamin, 50.
Simpson, Benjamin, 66.
Simpson, Danl, 72.
Simpson, Eben^s, 72.
Simpson, George, 71.
Simpson, Jabez, 31.
Simpson, James, 31.
Simpson, James, 41.
Simpson, John, 30.
Simpson, John, 31.
Simpson, John, 50.
Simpson, John, 50.
Simpson, John, 53.
Simpson, Joseph, 71.
Simpson, Joseph, 72.
Simpson, Joseph, 72.
Simpson, Joshua, 72.
Simpson, Josiah, 31.
Simpson, Josiah, 58.
Simpson, Lewis, 12.
Simpson, Nathl, 72.

Simpson, Paul, 31.
Simpson, Pelatiah, 72.
Simpson, Reuben, 50.
Simpson, Samuel, 31.
Simpson, Saml, 41.
Simpson, Simeon, 39.
Simpson, Tabitha, 72.
Simpson, Thos, 22.
Simpson, Thos, 71.
Simpson, Thos, 72.
Simpson, Timothy, 72.
Simpson, Webster, 64.
Simpson, William, 53.
Simpson, Willm, 64.
Simscott, Joseph, 20.
Simscott, Moses, 20.
Sinclair, Edward, 31.
Sinclair, Edward, 32.
Singly, Frederick, 53.
Sinkler, Adoniram, 35.
Sinkler, Benjamin, 69.
Sinkler, Nathl, 53.
Sinnet, Mich^l, 20.
Sinnet, Stephen, 20.
Sinnot, Thos, 66.
Skidmore, Elias, 34.
Skillens, Isaac, 21.
Skillens, Josiah, 22.
Skillin, Lewis, 44.
Skilling, Jno, 19.
Skilling, Thos, 19.
Skillings, Benjn, 19.
Skillings, Simeon, 19.
Skinner, Daniel, 30.
Skinner, Elisha, 30.
Skinner, Henry, 51.
Skinner, John, 14.
Skinner, Joseph, 49.
Slack, Thomas, 30.
Sleeper, Moses, 47.
Slemmons, Robert, 15.
Slemmons, Thomas, 15.
Slimmons, William, 14.
Sloman, John, 71.
Sloman, Simon, 51.
Sloman, William, 43.
Small, Benj^a, 64.
Small, Daniel, 15.
Small, Daniel, 24.
Small, Daniel, 24.
Small, Daniel, 54.
Small, Danl, 64.
Small, Danl, 64.
Small, David, 11.
Small, Ebenezer, 54.
Small, Edward, 13.
Small, Edward, 16.
Small, Elisha, 13.
Small, Elisha, 54.
Small, Ephrom, 35.
Small, Francis, 64.
Small, George, 24.
Small, Henry, 64.
Small, Isaac, 19.
Small, Isaac, 64.
Small, Jacob, 64.
Small, James, 19.
Small, James, 19.
Small, James, 24.
Small, James, 64.
Small, Jeremiah, 14.
Small, John, 14.
Small, John, 21.
Small, John, 46.
Small, John, 54.
Small, John, Junr, 54.
Small, John, 3^d, 54.
Small, Joseph, 35.
Small, Joseph, 53.
Small, Joshua, 64.
Small, Joshua, Jr, 64.
Small, Mark, 20.
Small, Reuben, 64.
Small, Saml, 19.
Small, Saml, 20.
Small, Taylor, 20.
Small, Taylor, 35.
Small, Timothy, 13.
Small, Willm, 64.
Small, Zachariah, 14.
Smallcorn, Cap^n Saml, 61.
Smalley, David, 35.
Smalley, Joshua, 36.
Smally, Andrew, 27.
Smally, Edward, 13.
Smally, Job, 27.
Smally, Thomas, 47.
Smally, Thomas, jun^r, 27.
Smart, Eliphelat, 49.
Smart, Hannah, 61.
Smart, James, 49.
Smart, John, 27.
Smart, John, 47.
Smart, Robert, 49.
Smellige, Josiah, 29.
Smellige, Timothy, 29.
Smiley, Alex^r, 47.
Smiley, David, 47.
Smiley, Hugh, 47.
Smiley, Thomas, 47.
Smiley, Willm, 47.
Smillidge, nathan, 48.
Smith, Aaron, 69.

Smith, Ablathar, 46.
Smith, Abraham, 44.
Smith, And^w, 58.
Smith, Anna, 64.
Smith, Archibald, 25.
Smith, Asa, 25.
Smith, Asa, 44.
Smith, Benjamin, 24.
Smith, Benj^a, 28.
Smith, Benj^a, 45.
Smith, Benj^a, 51.
Smith, Benj^a, 64.
Smith, Benj^a, 65.
Smith, Charles, 26.
Smith, Charles, 53.
Smith, Charles, 55.
Smith, Charles, 59.
Smith, Cheney, 44.
Smith, Comford, 51.
Smith, Cyril, 51.
Smith, Daniel, 36.
Smith, Daniel, 39.
Smith, Daniel, 49.
Smith, Daniel, 51.
Smith, Daniel, 53.
Smith, Danl, 55.
Smith, Danl, 56.
Smith, Danl, 64.
Smith, Danl, 72.
Smith, Danl, Jr, 64.
Smith, David, 23.
Smith, David, 27.
Smith, David, 55.
Smith, Dominicus, 58.
Smith, Dominicus, 64.
Smith, Ebenezer, 52.
Smith, Ebenezer, 53.
Smith, Ebenezer, 72.
Smith, Edward, 64.
Smith, Edward, 72.
Smith, Eliab, 50.
Smith, Elijah, 27.
Smith, Eliphelat, 45.
Smith, Mrs Eliphelat, 51.
Smith, Elisabeth, 56.
Smith, Elisha, 60.
Smith, Elisha, 64.
Smith, Elisha, jun., 60.
Smith, Ellis, 53.
Smith, Ellison, 58.
Smith, Eph^m, 19.
Smith, heneary, 67.
Smith, Henry, 42.
Smith, Herman, 35.
Smith, Hezekiah, 19.
Smith, Hozia, 61.
Smith, Ichabod, 63.
Smith, Isaac, 35.
Smith, Israel, 12.
Smith, Israel, 51.
Smith, Israil, 68.
Smith, Israil, jun^r, 68.
Smith, Jacob, 51.
Smith, Jacob, 68.
Smith, James, 23.
Smith, James, 28.
Smith, James, 32.
Smith, James, 42.
Smith, James, 49.
Smith, James, 53.
Smith, James, 59.
Smith, James, 62.
Smith, James, 69.
Smith, Jasael, 25.
Smith, Jedadiah, 64.
Smith, Jemima, 56.
Smith, Jere, 55.
Smith, Jeremiah, 20.
Smith, Jer^e, 58.
Smith, Jesse, 51.
Smith, Jethro, 68.
Smith, John, 20.
Smith, John, 28.
Smith, John, 29.
Smith, John, 32.
Smith, John, 32.
Smith, John, 34.
Smith, John, 36.
Smith, John, 41.
Smith, John, 55.
Smith, John, 58.
Smith, John, 63.
Smith, John, 64.
Smith, John, 68.
Smith, John, 69.
Smith, John, 72.
Smith, John, Junr, 58.
Smith, John, jun^r, 69.
Smith, John H., 14.
Smith, Jonah, 21.
Smith, Jonathan, 32.
Smith, Jonathan, 46.
Smith, Jon^a, 55.
Smith, Jon^a, 58.
Smith, Jonathan, 68.
Smith, Jon^a, Jr, 54.
Smith, Joseph, 27.
Smith, Joseph, 33.
Smith, Joseph, 34.
Smith, Joseph, 58.
Smith, Joshua, 35.

Smith, Josiah, 19.
Smith, Josiah, 20.
Smith, Josiah, 22.
Smith, Josiah, Ju^r, 25.
Smith, Jotham, 44.
Smith, Laban, 25.
Smith, Levi, 32.
Smith, Liddah, 50.
Smith, Manassa, 43.
Smith, Manuel, 50.
Smith, Mary, 52.
Smith, mathias, 51.
Smith, mathias, Jur., 51.
Smith, Merodick, 22.
Smith, Moses, 38.
Smith, Moses, 50.
Smith, Nathan, 49.
Smith, Nathl, 12.
Smith, Nathaniel, 31.
Smith, Nathaniel, 34.
Smith, Nathl, 64.
Smith, Nehemiah, 69.
Smith, Nicholas, 58.
Smith, Noah, 64.
Smith, Oliver, 46.
Smith, Peleg, 27.
Smith, Peter, 19.
Smith, Peter F., 26.
Smith, Rachel, 19.
Smith, Richard, 53.
Smith, Roger, 58.
Smith, Rogers, 43.
Smith, Saml, 19.
Smith, Samuel, 45.
Smith, Samuel, 50.
Smith, Samuel, 55.
Smith, Saml, 58.
Smith, Sarah, 57.
Smith, Seabury, 12.
Smith, Silas, 43.
Smith, Simon, 28.
Smith, Sol^m, 59.
Smith, Stephen, 53.
Smith, Stephen, 70.
Smith, Stephen, jun^r, 53.
Smith, Steven, 35.
Smith, Theo^s, 58.
Smith, Theophelus, 60.
Smith, Theo^s, Junr, 58.
Smith, Thial, 68.
Smith, Thial, Junr, 68.
Smith, Thomas, 22.
Smith, Thomas, 30.
Smith, thomas, 38.
Smith, Thomas, 45.
Smith, Thomas, 45.
Smith, Thomas, 47.
Smith, Thomas, 56.
Smith, Thos, 59.
Smith, Thos, 68.
Smith, thomas, 69.
Smith, thomas, Jr., 45.
Smith, thomas, Junr, 68.
Smith (Widow), 55.
Smith, William, 15.
Smith, Willm, 55.
Smith, Willm, 55.
Smith, W^m, 55.
Smith, W^m, 58.
Smith, W^m, 61.
Smith, W^m, 62.
Smith, Winthrop, 26.
Smith, Wolden, 50.
Smith, Zebulon, 27.
Smith, Zebulon, 40.
Smith, Zebulon, 52.
Smith, Zoeth, 32.
Smullin, John, 35.
Snaudel, william, 42.
Snell, David, 49.
Snell, James, 51.
Snell, Thaddeus, 39.
Snell, Thos, 51.
Snipe, John, 38.
Snouteigle, John, 42.
Snow, Aaron, 20.
Snow, Abizah, 20.
Snow, Amasa, 30.
Snow, Amasa, jun^r, 30.
Snow, Ambrose, 46.
Snow, Benj^a, 30.
Snow, Benj^a, 32.
Snow, Daniel, 35.
Snow, Ebenezer, 23.
Snow, Edward, 30.
Snow, Elisha, 46.
Snow, Ephraim, 46.
Snow, Gideon, 19.
Snow, Hannah, 20.
Snow, Harding, 28.
Snow, Isaac, 12.
Snow, Isaac, 20.
Snow, Isaac, 20.
Snow, James, 71.
Snow, John, 20.
Snow, John, 20.
Snow, Joseph, 12.
Snow, Joseph, 38.
Snow, Joshua, 14.
Snow, Joshua, 31.
Snow, Nickolas, 31.
Snow, Paul, 19.
Snow, Philip, 50.

INDEX.

Snow, Philip, 50.
Snow, Reuben, 32.
Snow, Sam¹, 20.
Snow, Thoˢ, 19.
Snow, Thomas, 28.
Snow, Wᵐ, 19.
Snow, Willᵐ, 20.
Snowman, John, 30.
Snowman, William, 30.
Soames, Jonathan, 20.
Soaper, Salter, 19.
Sofford, Reuben, 26.
Sole, Amasa, 44.
Sole, Asa, 19.
Sole, Barnabas, 16.
Sole, Cornelius, 16.
Sole, Ichabod, 16.
Sole, James, 16.
Sole, James, 24.
Sole, Jedediah, 16.
Sole, John, 16.
Sole, John, 16.
Sole, John, 51.
Sole, Jonˢ, 16.
Sole, Moses, 16.
Sole, Robert, 16.
Sole, Samˡ, 16.
Sole (widow), 42.
Sole, Willᵐ, 16.
Some, David, 41.
Somes, Abraham, 29.
Somes, Daniel, 53.
Sommers, Thomas, 29.
Soper, Justus, 28.
Soper, Samuel, 28.
Soper, Seth, 42.
Sottel, Nathˡ, 11.
Sottle, Henry, 11.
Soul, Asa, 50.
Soul, Jonathan, 50.
Soul, Joshua, 45.
Southard, John, 34.
Southard, John, 35.
Southeslin, Alexᵈ, 40.
Southgate, Robᵗ, 19.
Southward, Arbaᵐ, 43.
Southword, Constant, 41.
Southword, thomas, 41.
Southworth, John, 22.
Soward, Joseph, 72.
Soward, Theodore, 33.
Soward, Willᵐ, 71.
Sowards, Elizʰ, 62.
Sowards, Richᵈ, 61.
Spafford, Nathˡ, 68.
Spafford, Phinehas, 14.
Spalding, Ezekiel, 38.
Spalding, John, 48.
Spark, David, 12.
Sparkes, James, 35.
Sparks, Nicholas, 34.
Sparrow, Joseph, 64.
Sparrow, Stephen, 25.
Spaulding, Benjˢ, Jr., 12.
Spaulding, Benjˢ, second, 12.
Spaulding, Benjˢ Senior, 12.
Spaulding, Jedidiah, 46.
Spaulding, Samˡ, 12.
Spaulding, Timothy, 46.
Spear, John, 49.
Spear, Jonathan, 46.
Spear, Jonathan, Junʳ, 46.
Spear, Joshua, 21.
Spear, Robert, 12.
Spear, Robert, 49.
Spear, William, 46.
Spears, Ebenezer, 66.
Spears, Isrul, 66.
Speed, Benjˢ, 41.
Speed, Joseph, 33.
Spencer, Daniel, 27.
Spencer, Daniel, 28.
Spencer, Frithe, 56.
Spencer, Humpʸ, 57.
Spencer, Joseph, 56.
Spencer, Nathaniel, 28.
Spencer, Nathaniel, jun., 28.
Spencer, Phillip, 28.
Spencer, Simeon, 57.
Spencer, Thomas, 56.
Spencer, Wᵐ, 56.
Spencer, Wᵐ, Junʳ, 56.
Spener, Ichabod, 66.
Spensor, David, 39.
Spensor, Isaac, 39.
Spensor, Solomon, 37.
Spern, Benjamin, 39.
Sperring, John, 37.
Spinney, Ebenezʳ, 62.
Spinney, Edmund, 62.
Spinney, Geo., 62.
Spinney, Jerˢ, 37.
Spinney, Jerˢ, 38.
Spinney, John, 38.
Spinney, John, 62.
Spinney, John, Juʳ, 62.
Spinney, Nathˡ, 70.
Spinney, Samˡ, 62.
Spinney, Timoʸ, 62.
Spinney, Willᵐ, 62.
Spinny, Hannah, 38.
Spinny, John, 61.
Spinny, John, 62.

Spinny, Nicholas, 62.
Spinny, Samson, 61.
Spofford, Daniel, 26.
Spokin, Joseph, 34.
Spolden, Elezer, 42.
Spolden, Elezer, Jur, 42.
Spolden, Josiah, 42.
Spolden, Seth, 42.
Spolden, Thomas, 42.
Spolden, Willᵐ, 42.
Spolden, William, Ju., 42.
Spoldin, John, 50.
Spoldin, John, 50.
Spoldin, Nathˡ, 35.
Spoldin, Willard, 50.
Spotzeswell, Dorothy, 60.
Sprage, John, 19.
Sprage, William, Ju., 38.
Sprages, William, 38.
Sprags, Jamas, 38.
Sprague, Abiel, 53.
Sprague, Eli, 53.
Sprague, James, 53.
Sprague, John, 29.
Sprague, Joseph, 46.
Sprague, michel, 42.
Sprague, nathan, 42.
Sprague, Nathan, 49.
Sprague, Nathˡ, 12.
Sprague, Samuel, 53.
Sprague, William, 37.
Sprague, Willᵐ, 38.
Sprague, William, 39.
Spratt, George, 47.
Spreague, Samuel, 45.
Spring, Revᵈ Alpheus, 62.
Spring, Daniel, 44.
Spring, Josiah, 58.
Spring, Seth, 58.
Spring, Thomas, 26.
Springer, Andrew, 45.
Springer, David, 31.
Springer, David, 45.
Springer, David, ju., 45.
Springer, Edward, 39.
Springer, Edward, 50.
Springer, Jacob, 31.
Springer, James, 31.
Springer, James, 38.
Springer, Job, 50.
Springer, Job, 50.
Springer, John, 32.
Springer, John, 35.
Springer, John, 55.
Springer, Stutely, 50.
Springer, Thomas, 42.
Springer, Thoˢ, 35.
Springer, Willᵐ, 43.
Springet, Nathˡ, 20.
Sproul, James, 48.
Sproul, James, jun., 48.
Sproul, robert, jun., 48.
Sproul, william, 48.
Sprouls, Robert, 48.
Sprouls, william, 48.
Sprouls, william, 48.
Spurlin, Benjˢ, 29.
Spurlin, James, 29.
Spurr, Enoch, 22.
Spurr, Joseph, 22.
Spurr, William, 24.
Staboard, John, 35.
Stacey, Ebenezer, 58.
Stacey, George, 58.
Stacey, Nimphar, 43.
Stacey, Wᵐ, 72.
Stackpole, James, 46.
Stackpole, John, 20.
Stackpole, Joseph, 39.
Stacy, Benjˢ, 65.
Stacy, Ecabod, 62.
Stacy, Ellis, 62.
Stagpole, James, 50.
Stagpole, James, Jʳ, 50.
Stagpole, Samuel, 50.
Stair, John, 50.
Stakepole, Aaron, 56.
Stall, henry, 41.
Stall, philip, 41.
Standish, James, 49.
Standish, Lemuel, 33.
Standley, Adam, 51.
Standley, Edward, 66.
Standley, James, 56.
Standley, John, 56.
Standley, John, 66.
Standley, John, 68.
Standley, Nathaniel, 51.
Standley, Reah, 51.
Standley, Samˡ, 56.
Standley, Wᵐ, 68.
Standly, Jacob, 51.
Standly, Mary, 68.
Standly, Solomon, 51.
Stanford, Abigail, 13.
Stanford, Benjamin, 13.
Stanford, Christopher, 13.
Stanford, John, 13.
Stanford, John, 33.
Stanford, Joseph, 13.
Stanford, Sarah, 13.
Stanley, David, 27.
Stanley, John, 29.

Stanley, Kenny, 31.
Stanley, Margaret, 29.
Stanley, Mark, 62.
Stanley, Nathaniel, 32.
Stanley, Peter, 29.
Stanley, Samuel, 29.
Stanley, Sans, 29.
Stanley, Thomas, 29.
Stanton, Benjˢ, 56.
Stanton, Benjmin, 67.
Stanton, George, 56.
Stanton, paul, 67.
Stanwood, Benjˢ, 29.
Stanwood, Ebenezer, 12.
Stanwood, Humphry, 29.
Stanwood, Robert, 12.
Stanwood, Samˡ, 12.
Stanwood, Willᵐ, 12.
Stanwood, Willᵐ, 12.
Stanwood, Willᵐ, Junʳ, 12.
Stanyan, John, 66.
Staple, Benjˢ, 68.
Staple, Carrel, 64.
Staple, Daniel, 21.
Staple, David, 68.
Staple, Gedion, 57.
Staple, Jere, 19.
Staple, John, 57.
staple, Joshua, 57.
Staple, Josiah, 57.
Staple, Nathan, 60.
Staple, Peter, 57.
Staple, Peter, Junʳ, 57.
Staple, Ricᵈ, 57.
Staple, Stephen, 57.
Staple, William, 66.
Staples, Andʷ, 58.
Staples, Benjˢ, 58.
Staples, Daniel, 22.
Staples, David, 62.
Staples, Edwᵈ, 62.
Staples, Elisha, 66.
Staples, Enoch, 67.
Staples, Francis, 71.
Staples, Isaac, 62.
Staples, James, 48.
Staples, John, 11.
Staples, John, 28.
Staples, John, 31.
Staples, John, 58.
Staples, John, 69.
Staples, Joseph, 14.
Staples, Joseph, 16.
Staples, Joseph, 64.
Staples, Joshua, 27.
Staples, Josiah, 25.
Staples, Jotham, 28.
Staples, Mary, 62.
Staples, Miles, 28.
Staples, Moses, 27.
Staples, Nathaniel, 13.
Staples, Noah, 62.
Staples, Pertor, 24.
Staples, Peter, 62.
Staples, Robert, 64.
Staples, Ruth, 62.
Staples, Samˡ, 19.
Staples, Samuel, 27.
Staples, Samˡ, 46.
Staples, Samˡ, Jr., 19.
Staples, Soloman, 62.
Staples, Stephen, 35.
Staples, Stephen, 47.
Staples, William, 28.
Staples, Willᵐ, 54.
Staples, Wᵐ, 62.
Staples, Willᵐ, 71.
Stapole, Lenord, 55.
Starberd, Anthony, 15.
Starberd, Ebenezer, 23.
Starberd, Hannah, 25.
Starberd, Jethro, 19.
Starberd, John, 15.
Starberd, John, 15.
Starberd, Thomas, 15.
Starbird, Moses, 24.
Starboard, Samuel, 11.
Starboard, Willᵐ, 12.
Starbord, Samuel, 34.
Starbord (Widow), 19.
Starcy, John, 62.
Starling, Josiah, 36.
Starling, Moses, 44.
Starling, Richard, 36.
Starns, Ebennesor, 33.
Starow, andrew, 42.
Starow, mathias, 42.
Starpole, Absalom, 57.
Starrde, Edward, 45.
Starret, Thomas, 49.
Starret, Thomas, Junʳ, 49.
Starrot, David, 23.
Stasey, Benjˢ, 57.
Staycy, Wᵐ, Junʳ, 62.
Stearns, Benjˢ, 68.
Stearns, Dudley, 58.
Stearns, John, 68.
Stearns, Thomas, 68.
Stedman, James, 47.
Steel, Andrew, 30.
Steel, Clement, 67.
Steel, Robert, 26.
Steele, Jno, 59.

Steele, Peter, 59.
Steele, Reuben, 54.
Steele (Widow), 54.
Steper, John, 51.
Stephens, Abraham, 29.
Stephens, Amos, 51.
Stephens, Benjˢ, 19.
Stephens, Benjamin, 60.
Stephens, Benjˢ, Jr., 19.
Stephens, Revᵈ Benjˢ, 61.
Stephens, Hubbard, 37.
Stephens, Jerˢ, 69.
Stephens, Johanˢ, 61.
Stephens, John, 61.
Stephens, Jno, 61.
Stephens, Jonathan, 46.
Stephens, Joseph, 19.
Stephens, Joseph, 43.
Stephens, Moses, 61.
Stephens, Nance, 62.
Stephens, Nathˡ, 19.
Stephens, Pelatiah, 73.
Stephens, Samuel, 51.
Stephens, Thoˢ, 37.
Stephens, Thomas, 38.
Stephenson, Jerom, 26.
Stephenson, John, 22.
Stephenson, Nathˡ, 51.
Stephenson, Solon, 26.
Sterer, christian, 41.
Sterling, John, 60.
Sterrey, David, 43.
Stetson, Hezekiah, 13.
Stetson, William, 46.
Stevans, Daniel, 39.
Stevans, Joel, 71.
Stevans, John, 73.
Stevans, John, 73.
Stevans, Jonˢ, 73.
Stevans, Joseph, 58.
Stevans, Moses, 71.
Stevens, A. Hovey, 19.
Stevens, Aaron, 67.
Stevens, Abraham, 23.
Stevens, Alexander, 48.
Stevens, Asa, 23.
Stevens, Benjˢ, 70.
Stevens, Chase, 74.
Stevens, Christopher, 41.
Stevens, Daniel, 46.
Stevens, Danˡ, 56.
Stevens, David, 67.
Stevens, Ebenezer, 50.
Stevens, Ephraim, 51.
Stevens, hubbard, 67.
Stevens, Isaac S., 15.
Stevens, Jacob, 11.
Stevens, Jacob, 11.
Stevens, Jacob, 38.
Stevens, Jacob, Jʳ, 11.
Stevens, Joel, 19.
Stevens, John, 49.
Stevens, John, 51.
Stevens, John, 60.
Stevens, John, 61.
Stevens, John, Junʳ, 60.
Stevens, Jonas, 24.
Stevens, Jonas, 51.
Stevens, Jonathan, 19.
Stevens, Jonathan, 25.
Stevens, Jonathan, 53.
Stevens, Jonˢ, 70.
Stevens, Joseph, 24.
Stevens, Joseph, 51.
Stevens, Joshua, 14.
Stevens, Mary, 19.
Stevens, Moses, 12.
Stevens, Moses, 25.
Stevens, Nathaniel, 21.
Stevens, Nathˡ, 24.
Stevens, Nehemiah, 46.
Stevens, Paul, 20.
Stevens, Paul, 21.
Stevens, Richard, 26.
Stevens, Samuel, 63.
Stevens, Samˡ, 70.
Stevens, Solomon, 70.
Stevens, Thoˢ, 22.
Stevens, Thomas, 31.
Stevens, Thomas, 46.
Stevens, Thomas, Jun., 46.
Stevens, Trustum, 14.
Stevens (Widow), 54.
Stevens, William, 40.
Stevens, William, 51.
Stevens, Wᵐ, 63.
Stevenson, Willᵐ, 58.
Steward, Abraham, 35.
Steward, Jno, 19.
Steward, John, 32.
Steward, Jno, Jr., 19.
Steward, Joseph, 19.
Steward, Peeter, 14.
Steward, Phinihas, 35.
Steward, Phinihas, 35.
Steward, Samˡ, 19.
Steward, Samuel, 35.
Steward, Timo, 19.
Steward, Timothy, 47.
Steward, William, 35.
Stewart, Charles, 32.
Stewart, Daniel, 42.

Stewart, Solomon, 36.
Stewart, Solomon, Jr., 35.
Stewart, Steven, 48.
Stewart, William, 35.
Stickney, Bailey, 12.
Stickney, Benjamen, 33.
Stickney, John, 58.
Stickney, Jonˢ, 25.
Stiflen, George, 43.
Stiles, Ezra, 58.
Stilfan, Michˡ, 44.
Stillens, Isaac, 63.
Stillens, Luke, 57.
Stillens, Mary, 57.
Stillens, Peter, 57.
Stillens, Samˢˡ, 57.
Stillman, George, 53.
Stimplon, Stephen, junʳ, 59.
Stimpson, Alexʳ, 19.
Stimpson, Ephraim, 29.
Stimpson, Joseph, 72.
Stimpson, Loammi, 58.
Stimpson, Richard, 26.
Stimpson, Stephen, 60.
Stimson, Jeremiah, 64.
Stimson, Joseph, 64.
Stinchfield, Ephraim, 20.
Stinchfield, James, 20.
Stinchfield, John, 20.
Stinchfield, John, 21.
Stinchfield, John, 21.
Stinchfield, Josiah, 11.
Stinchfield, Mary, 21.
Stinchfield, Roger, 40.
Stinchfield, thomas, 40.
Stinson, James, 32.
Stinson, James, 38.
Stinson, James, 52.
Stinson, James, 52.
Stinson, John, 38.
Stinson, John, 38.
Stinson, Robert, 34.
Stinson, Robert, 52.
Stinson, Samuel, 27.
Stinson, Samˡ, 52.
Stinson, Thomas, 27.
Stinson, Thoˢ, 52.
Stinson, Thomas, jun., 27.
Stinson, William, 27.
Stinson, William, 35.
Stinson, Willᵐ, 38.
Stinson, Willᵐ, 38.
Stinson, Willᵐ, 44.
Stockbridge, Benjˢ, 27.
Stockbridge, John, 16.
Stockbridge, Joseph, 16.
Stockbridge, Michael, 16.
Stocker, John, 61.
Stocking, Thomas, 49.
Stockman, Jacob, 46.
Stockman, Samˡ, 47.
Stockman, Thoˢ, 46.
Stockpole, Andʷ, 58.
Stockpole, John, 58.
Stodard, David, 23.
Stodard, Phinhas, 38.
Stoddard, Baley C., 53.
Stoddard, Nathˡ, 53.
Stoddard, Willᵐ, 14.
Stone, Benjˢ, 12.
Stone, Benjamin, 23.
Stone, Benjˢ, 55.
Stone, Benjˢ, 55.
Stone, Dix, 55.
Stone, Dudley, 55.
Stone, Gabriel, 37.
Stone, George, 64.
Stone, Gidon, 67.
Stone, Hannah, 24.
Stone, John, 36.
Stone, John, 54.
Stone, John, 55.
Stone, John, 57.
Stone, John, 63.
Stone, John, 64.
Stone, Jonˢ, 19.
Stone, Jonˢ, 55.
Stone, Jonˢ, 55.
Stone, Jonathan, 57.
Stone, Jonˢ, Jr, 55.
Stone, Joseph, 67.
Stone, Josiah, 71.
Stone, Judah, 68.
Stone, Levi, 68.
Stone, Moses, 64.
Stone, Nehemiah, 55.
Stone, Paul, 57.
Stone, Paul, 57.
Stone, Robert, 55.
Stone, Samˡ, 71.
Stone, Solo, 19.
Stone, Solomon & Son, 53.
Stone (Widow), 55.
Storer, Abraᵐ, 71.
Storer, Amos, 69.
Storer, Benjˢ, 60.
Storer, Ebenezer, 24.
Storer, Isaac, 69.
Storer, Isaac, 69.
Storer, Jere, Jʳ, 69.
Storer, Jerˢ, 69.
Storer, Johanna, 15.

INDEX.

Storer, John, 71.
Storer, John, 71.
Storer, Joseph, 70.
Storer, Matthias, 22.
Storer, Nathl, 69.
Storer, Seth, 66.
Storer, Wm, 60.
Storer, Willm, 69.
Storer, Willm, 71.
Storer, Woodberry, 23.
Storey, Abram, 58.
Story, John, 12.
Story, Sam., 48.
Story (widow), 48.
stotson, Joseph, 48.
Stout, Benjamin, 54.
Stout, David, 13.
Stout, Eleazer, 13.
Stout, Eleazer, 13.
Stout, George, 13.
Stout, George, 13.
Stout, Jeremiah, 53.
Stout, John, 64.
Stout, Joseph, 54.
Stout, Joshua, 14.
Stout, Levi, 13.
Stout, Levi, 13.
Stout, Nathaniel, 13.
Stout, Prince, 64.
Stout, Richard, 64.
Stout, Saml, 64.
Stout, Simon, 64.
Stout, Thomas, 54.
Stout, William, 14.
Stout, William, 23.
Stoutley, Keturah, 62.
Stovar, Johnson, 20.
Stover, Abraham, 30.
Stover, Alcot, 20.
Stover, Dependence, 36.
Stover, George, 71.
Stover, Hannah, 23.
Stover, Huldah, 71.
Stover, Isaac, 30.
Stover, Jeremiah, 30.
Stover, John, 20.
Stover, John, 34.
Stover, John, 71.
Stover, John, Jr, 71.
Stover, Joseph, 34.
Stover, Jotham, 30.
Stover, Mary, 71.
Stover, Nathaniel, 30.
Stover, Saml, 71.
Stover, Timothy, 36.
Stover, William, 30.
Stover, William, 30.
Stow, Willm, 39.
Stowel, Daniel, 22.
Stowel, Elias, 25.
Stowel, Nathl, 22.
Stowel, Samuel, 19.
Stowel, Wllm, 22.
Stowers, Samuel, 28.
Stratton, Hezekiah, 50.
Straw, Daniel, 59.
Straw, Valintine, 69.
Straw, William, 60.
Streter, John, 49.
Streter, John, ju., 51.
Strickland, John, 25.
Strout, Elisha, 19.
Strout, Enoch, 64.
Strout, George, 19.
Strout, Gilbart, 64.
Strout, Isaac, 64.
Strout, Jacob, 11.
Strout, Joshua, 11.
Strout, Nehemiah, 11.
Strout, Willm, 64.
Stuard, James, 48.
Stuard, thomas, 48.
Stuart, Charles, 31.
Stuart, Danl, 70.
Stuart, David, 70.
Stuart, Elijah, 70.
Stuart, Elijah, Jr, 70.
Stuart, Elijah, 3d, 70.
Stuart, Isaac, 35.
Stuart, Joseph, 19.
Stuart, Josiah, 69.
Stuart, Reuben, 70.
Stuart, Saml, 70.
Stuart, Wentworth, 19.
Stubs, Benja, 21.
Stubs, Jera, 21.
Stubs, Jona, 21.
Stubs, Moses, 21.
Stubs, Richd, 21.
Stubs Saml, 22.
Stubbs, James, 28.
Stubbs, James, 32.
Stubbs, Samuel, 32.
Studle, sichl (long Island), 48.
Studley, dan., 28.
Studley, John, 28.
Studley, John, 41.
Studley, Lemuel, 28.
Studson, Elijah, 14.
Studson, Elisha, 14.
Sturdevant, andrew, 45.
Sturdevent, abisha, 45.
Sturdevent, Gamaah, 41.

Sturdifent, Lot, 37.
Sturdifent, Lot, 50.
Sturdivant, Asa, 22.
Sturdivant, David, 13.
Sturdivant, David, 22.
Sturdivant, Frances, 22.
Sturdivant, Isaac, 13.
Sturdivant, John, 22.
Sturgis, Edward, 32.
Sturgis, Jona, 19.
Stutson, Zealous, 43.
Stvens, Abijah, 63.
Stvens, Henery, 67.
Stvens, Jona, 63.
Stvens, Thomas, 63.
Styles, Enoch, 11.
Styles, Ezra, 11.
Styles, Noah, 11.
Suchfort, Andrass, 26.
Sullivan, Abigail, 31.
Sullivan, Amos, 12.
Sullivan, Benja, 63.
Sullivan, Danl, 38.
Sullivan, Ebenezer, 55.
Sullivan, John, 37.
Sullivan, John, 56.
Sullivan, William, 28.
Summer, David, 33.
Sumner, Ezra, 49.
Sumner, Hopestill, 49.
Sunders, Sam., 48.
Surline, John, 13.
Surtain, John, 44.
Sutten, ——, 64.
Swain, Elizabeth, 66.
Swain, Meriam, 30.
Swan, Caleb, 60.
Swan, Elijah, 68.
Swan, Gustavus, 27.
Swan, James, 68.
Swan, James, Junr, 68.
Swan, John, 23.
Swan, Joseph Frye, 60.
Swan, Joseph G., 68.
Swan, William, 22.
Swanson, Robert, 59.
Swanton, Robert, 38.
Swanton, Willm, 33.
Swanton, Willm, 33.
Swatland, Samuel, 42.
Sweat, Daniel, 53.
Sweat, Shebna, 27.
Sweat, Shebna, 30.
Sweat, Solomon, 30.
Sweet, Arnol, 51.
Sweet, Benja, 16.
Sweet, Ebenezer, 44.
Sweet, Elias, 51.
Sweet, John, 12.
Sweet, Jona, 25.
Sweetland, David, 46.
Sweetland, James, 36.
Sweetland, Sampson, 36.
Sweetland, Stephen, 36.
Sweetser, John, 23.
Sweetser, John, 28.
Sweetser, John, junr, 28.
Swet, Moses, 66.
Swett, Benja, 38.
Swett, Israel, 14.
Swett, John, 12.
Swett, John, 26.
Swett, John, 58.
Swett, John, 72.
Swett, Jonathan, 23.
Swett, Joseph, 26.
Swett, Josiah, 19.
Swett, Moses, 14.
Swett, Moses, 19.
Swett, Moses, Junr, 67.
Swett, Nathl, 71.
Swett, Samuel, 15.
Swett, Samuel, 25.
Swett, Saml, 39.
Swett, Saml, 72.
Swett, Sarah, 72.
Swett, Stephen, 15.
Sweft, Stepn, 19.
Swicher, Wm, 19.
Swicker, Richard, 19.
Swift, John, 47.
Swift, Joseph, 22.
Swift, Turner, 44.
Switcher, Seth, 21.
Switcher, Willm, 22.
Switland, Nathl, 39.
Switzer, Benja, 21.
Switzer, John, 21.
Sylly, John, 19.
Sylvester, Joseph, 23.
Sylvester, Nathl, Junr, 37.
Symes, Ebenezer, 68.
Symes, Wm, 68.
Symonds, Óliver, 26.
Symonds, Peleg, 26.
Sympson, Zebediah, 61.

Taber, Bathw, 47.
Taber, Jacob, 47.
Taber, Jacob, 47.
Taber, John, 47.
tabet, henry, 48.
tabet, Steven, 48.

Taggot, James, 43.
Takins, Thomas, 35.
Talbot, Peter, 53.
Talbot, William, 51.
Talckut, Jona, 57.
talhelm, george, 42.
Tapley, Job, 66.
Tapley, John, 66.
Tapley, Peletiah, 30.
Tappen, Wiglesworth, 66.
Tarbble, David, 40.
Tarbell, ——, 47.
Tarble, Joseph, 42.
Tarble, Joseph, 42.
Tarbox, Abijah, 58.
Tarbox, Benja, 58.
Tarbox, Benja, 64.
Tarbox, Carol, 64.
Tarbox, Conelius, 37.
Tarbox, Danl, 58.
Tarbox, Eleazer, 42.
Tarbox, Elisabeth, 58.
Tarbox, Ezekiel, 58.
Tarbox, Jerea, 58.
Tarbox, John, 58.
Tarbox, Jona, 58.
Tarbox, Lemuel, 54.
Tarbox, Loring, 66.
Tarbox, Rufus, 58.
Tarbox, Thos, 58.
Tarr, Abraham, 33.
Tarr, Andrew, 29.
Tarr, Benja, 37.
Tarr, Henry, 14.
Tarr, Henry, Junr, 14.
Tarr, Joseph, 35.
Tarr, Joseph, 38.
Tarr, Sarah, 38.
Tarr, Seth, 38.
Tarr, William, 27.
tarrow, John, 48.
tarrow, John, jun., 48.
Tarry, David, 33.
Tate, George, 14.
Tate, Robert, 15.
Taxbox, Samuel, 20.
Tayler, Elias, 50.
Tayler, James, 46.
Tayler, Joseph, 40.
Tayler, Phinhas, 49.
Tayler, Thomas, 51.
tayler, Wilebe, 50.
Tayler, wilebey, 49.
Taylor, Amos, 45.
taylor, Daniel, 68.
Taylor, Ebenezer, 39.
taylor, Elifilate, 67.
Taylor, Ezra, 44.
Taylor, James, 31.
taylor, Jerimiah, 60.
Taylor, John, 45.
Taylor, John, 47.
Taylor, John, 69.
Taylor, John, 69.
Taylor, Jonas, 50.
Taylor, Jona, 70.
Taylor, Joseph, 43.
Taylor, Joseph, 45.
Taylor, Joseph, 59.
taylor, Joseph, 60.
Taylor, Joseph, Ju., 45.
taylor, Joshua, 67.
Taylor, Nathl, 39.
Taylor, Nathaniel, 45.
Taylor, Nathl, 71.
Taylor, Nathaniel, Ju., 45.
taylor, Noah, 66.
Taylor, Robert, 45.
Taylor, Samuel, 12.
Taylor, Samuel, 50.
Taylor, Saml, Jr., 13.
Taylor, Thomas, 40.
Taylor, Timothy, 50.
Taylor, Willm, 70.
Teague, Benj, 12.
Teal, Robert, 63.
Tedderly, Saml, 62.
Tedderly, Wm, 62.
Teel, Adam, 36.
Teel, Thos, 72.
temesson, Joseph, 35.
Temple, Ebenezer, 34.
Temple, Ichabod, 34.
Temple, Isaac, 50.
Temple, Jacob, 50.
Temple, John, 34.
Temple, Levi, 34.
Temple, Nathaniel, 26.
terral, isaac, 48.
terral, isaac, jun., 48.
Tetherly, John, 60.
Tetherly, Willm, 61.
Thatcher, George, 58.
Thatcher, Josiah, 19.
Thaxter, Marshal, 53.
Thaxter, William, 43.
Thayer, Lemuel, 28.
Thayer, Lemuel, junr, 28.
Thayer, Ruth, 24.
Theobald, Philip, 44.
thing, Catharine (Widw), 68.
thing, Coffin, 68.
Thing, Nathaniel, 68.

Thing, Wintrop, 67.
Tholl, Jeremiah, 16.
Thomas, Abigail, 13.
Thomas, Amos, 29.
Thomas, Asa, 40.
Thomas, Benja, 29.
Thomas, Charles, 12.
Thomas, Charles, 19.
Thomas, Charles, 27.
Thomas, Concider, 12.
Thomas, Danl, 58.
Thomas, David, 29.
Thomas, David, 39.
Thomas, David, 58.
Thomas, Geo., 19.
Thomas, George, 29.
Thomas, George, 35.
Thomas, Henry, 33.
Thomas, Holmes, 24.
Thomas, Ichabod, 47.
Thomas, James, 20.
Thomas, James, 37.
Thomas, James, Junr, 37.
Thomas, Jesse, 40.
Thomas, John, 29.
Thomas, John, 30.
Thomas, John, 66.
Thomas, John, junr, 29.
Thomas, Joseph, 27.
Thomas, Joseph, 47.
Thomas, Joshua, 28.
thomas, Joshua, 42.
Thomas, Josh, 59.
Thomas, Lewis, 12.
thomas, Nathaieh, 51.
Thomas, Nathan, 49.
Thomas, Nickolas, 29.
Thomas, Peeter, 23.
Thomas, Richard, 27.
Thomas, Richard, 46.
Thomas, Richard, 50.
Thomas, Saml, 19.
Thomas, Samuel, 32.
Thomas, Stephen, 22.
Thomas, Thos, 19.
Thomas, Turf, 19.
thomas, waterman, 42.
Thombs, Amos, 25.
Thombs, Benjamin, 13.
Thombs, Benjamin, 14.
Thombs, Cezar, 15.
Thombs, Joseph, 23.
Thombs, Joseph, 23.
Thombs, Samuel, 14.
Thomes, Thos, 28.
Thompson, Aaron, 46.
Thompson, Abraham, 53.
Thompson, Alexander, 46.
Thompson, Alexander, 46.
Thompson, Alexander, 73.
Thompson, Allexr, 57.
Thompson, Amos, 34.
Thompson, Amos, 56.
Thompson, Benjamin, 42.
Thompson, Benjamin, 46.
Thompson, Benja, 46.
Thompson, Benja, 54.
Thompson, Benja, 54.
Thompson, Benja, 72.
Thompson, Caleb, 69.
Thompson, Cornelius, 12.
Thompson, Cornelius, 29.
Thompson, Danl, 72.
Thompson, David, 69.
Thompson, Dodiford C., 72.
Thompson, Ebenezer, 45.
thompson, Ebenezer, 66.
Thompson, Ebenezer, 72.
Thompson, Edward, 15.
Thompson, Ephraim, 55.
Thompson, Ezekiel, 47.
thompson, Ezra, 66.
Thompson, George, 53.
Thompson, George, 68.
Thompson, Isaa S., 25.
Thompson, Isaac, 45.
Thompson, Isaac, 60.
Thompson, James, 40.
Thompson, James, 54.
Thompson, Jesse, 56.
Thompson, Joel, 40.
Thompson, John, 20.
Thompson, John, 26.
Thompson, John, 26.
Thompson, John, 34.
Thompson, John, 44.
Thompson, John, 46.
Thompson, John, 55.
Thompson, John, 56.
Thompson, Jno, 58.
Thompson, John, 68.
Thompson, Rev. John, 55.
Thompson, Jonathan, 15.
Thompson, Jona, 55.
Thompson, Jona, 72.
Thompson, Joseph, 15.
Thompson, Joseph, 35.
Thompson, Joseph, 40.
Thompson, Joseph, 45.
Thompson, Joseph, 60.
Thompson, Joseph, 72.
Thompson, Miles, 67.
Thompson, Moses, 46.

Thompson, Nathaniel, 15.
Thompson, Noah, 56.
Thompson, Paul, 58.
Thompson, Peleg, 29.
thompson, phiness, 66.
Thompson, Richd, 68.
Thompson, Richd, Jr, 69.
Thompson, Robert, 12.
Thompson, Robert, 13.
Thompson, Robert, 26.
Thompson, Robt, 68.
Thompson, Ruben, 66.
Thompson, Samuel, 19.
Thompson, Saml, 21.
Thompson, Saml, 46.
Thompson, Saml, 59.
thompson, Solomon, 66.
Thompson, Stephen, 54.
Thompson, Theodore, 59.
Thompson, Thomas, 12.
Thompson, Thomas, 23.
Thompson, Thomas, 27.
Thompson, Thos, 58.
Thompson, William, 15.
Thompson, Willm, 20.
Thompson, Wm, 68.
Thoms, William, 60.
Thomson, Alexander, 12.
Thomson, David, 14.
Thomson, Ebenezer, 46.
Thomson, Joseph, 34.
thomson, Joseph, 59.
Thomson, Mary, 36.
Thomson, Saml, 34.
Thomson, William, 46.
Thorlo, John, 22.
Thorn, Bartholomew, 16.
Thorn, Ebenezer, 21.
Thorn, Israel, 25.
Thorn, Joseph, 16.
Thorn, Samuel, 40.
Thorn, Susanna, 33.
Thorndike, Christian, 13.
Thorndike, Ebenezer, 13.
Thorndike, Joshua, 36.
Thorndike, Paul, 26.
Thorndike, Robert, 26.
Thorndike, Robert, 36.
Thorp, Thomas, 53.
Thrasher, Benjamin, 13.
Thrasher, Ebenezer, 13.
Thrasher, John, 23.
Thrasher, Joseph, 15.
Thrasher, Sarah, 23.
Thurel, Jona, 56.
Thurlo, John, 12.
Thurrel, Jacob, 56.
Thurrel, Jno, 56.
Thurrel, Jona, 56.
Thurrill, Asaph, 11.
Thurrill, Davis, 11.
Thursten, Jonr, 49.
Thurstin, Paul, 15.
Thurston, David, 22.
Thurston, John, 27.
Thurston, John, 57.
Thurston, Peter, 49.
Thurston, Thos, 19.
Thurston, Thomas, 22.
Tibbets, Danl, 67.
Tibbets, Ebenezer, 67.
Tibbets, Ephrim, 56.
Tibbets, Ephrim, 63.
Tibbets, Ichabod, 56.
Tibbets, Ichabod, 67.
Tibbets, Ichabod, Jr, 56.
tibbets, Jacob, 48.
Tibbets, Jedediah, 56.
Tibbets, John, 70.
Tibbets, Joseph, 54.
Tibbets, Joseph, 54.
tibbets, Joseph, 59.
Tibbets, Obidiah, 66.
Tibbets, Phillip, 67.
Tibbets, Saml, 66.
Tibbets, Stephen, 63.
Tibbets, Stephen, 66.
Tibbets, Timothy, 67.
Tibbets, William, 54.
Tibbets, Wm, 67.
Tibbetts, Abner, 27.
Tibbetts, Ebenezer, 57.
Tibbetts, John, 30.
Tibbits, Benjamin, 34.
Tibbits, Edward, 44.
Tibbits, Esther, 35.
Tibbits, Ichabod, 34.
Tibbits, Isaac, 35.
Tibbits, James, 34.
tibbits, Jonathan, 66.
Tibbits, Nathl, 34.
Tibbits, Nathaniel, 36.
Tibbits, Nathl, 51.
Tibbits, Samuel, 35.
Tibbits, Thomas, 35.
Tibbits, Timothy, 35.
Tibbitts, Benja, 28.
Tibbitts, Daniel, 27.
Tibbitts, George, 27.
Tibbitts, John, 27.
Tibbitts, Nathaniel, 28.
Tibbitts, Solomon, 28.
Tibbitts, Thomas, 26.

INDEX.

Tibbitts, William, 27.
tibbls, Moses, 66.
Tibits, Giles, 34.
tibits, James, 69.
tibits, Joshua, 69.
tibits, Mary (Wid^w), 69.
tibits, Simeon, 69.
tibits, William, 69.
Ticket, Benjamin, 14.
Ticket, Jonathan, 14.
Ticket, Mary 15.
Tiffany, Daniel, 47.
Tiffany, Saml, 47.
tigue, Daniel, 35.
Tilden, Elisha, 50.
Tiler, Humphrey, 66.
Tiler, James, 66.
Tillton, John, 47.
Tilly, Willm, 13.
Tilson, Josiah, 12.
Tilton, Abraham, 37.
Tilton, Cornelias, 50.
tilton, David, 45.
Tilton, Samuel, 40.
Tinglen, Paletiah, 69.
Tings, John, 46.
tinkam, elen, 49.
Tinker, David, 29.
Tinker, John, 31.
Tinkham, John, 39.
Tinkham, Seth, 43.
Tinney, John, 71.
Tinney, Samuel, 23.
Tinney, Samuel, 24.
Tinney, Seth, 20.
Tinny, David, 54.
Tinny, George, 54.
Tinny, George, jun^r, 54.
Tinny, John, 54.
Tinny, Samuel, 54.
Tissaker, John, 36.
Titas, Saml, 49.
titas, William, 49.
Titcomb, Andrew, 14.
Titcomb, Benjamin, 23.
Titcomb, Benjamin, 24.
Titcomb, Benj^a, 69.
Titcomb, Edmund, 21.
Titcomb, John, 20.
Titcomb, Joseph, 21.
Titcomb, Joseph, 23.
Titcomb, Stephen, 70.
Titcomb, William, 15.
Titton, Cornelius, 50.
Toal, Micael, 21.
Tobb, Jacob, 24.
Tobey, Barnabas, 44.
Tobin, Matthew, 26.
Toby, Betty, 61.
Toby, John, 61.
Toby, Joseph, 61.
Toby, Matthias, 53.
Toby, Nath^n, 62.
Toby, Page, 15.
Toby, Page, 21.
Toby, Richard, 21.
Toby, Samuel, 24.
Toby, Samuel, 37.
Toby, Samuel, 37.
Toby, Saml, 62.
Toby, Sarah, 23.
Toby, Steph^n, 62.
Toby, William, 23.
Toby, William, 33.
Tod, John, 11.
Tod, Saml, 33.
Todd, Eliz^h, 61.
Todd, James, 53.
Todd, John, 53.
Todd, John, 61.
Todd, Joseph, 72.
Todd, Willm, 16.
Todd, W^m, 61.
Todd, Willm, 61.
Tolbart, Ambros, 16.
Tolbart, Ambros, 16.
Tolbart, Saml, 16.
Tolbart, Trecott, 16.
Tole, Jere^h, 19.
Tole, Jonathan, 65.
Tole, Levi, 65.
Tole, Phinehas, 58.
Tole, Stephen D., 65.
Toler, Samuel, 25.
Tolman, Curtis, 46.
Tolman, Isaiah, 32.
Tolman, Isaiah, 46.
Tolman, Jeremiah, 46.
Tolman, Reuben, 49.
Tolman, Saml, 39.
Tolman, Samuel, 46.
Tolpy, Henry, 71.
Tolpy, Thos, 71.
Tombly, Andrew, 25.
Tompson, David, 41.
Tompson, Elick, 38.
tompson, george, 48.
Tompson, John, 66.
tompson, Jonathan, 49.
Tompson, Mary, 49.
tompson, mills, 48.
tompson, nat^l, 48.
tompson, Richard, 40.
tompson, Robert, 48.

tompson, thomas, 48.
tompson, William, 49.
Tomson, Jno & Thos, 19.
Tomson, Paul, 19.
Tomson, Thos. See Tomson, Jno & Thos, 19.
Tomson, W^m, 19.
Toner, Elias, 50.
Tongue, John, 58.
Toothacher, Mary, 35.
Toothaker, Abraham, 12.
Toothaker, Eben^r, 20.
Toothaker, Eben^r, 20.
Toothaker, Elijah, 27.
Toothaker, Gideon, 12.
Toothaker, Joanna, 20.
Toothaker, Nathl, 20.
Toothaker, Roger, 12.
Toothaker, Seth, 20.
Toppin, John, 15.
Topping, Luther, 25.
Torrey, David, 27.
Torrey, David, jun^r, 27.
Torrey, James, 15.
Torrey, Jonathan, 27.
Torrey, William, 27.
Tory, Elisha, 16.
Tosier, Amos, 37.
Tosier, Benjamin, 37.
Tosier, Jeremiah, 37.
Tosier, John, 37.
Tosier, John, Jur, 37.
Tosier, Jonathan, 37.
Tosier, Simeon, 50.
Totman, Henry, 20.
Totman, Henry, 38.
Totman, Joseph, 20.
Totman, Josiah, 20.
Tourtellott, Abraham, 27.
Tourtellott, Abraham, jun^r, 32.
Tourtellott, Reuben, 27.
Tower, Elizabeth, 28.
Towl, Josiah, 66.
Towle, Francies, 50.
Town, Willm, 20.
Townes, Ephrom, 50.
Townes, Isreal, 34.
Townes, Joseph, 35.
Townes, Joseph, 37.
Townes, Noah, 34.
Towns, Amos, 55.
Towns, Danl, 54.
Towns, Jacob, 70.
Towns, Josiah, 54.
Towns, Robert, 55.
Towns, Saml, 70.
Towns, Thomas, 43.
Townsand, Robert, 50.
Townsen, Daniel, 47.
Townsend, Abra^m, 64.
Townsend, Abra^m, Jr, 64.
Townsend, Beley, 16.
Townsend, Benj^a, 16.
Townsend, Danl, 64.
Townsend, Isaac, 64.
Townsend, John, 16.
Townsend, Joseph, 16.
Townsend, Nathan, 64.
Townsend, Robert, 16.
Townsend, Thos, 58.
Townsley, Gad, 54.
Townsley, Jacob, 53.
Toworgy, John, 59.
Towsanden, Robert, 50.
Towsend, Dodifer, 47.
Tozler, Lemuel, 27.
Traccy, Christopher, 14.
Tracey, Solomon, 14.
Tracey, Wheeler, 53.
Tracy, Asa, 29.
Tracy, Elizabeth, 29.
Tracy, Jonathan, 29.
Tracy, Samuel, 29.
trafen, Benjamin, 67.
trafen, Jeremiah, 67.
Trafton, Abiah, 71.
Trafton, Charles, 60.
Trafton, James, 72.
Trafton, Joseph, 38.
Trafton, Joshua, 67.
Trafton, Josiah, 67.
Trafton, Jotham, 67.
Trafton, Lemuel, 67.
Trafton, Saml, 72.
Trafton, Thaddeus, 71.
Trafton, Thos, 37.
Trafton, Thomas, 38.
Trafton (Widow), 72.
Trafton, Zachariah, 68.
Train, Jon^a, 34.
Trask, David, 36.
Trask, David, 37.
Trask, Eben^r, 47.
Trask, John, 41.
Trask, John, 47.
Trask, Jonathan, 33.
Trask, Joseph, 33.
Trask, Joseph, 36.
Trask, Joseph, 40.
Trask, Joseph, Juner, 33.
Trask, Moses, 36.
Trask, Obadiah, 34.
Trask, Saml, 36.
Trask, Solomon, 37.

Trask, Thomas, 32.
Trask, Thomas, Juner, 32.
Trask, Willm, 37.
Treadwel, Marsters, 60.
Treadwell, James, 69.
Treadwell, Nathl, 69.
Treadwell, Saml, 69.
Treat, James, 27.
Treat, Joseph, 28.
Treat, Joshua, 28.
Treat, Joshua, jun^r, 28.
Treat, Robert, 27.
Treat, Samuel, 28.
Trebbie, Joseph, 28.
Treeman, Joseph, 40.
Treferten, Danl, 61.
Treferton, Henry, 61.
Trescutt, Lemuel, 53.
Trevitt, Rich^d, 71.
Trew, Jabes, 21.
Trew, William, 21.
Tricet, John, 71.
Trickey, David, 15.
Trickey, Willm, 70.
Trickey, Zebulon, 13.
Trim, Godfrey, 29.
Trim, Godfrey, jun^r, 29.
tripe, Benjamin, 67.
Tripe, Eliz^h, 61.
tripe, Jonthan, 66.
tripe, Robt, 66.
tripe, Samuel, 66.
Tripe, Sarah, 62.
tripe, William, 66.
Tripp, Abner, 14.
Tripp, Nathaniel, 15.
Tripp, Peleg, 15.
Tripp, Richard, 11.
Trivet, Saml, 71.
Trott, Benjamin, 24.
Trott, Benj^a, 52.
Trott, Joanna, 52.
Trott, John, 61.
Trott, Thomas, 26.
Trough, Solomon, 22.
Truant, Job, 34.
Truant, Stephen, 34.
True, Abel, 14.
True, Abner, 45.
True, Aron, 45.
True, Benj^a, 25.
True, Daniel, 45.
True, David, 21.
True, Hannah, 21.
True, Henry, 26.
True, Israel, 21.
True, John, 21.
True, John, 45.
True, Jon^a, 21.
true, Obdiah, 66.
True, William, 11.
True, Willm, 14.
True, Willm, 21.
True, Winthrop, 22.
True, Zebulon, 39.
Trueworthy, Daniel, 32.
Trueworthy, James, 32.
Trueworthy, John, 58.
Trufaut, David, 33.
Trumbal, John, 40.
Trumbul, William, 36.
Trundy, George, 13.
Trundy, Jno, 59.
Trundy, Samuel, 27.
Trussell, Joshua, 31.
Tryon (Widow), 19.
Tuck, John M., 19.
Tuck, Samuel, 45.
Tucker, Andrew, 29.
Tucker, Catharine, 66.
Tucker, Daniel, 23.
Tucker, Francis, 66.
Tucker, Jane, 62.
Tucker, Job, 11.
Tucker, John, 40.
Tucker, John, 55.
Tucker, John, 66.
Tucker, Jonah, 23.
Tucker, Joseph, 72.
Tucker, Josiah, 54.
Tucker, Lemuel, 21.
Tucker, Lemuel, 24.
Tucker, Samuel, 54.
Tucker, Saml, 62.
Tucker, Stephen, 62.
Tucker, Stephen, 70.
Tucker, Susanna, 72.
Tucker, Willm, 13.
Tucker, William, 21.
Tuckes, abraham, 45.
Tuckfield, Mary, 23.
Tufts, Barnabas, 47.
Tufts, Francis, 44.
Tufts, John, 20.
Tufts, John, 21.
Tufts, John, 26.
Tufts, Moses, 41.
Tufts, Moses, 41.
Tugal, Elkanah, 41.
Tukesberry, John, 15.
Tukey, Hannah, 23.
Tukey, John, 23.
Tukey, John, 23.
Tukey, John, 23.

Tukey, Stephen, 23.
Tukey, William, 23.
Tupper, James, 44.
Tupper, Joseph, 54.
Tupper, Peleg, 50.
Tupper, William, 54.
turner, alexander, 42.
Turner, Benjamen, 38.
Turner, Briggs, 41.
turner, calab, 49.
Turner, Calvin, 28.
turner, Christopher, 51.
Turner, Concider, 33.
turner, cornelius, 42.
Turner, David, 38.
Turner, Ebenezer, 50.
Turner, Elisha, 22.
Turner, Elisha, 23.
Turner, Forbs, 38.
Turner, Gorge, 40.
Turner, Isaac, 14.
Turner, Isaac, 29.
Turner, James, 13.
Turner, James, 35.
Turner, Joseph, 40.
Turner, Joseph, 40.
Turner, Lemuel, 16.
Turner, Melzer, 15.
Turner, Nehemiah, 41.
Turner, Nichlass, 33.
Turner, Reuben, 44.
turner, Robt, 49.
Turner, Samuel, 28.
Turner, Simeon, 33.
Turner, Stabert, 68.
Turner, Thomas, 33.
turney, Edmond, 35.
Turnner, John, 51.
turrner, Oliver, 38.
Tusk, Lemuel, 21.
Tusker, Betty, 57.
Tuttel, Ebenezer, 57.
Tuttel, Job, 56.
Tuttle, Benj^a, 63.
Tuttle, Burrel, 21.
Tuttle, Elijah, 21.
Tuttle, Libius, 16.
Tuttle, Libius, 16.
Tuttle, Reuben, 14.
Tuttle, Samuel, 53.
Twamley, Daniel, 15.
tweed, Samuel, 67.
Twichel, Moses, 22.
Twichel, Moses, 24.
Twitchel, Eleazar, 68.
Twitchel, Eli, 68.
Twitchel, Ezra, 68.
Twitchel, Jeremiah, 19.
Twing, Nathl, 39.
Twing, Nathl, 51.
Twombley, Mercy, 57.
Tyler, Ab^m, 19.
Tyler, Abraham, 64.
Tyler, Ab^m, Jr., 19.
Tyler, Ab^m, 3^d, 19.
Tyler, Andrew, 28.
Tyler, Belcher, 27.
Tyler, George, 27.
Tyler, Joseph, 27.
Tyler, Joseph, 37.
Tyler, Joseph, 64.
Tylor, John, 21.
Tylor, Joseph, 21.
Tynan, Joseph, 67.
Tynan, Mary, 68.
Tynan, Ric^d, 60.
Tynan, Ric^d, 67.
Tyng, W^m, 19.

Ulmer, George, 28.
Ulmer, George, 46.
ulmer, John, 42.
Ulmer, John, 46.
Ulmer, Phillip, 28.
umbehind, Charles, 35.
Underhand, ——, 66.
Underwood, David, 15.
Underwood, Cap^n Job, 61.
Underwood, John, 66.
Underwood, Joseph, 15.
upham, Jabiz, 48.
Upham, William, 26.
Urann, John, 31.
Usher, Willm, 39.
Uslis, William, 44.

Varnam, Stevan, 50.
Varney, Francis, 70.
Varney, Ichabod, 11.
Varney, Jon^a, 70.
Varney, Nicholas, 14.
Varney, Peter, 61.
Varnham, Jon^a, 72.
Varnham, Jon^a, 73.
Varnum, Gershom, 31.
Varnum, John, 34.
Varnum, John, 35.
Varnum, John, Jur, 34.
Varnum, Jon^a, 72.
Varnum, Mathew, 30.
Varnum, Samuel, 35.
Varnum, Wanton, Jur, 34.

Varnum, William, 42.
Varrel, Jeremiah, 11.
Varrel, Joseph, 11.
Varrel, Richard, 11.
Varrel, Richard, Jur., 11.
Varrel, Saml, Jur, 11.
Varrel, Willm, 11.
Varrell, Davis, 11.
Varrell, Saml, 11.
Vaughn, William, 23.
Vening, Benj^a, 14.
Verney, Davis, 55.
Verney, Hezekiah, 56.
Verney, Hump^y, 63.
Verney, Jonathan, 57.
Verney, Ric^d, 56.
Verney, Tim^o, 57.
Verril, Solomon, 71.
Verrill (Widow), 71.
Verrill (Widow), 71.
Vezie, John, 23.
Vezie, Moses, 30.
Vezie, Nathaniel, 30.
Vezie, Samuel, 29.
Vezie, Samuel, 30.
Vezies, Jeremiah, 23.
Vicker, Ambros, 57.
Vickery, David, 19.
Vickery, Stephen, 36.
Videto, Comfort, 21.
Videto, Joseph, 21.
Videto (Widow), 21.
Viles, Joseph, 28.
Viles, Joseph, jun^r, 28.
Vinal, William, 32.
Vining, John, 14.
Vining, Jonah, 33.
Vitterin, Benjemin, 67.
Vose, Elijah, 36.
Vose, Jesse, 39.
Vose, Seth, 36.
Vose, Spencer, 46.
Vose, Thomas, 46.
Vrine, James, 69.

Wade, Abner, 51.
Wade, Charles, 45.
Wade, David, 50.
wade, jacob, 42.
Wade, John, 28.
Wade, Samuel, 50.
Wadley, Hannah, 56.
Wadley, John, 56.
Wadley, John, 64.
Wadley, Moses, 56.
Wadley, Moses, 64.
Wadley, Moses, j^r, 64.
Wadley, Thos, 70.
Wadley, Willm, 64.
Wadsworth, Peleg, 23.
Wadsworth, Sedate, 26.
Wadworth, John, 51.
Wag, John, 14.
wagner, andrew, 42.
wagner, william, 42.
Wald, Calvan, 47.
Wait, Daniel, 22.
Wait, Danl, 22.
Waite, Benjamin, 14.
Waite, Benjamin, 22.
Waite, Enoch, 26.
Waite, John, 15.
Waite, John, 23.
Waite, Stephen, 23.
Waite, Thomas B., 23.
Wakefield, Benj^a, 71.
Wakefield, Dominicus, 43.
Wakefield, Ezekiel, 69.
Wakefield, Gibbins, 60.
Wakefield, hazakiah, 67.
Wakefield, Israel, 59.
Wakefield, James, 70.
Wakefield, Jere^h, 43.
Wakefield, John, 70.
Wakefield, John, j^r, 70.
Wakefield, Jos., 19.
Wakefield, Josiah, 70.
Wakefield, Nathl, 55.
Wakefield, Samuel, 54.
Walcott, Spencer, 47.
Waldo, Benjamin, 43.
Waldo, Samuel, 23.
Waldron, Ebenezer, 67.
waliser, John, 41.
walk, henry, 41.
walk, peter, 42.
Walker, Abraham, 44.
Walker, And^w, 52.
Walker, And^w, 55.
Walker, Benj^a, 39.
Walker, Charles, 31.
Walker, Charles, 31.
Walker, Danl, 55.
Walker, Edward, 73.
Walker, Eleazer, 30.
Walker, Elephalet, 69.
Walker, Ezekiel, 60.
Walker, Gedeon, 69.
Walker, Gideon, 46.
Walker, Isaac, 60.
Walker, James, 21.
Walker, Jeremiah, 16.
Walker, Jesse, 46.

INDEX.

Walker, John, 25.
Walker, John, 29.
Walker, John, 31.
Walker, John, 52.
Walker, John, 55.
Walker, John, 55.
Walker, John, 60.
Walker, Jonª, 55.
Walker, Jonª, 56.
Walker, Joseph, 52.
Walker, Joseph, 58.
Walker, Joseph, 60.
Walker, Josiah, 15.
Walker, Micael, 21.
Walker, Nathˡ, 55.
Walker, Natheˡ, 56.
Walker, Nathˡ, 60.
Walker, Peeter, 23.
Walker, Richard, 43.
Walker, Samˡ, 55.
Walker, Samuel, 60.
Walker, Solomon, 52.
Walker, Stephen, 52.
Walker, Supply, 58.
Walker, William, 15.
Wall, Andʷ, 34.
Wall, David, 30.
Wall, Patrick, 36.
Wallace, David, 34.
Wallace, John, 12.
Wallace, John, 13.
Wallace, John, 37.
Wallace, John, 37.
Wallace, Jonah, 13.
Wallace, Samˡ, 38.
Wallace, Willᵐ, 38.
Wallace, Willᵐ, 38.
Walley, John, 67.
Wallingford, Abigˡ, 61.
Wallingford, John, 56.
Wallingford, Jnº, 63.
Wallingford, Joshua, 63.
Wallingford, Moses, 63.
Wallingford, Tobias, 63.
Wallis, Benjamin, 54.
Wallis, James, 54.
Wallis, Joseph, 54.
Wallis, Joseph, Junʳ, 54.
Walsh, William, 46.
Walten, John, 38.
walter, peter, 42.
Walton, Moses, 45.
Walton, Moses, 51.
Walton, Paul, 32.
Walton, William, 41.
Wamoth, Benjⁿ, 49.
Wamoth, Joseph, 49.
Wamoth, Samuel, 49.
Ward, Benjª, 29.
Ward, Benjª, 39.
Ward, Danˡ, 59.
Ward, Elijah, 15.
Ward, Ephrom, 42.
Ward, John, 19.
Ward, John, 47.
Ward, John, 54.
Ward, Joseph, 19.
Ward, Josiah, 39.
Ward, Mijah, 19.
Ward, Nathaniel, 30.
Ward, Nathˡ, 55.
Ward, Nehemiah, 12.
Ward, Nehemiah, 20.
Ward, Samuel, 47.
Ward, Thˢ, 39.
Wardwell, Daniel, 30.
Wardwell, Daniel, junʳ, 30.
Wardwell, Jeremiah, 30.
Wardwell, Jeremiah, junʳ, 30.
Wardwell, Joseph, 30.
Wardwell, Josiah, 30.
Wardworth, Samuel, 51.
Ware, Jason, 47.
Ware, Nathan, 33.
Warmwood, Amous, 66.
warner, george, 42.
warner, John, Jun., 42.
Warren, Aaron, 68.
Warren, Abijah, 22.
Warren, Alden, 57.
Warren, Benjⁿ, 19.
Warren, Chadbourne, 56.
Warren, Danˡ, 64.
Warren, David, 12.
Warren, David, 66.
Warren, Ebenʳ, 14.
Warren, Gedion, 57.
Warren, George, 23.
Warren, George, 63.
Warren, Gilbert, 56.
Warren, Gilbert, 68.
Warren, Henry, 14.
Warren, Ichabod, 58.
Warren, Jaˢ, 19.
warren, james, 48.
Warren, James, 56.
Warren, John, 12.
Warren, John, 15.
Warren, John, 56.
Warren, Joshua, 64.
Warren, Joshua, Jʳ, 64.
Warren, Moses, 73.
Warren, Nathˡ, 19.

Warren, Peeter, 23.
Warren, Pelatiah, 14.
Warren, Petten, 43.
Warren, Richard, 47.
Warren, Samˡ, 19.
Warren, Samˡ, 25.
Warren, Samuel, 29.
Warren, Samuel, 66.
Warren, Thomas, 27.
Warren, Tristram, 12.
Warren, Walter, 19.
Warren, Wᵐ, 56.
Warren, Wᵐ, 56.
Warrin, George, 50.
Warrin, Josiah, 42.
Warry, John, 38.
Washbane, Edward, 51.
Washborn, Stephen, 20.
Washborn, Stephen, 21.
Washbourn, Joseph, 55.
Washburn, Eliab, 11.
washburn, hosea, 41.
Washburn, Jacob, 22.
Washburn, John, 24.
Wason, Nathⁿ, 61.
Wass, Christoʳ, 54.
Wass, David M., 54.
Wass, Willmot, 3ᵈ, 54.
Wass, Wilmot, 54.
Wass, Wilmot, junʳ, 54.
Wasson, John, 30.
Wasson, Samuel, 33.
Wasson, Thomas, 30.
Waterhouse, Enoch, 53.
Waterhouse, George, 19.
Waterhouse, Jacob, 23.
Waterhouse, Jacob, 60.
Waterhouse, John, 14.
Waterhouse, Jnº, 19.
Waterhouse, John, 60.
Waterhouse, Josᵃ, 19.
Waterhouse, Joseph, 25.
Waterhouse, Nathˡ, 19.
Waterhouse, Samˡ, 19.
Waterhouse, Samˡ, 69.
Waterhouse, Samˡ, Jʳ, 69.
Waterhouse, Theoˢ, 19.
Waterhouse, Tinyʳ, 19.
Waterhouse, William, 14.
Waterhouse, William, 14.
Waterman, John, 11.
Waterman, Joseph, 11.
Waterman, Joseph, 32.
Waterman, Malchʳ, 19.
Waterman, Nathaniel, 46.
Waterman, Noah, 11.
Waterman, Primes, 38.
Waterman, Robert, 11.
Waters, Daniel, 41.
Waters, Samuel, 33.
Waters, Samuel, 38.
Watlon, Abiah, 41.
Watson, ——, 58.
Watson, Danˡ, 19.
Watson, Daniel, 45.
Watson, Daniel, ju., 45.
Watson, David, 46.
Watson, Ebenʳ, 19.
Watson, Eliphˡ, 19.
Watson, James, 49.
Watson, John, 11.
Watson, John, 19.
Watson, Jnº, 19.
Watson, John, 58.
Watson, Jonª, 19.
Watson, Samˡ, 54.
Watson, Shadrach, 31.
Watson, William, 49.
Watt, John, 49.
Watt, Samuel, 36.
Watts, David, 19.
Watts, David, 54.
Watts, Edward, 14.
Watts, John, 53.
Watts, Samuel, 15.
Watts, Samuel, 54.
Waugh, James, 44.
Waugh, Robert, 51.
Waugh, Thomas, 44.
Waymoth, Benjª, 57.
Waymoth, Benjª, Jʳ, 57.
Waymoth, Francis, 57.
Waymoth, James, 60.
Waymoth, Joshua, 68.
Waymoth, Moses, 57.
Waymouth, Edmond, 34.
Waymouth, James, 34.
Waymouth, Jonathan, 34.
Waymouth (Widʷ), 59.
Weaks, John, 33.
Weaks, John, Junʳ, 33.
Weaks, Joseph, 33.
Weaks, Mark, 33.
Weaks, Thomas, 33.
Weaks, Winteig, 33.
Wear, Abel, 36.
Wear, David, 50.
Wear, Ephrom, 42.
Wear, Danˡ, 71.
Weare, Elijah, 21.
Weare, Jerᵉ, 71.
Weare, Jerᵉ, Jʳ, 71.
Weare, John, 71.

Weare, Joseph, 71.
Weare, Joseph, Jʳ, 71.
Weare, Peter, 21.
Weare, Robert, 20.
Weathern, Benjamin, 44.
Webb, Christopher, 36.
Webb, Edward, 19.
Webb, Eli, 19.
Webb, Elisabeth, 15.
Webb, Hannah, 27.
Webb, Henry, 14.
Webb, James, 14.
Webb, James, 34.
Webb, James, 35.
Webb, John, 15.
Webb, Jonathan, 15.
Webb, Josiah, 26.
Webb, Micael, 23.
Webb, Nathˡ, 41.
Webb, Samˡ, 14.
Webb, Sarah, 13.
Webb (Widow), 52.
Webb, William, 15.
Webb, Willᵐ, 33.
Webb, William, 46.
Webb, William, 53.
Webber, ——, 47.
Webber, Benjⁿ, 61.
Webber, Benjª, 68.
Webber, Daniel, 66.
Webber, David, 20.
Webber, Edmond, 70.
Webber, Edmond, Jʳ, 70.
Webber, Edwᵈ, 61.
Webber, Ezekiel, 44.
Webber, George, 70.
Webber, Gersham, 34.
Webber, Isaac, 30.
Webber, John, 21.
Webber, John, 36.
Webber, John, 70.
Webber, John, 70.
Webber, Jonª, 22.
Webber, Joseph, 30.
Webber, Joseph, 40.
Webber, Joseph, 45.
Webber, Joseph, 47.
Wehber, Lewis, 40.
Webber, Mary, 20.
Webber, Matthias, 71.
Webber, Micael, 21.
Webber, Nathˡ, 71.
Webber, Nathˡ, 71.
Webber, Nicholas, 43.
Webber, Paul, 67.
Webber, Richard, 27.
Webber, Samuel, 23.
Webber, Samˡ, 37.
Webber, Samˡ, 70.
Webber, Stephen, 70.
Webber, Theodore, 71.
Webber, William, 30.
Weber, Daniel, 20.
weber, george, 41.
Weber, Stephen, 45.
Webster, Andrew, 27.
Webster, Andrew, 31.
Webster, Daniel, 30.
Webster, Daniel, 37.
Webster, David, 37.
Webster, Ebenezer, 27.
Webster, James, 13.
Webster, James, 13.
Webster, John, 13.
Webster, John, 22.
Webster, John, 60.
Webster, Joseph, 66.
Webster, Joshua, 69.
Webster, Nathˡ, 70.
Webster, Revᵈ Nathˡ, 58.
Webster, Thomas, 24.
Webster, Waldren, 19.
Webster (Widow), 19.
Webster, William, 19.
Wedgwood, Jesse, 65.
Wedgwood, Lot, 65.
Wedgwood, Noah, 65.
Weed, Benjamin, 27.
Weed, James, 46.
Weeds, Jonª, 67.
Weekes, James, 35.
Weeks, Abner, 40.
Weeks, Abrahᵐ, 61.
Weeks, Benjⁿ, 19.
Weeks, Benj., 47.
Weeks, Elihu, 61.
Weeks, John, 55.
Weeks, John, 61.
Weeks, John, 61.
Weeks, Joseph, 19.
Weeks, Joseph, 22.
Weeks, Joseph, 61.
Weeks, Lemuel, 22.
Weeks, Lemuel, 26.
Weeks, Lucy, 54.
Weeks, Nathˡ, 21.
Weeks, Nicholas, 55.
Weeks, Nickˢ, 61.
Weeks, Pellenak, 61.
Weeks, Phinias, 47.
Weeks, Samuel, 65.
Weeks, Capⁿ Samˡ, 61.
Weeks, Shubiaˡ, 38.
Weeks, Silvanus, 33.

Weeks, Solomon, 40.
Weeks, Solomon, Jʳ, 40.
Weeks, Willᵐ, 22.
Weeks, Wᵐ (Widʷ), 19.
Weeks, Wᵐ (Widʷ), 19.
Weels, James, 49.
Weels, Joshua, 49.
Weitherill, James, 63.
Weitherill, Thoˢ, 63.
Welch, Benjª, 72.
welch, Charles, 41.
welch, christopher, 41.
Welch, David, 61.
Welch, David, 61.
Welch, David, 66.
Welch, David, 72.
Welch, Edmand, 66.
Welch, Edmend, Juʳ, 66.
Welch, Edward, 33.
Welch, James, 13.
Welch, James, 24.
Welch, James, 37.
Welch, John, 62.
welch, John, jun., 41.
Welch, Joseph, 21.
Welch, Joseph, 66.
Welch, Joseph, 71.
Welch, Mark, 38.
Welch, Mary, 13.
Welch, Molley, 16.
Welch, Moses, 72.
Welch, Patrick, 14.
Welch, Paul, 72.
Welch, Samˡ, 39.
Welch, Sam., 62.
Welch, Sarah, 72.
Welch, Tabitha, 71.
Welch, Thoˢ, 16.
Welch, thomas, 69.
Welch (Widow), 73.
Welch, Wᵐ, 62.
Welch, Willᵐ, 71.
Weldridge, James, 23.
Wells, Danˡ, 71.
Wells, David, 39.
Wells, Dependence, 71.
Wells, Edward, 70.
Wells, John, 36.
Wells, John N., 71.
Wells, Joshª, 71.
Wells, Nathan, 71.
Wells, Richard, 31.
Wells, Robert, 69.
Wells, Simeon, 21.
Wells (Widow), 71.
Wells, William, 31.
Wells, Willᵐ, 70.
Welsh, Benjamin, 31.
Welsh, Henry, 28.
Welsh, John, 28.
Welsh, John, 68.
Welsh, Jonª, 56.
Welsh, Jonª, 68.
Welsh, Mark, 28.
Welsh, Paul, 56.
Welsh, Samˡ, 33.
welt, pleosus, 41.
Welts, John, 36.
Welts, Nathaniel, 36.
Wench, Joseph, 16.
Wengate, Simon, 58.
Wentworth, Ebenʳ, 59.
Wentworth, Enoch, 29.
Wentworth, Grant, 28.
Wentworth, Lemuel, 26.
Wentworth, Moses, 30.
Wentworth, Shubael, 26.
Wentworth, Silas, 16.
Wentworth, Sion, 26.
Wentworth, Wᵐ, 28.
Wentworth, Willᵐ, 64.
werner, andrew, 41.
werner, charles, 42.
werner, george, 42.
werner, John, 41.
werner, John, 42.
werner, John, jun., 41.
Wescoat, Benjª, 53.
Wescot, Daniel, 11.
Wescot, Joshua, 12.
Wescot, Reuben, 19.
Wescot, Richᵈ, 19.
Wescot, Wᵐ, 57.
Wescot, Zebulon, 19.
Wescott, Andrew, 31.
Wescott, Davis, 29.
Wescott, Elizabeth, 30.
Wescott, Samuel, 31.
Wescott, Thomas, 29.
Wescott, Thomas, junʳ, 29.
Wescott, William, 30.
Wessen, Josiah, 54.
Wesson, Benjamin, 52.
Wesson, Edmond, 47.
Wesson, Ely, 36.
Wesson, John, 36.
Wesson, Joseph, 36.
Wesson, Nathan, 39.
Wesson, Samuel, 35.
Wesson, William, 42.
West, Desper, 24.

West, Isaac, 44.
West, James, 70.
West, John, 46.
West, Judah, 51.
West, Nicholas, 70.
West, Nicholas, Jʳ, 70.
west, Obediah, 44.
West, Peleg, 16.
West, Samuel, 45.
West, Thomas, 53.
West (widow), 40.
Westcoat, Isaac, 61.
Westcot, Ellakim, 15.
Westcot, Josiah, 13.
Westcot, Richard, 15.
Westcot, Samuel, 13.
Western, Job, 53.
Western, John, 24.
Weston, abraham, 44.
weston, arona, 48.
Weston, Benlah, 13.
Weston, Caleb, 35.
Weston, Jacob, 12.
Weston, Joseph, 19.
Weston, Nathan, 16.
Weston, Samuel, 49.
Weston, Stephen, 14.
Westson, James, 24.
Wetch, John, 49.
Wetherby, Elisabeth, 58.
wethren, arnold, 35.
Wewer, John, 41.
Weymouth, Cathʳ, 19.
Weymouth, Moses, 52.
Weymouth, Timᵉ, 12.
Whalen, John, 37.
Whalen, Joseph, 38.
Whalen, Thomas, 37.
Whaling, James, 32.
Whaling, Patrick, 20.
Whaling, William, 32.
Wheaton, Mason, 46.
Wheeler, Benjª, 27.
Wheeler, Daniel, 37.
Wheeler, David, 20.
Wheeler, Hannah, 34.
Wheeler, John, 13.
Wheeler, John, 34.
Wheeler, John, 72.
Wheeler, Joseph, 34.
Wheeler, Joseph, 34.
Wheeler, Joseph, 34.
Wheeler, Mary, 22.
Wheeler, William, 36.
Wheeles, Enos, 37.
Wheeller, David, 20.
Wheelright, Aaron, 69.
Wheelright, Benjª, 70.
Wheelright, John, 71.
Wheelright, Joseph, 70.
Wheelright, Joseph, 70.
Wheelright, Joseph, Jʳ, 70.
Wheelright, Ralph, 71.
Wheelrite, Snell, 68.
Wheelwright, Benjª, 70.
Whelden, Ebenezer, 30.
Whelden, Joseph, 30.
Wheler, Moris, 51.
Wherren, Wᵐ, 62.
Whetcomb, Silas, 25.
Whettum, Martha, 15.
Whicher, Foxwell, 57.
Whicher, Moses, 51.
Whicher, Moses, Ju., 51.
Whicher, Nathaniel, 51.
Whicher, Ricᵈ, 57.
Whicher, Thomas, 51.
Whicher, William, 51.
Whidden, Israel, 55.
Whidden, John, 46.
Whidden, John, 46.
Whidden, Joseph, 55.
Whidden, Mark, 42.
Whidden, Ricᵈ, 56.
Whipple, Elezer, 36.
Whitaker, Elisha, 31.
whitcker, Nanse, 40.
Whitcomb, Abner, 26.
Whitcomb, David, 25.
Whitcomb, Ebenezer, 26.
Whitcum, Robart, 42.
Whitcum, Stephen, 36.
Whitcum, Thomas, 42.
Whitcum, Thomas, 44.
White, Abel, 21.
white, Benjª, 39.
White, Benjª, 44.
White, Benjª, 51.
White, Charles, 59.
White, Charles, 67.
White, Daniel, 26.
White, Danˡ, 55.
White, Edward, 26.
White, Elias, 16.
White, Elijah, 46.
White, George, 32.
White, Hugh, 35.
White, Hugh, 35.
White, Jacob, 16.
White, James, 35.
White, James, 35.
White, Jesse, 43.
White, Joab, 51.

INDEX.

White, John, 26.
White, John, 35.
White, John, 36.
White, John, 36.
White, John, 38.
White, John, 44.
White, John, 46.
White, John, 50.
White, John, 58.
White, John, 67.
White, John, Junor, 67.
White, Joseph, 22.
White, Joseph, 22.
White, Joseph, 33.
White, Joseph, 33.
White, Joseph, 59.
White, Joshua, 37.
White, Luther, 21.
White, Moses, 39.
White, Nath¹, 37.
White, Peter, 25.
White, Robert, 52.
White, Robert, 55.
White, Samuel, 27.
White, Sam¹, 44.
White, Samuel, 67.
White, Silas, 63.
White, Solomon, 35.
White, Thomas, 19.
White, Thomas, 31.
White, Tilly, 54.
White, William, 20.
White, William, 21.
White, William, 44.
Whiteher, Benjamin, 44.
Whiteher, Clerk, 44.
Whiteher, Moses, 44.
Whitehorn, William, 29.
Whitehouse, Abigail, 55.
Whitehouse, Dan¹, 56.
Whitehouse, John, 50.
Whitehouse, John, Jur, 50.
Whitehouse, Nat., 63.
Whitehouse, Pomphrit, 25.
Whitehouse, Robart, 50.
Whitehouse, Sam¹, 69.
Whitehouse, Zadock, 22.
Whitelaw, James, 27.
Whiteman, Samuel, 36.
Whiten, Joseph, 32.
Whitham, Benj³, 28.
Whitham, Joshua, 27.
Whithous, Samuel, Ju., 33.
Whithouse, Jacob, 33.
Whitiker, Nathaniel, 36.
whiting, John, 40.
Whiting, John, 60.
Whiting, Jonathan, 51.
Whiting, Jonathan, Jur., 51.
Whiting, Joshua, 68.
Whiting, Oliver, 68.
Whiting, Thurston, 49.
Whiting, William, 34.
Whitman, Abel, 32.
Whitman, Jacob 13.
Whitman, Willm, 64.
Whitmore, Abraham, 35.
Whitmore, Dan¹, 19.
Whitmore, Francis, 35.
Whitmore, John, 33.
Whitmore, Joseph, 27.
Whitmore, Sam¹, 19.
Whitmore, Sam¹, 24.
Whitmore, Stephen, 35.
Whitmore, W^m., 19.
Whitney, Abel, 19.
Whitney, Abraham, 40.
Whitney, Amos, 19.
Whitney, Amos, 59.
Whitney, Asa, 19.
Whitney, Barnibas, 16.
Whitney, Benjamin, 40.
Whitney, Clark, 22.
Whitney, Dan¹, 19.
Whitney, Dan¹, 22.
Whitney, Daniel, 28.
Whitney, David, 25.
Whitney, Eben³, 33.
Whitney, Elias, 16.
Whitney, Isaac, 19.
Whitney, Isaac, 34.
Whitney, Isaac, 59.
Whitney, Jacob, 40.
Whitney, Ja³, 19.
Whitney, Jesse, 66.
Whitney, Joel, 54.
Whitney, John, 26.
whitney, John, 40.
Whitney, Jonathan, 34.
Whitney, Jon³, 46.
Whitney, Jon³, 59.
Whitney, Joseph, 19.
Whitney, Joshua, 25.
Whitney, Joshua, 69.
Whitney, Jotham, 19.
Whitney, Matthias, 54.
Whitney, Micah, 19.
Whitney, Moses, 19.
Whitney, Moses, 24.
Whitney, Napth^m, 54.
Whitney, Nath¹, 19.
Whitney, Nath³, 54.
Whitney, Phineas, 25.

Whitney, Phinehas, 19.
Whitney, Phinehas, 69.
Whitney, Priscilla, 19.
Whitney, Samuel, 14.
Whitney, Sam¹, 33.
Whitney, Sarah, 58.
Whitney, Steph^n, 58.
Whitney, Thomas, 28.
Whitney, Uriel, 19.
Whitney, Zebulon, 19.
Whitny, Benjamin, 47.
Whiton, Aaron, 67.
Whitrage, Jacob, 35.
Whitrow, James, 56.
Whittam, Bartholomew, 71.
Whittam, John, 69.
Whittem, Elisabeth, 71.
Whittem, John S., 72.
Whittem, Reuben, 72.
Whittemore, Isaac, 24.
Whitten, Asa, 52.
Whitten, Ebenezer, 41.
Whitten, George, 47.
Whitten, George, 50.
Whitten, James, 67.
Whitten, John, 41.
Whitten, Joseph, 37.
Whitten, Phineas, 29.
Whitten, Sam¹, 55.
Whitten, Samuel, 67.
Whitten, Thomas, 68.
Whitten, Tobolas, 35.
Whitten, Umpery, 67.
Whittier, Ebenezer, 43.
Whittier, Jacob, 56.
Whittier, Joseph, 44.
Whittier, Nath¹, 64.
Whittimore, Stephen, 35.
Whittom, Andrew, 57.
Whitton, Jn°, 58.
Whitton, Rich^d, 68.
Whittum, Benjamin, 45.
Whittum, Benjamin, Jur, 45.
Whittum, Benjamin, Ju., 45.
Whittum, Caleb, 45.
Whittum, Daniel, 45.
Whittum, Ebenezer, 45.
Whittum, Jedadiah, 16.
Whorfe, Joseph, 21.
whrorter, Roling, 51.
wickly, bernhard, 41.
Widgery, William, 21.
Wiggen, Bradstreet, 65.
Wiggen, Nathan, 65.
Wiggen, Nath¹, 65.
wiggens, Asa, 45.
Wiggins, Benj³, 31.
Wiggins, Nath¹, 39.
Wiggins, Nicholas, 49.
Wiggins, Phinehas, 15.
Wight, John Morse, 47.
Wightman, Robert, 22.
wihal, francis, 41.
Wiket, Abraham, 41.
Wilber, Jn°, Jr., 19.
Wilbert, John, 19.
Wilborn, Robert, 24.
Wilcom, Michael, 11.
Wilcot, Solomon, 11.
Wilder, Benj³, 55.
Wilder, Theophilus, 53.
Wilder, Theo³, jun^r, 53.
Wile, Timothy, Ju., 49.
Wilee, Robert, 34.
Wiles, Benj³, 55.
Wiles, Ephraim, 55.
Wiles, Israel, 55.
Wiles, Jacob, 55.
Wiles, Ruth, 55.
Wiles, Sam¹, 55.
Wiles, Sam¹, Jr, 55.
Wiley, Benjamin, 60.
Wiley, David, 25.
Wiley, Isaac, 36.
Wiley, John, 49.
Wiley, Willm, 25.
Wiley, William, 36.
Wiley, William, 60.
Wilham, Morris, 60.
Wilkeson, Joseph, 66.
Wilkins, David, 40.
Wilkison, George, 56.
Wilkison, James, 56.
Wilkison, Samuel, 56.
Wilkison, W^m, 56.
Willard, anna (Widow), 66.
Willard, Jesse, 13.
Willard, John, 66.
Willard, Samuel, 66.
Willbee, Thomas, 24.
wille, James, 48.
Willee, Edward, 12.
Willee, John, 34.
Willee, Martha, 34.
Willee, Robert, 34.
Willey, Alexander, 34.
Willey, Ichabod, 54.
Willey, Sam¹, 67.
Williams, Amos, 29.
Williams, Amos, 61.
Williams, Asa, 39.
Williams, Benj³, 20.
Williams, Ebenezer, 15.

Williams, George, 33.
Williams, George, 35.
Williams, Hart, 19.
Williams, Henry, 37.
Williams, Jacob, 36.
Williams, James, 38.
Williams, Jere^h, 19.
Williams, Johan³, 61.
Williams, John, 31.
Williams, John, 33.
Williams, John, 33.
Williams, John, 33.
Williams, Jonathan, 35.
Williams, Joseph, 22.
Williams, Joseph, 69.
Williams, Joshua, 39.
Williams, Nathaniel, 14.
Williams, Nath¹, 52.
Williams, Obediah, 50.
Williams, Peter, 27.
Williams, Sam¹, 20.
Williams, Samuel, 29.
Williams, Samuel, 45.
Williams, Sam¹, 69.
Williams, Seth, 39.
Williams, Shubael, 29.
williams, Simien, 67.
Williams, Thomas, 31.
Williams, Tho³, 33.
Williams, Thomas, 67.
Williams, Tim°, 52.
Williams, William, 34.
Williamson, Jonathan, 43.
Williamson, Jonathan, 45.
Williamson, Samuel, 45.
Williamson, Sarah, 43.
Williamson, Stephen, 45.
Willis, James, 11.
Willis, Thomas, 36.
Willman, Abraham, 50.
Wills, Benajah, 57.
Willson, David, 30.
Willson, Gawing, 54.
Willson, Gowen, 54.
Willson, Ichabod, 14.
Willson, James, 14.
Willson, John, 30.
Willson, Jonathan, 26.
Willson, Jonathan, 26.
Willson, Jonathan, 67.
Willson, Joseph, 54.
Willson, Joseph, Jr., 54.
Willson, Joshua, 53.
Willson, Joseph, 24.
Willson, Mark, 15.
Willson, Nathaniel, 15.
Willson, Samuel, 27.
Willson, William, 53.
Wilman, Asa, 47.
wilman, benjamin, 41.
wilman, ben, 49.
wilman, Joseph, 49.
wilman, Samuel, 41.
wilman, Sam, 49.
Wilmy, Daniel, 38.
Wilson, Aaron, 61.
Wilson, Alexander, 20.
Wilson, Benj³, 70.
Wilson, Dan¹, 61.
Wilson, Dan¹, 68.
Wilson, David, 16.
Wilson, David, 20.
Wilson, David, 34.
Wilson, Edmund, 61.
Wilson, Elihu, 61.
Wilson, Eliz^b, 61.
Wilson, Ephrom, 50.
Wilson, Gonen, 11.
Wilson, Hugh, 46.
Wilson, Humpy, 67.
Wilson, James, 20.
Wilson, James, 46.
Wilson, James, 49.
Wilson, John, 36.
Wilson, John, 40.
Wilson, John, 43.
Wilson, John, 47.
Wilson, Jon³, 71.
Wilson, Joseph, 61.
Wilson, Joseph, 71.
Wilson, Michael, 71.
Wilson, Miles, 71.
Wilson, Noah, 71.
Wilson, oliver, 44.
Wilson, Samuel, 34.
Wilson, Samuel, 40.
Wilson, Sam¹, 46.
Wilson, Sam¹, 61.
Wilson, Tho³, 61.
Wilson, Willm, 20.
Wilson, Willm, 46.
Wilton, Edmond, 70.
Wiman, henry, 51.
Wiman, James, 50.
Wiman, John, 64.
Wiman, Jon³, 50.
Wiman, Nathan, 46.
Wiman, Simon, 50.
Wiman, thomas, 44.
winal, david, 42.
winal, ezechial, 42.
winchafsaw, henry, 42.
winchapaw, John, 42.

Winchel, Anna, 46.
Winchel, Job, 57.
Winchel, John, 46.
Winchester, Silas, 30.
Windship, Ephraim, 26.
Windship, Gersham, 26.
Windship, John, 26.
Wing, Alan, 41.
Wing, Aron, 41.
wing, Benjn, 45.
Wing, Daniel, 51.
Wing, Daniel, Ju., 51.
Wing, Ebnezer, 41.
Wing, Gidion, 47.
Wing, Ichabod, 51.
wing, Isral, 45.
Wing, Moses, 41.
Wing, Nathan, 64.
wing, Paul, 51.
Wing, Phillip, 37.
Wing, Reuben, 40.
Wing, Reuben, 51.
Wing, Simeon, 41.
Wing, Simeon, Jr., 41.
Wing, Willm, 47.
Wing, Willm, Junr, 47.
Wingat, John, 63.
Wingate, Jon³, 19.
Wingate, Jon³, Jr, 19.
Wingate, Sam¹, 45.
Wingate, Snell, 59.
Wingumpaugh, John, 40.
winkenbach, Jacob, 41.
Winkley, Emerson, 61.
Winkley, John, 61.
Winkley, Thomas, 39.
Winn, Benj³, 71.
Winn, Dan¹, 70.
Winn, John, 70.
Winn, John, 70.
Winn, Jon³, 71.
Winn, Joseph, 70.
Winn, Joseph, 71.
Winn, Josiah, 70.
Winn, Nathan, 69.
Winn, Sam¹, 69.
Winn, Stephen, 70.
Winn, Stephen, 71.
Winshop, Josiah, 52.
Winslow, Barnabas, 20.
Winslow, Benjamin, 15.
Winslow, Benj³, 16.
Winslow, Benj³, 21.
Winslow, Benjamin, 33.
Winslow, Carpenter, 42.
winslow, David, 35.
Winslow, Ebenezer, 14.
Winslow, Elijah, 30.
Winslow, Else, 21.
winslow, Ez¹, 35.
Winslow, George, 12.
Winslow, Gilbert, 16.
Winslow, Hezekiah, 14.
Winslow, James, 14.
Winslow, James, 44.
Winslow, Job, 15.
Winslow, John, 14.
Winslow, John, 16.
winslow, John, 35.
Winslow, Jon³, 42.
Winslow, Joseph, 25.
Winslow, Joseph, 32.
Winslow, Kernelm, 40.
Winslow, Mary, 40.
Winslow, Nathan, 14.
Winslow, Nath¹, 37.
winslow, nicklas, 48.
Winslow, Olive, 15.
Winslow, Penelope, 32.
Winslow, Phebe, 60.
Winslow, Samuel, 14.
Winslow, Samuel, 15.
Winslow, Sam¹, 16.
Winslow, Samuel, 23.
Winslow, Thomas, 15.
Winslow, William, 14.
Winter, John, 44.
Wintworth, Amaziah, 63.
Wintworth, Benj³, 63.
Wintworth, Caleb, 63.
Wintworth, Ezekil, 56.
Wintworth, Gersham, 63.
Wintworth, Grant, 67.
Wintworth, Jedediah, 63.
Wintworth, Judah, 56.
wintworth, juke, 48.
Wintworth, Paul, 67.
Wintworth, Ric^d, 56.
Wintworth, Ruben, 67.
Wintworth, Samuel, 56.
Wintworth, Silas, 63.
Wintworth, Stimson, 63.
Wintworth, Thomas M., 63.
Wintworth, Timothy, 56.
wintworth (widow), 48.
Wintworth, W^m, 65.
Wire, John, 33.
Wire, John, 34.
Wire, John, 57.
Wire, Obed, 33.
Wirthwill, John, 56.
Wise, Amaziah, 15.
Wise, Dan¹, 70.

Wise, Jeremiah, 66.
Wissel, Tho³, 55.
Wiswall, David, 30.
Wiswall, Enoch, 23.
Wiswall, John, 24.
Wiswall, Samuel, 30.
Wite, Timothy, 49.
Withain, Robert, 66.
Witham, Aaron, 62.
Witham, Abner, 62.
Witham, Abraham, 30.
Witham, Benjamin, 21.
Witham, James, 60.
Witham, Jeremiah, 20.
Witham, Kezia, 62.
Witham, Magdalan, 61.
Witham, Mary, 66.
Witham, Moses, 62.
Witham, Thomas, 20.
Witham, Thomas, 20.
Witham, Tobias, 60.
Witham, William, 46.
Witherby, Jon³, 52.
Withern, Arnold, 44.
Withern, Michal, 45.
Withers, Longly, 42.
Withers, Obediah, 42.
Withers, Zoe, 44.
Witherton, Robert, 49.
Withey, Luke, 42.
Withey, Nathaniel, 42.
Withey, Uziel, 42.
Withey, William, 42.
withouse, Samuel, 33.
Withum, Edmond, 66.
Withum, Ganzbury, 66.
Withum, Ichabod, 67.
Withum, Jacob, 66.
Withum, Jeremiah, 66.
Withum, John, 66.
Withum, Jonathan, 66.
Withum, Mouses, 66.
Withum, Zeblion, 66.
Witt, Benjn, 24.
Witten, Tho³, 19.
Witlny, Joseph, 51.
Wodley, Daniel, 66.
Wodley, John, 68.
Wodword, Sarah (Wid^w), 69.
wolfgruber, Stofel, 41.
Wolpgrover, John, 40.
Wolton, Joshua, 45.
wolts, Andrew, 35.
woltz, andrew, 41.
Wood, Abiel, 43.
Wood, Bennit, 50.
Wood, Bethuel, 22.
Wood, Charles, 19.
Wood, Dan¹, 55.
Wood, Elijah, 51.
Wood, Ephrom, 36.
Wood, Isaac, 46.
Wood, Israel, 26.
Wood, James, 53.
Wood, Jean, 50.
Wood, John, 25.
Wood, John, 33.
Wood, John, 44.
Wood, Joseph, 26.
Wood, Joseph, 34.
Wood, Joseph, jun^r, 26.
Wood, Moses, 51.
Wood, Nathan, 44.
Wood, Oliver, 42.
Wood, Robert, 35.
Wood, Robert H., 26.
Wood, Samuel, 51.
Wood, Silas, 41.
wood, Simeon, 40.
Wood, Stephen, 68.
Wood, W^m, 19.
Woodard, David, 35.
Woodard, John, 35.
woodard, Sam., 48.
Woodberry, Hugh, 15.
Woodberry, Israel, 13.
Woodberry, John, 13.
Woodberry, Joseph, 20.
Woodberry, Joshua, 15.
Woodberry, Lucy, 13.
Woodberry, Peeter, 13.
Woodberry, Samuel, 24.
woodbery, ephram, 48.
Woodbridge, Benj³, 41.
Woodbridge, Benj³, Jur., 41.
Woodbridge, Christopher, 41.
Woodbridge, John, 7.
Woodbridge, Norton, 71.
Woodbridge, Paul D., 71.
Woodbrige, Tho^m, 41.
Woodbury, Ebenezer, 14.
Woodcock, David, 47.
Woodcock, David, 51.
Woodcock, Nathaniel, 46.
Woodhouse, George, 31.
Woodman, Benj³, 28.
Woodman, Benj³, 59.
Woodman, Benj³, 62.
Woodman, David, 20.
Woodman, David, 23.
Woodman, David, 63.
Woodman, Ep^m, 59.
Woodman, Jacob, 43.

INDEX.

Woodman, Jam^s, 59.
Woodman, Jer^h, 59.
Woodman, John, 11.
Woodman, John, 21.
Woodman, John, 33.
Woodman, Jno, 59.
Woodman, John, 63.
Woodman, Jon^a, 16.
Woodman, Joseph, 21.
Woodman, Joseph, 64.
Woodman, Joshua, 30.
Woodman, Joshua, 58.
Woodman, Jos^h, Junr, 59.
Woodman, Jos^h, 2nd, 59.
Woodman, Mary, 57.
Woodman, Merry, 23.
Woodman, Molly, 28.
Woodman, Nathan, 25.
Woodman, Nathl, 59.
Woodman, Sarah, 23.
Woodman, Stephⁿ, 59.
Woodman, Thomas, 43.
Woodman, True, 11.
Woodruff, Jonathan, 53.
Woods, John, 58.
Woods, Joseph, 25.
Woodside, Anthony, 12.
Woodside, Vincent, 12.
Woodside, Willm, 12.
Woodside, Willm, Junr, 12.
Woodsom, Abiath, 59.
Woodsom, Benj^a, 66.
Woodsom, John, 66.
Woodsom, Mich^l, 59.
Woodsom, Samuel, 66.
Woodson, Caleb, 14.
Woodsum, Daniel, 58.
Woodsum, David, 63.
Woodsum, John, 58.
Woodward, Davis, 21.
Woodward, Joseph, 29.
Woodward, Lem^l, 72.
Woodward, Noah, 39.
Woodward, Peter, 29.
Woodward, Saml, 12.
Woodward, Saml, 44.
Woodward, Willm, 33.

Woodword, William, 69.
Woodworth, James, 16.
Woodworth, James, 16.
Woollins, John, 30.
Wooster, David, 31.
Wooster, David, 32.
Wooster, Joseph, 32.
Wooster, Nathaniel, 32.
Wooster, Oliver, 31.
Wooster, William, 31.
Worcester, John, 11.
Worit, Josiah, 44.
Work, Eben^r, 46.
Works, James, 51.
Wormwell, John, 15.
Wormwell, Nathaniel, 15.
Wormwood, Abner, 70.
Wormwood, Benj^a, 32.
Wormwood, Benj^a, 70.
Wormwood, Eben^r, 69.
Wormwood, Eli, 32.
Wormwood, James, 60.
Wormwood, John, 67.
Wormwood, Joseph, 32.
Wormwood, Joseph, 69.
Wormwood, Thos, 70.
Wormwood, Willm, 70.
Worrim, Benjamin, 69.
Worseter, Moses, 54.
Worster, Francis, 33.
Worster, George, 57.
Worster, John, 63.
Worster, Lemuel, 56.
Worster, Luke H., 14.
Worster, Lydia, 56.
Worster, Phillip, 56.
Worster, Samuel, 56.
Worth, Saml, 64.
Worthley, Daniel, 21.
Worthley, Saml, 21.
Wortley, John, 21.
Woster, Thomas, 66.
Woster, William, 66.
Wotson (Wid^w), 68.
Wough, Robert, 45.
Wright, Boston, 15.
Wright, Daniel, 29.
Wright, John, 52.
Wright, Joseph, 52.

Wright, Joseph, Junr, 52.
Wright, Oliver, 44.
Writne, Josiah, 67.
Wuman, Volentine, 13.
Wutton, Benjamin, 40.
Wyer, Daniel, 23.
Wyer, Elijah, 15.
Wyley, James, 23.
Wyman, Abraham, 36.
Wyman, Daniel, 36.
Wyman, Daniel, 37.
Wyman, Dean, 39.
Wyman, Francis, 38.
Wyman, Francis, 47.
Wyman, James, 50.
Wyman, Jonas, 60.
Wyman, Josiah, 21.
Wyman, Martha, 38.
Wyman, Moses, 50.
Wyman, Reuben, 39.
Wyman, Reuben, Jr., 37.
Wyman, Seth, 35.
Wyman, Simon, 50.
Wyman, Willm, 21.
Wyman, Willm, 37.

Yates, Francis, 54.
Yates, John, 25.
Yates, Timothy, 11.
Yeaton, John, 53.
Yeaton, John, 63.
Yeaton, Jonathan, 56.
Yeaton, Phillip, 58.
Yeaton, Richard, 59.
Yeaton, Saml, 11.
Yeaton, Stephen, 11.
Yetton, James, 20.
Yongill, Enoch, 36.
Yongiue, David, 45.
Yongue, Joshua, 45.
Yongue, William, 45.
York, Bartholomew, 31.
York, Benj^a, 27.
York, Benj^a, jun^r, 31.
York, Ebenezer, 25.
York, Edward, 67.
York, Isaac, 68.
York, Isaas, 25.

York, Jacob, 13.
York, Jacob, 25.
York, Job, 25.
York, John, 13.
York, John, 36.
York, John, 68.
York, Joseph, 13.
York, Joseph, 14.
York, Joseph, 15.
York, Joseph, 30.
York, Nicholas, 67.
York, Robert, 19.
York, Samuel, 13.
York, Saml, 14.
York, Samuel, 15.
York, Saml, 22.
York, Solomon, 31.
York, William R., 15.
Young, Abner, 56.
Young, Abraham, 19.
Young, Abraham, 23.
Young, Abraham, 32.
Young, Alexander, 28.
Young, Benaiah, 37.
Young, Benj^a, 32.
Young, Benj^a, 44.
Young, Cabel, 12.
Young, Danl, 64.
Young, Daniel, 66.
Young, Danl, Jr, 64.
Young, David, 42.
Young, David, 64.
Young, David, 64.
young, Edward, 48.
Young, Eliphelet, 63.
Young, Elkanah, 29.
Young, Ezra, 29.
Young, Francis, 49.
Young, George, 36.
Young, Gideon, 26.
Young, Henry, 36.
Young, Hezekiah, 64.
Young, Isaac, 43.
Young, Job, 19.
Young, Job, 25.
Young, Joel, 72.
Young, John, 19.
Young, John, 56.

Young, John, 64.
Young, John, 71.
Young, John, Jr, 71.
Young, Jon^a, 72.
Young, Joseph, 21.
Young, Joseph, 21.
Young, Joseph, 13.
Young, Joseph, 30.
Young, Joseph, 32.
Young, Joseph, 72.
Young, Joseph, Jr., 19.
Young, Joseph, Senr, 19.
Young, Joshua, 12.
Young, Joshua, 43.
Young, Joshua, 72.
Young, Marstinson, 72.
Young, Martha, 25.
Young, Matthias, 72.
Young, Nathaniel, 19.
Young, Nathl, 22.
Young, Noah, 29.
Young, Reuben, 43.
Young, Richard, 36.
Young, Robert, 29.
Young, Rowland, 71.
Young, Samuel, 28.
Young, Samuel, 29.
Young, Samuel, 32.
Young, Samuel, 32.
Young, Saml, 72.
Young, Sarah, 36.
Young, Solomon, 71.
Young, Stephen, 31.
Young, Stephen, 55.
Young, Theodore, 37.
Young, Thos, 64.
Young, William, 36.
Young, Zebulon, 28.
Yourk, Nathan, 67.

Zentner, philliss, 35.
——, ——, 39.
——, ——, 47.
——, ——, 67.
——oston, Daniel, 60.
——, John, 62.
——, John, 67.
——sman, Solomon, 60.
——, W^m, 62.

www.ingramcontent.com/pod-product-compliance
Lightning Source LLC
Chambersburg PA
CBHW082052230426
43670CB00016B/2867